Mathcad7

Official User's Guide

Mathcad7 Student

Mathsoft, Inc.
101 Main Street
Cambridge
Massachusetts 02142
USA
http://www.mathsoft.com/

M a t h S o f t
Σ + √ − = × ∫ ÷ δ

INTERNATIONAL THOMSON PUBLISHING
I Ⓣ P® An International Thomson Publishing Company

London • Bonn • Boston • Johannesburg • Madrid • Melbourne • Mexico City • New York • Paris
Singapore • Tokyo • Toronto • Albany, NY • Belmont, CA • Cincinnati, OH • Detroit, MI

Mathcad 7 Official User's Guide

Copyright © 1998 Mathsoft Inc., All Rights Reserved

 I(T)P A division of International Thomson Publishing Inc.
The ITP logo is a trademark under licence

British Library Cataloguing-in-Publication Data
A catalogue record for this book is available from the British Library

First published 1998

Printed in the UK by The Alden Press, Oxford

ISBN 1-86152-266-5

International Thomson Publishing
Berkshire House
168–173 High Holborn
London WC1V 7AA
UK

http://www.itpe.com

Warning: MATHSOFT, INC. IS WILLING TO LICENSE THE ENCLOSED SOFTWARE TO YOU ONLY UPON THE CONDITION THAT YOU ACCEPT ALL OF THE TERMS CONTAINED IN THIS LICENSE AGREEMENT. PLEASE READ THE TERMS CAREFULLY BEFORE OPENING THE PACKAGE WITH THE CD-ROM OR OTHER MEDIA, AS OPENING THE PACKAGE WILL INDICATE YOUR ASSENT TO THEM. IF YOU DO NOT AGREE TO THESE TERMS, THEN MATHSOFT IS UNWILLING TO LICENSE THE SOFTWARE TO YOU, IN WHICH EVENT YOU SHOULD RETURN THIS COMPLETE PACKAGE WITH ALL ORIGINAL MATERIALS AND THE UNOPENED PACKAGE WITH THE CD-ROM OR OTHER MEDIA AND YOUR MONEY WILL BE REFUNDED.

MATHSOFT, INC. LICENSE AGREEMENT

Both the Software and the documentation are protected under applicable copyright laws, international treaty provisions, and trade secret statutes of the various states. This Agreement grants you a limited non-exclusive, non-transferable license to use the Software and the documentation. This is not an agreement for the sale of the Software or the documentation or any copies or part thereof. Your right to use the Software and the documentation is limited to the terms and conditions described therein.

You may use the Software and the documentation solely for your own personal or internal purposes, for non-remunerated demonstrations (but not for delivery or sale) in connection with your personal or internal purposes: (a) if you have a single license, on only one computer at a time and by only one user at a time, the user of the computer on which the Software is installed may make a copy for his or her exclusive use on a portable computer so long as the Software is not used on both computers at the same time; (b) if you have acquired multiple licenses, the Software may be used on either stand alone computers, or on computer networks, by a number of simultaneous users equal to or less than the number of licenses that you have acquired; and, (c) if you maintain the confidentiality of the Software and documentation at all times.

You may make copies of the Software solely for archival purposes, provided you reproduce and include the copyright notice on any backup copy.

You must have a reasonable mechanism or process that the number of users at any one time does not exceed the number of licenses you have paid for and to prevent access to the Software to any person not authorized under the above license to use the Software. Any copy which you make of the Software, in whole or in part, is the property of MathSoft. You agree to reproduce and include MathSoft's copyright, trademark and other proprietary rights notices on any copy you make of the Software.

You may receive the Software in more than one medium. Regardless of the type or size of media you receive, you may use only one medium that is appropriate for your single computer. You may not use or install the other medium on another computer. You may not loan, rent, lease, or otherwise transfer the other medium to another user, expect as part of the permanent transfer (as provided below) of the Software.

You may permanently transfer all of your rights under this license, provided that (i) you retain no copies, (ii) you transfer all of the Software (including all the media and all documentation, any upgrades and this license), and (iii) the recipient agrees to the terms of this license. If the Software is an upgrade, any transfer must include all prior versions of the Software.

If the Software is labeled as an upgrade, you must be properly licensed to use a product identified by MathSoft as being eligible for the upgrade in order to use the Software. Software labeled as an upgrade replaces and/or supplements the product that formed the basis of your eligibility for the upgrade. You may use the resulting upgraded product only in accordance with the terms of this license, which supersedes all prior agreements.

MathSoft, Inc. reserves all rights not expressly granted to you by this License Agreement. The license granted herein is limited solely to the uses specified above and, without limited the generality of the foregoing, you are NOT licensed to use or to copy all or any part of the Software or the documentation in connection with the sale, resale, license, or other for-profit personal or commercial reproduction or commercial distribution or computer programs or other materials without the prior written consent of MathSoft, Inc. In particular, the DLL interface specifications, the HBK file format and other confidential information and copyrighted materials may not be used for creating computer programs or other materials for sale, resale, license, or for remunerated personal or commercial reproduction or commercial distribution without the prior written consent of MathSoft, Inc.

Your license to use the Software and documentation will automatically terminate if you fail to comply with the terms of the Agreement. If this license is terminated, you agree to destroy all copies of the Software and documentation in your possession.

MATHSOFT, INC. LIMITED WARRANTY

MathSoft, Inc. warrants to the original licensee that the media on which the Software is recorded will be free from defects in materials and workmanship under normal use for a period of ninety (90) days from the date of purchase as evidenced by a copy of your receipt. The liability of MathSoft, Inc. pursuant to this limited warranty shall be limited to the replacement of the defective media. If failure of the media has resulted from accident, abuse, or misapplication of the product, then MathSoft, Inc. shall have no responsibility to replace the media under this limited warranty.

THIS LIMITED WARRANTY AND RIGHT OF REPLACEMENT IS IN LIEU OF, AND YOU HEREBY WAIVE, ANY AND ALL OTHER WARRANTIES BOTH EXPRESS AND IMPLIED, RELATING TO THE SOFTWARE, DOCUMENTATION, MEDIA OR THIS LICENSE, INCLUDING BUT NOT LIMITED TO WARRANTIES OF MERCHANTABILITY AND FITNESS FOR A PARTICULAR PURPOSE. IN NO EVENT SHALL MATHSOFT, INC. BE LIABLE FOR INCIDENTAL OR CONSEQUENTIAL DAMAGES, INCLUDING BUT NOT LIMITED TO LOSS OF USE, LOSS OF REVENUES OR PROFIT, LOSS OF DATA OR DATA BEING RENDERED INACCURATE, OR LOSSES SUSTAINED BY THIRD PARTIES EVEN IF MATHSOFT, INC. HAS BEEN ADVISED OF THE POSSIBILITIES OF SUCH DAMAGES. This warranty gives you specific legal rights which may vary from state to state. Some states do not allow the limitation or exclusion of liability for consequential damages, so the above limitation may not apply to you.

This License agreement shall be governed by the laws of the Commonwealth of Massachusetts and shall inure to the benefit of MathSoft, its successors, representatives and assigns. The license granted hereunder may not be assigned, sublicensed or otherwise transferred by you without the prior written consent of MathSoft, Inc. If any provisions of this Agreement shall be held to be invalid, illegal or unenforceable, the validity, legality and enforceability of the remaining provisions shall in no way be affected or impaired thereby.

Table of Contents

What is Mathcad? 1
Mathcad features 2
How to use this User's Guide 5

Getting Started

1: The Basics 9
First principles.. 10
What you can do with Mathcad.......................... 11
Working with windows 13
A simple calculation 15
Definitions and variables............................... 16
Entering text.. 18
Regions and menus.. 20
Iterative calculations 21
Graphs... 24
Saving, printing, and quitting 28

2: On-line Resources.. 31
Internet access in Mathcad............................... 32
The Collaboratory 33
Resource Center....................................... 37
Using Electronic Books 40
Help and context sensitive help 46

Editing and Worksheet Features

3: Editing Equations.. 49
Building expressions.. 50
Editing an existing expression 55
Rearranging your worksheet........................ 64

4: Worksheet Management 71
Worksheets and templates 72
Layout.. 76
Printing.. 79
Mailing 83
Safeguarding your calculations........................ 83
References and hyperlinks 86
Using OLE 91

5: Text 97
Inserting text 98
Equations in text 100
Text editing 102
Text styles 108
Text region properties 112
Find and Replace 113
Spell-checking 115

6: Equation and Result Formatting 117
Formatting results 118
Math styles 122
Highlighting equations 127

Computational Features

7: Equations and Computation 131
Defining variables and functions 132
Evaluating expressions 141
Copying numerical results 142
Controlling calculations 144
Disabling equations 148
Error messages 148

8: Variables and Constants 153
Names 154
Predefined variables 158
Numbers 159
Complex numbers 161
Strings 164

9: Units and Dimensions 167
Computing with units 168
Displaying units of results 171
Built-in units 175
Changing dimension names 177

10:Vectors and Matrices 179
Creating a vector or matrix 180
Computing with arrays 183
Subscripts and superscripts 185
Displaying vectors and matrices 190
Limits on array sizes 192

Vector and matrix operators 193
Vector and matrix functions 196
Doing calculations in parallel 204
Simultaneous definitions... 207
Arrays and user-defined functions 208
Nested arrays 209

11:Range Variables **213**
Range variables... 214
Output tables 217
Entering a table of numbers.. 220
Iterative calculations 222
Seeded iteration.. 226
Vector or subscript notation 230

12:Operators **233**
List of operators 234
Summations and products.. 237
Derivatives 241
Integrals 246
Boolean operators 250
Customizing operators... 252

13:Built-in Functions... **257**
Inserting built-in functions 258
Transcendental functions... 259
Truncation and round-off functions 264
Discrete transform functions 266
Sorting functions 270
Piecewise continuous functions....................................... 271
String functions 276

14:Statistical Functions **279**
Population and sample statistics 280
Probability distributions... 281
Histogram function... 287
Random numbers 288
Interpolation and prediction functions................................ 291
Regression functions 299
Smoothing functions 306

15:Solving Equations **309**
 Solving one equation.. 310
 Systems of equations.. 315
 Using the solver effectively 325

16:Solving Differential Equations........................... **333**
 Solving ordinary differential equations 334
 Systems of differential equations 338
 Specialized differential equation solvers 340
 Boundary value problems 344

17:Symbolic Calculation **351**
 What is symbolic math? 352
 Live symbolic evaluation 353
 Using the Symbolics menu............................. 360
 Symbolic algebra.. 362
 Symbolic calculus.. 374
 Solving equations symbolically 379
 Symbolic matrix manipulation 382
 Symbolic transforms.. 384
 Symbolic optimization 388
 Using functions and variables 390
 Limits to symbolic processing 395

18:Programming **399**
 Defining a program.. 400
 Conditional statements.................................... 402
 Looping 405
 Controlling program execution 407
 Error handling.. 411
 Programs within programs 413
 Evaluating programs symbolically.................... 416
 Programming examples 418

19:Data Management **421**
 Introduction to components............................. 422
 Importing data 425
 Exporting data 431
 Exchanging data with other applications........................ 435
 Functions for reading and writing ASCII data files 447

Graphics Features

20:Graphs.. **459**
    Creating a graph.. 460
    Graphing functions.................................... 464
    Graphing a vector 465
    Graphing more than one expression 470
    Formatting the axes.................................. 472
    Formatting individual curves...................... 478
    Setting default formats............................. 479
    Labeling your graph 481
    Modifying your graph's perspective 484
    Gallery of graphs 489

21:Polar Plots... **493**
    Creating a polar plot 494
    Graphing more than one expression 496
    Formatting the axes.................................. 498
    Formatting individual curves...................... 502
    Setting default formats............................. 504
    Labeling your polar plot 506
    Modifying your polar plot's perspective......... 508
    Gallery of polar plots 512

22:Surface Plots **515**
    Creating a surface plot.............................. 516
    Resizing surface plots............................... 518
    Formatting surface plots 519

23:Contour Plots.. **529**
    Creating a contour plot 530
    Resizing a contour plot 532
    Formatting contour plots 532

24:3D Bar Charts **539**
    Creating a 3D bar chart 540
    Resizing 3D bar charts 541
    Formatting 3D bar charts 542

25:3D Scatter Plots **551**
    Creating a 3D scatter plot.......................... 552
    Resizing scatter plots................................ 553
    Formatting scatter plots 553

26:Vector Field Plots **563**
    Creating a vector field plot 564
    Resizing vector field plots 566
    Formatting vector field plots 567

27:Animation **571**
    Creating an animation clip... 572
    Playing an animation clip 574
    Gallery of animations 576

28:Importing and Exporting Graphics **581**
    Reading and writing graphics files 582
    Creating pictures 587
    Formatting pictures 589

Appendices
A: Reference **593**
    Menu commands... 594
    Function keys 602
    Greek letters.. 603
    Operators 604
    Built-in functions listed alphabetically.......................... 607
    Predefined variables 621
    Suffixes for numbers 622
    Arrow and movement keys.. 623

B: Unit Tables **627**
    SI units 628
    CGS units.. 630
    U.S. customary units 632
    MKS units.. 634
    Alphabetical list of units... 636

C: Creating a User DLL **641**
    Creating dynamically linked libraries............................ 642
    A sample DLL.. 643
    Examining a sample DLL 646
    Handling arrays 649
    Allocating memory.. 649
    Exception handling... 649
    Structure and function definitions................................. 650

Index **657**

What is Mathcad?

Mathcad is the choice of professionals and academics around the world for technical calculations. Mathcad is as versatile and powerful as programming languages, yet it's easy to learn as a spreadsheet. Plus, it is fully wired to take advantage of the Internet and other applications you use every day.

Mathcad lets you type equations as you're used to seeing them, expanded fully on your screen. In a programming language, equations look something like this:

$$x=(-B+SQRT(B**2-4*A*C))/(2*A)$$

In a spreadsheet, equations go into cells looking something like this:

$$+(B1+SQRT(B1*B1-4*A1*C1))/(2*A1)$$

And that's assuming you can see them. Usually all you see is a number.

In Mathcad, the same equation looks the way you might see it on a blackboard or in a reference book. And there is no difficult syntax to learn; you simply point and click and your equations appear:

$$x := \frac{-b + \sqrt{b^2 - 4 \cdot a \cdot c}}{2 \cdot a}$$

But Mathcad equations do much more than look good. You can use them to solve just about any math problem you can think of, symbolically or numerically. You can place text anywhere around them to document your work. You can show how they look with Mathcad's two and three dimensional plots. You can even illustrate your work with graphics taken from another Windows application.

Mathcad comes with its own on-line reference system called the Resource Center. It gives you access to many useful formulas, data values, reference material, and diagrams at the click of a button.

By combining text, graphics and equations in a single worksheet, Mathcad makes it easy to keep track of the most complex calculations. The document formatting and preparation features make it even easier, and by printing the worksheet exactly as it appears on the screen, Mathcad lets you make a permanent and accurate record of your work.

Mathcad features

Mathcad provides hundreds of operators and built-in functions for solving technical problems from the simple to the very complex. Mathcad can be used to perform numeric calculations or to find more general and precise symbolic solutions.

Advanced math functionality

■ Handle real, imaginary, and complex numbers, as well as dimensional values

■ Operators and built-in functions for manipulating numbers, vectors, and matrices

■ Numeric systems solving and minimization

■ Derivatives, integrals, summations, and products

■ Trigonometric, hyperbolic, exponential, and Bessel functions

■ Fast Fourier transforms and inverses

Pro ■ Wavelet transform and inverse

■ Symbolic calculations are "live": make a change, and Mathcad updates the symbolic result

■ Symbolic solutions to individual equations or systems of equations

■ Symbolic integration and differentiation, limits, and series

■ Expand, simplify, and factor expressions

■ Laplace, z, Fourier integral transforms and their inverses

■ Inverse, transpose and determinant of a matrix, and eigenvalues and eigenvectors

■ 20 operators to manipulate arrays, nested arrays and matrices, and 6 functions to find the size and scope of an array

Pro ■ Advanced linear algebra functions, including Cholesky, QR, LU and SV decomposition

Pro ■ 13 ordinary and partial differential equation solvers to solve ordinary differential equations, systems of differential equations, and boundary value problems (*rkfixed* also available in Mathcad 7 Standard)

■ 64 statistical functions support standard and advanced methods of analysis, including parametric and non-parametric hypothesis testing, analysis of variance, and Monte Carlo techniques

■ Compute the frequency distribution for histograms

■ Curve fitting and surface interpolation

■ Data smoothing functions are provided for smoothing time series with either a running median, a Gaussian kernel, or an adaptive linear least-squares method

Improved usability

- New Windows NT and 95 user interface and conventions, including context menus
- Easier equation entry and editing
- OLE2 client and server support
- OLE2 automation support using VBScript
- New ways to format regions.

Smart automatic unit conversion

- Automatically tracks and converts your units
- Complete SI unit system
- MKS, CGS, and U.S. customary units

New data input/output

- Move data in and out of Mathcad quickly
- Data filters for Excel files, MATLAB .mat files, ASCII and more
- *Pro*   Dedicated components for Excel, MATLAB, and Axum

Powerful functional programming (*Mathcad Professional only*)

- Procedural operators for building functional programs
- Define local variables, string variables, complex data structures, and nested arrays
- Looping, recursion, and conditional branching, with Return and Continue statements
- Run-time error-handling with On Error statement
- Program with live symbolic expressions

New MathConnex™ (*Mathcad Professional only*)

- Define and link drag-and-drop MathConnex components, including data input and output tables, Mathcad, Excel, MATLAB, and conditionals
- Integrate and manage data and computations between different applications
- Analyze and debug calculations
- ConnexScript™ math scripting language
- Script embedded OLE components using VBScript or JScript

Intelligent visualization tools

- Interactive 2D and 3D graphs, including X-Y, scatter, bar, polar, vector, contour, and parametric surface

- Trace and zoom, animation, image viewing
- 2D QuickPlot

Extensive formatting and preparation

- Technical spell checker
- Document templates, style sheets, and region formatting
- Include equations in text and highlight equations
- Page setup control and print preview

Innovative Web integration

- Browse "live" math and HTML from within Mathcad seamlessly, using Microsoft Internet Explorer (included for free with Mathcad 7)
- MAPI-based e-mail support
- Define hyperlinks locally or to the Web
- Join the Collaboratory™, a free Internet forum serving the world-wide Mathcad community

Complete extensibility

Pro ■ Set up your own function libraries

Pro ■ User-definable math notation

Pro ■ Create your own functions using C or C++ programming language

Pro ■ Extend functionality with discipline-specific add-on packs

■ Access more 2D and 3D graph and plot types through a hotlink to Axum

New electronic content and guidance

- 300 QuickSheets covering standard analyses and tasks
- Technical reference tables and guide to practical statistics
- Guide to problem solving in Mathcad, excerpted from *The Mathcad Treasury*

Pro ■ Guide to programming in Mathcad, excerpted from *The Mathcad Treasury*

- Regularly updated Web Library of Mathcad worksheets and Electronic Books
- On-line help, tutorial, search-by-subject index, context-sensitive help, *User's Guide*, and free technical support

How to use this User's Guide

This *User's Guide* is organized into the following parts:

Getting Started

This section contains a quick introduction to Mathcad's features and workspace, including on-line resources and on the Internet for getting more out of Mathcad. Be sure to read this section if you are a new Mathcad user.

Editing and Worksheet Features

This section describes how to edit equations and worksheets. It leads you through the basic features of the Mathcad document-style interface. This section covers editing and formatting equations and text, as well as opening, editing, saving, and printing Mathcad worksheets and templates.

Computational Features

This section describes how Mathcad interprets equations and explains Mathcad's computational features: units of measurement, complex numbers, matrices, built-in functions, equation-solving, programming and so on. This section also describes how to do symbolic calculations.

Graphics Features

This section describes how to create and format a variety of two and three dimensional plots. It also describes how to import graphics into Mathcad and how to create an animation clip of anything in your worksheet.

The *User's Guide* ends with some useful reference appendices and a comprehensive index.

As far as possible, the topics in this manual are described independently of each other. This means that once you are familiar with the basic workings of the program, you can just select a topic of interest and read about it.

If you're trying to learn by reproducing screenshots from this *User's Guide*, keep in mind that some of them may be difficult to recreate because they contain equations other than those displayed, because default plot formats and numerical formats are not always used, because they involve random number generation, or because they use data files not available to you.

Notations and conventions

This *User's Guide* uses the following notations and conventions:

Italics represent scalar variable names, function names, and error messages.

`Bold Courier` represents keys you should type.

■ Filled squares indicate steps you should follow.

Bold represents a menu command. It is also used to denote vector and matrix valued variables.

An arrow such as that in "**Change Defaults⇒Text**" indicates a pull-right menu command.

Function keys and other special keys are enclosed in brackets. For example, [↑], [↓], [←], and [→] are the arrow keys on the keyboard. [**F1**], [**F2**], etc., are function keys; [**BkSp**] is the Backspace key for backspacing over characters; [**Delete**] is the Delete key for deleting characters to the right; and [**Tab**] is the Tab key.

[**Ctrl**], [**Shift**], and [**Alt**] are the Control, Shift, and Alt keys. When two keys are shown together, for example, [**Ctrl**]**V**, press and hold down the first key, and then press the second key.

The symbol [↵] and [**Enter**] refer to the same key.

When this *User's Guide* shows spaces in an equation, you need not type the spaces. Mathcad automatically spaces the equation correctly.

A Mathcad window takes on a variety of appearances depending on how you've configured the Math Palette, other operator palettes, the Toolbar, and the Format Bar. To maximize available space, nearly all screenshots in this *User's Guide* are taken with these elements hidden.

Pro

This *User's Guide* applies to Mathcad Professional, Mathcad Standard and Mathcad Student, as well as certain specialized editions of Mathcad. If you're not using Mathcad Professional, certain features described in this *User's Guide* will not be available to you. The word "*Pro*" appears:

■ In the page margin, as it does above, whenever a section in a chapter describes a feature or a function that is unique to Mathcad Professional.

■ In the page footer, whenever all features described in that chapter are unique to Mathcad Professional.

Getting Started

Chapter 1
The Basics

This chapter describes everything you need to get started working with Mathcad. The following sections make up this chapter:

First principles

Mathcad's design and interface.

What you can do with Mathcad

Starting Mathcad.

Working with windows

How to scroll a window, how to move and resize windows, and how to open several worksheets at once.

A simple calculation

Calculating with Mathcad.

Definitions and variables

Creating simple Mathcad equations.

Entering text

Adding notes and labels to a worksheet.

Regions and menus

How equations, text, and plots make up a worksheet; Mathcad's menu commands.

Iterative calculations

Using range variables to repeat an equation for several values.

Graphs

Building a simple two-dimensional plot.

Saving, printing, and quitting

The Save, Print, and Exit commands from the File menu.

First principles

Mathcad looks simple, and it is. It was created according to basic design principles to make it powerful, flexible, and easy to use. In Mathcad:

- **Everything appears in familiar math notation.** If there's a standard mathematical way to show an equation, operation, or graph, Mathcad uses it.

- **What you see is what you get.** There is no hidden information; everything appears on the screen. When you print, the output looks just like the screen display.

- **To create simple expressions, just type them.** Mathcad uses the standard keys for standard mathematical operations.

- **Typing aids make equations easier to enter.** There are palettes for most mathematical operators and symbols.

- **Fill in the blanks.** Mathcad guides you through the creation of plots, integrals, and other mathematical expressions by laying down the framework and letting you fill in the blanks.

- **Calculation features are modular.** If you don't want to use a feature—like complex numbers, units, or matrices—you can just pretend it isn't there.

- **The numerical algorithms are robust, standard, and predictable**. Mathcad's numerical algorithms for features like integrals, matrix inversion, and equation solving are reliable, standard methods.

- **OLE support**. Mathcad is an OLE2 application, providing drag and drop support of Mathcad objects into applications like Microsoft Word, in-place activation of Mathcad objects in client applications, and enhanced support for embedded OLE objects in Mathcad worksheets.

- **Exchange data with other applications.** Mathcad gives you easy-to-use tools to exchange data with spreadsheets, graphing packages, and other calculation applications.

- **On-line help.** Pressing [F1] brings up an extensive on-line help system. Click on error messages, operators and functions and press [F1] to display the relevant help screen. There's no need to search for the topic you're interested in. The *User's Guide* includes more detail on all the features, with step-by-step instructions and illustrative examples. At the back of the *User's Guide* is a complete cross-referenced index.

- **Collaboration features.** If you're connected to an electronic mail system compatible with Microsoft Mail, mail worksheets to colleagues from right within Mathcad. And you have access to MathSoft's Collaboratory server, a unique Web-based resource where you can exchange text messages, upload and download Mathcad files, and connect to a community of Mathcad users.

- **Resource Center.** A collection of Mathcad worksheets in an interactive, searchable Electronic Book, with links to resources on the World Wide Web. The Resource

Center includes an Overview, Tutorial, Reference Tables, QuickSheets—prefab working templates for completing common mathematical tasks, ready for customization and dragging into your own worksheets—and Practical Statistics, an overview of hypothesis testing and data analysis in Mathcad. Mathcad Professional includes in-depth sections on Solving and Programming drawn from *The Mathcad Treasury*, our best-selling Electronic Book. Visit MathSoft's home page (`www.mathsoft.com`) directly from the Resource Center, or browse to any other resources on the World Wide Web.

This chapter provides a quick introduction to Mathcad and demonstrates a few more advanced features like iterative calculation and plotting. After you read this chapter, you'll have enough information to begin to solve your own problems in Mathcad. The rest of this *User's Guide* describes all the features in detail, so you can learn more about any selected topic. For more information about on-line resources like the Collaboratory, Resource Center, and on-line Help system, see Chapter 2, "On-line Resources."

What you can do with Mathcad

Mathcad combines the live document interface of a spreadsheet with the WYSIWYG interface of a word processor. With Mathcad, you can typeset equations on the screen exactly the way you see them in a book. But Mathcad equations do more than look good on the screen. You can use them to actually do math.

Like a spreadsheet, as soon as you make a change anywhere in your worksheet, Mathcad goes straight to work, updating results and redrawing graphs. With Mathcad, you can easily read data from a file and do mathematical chores ranging from adding up a column of numbers to evaluating integrals and derivatives, inverting matrices and more. In fact, just about anything you can think of doing with math, you can do with Mathcad.

Like a word processor, Mathcad comes with a WYSIWYG interface, multiple fonts, and the ability to print whatever you see on the screen. This, combined with Mathcad's live document interface, makes it easy to produce up-to-date, publication quality reports.

Starting Mathcad

For information on system requirements and how to install Mathcad on your computer, see the instructions that accompanied your installation media.

When you start Mathcad, you'll see the window shown in Figure 1-1. You can view or hide the Math Palette, the Toolbar, and the Format Bar by choosing corresponding commands from the **View** menu.

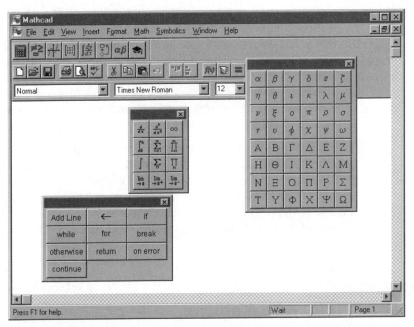

Figure 1-1: Mathcad Professional window with some math palettes displayed.

You can place equations anywhere in the Mathcad worksheet. To get to places not visible in the window, use the scroll bars as you would in any Windows application.

Each button in the Math Palette opens a palette of operators or symbols. You can insert many operators, Greek letters, and plot regions by clicking on the buttons found on these palettes. From left to right, these palettes are:

Button   Opens palette...

Common arithmetic operators.

Equal signs for evaluation and definition. Boolean expressions.

Various two and three dimensional plot types.

Matrix and vector operators.

Derivatives, integrals, limits and iterated sums and products.

Programming constructs (*Mathcad Professional only*).

Greek letters.

Symbolic keywords.

The Toolbar is the strip of buttons shown just below the Math Palette in Figure 1-1. Many menu commands can be accessed more quickly by clicking a button on the Toolbar. To learn what a button does, click on the button and read the message line. If you don't want to activate the button, move the pointer away without releasing the mouse button. If you just want to know what the button does, let the pointer rest on the button momentarily. You'll see some text beside the pointer telling you what that button does.

The Format Bar is shown immediately under the Toolbar in Figure 1-1. This contains scrolling lists and buttons used to specify font characteristics in equations and text.

To conserve screen space, you can show or hide each of these elements individually by choosing the appropriate command from the **View** menu. Throughout the figures in this *User's Guide*, the symbol palette, the toolbar, and the format bar have all been hidden to allow more space for examples.

You can also detach each of these window elements and drag them around your window. To do so, place the mouse pointer anywhere other than on a button or a text box. Then press and hold down the mouse button and drag. You'll find that the toolbar and the symbol palette will rearrange themselves appropriately depending on where you drag them. The format bar, on the other hand, will retain its shape no matter where you drag it. And Mathcad remembers where you left your palettes the next time you open the application.

Working with windows

When you start Mathcad you'll open up a window on a Mathcad *worksheet*. There are times when a Mathcad worksheet cannot be displayed in its entirety because the window is too small. To bring unseen portions of a worksheet into view, you can:

■ Use the scroll bars and arrow keys to move around the worksheet.

■ Make the window larger.

■ Choose **Zoom** from the **View** menu and choose a number smaller than 100%.

Mathcad windows work very much like those of most Windows applications. If you've worked with Windows applications before, much of the material in this section will already be familiar to you.

There are several ways to move the window from one part of a worksheet to another:

■ Move the mouse pointer and click the mouse button. The cursor jumps from wherever it was to wherever you clicked.

■ Use the arrow keys [↑], [↓], [→], and [←] to move the crosshair up, down, right and left respectively. Mathcad scrolls the window whenever necessary.

■ Click in the scroll bar to position the scroll box.

■ With the mouse pointer on the scroll box, press and hold down the mouse button and move the mouse to drag the scroll box to another part of the scroll bar.

■ Click on the arrows at the ends of the scroll bars to nudge the scroll box in the directions indicated by the arrows.

■ Press [PgUp] and [PgDn] to move the cursor up and down by about one fourth the height of the window. You can also use [Ctrl][PgUp] and [Ctrl][PgDn] to move the cursor up and down by about 80% of the height of the window.

■ Press [Ctrl][Home] to go to the first region of the worksheet, and [Ctrl][End] to go to the last region of a worksheet.

■ Press [Shift][PgUp] and [Shift][PgDn] to position the preceding or following pagebreak at the top of the window.

■ Choose **Go to Page** from the **Edit** menu and enter the page number you want to go to in the dialog box below. When you click "OK," Mathcad places the top of the page you specify at the top edge of the window.

The position of the scroll box within the scroll bar serves as a rough guide to the position of the window relative to the rest of the worksheet. If the top of the window is a third of the way down from the top of the worksheet, the scroll box will be about a third of the way down the vertical scroll bar. The page number for whatever page is visible in the window is shown on the message line at the bottom of the window.

Multiple windows

You can have as many windows open as your available system resources will allow. This allows you to work on several worksheets at once by simply clicking the mouse in whatever document window you want to work in. If the worksheet you want to work in is buried behind many other windows, pull down the **Window** menu and choose its name.

To open a new document window, choose **New** from the **File** menu. To open a window into a previously saved worksheet, choose **Open** from the **File** menu. For more information about opening new worksheets and templates, see Chapter 4, "Worksheet Management."

A simple calculation

Although Mathcad can perform sophisticated mathematics, you can just as easily use it as a simple calculator. To try your first calculation, follow these steps:

- Click anywhere in the worksheet. You see a small crosshair. Anything you type appears at the crosshair.

- Type `15-8/104.5=`. When you press the equals sign, Mathcad computes and shows the result.

$$15 - \frac{8}{104.5} = 14.923$$

This calculation demonstrates the way Mathcad works:

- Mathcad shows equations as you might see them in a book or on a blackboard, expanded fully in two dimensions. Mathcad sizes fraction bars, brackets, and other symbols to display equations the same way you would write them on paper.

- Mathcad understands which operation to perform first. In this example, Mathcad knew to perform the division before the subtraction and displayed the equation accordingly.

- As soon as you type the equal sign, Mathcad returns the result. Unless you specify otherwise, Mathcad processes each equation as you enter it. See the section "Controlling calculations" in Chapter 7 to learn how to change this.

- As you type each operator (in this case, – and /), Mathcad shows a small rectangle called a *placeholder*. Placeholders hold spaces open for numbers or expressions not yet typed. As soon as you type a number, it replaces the placeholder in the equation. The placeholder that appears at the end of the equation is used for unit conversions. Its use is discussed in the section "Displaying units of results" in Chapter 9.

Once an equation is on the screen, you can edit it by clicking in the appropriate spot and typing new letters, digits, or operators. You can type many operators and Greek letters by clicking in the symbol palette located just below the menu bar. Chapter 3, "Editing Equations," explains in detail how to edit Mathcad equations.

Definitions and variables

Mathcad's power and versatility quickly become apparent once you begin to use *variables* and *functions*. By defining variables and functions, you can link equations together and use intermediate results in further calculations.

The following examples show how to define and use several variables.

Defining variables

To clear the previous equation and define a variable *t*, follow these steps:

■ Click in the equation you just typed and press [**Space**] until the entire expression is held between the two editing lines. Then choose **Cut** from the **Edit** menu.

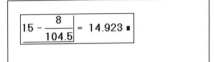

■ Now begin defining *t*. Type **t :** (the letter *t*, followed by a colon). Mathcad shows the colon as the definition symbol **:=**.

■ Type **10** in the empty placeholder to complete the definition for *t*.

If you make a mistake, click on the equation and press [**Space**] until the entire expression is between the two editing lines, just as you did earlier. Then delete it by choosing **Cut** from the **Edit** menu.

These steps show the form for typing any definition:

■ Type the variable name to be defined.

■ Type the colon key to insert the definition symbol.

■ Type the value to be assigned to the variable. The value can be a single number, as in the example shown here, or a more complicated combination of numbers and previously defined variables.

Mathcad worksheets read from top to bottom and left to right. Once you have defined a variable like *t*, you can compute with it anywhere *below and to the right* of the equation that defines it.

Now enter another definition.

■ Press [↵]. This moves the crosshair below the first equation.

■ To define *acc* as –9.8, type: `acc:-9.8`. Then press [↵] again.

Figure 1-2 shows the two definitions you just entered.

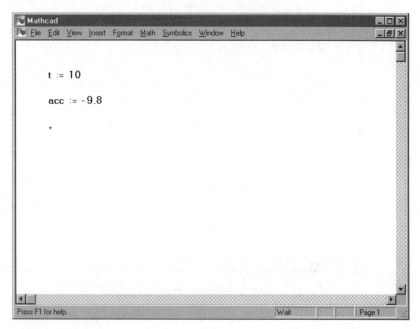

Figure 1-2: Equations to define acc and t.

Calculating results

Now that the variables *acc* and *t* are defined, you can use them in other expressions.

■ Click the mouse a few lines below the two definitions (see Figure 1-2).

■ Type `acc/2[Space]*t^2`. The caret symbol (`^`) represents raising to a power, the asterisk (`*`) is multiplication, and the slash (`/`) represents division.

■ Press the equal sign (=).

This equation calculates the distance traveled by a falling body in time *t* with acceleration *acc*. When you enter the equation, Mathcad returns the result as shown in Figure 1-3. The window now contains two *definitions*, which define variables, and one *evaluation*, which computes a result.

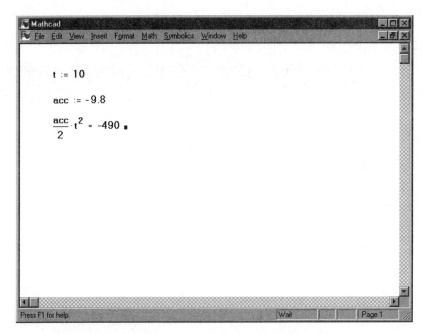

Figure 1-3: Calculating with variables.

Mathcad updates results as soon as you make changes. For example, If you click on the 10 on your screen and change it to some other number, Mathcad changes the result as soon as you press [⏎] or click outside of the equation.

Entering text

Mathcad handles text as easily as it does equations, so you can make notes about the calculations you are doing. To begin typing text, click in an empty space and do any one of the following: choose **Text Region** from the **Insert** menu, press the double-quote key (`"`), or click on the text region button on the toolbar.

Here's how to enter some text:

■ Click in the blank space to the right of the equations you entered. You'll see a small crosshair.

■ Press `"` to tell Mathcad that you're about to enter some text. Mathcad changes the crosshair into a vertical line called the insertion point. Characters you type appear behind this line. A box surrounds the insertion point, indicating you are now in a text region. This box is called a text box. It will grow as you enter text.

■ Type `Equations of motion`

Mathcad shows the text in the worksheet, next to the equations (Figure 1-4).

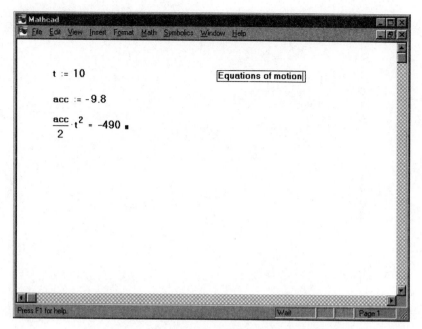

Figure 1-4: Entering text. Notice the text box surrounding it.

To enter a second line of text, just press [↵] and continue typing:

■ Press [↵].

■ Then type `for falling body under gravity.`

■ Click in a different spot in the worksheet or press [Shift][↵] to move out of the text region. The text box will disappear once you have done this. Don't use the [↵] key. If you press [↵], Mathcad will insert a line break in the text instead of leaving the text region.

Figure 1-5 shows the worksheet with two lines of text and the cursor outside the text region. Since you are outside the text region, the cursor appears as a small cross, and the text box is no longer visible.

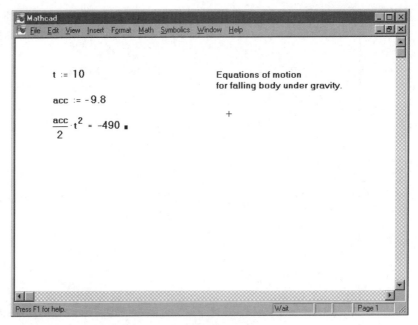

Figure 1-5: After clicking outside of a text region.

You can set the width of a text region and change the font, size, and style of the text in it. For more information on how to do these things, see Chapter 5, "Text."

Regions and menus

Mathcad lets you enter equations and text anywhere in the worksheet. Each equation or piece of text is a *region*. Mathcad creates an invisible rectangle to hold each region. A Mathcad worksheet is a collection of such regions. To see these regions, choose **Regions** from the **View** menu. Mathcad will display blank space in gray and leave any regions in the default color. To turn the blank space back into the default color, choose **Regions** from the **View** menu again.

To start a new region, you must first click in blank space. This leaves a small crosshair wherever you clicked the mouse. To start an equation, just start typing anywhere you put the crosshair, or choose **Math Region** from the **Insert** menu. To create a text region, first choose **Text Region** from the **Insert** menu. Whichever you do, Mathcad will place a box around the region you're working with.

In addition to equations and text, Mathcad supports a variety of plot regions. Plots are introduced in "Graphs" on page 24.

Iterative calculations

Mathcad can do repeated or iterative calculations as easily as individual calculations. Mathcad uses a special variable called a *range variable* to perform iteration.

Range variables take on a range of values, such as all the integers from 0 to 10. Whenever a range variable appears in a Mathcad equation, Mathcad calculates the equation not just once, but once for each value of the range variable.

This section describes how to use range variables to do iterative calculations.

Creating a range variable

To compute equations for a range of values, first create a range variable. In the problem shown in Figure 1-5, for example, you can compute results for a range of values of *t* from 10 to 20 in steps of 1. To do so, follow these steps:

- First, change *t* into a range variable by editing its definition. Click on the **10** in the equation **t := 10**. The insertion point should be next to the 10 as shown on the right.

  $$t := 10$$

- Type **,11**. This tells Mathcad that the next number in the range will be 11.

  $$t := 10, 11$$

- Type **;20**. This tells Mathcad that the last number in the range will be 20. Mathcad shows the semicolon as a pair of dots.

  $$t := 10, 11 .. 20$$

- Now click outside the equation for *t*. Mathcad begins to compute with *t* defined as a range variable. Since *t* now takes on eleven different values, there must also be eleven different answers. These are displayed in the table shown in Figure 1-6. You may have to resize your window or scroll down to see the whole table.

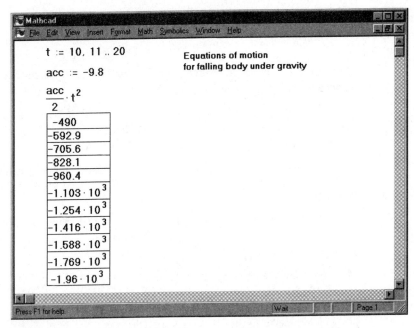

Figure 1-6: Generating a table of answers with a range variable.

Defining a function

You can gain additional flexibility by defining functions. Here's how to add a function definition to your worksheet:

- First delete the table. To do so, click anywhere in the table press [**Space**] until you've enclosed everything between the two editing lines.

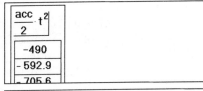

- Now define the function *d(t)* by typing **d(t):**

- Complete the definition by typing this expression: **1600+acc/2[Space]*t^2[⏎]**

$$d(t) := 1600 + \frac{acc}{2} \cdot t^2$$

The definition you just typed defines a function. The function name is *d*, and the argument of the function is *t*. You can use this function to evaluate the above expression for different values of *t*. To do so, simply replace *t* with an appropriate number. For example:

■ To evaluate the function at the value 3.5, type **d (3 . 5) =**. Mathcad returns the correct value as shown on the right.

d(3.5) = ~~939.975~~
            1539.975

■ To evaluate the function once for each value of *t* you defined earlier, click below the other equations and type **d (t) =**.

Mathcad shows a table of values (Figure 1-7). The first two values, $1.11 \cdot 10^3$ and $1.007 \cdot 10^3$, are in exponential (powers of 10) notation.

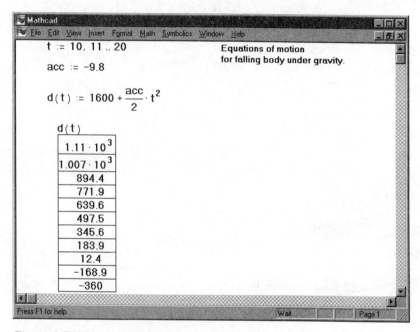

Figure 1-7: Using a function to return a table of answers.

Formatting a result

You can set the display format for any number Mathcad calculates and displays. This means changing the number of decimal places shown, changing exponential notation to ordinary decimal notation, and so on.

For example, here's how to change the table in Figure 1-7 so that none of the numbers in it are displayed in exponential notation:

■ Click on the table with the mouse.

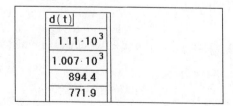

- Choose **Number** from the **Format** menu. You see the Format Number dialog box. This box contains settings that affect how results are displayed, including the number of decimal places, the use of exponential notation, and whether the number is shown in decimal, octal, or hexadecimal. The option button beside "Set for current region only" should be filled in. This indicates that whatever you do in this dialog box affects only the result you've selected.

- The default setting for Exponential Threshold is 3. This means that only numbers greater than or equal to 10^3 are displayed in exponential notation. Click to the right of the 3, press [**BkSp**] and type **6**.

- Click the "OK" button. The equation changes to reflect the new result format— 1110 is no longer shown in exponential notation.

d(t)
1110
1007.1
894.4
771.9
639.6
497.5

When you format a result, only the display of the result is affected. Mathcad maintains full precision internally.

Graphs

Mathcad can show both two-dimensional Cartesian and polar graphs, contour plots, surface plots, and a variety of other three-dimensional plots. These are all examples of *plot regions*.

This section describes how to create a simple two-dimensional graph showing the points calculated in the previous section.

Creating a graph

To create a graph in Mathcad, click in blank space where you want the graph to appear and choose **Graph⇒X-Y Plot** from the **Insert** menu. An empty graph appears with placeholders on the *x*-axis and *y*-axis for the expressions to be graphed. X-Y and polar plots are ordinarily driven by range variables you define: Mathcad graphs one point for each value of the range variable used in the graph. In most cases you will enter the range variable, or an expression depending on the range variable, on the *x*-axis of the plot. But the QuickPlot feature in Mathcad lets you plot expressions even when you don't specify the range variable directly in the plot.

For example, here's how to create a QuickPlot of the function *d(t)* defined in the previous section:

- Position the crosshair and type **d(t)**. Make sure the editing lines remain displayed on the expression.

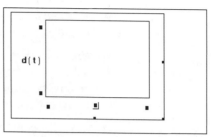

- Now choose **Graph⇒X-Y Plot** from the **Insert** menu, or click the X-Y Plot button on the Graphing palette. Mathcad displays the frame of the graph.

- Click anywhere outside the graph. Mathcad calculates and graphs the points as shown in Figure 1-8. A sample line appears under the "*d(t)*." This helps you identify the different curves when you plot more than one function. Unless you specify otherwise, Mathcad draws straight lines between the points and fills in the missing axis limits.

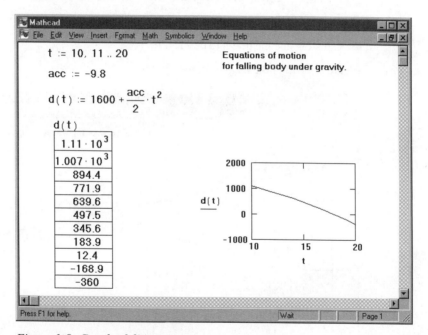

Figure 1-8: Graph of d(t) versus t.

For detailed information on creating and formatting graphs, see Chapter 20, "Graphs."

Resizing a graph

The graph shown in Figure 1-8 is the default size. It's easy to make a graph in Mathcad any size you want: just select the graph and stretch it to the desired size.

To resize a graph, follow these steps:

■ Click the mouse just outside the graphics region. This anchors one corner of the selection rectangle.

■ Press and hold down the mouse button. With the button still held, drag the mouse toward the plot region. A dashed selection rectangle emerges from the anchor point.

■ When the selection rectangle just enclos- es the graphics region, let go of the mouse button. The dashed rectangle will turn into a solid rectangle with handles.

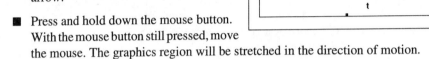

■ Move the mouse pointer to any of the handles. It will change to a double-headed arrow.

■ Press and hold down the mouse button. With the mouse button still pressed, move the mouse. The graphics region will be stretched in the direction of motion.

■ Once the graphics region is the right size, let go of the mouse button.

■ Click outside the graph to deselect it.

Figure 1-9 shows the result: a larger graph.

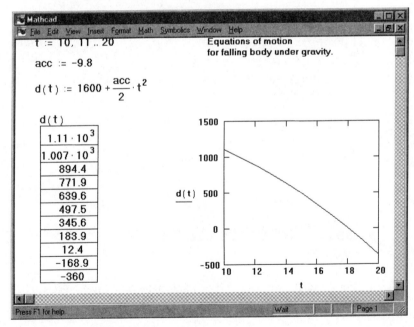

Figure 1-9: New graph, after resizing.

Formatting a graph

The graph in Figure 1-9 still has the default characteristics: numbered linear axes, no grid lines, and points connected with solid lines. You can change these characteristics by *formatting* the graph, just as you earlier formatted a number.

To format the graph, follow these steps:

■ Double-click on the graph to bring up the appropriate dialog box. This box contains settings for all available plot format options. To learn more about these settings, see Chapter 20, "Graphs."

■ Click on the Traces tab in the dialog box to see the correct page.

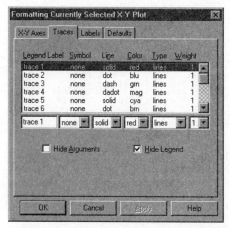

■ Click on "trace 1" in the scrolling list under "Legend Label." Mathcad places the current settings for trace 1 in the boxes under the corresponding columns of the scrolling list.

■ Click on the arrow under the "Type" column to see a drop-down list of trace types.

■ Choose "bar" from this drop-down list by clicking on it.

■ Click on the "OK" button to show the result of changing the setting. Mathcad shows the graph as a bar chart instead of connecting the points with lines (Figure 1-10). Note that the sample line under the $d(t)$ now has a bar on top of it.

■ Click outside the graph to deselect it.

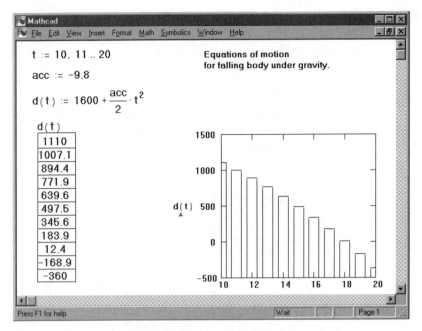

Figure 1-10: Graph formatted as a bar chart.

Saving, printing, and quitting

Once you've created a worksheet, you will probably want to save or print it. This section explains how to save and print in Mathcad.

Saving a worksheet

To save the file,

■ Choose **Save** from the **File** menu or click on the disk icon in the toolbar. If the file has never been saved before, the **Save As** dialog box appears. Otherwise, Mathcad saves the file with no further prompting.

■ Type the name of the file in the text box provided. By default, Mathcad saves the file either in the folder in which Mathcad is installed or in the folder from which you most recently opened a worksheet during the current session. To save to another folder, locate the folder using the Save As dialog box.

By default Mathcad saves the file in Mathcad (MCD) format, but you have the option of saving in RTF format to be able to open the file in a word processor. You may also save the file as a template for future Mathcad worksheets, or in a format compatible with earlier Mathcad versions. For more information on saving and opening files, see Chapter 4, "Worksheet Management."

Printing

To print, choose **Print** from the **File** menu or click on the printer icon in the toolbar. You may preview the printed page by choosing **Print Preview** from the **File** menu

For more information on printing, see Chapter 4, "Worksheet Management."

Quitting Mathcad

When you're done using Mathcad, choose **Exit** from the **File** menu. Mathcad closes down all its windows and returns you to the Desktop. If you've made any changes in your worksheets since the last time you saved, a dialog box appears asking if you want to discard or save your changes. If you have moved the toolbar, font bar, or math palettes, Mathcad remembers their locations for the next time you open the application.

Chapter 1 The Basics

Chapter 2
On-line Resources

Mathcad has a full on-line Help system, but with Mathcad you can also access mathematical and technical content located on your computer or on the World Wide Web. Mathcad gives you a direct link to the *Collaboratory*, a unique Web-based messaging system that connects you to the community of Mathcad users. Mathcad also comes with the *Resource Center*, a Mathcad Electronic Book containing an extensive collection of tutorials, examples, and reference information, with links to further resources on the World Wide Web. Additional Mathcad Electronic Books are available from MathSoft or your local software distributor.

The following sections make up this chapter:

Internet access in Mathcad

What you need to connect to Web-based resources from within Mathcad.

The Collaboratory

How to retrieve and post files to the Collaboratory, a Web-based service for communicating with other Mathcad users.

Resource Center

The Electronic Book that is both a library of reference content on your desktop and a gateway to resources on the World Wide Web.

Using Electronic Books

Opening, navigating, and annotating Mathcad Electronic Books.

Help and context sensitive help

On-line Help on product features.

Internet access in Mathcad

A number of the on-line Mathcad resources described in this chapter are located not on your own computer or on a local network but on the Internet, the global network that includes the World Wide Web. When you choose **Collaboratory** from the **File** menu, for example, you are requesting information from a file server on the World Wide Web.

To access these resources on the Internet you need:

■ Networking software to support a 32-bit Internet (TCP/IP) application. Such software is usually part of the networking services of your operating system; see your operating system documentation for details.

■ A direct or dial-up connection to the Internet, with appropriate hardware and communications software. Consult your system administrator or Internet access provider for more information about your Internet connection.

Before accessing the Internet through Mathcad, you also need to know whether you must use a proxy server to access the Internet. If you use a proxy, ask your system administrator for the proxy machine's name or Internet Protocol (IP) address, as well as the port number (socket) you use to connect to it. You may specify separate proxy servers for each of the three Internet protocols understood by Mathcad: HTTP, for the World Wide Web; FTP, an older file transfer protocol; and GOPHER, an older protocol for access to information archives. Once you have this information, choose **Internet Setup** from the **File** menu. Then enter this information in the appropriate places in the Internet Setup dialog box.

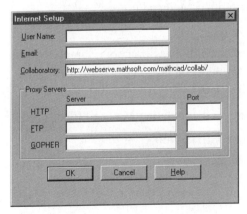

The remaining information in the Internet Setup dialog box was entered at the time you installed Mathcad, but you may modify it here at any time:

■ Your name, which will appear on any Collaboratory messages you send from within Mathcad.

■ Your Internet electronic mail address, which will appear on any Collaboratory messages you send from within Mathcad.

■ The URL for the Collaboratory server you contact when you choose **Collaboratory** from the **File** menu.

The Collaboratory

If you have a dial-up or direct Internet connection, you can access the MathSoft Collaboratory server. The Collaboratory is an interactive World Wide Web service that puts you in contact with a community of Mathcad users. The Collaboratory consists of a group of forums where you can contribute files, post messages, download files contributed by other users, and read messages posted by other Mathcad users. You'll find that the Collaboratory combines some of the best features of a computer bulletin board or an on-line news group with the convenience of sharing worksheets or other files created using Mathcad.

To access the Collaboratory, choose **Collaboratory** from the **File** menu. Mathcad displays the Collaboratory dialog box as shown in Figure 2-1.

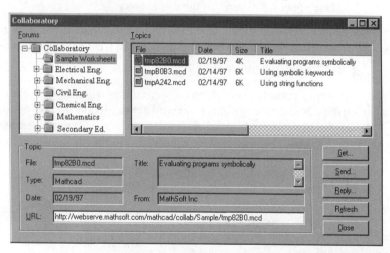

Figure 2-1: Opening the Collaboratory from Mathcad. Available forums and topics will change over time.

■ **Forums and Topics:** You can post and retrieve messages from the available forums, which will evolve over time. Each forum contains one or more topics. Click on a forum name to display the available topics in the "Topics" scrolling list to the right. If a title is indented, it's a reply to the previous topic.

■ **Topic Information:** When you click on a topic, information about it displays in the lower part of the Collaboratory dialog box. You'll see the name of the file, the format of the file, the date it was posted, its location on the Collaboratory server, the title given to it by its author, and the author's name.

- **Buttons:** The "Get," "Send," and "Reply" buttons are used to retrieve, post, and reply to files on the Collaboratory, respectively. You can post and retrieve a worksheet, another type of file, or a text message. Use the "Refresh" button to redisplay the list of topics and forums. The "Close" button closes the Collaboratory dialog box.

Note: MathSoft maintains the Collaboratory server as a free service, open to all in the Mathcad community. Be sure to read the Collaboratory Agreement posted in the top level of the Collaboratory for important legal information and disclaimers. Although the Collaboratory is monitored by MathSoft, it is not designed for product technical support. If you need technical support, see the contact information that accompanied your Mathcad installation media.

Opening a worksheet or other file stored in the Collaboratory

To open a worksheet or other file stored in the Collaboratory:

- Choose **Collaboratory** from the **File** menu.

- Click on the appropriate forum from the list of forums in the upper left corner of the dialog box.

- Once you've selected a forum, click on one of the topics shown in the scrolling list at the upper right corner of the dialog box.

- You'll see some additional information on that topic in the lower half of the dialog box. Examine this information to see if you want to go ahead and open the topic.

- Click the "Get" button.

Depending on the type of file, one of three things will happen. If the file is text, you'll see the text in a message box as shown below. Use the "Reply" button to reply to the message. If the file is a worksheet it will open in its own worksheet window. If the file is binary, you'll be prompted for a place to save the file.

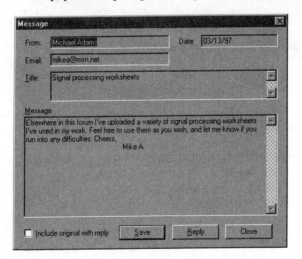

Sending a worksheet to the Collaboratory

If you want to send a worksheet you've created, or any other file, to the Collaboratory:

■ Choose **Collaboratory** from the **File** menu.

■ Check the list of forums in the upper left corner of the dialog box. Click on the forum to which you want to send your file.

■ Click the "Send" button.

■ Click on the "Send my Current File" if the worksheet you'd like to post is currently open. If it isn't, click on the "Send Another File" button.

■ Enter the path to the file in the File text box. Alternatively, click the "Browse" button to locate the file.

■ Enter a title in the Title text box. This is the text that will appear whenever anyone clicks on this file.

■ Click the "Send" button.

You'll see your file appear in the Topics window on the upper right corner of the dialog box. The "From:" text box will contain your "User Name" as it is specified in the Internet Setup dialog box. Choose **Internet Setup** from the **File** menu to change the user name as described in the section "Internet access in Mathcad" on page 32.

Sending a text message to the Collaboratory

If you'd like to write a text message and send it to the Collaboratory:

■ Choose **Collaboratory** from the **File** menu.

■ Check the list of forums in the upper left corner of the dialog box. Click on the forum to which you want to send your text message.

■ Click the "Send" button to see the Send dialog box.

■ Click on the "Send a Message" button.

■ Enter a title in the Title text box. This is the text that will appear whenever anyone scrolls through the Topics list of the forum.

■ Type your message into the Message text box, as shown below:

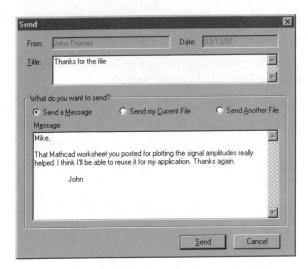

■ Click the "Send" button.

You'll see your message appear in the Topics window on the upper right corner of the dialog box.

Deleting a topic from the Collaboratory

If you posted a file or a message to the Collaboratory but would like to remove it:

■ Choose **Collaboratory** from the **File** menu.

■ Check the list of forums in the upper left corner of the dialog box. Click on the forum containing the topic you want to delete.

■ Once you've selected the forum, click on the topic you want to delete. The topics are in the scrolling list at the upper right corner of the dialog box.

■ Press [**Del**].

After you confirm that you want to delete the topic, you'll see your topic disappear from the Topics window on the upper right corner of the dialog box. Note that if your file or message has received any responses, you won't be able to delete it.

Opening a worksheet from another World Wide Web server

If you know the address of a Mathcad worksheet on the World Wide Web, you can use the Collaboratory dialog box to open that worksheet:

■ Choose **Collaboratory** from the **File** menu.

■ In the "URL" box at the bottom, delete any address that you see and then type the URL of the worksheet you want to open. The URL is typically of the form
`http://some.server.name/directories/worksheet.mcd`

- Click the "Get" button.

The Mathcad worksheet will appear in its own worksheet window.

See "Web browsing in the Resource Center" on page 38 for a more generic method of browsing the Web from within Mathcad.

Resource Center

If you learn best from examples, want information you can put to work immediately in your Mathcad worksheets, or wish to access any page on the World Wide Web from within Mathcad, choose **Resource Center** from the **Help** menu. You will see a Mathcad Electronic Book in a custom window with its own toolbar, as shown in Figure 2-2.

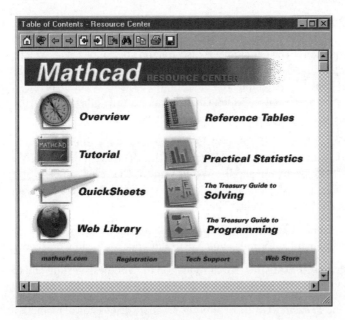

Figure 2-2: Resource Center for Mathcad Professional. Topics available in Mathcad Standard or other editions differ slightly.

The Resource Center offers:

- A comprehensive Mathcad Electronic Book containing a collection of tutorials, examples, and reference information. Simply drag and drop information from the Resource Center into your own Mathcad worksheets.

- Immediate access to Mathcad worksheets on MathSoft's World Wide Web site or other Internet sites.

■ Access to the full Web-browsing functionality of Microsoft Internet Explorer from within the Mathcad environment.

Browsing the Resource Center

The Resource Center is a *Mathcad Electronic Book*—a hyperlinked collection of Mathcad worksheets. As in other hypertext systems, you move around a Mathcad Electronic Book just by clicking on icons or underlined text. You can also use the toolbar buttons at the top of the Resource Center window. For more information about using the toolbar buttons to move around an Electronic Book and copying information from the Electronic Book to your worksheets, see "Using Electronic Books" on page 40.

Here are brief descriptions of the topics available in the Resource Center:

■ **Overview**. A high level introduction to Mathcad's computational features.

■ **Tutorial**. Step-by-step guidance for new users on creating math, text, and graphics regions.

■ **QuickSheets**. A collection of hundreds of pre-made Mathcad worksheets, from factoring a number or computing a mortgage payment to solving a system of equations. The QuickSheets also contain special pages on which you can save any text or math you want quick access to. Look for "Personal QuickSheets" in the table of contents. Anything you enter in these sheets is automatically saved when you close the Resource Center. Changes made to any other pages in the Resource Center are discarded when you close the Resource Center.

■ **Web Library**. If you have Internet access, jump directly to a growing library of Mathcad worksheets and Electronic Books on the World Wide Web. See "Opening a worksheet from another World Wide Web server" on page 36 for information about accessing other Mathcad worksheets on the Web. See also "Web browsing in the Resource Center" below.

■ **Reference Tables**. Look up physical constants, chemical and physical data, and mathematical formulas you can use in your Mathcad worksheets.

■ **Practical Statistics**. An introduction to hypothesis testing and data analysis in Mathcad.

■ **The Treasury Guide to Solving**. In-depth discussion of methods to solve equations in Mathcad, excerpted from *The Mathcad Treasury*, the best-selling Mathcad Electronic Book by Paul R. Lorczak.

Pro   ■ **The Treasury Guide to Programming**. In-depth discussion of programming operators and programming techniques in Mathcad Professional, also excerpted from *The Mathcad Treasury*.

Web browsing in the Resource Center

If you have Internet access, the Web Library button in the Resource Center connects you to a collection of Mathcad worksheets on the World Wide Web. You can also use the Resource Center window to browse to any location on the World Wide Web and open standard Hypertext Mark-up Language (HTML) and other Web pages, like those you can view with a standard Web-browsing application, in addition to Mathcad worksheets. You have the convenience of accessing all of the rich information resources of the Internet without leaving the Mathcad environment.

To browse to any World Wide Web page from within the Resource Center window:

- Click on the *Web Toolbar* button (the one that looks like a globe) on the Resource Center toolbar. As shown below, an additional toolbar with an "Address" line appears below the Resource Center toolbar to indicate that you are now in a Web-browsing mode:

- In the "Address" box type a Uniform Resource Locator (URL) for a document on the World Wide Web. To visit the MathSoft home page, for example, type `http://www.mathsoft.com/`. If you have Internet access and the server is available, you will load the requested page in your Resource Center window, as shown in Figure 2-3. Under Windows NT 3.51, you will launch a Web browser instead.

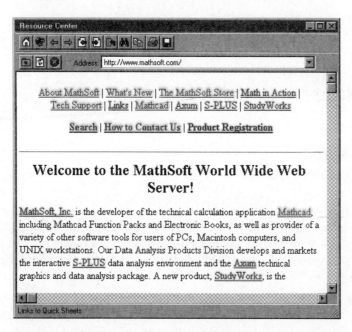

Figure 2-3: Browsing the World Wide Web from within the Resource Center.

The remaining buttons on the Web Toolbar let you bookmark the page for a later visit. reload the current page, and interrupt the current file transfer. When you are in Web-browsing mode and click with the right mouse button on the Resource Center window, Mathcad displays a context menu with commands appropriate for viewing Web pages.

Many of the buttons on the Resource Center toolbar remain active when you are in Web-browsing mode, so that you can copy, save, or print material you locate on the Web, or backtrack to pages you previously viewed. When you click on the Table of Contents button you return to the Table of Contents for the Resource Center.

You may use the Resource Center in Web-browsing mode to open Mathcad worksheets on the Web. Simply type the URL of a Mathcad worksheet in the "Address" box in the Web Toolbar.

When the Resource Center window is in Web-browsing mode, Mathcad is actually using a Web-browsing OLE control provided by Microsoft Internet Explorer. Web browsing in Mathcad requires Microsoft Internet Explorer version 3.02 or later to be installed on your system. Although Microsoft Internet Explorer is installed when you install Mathcad, you can refer to Microsoft Corporation's Web site at

$$\texttt{http://www.microsoft.com/}$$

for licensing and support information about Microsoft Internet Explorer and to download the latest version.

Use the buttons at the bottom of the Resource Center Table of Contents as shortcuts to the following pages on MathSoft's World Wide Web site:

■ **mathsoft.com**: MathSoft home page.

■ **Registration**: On-line product registration form.

■ **Tech Support**: Technical support pages.

■ **Web Store:** Purchase additional MathSoft products on-line.

Using Electronic Books

MathSoft and selected third-party publishers produce Mathcad Electronic Books, which are disk- and CD-based electronic publications that provide technical professionals, professors, and students with a wide range of technical reference and educational content, all created with Mathcad. Electronic Books help you get more out of Mathcad, because:

■ Every page of an Electronic Book is a live Mathcad worksheet. You can change values, calculate results, and experiment right on the electronic "page."

■ If you have your own Mathcad worksheet open, you can copy working examples and formulas from the Electronic Book simply by dragging and dropping them into your worksheet.

The Resource Center, which comes with Mathcad, is itself an Electronic Book, and more than 50 additional titles are now available, including the best-selling *The Mathcad Treasury*, by Paul R. Lorczak. If you are using Mathcad Professional, your Resource

Center includes two chapters excerpted from this Book. For more information about Mathcad Electronic Books and other products, contact MathSoft or your local software distributor or reseller, or click on the Web Store button in the Resource Center.

Opening an Electronic Book

To open an Electronic Book you have installed,

■ Choose **Open Book** from the **Help** menu.

■ Use the Open Book dialog box to locate the book. The file extension `.hbk` is used for Mathcad Electronic Book files. The title for any book you locate is displayed at the bottom of the dialog box.

■ Click "Open."

You may also open an Electronic Book you have installed via the **File** menu:

■ Choose **Open** from the **File** menu.

■ Set the "Files of Type" box to "Mathcad Electronic Book (*.hbk)." The file extension `.hbk` is used for Mathcad Electronic Book files.

■ Browse to find one of the available Electronic Books you have installed.

■ Click "Open."

The Electronic Book opens in its own window with a navigational toolbar at the top, as shown in Figure 2-4.

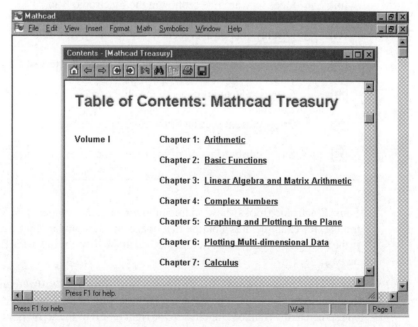

Figure 2-4: A Mathcad Electronic Book opens in its own window with a custom toolbar.

When you click in the book with the *right* mouse button, you will see a Books context menu with commands appropriate for using your Book.

Moving around an Electronic Book

As in other hypertext systems, you click on underlined text or icons to move from section to section. The mouse pointer automatically changes into the shape of a hand when you let it hover over a hypertext link, and a message appears at the bottom of the window that tells you what will happen when you click on the link. Then, when you click on a link or cross-reference, you automatically open the appropriate section or display information in a pop-up window, depending on how the book is organized.

You can also use the buttons on the toolbar at the top of the Electronic Book window to navigate the Electronic Book and take advantage of the content you find there:

Button	Function
🏠	Jumps to the Table of Contents, the page that displays when you first open the Electronic Book.
⇐	Backtracks to whatever document was last viewed.
⇒	Reverses the last backtrack.
◉	Goes backward one section in the Electronic Book.
◉	Goes forward one section in the Electronic Book.
🔖	Displays list of documents most recently viewed.
🔍	Searches the Electronic Book for a particular term.
📋	Copies selected regions to the clipboard.
🖨	Prints current section of the Electronic Book.
💾	Saves current section of the Electronic Book.

Some Electronic Books show additional buttons in the toolbar. The Resource Center toolbar, for example, has a button that opens an additional toolbar for Web browsing in the Resource Center window, as described in "Web browsing in the Resource Center" on page 38.

Use the key combinations [**Shift**][**PgDn**] and [**Shift**][**PgUp**] to move down or up in increments of one page within the current section of the Electronic Book. To move one screen to the right or left, click to the right or left of the scroll box in the horizontal scroll bar.

Mathcad keeps a record of where you've been in the Electronic Book. When you click on the *Back* button, Mathcad goes back to the last section you opened and the page you were on when you left it. Backtracking is especially useful when you have clicked to look at a cross reference and you want to go back to the section you just came from.

If you don't want to go back one section at a time, click on the *History* button in the Electronic Book toolbar. This opens a window listing all the sections you've viewed since you first opened the Electronic Book. And if your Book has a Web Toolbar, you can use the Bookmark button to save the location of a section to visit at a later date.

Finding information in an Electronic Book

In addition to using the Table of Contents to find topics in the Electronic Book, you can search for topics or phrases. To do so:

■ Click on the *Search* button in the Electronic Book toolbar to open the Search dialog box shown below.

■ Type a word or phrase in the "Search for" text box. As you type, the scrolling list displays words or phrases that closely match the letters you type.

■ Select a word or phrase and click "Search" to see a list of topics containing that entry and the number of times it occurs in each topic.

■ Choose one of these topics and click on "Go To." Mathcad opens the Electronic Book section containing the entry you want to search for.

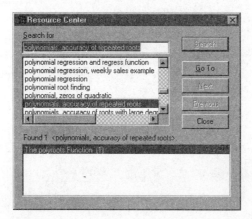

Click on "Next" or "Previous" to bring the next or previous occurrence of the entry into the window. If "Next" is grayed out, the last occurrence of that word is currently visible. If "Previous" is grayed out, the first occurrence of that word is currently visible.

Note that this feature will not locate any annotations you may have saved using the **Annotate Book** command, described in "Annotating an Electronic Book" on page 45.

Copying information from an Electronic Book

There are two ways to copy information from an Electronic Book into your Mathcad worksheet:

- You can use the clipboard by selecting text or equations in the Electronic Book, using the *Copy* button on the toolbar in the Electronic Book window, clicking on the appropriate spot in your worksheet and choosing **Paste** from the **Edit** menu, or

- You can drag regions from the Book window and drop them into your worksheet.

To drag regions from an Electronic Book to your worksheet, first select them. To do so:

- Press and hold down the mouse button to anchor one corner of the selection rectangle.

- Without letting go of the mouse button, move the mouse so as to enclose everything you want to select inside the selection rectangle.

- Release the mouse button. Mathcad encloses the regions you have selected in dashed selection rectangles. If you select only one region, Mathcad surrounds it with a selection box.

Now drag a copy of the selected regions into your worksheet, as shown in Figure 2-5.

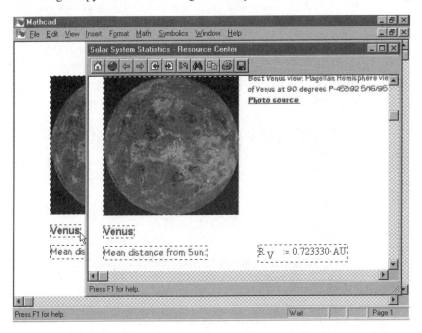

Figure 2-5: Copying selected regions from an Electronic Book to a worksheet.

To do so:

- Place the pointer over any selected region in the Electronic Book. The pointer will turn into a small hand.

- Hold down the mouse button. Without letting go of the button, move the mouse. You will see the rectangular outlines of the selected regions move as you move the mouse.

- Drag the regions in to the destination worksheet. Let go of the mouse button when you have positioned the regions to your liking.

Printing and saving a section from an Electronic Book

To print the current section of the Electronic Book,

- Click on the *Print* button in the Electronic Book toolbar.

- Use the Print dialog box to control what pages to print and what printer to print on.

To save the current section of the Electronic Book,

- Click on the *Save* button in the Electronic Book toolbar.

- Use the Save As dialog box to specify a location and format for the worksheet you want to save.

For more information about printing and saving Mathcad worksheets, see Chapter 4, "Worksheet Management."

Annotating an Electronic Book

While you have an Electronic Book open, you may edit any of the math you see, enter text, and create graphs directly in the Electronic Book window. By default, when you make changes in an Electronic Book, Mathcad remembers those changes as long as the book is open. When you close the book, whatever changes you make are lost. The next time you open that Electronic Book, it will appear as if it had never been changed at all.

To save a copy of your edited Electronic Book, choose **Annotate Book** from the context menu before making any changes. (Click on the Electronic Book window with the right mouse button to see the context menu.) This places a checkmark beside the menu command to indicate that you can now save an annotated copy of your Electronic Book. The original copy of your Electronic Book will, of course, remain untouched.

As you make changes and type in your Electronic Book, you may want to mark the regions you change. To do so, choose **Highlight Changes** from the Books context menu. After you've done so, Mathcad displays any changed regions in a different color. You can set this color by choosing **Color⇒Annotation** from the **Format** menu. To stop highlighting regions, choose **Highlight Changes** from the context menu again. This removes the checkmark from beside the menu command and disables this feature.

Once you've made changes in your Electronic Book, choose one of the following from the Books context menu. You will have the option of:

- Choosing **Save Section** to save the changes you've made in the section you're working on, or

- Choosing **Save All Changes** to save all changes since you last opened the book.

Once Mathcad saves an annotated copy of the Electronic Book, you'll see an asterisk beside the title whenever you turn to an annotated section. The next time you open that Electronic Book, Mathcad will open the annotated rather than the original copy.

If you've made changes to an Electronic Book and you *haven't* chosen one of the above options, you'll be given the option of saving all changes you have made or of reviewing the changed sections, one at a time, and deciding whether to save or discard the changes.

Deleting your annotations

Once you've saved an edited copy of an Electronic Book, Mathcad will open up that copy rather than the original unedited copy. Whenever you turn to a section that's been annotated and saved, you'll see a "*" in the title bar beside that section's title.

To see the original section, as it appeared in the original copy of the Electronic Book before you made any changes, choose **View Original Section** from the Books context menu. If you want to go back to the corresponding section in the annotated copy of the Electronic Book, choose **View Edited Section** from the context menu.

To delete the annotations permanently in a particular section, choose **Restore Section** from the Books context menu. To delete your annotated copy of the Electronic Book altogether, choose **Restore All**.

Help and context sensitive help

Mathcad provides several ways to get help on product features through a traditional on-line Help system. To see Mathcad's on-line Help at any time, choose **Mathcad Help** from the **Help** menu, or press [**F1**].

Choose **Tip of the Day** from the **Help** menu for a series of helpful hints on using Mathcad. Mathcad automatically displays one of these tips whenever you start it if "Show Tips at Startup" is checked.

You can get context sensitive help while using Mathcad. For menu commands, click on the command and read the message line at the bottom of your window. For toolbar or palette buttons, hold the pointer over the button momentarily to see a tool tip.

You can also get more detailed help on menu commands or on many operators and error messages. To do so:

■ Click on an error message, a built-in function or variable, or an operator.

■ Press [**F1**] to bring up the relevant Help screen.

To get help on menu commands or on any of the palette buttons:

■ Press [**Shift**][**F1**]. Mathcad changes the pointer into a question mark.

■ Choose a command from the menu. Mathcad shows the relevant Help screen.

■ Click on any palette button. Mathcad displays the operator's name and a keyboard shortcut on the message line.

To resume editing, press [**Esc**] or [**Shift**][**F1**]. The pointer turns back into an arrow.

Editing and Worksheet Features

Chapter 3
Editing Equations

This chapter describes the mechanics of creating mathematical expressions and making changes in existing mathematical expressions.

The following sections make up this chapter:

Building expressions

How to create mathematical expressions in a straightforward way by just typing a stream of characters. How to create expressions by exploiting their structure.

Editing an existing expression

Inserting and deleting operators, changing the names of variables, using Cut, Delete, Paste, and Copy to streamline your editing. How to add a line break to a lengthy expression.

Rearranging your worksheet

How to move one or more expressions to another part of your worksheet.

Building expressions

You can create many mathematical expressions by simply typing in a stream of characters. Certain characters, like letters and digits, make up parts of names and numbers. Other characters, like * and +, represent "operators." For example, if you type the characters

$$3/4+5\wedge2=$$

you get the result shown below:

$$\frac{3}{4+5^2} = 0.103$$

Figure 3-1: An expression and its computed value.

You can type many of these operators by clicking on the appropriate button in the various operator palettes. Each button on the Math Palette, described on page 11, calls up one of these operator palettes. Most of the operators used in this chapter are on the *arithmetic palette* which you can open by clicking on the left-most button (the one with a calculator on it). For example, instead of typing $5\wedge2$, type 5, click on the button labeled x^y on the arithmetic palette, and type 2 in the placeholder.

On the surface, Mathcad's equation editor seems very much like a simple text editor, but there's more to it than this. Mathematical expressions have a well-defined structure and Mathcad's equation editor is designed specifically to work within that structure. In Mathcad, mathematical expressions are not so much typed in as they are built.

Mathcad automatically assembles the various parts that make up an expression using the rules of precedence and some additional rules that simplify entering denominators, exponents, and expressions in radicals. For example, when you type / to create a fraction, Mathcad stays in the denominator until you explicitly tell it to leave by clicking on the fraction bar. This means that the characters $3/4+5\wedge2$ generate what you see in Figure 3-1 rather than

$$\frac{3}{4} + 5^2$$

Typing in names and numbers

When you type in names or numbers, Mathcad behaves very much like a standard word processor. As you type, you'll see the characters you type appear behind a vertical editing line. The left and right arrow keys move this vertical editing line to the left or to the right a character at a time, just as they would in a word processor. There are, however, two important differences.

- As it moves to the right, the vertical editing line leaves behind a trail. This trail is a "horizontal editing line." Its importance will become apparent in the next section when you begin working with operators.

- Unless the equation you've clicked in already has an operator in it, pressing [**Space**] will turn the math region into a text region. It is not possible to turn a text region back into a math region.

Typing in operators

Operators are symbols like "+" and "−" that link variables and numbers together to form expressions. The variables and numbers linked together by operators are called "operands." For example, in an expression like:

$$a^{x+y}$$

the operands for the "+" are x and y. The operands for the *exponent* operator are a and the expression $x + y$.

The key to working with operators is learning to specify what variable or expression is to become an operand. There are two ways to do this:

- You can type the operator first and fill in the placeholders with operands, or

- You can learn how to use the editing lines to specify what variable or expression you want to turn into an operand.

The first method feels more like you're building a skeleton and filling in the details later. You may find this method easier to use when you're either building very complicated expressions, or when you're working with operators like summation and integration which require many operands and lack a natural typing order.

The second method feels more like straight typing and can be much faster when expressions are simple. In practice, you may find yourself switching back and forth as the need arises.

Here's how to create the expression a^{x+y} using the first method:

- Press ^ to create the exponent operator. You'll see two placeholders.

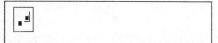

- Click in the lower placeholder and type **a**.

- Click in the upper placeholder.

■ Type **+**.

■ Click in the remaining placeholders and type **x** and **y**.

To use the editing lines to create the expression a^{x+y}, proceed as follows:

■ Type **a**. The line beneath the *a* indicates that *a* will become the first operand of whatever operator you type next.

■ Press **∧** to create the exponent operator. As promised, *a* becomes the first operand of the exponent. The editing lines now surround another placeholder.

■ Type **x+y** in this placeholder to complete the expression.

Note that in this example, you could type the expression the same way you'd say it out loud. However, even this simple example already contains an ambiguity. When you say "*a* to the *x* plus *y*" there's no way to tell if you mean a^{x+y} or $a^x + y$. For more complicated expressions, the number of ambiguities increases dramatically.

Although you could resolve any of these ambiguities by using parentheses, doing so can quickly become cumbersome. A better way is to use the editing lines to specify the operands of whatever operator you type. The following example illustrates this by describing how to create the expression $a^x + y$ instead of a^{x+y}.

■ Type **a∧x** as you did in the previous example. Note how the editing lines hold the *x* between them. If you were to type **+** at this point, the *x* would become the first operand of the plus.

■ Press [**Space**]. The editing lines now hold the entire expression a^x.

■ Now type **+**. Whatever was held between the editing lines now becomes the first operand of the plus.

■ In the remaining placeholder, type **y**.

$$a^x + y$$

Multiplication

A common way to show multiplication between two variables on a piece of paper is to place them next to each other. For example, expressions like ax or $a(x + y)$ are easily understood to mean "a times x" and "a times the quantity x plus y," respectively.

This cannot be done with Mathcad variables for the simple reason that when you type **ax**, Mathcad has no way of knowing whether you mean "a times x" or "the variable named ax." Similarly, when you type **a(x+y)**, Mathcad cannot tell if you mean "a times the quantity x plus y" or whether you mean "the function a applied to the argument $x + y$."

In the special case when you type a numerical constant followed immediately by a variable name, such as **4x**, Mathcad interprets the expression to mean the constant multiplied by the variable: $4 \cdot x$. Mathcad displays a space between the constant and the variable to indicate that the multiplication is implied. You can produce math notation in this way that closely approximates the notation you see in textbooks and reference books. Note that Mathcad reserves certain letters, such as "i" for the imaginary unit and "o" for octal, as suffixes for numbers, and in these cases will not attempt to multiply the number by a variable name but rather will treat the expression as a single number with a suffix.

To avoid ambiguity, we recommend that you press ***** explicitly to indicate multiplication, as shown in the following example:

■ Type **a** followed by *****. Mathcad inserts a small dot after the "a" to indicate multiplication.

$$a \cdot \blacksquare$$

■ In the placeholder, type the second factor, **x**.

$$a \cdot x$$

An annotated example

When it comes to editing equations, knowing how to use the editing lines assumes an importance similar to knowing where to put the flashing vertical bar you see in most word processors. A word processor can get away with a vertical bar because text is inherently one-dimensional, like a line. New letters go either to the left or to the right of old ones. Equations, on the other hand, are really *two-dimensional*. Their structure is more like a trees with branches than like a line of text. As a result, Mathcad has to use a *two-dimensional* version of that same vertical bar. That's why there are two editing lines: a vertical line and a horizontal line.

Suppose, for example, that you want to type the slightly more complicated expression

$$\frac{x - 3 \cdot a^2}{-4 + \sqrt{y + 1}}$$

Watch what happens to the editing lines in the following steps:

- Type **x-3*a^2**. Since the editing lines contain just the "2," only the "2" becomes the numerator when you press the **/**. Since we want the whole expression,

  $x - 3 \cdot a^2$, to be the numerator, we must make the editing lines hold that entire expression.

- To do so, press the [**Space**]. Each time you press the [**Space**], the editing lines hold more of the expression. You'll need to press [**Space**] three times to enclose the entire expression.

- Now press **/** to create a division bar. Note that the numerator is whatever was enclosed between the editing lines when you pressed **/**.

- Now type **-4+** and click on the button labeled "$\sqrt{}$" on the arithmetic palette. Then type **y+1** under the radical to complete the denominator.

- To add something *outside* the radical sign, press [**Space**] twice make the editing lines hold the radical. For example, to add the number π to the denominator, press [**Space**] twice.

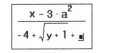

- Press **+**. Since the editing lines were holding the entire radical, it is the entire radical that becomes the first operand when you press **+**.

$$\frac{x - 3 \cdot a^2}{-4 + \sqrt{y + 1} + \blacksquare}$$

- Click on the button labeled "π" on the arithmetic palette. This is one of Mathcad's built-in variables.

$$\frac{x - 3 \cdot a^2}{-4 + \sqrt{y + 1} + \pi}$$

Editing an existing expression

This section describes how to make changes to an existing expression.

The simplest changes you can make are discussed in "Changing a name or number" on page 55. Here, the underlying tree structure of a math expression doesn't matter. As a result, the equation editor behaves very much like a text editor.

Most difficulties in editing equations arise from working with operators. That's because it's only when you start working with operators that the underlying tree structure of a math expression shows up.

The next few sections describe the three things you can do with an operator: inserting an operator, deleting an operator, or replacing one operator with another.

The equation editor normally works from left to right. If you want to insert an operator *before* an existing expression, or if you want to apply a function to an existing expression, see "Inserting an operator" on page 56 and "Applying a function to an expression" on page 60.

Although Mathcad inserts parentheses wherever required to prevent ambiguity, you may at times want to add parentheses to clarify an expression or delete extraneous parentheses. To do so, use the techniques described in the sections "Inserting parentheses" on page 61 and "Deleting parentheses" on page 62.

When working with a complicated expression, it is often easier to work with more manageable subexpressions within it. The sections "Moving parts of an expression" on page 62 and "Deleting parts of an expression" on page 63 describe how to use **Cut**, **Copy**, and **Paste** to do so.

Changing a name or number

To edit a name or number:

- Click on it with the mouse. This places the editing lines wherever you clicked the mouse.

- Move the editing lines if necessary by pressing the [→] and [←] keys. Alternatively, place the mouse pointer wherever you want the editing lines to go, and click the mouse.

- If you type a character, it will appear just to the left of the editing lines. Pressing [**Bksp**] removes the character to the left of the editing lines. Pressing [**Delete**] removes the character to the right of the editing lines.

If you need to change several occurrences of the same name or number, you may find it useful to choose **Replace** from the **Edit** menu. To search for a sequence of characters, choose **Find** from the **Edit** menu. These commands are discussed further in Chapter 5, "Text."

Inserting an operator

The easiest place to insert an operator is between two characters in a name or two numbers in a constant. For example, here is how to insert a plus sign between two characters:

■ Place the editing lines where you want the plus sign to be.

■ Press the **+** key.

Note that Mathcad automatically inserts a space on either side of the plus sign. You should never need to insert a space when typing an equation. Mathcad inserts spaces automatically wherever doing so is appropriate. In fact, if you do try to insert a space, Mathcad assumes you meant to type text rather than math and converts your math region into a text region accordingly.

Operators such as division and exponentiation result in more dramatic formatting changes. For example, when you insert a divide sign, Mathcad moves everything that comes after the divide sign into the denominator. Here's how you insert a divide sign.

■ Place the editing lines where you want the divide sign to be.

■ Press the **/** key. Mathcad reformats the expression to accommodate the division.

Some operators require only one operand. Examples are the square root, absolute value, and complex conjugate operators. To insert one of these, place the editing lines on either side of the operand and press the appropriate keystroke. Many of these operators are available on the arithmetic palette as well. For example, to turn x into $\sqrt{x}$ do the following:

■ Place the editing lines around the "x," either preceding or following the character.

■ Press **** to insert the square root operator.

Applying an operator to an expression

The methods described in the previous section work most predictably when you want to apply an operator to a variable or a number. If, however, you want to apply an operator to an *entire expression* there are two ways to proceed:

■ You can surround that expression in parentheses and proceed as described in the previous section, or

■ You can use the editing lines to specify the expression you want to apply the operator to.

Although the first method may be more intuitive, it is definitely slower since you will need to type pairs of parentheses. The more efficient second method is the subject of this section. The sections "Inserting parentheses" on page 61 and "Deleting parentheses" on page 62 describe ways to work with parentheses more efficiently.

The editing lines consist of a horizontal line and a vertical line that moves left to right along the horizontal line. To make an operator apply to an expression, select the expression by placing it between the two editing lines. The following examples show how typing *c results in completely different expressions depending on what was selected.

■ Here, the two editing lines hold only the numerator. This means any operator you type will apply only to the numerator.

$$\frac{a + b}{x + d}$$

■ Typing *c results in this expression. Note how the expression held between the editing lines became the first operand of the multiplication.

$$\frac{(a + b) \cdot c}{x + d}$$

■ Here, the editing lines hold the entire fraction. This means any operator you type will apply to the entire fraction.

$$\frac{a + b}{x + d}$$

■ Typing *c results in this expression. Note how the everything between the editing lines became the first operand of the multiplication.

$$\frac{a + b}{x + d} \cdot c$$

■ Here, the editing lines hold the entire fraction as they did in the previous example. However, this time the vertical editing line is on the *left* side instead of on the right side.

$$\frac{a + b}{x + d}$$

■ Typing ***c** results in this expression. Note how the expression enclosed by the editing lines became the *second* rather than the first operand of the multiplication. This happened because the vertical editing line was on the *left* side rather than the right side.

editing line was on the *left* side rather than the right side.

Now that you know the significance of what's held between these two editing lines, the pertinent question becomes "How do I control what's held between the two editing lines?"

One way to control the length of the editing lines is to click on an operator. When you click on an operator, you make the pair of editing lines hold that operator together with everything that operator applies to. Depending on exactly where on the operator you click, you'll find the vertical editing line either on the left or on the right. Use the [**Insert**] key to move it from one side completely to the other, or use the left and right arrow keys to move a character at a time.

A second way to control the length of the two editing lines is to press [**Space**] to cycle through all possible positions of the editing lines. Each time you press [**Space**] the editing lines grow progressively longer. As they do so, they enclose more and more of the expression, until eventually, they enclose the entire expression. Pressing [**Space**] one more time brings the editing lines back to where they were when you started.

The following example walks you through a short cycle:

■ This is the starting position. The two editing lines hold just the single variable "*d*."

■ Pressing [**Space**] makes the editing lines grow so that they now hold the entire denominator.

■ Pressing [**Space**] once makes the editing lines grow again so that they now hold the entire expression.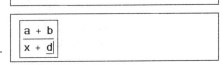

■ At this point, the editing lines can't become any longer. Pressing [**Space**] brings the editing lines back to the starting point of the cycle.

You'll notice that in stepping through the previous cycle there was never an intermediate step in which the editing lines held just the numerator. Nor was there ever a step in which the editing lines held just the *a* or just the *b* in the numerator. That's because the sequence of steps the editing lines go through as you press [**Space**] depends on the starting point of the cycle.

To set the starting point of the cycle, you can either click on the appropriate part of the expression as described earlier, or you can use the arrow keys to move around the expression. The arrow keys walk the editing lines through the expression in the indicated direction. Keep in mind however that the idea of "up" and "down" or "left" and "right" may not always be clear, particularly when the expression becomes very complicated or when the expression involves summations, integrals and other advanced operators.

Deleting an operator

To delete an operator connecting two variable names or constants:

■ Place the editing lines after the operator.

> a + b

■ Press the [BkSp] key.

> ab

Now you can easily insert a new operator to replace the one you deleted just by typing it in.

You can also delete an operator by placing the editing lines before it and pressing the [Delete] key instead. For example:

■ Place the editing lines before the operator.

> a + b

■ Press the [Delete] key.

> ab

In the above examples, it is easy to see what "before" and "after" mean because the expressions involved naturally flow from left to right, the same way we read. Fractions behave the same way. Since we would naturally say "*a* over *b*," putting the editing lines "after" the division bar means putting them just before the *b*. Similarly, putting the editing lines "before" the division bar means putting them immediately after the *a*. The following example illustrates this:

■ Place the editing lines *after* the division bar.

> $\frac{a}{b}$

■ Press the [BkSp] key.

> ab

To delete an operator having only one operand (for example, $\sqrt{x}$, $|x|$ or $x!$):

- Position the editing lines just after the operator.

- Press the [**BkSp**] key.

For certain operators, it may not be clear where to put the editing lines. For example, it is not clear when looking at $|x|$ or $\bar{x}$ what "before" and "after" mean. When this happens, Mathcad resolves the ambiguity by referring to the spoken form of the expression. For example, since you would read $\bar{x}$ as "x conjugate," the bar is treated as being *after* the x.

Inserting a minus sign

The minus sign that means "opposite of" uses the same keystroke as the one that means "subtract." To determine which one to insert, Mathcad looks at where the vertical editing line is. If it's on the left, Mathcad inserts the "opposite of" minus sign. If it's on the right, Mathcad inserts the "subtract" minus sign. To move the vertical editing line from one side to the other, use the [**Insert**] key.

The following example shows how to insert a minus sign in front of the expression "sin(a)."

- Click on the sin(a).

- If necessary, press [**Insert**] to move the vertical editing line all the way to the left.

- Type - to insert a minus sign.

If what you really want to do is turn $\sin(a)$ into $1 - \sin(a)$, insert another operator (say, "+") as described in the section "Inserting an operator" on page 56. Then replace the operator with a minus sign as described in the section "Deleting an operator" on page 59. Notice that in Mathcad the unary minus sign in the expression $-\sin(a)$ appears smaller than the minus sign in expressions such as $1 - \sin(a)$.

Applying a function to an expression

To turn an expression into the argument of a function, follow these steps:

- Click in the expression and press [**Space**] until the entire expression, $w \cdot t - (k \cdot z)$, is held between the editing lines.

Chapter 3 Editing Equations

- Type the single-quote key (the same as the double-quote key, but unshifted). The selected expression is enclosed by parentheses.

- Press [**Space**]. The editing lines now hold the parentheses as well.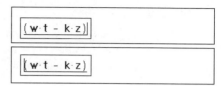

- If necessary, press the [**Insert**] key. The vertical editing line switches to the left side. If the vertical editing line is already on the left side, skip this step.

- Now type the name of the function. If the function you wish to use is a built-in function, you can choose **Function** from  the **Insert** menu and double-click on the name of the function.

Inserting parentheses

Mathcad places parentheses automatically as needed to maintain the precedence of operations. There may be instances however, when you want to place parentheses to clarify an expression or to change the overall structure of the expression. You can either insert a matched pair of parentheses all at once or you can insert the parentheses one at a time. We recommend you insert a matched pair since this avoids the possibility of unmatched parentheses.

To enclose an expression with a matched pair of parentheses:

- Select the expression by placing it between the editing lines. You can do this by clicking on the expression and pressing [**Space**] one or more times.

- Type the single-quote key. The selected expression is now enclosed by parentheses.

It is sometimes necessary to insert parentheses one at a time using the (and) keys. For example, to change $a - b + c$ to $a - (b + c)$ do the following:

- Move the editing lines just to the left of the b. Make sure the vertical editing line is on the left as shown. Press [**Insert**] if necessary to move it over.

- Type (. Now click to the right of the c. Make sure the vertical editing line is to the right as shown. Press [**Insert**] if necessary to move it over.

■ Type).

$$a - (b + c)|$$

Deleting parentheses

You cannot delete one parenthesis at a time. Whenever you delete one parenthesis, Mathcad deletes the matched parenthesis as well. This prevents you from inadvertently creating an expression having unmatched parentheses.

To delete a matched pair of parentheses:

■ Move the editing lines to the right of the "(".

$$a - (\underline{b} + c)$$

■ Press the [**BkSp**] key. Note that you could also begin with the editing lines to the left of the ")"and pressing the [**Delete**] key instead.

$$a - \underline{b} + c$$

Moving parts of an expression

The menu commands **Cut**, **Copy**, and **Paste** from the **Edit** menu are useful for editing complicated expressions. They function as follows:

■ **Cut** deletes whatever is between the editing lines and copies it to the clipboard.

■ **Copy** takes whatever is between the editing lines and copies it to the clipboard.

■ **Paste** takes whatever is on the clipboard and places it into your worksheet, either into a placeholder or into the blank space between equations.

The following example shows how to use **Copy** and **Paste** to eliminate retyping.

Suppose you want to build the expression

$$\cos(wt + x) + \sin(wt - x)$$

The argument to the sine function is nearly identical to that of the cosine function. You can take advantage of the similarity between the arguments of these two functions by doing the following:

■ Build the first term, then leave a placeholder where the argument to the sine should go. Type **sin()** to do this.

$$\cos(w \cdot t + x) + \sin(\blacksquare)$$

■ Click in the argument to the cosine function and press [**Space**] until the editing lines hold the argument between them. The expression looks like that shown on the right.

$$\cos(\underline{w \cdot t + x}) + \sin(\blacksquare)$$

■ Choose **Copy** from the **Edit** menu.

Chapter 3 Editing Equations

- Click on the placeholder inside the sine function.

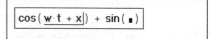

$$\cos(\underline{w \cdot t} + x) + \sin(\blacksquare)$$

- Choose **Paste** from the **Edit** menu. The expression now looks like that shown on the right.

$$\cos(w \cdot t + x) + \sin(\underline{w \cdot t} + x)$$

Now replace the "+" with a "−".

Deleting parts of an expression

You can avoid having to repeatedly backspace over parts of an expression by choosing **Cut** from the **Edit** menu. This will delete whatever is between the editing lines place it on the clipboard.

The following example shows how you can use the cut command to delete a significant part of an expression.

Suppose you want to change the expression

$$\cos\left(\frac{w \cdot t + x}{2}\right)$$

into

$$\cos\left(\frac{x}{2}\right)$$

Rather than repeatedly backspacing, you can do the following:

- Select the numerator as shown on the right.

$$\cos\left(\frac{\underline{w \cdot t} + x}{2}\right)$$

- Choose **Cut** from the **Edit** menu. This removes the numerator and leaves behind a placeholder.

$$\cos\left(\frac{\blacksquare}{2}\right)$$

- Type **x** in the placeholder.

$$\cos\left(\frac{\underline{x}}{2}\right)$$

You can also delete part of an expression by using either the [`Delete`] key or the [`BkSp`] key. If you use this method however, whatever you delete will *not* go to the clipboard. This is useful when you intend to replace whatever you delete with whatever is currently on the clipboard.

To delete part of an expression *without* placing it on the clipboard:

- Select the numerator as shown on the right. Note that the vertical editing line is to the right.

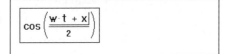

- Press [**BkSp**]. Mathcad highlights your selection to indicate what you've proposed to delete. Mathcad takes this extra step since once you delete, you'll have to retype the expression to get it back.

- Press [**BkSp**] one more time. This removes the numerator and leaves behind a placeholder.

To use the [**Delete**] key instead of the [**BkSp**] key, follow the preceding instructions but place the vertical editing line on the *left* side of the expression.

Rearranging your worksheet

This section describes how to rearrange expressions, graphics and text in your worksheets. The techniques described here work equally well for everything in your worksheet: equations, plots, sketches and text. Before you use the methods in this section, click in the empty space between regions to turn the cursor into a crosshair.

You can get an overall view of how your worksheet looks by choosing **Zoom** from the **View** menu and choosing a magnification from the Zoom dialog box. Set the magnification:

- Less than 100% to zoom out for an overall view.

- Greater than 100% to zoom in for a close-up view.

Selecting, cutting, pasting and aligning regions work the same way regardless of the magnification you choose.

Selecting regions

Before you can move or copy one or more regions, you must select them. To do so:

- Press and hold down the mouse button to anchor one corner of the selection rectangle.

- Without letting go of the mouse button, move the mouse so as to enclose everything you want to select inside the selection rectangle.

■ Once the selection rectangle encloses everything you want to select, release the mouse button. Mathcad encloses those regions you have selected.

Figure 3-2 shows how the worksheet might look just before you release the mouse button.

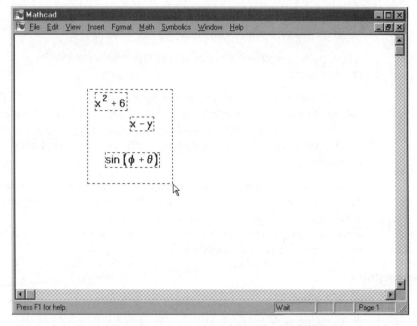

Figure 3-2: Several regions enclosed in a selection rectangle.

Copying regions

Once the regions are selected, you can copy them:

■ by using **Copy** and **Paste**, or

■ if the regions start out in either an Electronic Book or in a locked area, by dragging them with the mouse

To use the **Copy** and **Paste** commands:

■ Select the regions as described in the previous section.

■ Choose **Copy** from the **Edit** menu. This copies the selected regions into the clipboard.

■ Click the mouse wherever you want to place a copy of the regions. You can click either someplace else in your worksheet or in a different worksheet altogether. Make sure you've clicked in an empty space. You should see the crosshair.

■ Choose **Paste** from the **Edit** menu.

If the regions you want to copy are coming from a locked area or from an Electronic Book, you can also copy them by dragging them with the mouse. To do so:

- Select the regions as described in the previous section.

- Place the pointer on the border of any selected region. It should turn into a small hand.

- Hold down the mouse button.

- Without letting go of the button, move the mouse. You'll see the rectangular outlines of the selected regions move as you move the mouse.

At this point, you can either copy the selected regions to another spot in the worksheet, or you can copy them into another worksheet.

To copy the selected regions to another spot in the worksheet, move the rectangular outlines to wherever you want to place the regions and let go of the mouse button. If you want to copy the region to a spot beyond what you can see in the window, just drag the regions in the appropriate direction. Mathcad will automatically scroll in that direction.

To copy the selected regions into another worksheet, press the mouse button and drag the rectangular outlines toward the destination worksheet. Do not linger near the window's frame; drag the regions decisively across the frame and into the destination worksheet. Mathcad responds to hesitation near the window's frame by autoscrolling the document in the indicated direction.

Moving regions

Once the regions are selected, you can move them by:

- dragging with the mouse or,

- using **Cut** and **Paste**.

To drag regions with the mouse:

- Select the regions as described in the previous section.

- Place the pointer on the border of any selected region. The pointer will turn into a small hand.

- Press and hold down the mouse button.

- Without letting go of the button, move the mouse. You'll see the rectangular outlines of the selected regions following the mouse pointer.

At this point, you can either drag the selected regions to another spot in the worksheet, or you can drag them to another worksheet.

To move the selected regions to another spot in the worksheet, move the rectangular outlines to wherever you want to place the regions and let go of the mouse button. If you want to move the region to a spot beyond what you can see in the window, just drag the regions in the appropriate direction. Mathcad will automatically scroll in that direction.

To copy the selected regions into another worksheet, press the mouse button and drag the rectangular outlines toward the destination worksheet. Do not linger near the window's frame; drag the regions decisively across the frame and into the destination worksheet. Mathcad responds to hesitation near the window's frame by autoscrolling the document in the indicated direction.

You can also move the selected regions by using **Cut** and **Paste**. To do so:

- Select the regions as described in the previous section.

- Choose **Cut** from the **Edit** menu. This deletes the selected regions and puts them on the clipboard.

- Click the mouse wherever you want the regions moved to. Make sure you've clicked in an empty space. You can click either someplace else in your worksheet or in a different worksheet altogether. Make sure the cursor looks like a crosshair.

- Choose **Paste** from the **Edit** menu.

Aligning Regions

Once regions are selected, you can align them either horizontally or vertically by choosing **Align Regions** from the **Format** menu. This is a pull-right menu. Drag the mouse to the right to display two additional choices: **Across** and **Down**. You can also choose these commands by clicking on the appropriate button on the toolbar.

When you choose **Align Regions⇒Down** from the pull-right menu, Mathcad does the following:

- Mathcad draws an invisible vertical line halfway between the right edge of the right-most selected region and the left edge of the left-most selected region.

- All selected regions to the right of this line are moved left until their left edges are aligned with this line.

- All selected regions to the left of this line are moved right until their left edges are aligned with this line.

Choosing **Align Regions⇒Across** works in much the same way. Mathcad draws an invisible horizontal line halfway between the top edge of the uppermost region and the bottom edge of the lowest region. Selected regions below and above this line are moved up and down respectively until the midpoints of their left edges are on this line.

Note that this means it is possible to inadvertently make regions overlap. If, for example, the regions you select are almost horizontally aligned, choosing **Align Regions⇒Down** may result in overlapping regions.

Deleting regions

To delete one or more regions:

- Select the regions by dragging.

- Choose **Cut** from the **Edit** menu.

Choosing **Cut** removes the selected regions from your worksheet and puts them on the clipboard. If you don't want to disturb the contents of your clipboard or if you don't want to save the selected regions, choose **Delete** from the **Edit** menu instead.

Alternative ways to select regions

There are actually three different ways to select regions. Which one you choose depends on the arrangement of the regions you want to select.

The most common, selection by dragging the mouse, was discussed in a previous section. This is useful when the regions you want to select are not too far apart, and can be enclosed in a rectangle.

The two additional methods are:

■ Shift-clicking on the regions you want to select.

■ Marking the two endpoints of a selection by clicking on them with the [Ctrl] key held down.

Shift-clicking is useful when you want to select or deselect a region without affecting any other regions. For example, you should shift-click when:

■ You can't easily enclose the regions you want to select inside a rectangle. For example, if one region is near the top of a worksheet and the other is near the bottom, you cannot enclose them both in a rectangle without also enclosing many other regions in between.

■ You want to add several more regions to a collection of regions you may have selected some other way.

■ Several regions are selected and you want to deselect one of them.

To select regions by shift-clicking, do the following:

■ Move the mouse pointer to the first region you want to select,

■ Press and hold down the [Shift] key and click the mouse button.

Mathcad surrounds the selected region in a selection rectangle. To select additional regions, repeat these steps with the mouse on the region you want to select. Make sure you hold down the [Shift] key while clicking. If you don't, Mathcad will select whatever you shift-click on, but deselect all other selected regions.

When there are a lot of regions to select, the selection rectangle may become unwieldy. In such cases, you can fill in your selection by control-clicking as follows:

■ Select one or more regions either by shift-clicking, or by using the selection rectangle.

■ With the [Ctrl] key held down, click on the last region in your selection.

Mathcad selects all regions between the first selected region and whatever region you control-clicked on. This may include regions beyond the right or left edges of your window. You can think of control-clicking as a quick way to shift-click every region between the first and last regions selected.

The last region selected need not be the one you control-click on. If you control-click on a region between two selected regions, Mathcad selects all regions between the two selected regions.

Inserting or deleting blank lines

You can easily insert one or more blank lines into your worksheet. The procedure is as follows:

■ Click on the blank line below which you want to insert one or more blank lines. Make sure the cursor looks like a crosshair.

■ Press [↵] to insert a blank line and move the cursor to the left margin. Do this as many times as you want to insert lines.

To delete one or more blank lines from your worksheet:

■ Click above the blank lines you want to delete. Make sure the cursor looks like a crosshair and that there are no regions to the right or left of the cursor.

■ Press [`Delete`] as many times as there are lines you want to delete. Mathcad deletes blank lines below your cursor.

■ Alternatively, press [`BkSp`] as many times as there are lines you want to delete. Mathcad deletes blank lines *above* your cursor.

If you press either [`Delete`] or [`BkSp`] and nothing seems to be happening, check to make sure that the cursor is on a line all by itself. If any region in your worksheet extends into the line you are trying to delete, Mathcad won't be able to delete that line.

Separating regions

As you move and edit the regions in a Mathcad worksheet, they may end up overlapping one another. Overlapping regions don't interfere with each other's calculations, but they do make worksheets hard to read.

A good way to determine whether regions overlap is to choose **Regions** from the **View** menu. Mathcad will display blank space in gray and leave the regions in white. Figure 3-3 shows an example.

To separate all overlapping regions, choose **Separate Regions** from the **Format** menu. Wherever regions overlap, this command will move the regions in such a way as to avoid overlaps while preserving the order of the calculations.

Be careful with the **Separate Regions** menu command since not only can it have far-reaching effects, it also cannot be undone. As an alternative, consider dragging regions individually, adding lines by pressing [`Insert`], or cutting and pasting the equations so they don't overlap.

Figure 3-4 shows the worksheet from Figure 3-3 after having chosen **Separate Regions** from the **Format** menu. To turn the blank space back into white, choose **Regions** from the **View** menu again.

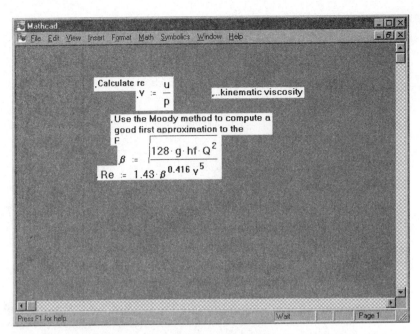

Figure 3-3: Worksheet with overlapping regions.

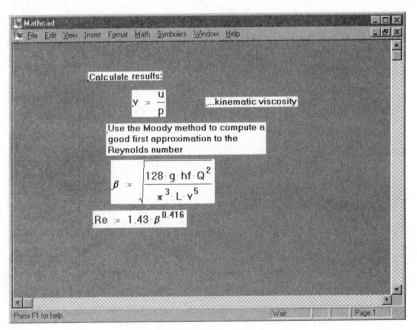

Figure 3-4: After separating the regions.

Chapter 4
Worksheet Management

This chapter describes how to manipulate and format Mathcad worksheets and templates, including how to save and print worksheets, send a worksheet by electronic mail, lock regions in a worksheet, and create file references and hyperlinks between worksheets. It also introduces Object Linking and Embedding (OLE) as a way of inserting other objects into a Mathcad worksheet and embedding Mathcad worksheets or regions into files created by other applications.

The following sections make up this chapter:

Worksheets and templates

How to use worksheets and templates. How to save worksheets in various formats.

Layout

How to adjust margins, insert page breaks, and create headers and footers.

Printing

How to print all or part of a worksheet. Includes a discussion of previewing your printed output.

Mailing

How to e-mail a Mathcad worksheet.

Safeguarding your calculations

How to write-protect selected areas of your worksheet.

References and hyperlinks

How to include a reference to a worksheet inside another worksheet. How to make Mathcad jump to another worksheet, open a pop-up window, or launch another application when you double-click on a region.

Using OLE

How to insert objects from other applications into a worksheet. How to embed a Mathcad worksheet or part of a worksheet into other applications.

Worksheets and templates

As you use Mathcad and save your work for later use, you usually are creating *worksheets,* each of which contains unique text, math, and graphic regions. You typically create a separate worksheet, or group of worksheets, for each of your different calculation procedures or projects. Mathcad uses ".mcd" as the default file extension for worksheets.

When you create a new worksheet in Mathcad, you can start with the equivalent of a blank piece of paper with Mathcad's default choices for formats and layout, or you can use a *template* that contains customized information for laying out and formatting the worksheet. When you create a worksheet based on a template, all of the formatting information and any text, math, and graphic regions from the template are copied to the new worksheet. The new worksheet therefore inherits the appearance and formatting instructions of the template, allowing you to maintain consistency in the appearance of your work.

Mathcad comes with a variety of predefined templates for you to use as you create new Mathcad worksheets. You may extend the collection of templates by saving any of your Mathcad worksheets as a template. Mathcad uses ".mct" as the default file extension for templates.

Other saving options are available in Mathcad. You can save a worksheet in rich-text format (RTF), so that many word processors can open it. You can also save a worksheet in a format that can be read by Windows and Macintosh versions of Mathcad 6.

Creating and saving a new worksheet

When you open Mathcad, you'll see an empty window to work in—this is the *blank worksheet template.* You can enter and format equations, graphs, text, and graphics in this space, and you can modify worksheet attributes such as the page margins, numerical format, headers and footers, and text and math styles. When you want to save the worksheet, choose either **Save** or **Save As** from the **File** menu. The **Save As** dialog box appears, prompting you for a file name with the extension .mcd under which to save the worksheet. After the first time you save the worksheet, simply choosing **Save** from the **File** menu updates the saved copy of the worksheet.

The blank worksheet template is only one of the templates Mathcad provides. Other built-in templates are specific to types of worksheets you'll be creating. For example, there is a template for homework assignments, one for engineering reports, and so on.

To create a new worksheet based on a template other than the blank worksheet template:

■ Choose **New** from the **File** menu. You will see a dialog box like the one below (the exact templates available will differ depending on your version of Mathcad):

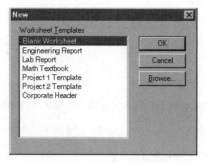

- Choose a template other than "Blank Worksheet." By default Mathcad displays worksheet templates in the `template` subdirectory of whatever directory you used to install Mathcad. Click the "Browse" button to find a template in another directory or on another drive.

- Click "OK."

- Create and edit the necessary equations, text, and other regions for your worksheet.

- Choose **Save** or **Save As** from the **File** menu. The **Save As** dialog box appears, prompting you for a filename with the extension `.mcd` under which to save the worksheet. After the first time you save the worksheet, simply choosing **Save** from the **File** menu updates the saved copy of the worksheet.

Creating a new template

Although Mathcad provides a variety of built-in templates, you can extend the collection of templates by creating your own. For example, you may want to use a template for a project that contains specific information in the worksheet header and footer, or you may want to customize the formatting in one of the predefined templates. The template you create can have equations, text, and graphics in certain places. The template also specifies:

- Default text properties (Chapter 5).

- Definitions of all math styles (Chapter 6).

- Definitions of all text styles (Chapter 5).

- Headers and footers (see "Layout" on page 76).

- Margins for printing (see "Printing" on page 79).

- Numerical result formats (Chapter 6).

- Values for Mathcad's built-in variables (Chapter 8).

- Names of Mathcad's basic units (Chapter 9).

- The default unit system (Chapter 9).

- The default calculation mode (Chapter 7).

To create a new template, first create a new worksheet having the options listed above set the way you want. The worksheet should also contain any equations, text, and graphics that you want in the template. The next step is to save this worksheet as a template. To do so:

■ Choose **Save As** from the **File** menu.

■ Double-click on the `Template` folder in the Save As dialog.

■ In the "Files of type" drop-down list, select "Mathcad Template."

■ Type a name for the template in the "File name" box.

■ Click "Save." The file is saved as a Mathcad template file (with the extension `.mct`) in the `template` subdirectory by default, but you may save it in another location if you wish.

Your template will now be added to the list of templates available in the dialog box that appears when you choose **New** from the **File** menu. To make a new worksheet based on a template you've created, simply choose **New** from the **File** menu and select your template from the list; if you did not save your template to the `template` subdirectory, you will need to browse to find the template.

Opening a worksheet

To work on a worksheet that you saved before, choose **Open** from the **File** menu. Mathcad prompts you for a name by displaying the Open dialog box. You can locate and open a Mathcad worksheet from other directories or drives just as you would in any other Windows application.

At the bottom of the **File** menu, Mathcad maintains a list of the most recently opened worksheets. You can bypass the Open dialog box by choosing from this list.

Opening a worksheet stored on the World Wide Web

If you are connected to the Internet and know the address of a Mathcad worksheet on a World Wide Web server, you can open it using the URL (Uniform Resource Locator) text box in the Collaboratory:

■ Choose **Collaboratory** from the **File** menu to open the Collaboratory dialog box.

■ Select the text that is in the URL text box at the bottom of the dialog box and press [`Del`] to delete it.

■ Type the URL of the worksheet you want to open in the URL text box. This identifies the name of the server computer on which the worksheet is saved together with the path to that worksheet within that computer's file system.

MathSoft maintains a collection of linked Mathcad worksheets on its World Wide Web server. To access these, choose **Resource Center** from the **Help** menu and click on "Web Library."

For more information about Internet access, the Collaboratory, and the Resource Center, see Chapter 2, "On-line Resources."

Editing a worksheet

Edit a worksheet by opening it by using **Open** from the **File** menu and then making any changes you choose. Then, to overwrite the original worksheet with the revised one, choose **Save**. Mathcad overwrites the original copy of the worksheet with the new copy that is currently shown in the worksheet window.

To make changes to an existing worksheet without modifying the original, choose **Save As** from the **File** menu instead. You will be prompted for a new name under which to save the worksheet.

Modifying a template

To modify an existing worksheet template,

- Choose **Open** from the **File** menu.

- In the "Files of type" drop-down list, select "Mathcad Template."

- Type the name of the template in the "File name" box, or browse to locate it in the dialog box. Worksheet templates are saved by default in the `template` subdirectory.

- Click "Open." The template opens in the Mathcad window.

You may now edit the template as you would modify any Mathcad worksheet. To save your changes under the current template name, choose **Save** from the **File** menu. If you wanted to give a new name to the modified template, choose **Save As** from the **File** menu instead and enter a new name for the template in the dialog box.

Note that when you modify a template, your changes will affect only new files created from the modified template. The changes will not affect any worksheets created with the template before the template was modified.

Saving your worksheet in RTF format

In addition to saving Mathcad worksheets and templates, Mathcad can save your entire worksheet in RTF format so that a word processor capable of reading an RTF file with embedded graphics might be able to open it. To do so:

- Scroll to the bottom of your worksheet to update all calculated results.

- Choose **Save As** from the **File** menu.

- In the Save As dialog box, choose "Rich Text Format Files" from the "Save as type" drop-down list.

- Enter a file name and then click "Save."

When you open this RTF file with a word processor such as Microsoft Word, you'll find all the Mathcad regions lined up one above the other at the left edge of the document. You can then use your word processor to move these regions wherever you want to.

Once the Mathcad regions saved in an RTF file have been loaded into a word processor, you'll no longer be able to edit equations and graphs—these will display as embedded graphics in your word processor. You will, however, still be able to edit the text.

To embed Mathcad worksheets or regions in a word processing document in a form that allows you to continue to edit the original Mathcad worksheets, see the section "Using OLE" on page 91.

Saving a worksheet as a Mathcad 6 file

In general, Mathcad worksheets are upwardly but not downwardly compatible. That is, worksheets created in an earlier version of Mathcad *will* open in the current version, but files created in the current version of Mathcad *will not* open in earlier versions. Mathcad 7, however, allows you to save a worksheet as a Mathcad 6 worksheet so that it will open in Mathcad version 6 for Windows or Macintosh. The caveat, of course, is that features in your worksheet new to Mathcad 7 will not be recognized in Mathcad 6. Regions or features that won't work in Mathcad 6 are rendered as bitmaps.

To save a worksheet as a Mathcad 6 worksheet:

■ Choose **Save** or **Save As** from the **File** menu.

■ In the "Save as type" drop-down list, select "Mathcad 6 Files" and provide a file name.

■ Click "Save." A message will appear warning you that certain features available only in Mathcad 7 will not work in Mathcad 6.

When you open a Mathcad 7 worksheet saved as a Mathcad 6 file in Mathcad 6 for Windows or Macintosh, you may see an additional warning indicating that certain features are not supported. For a list of product features, including features that are new in Mathcad 7, see "Mathcad features" on page 2.

Layout

Before printing a worksheet, you may need to adjust the margins, paper options, page breaks, and headers and footers so that pages of the worksheet are printed appropriately. This section describes how to change these worksheet attributes.

Once you've set these characteristics for a worksheet, you can easily apply these characteristics to future worksheets by saving your worksheet as a template, as described in the previous section.

Setting margins, paper size, source, and orientation

Mathcad worksheets have four user-specifiable margins, at the left, right, top, and bottom of the worksheet. To set these margins, choose **Page Setup** from the **File** menu. This brings up the Page Setup dialog box, shown below:

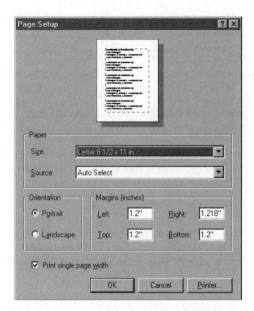

The four text boxes in the lower right of this dialog box show the distances from the margin to the corresponding edge of the actual sheet of paper on which you will be printing.

- **Left:** This is the distance from the left edge of the physical sheet of paper to the left edge of the print area.

- **Right:** This appears as a solid vertical line in your window. You may have to scroll to the right to see it. In addition to marking the right edge of the printed area, the right margin serves as a wrap margin for all text regions.

   Don't confuse the solid vertical line marking the right margin with the dashed vertical line marking the right page boundary. This line marks the right-hand edge of the sheet of paper itself. Its location depends on your choice of printer. If you haven't chosen a printer, you won't see this dashed line at all.

- **Top:** This is the distance from the top edge of the physical sheet of paper to the top edge of the print area. If your worksheet has a header, it appears just above this margin.

- **Bottom:** This is the distance from the bottom edge of the physical sheet of paper to the bottom edge of the print area. If your worksheet has a footer, it appears just below this margin.

You can also use settings in the Page Setup dialog box to change the size, source, or orientation of the paper on which you will print your worksheet:

- **Paper, Size:** This should correspond to the size of the paper in your printer.

- **Paper, Source:** This is the area in your printer supplying the paper.

- **Orientation, Portrait:** The paper is positioned vertically, with the longest dimension running from top to bottom.

- **Orientation, Landscape:** The paper is positioned horizontally, with the longest dimension running from left to right. This is useful if your worksheet is wider than a single page.

Click on the "Printer" button in the Page Setup dialog box to access your current printer settings. See "Printing" on page 79 for more about printing your Mathcad worksheets.

If you want the margin and other page setup settings in the current worksheet to be used in other worksheets, save the worksheet as a template as discussed in "Worksheets and templates" on page 72.

Pagebreaks

Mathcad provides two kinds of pagebreaks:

- **Soft pagebreaks**: Mathcad uses your default printer settings and your top and bottom margins to insert these pagebreaks automatically. These show up as dotted horizontal lines, and you see them as you scroll down in your worksheet. You cannot add or remove soft pagebreaks.

- **Hard pagebreaks**: You can insert a hard pagebreak by placing the cursor at the appropriate place in your worksheet and choosing **Page Break** from the **Insert** menu. Hard pagebreaks display as solid horizontal lines in your worksheets.

When Mathcad prints your worksheet, it begins printing on a new page whenever it encounters either a soft or a hard pagebreak.

To delete a hard pagebreak:

- Drag-select the hard pagebreak as you would select any other region in your Mathcad worksheet. A dashed selection box appears around the pagebreak.

- Choose **Cut** or **Delete** from the **Edit** menu.

Headers and Footers

To add a header or a footer to every printed page, choose **Headers/Footers** from the **Format** menu. This opens the Headers/Footers dialog box shown below:

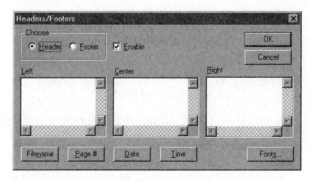

To add a header:

■ Click on the Header radio button.

■ Type the header into one or more of the text boxes. Whatever you type into the Left, Center, and Right text boxes will appear left-justified, centered, and right-justified on the page respectively.

■ To automatically insert the page number, current date, time, or filename wherever the insertion point is, click on the appropriate button below the text boxes. Mathcad inserts a special code into the text box. This will be replaced by the correct page number, date, time, or filename when you print the worksheet. Note that Mathcad always begins numbering at page 1.

■ Make sure the Enable check box is checked. When this is unchecked, Mathcad suppresses the display of headers and footers.

To add a footer:

■ Click on the Footer radio button.

■ Follow the rest of the instructions for inserting headers.

Printing

To print a Mathcad worksheet, choose **Print** from the **File** menu. The dialog box you see will depend on the particular printer you've selected. A typical dialog box is shown below:

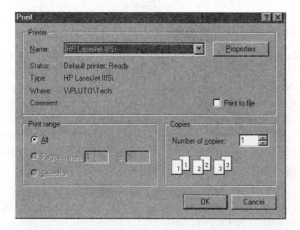

The Print dialog box lets you control whether to print the entire worksheet, selected pages, or selected regions; what printer to print on; and the number of copies to print. This section describes these various printing options in detail.

The "Properties" button in the Print dialog box gives you access to printing options for the paper, graphics, and fonts used by your printer. This allows you to change these options just before you print. If you don't want to print the worksheet immediately, you can change some of these options in the Page Setup dialog box as described in "Layout" on page 76.

Choosing what to print

You can choose to print the entire worksheet, selected pages, or even just selected regions. To control what Mathcad prints, click on one of the following radio buttons in the Print dialog box:

■ **All:** Click this button to print all pages in the worksheet.

■ **Pages:** Click this button to print a range of pages. Then fill in the two text boxes to indicate your selection. If you've selected a plotter as your output device, you'll only be able to print one page; the text box beside "To:" will be grayed out.

■ **Selection:** Click this button to print only the currently selected regions. If the button is gray, you have not selected any regions with the dashed rectangle.

If you find more pages than you expect coming out of the printer, keep in mind that Mathcad worksheets may be *wider* than a sheet of paper as well as longer. See "Printing wide worksheets" below.

Choosing what to print on

By default, Mathcad sends its output to whatever printer you installed as a default printer under your operating system. The installed printer is shown in the "Name" drop-down list. You may send your output to any printer you have installed under your operating system; simply choose another printer from the "Name" drop-down list. To redirect your output to a file, click the "Print to File" checkbox.

Printing wide worksheets

Because Mathcad worksheets can be wider than a sheet of paper, the idea of a "page" is not as clear as it would be in, for example, a word processor. You can scroll as far to the right as you like in a Mathcad worksheet and place equations, text, and graphics wherever you like. As you scroll horizontally, however, you will see dashed vertical lines appearing to indicate the right margins of successive "pages" corresponding to the settings for your printer. The sections of the worksheet separated by the dashed vertical line will print on separate sheets of paper, yet the page number at the bottom of the Mathcad window does not change as you scroll to the right.

You can think of the worksheet as being divided into vertical strips as shown in Figure 4-1. Mathcad begins printing at the top of the left-most strip and continues until it reaches the last region in this strip. It then goes to the top of the adjacent strip and prints every page down to the last region in that strip. This procedure is repeated until everything in the worksheet has been printed. Note that certain layouts will produce one or more blank pages.

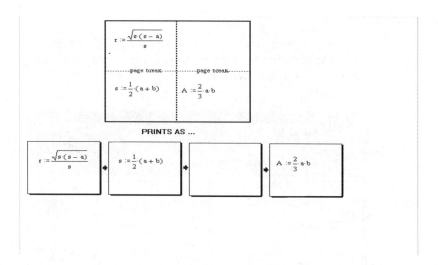

Figure 4-1: Mathcad divides very wide worksheets into strips for printing.

You can control whether or not Mathcad prints the entire worksheet or just the left-most strip shown in Figure 4-1. To do so, choose **Page Setup** from the **File** menu to open the Page Setup dialog box. Then:

■ To suppress printing of anything to the right of the right margin, click in the "Print single page width" box to put a check in it.

■ To print all the regions in the worksheet, even those to the right of the right margin, click in the "Print single page width" box to uncheck it.

As mentioned earlier in this section, you can ask Mathcad to print a range of pages in the worksheet by typing the page range in the Print dialog box. The page numbers in the dialog box refer only to horizontal divisions. For example, if your worksheet looks like that shown in Figure 4-1, and you ask Mathcad to print page 2, you will see two sheets of paper corresponding to the lower-left and lower-right quadrants in Figure 4-1.

To print only the lower left-hand page shown in Figure 4-1:

■ Choose **Print** from the **File** menu.

■ Type "2" in the boxes next to the words "From" and "To." This suppresses printing of the upper-left and upper-right quadrants.

■ Choose **Page Setup** from the **File** menu and make sure there is a check in the "Print single page width" box. This suppresses printing of the lower-right quadrant.

■ Click on "OK."

Note that this makes it impossible to print the upper- or lower-right quadrants by themselves.

Print preview

To check your worksheet's layout before printing, choose **Print Preview** from the **File** menu. The Print Preview window displays the current section of your worksheet, in miniature, as it will appear when printed. See Figure 4-2.

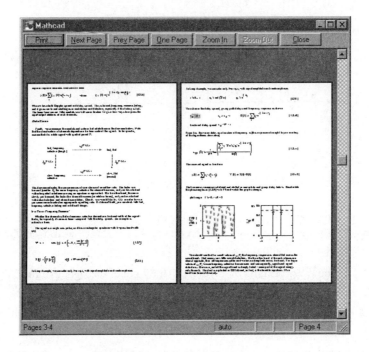

Figure 4-2: Previewing the printed output.

To print your worksheet from this screen, click on the "Print" button at the top of the window. Click "Close" to go back to the main worksheet screen. The remaining buttons at the top of the Print Preview screen give you more control over the preview:

- **Next Page:** Click this button to preview the next page of the worksheet. If this button is gray, there are no further pages in the worksheet.

- **Prev Page:** Click this button to preview the previous page of the worksheet. If this button is gray, there are no preceding pages in the worksheet.

- **Zoom In:** Click this button to magnify a portion of the worksheet.

- **Zoom Out:** Click this button to cancel any magnification so that you see your document in the normal size used in the Print Preview screen.

- **Two Page or One Page:** Click "Two Page" to show two pages of the worksheet at a time, as was done in Figure 4-2. Click "One Page" to show only one.

Although you can use the "Zoom In" and "Zoom Out" buttons to magnify the worksheet, you can also magnify the worksheet by moving the cursor onto the previewed page so that the cursor changes to a magnifying glass. Then click the mouse. You can click again to magnify your worksheet even more. Once you're at the maximum magnification, clicking on the page de-magnifies it.

You cannot edit the current page or change its format in the Print Preview screen. To edit the page or change its format, return to the normal worksheet view by clicking the "Close" button. You can then edit the worksheet or change its format as described in the previous section, "Layout."

Mailing

If you're connected to a mail system that's compatible with Microsoft Mail, you'll be able to use Mathcad to direct that system to send an electronic mail message and your current Mathcad worksheet. This saves you the work of opening a separate mail application to e-mail a Mathcad worksheet.

Mathcad supports any electronic mail system compatible with Microsoft's Mail API (MAPI). When you use Mathcad to send a worksheet by electronic mail, the recipient of the message will receive the worksheet as a file attached to an ordinary e-mail message, provided that the recipient's mail system uses the same encoding technique as yours.

To send a Mathcad worksheet by electronic mail:

■ Open the worksheet you want to send.

■ Choose **Send** from the **File** menu.

Once you do so, your mail system will launch and create a new message with your worksheet as an attachment. You should then enter the text of your mail message, the address of the recipient, and any other information allowed by your mail system.

The settings in your mail system determine how Mathcad worksheets are attached to the mail message. We recommend that you use an encoding method such as MIME or UUENCODE, if available, to attach Mathcad worksheets to mail messages.

If you're not connected to a MAPI-compatible mail system, the **Send** command on the **File** menu will be grayed out, but you can send a Mathcad worksheet by manually making it an attachment to a mail message.

Safeguarding your calculations

The ease with which you can alter a Mathcad worksheet can present a problem. It is all too easy to alter a worksheet and to change things which are not meant to be changed.

For example, if you've developed and thoroughly tested a set of equations, you may want to prevent anyone from tampering with them.

To avoid this, you may want to safeguard these equations by locking them up in such a way that you'll still be able to use them even though nobody will be able to change them.

Pro   You can use Mathcad Professional to lock a set of equations. To do so:

- You designate a particular area in your worksheet as a lockable area.

- You place the calculations that you want to safeguard into that lockable area.

- You lock the area.

Once an equation is safely inside a locked area, nobody will be able to edit it. That equation will, however, continue to affect other equations in the document. For example, if you define a function inside a locked area, you'll still be able to use that function anywhere below and to the right of its definition. You will not, however, be able to change the function's definition itself.

The remainder of this section describes how to specify the beginning and the end of the lockable area as well as how to lock and unlock that area once you've created it.

Specifying the lockable area

A lockable area is designated by two lines as shown in Figure 4-3. The open padlocks above and below these lines indicate that the area is now unlocked. As long as this area remains unlocked, you can edit equations and text within it as freely as you would anywhere else in the worksheet.

To designate a lockable area:

- Choose **Lock Regions**⇒**Set Lock Area** from the **Format** menu. Mathcad inserts a pair of lines like those in Figure 4-3. These mark the boundaries of the lockable area.

- Select either of these boundary lines just as you'd select any region: by dragging the mouse across the line or by shift-clicking on the line itself.

- Once you've selected the boundary line, drag it just as you'd drag any other region.

You should position the boundaries so that there's enough space between them for whatever equations you want to lock. You can have any number of lockable areas in your worksheet. The only restriction is that you cannot have one lockable area inside another.

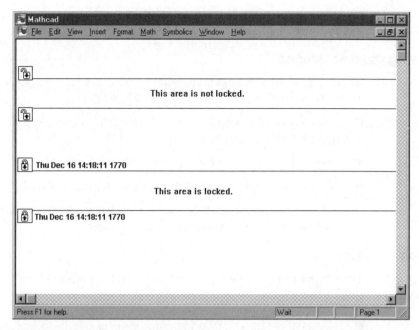

Figure 4-3: The area between the two lines is a lockable area. The first pair is still unlocked; the second pair was locked on the date shown.

Locking up the calculations

Once you've placed whatever equations you want to lock up inside the lockable area, you are ready to lock it up. You'll be able to lock it up either with or without a password. To do so:

■ Click in the lockable area.

■ Choose **Lock Regions⇒Lock Area** from the **Format** menu.

■ You'll see a dialog box asking you if you want to set a password. Click "Yes" if you want to require a password to unlock the area. Otherwise click "No."

■ If you clicked "Yes," you'll be prompted for a password. Type any combination of letters and numbers. Keep in mind that the password is case sensitive.

Once locked, the locked area looks like the lower pair of lines in Figure 4-3. The date and time the area was last locked is shown above and below the boundary lines.

Locking without a password is useful when you just want to prevent yourself from absent-mindedly changing something, and you don't want to worry about having to remember a password. When a region is locked without a password, anyone will be able to unlock it by simply choosing **Lock Regions⇒Unlock Area** from the **Format** menu.

Locking with a password is useful when you want to prevent unauthorized changes to a worksheet. When you choose this option, make sure you remember your password.

If you forget your password, you may find yourself permanently locked out of that lockable area.

Unlocking the calculations

If you want to make changes to an equation inside a locked area, you'll have to unlock it first. To do so:

■ Click on one of the boundary lines of the region you want to unlock. Mathcad highlights the boundary line.

■ Choose **Lock Regions**⇒**Unlock Area** from the **Format** menu.

■ If a password is required, you'll be prompted for the password.

Once an area is unlocked, you'll be able to make whatever changes you want to just as freely as you would anywhere else in your worksheet.

Deleting a lockable area

You can delete a lockable area just as you would any other region. To do so:

■ Make sure the area is unlocked. You cannot delete a locked area.

■ Select either of the two lines indicating the extent of the locked area by dragging the mouse across it.

■ Choose **Cut** from the **Edit** menu.

References and hyperlinks

Mathcad allows you to establish connections between Mathcad worksheets in two ways. One type of connection allows you to *reference* one worksheet from another—that is, to access the computational machinery in the other worksheet without opening it or typing its equations or definitions directly in the current worksheet. Mathcad also allows you to set up *hyperlinks* between Mathcad worksheets—that is, to create "hotspots" in your Mathcad worksheets that, when you double-click on them, bring up other Mathcad worksheets. You can also create simple hyperlinks in Mathcad worksheets in order to view arbitrary file types, such as word processing documents, help files, or animation files. These connections are explored in more detail below.

Pro Mathcad Professional also gives you MathSoft's MathConnex application to link Mathcad worksheets and other computational components to create heterogeneous computational systems. In MathConnex you draw "wires" between components, specifying which computational outputs from one component become the inputs for the next component. In this way you chain together computation procedures from Mathcad worksheets and other sources. See the *MathConnex Getting Start Guide* for more information. And for general information about establishing OLE links between Mathcad and other applications, see the section "Using OLE" on page 91 and Chapter 19, "Data Management."

Making equations of one worksheet available in another

There may be times when you want to use formulas and calculations from one Mathcad worksheet inside another. You can, of course, simply open both worksheets and use **Copy** and **Paste** from the **Edit** menu to move whatever you need to move, or drag regions from one worksheet and drop them in the other. However, when entire worksheets are involved, this method may be cumbersome or may result in unnecessary clutter, obscuring the main computations of your worksheet.

A simple way to make formulas from one worksheet available in another one is to insert a *reference* in the current worksheet. When you insert a reference to a worksheet, you won't see the formulas of the referenced worksheet, but the current worksheet behaves *as if* you could.

To insert a reference to a worksheet:

■ Click the mouse wherever you want to insert the reference. Make sure you click in empty space and not in an existing region. The cursor should look like a crosshair.

■ Choose **Reference** from the **Insert** menu. You'll see the following dialog box:

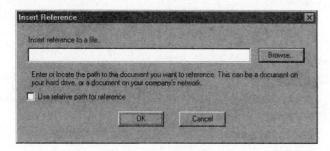

■ Click the "Browse" button to locate and select a worksheet. Alternatively, you may type the complete path to a worksheet in the empty text box. For example, you would type `c:\Program Files\MathSoft\Mathcad\conform.mcd` to insert a reference to the file `conform.mcd` located in the `Mathcad` folder. You can also enter an Internet address (URL) to insert a reference to a Mathcad file that is located on the World Wide Web.

■ Click "OK" to insert the reference into your worksheet.

To indicate that a reference has been inserted, Mathcad pastes a small icon wherever you had the crosshair as shown in Figure 4-4. The path to the referenced worksheet is to the right of the icon. All definitions in the referenced worksheet will be available below or to the right of this icon. If you double-click on this icon, Mathcad opens the referenced worksheet in its own window for editing. You can move or delete this icon just as you would any other Mathcad region.

By default, the location of the referenced file is stored in the worksheet as an absolute system path (or URL). This means that if you copy the main worksheet and the referenced worksheet to a different file system with a different directory structure, Mathcad will not be able to locate the referenced file. If you want the location of the referenced file to be stored relative to the Mathcad worksheet containing the reference, however, click the "Use relative path for reference" box in the Insert Reference dialog box. This allows the reference to be valid even if you move the referenced file and the main worksheet, but keep the *relative* directory structure between the two the same. To use a relative path, the two worksheets must be on the same local or network drive. If you specify a relative path, Mathcad displays a capital "R" in parentheses at the end of the path for the reference in your worksheet.

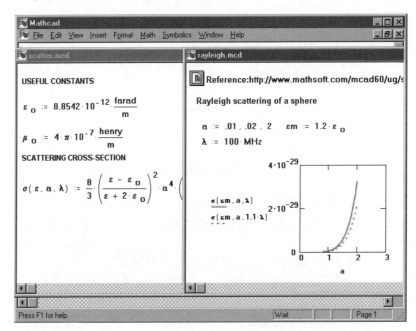

Figure 4-4: An icon representing a referenced worksheet, here from the World Wide Web. Definitions in the referenced worksheet are available below and to the right of this icon.

This mechanism will work for worksheets stored on a local or network drive or on the World Wide Web. Of course, if you move the referenced worksheet *after* having inserted a reference to it in another worksheet, Mathcad will display an error message in the main worksheet indicating that it can no longer find the referenced worksheet.

If you edit the contents of a referenced file so that any calculations change, you must re-open any worksheets that contain references to that file for any calculations to update. The calculations in those worksheets do not update automatically.

Creating hyperlinks between worksheets

You can create a hyperlink from any Mathcad region, such as a text region or a graphic element, to any Mathcad worksheet or template. When you or a reader double-clicks on this hyperlink, Mathcad will display the Mathcad worksheet designated by the hyperlink. In this way you can connect groups of related worksheets into a form similar to Mathcad's Electronic Books, or simply cross-reference a related Mathcad worksheet from within the current worksheet.

You have two options for the display of the linked worksheet when you double-click on the hyperlink:

■ The hyperlinked worksheet can open in a complete Mathcad worksheet window that overlays the current worksheet window and that allows you to edit its contents as you would any other worksheet, or

■ The hyperlinked worksheet can open in a small pop-up window that simply displays the contents of the worksheet, but does not allow you to edit its contents.

In either case the worksheet that contains the original hyperlink remains open for you to view and edit. Mathcad can follow a hyperlink to any worksheet, whether it is stored on a local drive, a network drive, or the World Wide Web.

To create a hyperlink, you must specify:

■ What to double-click on in order to go to another worksheet. This is the "gateway," and it can be a piece of text, an equation, or a graphics region.

■ What worksheet to go to. This is the "target worksheet."

First, specify the gateway by doing one of the following:

■ Select a piece of text, or

■ Click anywhere in an equation or graphics region, or

■ Place the insertion point anywhere within an entire text region.

The next step is to specify the target. To do so:

■ Choose **Hyperlink**⇒**New** from the **Insert** menu. You'll see the following dialog box:

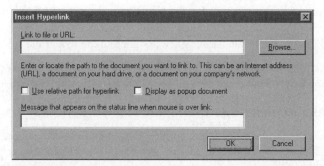

■ Click the "Browse" button to locate and select the target worksheet. Alternatively, you may type the complete path to a worksheet in the empty text box at the top of the dialog box. For example, type `c:\Program Files\MathSoft\Math-cad\conform.mcd` to insert a hyperlink to the file `conform.mcd` located in the `Mathcad` folder. You can also enter an Internet address (URL) to create a hyperlink to a file on the World Wide Web.

- Click the "Use relative path for hyperlink" box to store the location of the target worksheet relative to the Mathcad worksheet containing the hyperlink. This allows the hyperlink to be valid even if you move the target file and the worksheet containing the hyperlink, but keep the relative directory structure between the two the same. If you want the location of the target worksheet to be absolute instead, do not click the box for using a relative path. See the previous section, "Making equations of one worksheet available in another," for more information about relative and absolute paths.

- Click the "Display as pop-up document" checkbox if you want the target worksheet to open in a small pop-up window when you double-click on the gateway.

- If you want a message to appear on the status line at the bottom of the window when the mouse hovers over the gateway to the hyperlink, type the message in the text box at the bottom of the Insert Hyperlink dialog box.

- Click "OK."

Mathcad then establishes the hyperlink. If you used selected text as the gateway, Mathcad underlines the text and makes it bold to indicate the existence of a hyperlink. Other gateways won't be marked in any way, but if you use a graphic element as a "button" for the gateway, the existence of the hyperlink may be obvious. Mathcad will also now change the mouse pointer to a "hand" cursor when you hover over the gateway, and any message you specified will appear on the status line at the bottom of the window when the cursor is over the gateway.

When you double-click on the gateway to the hyperlink, Mathcad opens the target worksheet in the kind of window (either pop-up or full) you specified. You close a pop-up window by clicking on the close box in the upper right corner.

To change any aspects of a hyperlink—for example, if you move the target worksheet and still want the hyperlink to work—click anywhere in the gateway and choose **Hyperlink⇒Edit** from the **Insert** menu. Then you can change the name or location of the target worksheet, whether the target worksheet displays in a pop-up window, and whether the location of the target file is stored as a relative or absolute path. You can also change the status bar message assigned to the hyperlink.

To remove a hyperlink, simply click anywhere in the gateway and choose **Hyperlink⇒Erase** from the **Insert** menu. Mathcad will remove all traces of the link.

Creating hyperlinks to files other than Mathcad worksheets

The methods described in the previous section will create a hyperlink not only from one Mathcad worksheet to another, but also from a Mathcad worksheet to any other file type, either on a local or network drive or on the World Wide Web. Use this feature to create more full-featured "Electronic Books" or compound documents that contain not only Mathcad worksheets but word processing files, animation files—any file type that you want.

You can create a hyperlink to any file type for which you have an appropriate "viewer" application. When you double-click on a hyperlink to a file other than a Mathcad worksheet, you launch either the application that created the file or an application that is associated with a file of that type in the Windows Registry. You do not have the option of displaying such hyperlinked files within a pop-up window in the Mathcad application frame.

For example, to create a hyperlink from a Mathcad worksheet to an animation (AVI) file:

- Specify a gateway in your Mathcad worksheet as described in the previous section.

- Choose **Hyperlink⇒New** from the **Insert** menu.

- In the Insert Hyperlink dialog box, type the path or URL to the AVI file, or use the "browse" button to locate it on your file system.

- If you want a message to appear on the status line at the bottom of the window when the mouse hovers over the gateway to the hyperlink, type the message in the text box at the bottom of the Insert Hyperlink dialog box.

- Click "OK" when you are done.

Now when you double-click on the gateway, you will launch the Windows Media Player or a comparable application that can play AVI files, and you will see the animation.

Warning about hyperlinks from regions other than text

Although the gateway to a target worksheet can be any region, such as an equation or plot, there are two significant disadvantages to using a region other than selected text:

- When you use text as a gateway, Mathcad makes the selected text bold and underlined to indicate that a hyperlink exists there. No corresponding indication is possible when you choose something other than selected text as a gateway.

- The hyperlink preempts the normal response to double-clicking on the region. For example, if you choose a plot as a gateway, you will no longer be able to double-click on that plot to open a formatting dialog box.

For these reasons, we recommend that you use either selected text or an embedded graphic as a gateway to another worksheet.

Using OLE

As you develop a Mathcad worksheet, you may want to embellish it or extend its functionality by inserting *objects,* which are elements you create in another application such as a word processor or a drawing package. Conversely, you may want to insert Mathcad worksheets or regions from a Mathcad worksheet into another application. OLE (Object Linking and Embedding) technology in Microsoft Windows makes it possible not only to insert static pictures of such objects into your applications (or of

Mathcad objects into other applications), but to insert the objects in such a way that they can be fully edited in their originating applications.

You insert objects into Mathcad, which is an OLE2-compatible application, by using the **Object** command from the **Insert** menu, by drag-and-drop, or by copying and pasting. Each of these methods is explained in detail in this section. The method you choose depends on whether you want to create the object on the fly, whether the object has already been created, or whether you want the object to be an entire file. You can edit objects in a Mathcad worksheet simply by double-clicking on them, causing *in-place activation* of the originating application in most cases.

In general, you can also use these methods to insert Mathcad objects into other applications and edit them inside those applications. However, the details depend on the extent to which the application receiving a Mathcad object supports OLE2. This section, therefore, focuses on inserting objects into Mathcad and only briefly touches on inserting Mathcad objects into other OLE2-compatible applications.

For information about using Mathcad's components for importing and exporting data, as well as establishing dynamic connections with other applications, see Chapter 19, "Data Management." If you would like to import or export graphic files such as bitmaps into your Mathcad worksheets, turn to Chapter 28, "Importing and Exporting Graphics."

Embedded vs. linked objects

Objects can be either *embedded* in or *linked* to a Mathcad worksheet. For you to link an object, the object must exist in a saved file. An object that you embed, on the other hand, may be created at the time of insertion or it may be part of a saved file. The difference between an embedded object and a linked object is only important when you want to edit it. When you edit an embedded object, any changes you make to the object will affect it only in the context of the Mathcad worksheet. The original object in the source application, if there is one, is left undisturbed. When you edit a linked object, on the other hand, any changes you make to the object will affect the actual file containing the object.

Inserting an object into a worksheet

One way to insert an object from another application into Mathcad is to use the **Object** command from the **Insert** menu. Using this method, you can insert an object that you create on the fly at the time you are inserting it, or you can insert an entire file that you've already created.

To insert an object or a saved file, you should first:

■ Click in a blank area of your worksheet where you would like to insert the object. Make sure that you see the crosshair.

■ Choose **Object** from the **Insert** menu to bring up the Insert Object dialog box. By default the "Create New" radio button is selected:

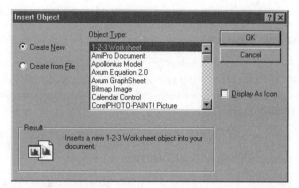

- Click the "Display as Icon" checkbox if you want an icon, rather than the actual object, to appear in your worksheet. The icon is typically the icon of the application that created the object.

Then, to create a new object:

- Select an application from the "Object Type" list in which to create the object. The available object types will depend on the applications you have installed on your system.

- Click "OK."

The source application opens so that you can create the object. When you are finished working to create the object, close the source application. The object you created will be embedded in your Mathcad worksheet.

If you want to insert a previously created file:

- Click the "Create from File" radio button in the Insert Object dialog box. The dialog box will then look like this:

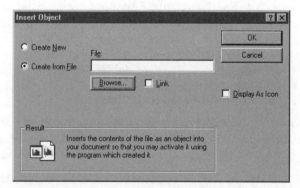

- Type the path to the object file or use the "Browse" button to locate it.

- Click the "Link" checkbox to insert a linked object. Otherwise, the object will be embedded.

- Click "OK."

The object will then be either linked or embedded in your Mathcad worksheet.

Pasting an object into a worksheet

Instead of inserting an object through the Insert Object dialog box, you can copy an object from a source application to the clipboard and paste it into Mathcad. This method is particularly useful when you've already created the object in another application and you don't want to insert an entire file.

To insert an embedded or linked object into a worksheet via the clipboard:

- Open the source application containing the object.

- Copy the object to the clipboard in the source application. You typically do this by choosing **Copy** from the **Edit** menu, or by pressing [**Ctrl**]C.

- Click in the Mathcad worksheet where you'd like to place the object.

- Choose **Paste** or **Paste Special** from Mathcad's **Edit** menu.

If you choose **Paste**, the object will be pasted in your Mathcad worksheet in a format that depends on what the source application has placed on the clipboard. The behavior may differ depending on whether you have selected a math placeholder or are pasting into a blank space in the worksheet. Mathcad will create one of the following:

- A *matrix,* if you are pasting numeric data from the clipboard into an empty math placeholder. (See Chapter 19, "Data Management.")

- A *text region,* if you are pasting text that does not contain numeric data exclusively.

- A *bitmap* or *picture (metafile),* if the originating application generates graphics. (See Chapter 28, "Importing and Exporting Graphics.")

- An embedded object, if the originating application supports OLE.

If you choose **Paste Special** from the **Edit** menu, you have the option of pasting the object in one of the available formats, which depend on the object you've copied. Typically you can choose to paste the object as an embedded or linked OLE object (if the object was stored in a saved file in an OLE-compatible source application), a picture (metafile), or a bitmap.

Dragging and dropping an object into a worksheet

A third way to insert an OLE object into a Mathcad worksheet is to drag it from the source application and drop it into the worksheet. This is very similar to copying and pasting, but does not allow you to create a link to an object. To do so:

- Open both Mathcad and the source application and arrange the two windows side by side on the screen.

- Select the object in the source application, usually by drag-selecting.

- Hold the mouse button down. For some applications, it may be necessary to press the [Ctrl] key and hold the mouse button down to ensure that the object will be copied (rather than cut) from the source application.

- Drag the cursor onto a blank space in the Mathcad worksheet.

- Let go of the mouse button to drop the object into the worksheet.

Editing an object

To edit either an embedded or linked object in a Mathcad worksheet, double-click the object. Mathcad's menus and toolbars will change to those of the source application, and a hatched border will surround the object so that you can edit it. This OLE editing mechanism is called in-place activation. For example, you can use in-place activation to edit objects created by Microsoft Office 95 or 97 applications such as Excel and Word inside Mathcad.

If the source application does not support in-place activation inside Mathcad, the behavior will differ. In the case of an embedded object, a copy of the object is placed into a window from the other application. If the object is linked, the source application opens the file containing the object.

Editing a link

If you've inserted a linked object into a Mathcad worksheet, you can update the link, eliminate it, or change the source file to which the object is linked. To do so, choose **Links** from the **Edit** menu. You'll see the following dialog box:

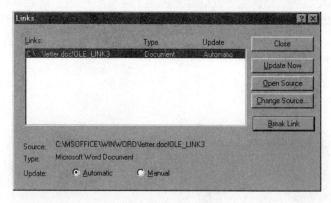

Choose the link you want to edit from the list of links. Then make any of the following changes:

Automatic: Click this radio button to make the link update whenever you open the worksheet and any time the source information changes while the worksheet is open.

Manual: Click this radio button to make the link update only when you press the "Update Now" button.

Update Now: Click this button to update a manual link.

Open Source: Opens the application in which the linked object was created.

Change Source: Links the object with a different source file. The new source file must have been created in the same application as the original source file.

Break Link: Breaks the link between an object's original source and the copy of the object in the worksheet.

Inserting Mathcad objects into other applications

Just as you can insert objects into a Mathcad worksheet from other OLE2-compatible applications, you can insert Mathcad objects—either entire Mathcad worksheets or selected Mathcad regions—into other applications. The methods of doing so are nearly the same as those outlined in the previous section for inserting objects into Mathcad. They depend, however, on the extent to which the other applications support OLE2.

For example, you may use any of the three methods of inserting OLE objects (choosing **Object** from the receiving application's **Insert** menu, copying and pasting, and drag-and-drop) to insert Mathcad objects into Microsoft Office 95 or 97 applications.

Once you've inserted a Mathcad object into another application, you can edit it by double-clicking on it. If the application supports in-place activation, as Microsoft Office applications do, the menus and toolbars will change to Mathcad's so that you can edit the object without exiting the application and launching Mathcad. Figure 4-5 shows the in-place activation of a Mathcad object inside Microsoft Word.

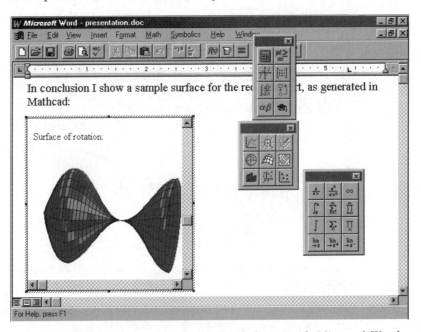

Figure 4-5: In-place activation of a Mathcad object inside Microsoft Word, giving you access to Mathcad's menus, toolbar, and palettes.

Chapter 5
Text

Text regions function as commentary in a Mathcad worksheet, explaining and annotating your computations and plots.

Mathcad supports many of the text editing and formatting features of word processors. Mathcad text can include any combination of fonts, sizes, and type and paragraph styles. Text automatically wraps, breaking lines according to margins that you specify. You can specify the alignment and indentation of text regions. You can define and apply text styles to maintain consistency in the appearance of your text.

This chapter describes Mathcad's commands for creating and editing text and for creating and applying text styles.

This chapter includes the following sections:

Inserting text

Creating and resizing text regions.

Equations in text

Embedding equations into text regions.

Text editing

Manipulating text that is already in a region: cutting and pasting; changing font properties, alignment and indentation; and typing Greek letters.

Text styles

Working with text styles to streamline text formatting. Creating and applying new text styles.

Text region properties

Highlighting text regions.

Find and Replace

Finding and replacing text strings and variable names.

Spell-checking

Using the **Check Spelling** command to find and correct spelling errors in text.

Inserting text

This section describes how to create text regions in Mathcad. Text regions are useful for inserting any kind of text into your worksheets and templates: comments around the equations and plots in your worksheet, blocks of explanatory text, background information, instructions for the use of the worksheet, and so on. There is no limit on the size of text regions. Mathcad ignores text when it performs calculations, but you can insert working math equations into text regions as described in "Equations in text" on page 100.

Creating a text region

To create a text region, follow these steps:

■ Click in blank space to position the crosshair where you want the text region to begin. Then choose **Text Region** from the **Insert** menu, or press the double quote (") key. Mathcad begins a text region. The crosshair changes into an insertion point and a text box appears.

■ Now begin typing some text. Mathcad displays the text and surrounds it with a text box. As you type, the insertion point moves and the text box grows.

■ When you've finished typing the text, click outside the text region. The text box disappears.

You cannot leave a text region by pressing [↵]. You must leave the text region by:

■ Clicking outside the region, or

■ By repeatedly pressing one of the arrow keys until the cursor leaves the region.

Figure 5-1 on the next page shows a Mathcad worksheet containing several text regions followed by an equation.

To insert text into an existing text region:

■ Click between two characters in a text region. A text box will surround your text. Anything you type gets inserted at the insertion point.

To delete text from an existing text region, click in the text region and:

■ Press [BkSp] to delete the character to the left of the insertion point, or

■ Press [Del] to delete the character to the right of the insertion point.

To overtype text:

■ Place the insertion point to the left of the first character you want to overtype.

■ Press the [Ins] key and begin typing. The vertical bar now has a break in the middle to indicate that you are in *overtype* mode. To return to the default *insert* mode, press [Ins] again.

To break a line or start a new line in a text region, press [⏎]. Mathcad inserts a *hard line break* and moves the insertion point down to the next line. When you rewrap the text by changing the width of the text region, Mathcad will maintain a line break at this spot in the text.

To delete a hard line break, click at the beginning of the next line in the text region and press [BkSp].

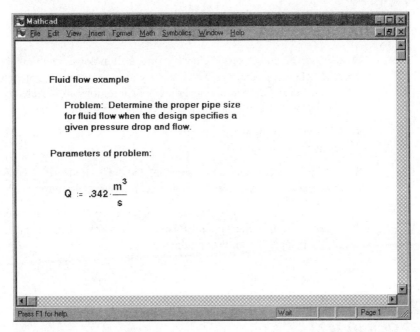

Figure 5-1: Text regions above an equation in a Mathcad worksheet.

Changing the width of a text region

When you start typing in a text region, the region grows as you type, wrapping only when you reach the right margin or page boundary. (The location of the right margin is determined by the settings in the Page Setup dialog box, which you can modify by choosing **Page Setup** from the **File** menu.) Press [⏎] whenever you want to start a new line. Often you would like to set a width for your whole text region, and have lines wrap to stay within that width as you type. To do this:

■ Type normally until the first line reaches the width you want.

■ Type a space and press [Ctrl][⏎].

All other lines will break to stay within this width. When you add to or edit the text, Mathcad rewraps the text according to the width set by the line at the end of which you pressed [Ctrl][⏎].

To change the width of an existing text region, do the following:

- Drag-select the text region by clicking in the worksheet outside it and dragging the mouse pointer across the region and releasing it, or click anywhere in the text region. A selection box encloses the text region.

- Move the pointer to the middle of the right edge of the text region until it hovers over the "handle" on the selection rectangle. The pointer now changes to a double arrow. You can now change the size of the text region the same way you change the size of any window: by dragging the mouse.

Moving text regions

To move a single text region or group of regions, follow the same steps that you would with math regions:

- Click on an empty spot, hold the mouse button down, and drag the selection rectangle across the region or regions you want to select. When you release the mouse button, dashed outlines show which regions are selected or, if you have selected a single region, a selection box appears around the region.

- Now move the mouse pointer to the edge of a selected region so that its appearance changes to a hand.

- Hold down the mouse button and drag it to the desired spot. If you've selected more than one region, the selected regions will move as a group.

You can also cut, paste, and copy text regions as you would any other regions. Select the regions and then choose **Cut**, **Paste**, or **Copy** from the **Edit** menu. You can also use the corresponding buttons on the toolbar.

Equations in text

This section describes how to insert equations into your text regions. Equations inserted into text have the same properties as those in the rest of your worksheet. You can edit them using the methods described in Chapter 3, "Editing Equations."

Entering an equation into text can affect the spacing between the lines of a text paragraph. If the equation is taller than a single line, the spacing between all the lines in the paragraph adjusts to make room for the equation.

Inserting an equation into text

You can place an equation into text either by creating a new equation or by pasting an existing equation into a text region.

To add a new equation into a text region or a paragraph, follow these steps:

- Click in the text region or paragraph to place the insertion point where you want the equation to start.

> The universal gravitational constant, G, has the value | and can be used to determine the acceleration of a less massive object toward a more massive object.

- Choose **Math Region** from the **Insert** menu.

> The universal gravitational constant, G, has the value ▮ and can be used to determine the acceleration of a less massive object toward a more massive object.

- Type in the equation just as you would in a math region.

- When you've finished typing in the equation, click on any text to return to the text region. Mathcad adjusts the line spacing in the text region to accommodate the embedded math region.

> The universal gravitational constant, G, has the value $G := 6.67259 \cdot 10^{-11} \cdot \dfrac{m^3}{kg \cdot s^2}$ and can be used to determine the acceleration of a less massive object toward a more massive object.

To paste an existing equation into a text region, follow these steps:

- Select the equation you want to paste into the text.

- Choose **Copy** from the **Edit** menu.

- Click in the text region to place the insertion point where you want the equation to start.

- Choose **Paste** from the **Edit** menu.

Editing equations in text

Once you've embedded an equation into a text region, you can edit it in the same way you edit equations anywhere else. For detailed procedures, see Chapter 3, "Editing Equations."

Disabling embedded equations

When you first insert an equation into text, it behaves just like an equation in a math region; it affects calculations throughout the worksheet. If you want the equation to be purely cosmetic, you can disable it so that it no longer calculates. To do so:

- Click on the equation you want to disable.

- Choose **Properties** from the **Format** menu. Click on the Calculation tab.

- Click in the check box next to "Disable Evaluation."

- Click "OK."

Once you've done so, the equation will neither affect nor be affected by other equations in the worksheet. To turn it back on, remove the check box next to "Disable Evaluation" in the Properties dialog box.

For a more general discussion of disabling and locking equations, see the section "Disabling equations" in Chapter 7.

Text editing

This section describes Mathcad features for editing existing text. This includes changing the words themselves, either manually or by clicking and typing. It also includes changing the way the words look by changing various font properties, and changing the way they're arranged by changing the alignment within text regions.

Moving the insertion point in text

In general, the procedures in this *User's Guide* tell you to move the insertion point around text regions by clicking with the mouse wherever you want to put the insertion point. However, as an alternative, you can also use the arrow keys to move the insertion point. This section briefly describes these keys.

The arrow keys move the insertion point character by character or line by line within text. Pressing [Ctrl] and an arrow key moves the insertion point word by word or line by line. These and other ways of moving the insertion point are summarized in the table below.

Key	Action
[→]	Move right one character.
[←]	Move left one character.
[↑]	Move up to the previous line.
[↓]	Move down to the next line.
[Ctrl][→]	Move to the end of the current word. If the insertion point is already there, move to the end of the next word.
[Ctrl][←]	Move to the beginning of the current word. If the insertion point is already there, move to the beginning of the previous word.
[Ctrl][↑]	Move to the beginning of the current line. If the insertion point is already there, move to the beginning of the previous line.
[Ctrl][↓]	Move to the end of the current line. If the insertion point is already there, move to the end of the next line.
[Home]	Move to the beginning of the current line.
[End]	Move to the end of the current line.

Selecting text

The commands described in "Inserting text" on page 98 involve selecting the whole text region by dragging the selection rectangle. The commands described in this section on text editing involve working with selections of text *within* a text region. There are several ways to select text in a text region:

- Click in the text region so that the text box appears. Drag across the text holding the mouse button down. Mathcad highlights the selected text, including any full lines between the first and last characters you selected.

- Click in the text and press [**Shift**] and an arrow key. Mathcad highlights the text in the direction of the arrow key used.

- Click in the text and press [**Ctrl**][**Shift**] and an arrow key. If a left or right arrow is used, Mathcad highlights from the insertion point to the beginning of the current or next word. If an up or down arrow is used, Mathcad highlights text from the insertion point to the beginning or end of a line.

- Select just one word of text by double-clicking on it.

Once text is selected, you can delete it, copy it, check the spelling, or change its font, size, style, or color.

Cutting and copying text

To cut a sequence of characters from a text region, follow these steps:

- Click in the text region and select the desired string of text. The highlighted text is shown in "reverse video."

  > Problem: Assume a long pipe with turbulent frictional losses. Use the Moody method to estimate Reynolds number.

- Choose **Cut** from the **Edit** menu. Mathcad deletes the text from the text region, copies it to the clipboard, and rewraps the remaining text.

  > Problem: Assume a long pipe with turbulent frictional losses.

You could also copy text to the clipboard without deleting it. To do so, choose **Copy** instead of **Cut** from the **Edit** menu. You can use the appropriate toolbar buttons for these operations instead of using the **Edit** menu commands.

Once you've cut or copied text to the clipboard, you can paste it back into any text region or into an empty space to create a new text region. To do so:

- Click in the spot where you want to paste the text. This can be anywhere in an existing text region or in an empty area of your worksheet.

  > Problem: Assume a long pipe with turbulent frictional losses.

- Choose **Paste** from the **Edit** menu. Mathcad pastes the text from the clipboard into the text region.

  > Problem: Use the Moody method to estimate Reynolds number. Assume a long pipe with turbulent frictional losses.

Note that if you want to insert the entire contents of a text region into an existing region, you should select the material you want to insert as a text string by clicking in the text and dragging to highlight it. If you copy an entire region selected with the selection rectangle, you can paste this selection only into a blank area of your worksheet.

Changing text properties

When you first enter text, its properties are determined by the worksheet or template defaults for the style called "Normal." See the section "Text styles" on page 108 to find out about applying and modifying existing text styles and creating new ones for governing the default appearance of entire text regions.

To change the font, size, style, position, and color of a *portion* of the text within a text region, you can first select it and choose **Text** from the **Format** menu. Any properties that you define for selected text using this process override the properties associated with the style for that text region, even when you change those style properties.

To change the properties of selected text:

- Select some text using one of the methods described in the section "Selecting text" on page 103.

- Choose **Text** from the **Format** menu. Mathcad displays a dialog box showing available fonts, styles, sizes, effects, and color. Alternatively, use the Format Bar for choosing fonts, sizes, and some styles and effects.

- Change the appropriate properties in the dialog box and click "OK." You can change the following properties:

Font

To change the font of the selected text, scroll through the Font list in the dialog box and choose an available font.

Font Style

To change the style of the selected text, scroll through the Font Style list in the dialog box.

As you scroll through the Font Style list you'll notice that some style combinations are unavailable. For example, some fonts come in bold or italic, but not in bold and italic at the same time. If you're using the font bar buttons and nothing seems to be happening, check the dialog box to see if the style you want is available for the font family you're using.

Font Size

To change the size of the selected text, scroll through the Size list in the dialog box. Font sizes are in points. Note that some fonts are available in many sizes and others aren't. Remember that if you choose a bigger font, the text region you're in may grow and overlap nearby regions. Choose **Separate Regions** from the **Format** menu if necessary.

Effects

To make selected text superscripted, subscripted, underlined, or struck out, click on the appropriate Effects option in the dialog box.

Color

To change the color of the selected text, scroll through the color list in the dialog box. Note that you can't use the Format Bar to change color. You can only use the dialog box.

If you simply place the insertion point in text and then change the text properties by choosing **Text** from the **Format** menu, any text you now type at that insertion point will have the new properties you selected.

Changing paragraph properties

The paragraph properties of a text region consist of *alignment* and *indentation* for either the first or all lines in the text region. When you first create a text region in your worksheet, the lines in the region are left aligned and not indented. You can change these properties for an individual text region by doing the following:

■ Select the text region by clicking on it.

■ Choose **Paragraph** from the **Format** menu. Mathcad displays the following dialog box:

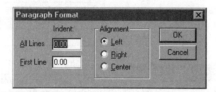

■ Change the appropriate properties in the dialog box and click "OK." You can change the following properties:

Alignment

To align the text at either the left or right edge of the text region, or to center the text within the text region, use these three alignment buttons. Alternatively, use one of the three alignment buttons on the Format Bar.

Indentation

To indent every line in the text region the same amount, enter a value in the All Lines text box. To indent the *first* line of the text region a different amount than the rest of the lines, as for a conventional or hanging indent, enter a different value in the First Line text box. Both these text boxes expect a number in inches.

Greek letters in text

To type a Greek letter in a text region, use one of these two methods:

■ Open the Greek Symbol Palette by clicking on the button labeled αβ on the Math Palette, then click on the appropriate button on the palette.

■ Type the roman equivalent of the Greek letter and immediately press [Ctrl]G.

The Greek Symbol Palette, shown below, provides a convenient way to insert a Greek symbol into your text. Just place the insertion point in a text region and click on the button in the palette. You can also use the Greek Symbol Palette to insert Greek letters into math expressions.

Once you've learned your way around Mathcad, however, you may find the [Ctrl]G keyboard shortcut method is faster. For example, to type the Greek symbol ϕ in a text region, follow these steps:

■ Type the roman equivalent of the letter. For the Greek lowercase letter ϕ, the roman equivalent is the letter "f."

> First, add the correction factor to the phase angle f used above.

■ Be sure to place the insertion point immediately to the *right* of the letter.

> First, add the correction factor to the phase angle f used above.

■ Type [Ctrl]G. The Greek symbol appears.

> First, add the correction factor to the phase angle ϕ used above.

The table on the following page lists all the Greek letters and their roman equivalents. These are the same roman equivalents used in the Windows Symbol font. To insert an uppercase Greek letter, use the uppercase roman equivalent. To insert a lowercase Greek letter, use the lowercase roman equivalent.

Typing [Ctrl]G after a letter in a math region also converts it to its Greek equivalent. In addition, [Ctrl]G converts a nonalphabetic character to its Greek symbol equivalent. For example, typing [Shift]2[Ctrl]G in a text region produces the "≅" character.

Name	Uppercase	Lowercase	Roman equivalent
alpha	A	α	A
beta	B	β	B
chi	X	χ	C
delta	Δ	δ	D
epsilon	E	ε	E
eta	H	η	H
gamma	Γ	γ	G
iota	I	ι	I
kappa	K	κ	K
lambda	Λ	λ	L
mu	M	μ	M
nu	N	ν	N
omega	Ω	ω	W
omicron	O	o	O
phi	Φ	φ	F
phi(alternate)		φ	J
pi	Π	π	P
psi	Ψ	ψ	Y
rho	P	ρ	R
sigma	Σ	σ	S
tau	T	τ	T
theta	Θ	θ	Q
theta(alternate)	ϑ		J
upsilon	Y	υ	U
xi	Ξ	ξ	X
zeta	Z	ζ	Z

To change a text selection into its Greek equivalent, select the text and then:

- Choose **Text** from the **Format** menu.

- From the Font list select the Symbol font.

Importing and exporting text

Mathcad's text is formatted using Microsoft's "Rich Text Format" (RTF) specification. This means you can export text from Mathcad text regions to word processing programs that read files in RTF format. For many word processing programs running under Windows concurrently with Mathcad, you can export directly via the clipboard. To do so:

- Click in a text region to place the insertion point (a vertical bar).

- Drag to highlight the text you want to export if you do not want to export the entire text region.

- Choose **Copy** from the **Edit** menu.

- Click in the target application's window and paste from the clipboard.

You can also import text from most other Windows applications. To do so:

- Place the text in the clipboard.

- Click in an empty region of the Mathcad worksheet. You should see the crosshair.

- Choose **Paste** from Mathcad's **Edit** menu.

Mathcad creates a text region containing the text on the clipboard. If the text contains RTF formatting codes, Mathcad formats the text as directed. Notice that Mathcad treats the imported text as a single text region, even if several separate paragraphs were selected in the original application.

You can also save the entire worksheet, including equations and plots, in RTF format, or choose to import text into Mathcad as an OLE object so that it can continue to be edited in its original application. For more information see Chapter 4, "Worksheet Management."

Text styles

Mathcad uses *text styles* to assign default text and paragraph properties to entire text regions. Text styles give you an easy way to create a consistent appearance in your worksheets: rather than choose particular text and paragraph properties for each individual region, you can apply an available text style, setting a range of text and paragraph properties at once.

Every worksheet has a default, "normal" text style with a particular choice of text and paragraph properties. Depending on your worksheet and the template from which the worksheet is derived, you may have other predefined text styles to choose from, and you can apply those styles to existing or new text regions. You can also modify existing text styles, create new ones of your own, and delete ones you no longer need.

This section describes the procedures for applying, modifying, creating, and deleting text styles. See the previous section, "Text editing," for details on the available text and paragraph properties and for instructions on formatting selected text *within* a text region.

Applying a text style to a text region

Your worksheet or worksheet template provides you with one or more text styles for determining the default appearance of text regions; each text style governs a constellation of text properties and paragraph properties. If you simply create a text region in your Mathcad worksheet, the region is tagged with the style called "Normal."

To apply a different text style to a text region:

■ Click in the text region.

■ Choose **Style** from the **Format** menu to see a list of the available text styles, as shown below:

Available text styles will differ depending on the worksheet template you based your worksheet on.

■ Select one of the available text styles and click "Apply." The default text in your region acquires the text and paragraph properties associated with that style.

As an alternative to choosing **Style** from the **Format** menu, you can apply a text style to a text region simply by clicking in the text region and choosing a style from the left-most drop-down list in the Format Bar:

When you apply a text style to a text region, the region's paragraph properties change to those of the applied text style, but only the default text in the region acquires the new text properties. Text you have previously selected and formatted by changing the font, font size, and color, as described in the section "Text editing," will retain its previous appearance. If you previously only modified text properties other than the font in the selected text, the selected text will now acquire the text properties of the style with the addition of the particular style, size, and effects chosen.

Figure 5-2 shows part of a Mathcad worksheet that contains text regions with different text styles.

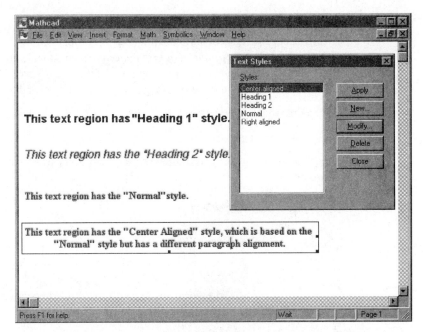

Figure 5-2: Applying different text styles to text regions in a worksheet.

Modifying an existing text style

You can change the definition of a text style—its text and paragraph properties—at any time.

To modify a text style:

■ Choose **Style** from the **Format** menu. Mathcad brings up the Text Styles dialog box showing the currently available text styles.

■ Select the name of the text style you want to modify and click "Modify."

■ You will see a dialog box, like the one below, displaying the definitions of that text style:

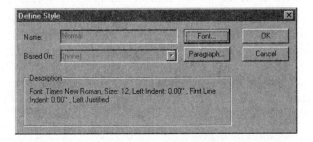

■ Click on the "Font" button to modify the text formats such as the font, font size, font styling, special effects, and color. Click on the "Paragraph" button to modify the indentation and alignment for that text style. See the section "Text editing" on page 102 for information about the available text and paragraph formatting options.

■ Click "OK" to save your changes.

Any new text regions to which you apply the modified text style will reflect the new definition for that text style. In addition, any text regions previously created with the text style will redisplay according to the definitions of the new text style.

Creating and deleting text styles

You can modify the list of available text styles in your worksheet by creating new ones and deleting ones you no longer use; any text style changes are saved with your worksheet. You can base a new text style on an existing text style, such that it inherits some text or paragraph properties but not others, or you can create the style entirely anew. For example, you may want to base a new "Subheading" style on an existing "Heading" style, but choose a smaller font size, keeping other text and paragraph properties the same.

To create a new text style:

■ Choose **Style** from the **Format** menu. Mathcad brings up the Text Styles dialog box showing the currently available text styles.

■ Click "New."

■ In the Define Styles dialog box, enter a name for the new style in the "Name" text box.

■ If you want to base the new style on one of the existing styles in the current worksheet or template, select a style from the "Based on" drop-down list.

■ Click on the "Font" button to make your choices for text formats for the new style. Click on the "Paragraph" button to choose alignment and indentation options for the new style.

■ Click "OK" when you have finished defining the new style.

Your new style will now appear in the Text Styles dialog box and can be applied to any text region as described in the section "Applying a text style to a text region" on page 109. When you save the worksheet, the new text style is saved with it. If you want to use the new text style in your future worksheets, save your worksheet as a template as described in Chapter 4, "Worksheet Management." You may also copy the text style into another worksheet that doesn't have the style simply by pasting in a region that has that text style.

If you base a new text style on an existing text style, any changes you later make to properties of the original text style that carry over to the new text style will be reflected in any text regions that have the new text style. In addition, the properties of the new text style will be updated for future applications of the style.

In the example of Figure 5-2 the "Center Aligned" style was created based on the "Normal" style but with center paragraph alignment instead of left alignment. Figure

5-3 shows how the appearance of the text with the "Center Aligned" style will change when the base "Normal" style is updated.

You may choose to delete a text style at any time. To do so:

■ Choose **Style** from the **Format** menu. Mathcad brings up the Text Styles dialog box showing the currently available text styles.

■ Select one of the available text styles from the list.

■ Click "Delete."

The text style is removed from the list of available text styles. Any text regions in your worksheet whose text and paragraph properties were defined in terms of that text style will continue to display the properties of that style, however.

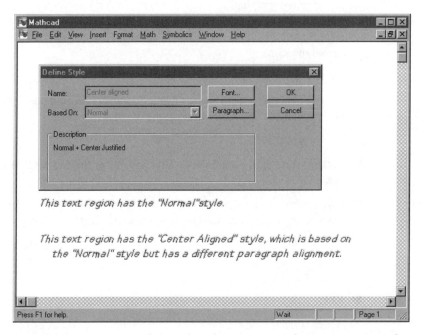

Figure 5-3: A new text style based on the properties of an existing text style.

Text region properties

Mathcad allows you to highlight the background of text regions so that they stand out from the rest of the equations and text in your worksheet.

To apply a background highlight color to a text region:

■ Click in the text region you want to highlight.

■ Choose **Properties** from the **Format** menu.

- Click on the Display tab.

- Click in the box next to "Highlight Region." Click "Choose Color" to choose a highlight color other than the default choice.

- Click "OK."

Mathcad fills a box around the text region with either the default background highlight color or the color you chose.

The appearance of a highlighted text region on printing will depend very much on the capabilities of your printer and the choice of highlight color. Some printers will render a color as black, obscuring the equation in the process. Others will render the exact same color as just the right gray to highlight the equation without obscuring it.

To change the default background color of a highlighted text region, do the following:

- Choose **Color** from the **Format** menu.

- Pull right and choose **Highlight** to bring up a dialog box containing a palette of colors.

- Click on the appropriate color.

Find and Replace

Mathcad's Find and Replace commands work in both text and equations. When you search for a sequence of characters, Mathcad looks for that sequence as part of a variable or function name or as a piece of text in a text region.

Searching for text

To find a sequence of characters,

- Choose **Find** from the **Edit** menu. Mathcad brings up the dialog box shown below:

- Enter the sequence of characters you want to find in the text box labeled "Find".

- Click on "Next" or "Previous" to find the occurrence of the character sequence immediately after or before the current insertion point location.

For example, to search for all occurrences of the letters **lb** in a worksheet:

- Choose **Find** from the **Edit** menu. Mathcad brings up a dialog box and prompts you for a string to find.

- Type **lb** and click on "Next".

Mathcad searches forward from the insertion point position for a region containing the letters **1b**, whether in text or in an equation. When Mathcad finds a match in a text region, it shows it in reverse video; when it finds a match in an equation it positions the insertion point in the string. The dialog box remains up so that you can continue searching. When you're done with the search, close the Find dialog box by clicking "Cancel."

Note that Mathcad's Find command is case-sensitive, but not font-sensitive. For example, if you're searching for **b**, you won't find **B**, but you will find β, since this is nothing more than a lowercase **b** in Greek or Symbol font.

Replacing characters

To search and replace, choose **Replace** from the **Edit** menu. For example, to replace instances of the name *rw* with *Rw*:

■ Choose **Replace** from the **Edit** menu to bring up the Replace dialog box shown in Figure 5-4.

■ Enter the string you want to find (the target string) in the text box labeled "Find".

■ Enter the string you want to replace it with in the text box labeled "Change to".

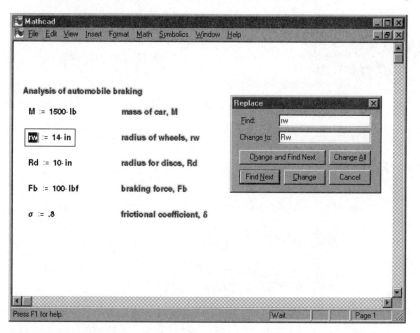

Figure 5-4: Replacing text or math characters via the Replace dialog box.

You now have four choices:

■ Click on "Change and Find Next" to replace this instance and find the next one.

■ Click on "Find Next" to find and select the next instance of your target string.

- Click on "Change" to replace the currently selected instance of the string.

- Click on "Change All" to replace all instances without further prompting.

Spell-checking

After creating text, you can have Mathcad search it for misspelled words and suggest replacements. You can also add words that you commonly use to your dictionary. Note that Mathcad will spell-check only text regions, not math or graphics regions.

Checking text for misspelled words

To begin spell-checking, you first have to tell Mathcad what portions of the worksheet to spell-check. There are two ways to do this:

- Click at the beginning of wherever you want to spell-check. Mathcad will spell-check starting from this point and continue to the end of the worksheet. Mathcad will then let you either continue the spell-check from the beginning of the worksheet or quit spell-checking.

- Alternatively, select the text you want to spell-check by dragging the mouse across the text.

Once you've defined a range over which to check spelling:

- Choose **Check Spelling** from the **Edit** menu. When Mathcad finds a misspelled word, it opens the dialog box shown below.

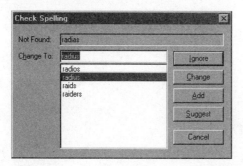

The dialog box shows the misspelled word along with a suggested replacement. It may also show a list of other suggested replacements. If Mathcad has no immediate suggestions, it will show only the misspelled word.

After the dialog box appears, you have several options:

- To change the word to the suggested replacement, click on "Change".

- To change the word to one from the list of replacements, select one and click "Change".

- To see additional but less likely replacements, click "Suggest". Note that if Mathcad can offer no additional suggestions, the "Suggest" button will be grayed out.

- To change the word to one not listed, type the replacement into the "Change to" box and click "Change".

- To leave the word as is, click "Ignore" or "Add". If you click "Ignore", Mathcad will leave the word alone and continue spell-checking, ignoring all future occurrences of the word as it does so. If you click "Add," Mathcad will add the word to your dictionary. The following section explains this dictionary in more detail.

Personal dictionaries

To determine whether a word is misspelled, Mathcad compares it with the words in the following dictionaries:

- A general dictionary of common English words supplemented by mathematical terms.

- A personal dictionary.

When a word is not found in either dictionary, Mathcad will warn you that it may be misspelled. If there are certain correctly spelled words throughout your worksheet which Mathcad nevertheless shows as being misspelled, you may want to add them to your personal dictionary. This will prevent Mathcad from considering them misspelled.

To add a word to your personal dictionary:

- When Mathcad shows the word in the Check Spelling dialog box, click "Add".

This will add the word to your dictionary. For future spell-checking, Mathcad will not show it as being misspelled.

Chapter 6
Equation and Result Formatting

You can specify how Mathcad displays answers, including specifying the number of decimal places, the base in which answers are displayed, and the use of scientific notation. And although Mathcad shows equations in standard math notation, you can apply math styles to control the font, font size, and font styles and effects used for names and numbers in equations.

The following sections make up this chapter:

Formatting results

Changing the display of computed values in equations.

Math styles

Changing the font, font size, and font styles and effects used in equations and plots.

Highlighting equations

Making a particular equation stand out from all the other equations and regions in your worksheet.

Formatting results

The way that Mathcad displays numbers (the number of decimal places, whether to use *i* or *j* for imaginary numbers, and so on) is called the *result format*. You can set the result format for a whole worksheet or for a single calculated result.

Setting worksheet default format

To change the default display of numerical results, click on an empty space and choose **Number** from the **Format** menu. You will see the dialog box shown below. Default values for the four precision settings are shown in parentheses. The range of values allowed for each setting is shown to the right of the corresponding text box.

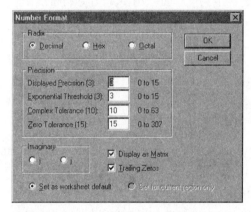

Change the desired settings and click "OK." Mathcad changes the display of all results whose formats have not been explicitly specified. You can control the display of a single result without affecting any others by setting the *local result format*. The section "Setting the format of a single result" on page 120 discusses how to do this.

This is the meaning of each of the settings in the dialog box:

Radix

This allows you to set the radix (base) in which results are displayed. The default is decimal. If you select "Octal" or "Hex," Mathcad truncates the number to an integer and displays it as octal or hexadecimal. Hexadecimal results are indicated by the letter "**h**" after the number, octal results by the letter "**o**." (Mathcad does not reliably show hexadecimal or octal numbers of magnitude greater than 2^{31}, or about $2 \cdot 10^9$).

Imaginary

Click on the *i* or *j* button. Mathcad uses the selected letter to indicate an imaginary result. The default is *i*. You can use either *i* or *j* in equations—Mathcad always understands both. The selection you make here tells Mathcad which one to use when it gives you a complex answer. See the section "Complex numbers" in Chapter 8 for more information on how to type complex numbers.

Display as Matrix

Check this box to suppress the use of scrolling output tables. Vectors and matrices having more than nine rows or columns are displayed as scrolling output tables unless this box is checked. See the section "Displaying vectors and matrices" in Chapter 10 for more information on scrolling output tables.

Trailing Zeros

Check this box to make all displayed results have as many digits to the right of the decimal point as required by the current choice of Displayed Precision. For example, with Displayed Precision set to 3, Mathcad displays 5 as 5.000.

Displayed Precision

Enter an integer between 0 and 15. This indicates how many decimal places to show in computed results. The default is 3. Numbers are rounded for display only. Mathcad maintains 15 digits of precision internally.

Exponential Threshold

Enter an integer n between 0 and 15. Mathcad shows computed results of magnitude greater than 10^n or smaller than 10^{-n} in exponential notation. When the threshold is 3, numbers like 30,000 are displayed as $3 \cdot 10^4$ instead of 30,000. The default is 3.

Complex Tolerance

Enter an integer n between 0 and 63. If the ratio between the real and imaginary part of a complex number is less than 10^n or greater than 10^{-n}, then the smaller part is not shown. The default setting is 10. This means that numbers like $1 + 10^{-12} i$ will appear simply as 1. Mathcad rounds only the displayed values. No change is made in the internally stored values.

Zero Tolerance

Enter an integer n between 0 and 307. Numbers less than 10^n are shown as zero. The default setting is 15. This means numbers of magnitude less than 10^{-15} appear as zero. Mathcad changes the displayed values only. No change is made in the internally stored values.

Changing the worksheet default result format affects only the worksheet you were in when you made the change. Any other worksheets that may have been open at the time retain their own default result formats.

If you want to re-use your default result formats in other Mathcad worksheets, save your worksheet as a template as described in Chapter 4, "Worksheet Management."

All of these formatting options affect only the display of a number. Mathcad continues to carry out all calculations in full precision regardless of formatting options. If you copy a result by choosing **Copy** from the **Edit** menu, Mathcad copies the answer to the precision displayed.

To see the number as it is stored internally:

■ Click anywhere on the result.

■ Press [Ctrl][Shift]N.

- Mathcad displays the number in full precision on the message line at the bottom of the application window, as shown in Figure 6-1.

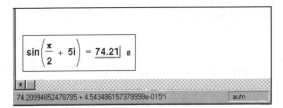

Figure 6-1: Full precision is maintained internally.

Setting the format of a single result

You can set the format for a single result—a number, table, vector, or matrix—independently of the worksheet default result format. To change the format with which a particular result is displayed, do the following:

- Click anywhere in the equation whose result you want to format.

$$\pi \cdot 10^5 = 3.142 \cdot 10^5 \ \blacksquare$$

- Choose **Number** from the **Format** menu. Alternatively, double-click on the equation itself. The dialog box shown below appears. Note that the option button "Set for current region only" is already selected.

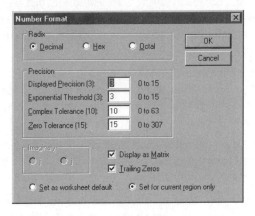

- Change the desired settings. See the section "Setting worksheet default format" on page 118 to learn what the various settings do and what their allowed values are. To display the six decimal places shown below, you would change "Displayed Precision" from 3 to 6.

- Click "OK." Mathcad redisplays the result using the new format.

$$\pi \cdot 10^5 = 3.141593 \cdot 10^5 \ \blacksquare$$

You can also apply local formats to all tables, vectors, or matrices. Just click on the table, vector, or matrix and choose **Number** from the **Format** menu. When you click on "OK," Mathcad applies the selected format to all the numbers in the table, vector, or matrix. It is not possible to format these numbers individually.

When you click the button labeled "Set for current region only," Mathcad disables the Imaginary Unit and Zero Tolerance settings. These settings can only be defined for the entire worksheet, not for individual regions.

To redisplay a result using the worksheet default result format settings:

■ Click on the result to enclose the result between the editing lines.

■ Delete the equal sign.

■ Press = to replace the equal sign. The result format has now been restored to the worksheet default settings.

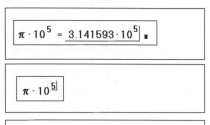

Figure 6-2 shows the same number formatted several different ways.

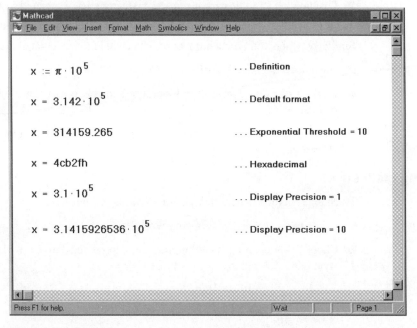

Figure 6-2: Several ways to format the same number.

Math styles

Just as you apply predefined styles and styles you create to modify the appearance of text regions in your worksheet, as described in Chapter 5, "Text," you apply math styles to assign particular fonts, font sizes, font styles and effects, and colors to the elements of your math regions. Mathcad has two predefined math styles that govern the default appearance of all the math in your worksheet, but you can define and apply additional styles to enhance the appearance of your equations.

Mathcad's predefined math styles are:

- **Variables**, which governs the default appearance of all variables and plots.

- **Constants**, which governs the default appearance of all numbers you type in math regions as well as all numbers that appear in results.

Whenever you type a variable name, Mathcad:

- Assigns to it a math style named "Variables."

- Looks up the font, font size, and font style and effects associated with that particular math style.

- Displays the variable name using the characteristics associated with the style named "Variables."

Similarly, when you type a number or when a result is calculated, Mathcad:

- Assigns to it a math style named "Constants."

- Looks up the font, font size, and font style and effects associated with that particular math style.

- Displays the number using the characteristics associated with the style named "Constants."

Editing math styles

To change Mathcad's default style for all variables and plots:

- Click on a variable name in your worksheet.

- Choose **Equation** from the **Format** menu to see the dialog box shown below. The style name "Variables" is selected.

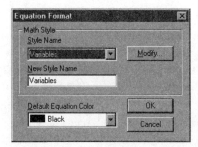

- To change the font associated with that variable's math style, click on "Modify." You'll see a dialog box for changing fonts.

- Click the "OK" button. Mathcad changes the font of all variables in the worksheet.

If you change the Variables style, you may also want to change the style used for numbers so that the two look good together. To do so:

- Click on a number.

- Choose **Equation** from the **Format** menu to see the Equation Format dialog box. The style name "Constants" is now selected.

- Follow the procedure given above for modifying the Variables style.

You can also use the Format Bar to change the font, font size, or font style associated with a math style. To use the Font Bar to modify some of the settings for the Variables math style, for example, click on a variable, then click on the appropriate Format Bar button to make variables bold, italic, or underlined or to specify the font or point size in the drop-down lists.

The font, font size, and font style you choose for the Variables and Constants styles (as well as any math styles you define) affect not only the appearance of equations, but the appearance of the entire worksheet. Mathcad's line-and-character grid does not respond to changes in the font sizes used in text and math. Therefore, changing font characteristics, particularly font sizes, may cause regions to overlap. You can separate these regions by choosing **Separate Regions** from the **Format** menu.

You may wish to have your equations display in a different color than your default text regions to avoid mixing the two up. To change the default color of all equations in your worksheet,

- Choose **Equation** from the **Format** menu.

- Select a color in the "Default Equation Color" drop-down list.

- Click "OK."

Applying math styles

As described in the previous section, variables in your Mathcad worksheet by default are assigned the "Variables" style, and numbers are assigned the "Constants" style. Answers displayed on the right of an equal sign are always assigned the "Constants" style. These two style names cannot be changed. You may, however, create and apply additional math styles, named as you choose, in your worksheets and templates.

To see what math style is currently assigned to a name or number, double-click on the name or number to select it, or simply click in the name or number, and look at the style window on the Format Bar.

Alternatively, you can double-click on the name or number and choose **Equation** from the **Format** menu. You'll see the dialog box shown in the previous section. The math style associated with whatever you clicked on will appear in the drop-down list as shown in Figure 6-3.

If you click on the button to the right of "Variables" in either the Format Bar or the Equation Format dialog box, you'll see a drop-down list of available math styles. If you now choose "User 1" and click "OK," a new math style is applied to the variable selected in Figure 6-3 and its appearance changes accordingly. Figure 6-4 shows the result.

In this way you can apply any of a variety of math styles to:

■ individual variable names in an expression, or

■ individual numbers in a math expression (but not in computed results, which always display in the "Constants" style).

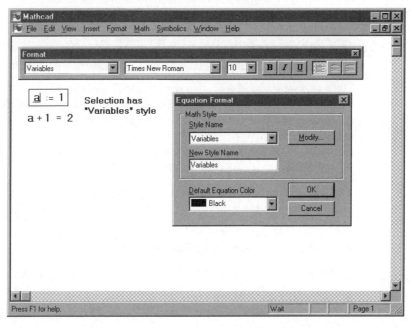

Figure 6-3: Scrolling list shows math style of selected math element.

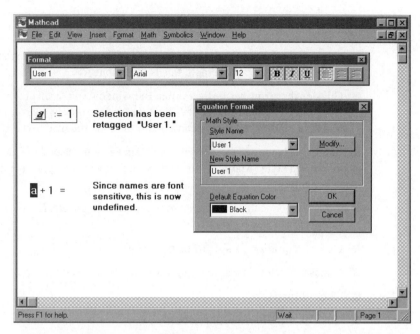

Figure 6-4: A different math style has been applied to the first variable name in Figure 6-3. Note change in font.

Applications of math styles

You may already have encountered the styles used for determining the appearance of Mathcad text regions, as described in Chapter 5, "Text." By making changes to text styles rather than to individual text regions, you can make sweeping and strikingly uniform changes in the way a worksheet looks. You can get this same kind of leverage in the display of equations by math styles.

For example, many math books show vectors in a bold, underlined font and matrices in a bold font. If you want to use this convention, do the following:

■ Choose **Equation** from the **Format** menu.

■ Click the down arrow beside the name of the current math styles to see a drop-down list of available math styles.

■ Click on an unused math style name like "User 1" to select it.

■ The name "User 1" should now appear in the "New Style Name" text box. Click in this text box and change the name to something like "Vectors."

■ Click on "Modify" to change this style to a bold, underlined font.

This creates a math style called "Vectors" with the desired appearance. Proceed in a similar way to create a math style named "Matrices" having a bold font. When you're done defining both styles, click "OK."

Now rather than individually changing the font, font size, and font style for names of

---

vectors and matrices, you can simply change their math styles. To do so, do the following:

- Click on the name of the vector or matrix. The style assigned to that name appears on the Format Bar. By default, this is "Variables."

- Click on the arrow beside the Format Bar window and scroll down to the math style "Vectors". The style changes to "Vectors" and the appearance of the name changes to a bold, underlined font because that's the font assigned to the Vectors style.

Repeat the previous two steps for all vectors in the worksheet. For matrices, choose the newly created style "Matrices" instead. Note that you can apply a style to only one name at a time.

If after having done this you decide to remove all the underlines from the vectors, you can simply:

- Choose **Equation** from the **Format** menu.

- Choose "Vectors" from the drop-down list of styles at the top of the dialog box.

- Click "Modify."

- Click on the Underline check box.

Once you click on the "OK" button, the underlines will be removed from every vector in the worksheet.

Note that this procedure changes the appearance of the *names* of vectors and matrices, not the individual vector or matrix elements themselves. The individual elements continue to have the "Variables" or "Constants" math style by default.

Saving math styles

Once you've completed a set of math styles that you like, you need not repeat the process for other worksheets. You can save math style information by saving a worksheet as a template.

To apply math style information to another worksheet, open your template from the **File** menu and copy the contents of the worksheet to the template. For more information about worksheet templates, see Chapter 4, "Worksheet Management."

Font sensitivity

All names, whether function names or variable names, are font sensitive. This means that x and x refer to different variables, and $f(x)$ and $f(x)$ refer to different functions.

In deciding whether two variable names are the same, Mathcad actually checks *math styles* rather than fonts. To avoid having distinct variables that look identical, don't create a math style with exactly the same font, size and style as another math style.

Highlighting equations

Mathcad allows you to highlight equations so that they stand out from the rest of the equations and text in your worksheet:

To apply a background highlight color to an equation:

■ Click in the equation you want to highlight.

■ Choose **Properties** from the **Format** menu.

■ Click on the Display tab.

■ Click in the box next to "Highlight Region." Click "Choose Color" to choose a highlight color other than the default choice.

■ Click "OK."

Mathcad fills a box around the equation with either the default background highlight color or the color you chose. This is a purely cosmetic change with no effect on the equation other than rendering it more conspicuous.

The appearance of a highlighted equation on printing will depend very much on the capabilities of your printer and the choice of highlight color. Some printers will render a color as black, obscuring the equation in the process. Others will render the exact same color as just the right gray to highlight the equation without obscuring it.

To change the default background color of a highlighted equation, do the following:

■ Choose **Color** from the **Format** menu.

■ Pull right and choose **Highlight** to bring up a dialog box containing a palette of colors.

■ Click on the appropriate color.

Computational Features

Chapter 7
Equations and Computation

This chapter describes how to define and evaluate variables and functions. This chapter discusses only numerical equations. To learn how to use Mathcad's symbolic processing features, turn to Chapter 17, "Symbolic Calculation."

The following sections make up this chapter:

Defining variables and functions

How to define variables and functions. How the relative placement of equations affects calculations.

Evaluating expressions

How to get a numerical answer.

Copying numerical results

How to copy numerical results from one worksheet to another or from Mathcad to other applications.

Controlling calculations

How to suppress the way Mathcad automatically updates the worksheet.

Disabling equations

Turning calculation or editing on and off for individual equations.

Error messages

What to do when Mathcad displays an error message.

Defining variables and functions

Whenever you type an equation into a worksheet, you are doing one of two things:

■ You could be typing an expression and asking Mathcad to give you the answer. This is discussed in the next section, "Evaluating expressions."

■ You could be typing a variable or function name and assigning some value to it. The remainder of this section discusses how to do this.

Defining a variable

A variable definition defines the value of a variable everywhere below the definition. To define a variable, you must follow these three steps:

■ Type the variable name to be defined. Chapter 8, "Variables and Constants," contains a description of valid variable names.

$\boxed{\underline{KE|}}$

■ Press the colon (:) key. The definition symbol (:=) appears.

$\boxed{KE := \blacksquare|}$

■ Type an expression to complete the definition. This expression can include numbers and any previously defined variables and functions.

$KE := \dfrac{1}{2} \cdot m \cdot v^{2}|$

Figure 7-1 shows several examples of a variable definition. The left hand side of a ":=" can contain any of the following:

■ A simple variable name like x.

■ A subscripted variable name like v_i.

■ A matrix whose elements are any of the above. For example:

$$\begin{bmatrix} x \\ y_1 \end{bmatrix}$$

■ A function name with an argument list of simple variable names. For example, $f(x, y, z)$. This is described further in the next section.

■ A superscripted variable name like $\mathbf{M}^{\langle 1 \rangle}$.

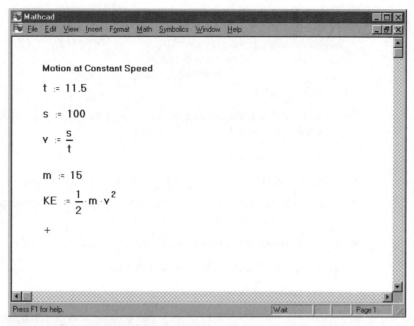

Figure 7-1: Defining variables.

Defining a function

You can also define your own functions in Mathcad. Unlike a variable, the value of a function depends on the values of its arguments.

You define a function in much the same way you define a variable. The name goes on the left, a ":=" goes in the middle, and an expression goes on the right. The main difference is that the name includes an *argument list*. The example below shows how to define a function called dist(*x*, *y*) which returns the distance between the point (*x*, *y*) and the origin.

To type such a function definition:

■ Type the function name.

■ Type a left parenthesis followed by one or more names separated by commas. Complete this argument list by typing a right parenthesis.

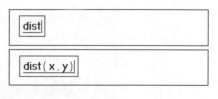

It makes no difference whether or not the names in the argument list have been defined or used elsewhere in the worksheet. What is important is that these arguments *must be names*. They cannot be more complicated expressions.

■ Press the colon (:) key. You see the definition symbol (:=).

Defining variables and functions

■ Type an expression to define the function. In this example, the expression involves only the names in the argument list. In general though, the expression can contain any previously defined functions and variables as well.

$$dist(x, y) := \sqrt{x^2 + y^2}$$

Once you have defined a function, you can use it anywhere below the definition, just as you would use a variable.

When you use a function in an equation, Mathcad:

■ evaluates the arguments you place between the parentheses,

■ replaces the dummy arguments in the function definition with the actual arguments you place between the parentheses,

■ performs whatever arithmetic is specified by the function definition, and

■ returns the result as the value of the function.

Figure 7-2 shows an example.

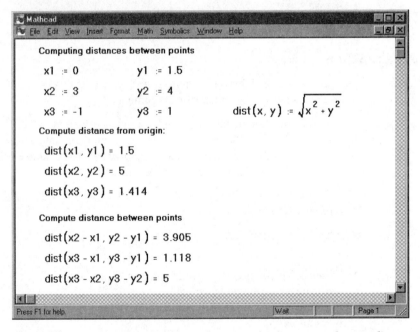

Figure 7-2: A user-defined function to compute the distance to the coordinate origin.

The arguments of a user function can represent scalars, vectors, or matrices. For example, you could define the distance function as

$$dist(\mathbf{v}) := \sqrt{v_0^2 + v_1^2}$$

Chapter 7 Equations and Computation

This is an example of a function that accepts a vector as an argument, and returns a scalar result. See the section "Arrays and user-defined functions" in Chapter 10 for more information.

Note that function names are font sensitive. This means that the function **f**(x) is different from the function f(x). Figure 7-3 shows an example.

Mathcad's built-in functions are defined for all fonts (except the Symbol font), sizes, and styles. This means that **sin**(x), sin(x), and `sin`(x) all refer to the same function.

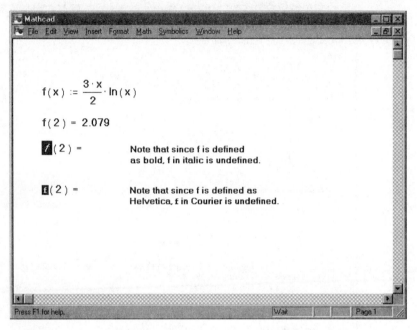

Figure 7-3: Function names are font sensitive. Undefined variables are marked in reverse video.

Variables in user-defined functions

When you define a function, you don't have to define any of the names in the argument list. This is because when you define a function, you are telling Mathcad *what to do* with the arguments, not what they are. When you define a function, Mathcad doesn't even have to know whether the arguments are scalars, vectors or matrices. All it needs to know is how many arguments there are and what to do with them. It is only when Mathcad actually *uses* a function that it needs to know what the arguments really are.

However, if in the process of defining a function you use a variable name that *is not* in the argument list, you must define that variable name above the function definition. The value of that variable at the time you make the function definition then becomes a permanent part of the function. This is illustrated in Figure 7-4.

When you evaluate a function, Mathcad:

■ evaluates the arguments,

- substitutes their values on the right side of the function definition,

- evaluates the values of the other variables *at the point where the function is defined*,

- computes and returns a result.

If you want a function to depend on the value of a variable, you must include that variable as an argument. If not, Mathcad will just use that variable's fixed value at the point in the worksheet where the function is defined.

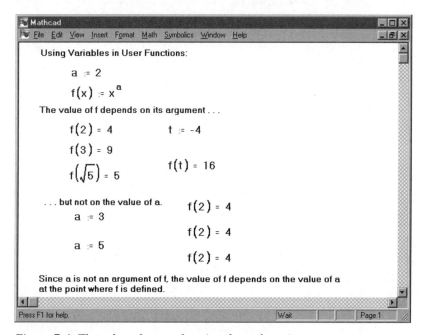

Figure 7-4: The value of a user function depends on its arguments.

Recursive function definitions

Mathcad supports *recursive* function definitions—you may define the value of a function in terms of a previous value of the function. As shown in Figure 7-5, recursive functions are useful for defining arbitrary periodic functions, as well as elegantly implementing numerical functions like the factorial function.

Note that a recursive function definition should always have at least two parts:

- An initial condition that prevents the recursion from going forever.

- A definition of the function in terms of some previous value(s) of the function.

If you do not specify an initial condition that stops the recursion, Mathcad will generate a "stack overflow" error message as described in "Error messages" on page 148.

Pro   The programming operators in Mathcad Professional also support recursion. See the section "Programs within programs" in Chapter 18 for examples.

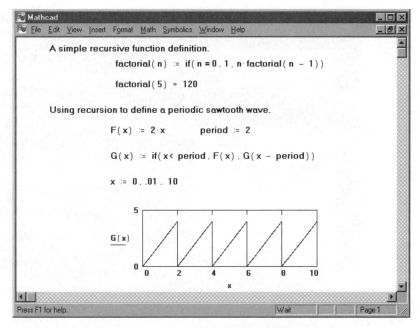

Figure 7-5: Mathcad allows recursive function definitions.

How Mathcad scans a worksheet

Mathcad scans a worksheet the same way you read it: left to right and top to bottom. This means that a variable or function definition involving a ": =" affects everything below and to the right of it.

To determine whether one equation is above or below another, Mathcad compares their *anchor points*. To see these anchor points, choose **Regions** from the **View** menu. Mathcad will display blank space in gray and leave regions white (or whatever your background color happens to be). Each region's anchor point will appear as a dot on the left.

Figure 7-6 shows an example of how not to place equations in a worksheet. In the first evaluation, both x and y are shown in red to indicate that they are undefined. This is because the definitions for x and y lie below where they are used. Because Mathcad scans from top to bottom, when it gets to the first equation, it has no idea what numbers to substitute in place of x and y.

The second evaluation, on the other hand, is below the definitions of x and y. By the time Mathcad gets to this equation, it has already assigned values to both x and y.

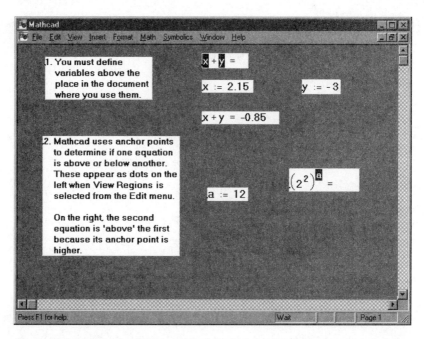

Figure 7-6: Mathcad evaluates equations from top to bottom in a worksheet. The small dot on the left side of each equation is an anchor point. Undefined variables are marked in reverse video.

You can define a variable twice in the same worksheet. Mathcad will simply use the first definition for all expressions below the first definition and above the second. For expressions below the second definition, Mathcad uses the second definition. Figure 7-7 illustrates a worksheet in which some variables are defined twice.

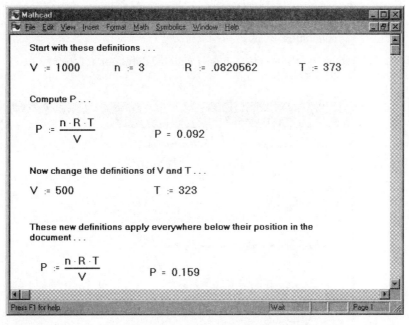

Figure 7-7: A worksheet in which V and T are both defined twice.

Global definitions

Global definitions are exactly like local definitions except that they are evaluated before any local definitions. If you define a variable or function with a global definition, that variable or function is available to all local definitions in your worksheet, regardless of whether the local definition appears above or below the global definition.

To type a global definition, follow these steps:

■ Type a variable name or function to be defined.

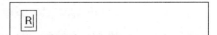

■ Press the tilde (~) key. The global definition symbol appears.

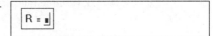

■ Type an expression. The expression can involve numbers or other globally defined variables and functions.

You can use global definitions for functions, subscripted variables, and anything else that normally uses the definition symbol ":=". Just type a tilde instead of a colon, and Mathcad will show the global definition symbol "≡" in place of ":=".

This is the algorithm that Mathcad uses to evaluate all definitions, global and otherwise:

■ First, Mathcad takes one pass through the entire worksheet from top to bottom. During this first pass, Mathcad evaluates global definitions only.

■ Mathcad then makes a second pass through the worksheet from top to bottom. This time, Mathcad evaluates all definitions made with ":=" as well as all equations containing "=".

Figure 7-8 shows the results of a global definition for the variable R which appears at the bottom of the figure.

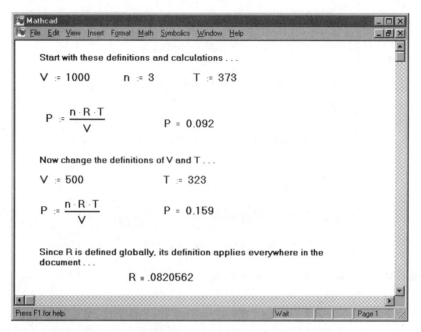

Figure 7-8: Using the global definition.

Although global definitions are evaluated before any local definitions, Mathcad evaluates global definitions the same way it evaluates local definitions: top to bottom and left to right. This means that whenever you use a variable to the right of a "≡":

■ that variable must also have been defined with a "≡," *and*

■ the variable must have been defined *above* the place where you are trying to use it.

Otherwise, the variable is marked in red to indicate that it is undefined.

It is good practice to allow only one definition for each global variable. Although you can do things like define a variable with two different global definitions or with one global and one local definition, this is never necessary and usually serves only to make your worksheet difficult to understand.

Evaluating expressions

To evaluate an expression, follow these steps:

■ Type an expression containing any valid combination of numbers, variables and functions. Any variables or functions in this expression should be defined earlier in the worksheet.

■ Press the "=" key. Mathcad computes the value of the expression and shows it after the equals sign.

$$\frac{1}{2} \cdot m \cdot v^2 = 567.108 \quad \blacksquare$$

Figure 7-9 shows some calculations using the definitions from Figure 7-1.

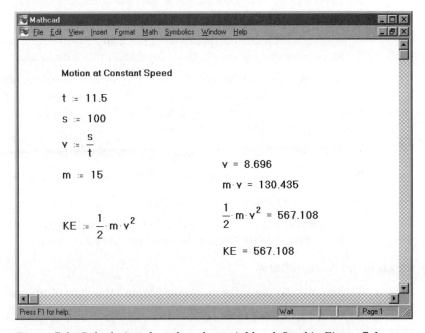

Figure 7-9: Calculations based on the variables defined in Figure 7-1.

Whenever you evaluate an expression, Mathcad shows a final placeholder at the end of the equation. You can use this placeholder for unit conversions, as explained in Chapter 9, "Units and Dimensions." As soon as you click outside the region, Mathcad hides the placeholder.

Copying numerical results

You can copy a numerical result and paste it either elsewhere in your worksheet or into another application. This allows you to copy an array of numbers directly from a spreadsheet or database into Mathcad where you can take advantage of its free-form interface and its advanced mathematical tools, and vice versa. Once you've performed the necessary computations, you can paste the resulting array of numbers back to where it came from or even into another application.

Copying a single number

To copy a single number appearing to the right of an equal sign:

- Click on the result to the right of the equal sign. This puts the result between the editing lines.

- Choose **Copy** from the **Edit** menu. This places the result on the clipboard.

- Click wherever you want to paste the result. If you're pasting into another application, choose **Paste** from that application's **Edit** menu. If you're pasting into a Mathcad worksheet, choose **Paste** from Mathcad's **Edit** menu.

The **Copy** command will copy the numerical result only to the precision displayed. To copy the result in greater precision, double-click on it and increase "Displayed Precision" on the Number Format dialog box. Note that **Copy** will not copy units and dimensions from a numerical result.

When you paste a numerical result into a Mathcad worksheet, it appears as:

- a math region consisting of a number if you paste it into empty space,

- a text string if you paste it into a text,

- a number if you paste it into a placeholder in a math region or if you paste it into text using the **Math Region** command on the **Insert** menu.

Copying an array of numbers

To copy an array (vector or matrix) appearing to the right of an equal sign:

- Click on the array to the right of the equal sign. This puts the array between the editing lines.

- Choose **Copy** from the **Edit** menu. This places the array on the clipboard.

- Click wherever you want to paste the result. If you're pasting into another application, choose **Paste** from that application's **Edit** menu. If you're pasting into a Mathcad worksheet, choose **Paste** from Mathcad's **Edit** menu.

When you paste an array into a Mathcad worksheet, it appears as:

- a vector or matrix if you paste it into empty space,

- a text string if you paste it into text,

- a vector or matrix if you paste it into a placeholder in a math region or if you paste it into text using the **Math Region** command on the **Insert** menu.

The **Copy** command will copy the numerical result to the precision with which it is displayed. You can view the current display settings by double-clicking on the result you want to copy and examining the dialog box. See Chapter 6, "Equation and Result Formatting," to learn more about formatting numbers for display. Note that **Copy** will not copy units and dimensions.

Copying numbers from a scrolling output table

When you display results in a scrolling output table as described in the section "Displaying vectors and matrices" in Chapter 10, you may want to copy some of the numbers from the table and use them elsewhere.

To copy just one number from a scrolling output table, simply click on the number and choose **Copy** from the **Edit** menu. To copy more than one number from a scrolling output table:

- Click on the first number you want to copy.

- Drag the mouse in the direction of the other values you want to copy while holding the mouse button down.

- Choose **Copy** from the **Edit** menu.

To copy all the values in a row or column, click on the column or row number shown to the left of the row or at the top of the column. All the values in the row or column will be selected. Then choose **Copy** from the **Edit** menu.

After you have copied one or more numbers from a scrolling output table, you can paste them into another part of your worksheet or into another application. Figure 7-10 shows an example of a new matrix created by copying and pasting numbers from a scrolling output table. Note that if you copied and pasted more than nine rows or columns of numbers from the table, they will be displayed as a new scrolling output table.

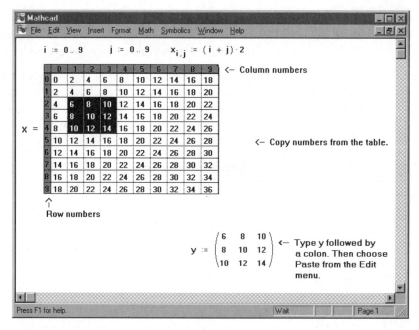

Figure 7-10: Creating a new matrix from numbers in a scrolling output table.

Controlling calculations

When you start Mathcad, you are in "automatic mode." This means that Mathcad updates results in the worksheet window automatically. You can tell you're in automatic mode because the word "Auto" appears in the message line.

If you don't want to wait for Mathcad to make computations as you edit, disable automatic mode by choosing **Automatic Calculation** from the **Math** menu or by clicking the light bulb on the toolbar. The word "Auto" disappears from the message line and the checkmark beside **Automatic Calculation** disappears to indicate that automatic mode is now off.

Automatic window update

The word "Auto" on the message line indicates that you are in automatic mode. This means that:

■ As soon as you press the equals sign, Mathcad displays a result.

■ As soon as you click outside of an equation having a ":=" or a "≡, " Mathcad performs all calculations necessary to make the assignment statement.

When you process a definition in automatic mode by clicking outside the equation region, this is what happens:

■ Mathcad evaluates the expression on the right side of the definition and assigns it to the name on the left.

■ Mathcad then takes note of all other equations in the worksheet that are in any way affected by the definition you just made.

■ Finally, Mathcad updates any of the affected equations that are currently visible in the worksheet window.

Although the equation you altered may affect equations throughout your worksheet, Mathcad performs only those calculations necessary to insure that whatever you can see in the window is up-to-date. This optimization makes sure you don't have to wait for Mathcad to evaluate expressions that are not visible.

In automatic mode, if you print or move to the end of the worksheet, Mathcad automatically updates the whole worksheet.

Whenever Mathcad needs time to complete computations, the mouse pointer changes its appearance and the word "WAIT" appears on the message line. This can occur when you enter or calculate an equation, when you scroll, during printing, or when you enlarge a window to reveal additional equations. In all these cases, Mathcad evaluates pending calculations from earlier changes.

As Mathcad evaluates an expression, it surrounds it with a green rectangle. This makes it easy to follow the progress of a calculation.

To force Mathcad to recalculate all equations throughout the worksheet, choose **Calculate Worksheet** from the **Math** menu.

Manual window update

In manual mode, Mathcad does not compute equations or display results until you specifically request it to recalculate. This means that you don't have to wait for Mathcad to calculate as you enter equations or scroll around a worksheet.

Mathcad keeps track of pending computations while you're in manual mode. As soon as you make a change that requires computation, the word "Calc" appears on the message line, as shown in Figure 7-11. This is to remind you that the results you see in the window are not up-to-date and that you must recalculate them before you can be sure they are updated.

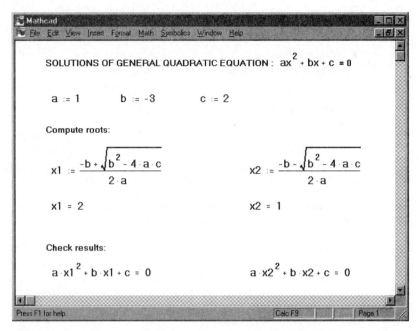

Figure 7-11: The word "Calc" on the message line indicates that recalculation is required.

You can update the screen by choosing **Calculate** from the **Math** menu. Mathcad performs whatever computations are necessary to update all results visible in the worksheet window. When you move down to see more of the worksheet, the word "Calc" reappears on the message line to indicate that you must recalculate to see up-to-date results.

To process the whole worksheet, including those portions not visible in the worksheet window, choose **Calculate Worksheet** from the **Math** menu.

To switch back to automatic mode, choose **Automatic Calculation** from the **Math** menu. Mathcad updates the entire worksheet and displays the word "auto" on the message line.

When you print a worksheet in manual calculation mode, the results on the printout are not necessarily up-to-date. When you're in manual mode, make sure to choose **Calculate Worksheet** from the **Math** menu before you print.

Interrupting calculations

To interrupt a computation in progress:

■ Press [**Esc**]. The dialog box shown below will appear.

■ Click "OK" to stop the calculations or "Cancel" to resume calculations.

If you click "OK," Mathcad displays a message on the message line to indicate that processing has been interrupted. The equation that was being processed when you pressed [Esc] is marked with an error message indicating that calculation has been interrupted. To resume an interrupted calculation, first click in the equation having the error message, then choose **Calculate** from the **Math** menu.

If you find yourself frequently interrupting calculations to avoid having to wait for Mathcad to recalculate as you edit your worksheet, you may wish to switch to manual mode. To do so, disable automatic mode by choosing **Automatic Calculation** from the **Math** menu. This will remove the checkmark from the menu. In manual mode, Mathcad recalculates only when you choose **Calculate** from the **Math** menu.

Starting in manual mode

The calculation mode—either manual or automatic—is a property saved in your Mathcad worksheet. If you often work in manual calculation mode, simply save your worksheets with Mathcad configured to work in manual mode; this way you do not have to disable automatic calculation each time you open your worksheets.

The calculation mode of Mathcad is also one of the properties saved in Mathcad template (MCT) files. As described in Chapter 4, "Worksheet Management," you use Mathcad templates to save layout and formatting information to re-use in worksheets you later create. When you create a Mathcad template file, the template will be in manual mode if you previously removed the checkmark from **Automatic Calculation** on the **Math** menu; otherwise it will be in automatic mode.

You may also change the calculation mode of a template file from automatic to manual, or vice versa. For example, to change the calculation mode of an existing Mathcad template file from automatic to manual, do the following:

■ Open the Mathcad template file, as described in the section "Worksheets and templates" in Chapter 4.

■ Choose **Automatic Calculation** from the **Math** menu. This command puts Mathcad into manual mode. The checkmark beside this menu item should now be gone.

■ Save the template file.

Thereafter, whenever you create a Mathcad worksheet based on this template, Mathcad will be in manual mode.

Disabling equations

You can *disable* a single equation so that it no longer calculates along with other regions in your worksheet, but you can still use Mathcad's equation editing, formatting, and display capabilities.

To disable calculation for a single equation in your worksheet, without affecting the calculation mode of the rest of the worksheet, follow these steps:

■ Click on the equation you want to disable.

■ Choose **Properties** from the **Format** menu, and click on the Calculation tab.

■ Under "Calculation Options" place a check in the box next to "Disable Evaluation."

■ Mathcad shows a small rectangle after the equation to indicate that it is disabled. An example is shown at right.

$$KE := \frac{1}{2} \cdot m \cdot v^2 \quad \blacksquare$$

You can edit a disabled equation just as you would any other equation. However, a disabled equation does not affect any other calculations, nor does it reflect changes you make to other equations in the worksheet.

To re-enable calculation for a disabled equation:

■ Click on the equation to select it.

■ Choose **Properties** from the **Format** menu, and click on the Calculation tab.

■ Under "Calculation Options" remove the check in the box next to "Disable Evaluation."

Mathcad removes the small rectangle beside the equation.

Note: If you disable a plot or an output table, Mathcad freezes the display for the plot or table. Changes you make to other parts of the worksheet will not affect the plot or table. If you move a disabled equation that happens to be displaying a result, the result will disappear. If you move a graph, whatever is inside the graph will disappear.

Error messages

Mathcad may encounter an error when evaluating an expression. If it does, it marks the offending expression with an error message and highlights the offending name or operator in a different color (red).

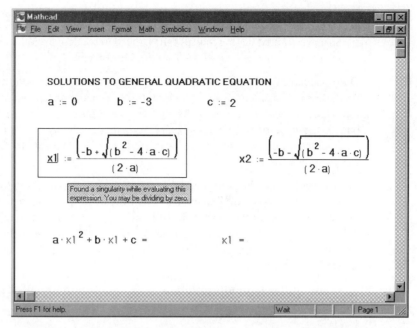

Figure 7-12: A worksheet containing an error message and several undefined variables.

An error message is visible only when you click on the associated expression. Figure 7-12 shows how an error message looks when you click on an expression. You'll always be able to get on-line help about the error message by clicking on it and pressing [Shift][F1].

Mathcad cannot process an expression containing an error. If the expression is a definition, the variable or function it is supposed to define will remain undefined. This can cause any expressions that reference that variable to be undefined as well. Mathcad indicates undefined variables and functions by displaying their names in red. In the example shown in Figure 7-12, an error in the definition of *x1* causes the variable to be undefined in three different places in the worksheet.

Note that in an expression in which zero is either a pre-factor or numerator (for example $0 \cdot x$ or $0/x$), Mathcad computes the result as zero, without evaluating or checking for errors in the *x* expression.

Fixing errors

If your worksheet contains several expressions with errors, as shown in Figure 7-12, this is what to do:

■ Determine which expression with an error is closest to the top of the worksheet. This error is probably the cause of many of the other errors.

■ If necessary, click on the error and press [Shift][F1] for help.

■ If you anticipate time-consuming calculations, switch to manual mode as described in "Controlling calculations" on page 144. This will allow you to make numerous changes without having to wait for Mathcad to recalculate. When you are ready to recalculate, choose **Calculate** from the **Math** menu.

Once you have determined which expression caused the error, edit that expression to fix the error, or change the variable definitions that led to the error. When you click in the expression and begin editing, Mathcad removes the error message. When you click outside the equation (or in manual calculation mode, when you recalculate), Mathcad recomputes the expression. If you have fixed the error, Mathcad then recomputes the other expressions affected by the expression you changed.

Note that when you see an error message attached to an expression, it doesn't necessarily mean that you should edit that expression. More often than not, the error arises as a result of functions or variables defined farther up in the worksheet. Edit these other definitions to fix the error. For example, in Figure 7-12, all five errors are caused by a division by zero. To fix all five error messages at once, change the definition for *a* as shown in Figure 7-13.

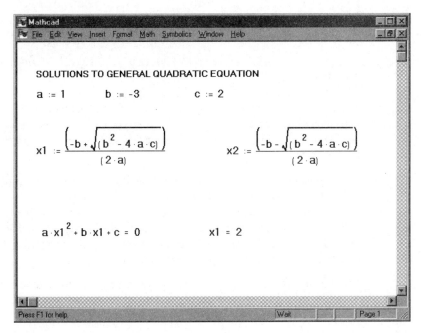

Figure 7-13: Changing the definition of the variable "a" fixes all errors at once.

A note about function definitions

When you define a function, Mathcad does not try to evaluate it until you use it later on in the worksheet. If there is an error, the use of the function is marked in error, even though the real problem may be in the definition of the function itself. Figure 7-14 shows two examples of this.

Chapter 7 Equations and Computation

When a user-defined function is marked in error, be sure to check the function definition to find the actual source of error. Note that the second example in shows a recursive definition generating a "stack overflow" error message. Although Mathcad supports recursive function definitions, as described in "Recursive function definitions" on page 136, you must supply an initial condition in your function definition that prevents the recursion from going on forever.

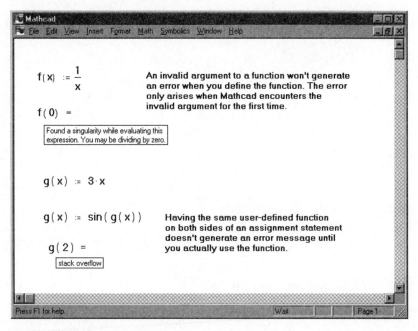

Figure 7-14: When an error message points to a function, go back and check the way the function was defined.

Chapter 8
Variables and Constants

This chapter describes valid Mathcad variable names, function names, and numbers, including predefined variables like π.

Mathcad handles imaginary and complex numbers as easily as it does real numbers. Mathcad variables can have imaginary or complex values, and most Mathcad built-in functions can take complex arguments. This chapter describes how to use complex numbers in Mathcad.

In addition to handling real and complex numbers, Mathcad supports *strings* in math: arbitrary sequences of characters such as letters, numbers, and punctuation marks. This chapter describes how to create strings and use them in variable definitions.

The following sections make up this chapter:

Names
 Valid variable and function names; how to type Greek letters.

Predefined variables
 List of variables that have values when you start Mathcad.

Numbers
 Real, imaginary, hexadecimal, and octal numbers; dimensional values.

Complex numbers
 How to use complex numbers in Mathcad.

Strings
 How to create and use string variables and string expressions in Mathcad.

Names

Mathcad lets you use almost any expression as a variable or function name.

Names in Mathcad can contain any of the following characters:

- Uppercase and lowercase letters.

- The digits 0 through 9.

- The underscore (_).

- a prime symbol ('). Note that this is not the same as an apostrophe. You'll find the prime symbol on the same key as the tilde (~).

- percent (%).

- Greek letters. To insert a Greek letter, type the equivalent roman letter and press [Ctrl]G. The section "How to type Greek letters" on page 155 contains a table of equivalent roman letters.

- The infinity symbol ∞, generated by typing [Ctrl]Z.

- Any other character provided you type [Ctrl][Shift]P before typing that character. This is discussed further in the section "Using an operator symbol in a name."

- Any math expression appearing between the brackets generated by typing [Ctrl][Shift]O. This is discussed further in the section "Chemistry notation" on page 157.

The following restrictions apply to variable names:

- A name cannot start with one of the digits 0 through 9. Mathcad interprets anything beginning with a number as either an imaginary number ($2i$ or $3j$), an octal or hexadecimal number (5o or 7h), or as a number *times* a variable ($3 \cdot x$).

- The infinity symbol, ∞, can only appear as the first character in a name.

- Any characters you type after a period (.) will appear as a subscript. This is discussed in the section "Literal subscripts" on page 156.

- All characters in a name must be in the same font, have the same point size, and be in the same style (italic, bold, etc.). Greek letters can, however, appear in any variable name.

- Mathcad does not distinguish between variable names and function names. Thus, if you define $f(x)$, and later on you define the variable f, you will find that you cannot use $f(x)$ anywhere below the definition for f.

- Certain names are already used by Mathcad for built-in constants, functions, and unit. (For a list of constants and functions, see Appendix A, "Reference." For a list of units, see Appendix B, "Unit Tables.") Although you can redefine these names, keep in mind that their built-in meanings will no longer exist after the definition.

For example, if you define a variable *mean*, Mathcad's built-in function *mean*(**v**) can no longer be used.

Mathcad distinguishes between uppercase and lowercase letters. For example, *diam* is a different variable from *DIAM*. Mathcad also distinguishes between names in different fonts, as discussed in Chapter 6, "Equation and Result Formatting." Thus, *Diam* is also a different variable from ***Diam***. The following are examples of valid names:

```
alpha                    b
xyz700                   A1_B2_C3_D4%%%
F1'                      a%%
```

How to type Greek letters

There are two ways to type a Greek variable name in Mathcad:

- Type the roman equivalent from the table below. Then press [**Ctrl**]**G**.

- Click on the appropriate letter on Greek Symbol Palette. To see this palette, click on the button labeled "αβ" on the Math Palette.

Note that although many of the uppercase Greek letters look like ordinary capital letters, they are *not* the same. Mathcad distinguishes between Greek and roman letters. If you use a Greek letter in place of the corresponding roman letter in a variable or function name, Mathcad will not recognize the two as equivalent.

Note: Because it is used so frequently, the Greek letter π can also be typed by pressing [**Ctrl**]**P**.

The following table lists all the Greek letters and their roman equivalents. These are the same roman equivalents used in the Symbol font. To insert an uppercase Greek letter, use the uppercase roman equivalent. To insert a lowercase Greek letter, use the lowercase roman equivalent.

Name	Uppercase	Lowercase	Roman equivalent
alpha	A	α	A
beta	B	β	B
chi	X	χ	C
delta	Δ	δ	D
epsilon	E	ε	E
eta	H	η	H
gamma	Γ	γ	G
iota	I	ι	I
kappa	K	κ	K
lambda	Λ	λ	L
mu	M	μ	M
nu	N	ν	N

omega	Ω	ω	W
omicron	O	o	O
phi	Φ	ϕ	F
phi(alternate)		φ	J
pi	Π	π	P
psi	Ψ	ψ	Y
rho	P	ρ	R
sigma	Σ	σ	S
tau	T	τ	T
theta	Θ	θ	Q
theta(alternate)	ϑ		J
upsilon	Y	υ	U
xi	Ξ	ξ	X
zeta	Z	ζ	Z

Literal subscripts

If you include a period in a variable name, Mathcad displays whatever follows the period as a subscript. You can use these *literal subscripts* to create variables with names like vel_{init} and u_{air}.

To create a literal subscript, follow these steps:

■ Type the portion of the name that appears before the subscript.

■ Type a period, followed by the portion of the name that is to become the subscript.

Do not confuse literal subscripts with *array* subscripts. Although they appear similar—a literal subscript appears below the line, like an array subscript, but with a slight space before the subscript—they behave quite differently in computations. A literal subscript, created by typing a period, is really just part of a variable name. An array subscript represents a reference to an array element. Array subscripts are generated with the left bracket key ([ ). See Chapter 10, "Vectors and Matrices," for a description of how to use subscripts with arrays.

Using an operator symbol in a name

When you're in a math region, certain keystrokes insert math operators rather than the characters you see imprinted on the keys. For example, when you type "$" in a math region, Mathcad displays a summation symbol with placeholders, not a dollar sign. Although this feature makes it easier to type math expressions, it also excludes certain characters from use in variable names.

To circumvent this problem, Mathcad lets you temporarily enter text mode while you're still in a math expression. When you're in text mode, all the keys lose their mathematical meaning. This lets you type exactly what you see imprinted on the keys on your keyboard. For example, here's how you define the variable $a\$$ to be equal to "1":

- Type **a**. Do not type **$** yet since, at this point, the "$" key will insert a summation sign.

- Type **[Ctrl][Shift]P** to enter a "text" mode.

- Now go ahead and type **$**. The insertion point turns red to show that you're in text mode.

- Type **[Ctrl][Shift]P** again to return to math mode.

- Type **:1** to complete the definition. Since you're now back in math mode, the ":" key has recovered its mathematical meaning.

Chemistry notation

Ordinarily, a name cannot contain other operators within it. There may be times, however, when you want to define a name which contains superscripts, subscripts, or other operators as part of it. For example, you may want assign a value to the variable named H_2O. To do this:

- Press **[Ctrl][Shift]O**. This inserts a pair of brackets with a placeholder between them.

- Type **H[2**.

- Press the **[Space]** key to place the H_2 between the editing lines.

- Now type **O**.

■ Press : and type a value in the placeholder. Mathcad always uses brackets as part of a variable name defined in this way.

$$\left[\, H_2\ O\, \right] \,:= \,\blacksquare$$

Predefined variables

Mathcad includes several variables that, unlike ordinary variables, are already defined when you start Mathcad. These variables are called *predefined* or *built-in variables*. Predefined variables either have a conventional value, like π and e, or are used as system variables to control how Mathcad works, like ORIGIN and TOL.

Variable = default value	Definition and use
$\pi = 3.14159...$	Pi. Mathcad uses the value of π to 15 digits in numerical calculations. In symbolic calculations, π is exact. To type π, press [Ctrl]P.
$e = 2.71828...$	The base of natural logarithms. Mathcad uses the value of e to 15 digits in numerical calculations. In symbolic calculations, e is exact.
$\infty = 10^{307}$	Infinity. In numerical calculations, this is an actual number of finite magnitude. In symbolic calculations, this represents a true infinity. To type ∞, press [Ctrl]Z.
$\% = 0.01$	Percent. Use this in expressions like $10 \cdot \%$ or as a scaling unit in the placeholder at the end of an equation with an equals sign.
$\text{TOL} = 10^{-3}$	Numerical tolerance for the various approximation algorithms (integrals, equation solving, etc.). See the sections on the specific operations for details.
$\text{ORIGIN} = 0$	Array origin: the index of the first element of an array.
$\text{PRNCOLWIDTH} = 8$	Column width used when writing files with the *WRITEPRN* function.
$\text{PRNPRECISION} = 4$	Number of significant digits used when writing files with the *WRITEPRN* function.
$\text{FRAME} = 0$	Used to drive animation. Set to zero when no animation is in progress.
Pro $\text{CWD} = \text{"<system path>"}$	String corresponding to the directory of the worksheet.
Pro $\text{in}n = 0, \text{out}n = 0$	Input and output variables (`in0`, `in1`, `out0`, `out1`, etc.) in a Mathcad component in a MathConnex system. See the *MathConnex Getting Started Guide* for details.

In addition to the predefined variables in the table above, Mathcad treats the names of all built-in units as predefined variables. See Chapter 9, "Units and Dimensions,"for more on using units in your calculations; a list of built-in units is in Appendix B, "Unit Tables."

Although Mathcad's predefined variables already have values when you start Mathcad, you can still redefine them. For example, if you want to use a variable called e with a value other than the one Mathcad provides, enter a new definition, like $e := 2$. The variable e takes on the new value everywhere in the worksheet below the new definition.

Mathcad's predefined variables are defined for all fonts, sizes, and styles. This means that if you redefine e as shown above, you can still use **e**, for example, as the base for natural logarithms. Note, however, that Greek letters are not included. This means that "ε", although it is typed as "e" in the Symbol font, is not the same number as e.

You can control the values of TOL, ORIGIN, PRNPRECISION, and PRNCOLWIDTH without having to explicitly define them in your worksheet. To do so, choose **Options** from the **Math** menu, and click on the Built-In Variables tab, as shown below:

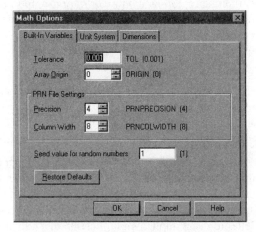

To set new starting values for any of these variables, enter a new value in the appropriate text box and click "OK." Then choose **Calculate Worksheet** from the **Math** menu to ensure that all existing equations take the new values into account.

The numbers in brackets to the right of the variable names represent the default values for those variables. To restore these default values, click on the "Restore Defaults" button and then click "OK."

Numbers

This section describes the various types of numbers that Mathcad uses and how to enter them into equations.

Types of numbers

Mathcad interprets anything beginning with a digit as a number. A digit can be followed by:

- other digits

- a decimal point

- digits after the decimal point

- one of the letters **h** or **o**, for hex and octal numbers, **i** or **j** for imaginary numbers, and **M**, **L**, **T**, **Q**, **K**, **C**, or **S** for numbers carrying units. These are discussed in more detail below.

Note that Mathcad uses the period (.) to signify the decimal point. The comma (**,**) is used both to show iteration and to separate values in an input table. These topics are discussed in Chapter 11, "Range Variables."

Imaginary numbers

To enter an imaginary number, follow it with i or j, for example, $1i$ or $2.5j$. You cannot use i or j alone to represent the imaginary unit. You must always type **1i** or **1j**. If you don't, Mathcad will think you are referring to a variable named either i or j. See the section "Complex numbers" on page 161.

Dimensional values

Dimensional values are numbers associated with one of the Mathcad dimensions: in the SI system, *mass, length, time, current, temperature, luminous intensity,* and *substance.* Mathcad uses these dimensions to keep track of units for dimensional analysis and unit conversions. See Chapter 9, "Units and Dimensions."

To enter a dimensional value, type a number followed by an upper or lowercase **M** for mass, **L** for length, **T** for time, **I** for current, **K** for temperature, **C** for luminous intensity, and **S** for substance. For example, **4.5M** represents 4.5 mass units. Because Mathcad by default treats most expressions involving a number followed immediately by a letter to mean implied multiplication of a number by a variable name, as described in Chapter 3, "Editing Equations," you will need to backspace over the implied multiplication operator to create expressions like **4.5M**.

Octal integers

To enter a number in octal, follow it with the upper or lowercase letter **O**. For example, **25636o** represents 11166 in decimal. Octal numbers must be integers less than 2^{31}.

Hexadecimal integers

To enter a number in hexadecimal, follow it with the upper or lowercase letter **H**. For example, **2b9eh** represents 11166 in decimal. To represent digits above 9, use the upper or lowercase letters **A** through **F**. To enter a hexadecimal number that begins with a letter, you must begin it with a leading zero. If you don't, Mathcad will think it's a variable name. For example, use **0a3h** rather than **a3h** to represent the decimal number 163 in hexadecimal. Hexadecimal numbers must be integers less than 2^{31}.

Exponential notation

To enter very large or very small numbers in exponential notation, just multiply a number by a power of 10. For example, to represent the number $3 \cdot 10^8$, type **3 * 10 ^ 8**.

Combining types of numbers

You can freely combine all types of numbers with various operators. Figure 8-1 shows some examples.

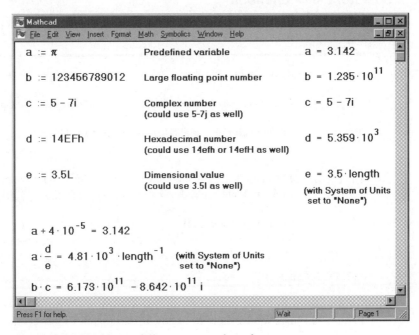

Figure 8-1: Combining different types of numbers.

Complex numbers

As described in the preceding section, Mathcad accepts complex numbers of the form $a + bi$, where a and b are ordinary numbers. You can use j instead of i if you prefer that notation.

Complex numbers can also arise if you enter an expression with a complex result. Even a Mathcad expression that involves only real numbers can have a complex value. For example, if you evaluate $\sqrt{-1}$, Mathcad will return i.

Although you can enter imaginary numbers followed by either i or j, Mathcad normally displays them followed by i. To have Mathcad display imaginary numbers with j, choose **Number** from the **Format** menu, click on the "Global" option button, and set

---

"Imaginary" to j. See Chapter 6, "Equation and Result Formatting," for a full description of the numerical formatting options.

When typing complex numbers, remember that you cannot use i or j alone to represent the imaginary unit. You must always type `1i` or `1j`. If you don't, Mathcad will interpret the i or j as a variable. When the cursor is outside an equation that shows $1i$ or $1j$, Mathcad hides the superfluous 1.

Complex operators and functions

Mathcad has the following functions and operators for working with complex numbers:

Re(z)   Real part of a number z.

Im(z)   Imaginary part of a number z.

arg(z)   Angle in complex plane from real axis to z. This returns a result between $-\pi$ and π radians.

$|z|$ The magnitude of the number z. To take the magnitude of an expression, click on it and press the vertical-bar key "│".

$\bar{z}$ Complex conjugate of z. To apply the conjugate operator to an expression, select the expression, then press the double-quote key ("). The conjugate of the complex number $a + b \cdot i$ is $a - b \cdot i$.

Figure 8-2 shows some examples of how to use complex numbers in Mathcad.

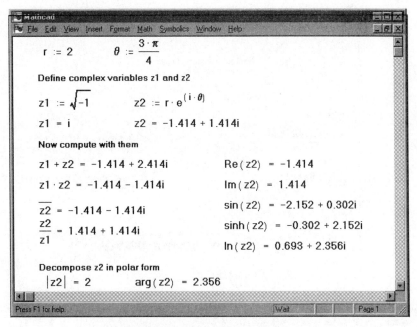

Figure 8-2: Complex numbers in Mathcad.

Multivalued functions

When complex numbers are available, many functions and operators we think of as returning unique results become multivalued. The impact of this on logarithmic and exponential functions is discussed more fully in Chapter 13, "Built-in Functions."

As a general rule, when a function or operator is multivalued, Mathcad always returns the value making the smallest positive angle relative to the positive real axis in the complex plane. This is the principal value.

For example, when asked to evaluate $(-1)^{1/3}$, Mathcad will return $.5 + .866i$ despite the fact that we commonly think of the cube root of -1 as being -1. This is because the number $.5 + .866i$ makes an angle of only 60 degrees from the positive real axis. The number -1, on the other hand, is all the way on the other side, 180 degrees from the positive real axis.

The single exception to this rule is the nth root operator described in Chapter 12, "Operators." This operator always returns a real root whenever one is available. Figure 8-3 compares these two alternatives.

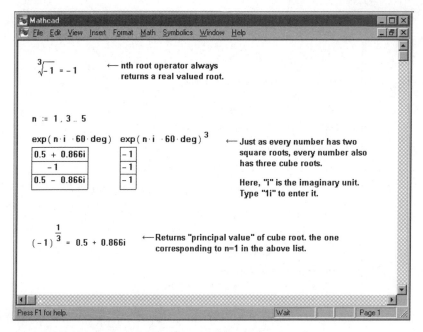

Figure 8-3: Finding real valued roots of a negative number.

Strings

Although in most cases the math expressions or variables you work with in Mathcad are real and complex numbers, you can also work with *string expressions* (also called *string literals* or *string variables*). String expressions can include any character you can type at the keyboard, including letters, numbers, punctuation, and spacing, as well as a variety of special symbols as listed in the table of ASCII codes in Appendix A, "Reference." Strings differ from variable names or numbers because Mathcad always displays them between double quotes. You may assign a string expression to a variable name, use a string expression as an element of a vector or matrix, or use a string expression as the argument to a function.

To create a string expression in math:

■ Click on an empty math placeholder in a math expression, usually on the right-hand side of a variable definition.

■ Type the double-quote (") key. Mathcad displays a pair of quotes and an insertion line between them.

- Type any combination of letters, numbers, punctuation, or spaces. Click outside the expression or press the right arrow key ($\rightarrow$) when you are finished.

$$s := \text{"The result 5 is valid|"}$$

To enter a special character corresponding to one of the ASCII codes, do the following:

- Click to position the insertion point in the string.

- Hold down the [**Alt**] key, and type the number "0" followed immediately by the number of the ASCII code *using the numeric keypad at the right of the keyboard* in number-entry mode.

- Release the [**Alt**] key to see the symbol in the string.

For example, to enter the degree symbol (°) in a string, press down [**Alt**] and type "0176" using the numeric keypad.

Notice that the double-quote key (") has a variety of meanings in Mathcad, depending on the exact location of the cursor in your worksheet. When you type this key in a blank placeholder, Mathcad begins a string expression. As described in "Complex numbers" on page 161, typing the double-quote key *after* you have selected a math expression creates the complex conjugate of the selected expression. And typing the double-quote key when you see a crosshair cursor in a blank space in the worksheet begins a text region, as described in Chapter 5, "Text." So when you want to enter a string variable, you must *always* have a blank placeholder selected.

Editing of strings differs from editing of other math expressions because you must use the arrow keys or click outside the string to move out of a string expression. Pressing [**Space**] or [**Tab**], which can be used in other expressions to change the position of the editing lines, is interpreted as just another character in string.

Figure 8-4 shows examples of strings in math expressions. Valid strings include expressions such as "The Rain in Spain Falls Mainly on the Plain," "Invalid input: try a number less than -5," and "Meets stress requirements." A string expression in Mathcad, while not limited in size, always appears as a single line of text in your worksheet. Note that a string such as "123," created in the way described above, is understood by Mathcad to be a string of characters rather than the number 123.

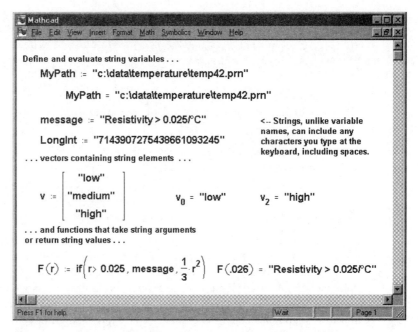

Figure 8-4: Using strings in math expressions.

Most of Mathcad's arithmetic operators and built-in functions expect numeric arguments and will issue error messages when you use string expressions with them. As described in Chapter 12, "Operators," however, you can use Mathcad's boolean operators to compare strings. Mathcad also includes a set of specialized string-manipulation functions as described in Chapter 13, "Built-in Functions." String expressions are especially useful for generating custom error messages in user-defined functions (see the example at the bottom of Figure 8-4) and in programs, as described in Chapter 18, "Programming." Use string expressions also to specify system paths for arguments to Mathcad's data and graphics input and output functions, as described in Chapter 19, "Data Management," and Chapter 28, "Importing and Exporting Graphics."

Chapter 9
Units and Dimensions

Units of measurement, while not required in Mathcad equations, can help detect errors and enhance the display of computed results. Mathcad's unit capabilities take care of many of the usual chores associated with using units and dimensions in scientific calculation. Once you enter the appropriate definitions, Mathcad automatically performs unit conversions and flags incorrect and inconsistent dimensional calculations.

This chapter describes how to use units and dimensions in Mathcad, including unit conversions and dimensional checking.

The following sections make up this chapter.

Computing with units

How to use units in an equation and how Mathcad catches any dimensional inconsistencies.

Displaying units of results

How Mathcad displays units and how to convert from one unit to another.

Built-in units

Choosing a system of units; defining your own units in terms of fundamental dimensions.

Changing dimension names

How to change the names of Mathcad's fundamental dimensions.

Computing with units

When you first start Mathcad, a complete set of units is available for your calculations. You can treat these units just like built-in variables. To assign units to a number, just multiply it by the name of the unit. For example, type expressions like the following:

```
mass:75*kg
acc:100*m/s^2
acc_g:9.8*m/s^2
F:mass*(acc + acc_g)
```

Figure 9-1 shows how these equations appear in a worksheet.

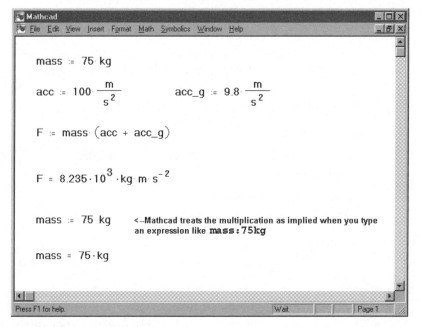

Figure 9-1: Equations using units.

If you define a variable which consists of a number followed immediately by a unit name, you can omit the multiplication symbol and Mathcad will treat the multiplication as implied, as you can see in the bottom-most example in Figure 9-1.

Mathcad recognizes most units by their common abbreviations. A list of all of Mathcad's built-in units is in Appendix B, "Unit Tables." By default Mathcad uses units from the SI unit system (also known as the International System of Units) in your worksheets. See the section "Built-in units" on page 175 for more information about selecting a unit system.

You can also use the Insert Unit dialog box to insert one of Mathcad's built-in units into any placeholder. The Insert Unit dialog box offers the following advantages:

- You won't have to remember the abbreviation Mathcad uses for a unit.

- You'll see at a glance all available units appropriate to the result you've clicked on.

- You can't make any typing mistakes.

To use the Insert Unit dialog box:

- Click in the empty placeholder and choose **Unit** from the **Insert** menu. Mathcad opens a dialog box with two scrolling lists.

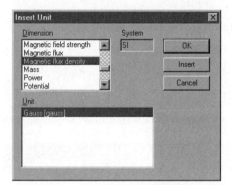

- The list at the bottom shows built-in units, along with their Mathcad names, corresponding to whatever physical quantity is selected in the top scrolling list. For convenience, when "Dimensionless" is selected at the top, a list of all available built-in units shows on the bottom.

- If necessary, use the top scrolling list to display only those units corresponding to a particular physical quantity. This makes it easier to find a particular unit or to see what choices are appropriate.

- In the bottom list, double-click on the unit you want to insert, or click on the unit you want and then click the "Insert" button. Mathcad inserts that unit into the empty placeholder.

For some engineering units—such as *hp*, *cal*, *BTU*, and *Hz*—Mathcad adopts one common definition for the unit name but allows you to use insert one of several alternative unit names, corresponding to alternative definitions of that unit, in your results. The alternative names are presented, where available, along with the standard unit name in the unit list at the bottom of the Insert Unit dialog box. Mathcad's preferred unit name is denoted in square brackets, and the alternative names are given in parentheses. In the case of horsepower, for example, Mathcad uses the U.K. definition of the unit for the name *hp* but gives you several variants, such as water horsepower, metric horsepower, boiler horsepower, and electric horsepower.

Note that Mathcad performs some dimensional analysis by trying to match the dimensions of your selected result with one of the common physical quantities in the top scrolling list. If it finds a match, you'll see all the built-in units corresponding to the highlighted physical quantity in the bottom scrolling list. If nothing matches, Mathcad simply lists all available built-in units on the bottom.

Dimensional checking

Whenever you enter an expression involving units, Mathcad checks it for dimensional consistency. If you add or subtract values with incompatible units, or violate other principles of dimensional analysis, Mathcad displays an appropriate error message.

For example, suppose you had defined acc as $100 \cdot m/s$ instead of $100 \cdot m/s^2$ as shown in Figure 9-2. Since acc is in units of velocity and acc_g is in units of acceleration, it is inappropriate to add them together. When you attempt to do so, Mathcad displays an error message.

Unit errors are usually caused by one of the following:

- An incorrect unit conversion.

- A variable with the wrong units, as shown in Figure 9-2.

- Units in exponents or subscripts (for example $v_{3 \cdot acre}$ or $2^{3 \cdot ft}$).

- Units as arguments to inappropriate functions (for example, $\sin(0 \cdot henry)$).

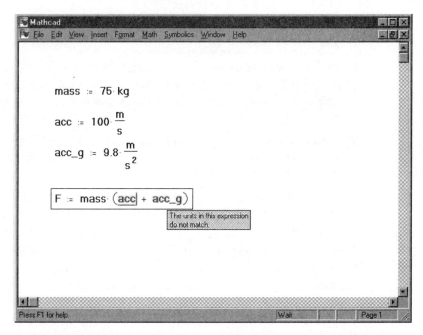

Figure 9-2: An equation with incompatible units.

Defining your own units

Although Mathcad recognizes many common units, you may need to define your own unit if:

- that unit isn't in the list of built-in units in Appendix B, "Unit Tables."

- you prefer to use your own abbreviation instead of that shown in Appendix B, "Unit Tables."

Chapter 9 Units and Dimensions

You define your own units in terms of existing units in exactly the same way you would define a variable in terms of an existing variable. Figure 9-3 shows how to define new units as well as how to redefine existing units.

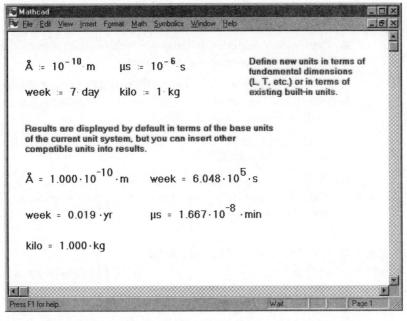

Figure 9-3: Defining your own units.

Since units behave just like variables, you may run into unexpected conflicts. For example, if you define the variable *m* in your worksheet, you won't be able to use the built-in unit *m* for meters anywhere below that definition. However, Mathcad will automatically display the unit *m* in any results involving meters.

Displaying units of results

Mathcad automatically displays results in terms of the fundamental units of the unit system you're working with. Mathcad offers several choices of unit system: SI, CGS, MKS, U.S. customary units, or no unit system. If you're using SI units, the default system in Mathcad, the base units are *meter, kilogram, second, ampere, Kelvin, candela*, and *mole*. If you're using the CGS system, for example, the base units are *centimeter, gram, second, coulomb*, and *Kelvin*. For details about the base units in MKS and U.S. customary units see Appendix B, "Unit Tables."

You can have Mathcad redisplay a particular result in terms of any of Mathcad's built-in units. To do so:

- Click in the result. You'll see an empty placeholder to its right. This is the *units placeholder*.

- Click on the units placeholder and choose **Unit** from the **Insert** menu. Mathcad opens the Insert Unit dialog box. This is described in detail in "Computing with units" on page 168.

- Double-click on the unit in terms of which you want to display the result. Mathcad inserts this unit in the units placeholder.

Another way to insert a unit is to type it directly into the units placeholder. This method is more general since it works not only for built-in units but for units you've defined yourself and for combinations of units.

For example, in Figure 9-1, *F* is displayed in terms of the fundamental units *kg*, *m* and *s*. To change this to *dyne:*

- Click in a displayed result to see the units placeholder to its right. Then click on this units placeholder.

$$F = 8235 \cdot kg \cdot m \cdot s^{-2} \ \blacksquare$$

- In the units placeholder, type **dyne**.

$$F = 8235 \cdot kg \cdot m \cdot s^{-2} \cdot dyne$$

- Click outside the equation. Mathcad displays the answer in terms of the units you entered.

$$F = 8.235 \cdot 10^{8} \cdot dyne$$

Unit conversions

There are two ways to convert from one set of units to another:

- By using the Insert Unit dialog box, or

- By typing the new units in the units placeholder itself.

If you want to display the result in terms of one of Mathcad's built-in units, the simplest method is to use the Insert Unit dialog box:

- Click on the unit you want to replace.

- Choose **Unit** from the **Insert** menu.

- In the scrolling list of units, double-click on the unit in terms of which you want to display the result.

As a quick shortcut, or if you want to display the result in terms of something not available through the Insert Unit dialog box—for example, a unit you defined yourself or an algebraic combination of units—you can edit the units placeholder directly. For example, to express the result in the previous example in terms of force-pounds rather than dynes:

■ Click in the name of the unit you want to replace.

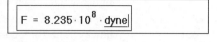

■ Delete the unit name by drag-selecting it and pressing [Del].

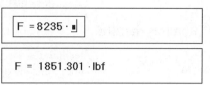

■ Type in the name of the new unit and click outside the equation.

Figure 9-4 shows *F* displayed both in terms of its fundamental SI units and in terms of several combinations of units.

When you enter an inappropriate unit in the units placeholder, Mathcad will display whatever combination of base units that make the result have the right units. For example, in the last equation in Figure 9-4, you see that $kW \cdot s$ is not a unit of force. Mathcad therefore inserts m^{-1} to cancel the extra length dimension.

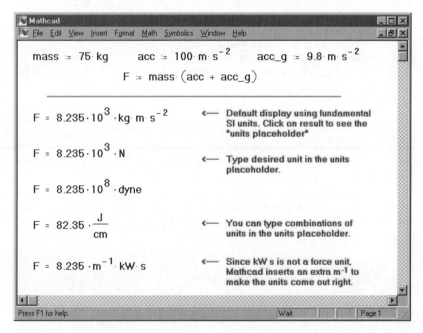

Figure 9-4: A calculated result displayed in terms of different units.

Whenever you enter units in the units placeholder, Mathcad divides the value to be displayed by whatever you enter in the units placeholder. This ensures that the complete displayed result—the number *times* the expression you entered for the placeholder—is a correct value for the equation.

Conversions involving an offset in addition to a multiplication, for example gauge pressure to absolute pressure, cannot be performed directly with Mathcad's unit conversion mechanism.

In particular, when working with temperature, keep in mind that you cannot use Mathcad's unit conversions to convert between Fahrenheit and Centigrade. You can, however, perform conversions of this type by defining suitable functions. See Chapter 7, "Equations and Computation," for more on defining your own functions.

Scaling results

The techniques described in this chapter are not restricted to units. You can put any variable, constant. or expression in a units placeholder. Mathcad will then redisplay the result in terms of the value of whatever is in the units placeholder. Just remember that whenever you type something in the units placeholder, Mathcad will change the calculated result so that the complete displayed result—the number *times* the expression you entered in the placeholder—is correct.

For example, you can use the units placeholder to display a result as a multiple of π. To do so:

■ Click on the units placeholder.

$$\frac{4509}{11750} = 0.384 \ \blacksquare$$

■ Click on π on the symbol palette. Then click outside the equation. Mathcad shows the result in terms of π.

$$\frac{4509}{11750} = 0.122 \cdot \pi$$

You can also use the units placeholder for dimensionless units like degrees and radians. Mathcad treats the unit *rad* as a constant equal to 1, so if you have a number or an expression in radians, you can type *deg* into the units placeholder to convert the result from radians to degrees. To convert an expression in degrees to radians, simply press the equal sign to evaluate it; Mathcad displays the results by default in radians. You may insert the unit name *rad* in the units placeholder if you wish. Figure 9-5 shows some examples of these techniques of converting and scaling results involving degrees and radians.

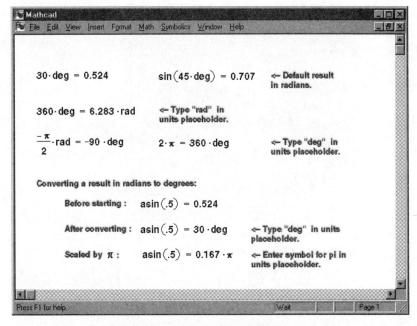

Figure 9-5: Using dimensionless units in placeholders.

Built-in units

When you start Mathcad, the SI system of units is automatically loaded by default. This means that when you use the equal sign to display a result having units, Mathcad automatically displays the units in the result in terms of some combination of the SI base units: *meter, kilogram, second, ampere, Kelvin, candela,* and *mole.* You can of course convert this combination of base units into a different unit by typing that unit into the units placeholder, as discussed in "Displaying units of results" on page 171. However, until you do so, Mathcad uses the fundamental units of the SI unit system to display your result.

You can have Mathcad display results in terms of the fundamental units of any of the other built-in unit systems in Mathcad: CGS, US customary, MKS, or no unit system at all. To do so, choose **Options** from the **Math** menu and click on the Unit System tab. You will see a dialog box like the one shown below:

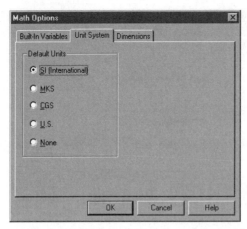

Click on the button corresponding to the default units in which you want to display results. The table below summarizes what each button does.

SI	Displays results in terms of *m*, *kg*, *s*, *A*, *K*, *cd*, and *mole*.
MKS	Displays results in terms of *m*, *kg*, *sec*, *coul*, and *K*.
CGS	Displays results in terms of *cm*, *gm*, *sec*, *coul*, and *K*.
U.S.	Displays results in terms of *ft*, *lb*, *sec*, *coul*, and *K*.
None	Displays results in terms of fundamental dimensions of length, mass, time, charge, and absolute temperature. All built-in units are disabled.

The SI unit system, widely used by scientists and engineers in many countries, is the preferred unit system in Mathcad and the one available to you by default in new Mathcad worksheets. SI provides two additional base units over the other systems, one for luminosity (*candela*) and one for substance (*mole*), and the base SI electrical unit (*ampere*) differs from the base electrical unit in the other systems (*coulomb*).

The standard SI unit names—such as *A* for *ampere*, *L* for *liter*, *s* for *second*, and *S* for *siemens*—are generally available only in the SI unit system. Many other unit names are available in all the available systems of units. For example, when CGS is selected, you'll still be able to use *kg* and *lb* even though these are not, strictly speaking, part of the CGS system of units. For a listing of which units are available in each system, see Appendix B, "Unit Tables." Mathcad includes most units common to scientific and engineering practice. Where conventional unit prefixes such as *m-* for *milli-*, *n-* for *nano-*, etc. are not understood by Mathcad, you can easily define custom units such as μm as described in "Defining your own units" on page 170. For examples of units with prefixes not already built into Mathcad, see the QuickSheets in the Resource Center.

If you click "None" in the Unit System tab of the Math Options dialog box, there will be no built-in units at all. You can, however, still define and use your own units. To do so, you use the special built-in constants: *1L*, *1M*, *1T*, *1Q*, and *1K*. These represent the dimensions *length*, *mass*, *time*, *charge*, and absolute *temperature*; you may also use the constants *1U* and *1S* for *luminosity* and *substance*. When you click "None," Mathcad displays answers in terms of the fundamental dimensions of *length*, *mass*, *time*, *charge*, and *temperature* rather than in terms of any system of units. Figure 9-6 shows how to define units using these built-in constants and how to carry out the analysis in Figure 9-1 after having done so. Notice that if you type the expression **kg:1M** in your worksheet Mathcad will display $kg := 1\ M$, treating the multiplication as implied on the right-hand side; so you will need to backspace over the implied multiplication to delete it to create the constant *1M*.

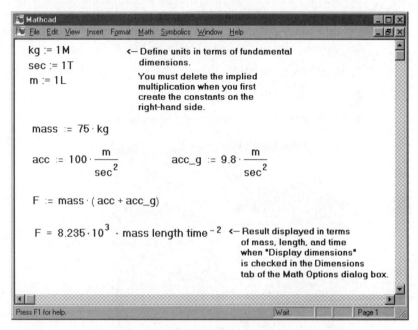

Figure 9-6: Using the constants 1L, 1M, and 1T to define a system of units.

Even if you are working in one of Mathcad's built-in unit systems, you can always choose to see results in your worksheet displayed in terms of fundamental dimensions like *mass* and *length* rather than the base units of the unit system. To do so:

■ Choose **Options** from the **Math** menu. Click on the Dimensions tab.

■ Click on the check box beside "Display dimensions."

■ Click "OK."

Changing dimension names

The previous section showed how you can display a result in terms of the fundamental units of either of four systems of units or in terms of the fundamental physical dimensions of *mass*, *length*, *time*, *charge*, *temperature*, *luminosity*, and *substance*. (The

---

latter two dimensions are used only in the SI unit system.) This section describes how to go even further and actually change the names of the fundamental dimensions altogether.

This may be useful if the nature of your work makes another set of fundamental dimensions more appropriate. Thus, a commodities trader may prefer to use *bushels* and *currency* rather than *charge* and *temperature*; a car salesman might define *trucks* and *sedans* rather than *length* and *mass*. In short, a dimension is nothing more than a way of tagging numbers so you can keep better track of them. It just so happens that in most physical problems, it's convenient to name these dimensions according to the fundamental dimensions in the SI unit system.

To change the names of the dimensions:

■ Choose **Options** from the **Math** menu.

■ Click on the Dimensions tab, as shown below:

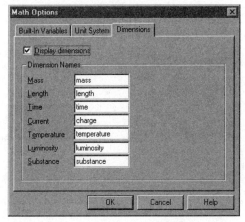

■ Click on the check box beside "Display dimensions" if it is not already checked.

■ To change a dimension name, edit the name shown in the appropriate text box.

■ Click "OK."

Renaming the dimensions in this dialog box changes the dimension names only for the Mathcad worksheet you are working on. To make these dimension names available in other worksheets, you can save your worksheet as a template as described in Chapter 4, "Worksheet Management."

Chapter 10
Vectors and Matrices

This chapter describes Mathcad arrays. While ordinary variables (scalars) hold a single value, arrays hold many values. As is customary in linear algebra, arrays having only one column will often be referred to as vectors. All others are matrices. The following sections make up this chapter.

Creating a vector or matrix

How to create or edit vectors and matrices

Computing with arrays

Defining variables as arrays and using them in expressions.

Subscripts and superscripts

Referring to individual array elements and columns.

Displaying vectors and matrices

How Mathcad displays answers involving matrices and vectors.

Limits on array sizes

Limits on the sizes of arrays to be stored, displayed, or entered.

Vector and matrix operators

Operators designed for use with vectors and matrices.

Vector and matrix functions

Built-in functions designed for use with vectors and matrices.

Doing calculations in parallel

Using Mathcad's "vectorize" operator to speed calculations.

Simultaneous definitions

Using vectors to define several variables simultaneously.

Arrays and user-defined functions

Using arrays as arguments to user defined functions.

Nested arrays

Arrays in which the elements are themselves arrays.

Creating a vector or matrix

A single number in Mathcad is called a *scalar*. A column of numbers is a *vector*, and a rectangular array of numbers is called a *matrix*. The general term for a vector or matrix is an *array*.

There are three ways to create an array:

■ By filling in an array of empty placeholders as discussed in this section. This technique is useful for arrays that are not too large.

■ By using range variables to fill in the elements as discussed in Chapter 11, "Range Variables." This technique is useful when you have some explicit formula for the elements in terms of their indices.

■ By reading data in from external files or applications as discussed in Chapter 19, "Data Management," and Chapter 28, "Importing and Exporting Graphics."

You may wish to distinguish between the names of matrices, vectors, and scalars by font. For example, in many math and engineering books, names of vectors are set in bold while those of scalars are set in italic. See the section "Math styles" in Chapter 6 for a description of how to do this.

Creating a vector

A vector is an array or matrix containing one column. To create a vector in Mathcad, follow these steps:

■ Click in either a blank space or on a placeholder.

■ Choose **Matrix** from the **Insert** menu, or click on the Vector or Matrix button on the Vectors and Matrices palette. A dialog box appears, as shown on the right.

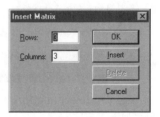

■ Enter the number of elements in the text box beside "Rows." For example, to create a three-element vector, type **3**.

■ Enter **1** in the text box beside "Columns." Then click "Create." Mathcad inserts a vector of placeholders.

The next step is to fill in these placeholders with scalar expressions. To do so, follow these steps:

- Click on the top placeholder and type **2**.

- Move the insertion point to the next place-holder. You can do this by clicking directly on the second placeholder.

- Type **3** on the second placeholder. Then move the insertion point to the third place-holder and type **4**.

If you're going to need several vectors in your calculation, you can leave the **Insert Matrix** dialog box up for later use.

Once you have created a vector, you can use it in calculations just as you would a number. For example, to add another vector to this vector, follow these steps:

- Press [**Space**] to enclose the entire vector is now between the editing lines. This ensures that the plus sign you type next will apply to the whole vector rather than to one of its elements.

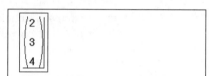

- Type the plus key (**+**). Mathcad shows a placeholder for the second vector.

- Use the **Insert Matrix** dialog box to create another three-element vector.

- Fill in this vector by clicking in each place-holder and typing in the numbers shown on the right.

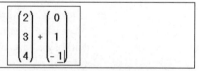

- Press the equal sign (**=**) to see the result.

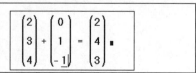

Addition is just one of Mathcad's vector and matrix operations. Mathcad also includes matrix subtraction, matrix multiplication, dot product, integer powers, determinants, and many other operators and functions for vectors and matrices. Complete lists appear in the sections "Vector and matrix operators" on page 193 and "Vector and matrix functions" on page 196.

Creating a matrix

To create a matrix, first click in a blank space or on a placeholder. Then:

■ Choose **Matrix** from the **Insert** menu. The dialog box shown on the right appears.

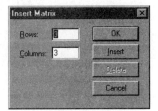

■ Enter a number of rows and a number of columns in the appropriate boxes. In this example, there are two rows and three columns. Then click on "Create." Mathcad inserts a matrix of placeholders.

$$\begin{pmatrix} \blacksquare & \bullet & \bullet \\ \bullet & \bullet & \bullet \end{pmatrix}$$

■ Fill in the placeholders to complete the matrix as described in the previous section for vectors.

$$\begin{pmatrix} 2 & 5 & 17 \\ 3.5 & 3.9 & -12.9 \end{pmatrix}$$

You can use this matrix in equations, just as you would a number or vector.

Throughout this *User's Guide*, the term "vector" refers to a column vector. A column vector is identical to a matrix with one column. You can also create a *row vector* by creating a matrix with one row and many columns. Operators and functions which expect vectors always expect column vectors. They do not apply to row vectors. To change a row vector into a column vector, use the transpose operator [**Ctrl**]**1**.

Changing the size of a matrix

You can change the size of a matrix by inserting and deleting rows and columns. To do so, follow these steps:

■ Click on one of the matrix elements to place it between the editing lines. Mathcad will begin inserting or deleting with this element.

$$\begin{pmatrix} 2| & 5 & 17 \\ 3.5 & 3.9 & -12.9 \end{pmatrix}$$

- Choose **Matrix** from the **Insert** menu. The dialog box as shown on the right appears.

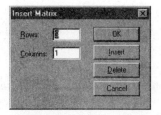

- Type the number of rows and/or columns you want to insert or delete. Then click on either "Insert" or "Delete." For example, to delete the column that currently holds the selected element, type **1** in the box next to "Columns," **0** in the box next to "Rows," and click on "Delete."

$$\begin{pmatrix} 5 & 17 \\ 3.9 & -12.9 \end{pmatrix}$$

Here's how Mathcad inserts or deletes rows or columns based on what you type in the dialog box:

- If you insert rows, Mathcad creates rows of empty placeholders below the selected element. If you insert columns, Mathcad creates columns of empty placeholders to the right of the selected element.

- To insert a row above the top row or a column to the left of the first column, first place the whole matrix between the editing lines. To do so, click in the matrix and press [**Space**]. Then choose **Matrix** and proceed as you would normally.

- If you delete rows or columns, Mathcad begins with the row or column occupied by the selected element. Mathcad deletes rows from that element downward and columns from that element rightward.

- If you type 0 as the number for "Rows," Mathcad neither inserts nor deletes rows. If you type 0 as the number for "Columns," Mathcad neither inserts nor deletes columns.

Note that when you delete rows or columns, Mathcad discards the information in the rows or columns you eliminate.

To delete an entire matrix or vector, place the entire matrix or vector between the editing lines and choose **Cut** from the **Edit** menu.

Computing with arrays

Variables can represent arrays as well as scalars. Defining a variable as an array is very much like defining a scalar. First type a variable name and a colon as you would with any other definition. Then create an array (vector or matrix) on the other side of the equation.

For example, to define a vector **v**, follow these steps:

- Click in empty space and type **v**, followed by the colon key (**:**).

- Choose **Matrix** from the **Insert** menu to bring up a dialog box. Type **3** in the box next to "Rows" and **1** in the box next to "Columns."

- Press "Create" and fill in the elements.

$$v := \begin{pmatrix} 2 \\ 3 \\ 4 \end{pmatrix}$$

You can now use the name **v** in place of the actual vector in any equation. Figure 10-1 demonstrates that the variable name **v** and the vector itself are interchangeable. Once you have defined a vector, you can of course define other vectors in terms of that vector, just as if you were doing mathematics on paper.

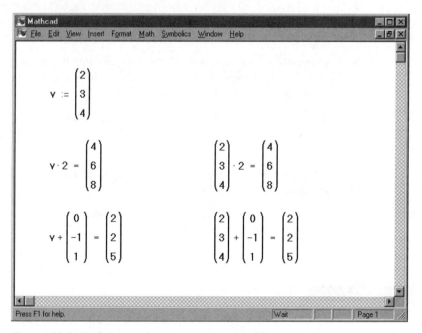

Figure 10-1: Defining and using a vector variable.

Do not use the same name for a scalar variable and a vector variable. This will simply redefine the variable.

Chapter 10 Vectors and Matrices

Subscripts and superscripts

You can refer to individual array elements by using subscripts. You can also refer to an entire column of an array by using a superscript. To type a subscript, use the left bracket key " [" and put an integer or a pair of integers in the placeholder. To insert a superscript operator, press [Ctrl]6 and place an integer in the placeholder.

Vector and matrix elements are ordinarily numbered starting with row zero and column zero. To change this, change the value of the built-in variable ORIGIN. See "Changing the array origin" on page 188.

Subscripts and vector elements

The top equation in Figure 10-1 defines the vector $\mathbf{v}$. To see the zeroth (top) element of the vector $\mathbf{v}$:

■ Type $\mathbf{v}$[0=

$$v_{0} = 2 \quad \blacksquare$$

You can also define individual vector elements by using a subscript on the left side of a definition. To change v_2 to 6:

■ Type $\mathbf{v}$[2:6

$$v_2 := 6$$

Figure 10-2 shows how this changes the value of $\mathbf{v}$.

When you define vector elements, you may leave gaps in the vector. For example, if $\mathbf{v}$ is undefined and you define v_3 as 10, v_0, v_1, and v_2 are all undefined. Mathcad fills these gaps with zeros until you enter specific values for them, as shown in Figure 10-3. Be careful of inadvertently creating very large vectors and matrices by doing this.

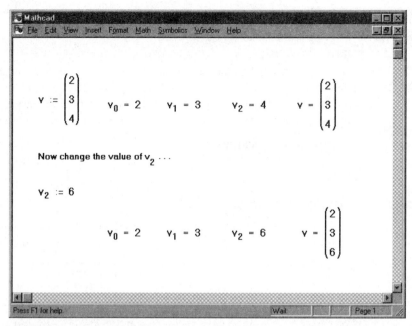

Figure 10-2: Defining a vector element.

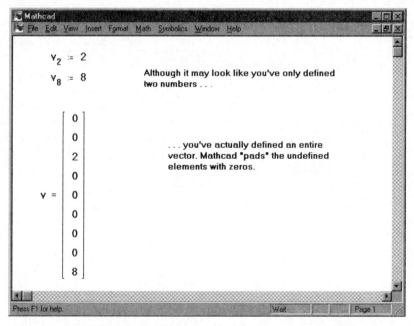

Figure 10-3: Mathcad places zeros into all elements you don't explicitly define.

Subscripts and matrix elements

To view or define a matrix element, use two subscripts separated by a comma. In general, to refer to the element in the ith row, jth column of matrix **M**, type:

        M[i,j

Note that the subscripts, like division and exponentiation, are "sticky." Whatever you type after [remains in the subscript until you press [**Space**] to leave.

If you want to add more to the equation, press [**Space**] to place the entire matrix element name, $M_{i,j}$, between the editing lines.

Figure 10-4 shows some examples of how to define individual matrix elements and how to view them. Notice that, as with vectors, Mathcad fills unspecified matrix elements with zeros.

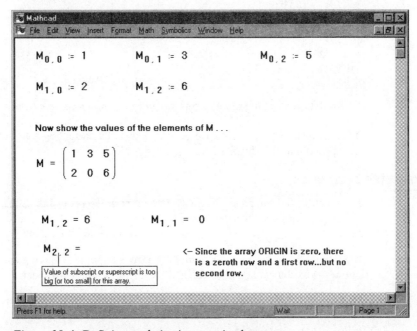

Figure 10-4: Defining and viewing matrix elements.

You can also define the elements of a vector or matrix with a definition like $v_i := i$, where i is a *range variable*. See Chapter 11, "Range Variables."

Superscripts with matrix columns

To refer to an entire column of an array, press [**Ctrl**]6 and place the column number in the resultant placeholder. Figure 10-5 shows how to place the third column of the matrix **M** in the vector **v**.

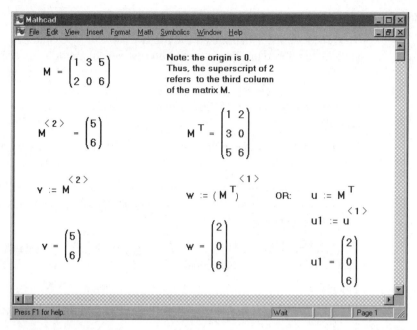

Figure 10-5: Using the superscript operator to extract a column from a matrix.

You can also extract a single row from a matrix by extracting a column from the transposed matrix. This is shown on the right-hand side of Figure 10-5.

Changing the array origin

By default, Mathcad arrays begin at element zero. To change this, change the value of the built-in variable ORIGIN. When you use subscripts to refer to array elements, Mathcad assumes the arrays begin at the current value of ORIGIN.

For example, suppose you want all your arrays to begin with element one. There are two ways to change the value of ORIGIN for the whole worksheet:

- Choose the **Options** command from the **Math** menu, click on the Built-In Variables tab, and change the value of ORIGIN.

- Enter a global definition for ORIGIN anywhere in your worksheet. For example, to change the ORIGIN to one, type: `ORIGIN~1`.

If you change ORIGIN to one, Mathcad no longer maintains an element zero for vectors or a zeroth row and column for matrices. Figure 10-6 shows a worksheet with the ORIGIN set to 1. Note that when you try to refer to v_0, Mathcad displays an appropriate error message.

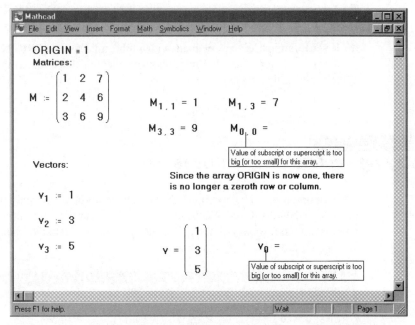

Figure 10-6: Arrays beginning at element one instead of at element zero.

When you redefine ORIGIN in a worksheet, keep in mind the following suggestions:

■ If you define ORIGIN with a definition in the worksheet rather than using the **Options** command on the **Math** menu, use a single global definition. Although you can redefine ORIGIN with a "$:=$" this will invariably lead to confusion. Changing ORIGIN in the middle of a worksheet can cause confusing effects. Array elements will seem to have shifted n positions, where n is the difference between the old ORIGIN and the new ORIGIN.

■ Don't forget to type ORIGIN in capital letters. Mathcad variable names are case-sensitive. Because ORIGIN is a built-in variable, its name is not font sensitive. It is however, still case-sensitive.

■ When you define an array, Mathcad assigns zero to any undefined elements. See Figure 10-3 for an example.

■ If you inadvertently define an array starting with element one when ORIGIN is set to its default value of zero, you will get unexpected answers with array functions like *mean* and *fft*. This is because Mathcad will automatically define $x_0 = 0$ for all these arrays. This extra element distorts the values returned by array functions. To avoid this problem, choose **Options** from the **Math** menu, click on the Built-In Variables tab, and set ORIGIN to 1.

■ When you set ORIGIN in the Built-In Variable dialog box, its value applies to all array variables. It is not possible to have some variables use one ORIGIN and others use a different ORIGIN.

- You can use ORIGIN to define variables with negative subscripts. If you set ORIGIN to –10, all arrays will begin with element –10.

- If you reference an array element with a subscript less than ORIGIN, Mathcad marks the array reference with an error message indicating that the array index goes beyond the ends of the array.

Displaying vectors and matrices

After computing with arrays in Mathcad, your resulting arrays may be large and unwieldy when displayed. Mathcad therefore displays matrices and vectors having more than nine rows or columns as scrolling output tables rather than as matrices or vectors. Figure 10-7 shows an example.

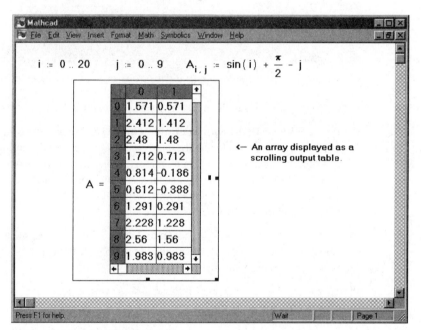

Figure 10-7: Displaying results in a scrolling output table.

A scrolling output table displays a portion of an array. To the left of each row and at the top of each column, there is a number indicating the index of the row or column. Use these row and column headers to determine the index of a particular value in the table.

If your results extend beyond the table, a scroll bar will appear along the appropriate edge of the table. You can scroll through the table using these scroll bars just as you would scroll through any window.

Another way to view more of a resulting array is to enlarge the table. To resize a scrolling output table:

■ Click the mouse just outside the equation region in which the scrolling output table appears. This anchors one corner of the selection rectangle.

■ Press and hold down the mouse button. With the button still held, drag the mouse across the scrolling output table. A selection rectangle emerges from the anchor point.

■ When the selection rectangle just encloses the equation region, release the mouse button.

■ Move the mouse pointer to the right or bottom edge of the selection rectangle. It will change to a double headed arrow.

■ Press and hold down the mouse button. With the mouse button still pressed, move the mouse. The scrolling output table will be stretched in the direction of the motion.

■ Once the scrolling output table is the right size, release the mouse button. Click outside the selection rectangle to deselect the equation region.

In addition to being able to resize and scroll through a scrolling output table, you can copy one or more values from it and paste them into another part of your worksheet or into another Windows application. For information on copying results from a scrolling output table, see the section "Copying numerical results" in Chapter 7.

Changing the display of arrays

Although matrices and vectors having more than nine rows or columns are automatically displayed as scrolling output tables, you can have Mathcad display them as matrices. To do so:

■ Click on the scrolling output table.

■ Choose **Number** from the **Format** menu.

■ Click on the box beside "Display as Matrix." The box should now be checked.

■ Click the "OK" button.

To display all the matrices and vectors of results in your worksheet as matrices regardless of their size:

■ Click on an empty part of your worksheet.

■ Choose **Number** from the **Format** menu.

■ Click on the box beside "Display as Matrix."

■ Make sure the "Set as worksheet default" radio button is filled and click "OK".

Graphical display of matrices

In addition to looking at the actual numbers making up an array, you can also see a graphical representation of those same numbers. There are three ways to do this:

- For an arbitrary array, you can use the various three dimensional plot types discussed starting at Chapter 22, "Surface Plots."

- For an array of integers between 0 and 255, you can look at a grayscale image by choosing **Picture** from the **Insert** menu and entering the array's name in the placeholder.

- For three arrays of integers between 0 and 255 representing the red, green, and blue components of an image, by choosing **Picture** from the **Insert** menu and entering the arrays' names, separated by commas, in the placeholder.

An example of viewing a matrix as a grayscale image is shown in Figure 18-19 of Chapter 18, "Programming." See Chapter 28, "Importing and Exporting Graphics," for more on viewing a matrix (or three matrices, in the case of a color image) in the picture operator.

Limits on array sizes

Mathcad has the following limits on the sizes of arrays to be defined, entered, or displayed:

Limit on input arrays

You cannot use the **Matrix** command on the **Insert** menu to create an array having more than 100 elements. This limitation applies whether you attempt to create a new array or add to an existing array. You can however, create larger arrays by either using the *augment* or *stack* functions to join arrays together, by using range variables, or by reading the numbers in directly from a disk file. An example of how to use the *augment* function is shown in Figure 10-8. The use of range variables to create arrays is discussed in Chapter 11, "Range Variables." Reading data files directly from a local or network drive, the clipboard, or another application is discussed in Chapter 19, "Data Management."

Limit on displayed arrays

If an array has more than nine rows or columns, Mathcad automatically displays it as a scrolling output table. You can enlarge the table or use the scroll bars provided in order to view all of the array. If, however, you change the local result format such that Mathcad displays it as an array rather than as a scrolling output table, Mathcad displays only the first two hundred rows or columns. Mathcad uses an ellipsis to indicate that rows and columns are present but not displayed. Although Mathcad does not display these rows or columns, it does continue to keep track of them internally.

Limit on array size

The effective array size limit depends on the memory available on your system. For most systems, it will usually be at least 1 million elements. In no system will it be higher than 8 million elements. If you try to define an array larger than your system will accommodate, you'll see an error message indicating that you have insufficient memory to do so. The elements can be distributed among any combination of rows and columns. When only limited memory is available and you define several very large arrays, the array size limit may decrease.

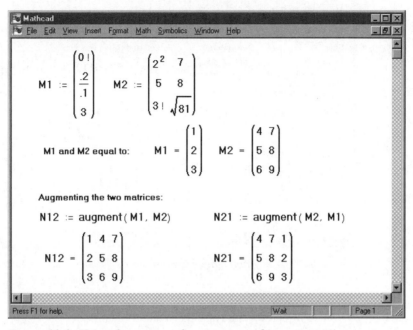

Figure 10-8: Using the augment function to combine two matrices.

Vector and matrix operators

Some of Mathcad's operators have special meanings for vectors and matrices. For example, the multiplication symbol means multiplication when applied to two numbers, but it means dot product when applied to vectors, and matrix multiplication when applied to matrices.

The table below describes Mathcad's vector and matrix operations. Many of these operators are available from the Vector and Matrices palette, available off the Math Palette. Note that operators which expect vectors always expect column vectors rather than row vectors. To change a row vector into a column vector, use the transpose operator [**Ctrl**]1.

Operators not listed in this table will not work for vectors and matrices. You can, however, use the "vectorize" operator to perform any scalar operation or function element by element on a vector or matrix. See "Doing calculations in parallel" on page 204. Figure 10-9 shows some ways to use vector and matrix operations.

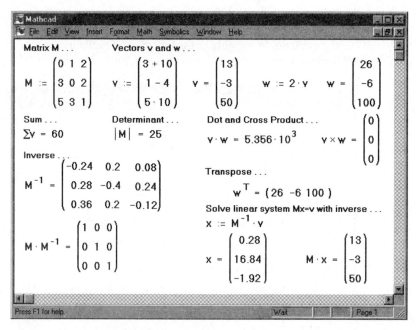

Figure 10-9: Vector and matrix operations.

In the following table,

- **A** and **B** represent arrays, either vector or matrix.

- **u** and **v** represent vectors.

- **M** represents a square matrix.

- u_i and v_i represent the individual elements of vectors **u** and **v**.

- z represents a scalar.

- m and n represent integers.

Operation	Appearance	Keystroke	Description
Scalar multiplication	$A \cdot z$	*	Multiplies each element of **A** by the scalar z.
Dot product	$u \cdot v$	*	Returns a scalar: $\Sigma u_i \cdot v_i$. The vectors must have the same number of elements.
Matrix multiplication	$A \cdot B$	*	Returns the matrix product of **A** and **B**. The number of columns in **A** must match the number of rows in **B**.
Vector/Matrix multiplication	$A \cdot v$	*	Returns the product of **A** and **v**. The number of columns in A must match the number of rows in **v**.
Scalar division	$\dfrac{A}{z}$	/	Divides each element of the array **A** by the scalar z.

Operation	Appearance	Keystroke	Description
Vector and matrix addition	$\mathbf{A} + \mathbf{B}$	+	Adds corresponding elements of $\mathbf{A}$ and $\mathbf{B}$. The arrays $\mathbf{A}$ and $\mathbf{B}$ must have the same number of rows and columns.
Scalar addition	$\mathbf{A} + z$	+	Adds z to each element of $\mathbf{A}$.
Vector and matrix subtraction	$\mathbf{A} - \mathbf{B}$	–	Subtracts corresponding elements of $\mathbf{A}$ and $\mathbf{B}$. The arrays $\mathbf{A}$ and $\mathbf{B}$ must have the same number of rows and columns.
Scalar subtraction	$\mathbf{A} - z$	–	Subtracts z from each element of $\mathbf{A}$.
Negative of vector or matrix	$-\mathbf{A}$	–	Returns an array whose elements are the negatives of the elements of $\mathbf{A}$.
Powers of matrix, matrix inverse	$\mathbf{M}^n$	^	nth power of square matrix $\mathbf{M}$ (using matrix multiplication). n must be an integer. $\mathbf{M}^{-1}$ represents the inverse of $\mathbf{M}$. Other negative powers are powers of the inverse. Returns a matrix.
Magnitude of vector	$|\mathbf{v}|$	|	Returns $\sqrt{\mathbf{v} \cdot \bar{\mathbf{v}}}$ where $\bar{\mathbf{v}}$ is the complex conjugate of $\mathbf{v}$.
Determinant	$|\mathbf{M}|$	|	$\mathbf{M}$ must be square matrix. Returns a scalar.
Transpose	$\mathbf{A}^{\mathsf{T}}$	[Ctrl]1	Interchanges row and columns of $\mathbf{A}$.
Cross product	$\mathbf{u} \times \mathbf{v}$	[Ctrl]8	$\mathbf{u}$ and $\mathbf{v}$ must be three-element vectors; result is another three-element vector.
Complex conjugate	$\bar{\mathbf{A}}$	"	Takes complex conjugate of each element of $\mathbf{A}$.
Sum	$\Sigma \mathbf{v}$	[Ctrl]4	Sum elements in $\mathbf{v}$.
Vectorize	$\overrightarrow{\mathbf{A}}$	[Ctrl]–	Treat all operations in $\mathbf{A}$ element by element. See the section "Doing calculations in parallel" on page 204 for a complete description.
Superscript	$\mathbf{A}^{\langle n \rangle}$	[Ctrl]6	nth column of array $\mathbf{A}$. Returns a vector.
Vector subscript	v_n	[	nth element of a vector.
Matrix subscript	$A_{m,n}$	[	(m, n)th element of a matrix.

Vector and matrix functions

Mathcad includes functions for manipulating arrays in ways that are common in linear algebra. These functions are intended for use with vectors and matrices. If a function is not explicitly set up to take a vector or matrix argument, it is inappropriate to supply one to it as an argument. Note that functions which expect vectors always expect column vectors rather than row vectors. To change a row vector into a column vector, use the transpose operator [Ctrl]1.

The following tables list Mathcad's vector and matrix functions. In these tables,

- **A** and **B** are arrays, either vector or matrix.

- **v** is a vector.

- **M** and **N** are square matrices.

- z is a scalar expression.

- Names beginning with m, n, i or j are integers.

Size and scope of an array

Mathcad provides several functions that return information about the size of an array and its elements. Figure 10-10 shows how these functions are used.

Function Name	Returns...
rows(**A**)	Number of rows in array **A**. If **A** is a scalar, returns 0.
cols(**A**)	Number of columns in array **A**. If **A** is a scalar, returns 0.
length(**v**)	Number of elements in vector **v**.
last(**v**)	Index of last element in vector **v**.
max(**A**)	Largest element in array **A**. If **A** has complex elements, returns the largest real part plus i times the largest imaginary part.
min(**A**)	Smallest element in array **A**. If **A** has complex elements, returns the smallest real part plus i times the smallest imaginary part.

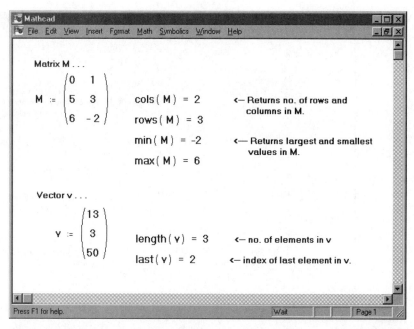

Figure 10-10: Vector and matrix functions for finding the size of an array and information about its elements.

Special types of matrices

You can use the following functions to derive from an array or scalar a special type or form of a matrix. Some of these functions are available only in Mathcad Professional.

Function Name	Returns...
identity(n)	An $n \times n$ matrix of 0's with 1's on the diagonal.
Re(**A**)	An array of the same size as **A** but with the imaginary parts of each element set to 0.
Im(**A**)	An array of the same size as **A** but with the real parts of each element set to 0.
diag(v)	A diagonal matrix containing on its diagonal the elements of **v**.
geninv(**A**)	The left inverse matrix **L** of **A**, such that $L \cdot A = I$, where **I** is the identity matrix having the same number of columns as **A**. Matrix **A** is an $m \times n$ real-valued matrix, where $m \geq n$.
rref(**A**)	The reduced-row echelon form of **A**.

The "Pro" labels appear to the left of the diag(v) and geninv(**A**) rows:

Pro diag(v)

Pro geninv(**A**)

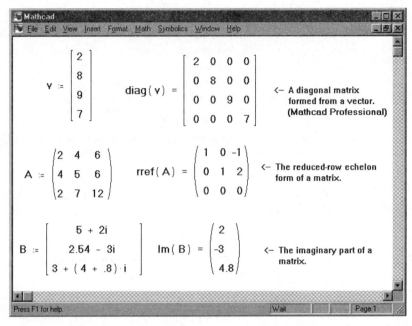

Figure 10-11: Functions for transforming arrays.

Special characteristics of a matrix

You can use the functions in the following table to find the trace, rank, norms, and condition numbers of a matrix. Most of these functions are available only in Mathcad Professional.

	Function Name	Returns ...
	tr(**M**)	The sum of the diagonal elements, otherwise known as the *trace*, of **M**.
	rank(**A**)	The rank of the real-valued matrix **A**.
Pro	norm1(**M**)	The L_1 norm of the matrix **M**.
Pro	norm2(**M**)	The L_2 norm of the matrix **M**.
Pro	norme(**M**)	The Euclidean norm of the matrix **M**.
Pro	normi(**M**)	The infinity norm of the matrix **M**.
Pro	cond1(**M**)	The condition number of the matrix **M** based on the L_1 norm.
Pro	cond2(**M**)	The condition number of the matrix **M** based on the L_2 norm.
Pro	conde(**M**)	The condition number of the matrix **M** based on the Euclidean norm.
Pro	condi(**M**)	The condition number of the matrix **M** based on the infinity norm.

Forming new matrices

Mathcad provides two functions for joining matrices together, either side by side, or one on top of the other. Mathcad also provides a function for filling in a matrix with values of a predefined function, and a function for extracting a smaller matrix from a larger one. Figure 10-12 and Figure 10-13 show some examples.

Function Name	Returns . . .
augment(**A**, **B**)	An array formed by placing **A** and **B** side by side. The arrays **A** and **B** must have the same number of rows.
stack(**A**, **B**)	An array formed by placing **A** above **B**. The arrays **A** and **B** must have the same number of columns.
matrix(m, n, f)	Creates a matrix in which the ijth element contains $f(i, j)$ where $i = 0, 1, ..., m - 1$ and $j = 0, 1, ..., n - 1$.
submatrix(**A**, ir, jr, ic, jc)	A submatrix of **A** consisting of all elements contained in rows ir through jr and columns ic through jc. To maintain order of rows and/or columns, make sure $ir \leq jr$ and $ic \leq jc$, otherwise order of rows and/or columns will be reversed.

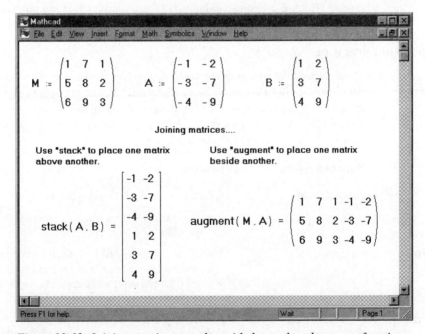

Figure 10-12: Joining matrices together with the stack and augment functions.

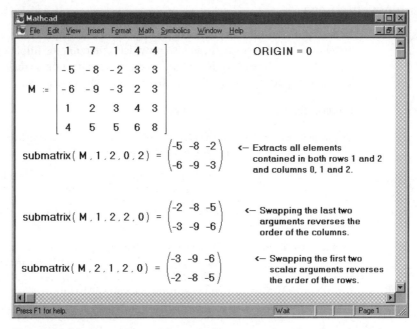

Figure 10-13: Extracting a submatrix from a matrix using the submatrix function.

Eigenvalues and eigenvectors

Mathcad provides functions for working with eigenvalues and eigenvectors of a matrix. The *eigenvecs* function, available in Mathcad Professional, obtains all the eigenvectors at once. If you're using Mathcad Professional, you'll also have access to *genvals* and *genvecs* for finding the generalized eigenvalues and eigenvectors. Figure 10-14 shows how some of these functions are used.

Function Name	Returns . . .
eigenvals(**M**)	A vector containing the eigenvalues of the matrix **M**.
eigenvec(**M**, z)	A matrix containing the normalized eigenvector corresponding to the eigenvalue z of the square matrix **M**.
Pro eigenvecs(**M**)	A matrix containing normalized eigenvectors corresponding to the eigenvalues of the square matrix **M**. The nth column of the matrix returned is an eigenvector corresponding to the nth eigenvalue returned by *eigenvals*.
Pro genvals(**M**, **N**)	A vector **v** of computed eigenvalues each of which satisfies the generalized eigenvalue problem $\mathbf{M} \cdot \mathbf{x} = v_i \cdot \mathbf{N} \cdot \mathbf{x}$. Matrices **M** and **N** contain real values. Vector **x** is the corresponding eigenvector. **M** and **N** are square matrices having the same number of columns.

Pro   genvecs(**M, N**)   A matrix containing the normalized eigenvectors corresponding
to the eigenvalues in **v**, the vector returned by *genvals*. The *n*th
column of this matrix is the eigenvector **x** satisfying the general-
ized eigenvalue problem $\mathbf{M} \cdot \mathbf{x} = v_n \cdot \mathbf{N} \cdot \mathbf{x}$. Matrices **M** and **N**
are real valued square matrices having the same number of col-
umns.

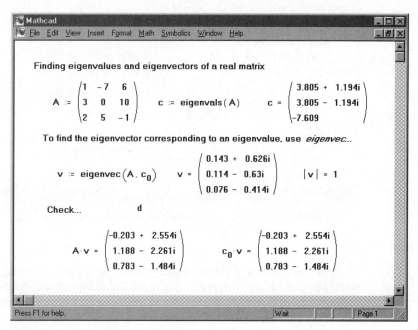

Figure 10-14: Finding eigenvalues and eigenvectors.

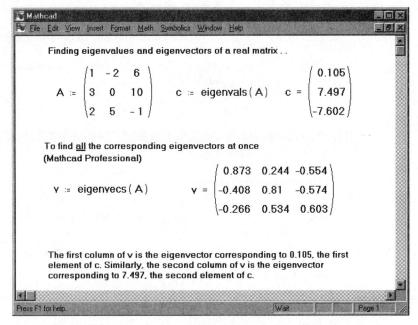

Figure 10-15: Using eigenvecs to find all the eigenvectors at once.

Decomposition

Mathcad Professional offers some additional functions for performing the cholesky decomposition, the QR decomposition, the LU decomposition, and the singular value decomposition of a matrix. Some of these functions return two or three matrices joined together as one large matrix. Use *submatrix* to extract these two or three smaller matrices. Figure 10-16 shows an example.

	Function Name	Returns ...
Pro	cholesky(**M**)	A lower triangular matrix **L** such that $\mathbf{L} \cdot \mathbf{L}^T = \mathbf{M}$. This uses only the upper triangular part of **M**. The upper triangular of **M**, when reflected about the diagonal, must form a positive definite matrix.
Pro	qr(**A**)	A matrix whose first n columns contain the square, orthonormal matrix **Q**, and whose remaining columns contain the upper triangular matrix, **R**. Matrices **Q** and **R** satisfy the equation $\mathbf{A} = \mathbf{Q} \cdot \mathbf{R}$, where **A** is a real-valued array.
Pro	lu(**M**)	One matrix containing the three square matrices **P**, **L**, and **U**, all having the same size as **M** and joined together side by side, in that order. These three matrices satisfy the equation $\mathbf{P} \cdot \mathbf{M} = \mathbf{L} \cdot \mathbf{U}$, where **L** and **U** are lower and upper triangular respectively.
Pro	svd(**A**)	One matrix containing two stacked matrices **U** and **V**, where **U** is the upper $m \times n$ submatrix and **V** is the lower $n \times n$ submatrix. Matrices **U** and **V** satisfy the equation $\mathbf{A} = \mathbf{U} \cdot \mathrm{diag}(\mathbf{s}) \cdot \mathbf{V}^T$, where **s** is a vector returned by svds(**A**). **A** is an $m \times n$ array of real values, where $m \geq n$.

Pro   svds(**A**)   A vector containing the singular values of the $m \times n$ real-valued
                                            array **A**, where $m \geq n$.

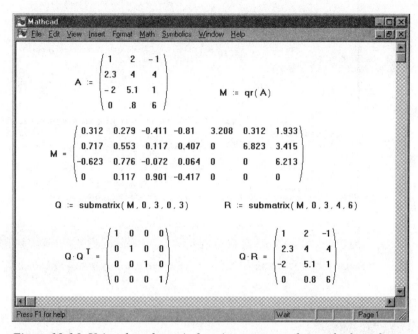

Figure 10-16: Using the submatrix function to extract the results from the qr function. Use submatrix in a similar way to extract results from the lu and svd functions.

Solving a linear system of equations

With Mathcad Professional, you'll be able to use the *lsolve* function to solve a linear system of equations. Figure 10-17 shows an example. Note that the argument **M** for *lsolve* must be a matrix that is neither singular nor nearly singular. A matrix is singular if its determinant is equal to zero. A matrix is nearly singular if it has a high condition number. You may want to use one of the functions described in"Special characteristics of a matrix" on page 198 to find the condition number of a matrix.

Function Name   **Returns . . .**

Pro   lsolve(**M**, **v**)   A solution vector **x** such that $\mathbf{M} \cdot \mathbf{x} = \mathbf{v}$.

Alternatively, you can solve a system of linear equations by using matrix inversion as shown in the lower right corner of Figure 10-9. For other numerical solving techniques in Mathcad, see Chapter 15, "Solving Equations." For symbolic solutions of systems of equations, see Chapter 17, "Symbolic Calculation."

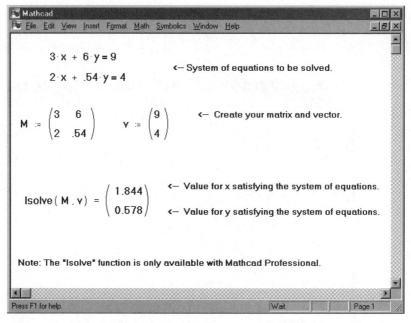

Figure 10-17: Using Isolve to solve two equations in two unknowns.

Doing calculations in parallel

Any calculation Mathcad can perform with single values, it can also perform with vectors or matrices of values. There are two ways to do this:

- By iterating over each element using range variables as described in Chapter 11, "Range Variables."

- By using the "vectorize" operator described in this chapter.

Mathcad's vectorize operator allows it to perform the same operation efficiently on each *element* of a vector or matrix.

Mathematical notation often shows repeated operations with subscripts. For example, to define a matrix **P** by multiplying corresponding elements of the matrices **M** and **N**, you would write:

$$\mathbf{P}_{i,j} = \mathbf{M}_{i,j} \cdot \mathbf{N}_{i,j}$$

Note that this is not matrix multiplication, but multiplication element by element. It *is* possible to perform this operation in Mathcad using subscripts, as described in Chapter 11, "Range Variables," but it is much faster to perform exactly the same operation with a vectorized equation.

How to apply the vectorize operator to an expression

Here's how to apply the vectorize operator to an expression like $\mathbf{M} \cdot \mathbf{N}$:

- Select the whole expression by clicking inside and pressing [**Space**] until the right-hand side is held between the editing lines.

$$P := \underline{M \cdot N}$$

- Press [**Ctrl**]– to apply the vectorize operator. Mathcad puts an arrow over the top of the selected expression.

$$P := \overrightarrow{(M \cdot N)}$$

How the vectorize operator changes the meaning of an expression

The vectorize operator changes the meaning of the operators and functions to which it applies. The vectorize operator tells Mathcad to apply the operators and functions with their scalar meanings, element by element.

Here are some examples of how the vectorize operator changes the meaning of expressions with vectors and matrices:

- If $\mathbf{v}$ is a vector, $\sin(\mathbf{v})$ is an illegal expression. But if you apply the vectorize operator, Mathcad applies the sine function to every element in $\mathbf{v}$. The result is a new vector whose elements are the sines of the elements in $\mathbf{v}$.

- If $\mathbf{M}$ is a matrix, $\sqrt{\mathbf{M}}$ is an illegal expression. But if you apply the vectorize operator, Mathcad takes the square root of every element of $\mathbf{M}$ and places the results in a new matrix.

- If $\mathbf{v}$ and $\mathbf{w}$ are vectors, then $\mathbf{v} \cdot \mathbf{w}$ means the dot product of $\mathbf{v}$ and $\mathbf{w}$. But if you apply the vectorize operator, the result is a new vector whose ith element is obtained by multiplying v_i and w_i. This is *not* the same as the dot product.

These properties of the vectorize operator let you use scalar operators and functions with array operands and arguments. In this *User's Guide*, this is referred to as "vectorizing" an expression. For example, suppose you want to apply the quadratic formula to three vectors containing coefficients a, b, and c. Figure 10-18 shows how to do this when a, b, and c are just scalars. Figure 10-19 shows how to do the same thing when $\mathbf{a}$, $\mathbf{b}$, and $\mathbf{c}$ are vectors.

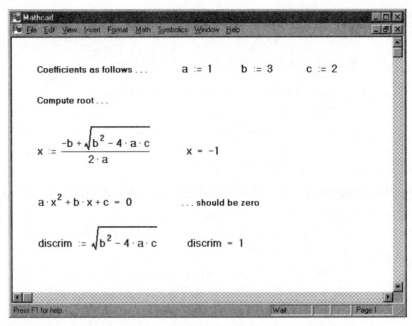

Figure 10-18: The quadratic formula.

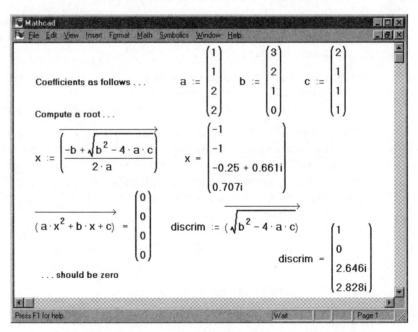

Figure 10-19: Quadratic formula with vectors and the vectorize operator.

The vectorize operator appears as an arrow above the quadratic formula in Figure 10-19. Its use is essential in this calculation. Without it, Mathcad would interpret $\mathbf{a} \cdot \mathbf{c}$ as a vector dot product and also flag the square root of a vector as illegal. But with the vectorize operator, both $\mathbf{a} \cdot \mathbf{c}$ and the square root are performed element by element.

Here are the properties of the vectorize operator:

■ The vectorize operator changes the meaning of the other *operators* and *functions* to which it applies. It does not change the meaning of the actual names and numbers. If you apply the vectorize operator to a single name, it simply draws an arrow over the name. You can use this arrow just for cosmetic purposes.

■ Since operations between two arrays are performed element by element, all arrays under a vectorize operator must be the same size. Operations between an array and a scalar are performed by applying the scalar to each element of the array. For example, if $\mathbf{v}$ is a vector and n is a scalar, applying the vectorize operator to $\mathbf{v}^n$ returns a vector whose elements are the nth powers of the elements of $\mathbf{v}$.

■ You cannot use any of the following matrix operations under a vectorize operator: dot product, matrix multiplication, matrix powers, matrix inverse, determinant, or magnitude of a vector. The vectorize operator will transform these operations into element-by-element scalar multiplication, exponentiation, or absolute value, as appropriate.

■ The vectorize operator has no effect on operators and functions that *require* vectors or matrices: transpose, cross product, sum of vector elements, and functions like *mean*. These operators and functions have no scalar meaning.

■ The vectorize operator applies only to the final, scalar arguments of *interp* and *linterp*. The other arguments are unaffected. See "Interpolation functions" in Chapter 14, "Statistical Functions."

Simultaneous definitions

You can use vectors and matrices to define several variables at once. You do this by placing an array of variable names on the left side of a : =, and a corresponding array of values to the right. Mathcad assigns the values on the right to the corresponding names on the left. Figure 10-20 shows two such definitions.

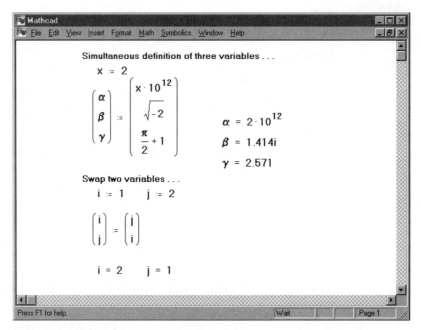

Figure 10-20: Simultaneous definitions.

The left side of a simultaneous definition is a vector or matrix whose elements are either names or subscripted variable names. The right side must be a vector or matrix expression having the same number of rows and columns as the left side. Mathcad defines each variable on the left side with the value of the expression in the corresponding position on the right side.

Mathcad evaluates all elements on the right-hand side before assigning any of them to the left hand side. Because of this, nothing on the right hand side of an expression can depend on what is on the left hand side. You also cannot have a variable appear more than once on the left hand side.

Simultaneous definitions are useful for iterating several equations simultaneously. Several examples are described in Chapter 11, "Range Variables."

Arrays and user-defined functions

The arguments in a function definition need not be scalar variables. They can also be vectors or matrices. Functions can return values that are scalars, vectors, or matrices.

Figure 10-21 shows some examples of functions with vector and matrix arguments and results.

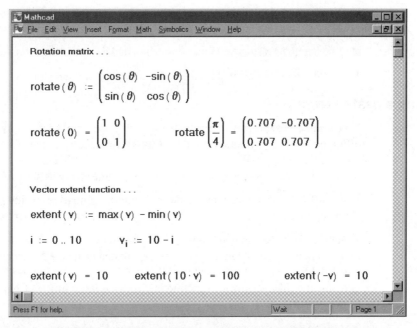

Figure 10-21: User functions used with vectors and matrices.

Note that if a function expects a vector or a matrix for an argument, it will not work on a scalar argument. In the example in Figure 10-21, trying to evaluate *extent*(3) will flag the equation with the an error message indicating that the argument must be an array.

If a function returns a vector or matrix as a result, you use the subscript and superscript operators to extract specific numbers. For example, in Figure 10-21, you could evaluate:

$$rotate(0)_{1,\,0} = 0$$

$$rotate(0)^{\langle 1 \rangle} = \begin{bmatrix} 0 \\ 1 \end{bmatrix}$$

Nested arrays

Pro An array element need not be a scalar. In Mathcad Professional it's possible to make an array element itself be another array. This allows you to create arrays within arrays.

These arrays behave very much like arrays whose elements are all scalars. However, there are some distinctions:

■ You cannot use the **Matrix** command from the **Insert** menu to insert an array into a placeholder that's already inside an array.

- You cannot display the entire nested array. You will instead see a notation like "{3,2}" to indicate that a 3×2 array is present in a particular array location.

- Most math operators and functions do not make sense in the context of nested arrays.

The following sections explore these differences in some detail.

Defining a nested array

You define a nested array in much the same way you would define any array. The only difference is that you cannot use the **Matrix** command from the **Insert** menu when you've selected a placeholder within an existing array. You can, however, click on a placeholder in an array and type the *name* of another array as shown in Figure 10-22.

Figure 10-22 shows three ways to define a matrix of matrices: using range variables, element by element, and with the **Matrix** command from the **Insert** menu.

In addition to those methods shown in Figure 10-22, you can also use the *READPRN* function in the array of empty placeholders created using the **Matrix** command. Keep in mind, however, that you can't use *READPRN* on the same file more than once in a given matrix. The *READPRN* function is discussed more fully in Chapter 19, "Data Management."

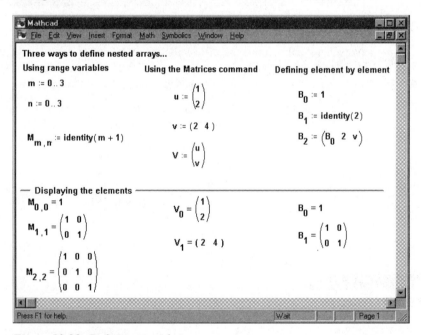

Figure 10-22: Defining nested arrays.

Displaying nested arrays

When you display a nested array using the equal sign, you won't actually see every element in every nested array. Such a display would be very cumbersome, especially when you consider that an array inside an array may itself contain arrays within it.

Instead, whenever an array element is itself an array, Mathcad indicates this by showing the number of rows and columns rather than the array itself. Figure 10-23 shows how the arrays created in Figure 10-22 would appear when displayed. Each array element is displayed either:

- As a number when the array element is simply a number, or

- As an ordered pair *m, n* where *m* and *n* are the number of rows and columns in the array which occupying that array element.

Note that the **B** array contains an element, B_2, which is itself a nested array. To view this array, you would simply nest your subscripts as shown in the lower-right corner of Figure 10-22.

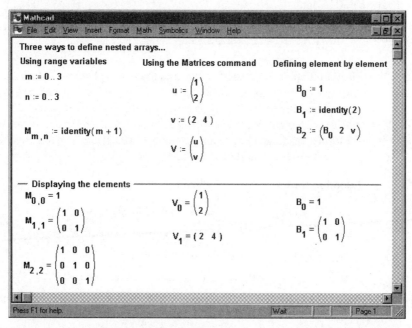

Figure 10-23: Displaying nested arrays.

Operators and functions for nested arrays

Most operators and functions do not work with nested arrays. This is because there is no universally accepted definition of what the correct behavior should be in this context. For example, there is no clear definition of what it means to "invert" such an array. When you attempt to perform the usual arithmetic operations on nested arrays, you will get either an error message or a meaningless result. For the most part, nested arrays are designed only for storing and accessing data in a convenient way.

Certain operators and functions are nevertheless useful and appropriate for nested arrays. For example, transpose does something meaningful as shown at the bottom of Figure 10-23. Operators which make sense in the context of nested arrays are:

Operation	Appearance	Keystroke	Description
Transpose	$\mathbf{A^T}$	[Ctrl]1	Interchanges row and columns of **A**.
Superscript	$\mathbf{A}^{\langle n \rangle}$	[Ctrl]6	nth column of array A. Returns a vector.
Vector subscript	v_n	[	nth element of a vector.
Matrix subscript	$A_{m,n}$	[	(m, n)th element of a matrix.
Boolean equals	$w = z$	[Ctrl]=	Boolean equals. Returns 1 if the two nested arrays, along with all nested arrays contained within them, are identical; otherwise returns 0.

Useful functions for nested arrays tend to be those having to do with the number of rows and columns in an array or those used for joining or dividing arrays. In particular, you can use the *rows* and *cols* functions to distinguish between scalar array elements and array elements which are themselves arrays. Both these functions return a zero in the former case and the appropriate number in the latter. The functions you'll find useful when working with nested arrays are:

Function Name	Returns . . .
rows(**A**)	Number of rows in matrix **A**.
cols(**A**)	Number of columns in matrix **A**.
length(**v**)	Number of elements in vector **v**.
last(**v**)	Index of last element in vector **v**.
augment(**A**, **B**)	An array formed by placing **A** and **B** side by side. The arrays **A** and **B** must have the same number of rows.
stack(**A**, **B**)	An array formed by placing **A** above **B**. The arrays **A** and **B** must have the same number of columns.
submatrix(**A**, ir, jr, ic, jc)	A submatrix of **A** consisting of all elements contained in rows ir through jr and columns ic through jc. To maintain order of rows and/or columns, make sure $ir \leq jr$ and $ic \leq jc$, otherwise order of rows and/or columns will be reversed.

Chapter 11
Range Variables

A range variable is a variable that takes on a range of values each time you use it. This chapter describes range variables and shows how to use them to perform iterative calculations, display tables of numbers, and facilitate the entry of many data values into a table.

The following sections make up this chapter.

Range variables

How to step through a range of numbers by defining a range variable.

Output tables

How to display a table of numbers.

Entering a table of numbers

How to use range variables to enter a table of numbers.

Iterative calculations

How to perform iteration with one or two range variables.

Seeded iteration

How to perform iteration when values in one step depend on the values in the previous step. Recursive techniques such as this provide the foundation for solving difference equations with Mathcad.

Vector or subscript notation

When to use the "vectorize" operator rather than subscripts.

Range variables

Iterative processes in Mathcad worksheets depend on *range variables*. Except for the way it's defined, a range variable looks just like a conventional variable. The difference is that a conventional variable takes on only one value. A range variable, on the other hand, takes on a range of values separated by uniform steps. For example, you could define a range variable to go from –4 through 4 in steps of 2. If you now use this range variable in an expression, Mathcad evaluates that expression five times, once for each value taken by the range variable.

Range variables are crucial to exploiting Mathcad's capabilities to their fullest. This section shows how to define and use range variables to perform iteration. For a description of more advanced iterative operations made possible by the programming operators in Mathcad Professional, turn to Chapter 18, "Programming."

Defining and using range variables

To define a range variable, type the variable name followed by a colon and a range of values. For example, here's how to define the variable *j* ranging from 0 to 15:

■ Type **j** and then press the colon key (**:**). The empty placeholder indicates that Mathcad expects a definition for *j*. At this point, Mathcad does not know whether *j* is to be a conventional variable or a range variable.

■ Type **0**. Then press the semicolon key (**;**). This tells Mathcad that you are defining a range variable. Mathcad shows the semi-colon as two periods ".." to indicate a range. Complete the range variable definition by typing **15** in the remaining placeholder.

This definition indicates that *j* now takes on the values $0, 1, 2 \ldots 15$. To define a range variable that changes in steps other than 1, see the section "Types of ranges" on page 216.

Once you define a range variable, it takes on its complete range of values *every time you use it*. If you use a range variable in an equation, for example, Mathcad must evaluate that equation once for each value of the range variable.

You must define a range variable exactly as shown above. There must be:

■ a variable name on the left,

■ either a ":=" or a "≡" in the middle, and

■ a valid range on the right.

In particular, you *cannot* define a variable in terms of a range variable. For example, if after having defined *j* as shown you now define $i := j + 1$, Mathcad assumes you are trying to set a scalar variable equal to a range variable and marks the equation with an appropriate error message.

One application of range variables is to fill up the elements of a vector or matrix. You can define vector elements by using a range variable as a subscript. For example, to define x_j for each value of j:

■ Type **x[j:j^2[Space]+1**.

$$x_j := j^2 + 1|$$

Figure 11-1 shows the vector of values computed by this equation. Since j is a range variable, the entire equation is evaluated once for each value of j. This defines x_j for each value of j from 0 to 15. The effect is exactly the same as if you had typed

$$x_0 := 0^2 + 1$$
$$x_1 := 1^2 + 1$$

.

.

$$x_{15} := 15^2 + 1$$

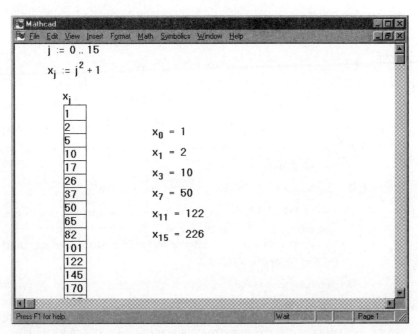

Figure 11-1: Using a range variable to define the values of the vector x.

To understand how Mathcad computes with range variables, keep in mind this fundamental principle:

*If you use a range variable in an expression, Mathcad evaluates the expression once
for each value of the range variable.*

This principle sums up the difference between expressions with and without range
variables. Expressions that involve no range variables have only one value. Expressions
that involve range variables take on many values, one for each value of each range
variable.

If you use two or more range variables in an equation, Mathcad evaluates the equation
once for each value of each range variable. The section "Iterative calculations" on page
222 discusses this in more detail.

Mathcad takes longer to compute equations with ranged expressions since there are
many computations for each equation. While Mathcad is computing, the mouse pointer
changes its appearance. To learn how to interrupt a calculation in progress, see the
section "Interrupting calculations" on page 146.

Types of ranges

The definition of j in the previous section, ranging from 0 to 15, is the simplest type of
range definition. Mathcad permits range variables with values ranging from any value
to any other value, using any constant increment or decrement.

To define an arbitrary range variable, type an equation of this form:

$$\mathtt{k:1,1.1;2}$$

This appears in your document window as:

$$k := 1, 1.1 .. 2$$

In this range definition:

■   The variable k is the name of the range variable itself. It must be a simple name.
    No subscripts or function definitions are allowed.

■   The number 1 is the first value taken by the range variable k.

■   The number 1.1 is the second value in the range. Note that this is *not* the step size.
    The step size in this example is 0.1, the difference between 1.1 and 1. If you omit
    the comma and the 1.1, Mathcad assumes a step size of one in whatever direction
    (up or down) is appropriate.

■   The number 2 is the last value in the range. In this example, the range values are
    constantly increasing. If instead you had defined $k := 10 .. 1$, then k would count
    down from 10 to 1. Even if the third number in the range definition is not an even
    number of increments from the starting value, the range will not go beyond it. For
    example, if you define $k := 10, 20 .. 65$ will take values 10, 20, 30 . . . 60.

You can use arbitrary scalar expressions in place of 1, 1.1, and 2. However, these values
must always be real numbers. Complex numbers do not make sense in range variable

definitions because given two complex numbers, there is an infinite number of paths connecting them. Figure 11-2 shows the results of various range variable definitions.

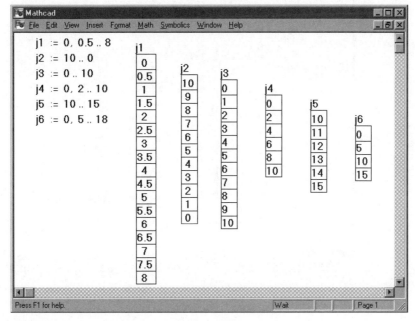

Figure 11-2: Some valid definitions for range variables.

Note that if you use a fractional increment for a range variable, you will not be able to use that range variable as a subscript. This is because subscripts must be integers.

Output tables

Whenever you type "=" after an expression involving range variables, Mathcad shows the computed values in an *output table*. Figure 11-2 shows the values of several range variables displayed as output tables.

Figure 11-3 shows some output tables for slightly more complicated expressions involving range variables.

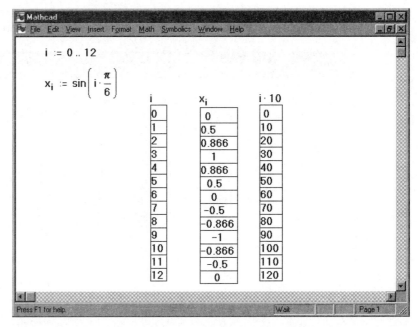

Figure 11-3: Typing "=" after an expression with range variables gives an output table.

To create the three tables in Figure 11-3, first define the range variable. Then type these equations:

```
i=
x[i=
i*10=
```

Whenever you type an expression followed by "=" Mathcad displays:

■ a number, if the result is a scalar (a single number).

■ a vector or a matrix, if the result is a vector or a matrix *and* the expression to the left of the "=" contains no range variables.

■ a table like that shown in Figure 11-3 if the expression to the left of the "=" contains range variables.

■ A scrolling output table if the result is a vector or a matrix, the expression to the left of the "=" contains no range variables, *and* the result has more than nine rows or columns. Scrolling output tables are discussed in the section "Displaying vectors and matrices" in Chapter 10.

Since both `x=` and `x[i=` display the same numbers, you can think of tables as another way of viewing the contents of a vector. Tables are particularly convenient for viewing selected parts of a vector. For example, if you've defined a vector **v**, you can view every other element of that vector by typing:

$$i := 0, 2 \; .. \; \text{last}(\mathbf{v})$$

$$v_i =$$

Here are some facts about output tables in Mathcad:

- Mathcad shows only the first 50 values of a ranged expression in a table. For example, even if i ranges from 1 to 100, typing `i^2=` will show only the values from 1^2 up to 50^2 in a table. To see more than 50 values, use several range variables and several tables. You could, for example, define $j1$ from 1 to 50 and $j2$ from 51 to 100, and then show tables for `j1^2=` and `j2^2=`, side by side.

- To format the numbers in a table, click in the table and choose **Number** from the **Format** menu. Then specify your formatting preferences in the dialog box as you would for an equation with a single numeric result. For more information on number formatting, see Chapter 6, "Equation and Result Formatting."

- There are three ways to show the values in a vector. If you use a vector name *with* a subscript like x_j =, Mathcad shows an output table. If instead you type a vector name *without* a subscript like x =, Mathcad shows the vector as a vector rather than as an output table. If you type a vector name without a subscript and the vector has more than nine elements, you see a scrolling output table as described in the section "Displaying vectors and matrices" in Chapter 10. Keep in mind that these are just three different ways of looking at the same thing: an ordered collection of numbers.

- You can't use units with a table as you would with a single scalar answer. If the results in a table have dimensions, Mathcad shows dimensions *on each value in the table*. To avoid this, divide the ranged expression by the units. See Figure 11-4.

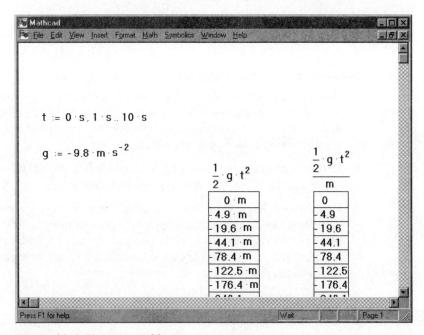

Figure 11-4: Units in a table.

Entering a table of numbers

When you enter a table of numbers, you are actually assigning elements to a vector. This section discusses how to do this using *input tables* and range variables. To enter an input table, enter a definition with a subscripted variable on one side and a sequence of values separated by commas on the other. For example:

■ To define *i* to run through four values, type **i:1;4**. Note that *i* must take integer values only. Otherwise it can't be used as a subscript in the next step.

■ Click in a new spot and type **x[i:** The placeholder indicates that Mathcad is expecting a value for x_1 .

■ Type **3** and press the comma key. Mathcad shows another placeholder to indicate that Mathcad now expects a value for x_2 .

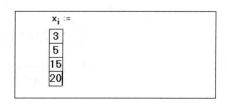

■ Type **5,15,20** to supply values for $x_2, x_3,$ and x_4 .

Once you have created an input table, you can do any of the following:

■ **Insert a value in the middle of a table**. Click on the value immediately above wherever you want to insert the new value. Then type a comma. Under the selected value in the table, Mathcad creates a placeholder surrounded by a box. To enter another number, just type it into this placeholder.

■ **Extend the table to hold additional values**. Click on the last value in the table and follow the steps above for inserting a value in the table.

■ **Replace or delete a value from the table**. Place the value you want to replace or delete between the two editing lines and choose **Cut** from the **Edit** menu. Mathcad replaces the value with an empty placeholder. Type a new value in this placeholder to replace the old one. To delete the value completely and decrease the array length by one in the process, backspace over the placeholder.

Some notes about input tables:

■ Each value in an input table must be either a number or an expression that returns a number, the name of an array or an expression that returns an array. Expressions involving range variables and expressions created by using the **Matrix** command on the **Insert** menu are not permitted.

■ All expressions in an input table must have the same dimensions if any. If you want each expression to be in meters, for example, you may have to include the abbreviation for meters in each table entry. A shortcut is to enter the numbers without units and redefine the vector with units by typing something like $x := x \cdot m/\sec^2$.

■ An input table ordinarily has one entry for each value of the range variable used in defining it. If the table has too few entries, Mathcad will define only as many values as are present. If the table has too many entries, the extra entries will be ignored.

■ Input tables assign values *only to those elements specified by the range variable*. If in the previous example, the range variable definition had been $i := 10, 20 .. 40$, Mathcad would have assigned values to x_{10}, x_{20}, x_{30} and x_{40}. Mathcad would then pad the unassigned entries, namely x_0 through x_9, x_{11} through x_{19}, and so on, with zeros. You will see these zeros if you display the vector by typing "**x=**." It is possible to inadvertently create large tables this way.

■ Input tables are limited to 50 elements. If you want to enter more than 50 elements, enter them using several tables. You could, for example, define *j1* from 1 to 50 and *j2* from 51 to 100, type **x[j1:** followed by the first fifty numbers, then type **x[j2:** followed by the second fifty numbers.

■ When confronted with a very large number of data values, consider reading them in from a data file stored on your disk as an alternative to typing them in with input tables. Chapter 19, "Data Management," discusses this in more detail.

Figure 11-5 shows some input tables. Note how typing **x=** and **y=** displays the elements of *x* and *y* in vector form. Mathcad ignores the last number in the input table for *y* since this entry would have index 5 and the range variable *i* stops at 4. Contrast this with typing **x[i=** as shown in Figure 11-3.

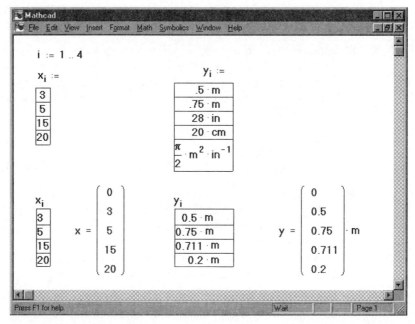

Figure 11-5: Input tables.

Note that the first element of both vectors is zero. This is because Mathcad's array origin is set to zero by default. Since the range variable *i* starts at 1, the zeroth element is never explicitly defined. In the absence of an explicit definition, Mathcad assumes a value of zero.

Iterative calculations

This section shows how to use range variables to perform iteration.

Iteration over a range

The simplest kind of iteration in Mathcad is just a generalization of scalar calculations. Any calculation you can perform once, you can perform over a range of values.

For example, suppose you want to create a list of *x* and *y* values for points on the polar curve $r = \cos(\theta) + 1$. The basic idea is as follows:

■ θ should take on values between 0 and 2π.

■ For each θ, the corresponding *r* is given by $r = \cos(\theta) + 1$.

■ For each *r* and θ, there is a corresponding *x* and *y* given by $x = r \cdot \cos(\theta)$ and $y = r \cdot \sin(\theta)$.

The strategy for solving this problem is simple: create a range variable i and then compute θ, r, x, and y for each value of i. The formula for $θ_i$ defines θ to run from 0 to 2π in steps of $2π/N$. To create the other formulas, just put the subscript i on each variable in the formula. Figure 11-6 shows the result.

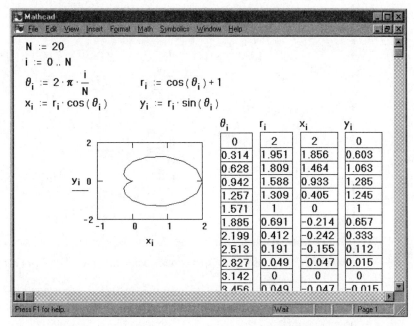

Figure 11-6: Using iteration to create a draw a polar curve using an X-Y plot.

Notice that in this example i, not θ, is defined as the range variable. Since i takes on only whole-number values, it is a valid subscript. On the other hand, θ takes on fractional values. It therefore cannot be used as a subscript. In many cases, you can avoid this extra step by using functions instead of vectors. Figure 11-7 shows how to generate the cardioid shown in Figure 11-6 with functions instead of vectors.

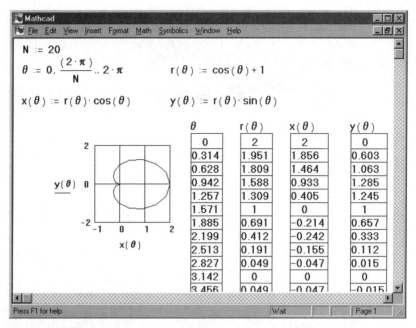

Figure 11-7: Using a function to do the same thing as shown in Figure 11-6.

By using vector notation and the vectorize operator, you can eliminate the use of a subscript in the last three equations in Figure 11-6. Figure 11-8 shows an example of how to do this.

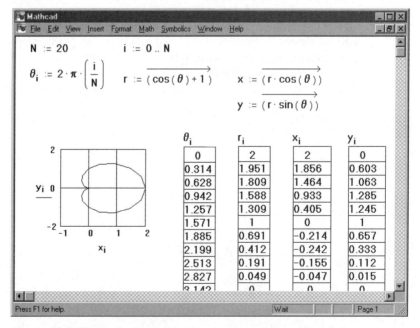

Figure 11-8: Using the vectorize operator to create a polar plot.

Equations that use vector notation instead of subscripts typically compute much more quickly. For more information, see Chapter 10, "Vectors and Matrices."

Multiple range variables and double subscripts

If you use two range variables in an equation, Mathcad runs through each value of each range variable. This is useful for defining matrices. For example, to define a 5×5 matrix whose i,jth element is $i + j$, type these equations:

```
i:0;4
j:0;4
x[i,j:i+j
```

Note that you don't need to type [**Space**] to leave the subscript in this case. Typing **:** leaves the subscript and creates the definition symbol.

Figure 11-9 shows the result of typing the above equations. It is usually best to display the matrix in the form shown in Figure 11-9. If instead of typing **x=** you were to type **x[i,j=**, Mathcad would show one long output table with 25 numbers. Such a table is often difficult to interpret. A similar problem arises when you use a pair of range variables in a graph.

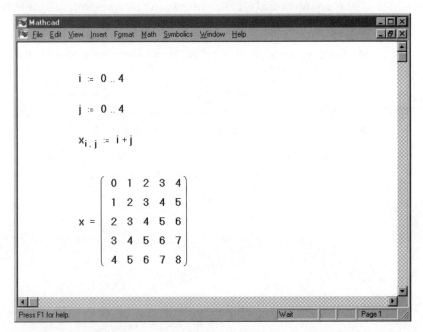

Figure 11-9: Defining a matrix.

The $x_{i,j}$ equation is evaluated for each value of each range variable, for a total of 25 evaluations. The result is the matrix shown at the bottom, with 5 rows and 5 columns. The element in the ith row and jth column of this matrix is $i + j$.

Note that if the two range variables have m and n values, respectively, then an equation using both range variables will calculate $m \cdot n$ results. If you try to use two range variables in an output table, Mathcad will show these $m \cdot n$ results in a long table with one entry for each result. If you use two range variables in a graph, Mathcad will plot one point for each of the $m \cdot n$ results.

Seeded iteration

Seeded iteration is a recursive technique for solving difference equations such as those that arise in compound interest problems, Markov processes, and many state variable equations. It can also be used for obtaining approximate solutions for certain differential equations. In a seeded iteration, you specify the first element of an array and then compute successive elements based on the first element. This section describes three types of seeded iteration: iterating a single variable, iterating multiple variables, and iterating a vector.

Seeded iteration on one variable

The classical method for estimating square roots arithmetically is as follows:

- To find $\sqrt{a}$, begin with a guess value.

- Compute a new guess based on the old guess, with this formula:

$$NewGuess = \frac{OldGuess + a/OldGuess}{2}$$

- Continue until the guesses converge to an answer.

Figure 11-10 shows how to implement this method in Mathcad.

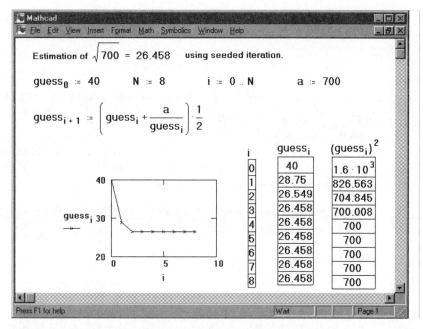

Figure 11-10: Using seeded iteration to estimate a square root.

The important characteristics of this example are:

■ The seed value is defined as the zeroth element of the array,   .

■ Each   is defined in terms of a previously computed element.

It is this dependence of array elements on previously computed array elements that distinguishes seeded iteration from the more straightforward iteration discussed in the previous section.

Seeded iteration on several variables

You can use Mathcad's vector notation to iterate several variables simultaneously. This variation on simple seeded iteration is a powerful method for solving a system of simultaneous difference equations.

When you iterate several variables, each step computes the value of the variables from all of their previous values. You can't accomplish this with several equations because when Mathcad sees an equation with range variables, it attempts to evaluate it for *each* value of the range variable before going on to the next equation. You must, therefore, create one equation that performs all the iterations simultaneously.

For example, consider an infection model with four variables: i for the number of individuals infected, s for the number susceptible, d for the number deceased, and r for the number recovered and hence immune. The four equations that relate these four variables over time are:

$$i_{t+1} = 0.0001 \cdot s_t \cdot i_t$$
$$s_{t+1} = s_t - 0.0001 \cdot s_t \cdot i_t$$
$$d_{t+1} = d_t + 0.55 \cdot i_t$$
$$r_{t+1} = r_t + 0.45 \cdot i_t$$

Figure 11-11 shows how to perform a simultaneous iteration using these equations.

The single most important thing about this example is that all the $t + 1$ subscripts are on the left-hand side of the matrix equation. The right-hand side contains only the subscript t. Mathcad evaluates all the expressions on the right-hand side before performing any assignments to the left-hand side. This means that nothing on the right-hand side can depend on something on the left-hand side.

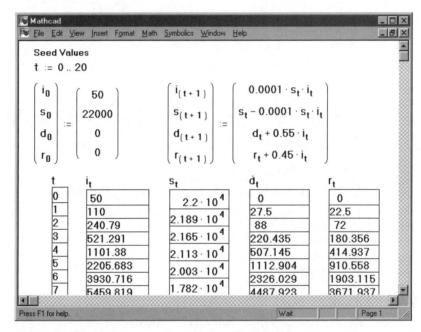

Figure 11-11: Simultaneous iteration to model an infection.

Seeded iteration on a vector

You can also perform seeded iteration starting with a vector and computing a new vector each time. This type of iteration uses a seed vector and Mathcad's superscript operator.

A *Markov process* is an example of a problem that involves iteration on a vector. A Markov process begins with a vector **v** that represents the starting values of some quantities, for example, the number of voters planning to vote for different candidates, the number of trucks at regional offices of a truck rental company, or the market share of different companies. Each step in the Markov process computes a new vector by multiplying the previous vector by a "state transition" matrix **A**.

Figure 11-12 shows how to set up a Markov process. This technique uses *superscripts* to index an entire column of a matrix at once. To create a superscript, press [**Ctrl**]**6**. This generates a placeholder between angle brackets: <>.

Here's how to enter the equations in Figure 11-12:

- First, define the state transition matrix **A**. Type **A**, press the colon key (**:**), and create a 3 × 3 matrix. To create a matrix, choose **Matrix** from the **Insert** menu.

$$A := \begin{pmatrix} .5 & 0 & .2 \\ .25 & .9 & .1 \\ .25 & .1 & .7 \end{pmatrix}$$

- Click to the right of the matrix and type **v**. Then press [**Ctrl**]**6**. Type **0** in the placeholder for the superscript.

- Now complete the definition of the initial vector. First press the colon key (**:**). Then choose **Matrix** from the **Insert** menu. Specify that you want to create a matrix with three rows and one column. Then fill in the matrix entries.

$$v^{\langle 0 \rangle} := \begin{pmatrix} 10 \\ 25 \\ 15 \end{pmatrix}$$

- Type **k:1;8**. This defines a range variable *k* to count eight iterations.

$$k := 1 .. 8$$

- To define the *k*th vector in terms of the $(k-1)$ st, type **v[Ctrl]6 k**. Then type a colon (**:**) for the definition symbol. Complete the equation by typing this expression after the definition symbol: **A*v[Ctrl]6 k-1** .

$$v^{\langle k \rangle} := A \cdot v^{\langle k-1 \rangle}$$

- To see the eighth (last) column of the matrix, type **v [Ctrl]6 8 =** .

$$v^{\langle 8 \rangle} = \begin{pmatrix} 6.017 \\ 29.124 \\ 14.859 \end{pmatrix}$$

- To see all the vectors as columns of a matrix, type **v=** . Note that not all the columns are displayed in the picture to the right.

$$v = \begin{pmatrix} 10 & 8 & 7.1 & 6.65 & 6.398 \\ 25 & 26.5 & 27.4 & 27.985 & 28.386 \\ 15 & 15.5 & 15.5 & 15.365 & 15.217 \end{pmatrix}$$

The superscript operator actually retrieves or defines one column in a matrix. When you define   in terms of   , you are actually defining each column of a matrix in terms of the preceding column. The last equation in Figure 11-12 shows the matrix composed from these columns.

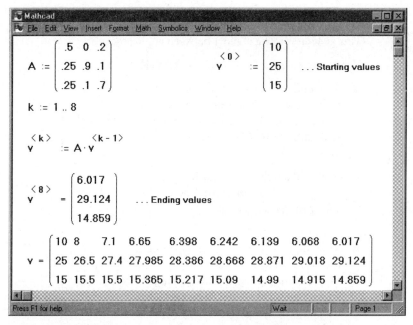

Figure 11-12: Iterating a vector to model a Markov process.

Vector or subscript notation

This chapter has shown many examples using subscript notation and range variables. Chapter 10, "Vectors and Matrices," showed many examples using vector notation without subscripts. This distinction is important. If you use subscripts when they are not required, or vice versa, you probably won't get the answer you're looking for.

Subscripts refer to individual array elements. When you use range variables as subscripts like $M_{i,j}$, Mathcad runs through the individual elements of the array one at a time.

Without subscripts, the variable name refers to the whole array.

Here are some rules of thumb for when to use subscripts:

■ To refer to an individual array element, use numbers as subscripts. For example, to see matrix element (2,3), type `M[2,3=`.

■ To refer to an array as a whole, use the array name without subscripts. (The term array means either a vector or a matrix.) The array name with no subscripts is appropriate for multiplying one matrix by another, applying the *mean* function to an array, or viewing a whole vector or matrix—all cases where you want to treat the array as a whole. For example, to view the whole matrix **M** in Figure 11-13, type `M=`.

■ To refer to each of the array elements in succession, use the array name with a range variable subscript. This is useful when defining the matrix elements using some sort of formula. For example, to define the matrix **M** in Figure 11-13, type three equations:

```
i:0;3
j:0;3
M[i,j:i*j
```

Figure 11-13 shows some examples of using array names with and without subscripts.

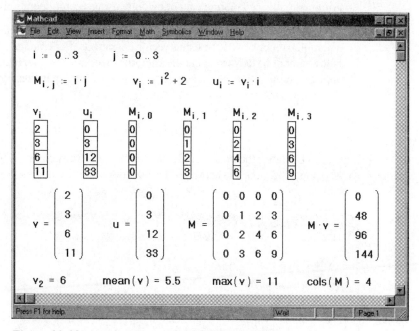

Figure 11-13: Array names with and without subscripts.

Iterative calculations with and without subscripts

It's often faster to use vector operations to perform iterative calculations than it is to do them element by element with a range variable. This is discussed in more detail in the section "Doing calculations in parallel" in Chapter 10. Unfortunately, not all iterative calculations can be done as vector operations. For example, the seeded iteration technique discussed earlier in this chapter cannot be done with vector operations.

To tell if an equation with subscripts could be rewritten using vector notation and the vectorize operator, check the following:

■ If all the subscripts in the calculation are the same, then the calculation can probably be done quickly using vector operations. For example, consider this equation:

$$x_i := r_i \cdot \cos(\theta_i)$$

Since this equation contains no subscript other than i, it can be rewritten with the vectorize operator ([Ctrl]-) instead of with subscripts:

$$x := \overrightarrow{(r \cdot \cos(\theta))}$$

■ If the subscripts in a calculation vary or if there is arithmetic involved in computing the subscript, then the calculation probably cannot be done using vector operations. For example, seeded iteration involves the subscripts i and $i-1$ in the same equation. Since the subscripts are not the same, and since the second subscript involves arithmetic, this calculation cannot be done using vector operations.

■ If the range variable appears anywhere in an equation other than in a subscript, the equation cannot be written using vector operations. For example, the variable θ below cannot be defined using the vectorize operator. Although the range variable appears on the left side as a subscript, its presence in an expression on the right disqualifies the entire equation.

$$\theta_i = 0.1 \cdot i$$

Figure 11-14 shows the polar coordinate conversions from Figure 11-6 computed two ways: using subscripts and using vector operations. The second method is much faster in Mathcad.

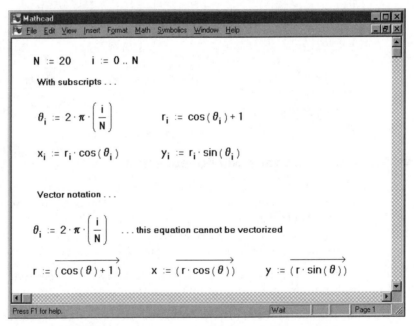

Figure 11-14: Changing an iterative process to vector operations.

Chapter 12
Operators

Mathcad includes ordinary operators like + and /, matrix operators like transpose and determinant, and special operators like iterated sum, iterated product, integrals, and derivatives.

This chapter contains a list of Mathcad operators and describes how to enter and use the special operators.

This chapter contains the following sections:

List of operators

List of Mathcad's operators in order of precedence.

Summations and products

How to use Mathcad's summation and product operators.

Derivatives

How to use Mathcad's derivative operators.

Integrals

How to use Mathcad's definite integral operator.

Boolean operators

How to use Mathcad's boolean operators such as ">" and "<."

Pro   **Customizing operators**

How to define your own operators just the way you define your own functions.

List of operators

This is a list of Mathcad operators in order of precedence. For details on vector and matrix operators, see Chapter 10, "Vectors and Matrices." Most of the following operators are available by clicking on one of the operator palettes, or by using the keystrokes listed in the table below. To open the operator palettes, click on the buttons on the Math Palette, which you can see by choosing **Math Palette** from the **View** menu:

In this table:

■ **A** and **B** represent arrays, either vector or matrix.

■ **u** and **v** represent vectors with real or complex elements.

■ **M** represents a square matrix.

■ *z* and *w* represent real or complex numbers.

■ *x* and *y* represent real numbers.

■ *m* and *n* represent integers.

■ *i* represents a range variable.

■ *S* and any names beginning with *S* represent string expressions.

■ *t* represents any variable name.

■ *f* represents a function.

■ *X* and *Y* represent variables or expressions of any type.

Operation	Appearance	Keystroke	Description
Parentheses	(X)	'	Grouping operator.
Vector Subscript	$\mathbf{v}_n$	[	Returns indicated element of a vector.
Matrix Subscript	$\mathbf{A}_{m,n}$	[	Returns indicated element of a matrix.
Superscript	$\mathbf{A}^{\langle n \rangle}$	[Ctrl]6	Extracts column *n* from array **A**. Returns a vector.
Vectorize	$\vec{X}$	[Ctrl]-	Forces operations in expression *X* to take place element by element. All vectors or matrices in *X* must be the same size.

Operation	Appearance	Keystroke	Description
Factorial	$n!$	!	Returns $n \cdot (n-1) \cdot (n-2)\ldots$ The integer n cannot be negative.
Complex conjugate	$\overline{X}$	"	Inverts the sign of the imaginary part of X.
Transpose	$\mathbf{A}^T$	[Ctrl]1	Returns a matrix whose rows are the columns of $\mathbf{A}$ and whose columns are the rows of $\mathbf{A}$. $\mathbf{A}$ can be a vector or a matrix.
Power	z^w	^	Raises z to the power w.
Powers of matrix, matrix inverse	$\mathbf{M}^n$	^	nth power of square matrix $\mathbf{M}$ (using matrix multiplication). n must be a whole number. $\mathbf{M}^{-1}$ is the inverse of $\mathbf{M}$. Other negative powers are powers of the inverse. Returns a square matrix.
Negation	$-X$	–	Multiplies X by -1.
Vector sum	$\Sigma\mathbf{v}$	[Ctrl]4	Sums elements of vector v; returns a scalar.
Square root	$\sqrt{z}$	\	Returns positive square root for positive z; principal value for negative or complex z.
nth root	$\sqrt[n]{z}$	[Ctrl]\	Returns nth root of z; returns a real valued root whenever possible.
Magnitude, Absolute value	$\lvert z \rvert$	|	Returns $\sqrt{\mathrm{Re}(z)^2 + \mathrm{Im}(z)^2}$.
Magnitude of vector	$\lvert \mathbf{v} \rvert$	|	Returns the magnitude of the vector $\mathbf{v}$: $\sqrt{\mathbf{v} \cdot \mathbf{v}}$ if all elements in $\mathbf{v}$ are real. Returns $\sqrt{\mathbf{v} \cdot \overline{\mathbf{v}}}$ if any element in $\mathbf{v}$ is complex.
Determinant	$\lvert \mathbf{M} \rvert$	|	Returns the determinant of the square matrix $\mathbf{M}$. Result is a scalar.
Division	$\dfrac{X}{z}$	/	Divides the expression X by the non-zero scalar z. If X is an array, divides each element by z.
Multiplication	$X \cdot Y$	*	Returns the product of X and Y if both X and Y are scalars. Multiplies each element of Y by X if Y is an array and X is a scalar. Returns the dot product (inner product) if X and Y are vectors of the same size. Performs matrix multiplication if X and Y are conformable matrices.
Cross product	$\mathbf{u} \times \mathbf{v}$	[Ctrl]8	Returns cross-product (vector product) for the three-element vectors $\mathbf{u}$ and $\mathbf{v}$.
Summation	$\displaystyle\sum_{i=m}^{n} X$	[Ctrl] [Shift]4	Performs summation of X over $= m, m+1, \ldots, r$. X can be any expression. It need not involve i but it usually does. m and n must be integers.
Product	$\displaystyle\prod_{i=m}^{n} X$	[Ctrl] [Shift]3	Performs iterated product of X for $= m, m+1, \ldots, r$. X can be any expression. It need not involve i but it usually does. m and n must be integers.

Operation	Appearance	Keystroke	Description
Range sum	$\displaystyle\sum_i X$	$	Returns a summation of X over the range variable i. X can be any expression. It need not involve i but it usually does.
Range product	$\displaystyle\prod_i X$	#	Returns the iterated product of X over the range variable i. X can be any expression. It need not involve i but it usually does.
Integral	$\displaystyle\int_a^b f(t)\,dt$	&	Returns the definite integral of $f(t)$ over the interval $[a, b]$. a and b must be real scalars. All variables in the expression $f(t)$, except the variable of integration t, must be defined. The integrand, $f(t)$, cannot return an array.
Derivative	$\dfrac{d}{dt}f(t)$	?	Returns the derivative of $f(t)$ evaluated at t. All variables in the expression $f(t)$ must be defined. The variable t must be a scalar value. The function $f(t)$ must return a scalar.
nth Derivative	$\dfrac{d^n}{dt^n}f(t)$	[Ctrl]?	Returns the nth derivative of $f(t)$ evaluated at t. All variables in $f(t)$ must be defined. The variable t must be a scalar value. The function $f(t)$ must return a scalar. n must be an integer between 0 and 5 for numerical evaluation or a positive integer for symbolic evaluation.
Addition	$X + Y$	+	Scalar addition if X, Y, or both are scalars. Element by element addition if X and Y are vectors or matrices of the same size. If X is an array and Y is a scalar, adds Y to each element of X.
Subtraction	$X - Y$	–	Performs scalar subtraction if X, Y, or both are scalars. Performs element by element subtraction if X and Y are vectors or matrices of the same size. If X is an array and Y is a scalar, subtracts Y from each element of X.
Addition with line break	$X...$ $+ Y$	[Ctrl][↵]	Same as addition. Line break is purely cosmetic.
Greater than	$x > y,$ $S1 > S2$	>	For real scalars x and y, returns 1 if $x > y$, 0 otherwise. For string expressions $S1$ and $S2$, returns 1 if $S1$ strictly follows $S2$ in ASCII order, 0 otherwise.
Less than	$x < y,$ $S1 < S2$	<	For real scalars x and y, returns 1 if $x < y$, 0 otherwise. For string expressions $S1$ and $S2$, returns 1 if $S1$ strictly precedes $S2$ in ASCII order, 0 otherwise.
Greater than or equal	$x \geq y,$ $S1 \geq S2$	[Ctrl]0	For real scalars x and y, returns 1 if $x \geq y$, 0 otherwise. For string expressions $S1$ and $S2$, returns 1 if $S1$ follows $S2$ in ASCII order, 0 otherwise.
Less than or equal	$x \leq y,$ $S1 \leq S2$	[Ctrl]9	For real scalars x and y, returns 1 if $x \leq y$, 0 otherwise. For string expressions $S1$ and $S2$, returns 1 if $S1$ precedes $S2$ in ASCII order, 0 otherwise.

Operation	Appearance	Keystroke	Description
Not equal to	$z \ne w$, $S1 \ne S2$	[Ctrl]3	For scalars z and w, returns 1 if $z \ne w$, 0 otherwise. For string expressions $S1$ and $S2$, returns 1 if $S1$ is not character by character identical to $S2$.
Equal to	$X = Y$	[Ctrl]=	Returns 1 if $X = Y$, 0 otherwise. Appears as a bold = on the screen.

Help with typing operators

You can avoid having to remember the keystrokes that go with each operator by using the operator palettes. To open the operator palettes, click on the buttons on the Math Palette. Each button opens a palette of operators grouped loosely by function.

The icons on the operator palette buttons indicate what operator appears when you click on that button. You can also hold the mouse pointer momentarily over a button to see a tool tip indicating what the button does.

To type any operator from the table on the previous pages, just click wherever you want to put the operator, then click on its button on the appropriate operator palette.

In general, operator palettes only work in math regions. To use the operator palettes in text, you must first click in the text and choose **Math Region** from the **Insert** menu. This will create a math placeholder in the text into which you can insert operators using the palettes.

Summations and products

The summation operator sums an expression over all values of an index. The iterated product operator works much the same way. It takes the product of an expression over all values of an index.

To create a summation operator in your worksheet:

■ Click in a blank space. Then type
[Ctrl][Shift]4. A summation sign
with four placeholders appears.

■ In the placeholder to the left of the equal
sign, type a variable name. This variable
is the index of summation. It is defined
only within the summation operator and
therefore has no effect on, and is not influ-

enced by, variable definitions outside the summation operator.

■ In the placeholder to the right of the equal
sign, type an integer or any expression that
evaluates to an integer.

$$\sum_{n=1}^{\blacksquare} \blacksquare$$

■ In the single placeholder above the sigma,
type an integer or any expression that evaluates to an integer.

$$\sum_{n=1}^{10} \blacksquare$$

■ In the remaining placeholder, type the expression you want to sum. Usually, this
expression will involve the index of summation. If this expression has several
terms, type an apostrophe (') to create a
pair of parentheses around the placeholder.

$$\sum_{n=1}^{10} n^2$$

Iterated products are similar. Just type [**Ctrl**][**Shift**]3 and fill in the placeholders
as described earlier.

Figure 12-1 shows some examples of how to use the summation and product operators.
You can use a summation or an iterated product just as you would any other expression.

To evaluate multiple summations, place another summation in the final placeholder of
the first summation. An example of this appears at the bottom of Figure 12-1.

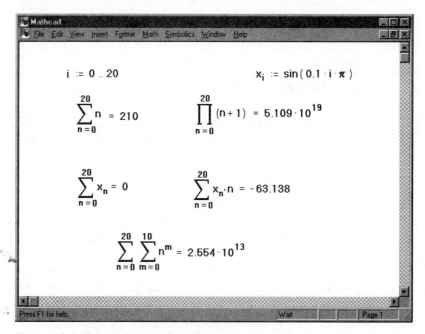

Figure 12-1: Summations and products.

Chapter 12 Operators

When you use the summation operator shown in Figure 12-1, the summation must be carried out over integers and in steps of one. Mathcad provides more general versions of these operators that can use any range variable you define as an index of summation. To use these operators, first define a range variable. In the following example type `i:1,2;10`. Then do the following:

- Click in a blank space. Then type `$`. A summation sign with two placeholders appears.

- Click on the bottom placeholder and type the name of a range variable. The range variable you use here should already have been defined earlier in the worksheet.

- Click on the placeholder to the right of the summation sign and type an expression involving the range variable. If this expression has several terms, type an apostrophe (`'`) to create a pair of parentheses around the placeholder.

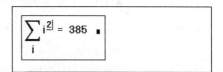

- Press the equal sign (`=`) to see the result.

$$\sum_i i^2 = 385$$

If you don't want to take the time to click in each placeholder, you can enter the previous expression by typing `i$i^2`.

A generalized version of the iterated product also exists. To use it, type `#`. Then fill in the two placeholders.

Figure 12-2 shows some examples of how to apply the range sum and range product operators. These operators, unlike the summation and product operators created with [Ctrl][Shift]4 and [Ctrl][Shift]3, cannot stand alone. They require the existence of a range variable. Note however, that a single range variable can be used with any number of these operators.

You can use summations and iterated products just as you would any other expression. To evaluate multiple summations, use two range variables as shown in Figure 12-2.

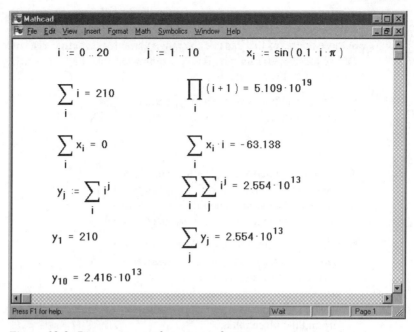

Figure 12-2: Range sums and range products.

Variable upper limit of summation

Mathcad's range summation operator runs through each value of the range variable you place in the bottom placeholder. It is possible, by judicious use of boolean expressions, to sum only up to a particular value. In Figure 12-3, the term $i \le x$ returns the value 1 whenever it is true and 0 whenever it is false. Although the summation operator still sums over each value of the index of summation, those terms for which $i > x$ are multiplied by 0 and hence do not contribute to the summation.

You can also use the four-placeholder summation and product operators to compute sums and products with a variable upper limit, but note that the upper limit in these operators must be an integer.

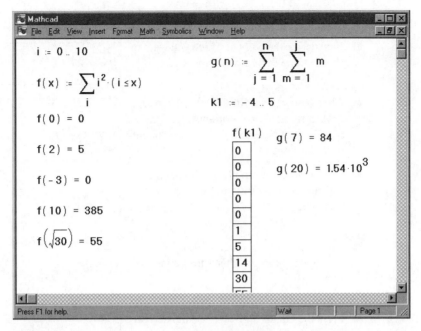

Figure 12-3: A variable upper limit of summation.

The vector-sum operator

The operation of summing the elements of a vector is so common that Mathcad provides a special operator for it. While the ordinary summation operator sums a ranged expression, the vector sum operator sums the elements of a vector without needing a range variable.

To sum all the elements of a vector **v** defined elsewhere in your worksheet, follow these steps:

■ Click in blank space or on a placeholder.
Then press [**Ctrl**]**4**.

$$\Sigma\blacksquare$$

■ Type the name of a vector or vector-valued expression. Mathcad returns the sum of all the elements in the vector. In

$$\Sigma y = 2.554 \cdot 10^{13}$$

this example, the vector used is that shown in Figure 12-2.

Derivatives

You can use Mathcad's derivative operator to evaluate the derivative of a function at a particular point.

As an example, here's how you would evaluate the derivative of x^3 with respect to x at the point $x = 2$:

■ First define the point at which you want to evaluate the derivative. Type **x : 2** .

■ Click below the definition of x. Then type **?**. A derivative operator appears, with a placeholder in the denominator and another to the right.

■ Click on the bottom placeholder and type **x**. You are differentiating with respect to this variable.

■ Click on the placeholder to the right of the d/dx and type **x ^ 3** . This is the expression to be differentiated.

■ Press the equals sign **=** to see the derivative of the expression at the indicated point.

$$\frac{d}{dx} x^3 = 12$$

Figure 12-4 shows examples of differentiation in Mathcad.

With Mathcad's derivative algorithm, you can expect the first derivative to be accurate to within 7 or 8 significant digits, provided that the value at which you evaluate the derivative is not too close to a singularity of the function. The accuracy of this algorithm tends to decrease by one significant digit for each increase in the order of the derivative (see the section "Derivatives of higher order" on page 245).

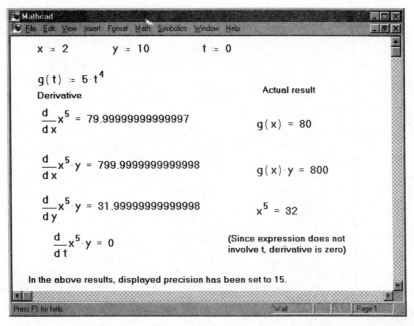

Figure 12-4: Examples of Mathcad differentiation.

Keep in mind that the result of differentiating is not a function, but a single number: the computed derivative at the indicated value of the differentiation variable. In the previous example, the derivative of x^3 is not the expression $3x^2$ but $3x^2$ evaluated at $x = 2$. If you want to evaluate derivatives symbolically, see Chapter 17, "Symbolic Calculation."

Although differentiation returns just one number, you can still define one function as the derivative of another. For example:

$$f(x) := \frac{d}{dx}g(x)$$

Evaluating $f(x)$ will return the numerically computed derivative of $g(x)$ at x.

You can use this technique to evaluate the derivative of a function at many points. An example of this is shown in Figure 12-5.

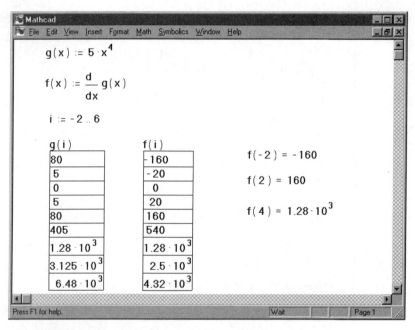

Figure 12-5: Evaluating the derivative of a function at several points.

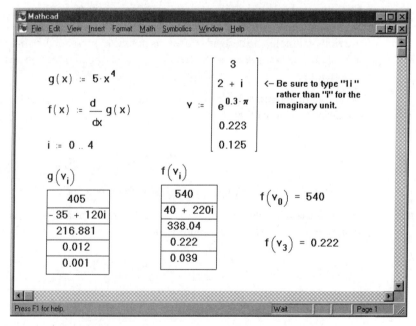

Figure 12-6: Evaluating the derivative of a function at several values stored as elements of a vector.

Chapter 12 Operators

There are some important things to remember about differentiation in Mathcad:

■ The expression to be differentiated can be either real or complex.

■ The differentiation variable must be a single variable name. If you want to evaluate the derivative at several different values stored in a vector, use the technique illustrated in Figure 12-6.

Derivatives of higher order

Mathcad has an additional derivative operator for evaluating the nth order derivative of a function at a particular point.

As an example, here's how you would evaluate the third derivative of x^9 with respect to x at the point $x = 2$:

■ First define the point at which you want to evaluate the derivative. Type **x:2**.

$$x := 2$$

■ Click below the definition of x. Then type **[Ctrl] ?**. A derivative operator appears, with two placeholders in the denominator, one in the numerator, and another to the right.

■ Click on the bottom placeholder and type **x**. You are differentiating with respect to this variable.

■ Click on the expression above and to the right of the previous placeholder and type **3**. This must be an integer between 0 and 5 inclusive. Note that the placeholder in the numerator automatically mirrors whatever you've typed.

$$\frac{d^3}{dx^3}\blacksquare$$

■ Click on the placeholder to the right of the d/dx and type **x^9**. This is the expression to be differentiated.

$$\frac{d^3}{dx^3}x^9$$

■ Press the equal sign (=) to see the third derivative of the expression at the indicated point.

For $n = 1$, this operator gives the same answer as the first-derivative operator discussed above. For $n = 0$, it simply returns the value of the function itself.

Integrals

You can use Mathcad's integral operator to numerically evaluate the definite integral of a function over some interval.

As an example, here's how you would evaluate the definite integral of $\sin(x)^2$ from 0 to $\pi/2$. Follow these steps:

■ Click in a blank space and type **&**. An integral appears, with placeholders for the integrand, the limits of integration, and the variable of integration.

$$\int_{\blacksquare}^{\blacksquare} \blacksquare \ d\blacksquare$$

■ Click on the bottom placeholder and type **0**. Click on the top placeholder and type **[Ctrl]p/4**. These are the upper and lower limits of integration.

$$\int_{0}^{\frac{\pi}{4}} \blacksquare \ d\blacksquare$$

■ Click on the placeholder between the integral sign and the "d." Then type **sin(x)^2**. This is the expression to be integrated.

$$\int_{0}^{\frac{\pi}{4}} \sin(x)^2 \ d\blacksquare$$

■ Click on the remaining placeholder and type **x**. This is the variable of integration. Then press the equal sign (=) to see the result.

$$\int_{0}^{\frac{\pi}{4}} \sin(x)^2 \ dx = 0.143$$

Mathcad uses a numerical algorithm called *Romberg integration* to approximate the integral of an expression over an interval of real numbers.

There are some important things to remember about integration in Mathcad:

■ The limits of integration must be real. The expression to be integrated can, however, be either real or complex.

■ Except for the integrating variable, all variables in the integrand must have been defined elsewhere in the worksheet.

■ The integrating variable must be a single variable name.

■ If the integrating variable involves units, the upper and lower limits of integration must have the same units.

Like all numerical methods, Mathcad's integration algorithm can have difficulty with ill-behaved integrands. If the expression to be integrated has singularities, discontinuities, or large and rapid fluctuations, Mathcad's solution may be inaccurate.

Because Mathcad's integration method divides the interval into four subintervals and then successively doubles the number of points, it can return incorrect answers for periodic functions with having periods $1/2^n$ times the length of the interval. To avoid this problem, divide the interval into two uneven subintervals and integrate over each subinterval separately.

In some cases, you may be able to find an exact numerical value for your integral by using Mathcad's symbolic integration capability. You can also use this capability to evaluate indefinite integrals. See Chapter 17, "Symbolic Calculation."

Variable limits of integration

Although the result of an integration is a single number, you can always use an integral with a range variable to obtain results for many numbers at once. You might do this, for example, when you set up a variable limit of integration. Figure 12-7 shows how to do this.

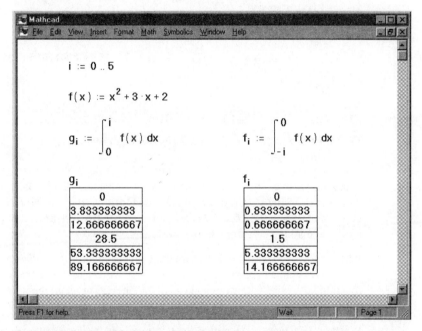

Figure 12-7: Variable limits of integration.

Keep in mind that calculations such as those shown in Figure 12-7 may require repeatedly evaluating an integral. This may take considerable time depending on the complexity of the integrals, the length of the interval, and the value of TOL (see below).

Changing the tolerance for integrals

Mathcad's numerical integration algorithm makes successive estimates of the value of the integral and returns a value when the two most recent estimates differ by less than the value of the built-in variable TOL. Figure 12-8 shows how changing TOL affects the accuracy of integral calculations. To display many digits of precision, see Chapter 6, "Equation and Result Formatting."

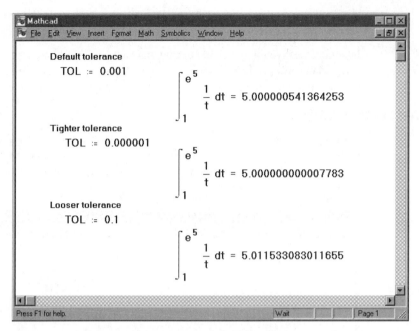

Figure 12-8: Effects of tolerance on integral calculations.

You can change the value of the tolerance by including definitions for TOL directly in your worksheet as shown on Figure 12-8. You can also change the tolerance by using the Built-In Variables tab when you choose **Options** from the **Math** menu. To see the effect of changing the tolerance, choose **Calculate Document** from the **Math** menu to recalculate all the equations in the worksheet.

If Mathcad's approximations to an integral fail to converge to an answer, Mathcad marks the integral with an appropriate error message. Failure to converge can occur when the function has singularities or "spikes" in the interval or when the interval is extremely long.

When you change the tolerance, keep in mind the trade-off between accuracy and computation time. If you decrease (tighten) the tolerance, Mathcad will compute integrals more accurately. However, because this requires more work, Mathcad will take longer to return a result. Conversely, if you increase (loosen) the tolerance, Mathcad will compute more quickly, but the answers will be less accurate.

Contour integrals and double integrals

You can use Mathcad to evaluate complex contour integrals. To do so, first parametrize the contour. Then integrate over the parameter. If the parameter is something other than arc length, you must also include the derivative of the parametrization as a correction factor. Figure 12-9 shows an example. Note that the imaginary unit i used in specifying the path must be typed as `1i`.

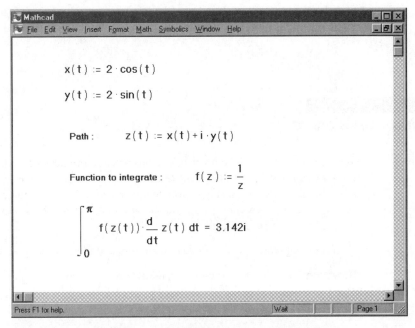

Figure 12-9: How to do a complex contour integral in Mathcad.

You can also use Mathcad to evaluate double or multiple integrals. To set up a double integral, press **&** twice. Fill in the integrand, the limits, and the integrating variable for each integral. Figure 12-10 shows an example.

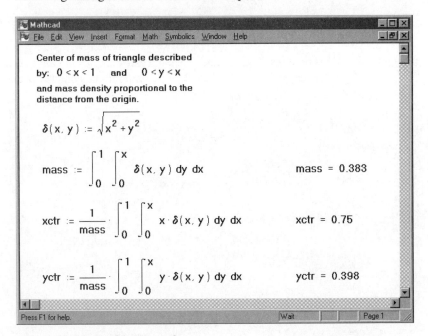

Figure 12-10: Double integrals.

Keep in mind that double integrals take much longer to converge to an answer than single integrals. Wherever possible, use an equivalent single integral in place of a double integral.

Boolean operators

Unlike other operators, the boolean operators can return only a zero or a one. Despite this, they can be very useful. You have already seen an example in Figure 12-3 showing how a boolean operator made a variable upper limit of summation possible. Chapter 12, "Operators," shows how a boolean operator makes it possible to determine the array index of a particular element.

The following table lists the boolean operators and their meaning with numbers:

Condition	How to type	Description
$w = z$	[Ctrl]=	Boolean equals. Returns 1 if expressions are equal; otherwise 0.
$x > y$	>	Greater than.
$x < y$	<	Less than.
$x \geq y$	[Ctrl]0	Greater than or equal to.
$x \leq y$	[Ctrl]9	Less than or equal to.
$w \neq z$	[Ctrl]3	Not equal to.

The four operators $>$, $<$, $\leq$, and $\geq$ cannot take complex numbers because the concepts of greater than and less than lose their meaning in the complex plane.

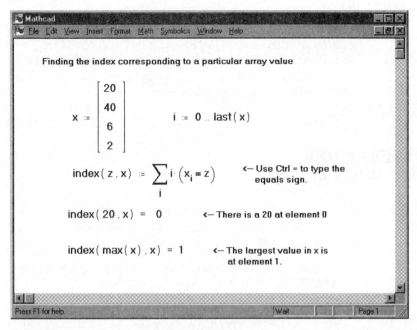

Figure 12-11: Using boolean operators.

As shown in Figure 12-12, the boolean operators can also be used to compare string expressions.

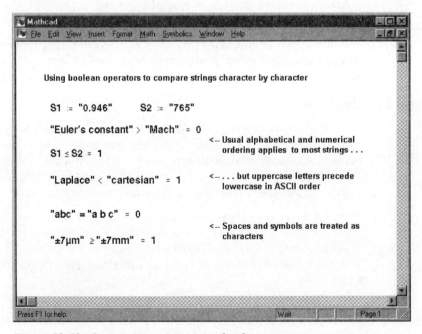

Figure 12-12: Comparing strings using boolean operators.

Mathcad compares two strings character by character by determining the ASCII codes of the component characters. For example, the string "Euler" precedes the string "Mach" in ASCII order and so the expression ("Euler"<"Mach") evaluates to 1. See the table of ASCII codes in Appendix A, "Reference." to determine the character ordering Mathcad uses in comparing strings. Using a boolean operator to compare a string to a number produces a type mismatch error.

Customizing operators

You can think of operators and functions as really being the same thing. A function takes "arguments" and returns a result. An operator, likewise, takes "operands" and returns a result. The differences are merely cosmetic:

- Functions have names you can spell, like *tan* or *spline*; operators are generally symbols like "+" or "×".

- Arguments to a function are enclosed by parentheses, they come after the function's name, and they're separated by commas. Operands on the other hand, can appear elsewhere. For example, you'll often see $f(x, y)$ but you'll rarely see $x f y$. Similarly, you'll often find "$x + y$" but you'll rarely find "$+(x, y)$".

Since operators and functions are fundamentally the same, and since you can define your own functions, there's no reason why you can't define your own customized operators as well. With Mathcad Professional, you'll be able to do just that.

The first section describes how to define a new operator. This is followed by a section on how to use the operator you've just defined. The last section brings together these ideas by showing how functions can themselves be displayed as if they were operators.

Defining a custom operator

You define an operator just as if you were defining a function. You'd type the operator name followed by a pair of parentheses. The operands (two at the most) would go between the parentheses. On the other side of the **:=** you'd type an expression describing what you want the operator to do with its operands. These steps are described in detail in the section "Defining variables and functions" in Chapter 7.

Since operators tend to have names that aren't found on a keyboard, a problem arises when you try and type the name. For example, suppose you want to define a new division operator using " ÷ ". You first have to know how to put a " ÷ " into your worksheet. The simplest way to do this is to drag the symbol from the "Math Symbols" QuickSheet.

We recommend that you save your custom operators by dragging them into a Quick-Sheet. Open the QuickSheets from the Resource Center as described in Chapter 2, "On-line Resources." Then click on "Personal QuickSheets" from the topics in the table of contents. Click on "My Operators." Then drag the definitions into the this QuickSheet.

The next time you need them, you'll be able to drag them off the same QuickSheet rather than having to redefine them.

- When you paste the character, it will appear in the default math font as shown on the right.

- To see the " ÷ ," you'll need to change this into the Symbol font. Press the **[Ins]** key if necessary to move the vertical arm of the insertion point directly in front of the character as shown.

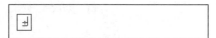

- Press **[Ctrl]G** to display the character in the Symbol font.

You can now continue as if you were defining a function of two variables that happens to have an unusual looking *"name"*.

- Type a left parenthesis followed by two names separated by a comma. Complete this argument list by typing a right parenthesis.

$$÷(x,y)$$

- Press the colon (**:**) key. You see the definition symbol, "**:=**," followed by a placeholder.

$$÷(x,y) := \blacksquare$$

- Type the function definition in the placeholder.

$$÷(x,y) := \frac{x}{y}$$

At this point, you've defined a function which behaves in every way like the user-defined functions described in Chapter 7, "Equations and Computation." You could, if you wanted to, type " ÷(1, 2)= " in your worksheet and see the result "0.5" on the other side of the equal sign.

The difference between functions and operators lies not so much in the way they're defined but in the way they're displayed. This is discussed further in the next section.

Using a custom operator

Once you've defined a new operator, you can use it in your calculations just as you would use one of Mathcad's built-in operators. You can't, however, just type the name of your operator since Mathcad has no way of knowing whether you intend to use your new operator or whether you just want to define a variable having the same name.

The procedure for inserting a custom operator depends on whether the operator has one operand (like "–1 " or "5!" for example) or two (like "1 ÷ 2"). In either case, you'll need to click on the button for the Evaluation and Boolean Palette on the Math Palette. This opens a palette that you'll need in the following procedures.

To insert an operator having two operands:

- Click on the button labelled "*xfy*" on the palette. You'll see three empty placeholders.

- In the middle placeholder, insert the name of the operator. You may find it more convenient to copy the name from the operator definition and paste it into the placeholder.

- In the remaining two placeholders, place the two operands.

- Press = to evaluate the expression.

Another way to display an operator having two operands is to use the other button showing the letters "x", "f" and "y" arranged like a water molecule. If you follow the preceding steps using this operator, you'll see the tree shaped display shown in the lower-left corner of Figure 12-13.

To insert an operator having only one operand, decide first whether you want the operator to appear before the operand, as in "−1 ", or after the operand as in "5!". The former is called a *prefix* operator; the latter is a *postfix* operator. The example below shows how to use a prefix operator. The steps for creating a postfix operator are almost identical.

In the following example, the symbol "¬" comes from the Symbol font. Before you can reproduce the steps in this example, you'll first have to define an operator "¬(*x*)". To do so, follow the steps for defining ÷(*x, y*) in the previous section, substituting the symbol "¬" for "÷" and using only one argument instead of two.

- To make a *prefix* operator click on the button labeled "*fx*" on the symbol palette. Otherwise, click on the "*xf*" button. In either case, you'll see two empty placeholders.

- If you clicked the "*xf*" button, put the operator name in the first placeholder. Otherwise put it in the second placeholder. In either case, you may find it more con-
venient to copy the name from the operator definition and paste it into the placeholder.

- In the remaining placeholder, place the operand.

■ Press **=** to evaluate the expression.

$$\neg 0 = 1$$

Be careful when you use operators this way. Since the placeholders look identical, there are no visual cues to tell you where the operands go and where the operator goes.

The most convenient way to use operators like this is create them once and then save them in a QuickSheet. To do this, open the QuickSheets from the Resource Center (choose **Resource Center** on the **Help** menu). Then click on "Math Symbols" to see a selection of common math symbols. You can drag any of these to your worksheet to help you define a new operator. Once you've defined the new operator, click on "Personal QuickSheets" and drag its definition into the QuickSheet. When you need to use this operator again, just open your Personal QuickSheet and drag it back off.

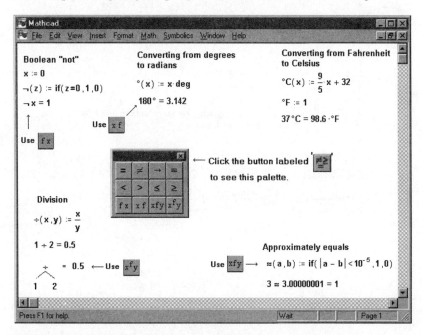

Figure 12-13: Defining your own operators.

Display of functions as operators

As noted earlier, there is really no fundamental difference between functions and operators. The steps given in the section "Defining a custom operator" on page 252 exactly parallel the steps given on page 133 for defining a function.

Since you *define* an operator just as if it were a function, you might expect to be able to *display* that operator as if it were a function as well. Figure 12-14 shows that this is indeed true. Although notation like "$\div(1, 2)$" is unconventional, nothing stops you from using it if you prefer it.

Conversely, you can display a function as if it were an operator. For example, many publishers prefer to omit parentheses around the arguments to certain functions (*sin* x rather than sin(*x*)). You can do the same thing by treating the *sin* function as an operator with one operand and following the steps in the section "Using a custom operator." The lower half of Figure 12-14 shows an example of this.

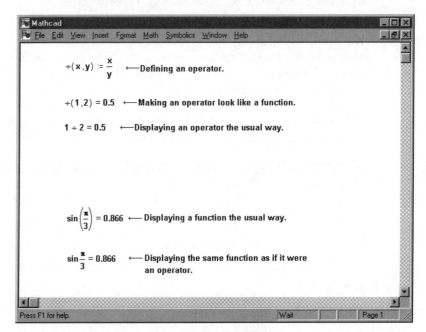

Figure 12-14: Displaying an operator as a function and a function as an operator.

Chapter 13
Built-in Functions

This chapter lists and describes many of Mathcad's built-in functions. Functions associated with Mathcad's statistical and data analysis features are described in Chapter 14, "Statistical Functions." Functions used for working with vectors are described in Chapter 10, "Vectors and Matrices." And for functions to solve differential equations, see Chapter 16, "Solving Differential Equations."

The following sections make up this chapter:

Inserting built-in functions

Using the **Insert Function** dialog box to see all available functions and get help on what they do.

Transcendental functions

Basic trigonometric, exponential, hyperbolic, and Bessel functions.

Truncation and round-off functions

Functions which extract something from a number, including the real or imaginary part, the mantissa, or the modulo function.

Discrete transform functions

Functions for discrete complex Fourier transforms and wavelet transforms.

Sorting functions

Functions to sort elements of vectors and matrices.

Piecewise continuous functions

Using piecewise continuous functions to perform conditional branching and iteration.

Pro　**String functions**

Functions for manipulating strings, converting strings to and from numbers and vectors, and creating customized error messages.

Inserting built-in functions

This section describes how to see a list of all functions available to you together with a brief description of each function. Mathcad's set of built-in functions can change depending on whether you've installed additional function packs or whether you've written your own built-in functions. These functions can come from four sources:

Built-in Mathcad functions

This is the core set of functions that come with Mathcad. These functions are all documented here and in other chapters of this *User's Guide*.

Mathcad Function Packs and Electronic Books

A Function Pack consists of a collection of advanced functions geared to a particular area of application. Documentation for these functions comes with the Function Pack itself. In addition, some but not all Electronic Books come with additional functions. Documentation for any of these functions is in the Electronic Book itself. The list of available Function Packs and Electronic Books is constantly expanding and includes collections for image processing, numerical analysis and advanced statistical analysis. To find out more about these products, contact MathSoft or your local distributor.

Pro
Built-in functions you write yourself

If you have Mathcad Professional and a supported 32-bit C compiler, you can write your own built-in functions. For details see Appendix C, "Creating a User DLL."

To see the list of built-in functions available with your copy of Mathcad, choose **Function** from the **Insert** menu. Although built-in function names are not font sensitive, they are case sensitive. You must type the names of built-in functions exactly as shown in the following tables: uppercase, lowercase, or mixed, as indicated. Alternatively, you can use the Insert Function dialog box to insert a function together with placeholders for its arguments. To do so:

■ Click in a blank area of your document or on a placeholder.

■ Choose **Function** from the **Insert** menu. Mathcad opens the Insert Function dialog box shown on the following page.

■ Double-click on the function you want to insert from the left-hand scrolling list, or click the "Insert" button.

■ Close the dialog box if you no longer need it by clicking the "Cancel" button.

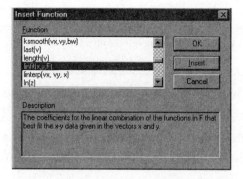

The scrolling list at the top of the Insert Function dialog box shows all of Mathcad's built-in functions along with their arguments. The box below gives a brief description of the currently selected function.

To apply a function to an expression you have already entered, place the expression between the two editing lines and follow the steps given on the preceding page.

Transcendental functions

This section describes Mathcad's trigonometric, hyperbolic, and exponential functions together with all their inverses. It also describes Mathcad's built-in cylindrical Bessel functions.

Trigonometric functions and their inverses

Mathcad's trig functions and their inverses accept any scalar argument: real, complex, or imaginary. They also return complex numbers wherever appropriate. Complex arguments and results are computed using the following identities:

$$\sin(z) = \frac{e^{i \cdot z} - e^{-i \cdot z}}{2 \cdot i}$$

$$\cos(z) = \frac{e^{i \cdot z} + e^{-i \cdot z}}{2 \cdot i}$$

$$e^{i \cdot z} = \cos(z) + i \cdot \sin(z)$$

If you want to apply one of these functions to every element of a vector or matrix, use the vectorize operator as described in the section "Doing calculations in parallel" in Chapter 10.

Note that all of these trig functions expect their arguments in *radians*. To pass degrees, use the built-in unit *deg*. For example, to evaluate the sine of 45 degrees, type `sin(45*deg)`.

Keep in mind that because of round-off errors inherent in a computer, Mathcad may return a very large number where you would ordinarily expect a singularity. In general, you should be cautious whenever you encounter any such singularity.

sin(z)	Returns the sine of z. In a right triangle, this is the ratio of the length of the side *opposite* the angle over the length of the hypotenuse.
cos(z)	Returns the cosine of z. In a right triangle, this is the ratio of the length of the side *adjacent* to the angle over the length of the hypotenuse.
tan(z)	Returns $\sin(z)/\cos(z)$, the tangent of z. In a right triangle, this is the ratio of the length of the side *opposite* the angle over the length of the side *adjacent* to the angle. z should not be an odd multiple of $\pi/2$.
csc(z)	Returns $1/\sin(z)$, the cosecant of z. z should not be an even multiple of π.
sec(z)	Returns $1/\cos(z)$, the secant of z. z should not be an odd multiple of $\pi/2$.
cot(z)	Returns $1/\tan(z)$, the cotangent of z. z should not be an even multiple of π.

The inverse trigonometric functions below all return an angle in radians between 0 and $2 \cdot \pi$. To convert this result into degrees, you can either divide the result by the built-in unit *deg* or type *deg* in the units placeholder as described in the section "Displaying units of results" in Chapter 9.

Because of roundoff error inherent in computers, you may find that *atan* of a very large number returns $\pi/2$. As a general rule, it's best to avoid numerical computations near such singularities.

asin(z)	Returns the angle (in radians) whose sine is z.
acos(z)	Returns the angle (in radians) whose cosine is z.
atan(z)	Returns the angle (in radians) whose tangent is z.

Hyperbolic functions

The hyperbolic functions *sinh* and *cosh* are given by:

$$\sinh(z) = \frac{e^z - e^{-z}}{2}$$

$$\cosh(z) = \frac{e^z + e^{-z}}{2}$$

Both these functions will accept and return complex arguments. As the above identities indicate, when you use complex arguments, the hyperbolic functions behave very much like trigonometric functions. In fact:

$$\sinh(i \cdot z) = i \cdot \sin(z)$$
$$\cosh(i \cdot z) = \cos(z)$$

$\sinh(z)$	Returns the hyperbolic sine of z.
$\cosh(z)$	Returns the hyperbolic cosine of z.
$\tanh(z)$	Returns $\sinh(z)/\cosh(z)$, the hyperbolic tangent of z.
$\operatorname{csch}(z)$	Returns $1/\sinh(z)$, the hyperbolic cosecant of z.
$\operatorname{sech}(z)$	Returns $1/\cosh(z)$, the hyperbolic secant of z.
$\coth(z)$	Returns $1(z)/\tanh(z)$, the hyperbolic cotangent of z.
$\operatorname{asinh}(z)$	Returns the number whose hyperbolic sine is z.
$\operatorname{acosh}(z)$	Returns the number whose hyperbolic cosine is z.
$\operatorname{atanh}(z)$	Returns the number whose hyperbolic tangent is z.

Log and exponential functions

Mathcad's exponential and logarithmic functions will accept and return complex arguments. Complex arguments to the exponential are given by:

$$e^{x + i \cdot y} = e^x \cdot (\cos(y) + i \cdot \sin(y))$$

In general, a complex argument to the natural log function returns:

$$\ln(x + i \cdot y) = \ln|x + i \cdot y| + \operatorname{atan}(y/x) \cdot i + 2 \cdot n \cdot \pi \cdot i$$

Mathcad's *ln* function returns the value corresponding to $n = 0$. Namely:

$$\ln(x + i \cdot y) = \ln|x + i \cdot y| + \operatorname{atan}(y/x) \cdot i$$

This is called the *principal branch* of the natural log function. Figure 13-1 illustrates some of the basic properties of log functions.

---

exp(*z*)   Returns *e* raised to the power *z*.

ln(*z*)   Returns the natural log of *z*. ($z \neq 0$).

log(*z*)   Returns the base 10 log of *z*. ($z \neq 0$).

Figure 13-1 shows how you can use these functions to easily find the log to any base.

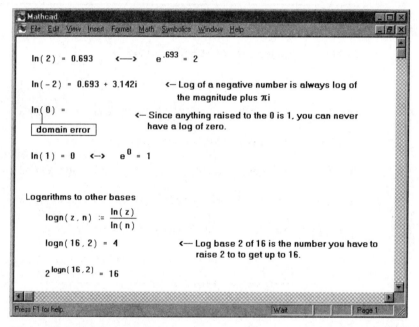

Figure 13-1: Using logarithmic functions.

Bessel functions

These functions typically arise as solutions to the wave equation subject to cylindrical boundary conditions.

Bessel functions of the first kind and second kind, $J_n(x)$ and $Y_n(x)$, are solutions to the following differential equation:

$$x^2 \cdot \frac{d^2 y}{dx^2} + x \cdot \frac{dy}{dx} + (x^2 - n^2) \cdot y = 0$$

Modified Bessel functions of the first and second kind, $I_n(x)$ and $K_n(x)$, are solutions to the slightly different differential equation:

$$x^2 \cdot \frac{d^2 y}{dx^2} + x \cdot \frac{dy}{dx} - ((x^2 - n^2) \cdot y) = 0$$

$J0(x)$	Returns $J_0(x)$. x real.
$J1(x)$	Returns $J_1(x)$. x real.
$J_n(m, x)$	Returns $J_m(x)$. x real, $0 \le m \le 100$.
$Y0(x)$	Returns $Y_0(x)$. x real, $x > 0$.
$Y1(x)$	Returns $Y_1(x)$. x real, $x > 0$.
$Y_n(m, x)$	Returns $Y_m(x)$. $x > 0$, $0 \le m \le 100$.
$I0(x)$	Returns $I_0(x)$. x real.
$I1(x)$	Returns $I_1(x)$. x real.
$I_n(m, x)$	Returns $I_m(x)$. x real, $0 \le m \le 100$.
$K0(x)$	Returns $K_0(x)$. x real, $x > 0$.
$K1(x)$	Returns $K_1(x)$. x real, $x > 0$.
$K_n(m, x)$	Returns $K_m(x)$. $x > 0$, $0 \le m \le 100$.

Special functions

The following functions arise in a wide variety of problems.

---

erf(x)   Returns the value of the error function at x:

$$\text{erf}(x) = \int_0^x \frac{2}{\sqrt{\pi}} e^{-t^2} dt$$

x must be real.

$\Gamma(z)$ Returns the value of the Euler gamma function at z. For real z, the values of this function coincide with the following integral:

$$\Gamma(x) = \int_0^\infty t^{z-1} e^{-t} dt$$

For complex z, the values are the analytic continuation of the real function. Euler's gamma function is undefined for $z = 0, -1, -2, \dots$

Euler's gamma function satisfies the recurrence relationship:

$$\Gamma(z+1) = z\Gamma(z)$$

which means that when z is a positive integer:

$$\Gamma(z+1) = z!$$

The error function arises frequently in statistics. You can also use it to define the complementary error function as:

$$\mathrm{erfc}(x) := 1 - \mathrm{erf}(x)$$

Truncation and round-off functions

These functions all have in common the fact that they extract something from their arguments.

The functions *Re*, *Im*, and *arg* extract the corresponding part of a complex number. For more information on these functions, see Chapter 8, "Variables and Constants."

The functions *ceil* and *floor* will return the next integer above and below their arguments respectively. You can use these functions to create a function that returns just the mantissa of a number:

```
mantissa(x) := x - floor(x)
```

Figure 13-2 shows how you can use the *floor* and *ceil* functions to round off numbers.

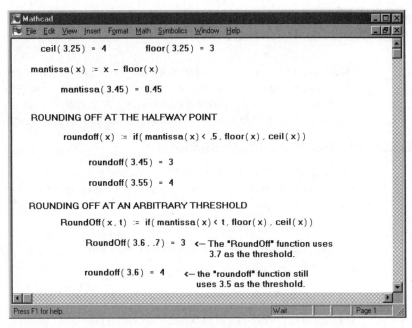

Figure 13-2: Creating a round-off function.

Re(z) Real part of z.

Im(z) Imaginary part of z.

arg(z) Argument of z: the value of θ when z is written as $r \cdot e^{i \cdot \theta}$. Result is between $-\pi$ and π.

floor(x) Greatest integer $\leq x$ (x real).

ceil(x) Least integer $\geq x$ (x real).

mod(x, y) Remainder on dividing x by y. Result has same sign as x.

angle(x, y) Angle (in radians) from positive x-axis to the point (x, y) in the x-y plane. Arguments must be real. Returns a value between zero and 2π.

Discrete transform functions

Mathcad contains a variety of functions for performing discrete transforms. All these functions require vectors as arguments. When you define a vector **v** for use with Fourier or wavelet transforms, be sure to start with v_0. If you do not define v_0, Mathcad automatically sets it to zero. This can distort the results of the transform functions.

Introduction to Discrete Fourier transforms

Mathcad comes with two types of Fourier transform pairs: *fft/ifft* and *cfft/icfft*. These functions are discrete: they apply to and return vectors and matrices only. You cannot use them with other functions.

Use the *fft* and *ifft* functions if:

■ The data values in the time domain are real, and

■ the data vector has 2^m elements.

Use the *cfft* and *icfft* functions in all other cases.

The first condition is required because the *fft/ifft* pair takes advantage of the fact that, for real data, the second half of the transform is just the conjugate of the first. Mathcad discards the second half of the result vector. This saves both time and memory. The *cfft/icfft* pair does not assume symmetry in the transform. For this reason, you *must* use this pair for complex valued data. Since the real numbers are just a subset of the complex numbers, you can use the *cfft/icfft* pair for real numbers as well.

The second condition is required because the *fft/ifft* Fourier transform pair uses a highly efficient fast Fourier transform algorithm. In order to do so, the vector you use with *fft* must have 2^m elements. The *cfft/icfft* Fourier transform pair uses an algorithm that permits vectors as well as matrices of arbitrary size. When you use this transform pair with a matrix, you get back a two-dimensional Fourier transform.

Note that if you used *fft* to get to the frequency domain, you *must* use *ifft* to get back to the time domain. Similarly, if you used *cfft* to get to the frequency domain, you *must* use *icfft* to get back to the time domain.

Different sources use different conventions concerning the initial factor of the Fourier transform and whether to conjugate the results of either the transform or the inverse transform. The functions *fft*, *ifft*, *cfft*, and *icfft* use $1/\sqrt{N}$ as a normalizing factor and a positive exponent in going from the time to the frequency domain. The functions *FFT*, *IFFT*, *CFFT*, and *ICFFT* use $1/N$ as a normalizing factor and a negative exponent in going from the time to the frequency domain. Be sure to use these functions in pairs. For example, if you used *CFFT* to go from the time domain to the frequency domain, you *must* use *ICFFT* to transform back to the time domain.

Fourier transforms on real data

With 2^m real-valued data points, you can use the *fft/ifft* Fourier transform pair. These functions take advantage of symmetry conditions present only when the data is real. This saves both time and memory.

---

fft(**v**)   This function returns the Fourier transform of a 2^m element vector of real data representing measurements at regular intervals in the time domain.

The vector **v** must have 2^m elements. The result is a vector of $1 + 2^{m-1}$ complex coefficients representing values in the frequency domain. If **v** contains other than 2^m elements, Mathcad returns an error message.

The elements of the vector returned by *fft* satisfy the following equation:

$$c_j = \frac{1}{\sqrt{n}} \sum_{k=0}^{n-1} v_k e^{2\pi i (j/n) k}$$

In this formula, n is the number of elements in **v** and i is the imaginary unit.

The elements in the vector returned by the *fft* function correspond to different frequencies. To recover the actual frequency, you must know the sampling frequency of the original signal. If **v** is an n element vector passed to the *fft* function, and the sampling frequency is f_s, the frequency corresponding to c_k is

$$f_k = \frac{k}{n} \cdot f_s$$

Note that this makes it impossible to detect frequencies above the sampling frequency. This is a limitation not of Mathcad, but of the underlying mathematics itself. In order to correctly recover a signal from the Fourier transform of its samples, you must sample the signal with a frequency of at least twice its bandwidth. A thorough discussion of this phenomenon is outside the scope of this manual but within that of any textbook on digital signal processing.

---

ifft(**v**)   This function returns the inverse Fourier transform of a vector of data representing values in the frequency domain. The inverse transform will be pure real.

The vector $\mathbf{v}$ must have $1 + 2^m$ elements for m integer. The result is a vector of 2^{m+1} complex coefficients representing values in the frequency domain. If $\mathbf{v}$ contains other than $1 + 2^m$ elements, Mathcad returns an error message.

The argument $\mathbf{v}$ is a vector similar to those generated by the *fft* function. To compute the result, Mathcad first creates a new vector $\mathbf{w}$ by taking the conjugates of the elements of $\mathbf{v}$ and appending them to the vector $\mathbf{v}$. Then Mathcad computes a vector $\mathbf{d}$ whose elements satisfy this formula:

$$d_j = \frac{1}{\sqrt{n}} \sum_{k=0}^{n-1} w_k e^{-2\pi i(j/n)k}$$

This is the same formula as the *fft* formula, except for the minus sign in the *exp* function. The *fft* and *ifft* functions are exact inverses. For all real $\mathbf{v}$, $\mathrm{ifft}(\mathrm{fft}(\mathbf{v})) = \mathbf{v}$.

Fourier transforms on complex data

There are two reasons why you may not be able to use the *fft/ifft* transform pair discussed in the previous section:

■ The data may be complex valued. This means that Mathcad can no longer exploit the symmetry present in the real valued case.

■ The data vector might not have 2^m data points in it. This means Mathcad cannot take advantage of the highly efficient FFT algorithm used by the *fft/ifft* Fourier transform pair.

Complex Fourier transforms require the following functions:

---

cfft($\mathbf{A}$)   Returns the fast Fourier transform of a vector or matrix of complex data representing equally spaced measurements in the time domain. The array returned is the same size as the array you used as an argument.

icfft($\mathbf{A}$)   Returns the inverse Fourier transform of a vector or matrix of data representing values in the frequency domain. The result is an array representing values in the time domain. The *icfft* function is the inverse of the *cfft* function. Like *cfft*, this function returns an array of the same size as its argument.

Although the *cfft/icfft* Fourier transform pair will work on arrays of any size, they work significantly faster when the number of rows and columns contains many smaller factors. Vectors with length 2^m fall into this category. So do vectors having lengths like 100 or 120. On the other hand, a vector whose length is a large prime number will slow down the Fourier transform algorithm.

The *cfft* and *icfft* functions are exact inverses. That is, $\text{icfft}(\text{cfft}(\mathbf{v})) = \mathbf{v}$. Figure 13-3 shows an example of Fourier transforms in Mathcad.

When you use the *cfft* with a matrix, the result is the two-dimensional Fourier transform of the input matrix

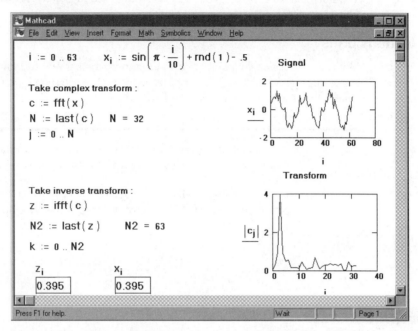

Figure 13-3: Use of fast Fourier transforms in Mathcad.

Alternate forms of the Fourier transform

The definitions for the Fourier transform discussed earlier are not the only ones used. For example, the following definitions for the discrete Fourier transform and its inverse appear in Ronald Bracewell's *The Fourier Transform and Its Applications* (McGraw-Hill, 1986):

$$F(\upsilon) = \frac{1}{n} \sum_{\tau = 1}^{n} f(\tau)e^{-2\pi i(\upsilon/n)\tau}$$

$$f(\tau) = \sum_{\upsilon = 1}^{n} F(\upsilon)e^{-2\pi i(\tau/n)\upsilon}$$

These definitions are very common in the engineering literature. To use these definitions rather than those presented in the last section, use the functions *FFT*, *IFFT*, *CFFT*, and *ICFFT*. These differ from those discussed in the last section as follows:

Discrete transform functions

- Instead of a factor of $1/\sqrt{n}$ in front of both forms, there is a factor of $1/n$ in front of the transform and no factor in front of the inverse.

- The minus sign appears in the exponent of the transform instead of in its inverse.

The functions *FFT*, *IFFT*, *CFFT*, and *ICFFT* are used in exactly the same way as the functions discussed in the previous section.

Wavelet transforms

Mathcad Professional includes two wavelet transforms for performing the one-dimensional discrete wavelet transform and its inverse. The transform is performed using the Daubechies four-coefficient wavelet basis.

Pro   wave(v)   Returns the discrete wavelet transform of **v**, a 2^m element vector containing real data. The vector returned is the same size as **v**.

Pro   iwave(v)   Returns the inverse discrete wavelet transform of **v**, a 2^m element vector containing real data. The vector returned is the same size as **v**.

Sorting functions

Mathcad includes three functions shown in Figure 13-4 for sorting arrays and one for reversing the order of their elements:

---

sort(**v**)   Returns the elements of the vector **v** sorted in ascending order.

csort(**A**, *n*)   Sorts the rows of the matrix **A** so as to place the elements in column *n* in ascending order. The result has the same size as **A**.

rsort(**A**, *n*)   Sorts the columns of the matrix **A** so as to place the elements in row *n* in ascending order. The result has the same size as **A**.

reverse(**v**)   Reverses the order of the elements of the vector **v** or the rows of the matrix
reverse(**A**)   **A**.

The above sorting functions accept matrices and vectors with complex elements. However in sorting them, Mathcad ignores the imaginary part.

To sort a vector or matrix in descending order, first sort in ascending order, then use *reverse*. For example, *reverse*(*sort*(**v**)) returns the elements of **v** sorted in descending order.

Unless you change the value of ORIGIN, matrices are numbered starting with row zero and column zero. If you forget this, it's easy to make the error of sorting a matrix on the wrong row or column by specifying an incorrect *n* argument for *rsort* and *csort*. To sort on the first column of a matrix, for example, you must use *csort*(**A**, 0).

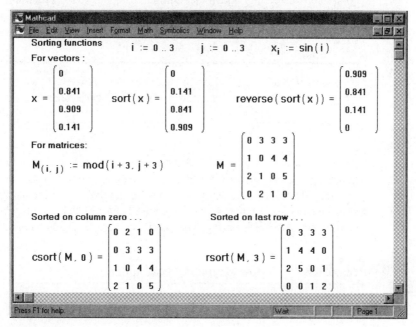

Figure 13-4: Sorting functions.

Piecewise continuous functions

Piecewise continuous functions are useful for branching and iteration. There are five Mathcad functions falling into this category. The *if* function is useful for choosing one of two values based on a condition. The Heaviside step function, $\Phi(x)$, and the Kronecker Delta function, $\delta(m, n)$, are special cases of the *if* function.

The *until* function is used to drive iteration. It is unique among Mathcad functions because it is designed to work only with range variables. This is the only Mathcad function which can actually halt iteration upon the occurrence of a condition. Mathcad Professional, however, also includes specialized programming operators that allow you to control iteration, as described in Chapter 18, "Programming."

The last function is ε, the completely anti-symmetric tensor function. This returns a 0, 1, or −1 depending on the permutation of its arguments. Although this function is of limited applicability, it would be difficult to perform this function using any other combination of Mathcad functions.

The if function

Use *if* to define a function that behaves one way below a certain number and behaves completely differently above that number. That point of discontinuity is specified by its first argument, *cond*. The remaining two arguments let you specify the behavior of the function on either side of that discontinuity.

---

if(*cond, tval, fval*)   Returns *tval* if *cond* is nonzero (true)

Returns *fval* if *cond* is zero (false).

Although the argument *cond* can be any expression at all, it is usually more convenient to use a boolean expression from the table below. The following table shows the meaning of boolean expressions with numbers (x and y can be real scalars, while w and z can be complex scalars). As explained in Chapter 12, "Operators," boolean operators can also be used to order string expressions character by character based on ASCII codes.

Condition	How to type	Description
$w=z$	[Ctrl]=	Boolean equals. Returns 1 if expressions are equal; otherwise 0.
$x>y$	>	Greater than.
$x<y$	<	Less than.
$x\geq y$	[Ctrl]0	Greater than or equal to.
$x\leq y$	[Ctrl]9	Less than or equal to.
$w\neq z$	[Ctrl]3	Not equal to.

Note that boolean expressions involving inequalities cannot be used with complex numbers. This is because it is meaningless to speak of one complex number being "larger" or "smaller" than another.

To save time, Mathcad only evaluates those arguments it has to. For example, if *cond* is false, there is no need to evaluate *tval* since it will not be returned anyway. Because of this, errors in the unevaluated argument can escape detection. For example, Mathcad will never detect the fact that $ln(0)$ is undefined in the expression below:

```
if(|x| < 0,ln(0),ln(x))
```

Figure 13-5 shows several equations using the *if* function. You can combine boolean operators to create more complicated conditions. For example, the condition

$$(x < 1) \cdot (x > 0)$$

acts like an "and" gate, returning 1 only if *x* is between 0 and 1. Similarly, the expression

$$(x > 1) + (x < 0)$$

acts like an "or" gate, returning a 1 if either $x > 1$ or $x < 0$, but not if *x* is between 0 and 1.

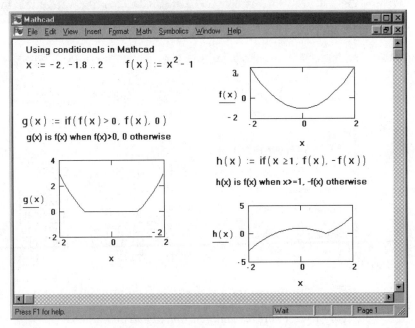

Figure 13-5: Conditionals in Mathcad.

The until function

Mathcad's *until* function allows you to halt an iteration when a particular condition is met. The *until* function has no effect when its first argument involves no range variables. When the first argument does involve a range variable, Mathcad will iterate until the first argument evaluates to a negative value. When this happens, Mathcad halts iteration.

---

until(*x*, *z*) Returns *z* until the test expression *x* becomes negative. *x* should be an expression involving a range variable.

Do not use the *until* function in equations with more than one range variable (for example, multiple summations). Mathcad will halt all iteration on all range variables the first time that the first argument of *until* is negative. This usually does not produce the desired result.

The *until* function is useful in iterative processes with a specified convergence condition. For example, Figure 13-6 shows how to use the *until* function to test an iterative process for convergence. The iteration in the equation for x_i continues until x_i is within *err* of *a*. Figure 13-6 also shows how to use the *last* function to detect when iteration has halted and to compute the size of the resulting array.

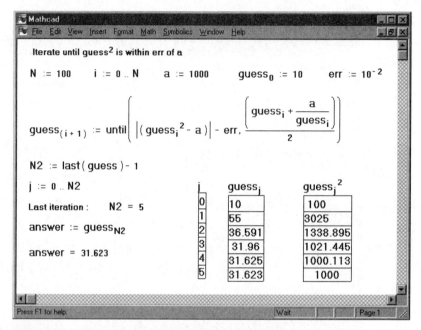

Figure 13-6: Using the until function to halt an iteration.

When you use the *until* function, be sure that the value of the test expression does in fact change somewhere in the iteration. Otherwise, you may find yourself in an infinite loop. If this does occur, press the [**Esc**] key to interrupt calculation.

Impulse and step functions

These two functions are special cases of the *if* function. The Heaviside step function is equivalent to:

$$\Phi(\text{x}) := \text{if}(\text{x} < 0, 0, 1)$$

For integer *m* and *n*, the Kronecker delta function is equivalent to

$$\delta(\text{m,n}) := \text{if}(\text{m} = \text{n}, 1, 0)$$

$\Phi(x)$ Heaviside step function. 1 if $x \geq 0$; otherwise, 0.

$\delta(m, n)$ Kronecker's delta function. Returns 1 if $m = n$; otherwise, 0. Both arguments must be integer.

You can use the Heaviside step function to define a pulse of width w by defining:

```
pulse(x,w) := Φ(x) - Φ(x-w)
```

A lowpass and highpass filter having width $2 \cdot w$ could then be defined as:

```
lowpass(x,w) := pulse(x+w, 2*w)

highpass(x,w) := 1 - pulse(x+w, 2*w)
```

Figure 13-7 illustrates the use of the Heaviside step function for creating filters.

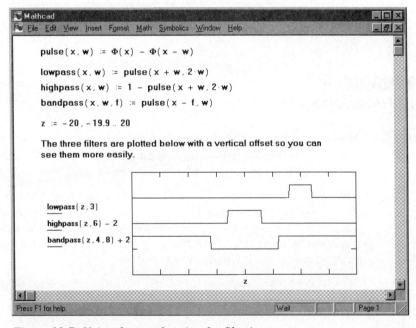

Figure 13-7: Using the step function for filtering.

Antisymmetric tensor function

The arguments to this function are three integers between 0 and 2 inclusive. It basically determines how many times you have to swap two numbers in order to get back to the sequence $[0, 1, 2]$ from whatever sequence $[i, j, k]$ you passed to it.

More generally, $\varepsilon(i, j, k) = 1$ if $[i, j, k]$ is an even permutation of $[0, 1, 2]$ (an even number of swaps), and $\varepsilon(i, j, k) = -1$ if $[i, j, k]$ is an odd permutation of $[0, 1, 2]$ (an odd number of swaps). This explains why $\varepsilon(0, 1, 2) = 1$.

For example, $\varepsilon(2, 0, 1) = 1$ because to get from $[2, 0, 1]$ back to $[0, 1, 2]$ you'll have to swap twice. On the other hand, $\varepsilon(0, 2, 1) = -1$ because to get from $[0, 2, 1]$ back to $[0, 1, 2]$ you only have to swap once. If two numbers are the same, for example $\varepsilon(0, 1, 1)$, you can never get back to $[0, 1, 2]$, so the function just returns 0.

Although this function is not used very often, it is truly indispensable when you need it. It is very difficult to perform this same feat using any other combination of Mathcad functions.

$\varepsilon(i, j, k)$ Completely antisymmetric tensor of rank 3. i, j, and k must be integers between 0 and 2 inclusive (or between ORIGIN and ORIGIN + 2 inclusive if ORIGIN≠0). Result is 0 if any two are the same, 1 for even permutations, -1 for odd permutations.

String functions

Pro

Most built-in functions and operators do not make sense when used with strings and will issue error messages if you use string arguments with them. Mathcad Professional, however, includes several specialized functions for working with strings.

The strings used and returned by most of the functions described below are typed in a math placeholder by pressing the double-quote key (") in a placeholder and entering any combination of letters, numbers, or other ASCII characters. Mathcad automatically places double quotes around the string expression, and will display quotes around a string whenever one is returned as a result.

See Chapter 8, "Variables and Constants," for more information on strings.

Manipulating strings

The following four functions are useful for combining strings, determining the length of a string, and locating and returning substrings.

When evaluating the functions *search* and *substr*, Mathcad assumes that the first character in a string is at position 0.

Pro   concat(*S1*, *S2*)   Returns a string formed by appending string *S2* to the end of string *S1*.

Pro	strlen(*S*)	Returns the number of characters in string *S*.
Pro	search(*S1*, *SubS*, *m*)	Returns the starting position of the substring *SubS* in string *S1* beginning from position *m*, or −1 if no substring is found. The argument *m* must be a nonnegative integer.
Pro	substr(*S*, *m*, *n*)	Returns a substring of *S* beginning with the character in the *m*th position and having at most *n* characters. The arguments *m* and *n* must be nonnegative integers.

Converting to and from strings

Use *num2str* and *str2num* to convert between numeric values and strings. These functions are useful when it is more convenient to manipulate a number as a string rather than mathematically, or when you need to perform numerical calculations on a string of numbers.

The *str2num* function requires a string consisting of characters which constitute an integer, a floating-point or complex number, or an e-format number such as 4.51e-3 (for $4.51 \cdot 10^{-3}$). For example, valid string arguments for *str2num* are "-16.5," "2.1+6i," "3.241 - 9.234j," and "2.418e3." Spaces are ignored.

Use *str2vec* and *vec2str* if you want to convert between the ASCII codes for characters and the characters themselves. For a list of ASCII codes see Appendix A, "Reference." For example, the ASCII code for letter "a" is 97, that for letter "b" is 98, and that for letter "c" is 99.

Pro	str2num(*S*)	Returns a constant formed by converting the characters in string *S* to a number. *S* must contain only characters which constitute an integer, a floating-point or complex number, or an e-format number such as 4.51e-3 (for $4.51 \cdot 10^{-3}$). Spaces are ignored.
Pro	num2str(*z*)	Returns a string formed by converting the real or complex number *z* into a decimal-valued string.
Pro	str2vec(*S*)	Returns a vector of ASCII codes corresponding to the characters in string *S*.
Pro	vec2str(**v**)	Returns a string formed by converting a vector **v** of ASCII codes to characters. The elements of **v** must be integers between 0 and 255.

Customized error messages

Just as Mathcad's built-in error messages appear as "error tips" when a built-in function is used incorrectly or could not return a result, you may want specialized error messages to appear when your user-defined functions are used improperly or cannot return answers.

Mathcad allows you to define your own error messages using the string function error. This function is especially useful for trapping erroneous inputs to Mathcad programs you write. See Chapter 18, "Programming," for details on using error in programs.

Pro   error(*S*)   Returns the string *S* as an error message.

When Mathcad encounters the *error* function in an expression, it highlights the expression in red. When you click on the expression, the error message appears in a tool tip that hovers over the expression. The text of the message is the string argument you supply to the *error* function.

Figure 13-8 shows examples of Mathcad's string manipulation, string conversion, and custom error message functions.

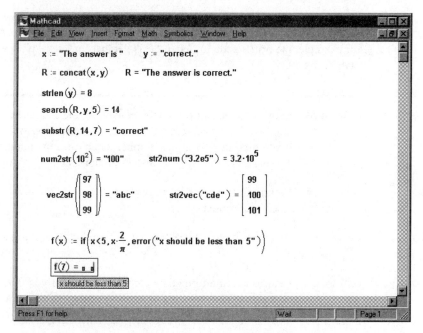

Figure 13-8: Using string functions to manipulate strings, convert to and from strings, and define error messages.

Chapter 14
Statistical Functions

This chapter lists and describes many of Mathcad's built-in statistical functions. These functions perform a wide variety of computational tasks, including statistical analysis, interpolation, regression, and smoothing.

The following sections make up this chapter:

Population and sample statistics

Functions for computing the mean, variance, standard deviation, and correlation of data.

Probability distributions

Functions for evaluating probability densities, cumulative probability distributions and their inverses for over a dozen common distribution functions.

Histogram function

How to count the number of data values falling into specified intervals.

Random numbers

Generating random numbers having various distributions.

Interpolation and prediction functions

Linear and cubic spline interpolation. Functions for multivariate interpolation.

Regression functions

Functions for linear regression, polynomial regression, and regression using combinations of arbitrary functions.

Smoothing functions

Functions for smoothing time series with either a running median, a Gaussian kernel, or an adaptive linear least-squares method.

Population and sample statistics

Mathcad includes eight functions for population and sample statistics. In the following descriptions, m and n represent the number of rows and columns in the specified arrays. In the formulas below, the built-in variable ORIGIN is set to its default value of zero.

---

mean(**A**)   Returns the mean of the elements of an $m \times n$ array **A** using the formula:

$$\text{mean}(\mathbf{A}) = \frac{1}{mn} \sum_{i=0}^{m-1} \sum_{j=0}^{n-1} A_{i,j}$$

median(**A**)   Returns the median of the elements of an $m \times n$ array **A**. This is the value above and below which there are an equal number of values. If **A** has an even number of elements, this is the arithmetic mean of the two central values.

var(**A**)   Returns the population variance of the elements of an $m \times n$ array **A** using the formula:

$$\text{var}(\mathbf{A}) = \frac{1}{mn} \sum_{i=0}^{m-1} \sum_{j=0}^{n-1} |A_{i,j} - \text{mean}(\mathbf{A})|^2$$

Var(**A**)   Returns the sample variance of the elements of an $m \times n$ array **A** using the formula:

$$\text{var}(\mathbf{A}) = \frac{1}{mn-1} \sum_{i=0}^{m-1} \sum_{j=0}^{n-1} |A_{i,j} - \text{mean}(\mathbf{A})|^2$$

cvar(**A**, **B**)   Returns the covariance of the elements in the $m \times n$ arrays **A** and **B** using the formula:

$$\text{cvar}(\mathbf{A}, \mathbf{B}) = \frac{1}{mn} \sum_{i=0}^{m-1} \sum_{j=0}^{n-1} [A_{i,j} - \text{mean}(\mathbf{A})]\overline{[B_{i,j} - \text{mean}(\mathbf{B})]}$$

where the bar indicates complex conjugation.

stdev(**A**)   Returns the population standard deviation (square root of the variance) of the elements of the $m \times n$ array **A**:

$$\text{stdev}(\mathbf{A}) = \sqrt{\text{var}(\mathbf{A})}$$

Stdev(**A**)   Returns the sample standard deviation (square root of the sample variance) of the elements of the $m \times n$ array **A**:

$$\text{Stdev}(\mathbf{A}) = \sqrt{\text{Var}(\mathbf{A})}$$

corr(**A**, **B**)   Returns a scalar: the correlation coefficient (Pearson's r) for the two $m \times n$ arrays **A** and **B**.

Probability distributions

Mathcad includes several functions for working with several common probability densities. These functions fall into three classes:

- **Probability densities:** These give the likelihood that a random variable will take on a particular value.

- **Cumulative probability distributions:** These give the probability that a random variable will take on a value *less than or equal to* a specified value. These are obtained by simply integrating (or summing when appropriate) the corresponding probability density over an appropriate range.

- **Inverse cumulative probability distributions:** These functions take a probability as an argument and return a value such that the probability that a random variable will be *less than or equal to* that value is whatever probability you supplied as an argument.

Probability densities

These functions return the likelihood that a random variable will take on a particular value. The probability density functions are the derivatives of the corresponding cumulative distribution functions discussed in the next section.

dbeta(x, s_1, s_2)   Returns the probability density for the beta distribution:

$$\frac{\Gamma(s_1 + s_2)}{\Gamma(s_1) \cdot \Gamma(s_2)} \cdot x^{s_1 - 1} \cdot (1 - x)^{s_2 - 1}$$

in which ($s_1, s_2 > 0$) are the shape parameters. ($0 < x < 1$).

dbinom(k, n, p)   Returns $P(X = k)$ when the random variable X has the binomial distribution:

$$\frac{n!}{k!(n-k)!}p^k(1-p)^{n-k}$$

in which n and k are integers satisfying $0 \le k \le n$. p satisfies $0 \le p \le 1$.

dcauchy(x, l, s)   Returns the probability density for the Cauchy distribution:

$$(\pi s(1 + ((x-l)/s)^2))^{-1}$$

in which l is a location parameter and $s > 0$ is a scale parameter.

dchisq(x, d)   Returns the probability density for the chi-squared distribution:

$$\frac{e^{-x/2}}{2\Gamma(d/2)}\left(\frac{x}{2}\right)^{(d/2-1)}$$

in which $d > 0$ is the degrees of freedom and $x > 0$.

dexp(x, r)   Returns the probability density for the exponential distribution:

$$re^{-rx}$$

in which $r > 0$ is the rate and $x > 0$.

dF(x, d_1, d_2)   Returns the probability density for the F distribution:

$$\frac{d_1^{d_1/2}d_2^{d_2/2}\Gamma((d_1+d_2)/2)}{\Gamma(d_1/2)\Gamma(d_2/2)} \cdot \frac{x^{(d_1-2)/2}}{(d_2+d_1x)^{(d_1+d_2)/2}}$$

in which $(d_1, d_2 > 0)$ are the degrees of freedom and $x > 0$.

dgamma(x, s)   Returns the probability density for the gamma distribution:

$$\frac{x^{s-1}e^{-x}}{\Gamma(s)}$$

in which $s > 0$ is the shape parameter and $x \ge 0$.

dgeom(k, p)   Returns $P(X = k)$ when the random variable X has the geometric distribution:

$$p(1-p)^k$$

in which $0 < p \le 1$ is the probability of success and k is a nonnegative integer.

dlnorm(x, μ, σ) Returns the probability density for the lognormal distribution:

$$\frac{1}{\sqrt{2\pi}\sigma x}\exp\left(-\frac{1}{2\sigma^2}(\ln(x)-\mu)^2\right)$$

in which μ is the logmean and σ is the logdeviation. $x > 0$.

dlogis(x, l, s) Returns the probability density for the logistic distribution:

$$\frac{\exp(-(x-l)/s)}{s(1+\exp(-(x-l)/s))^2}$$

in which l is the location parameter and $s > 0$ is the scale parameter.

dnbinom(k, n, p) Returns $P(X = k)$ when the random variable X has the negative binomial distribution:

$$\binom{n+k-1}{k}p^n(1-p)^k$$

in which $0 < p \leq 1$ and n and k are integers, $n > 0$ and $k \geq 0$

dnorm(x, μ, σ) Returns the probability density for the normal distribution:

$$\frac{1}{\sqrt{2\pi}\sigma}\exp\left(-\frac{1}{2\sigma^2}(x-\mu)^2\right)$$

in which μ and σ are the mean and standard deviation. $\sigma > 0$.

dpois(k, λ) Returns $P(X = k)$ when the random variable X has the Poisson distribution:

$$\frac{\lambda^k}{k!}e^{-\lambda}$$

in which $\lambda > 0$ and k is a nonnegative integer.

dt(x, d) Returns the probability density for Student's t distribution:

$$\frac{\Gamma((d+1)/2)}{\Gamma(d/2)\sqrt{\pi d}}\left(1+\frac{x^2}{d}\right)^{-(d+1)/2}$$

in which d is the degrees of freedom, $d > 0$ and x is real.

dunif(x, a, b) Returns the probability density for the uniform distribution:

$$\frac{1}{b-a}$$

in which b and a are the endpoints of the interval with $a < b$ and $a \le x \le b$.

dweibull(x, s)   Returns the probability density for the Weibull distribution:

$$sx^{s-1}\exp(-x^s)$$

in which $s > 0$ is the shape parameter and $x > 0$.

Cumulative probability distributions

These functions return the probability that a random variable is less than or equal to a specified value. The cumulative probability distribution is simply the probability density function integrated from $-\infty$ to the specified value. For integer random variables, the integral is replaced by a summation over the appropriate range.

The probability density functions corresponding to each of the following cumulative distributions are given in the section "Probability distributions" on page 281.

Figure 14-1 at the end of this section illustrates the relationship between these three functions.

cnorm(x)   Returns the cumulative standard normal distribution function. Equivalent to pnorm(x, 0, 1).

pbeta(x, s_1, s_2)   Returns the cumulative beta distribution with shape parameters s_1 and s_2. ($s_1, s_2 > 0$).

pbinom(k, n, p)   Returns the cumulative binomial distribution for k successes in n trials. n is a positive integer. p is the probability of success, $0 \le p \le 1$.

pcauchy(x, l, s)   Returns the cumulative Cauchy distribution with scale parameter s and location parameter l. $s > 0$.

pchisq(x, d)   Returns the cumulative chi-squared distribution in which $d > 0$ is the degrees of freedom.

pexp(x, r)   Returns the cumulative exponential distribution in which $r > 0$ is the rate.

pF(x, d_1, d_2)   Returns the cumulative F distribution in which ($d_1, d_2 > 0$) are the degrees of freedom.

pgamma(x, s)	Returns the cumulative gamma distribution in which $s > 0$ is the shape parameter.
pgeom(k, p)	Returns the cumulative geometric distribution. p is the probability of success. $0 < p \le 1$.
plnorm(x, μ, σ)	Returns the cumulative lognormal distribution having logmean $μ$ and logdeviation $σ > 0$.
plogis(x, l, s)	Returns the cumulative logistic distribution. l is the location parameter. $s > 0$ is the scale parameter.
pnbinom(k, n, p)	Returns the cumulative negative binomial distribution in which $0 \le p < 1$. n must be a positive integer.
pnorm(x, μ, σ)	Returns the cumulative normal distribution with mean $μ$ and standard deviation $σ$. $σ > 0$.
ppois(k, λ)	Returns the cumulative Poisson distribution. $λ > 0$.
pt(x, d)	Returns the cumulative Student's t distribution. d is the degrees of freedom. $d > 0$.
punif(x, a, b)	Returns the cumulative uniform distribution. b and a are the endpoints of the interval. $a < b$.
pweibull(x, s)	Returns the cumulative Weibull distribution. $s > 0$.

Inverse cumulative probability distributions

These functions take a probability p as an argument and return the value of x such that $P(X \le x) = p$.

The probability density functions corresponding to each of the following inverse cumulative distributions are given in the section "Probability distributions" on page 281.

qbeta(p, s_1, s_2)	Returns the inverse beta distribution with shape parameters s_1 and s_2. $0 \le p \le 1$ and $s_1, s_2 > 0$.
qbinom(p, n, r)	Returns the number of successes in n trials of the Bernoulli process such that the probability of at most that number of successes is p. r is the probability of success on a single trial. $0 \le r \le 1$ and $0 \le p \le 1$. n must be an integer greater than zero.
qcauchy(p, l, s)	Returns the inverse Cauchy distribution with scale parameter s and

location parameter l. $s > 0$. $0 < p < 1$.

qchisq(p, d)   Returns the inverse chi-squared distribution in which $d > 0$ is the degrees of freedom. $0 \le p < 1$.

qexp(p, r)   Returns the inverse exponential distribution in which $r > 0$ is the rate. $0 \le p < 1$.

qF(p, d_1, d_2)   Returns the inverse F distribution in which $(d_1, d_2 > 0)$ are the degrees of freedom. $0 \le p < 1$.

qgamma(p, s)   Returns the inverse gamma distribution in which $s > 0$ is the shape parameter. $0 \le p < 1$.

qgeom(p, r)   Returns the inverse geometric distribution. r is the probability of success on a single trial. $0 < p < 1$ and $0 < r < 1$.

qlnorm(p, μ, σ)   Returns the inverse lognormal distribution having logmean μ and logdeviation $\sigma > 0$. $0 \le p < 1$.

qlogis(p, l, s)   Returns the inverse logistic distribution. l is the location parameter. $s > 0$ is the scale parameter. $0 < p < 1$.

qnbinom(p, n, r)   Returns the inverse negative binomial distribution with size n and probability of success r. $0 < r \le 1$ and $0 \le p \le 1$.

qnorm(p, μ, σ)   Returns the inverse normal distribution with mean μ and standard deviation σ. $\sigma > 0$ and $0 < p < 1$.

qpois(p, λ)   Returns the inverse Poisson distribution. $\lambda > 0$ and $0 \le p \le 1$.

qt(p, d)   Returns the inverse Student's t distribution. d is the degrees of freedom. $d > 0$ and $0 < p < 1$.

qunif(p, a, b)   Returns the inverse uniform distribution. b and a are the endpoints of the interval. $a < b$ and $0 \le p \le 1$.

qweibull(p, s)   Returns the inverse Weibull distribution. $s > 0$ and $0 < p < 1$.

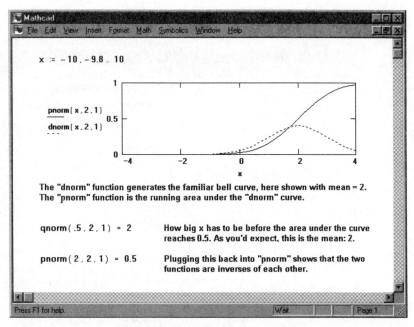

Figure 14-1: Relationship between probability densities, cumulative distributions, and their inverses.

Histogram function

Mathcad includes a function, *hist*, for computing frequency distributions for histograms:

hist(**int**, **A**)   Returns a vector representing the frequencies with which values in **A** fall in the intervals represented by the **int** vector. The elements in both **int** and **A** must be real. In addition, the elements of **int** must be in ascending order. The resulting vector is one element shorter than **int**.

Mathcad interprets **int** as a set of points defining a sequence of intervals in a histogram. The values in **int** must should be in ascending order. The result of this function is a vector **f**, in which f_i is the number of values in **A** satisfying the condition:

$$int_i \leq value \leq int_{i+1}$$

Mathcad ignores data points less than the first value in **int** or greater than the last value in **int**. Figure 14-2 shows how to use histograms in Mathcad.

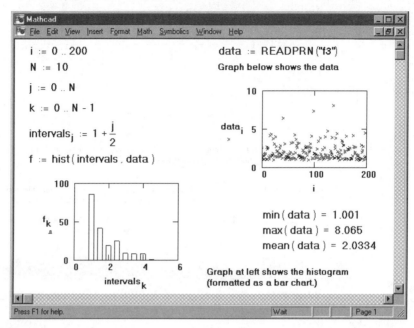

Figure 14-2: A histogram.

Random numbers

Mathcad comes with a number of functions for generating random numbers having a variety of probability distributions. The functional forms of the distributions associated with the following functions are given in the section "Probability distributions" on page 281.

---

rbeta(m, s_1, s_2) Returns a vector of m random numbers having the beta distribution. s_1, $s_2 > 0$ are the shape parameters.

rbinom(m, n, p) Returns a vector of m random numbers having the binomial distribution. $0 \leq p \leq 1$. n is an integer satisfying $n > 0$.

rcauchy(m, l, s) Returns a vector of m random numbers having the Cauchy distribution. $s > 0$ is the scale parameter. l is the location parameter.

rchisq(m, d) Returns a vector of m random numbers having the chi-squared distribution. $d > 0$ is the degrees of freedom.

rexp(m, r)	Returns a vector of m random numbers having the exponential distribution. $r > 0$ is the rate.
rF(m, d_1, d_2)	Returns a vector of m random numbers having the F distribution. $d_1, d_2 > 0$ are the degrees of freedom.
rgamma(m, s)	Returns a vector of m random numbers having the gamma distribution. $s > 0$ is the shape parameter.
rgeom(m, p)	Returns a vector of m random numbers having the geometric distribution. $0 < p \leq 1$.
rlnorm(m, μ, σ)	Returns a vector of m random numbers having the lognormal distribution in which μ is the logmean and $\sigma > 0$ is the logdeviation.
rlogis(m, l, s)	Returns a vector of m random numbers having the logistic distribution in which l is the location parameter and $s > 0$ is the scale parameter.
rnbinom(m, n, p)	Returns a vector of m random numbers having the negative binomial distribution. $0 < p \leq 1$. n is an integer satisfying $n > 0$.
rnorm(m, μ, σ)	Returns a vector of m random numbers having the normal distribution with mean μ and standard deviation $\sigma > 0$.
rpois(m, λ)	Returns a vector of m random numbers having the Poisson distribution. $\lambda > 0$.
rt(m, d)	Returns a vector of m random numbers having Student's t distribution. $d > 0$.
runif(m, a, b)	Returns a vector of m random numbers having the uniform distribution in which b and a are the endpoints of the interval and $a < b$.
rnd(x)	Returns a uniformly distributed random number between 0 and x. Equivalent to runif($1, 0, x$).
rweibull(m, s)	Returns a vector of m random numbers having the Weibull distribution in which $s > 0$ is the shape parameter.

Each time you recalculate an equation containing one of these functions, Mathcad generates new random numbers. To force Mathcad to generate new random numbers, click on the equation containing the function and choose **Calculate** from the **Math** menu. Figure 14-3 shows an example of how to use Mathcad's random number generator. Figure 14-4 shows how to generate a large vector of random numbers having a specified distribution.

These functions have a "seed value" associated with them. Each time you reset the seed, Mathcad generates new random numbers based on that seed. A given seed value will always generate the same sequence of random numbers. Choosing **Calculate** from the **Math** menu advances Mathcad along this random number sequence. Changing the seed value, however, advances Mathcad along an altogether different random number sequence.

To change the seed value, choose **Options** from the **Math** menu and change the value of "seed" on the Built-In Variables tab. Be sure to supply an integer.

To reset Mathcad's random number generator without changing the seed value, choose **Options** from the **Math** menu, click on the Built-In Variables tab, and click "OK" to accept the current seed. Then click on the equation containing the random number generating function and choose **Calculate** from the **Math** menu. Since the randomizer has been reset, Mathcad generates the same random numbers it would generate if you restarted Mathcad.

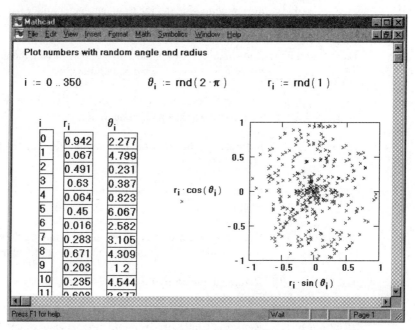

Figure 14-3: Uniformly distributed random numbers. Since the random number generator generates different numbers every time, it's unlikely that you'll be able to reproduce this example exactly as you see it here.

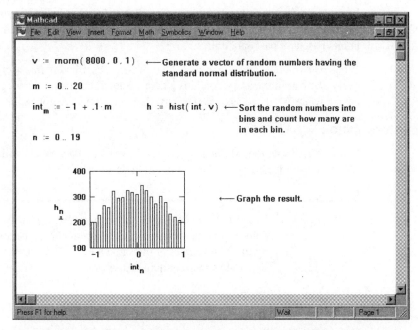

Figure 14-4: A vector of normally distributed random numbers. Since the random numbers are different every time, it's unlikely that you'll be able to reproduce this example exactly as you see it here.

If you want to check a test case several times with the same random numbers, reset the random number generator between calculations as described above.

To see a new set of random numbers, change the seed value as described above. This causes Mathcad to generate a different set of random numbers from what you see when you start Mathcad. Each time you want to reset Mathcad to regenerate these random numbers, reset the seed as described above. To see a different set of random numbers, change the seed value.

Interpolation and prediction functions

Interpolation involves using existing data points to predict values between these data points. Mathcad allows you to either connect the data points with straight lines (linear interpolation) or to connect them with sections of a cubic polynomial (cubic spline interpolation).

Unlike the regression functions discussed in the next section, these interpolation functions return a curve which must pass through the points you specify. Because of this, the resulting function is very sensitive to spurious data points. If your data is noisy, you should consider using the regression functions instead.

Linear prediction involves using existing data values to predict values beyond the existing ones. Mathcad provides a function which allows you to predict future data points based on past data points.

Whenever you use arrays in any of the functions described in this section, be sure that every element in the array contains a data value. Since every element in a array must have a value, Mathcad assigns 0 to any elements you have not explicitly assigned.

Linear interpolation

In linear interpolation, Mathcad connects the existing data points with straight lines. This is accomplished by the *linterp* function described below.

---

linterp(**vx**, **vy**, *x*) Uses the data vectors **vx** and **vy** to return a linearly interpolated *y* value corresponding to the third argument *x*. The arguments **vx** and **vy** must be vectors of the same length. The vector **vx** must contain real values in ascending order.

To find the interpolated value for a particular *x*, Mathcad finds the two points between which the value falls and returns the corresponding *y* value on the straight line between the two points.

For *x* values before the first point in **vx**, Mathcad extrapolates the straight line between the first two data points. For *x* values beyond the last point in **vx**, Mathcad extrapolates the straight line between the last two data points.

For best results, the value of *x* should be between the largest and smallest values in the vector **vx**. The *linterp* function is intended for interpolation, not extrapolation. Consequently, computed values for *x* outside this range are unlikely to be useful. Figure 14-5 shows some examples of linear interpolation.

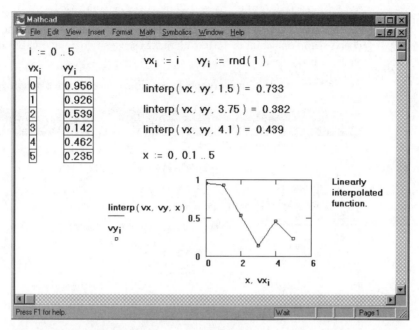

Figure 14-5: Examples of linear interpolation. Since the random number generator gives different numbers every time, you may not be able to recreate this example exactly as you see it.

Cubic spline interpolation

Cubic spline interpolation lets you pass a curve through a set of points in such a way that the first and second derivatives of the curve are continuous across each point. This curve is assembled by taking three adjacent points and constructing a cubic polynomial passing through those points. These cubic polynomials are then strung together to form the completed curve.

To fit a cubic spline curve through a set of points:

■ Create the vectors **vx** and **vy** containing the *x* and *y* coordinates through which you want the cubic spline to pass. The elements of **vx** should be in ascending order. (Although we use the names **vx**, **vy** and **vs**, there is nothing special about these variable names; you can use whatever names you prefer in your own work.)

■ Generate the vector **vs** := cspline(**vx**, **vy**). The vector **vs** is a vector of intermediate results designed to be used with *interp*.

■ To evaluate the cubic spline at an arbitrary point, say *x0*, evaluate (interp(**vs**, **vx**, **vy**, *x0*) where **vs**, **vx** and **vy** are the vectors described earlier.

Note that you could have accomplished the same task by evaluating:

$$\text{interp}(\text{cspline}(\textbf{vx}, \textbf{vy}), \textbf{vx}, \textbf{vy}, x0)$$

As a practical matter, though, you'll probably be evaluating *interp* for many different points. Since the call to *cspline* can be time-consuming, and since the result won't change from one point to the next, it makes sense to do it once and just reuse the result as described above.

Figure 14-6 shows how to compute the spline curve for the example in Figure 14-5.

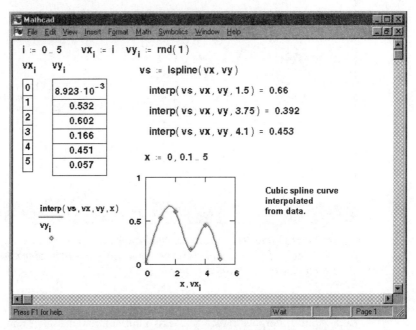

Figure 14-6: Spline curve for the points stored in x and y. Since the random number generator gives different numbers every time, you may not be able to recreate this example exactly as you see it.

Here is a description of the steps involved in the example in Figure 14-6:

■ The equation with the *cspline* function computes the array **vs** containing, among other things, the second derivatives for the spline curve used to fit the points in **vx** and **vy**.

■ Once the **vs** array is computed, the *interp* function computes the interpolated values.

Note that the **vs** array needs to be computed only once, even for multiple interpolations. Since the spline calculations that lead to **vs** are time-consuming, it is more efficient to store these intermediate results as a vector than it is to recalculate them as needed.

In addition to *cspline*, Mathcad comes with two other cubic spline functions, as described below:

cspline(**vx**, **vy**) pspline(**vx**, **vy**) lspline(**vx**, **vy**)	These all return a vector of intermediate results, **vs**, which is used in the *interp* function described below. Arguments **vx** and **vy** must be real vectors of the same length. The values in **vx** must be real and in ascending order.

These three functions differ only in the boundary conditions:

■ The *lspline* function generates a spline curve that approaches a straight line at the endpoints.

■ The *pspline* function generates a spline curve that approaches a parabola at the endpoints.

■ The *cspline* function generates a spline curve that can be fully cubic at the endpoints.

interp(**vs**, **vx**, **vy**, *x*)	Returns the interpolated *y* value corresponding to the argument *x*. The vector **vs** is a vector of intermediate results obtained by evaluating *lspline*, *pspline*, or *cspline* using the data vectors **vx** and **vy**.

To find the interpolated value for a particular *x*, Mathcad finds the two points between which it falls. It then returns the *y* value on the cubic section enclosed by these two points. For *x* values before the first point in **vx**, Mathcad extrapolates the cubic section connecting the first two points of **vx**. Similarly, for *x* values beyond the last point in **vx**, Mathcad extrapolates the cubic section connecting the last two points of **vx**.

For best results, do not use the *interp* function on values of *x* far from the fitted points. Splines are intended for interpolation, not extrapolation. Consequently, computed values for such *x* values are unlikely to be useful.

Interpolating a vector of points

You can use the vectorize operator to return a whole vector of interpolated values corresponding to a vector of data points. This works with both *interp* and *linterp*.

Figure 14-7 shows how to perform this operation. To apply the vectorize operator to the function, click on the function name and press [**Space**] until the function is between the two editing lines. Then press [**Ctrl**]- (hold down the [**Ctrl**] key and press the minus sign).

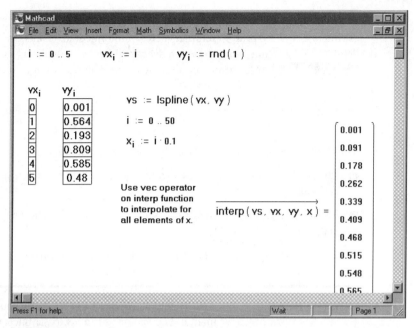

Figure 14-7: Interpolating a vector of points. Note that since these are random numbers, it's unlikely you'll be able to reproduce this example exactly as you see here.

Multivariate cubic spline interpolation

Mathcad handles two dimensional cubic spline interpolation in much the same way as the one-dimensional case discussed earlier. Instead of passing a curve through a set of points in such a way that the first and second derivatives of the curve are continuous across each point, Mathcad passes a surface through a grid of points. This surface corresponds to a cubic polynomial in x and y in which the first and second partial derivatives are continuous in the corresponding direction across each grid point.

The first step in two-dimensional spline interpolation is exactly the same as that in the one-dimensional case: specify the points through which the surface is to pass. The procedure, however, is more complicated because you now have to specify a grid of points:

■ Create the $n \times 2$ matrix **Mxy** whose elements, $Mxy_{i,0}$ and $Mxy_{i,1}$, specify the x and y coordinates along the *diagonal* of a rectangular grid. This matrix plays the exactly the same role as **vx** in the one-dimensional case described earlier. Since these points describe a diagonal, the elements in each column of **Mxy** be in ascending order ($Mxy_{i,k} < Mxy_{j,k}$ whenever $i < j$).

■ Create the $n \times n$ matrix **Mz** whose ijth element is the z coordinate corresponding to the point $x = Mxy_{i,0}$ and $y = Mxy_{j,1}$. This plays exactly the same role as **vy** in the one-dimensional case described earlier.

- Generate the vector **vs** := cspline(**Mxy, Mz**). The vector **vs** is a vector of intermediate results designed to be used with *interp*.

- To evaluate the cubic spline at an arbitrary point, say $(x0, y0)$, evaluate

$$\text{interp}\left(\textbf{vs, Mxy, Mz,} \begin{bmatrix} x0 \\ y0 \end{bmatrix}\right)$$

where **vs**, **Mxy** and **Mz** are the arrays described earlier. The result is the value of the interpolating surface corresponding to the arbitrary point $(x0, y0)$.

Note that you could have accomplished exactly the same task by evaluating:

$$\text{interp}\left(\text{cspline}(\textbf{Mxy, Mz}), \textbf{Mxy, Mz,} \begin{bmatrix} x0 \\ y0 \end{bmatrix}\right)$$

As a practical matter though, you'll probably be evaluating *interp* for many different points. Since the call to *cspline* can be time-consuming, and since the result won't change from one point to the next, it makes sense to call it once and just keep re-using the result as described above.

In addition to *cspline*, Mathcad comes with two other cubic spline functions. The three spline functions are:

cspline(**Mxy, Mz**) pspline(**Mxy, Mz**) lspline(**Mxy, Mz**)	These all return a vector of intermediate results which we'll call **vs**. This vector, **vs**, is used in the *interp* function described below. **Mxy** is an $n \times 2$ matrix whose elements $Mxy_{i,0}$ and $Mxy_{i,1}$ specify points on the diagonal of an $n \times n$ grid. The *ij*th element of the $n \times n$ matrix **Mz** specifies the value of the interpolating surface at $(Mxy_{i,0}, Mxy_{j,1})$.

These three functions differ only in the boundary conditions:

- The *lspline* function generates a spline curve that approaches a plane along the edges.

- The *pspline* function generates a spline curve that approaches a second degree polynomial in x and y along the edges.

- The *cspline* function generates a spline curve that approaches a third degree polynomial in x and y along the edges.

interp(**vs**, **Mxy**, **Mz**, **v**)	Returns the interpolated z value corresponding to the point $x = v_0$ and $y = v_1$. The vector **vs** comes from evaluating *lspline*, *pspline*, or *cspline* using the data matrices **Mxy** and **Mz**.

For best results, do not use the *interp* function on values of x and y far from the grid points. Splines are intended for interpolation, not extrapolation. Consequently, computed values for such x and y values are unlikely to be useful.

Linear prediction

The functions described so far in this section allow you to find data points lying between existing data points. However, you may need to find data points that lie beyond your existing ones. Mathcad provides the function *predict* which uses some of your existing data to predict data points lying beyond the existing ones. This function uses a linear prediction algorithm which is useful when your data is smooth and oscillatory, though not necessarily periodic. Linear prediction can be seen as a kind of extrapolation method but should not be confused with linear or polynomial extrapolation.

predict(**v**, m, n)	Returns n predicted values based on m consecutive values from the data vector **v**. Elements in **v** should represent samples taken at equal intervals.

The *predict* function uses the last m of the original data values to compute prediction coefficients. Once it has these coefficients, it uses the last m points to predict the coordinates of the $(m + 1)$st point, in effect creating a moving window m points wide.

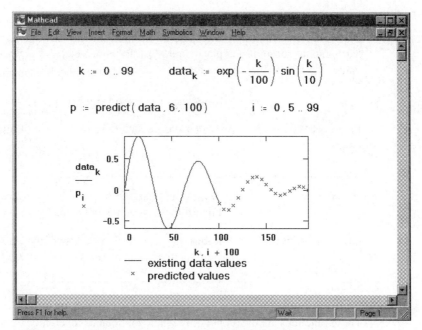

Figure 14-8: Using the predict function to find future data values.

Regression functions

Mathcad includes a number of functions for performing regression. Typically, these functions generate a curve or surface of a specified type which in some sense minimizes the error between itself and the data you supply. The functions differ primarily in the type of curve or surface they use to fit the data.

Unlike the interpolation functions discussed in the previous section, these functions do not require that the fitted curve or surface pass through the data points you supply. The regression functions in this section are therefore far less sensitive to spurious data than the interpolation functions.

Unlike the smoothing functions in the next section, the end result of a regression is an actual function, one that can be evaluated at points in between the points you supply.

Whenever you use arrays in any of the functions described in this section, be sure that every element in the array contains a data value. Since every element in a array must have a value, Mathcad assigns 0 to any elements you have not explicitly assigned.

Linear regression

These functions return the slope and intercept of the line that best fits your data in a least-squares sense. If you place your x values in the vector **vx** and your sampled y values in **vy**, that line is given by:

$$y = \text{slope}(\mathbf{vx}, \mathbf{vy}) \cdot x + \text{intercept}(\mathbf{vx}, \mathbf{vy})$$

Figure 14-9 shows how you can use these functions to fit a line through a set of data points.

---

slope(**vx, vy**)	Returns a scalar: the slope of the least-squares regression line for the data points in **vx** and **vy**.
intercept(**vx, vy**)	Returns a scalar: the y-intercept of the least-squares regression line for the data points in **vx** and **vy**.

These functions are useful not only when your data is inherently linear but when it is exponential as well. More specifically, if your x and y are related by:

$$y = Ae^{kx}$$

You can apply these functions to the log of your data values and make use of the fact that:

$$\log(y) = \log(A) + kx$$

In which case:

$$A = \exp(\text{intercept}(\mathbf{vx}, \mathbf{vy})) \ \text{ and } \ k = \text{slope}(\mathbf{vx}, \mathbf{vy})$$

The resulting fit weighs the errors differently from a least-squares exponential fit but is usually a good approximation.

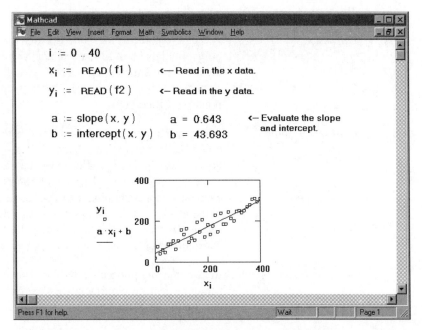

Figure 14-9: Using slope and intercept for linear regression.

Polynomial regression

These functions are useful when you have set of measured y values corresponding to x values and you want to fit a polynomial through those y values.

Use *regress* when you want to use a single polynomial to fit all your data values. The *regress* function lets you fit a polynomial of any order. However as a practical matter, you would rarely need to go beyond $n = 4$.

Since *regress* tries to accommodate all your data points using a single polynomial, it will not work well when your data does not behave like a single polynomial. For example, suppose you expect your y_i to be linear from x_1 to x_{10} and to behave like a cubic equation from x_{11} to x_{20}. If you use *regress* with $n = 3$ (a cubic), you may get a good fit for the second half but a terrible fit for the first half.

The *loess* function, available in Mathcad Professional, alleviates these kinds of problems by performing a more localized regression. Instead of generating a single polynomial the way *regress* does, *loess* generates a different second order polynomial depending on where you are on the curve. It does this by examining the data in a small neighborhood of the point you're interested in. The argument *span* controls the size of this neighborhood. As *span* gets larger, *loess* becomes equivalent to *regress* with $n = 2$. A good default value is $span = 0.75$.

Figure 14-10 shows how *span* affects the fit generated by the *loess* function. Note how a smaller value of *span* makes the fitted curve track fluctuations in data more effectively. A larger value of *span* tends to smear out fluctuations in data and therefore generates a smoother fit.

regress(**vx**, **vy**, *n*)		A vector required by the *interp* function to find the *n*th order polynomial that best fits data vectors **vx** and **vy**. **vx** is an *m* element vector containing *x* coordinates. **vy** is an *m* element vector containing the *y* coordinates corresponding to the *m* points specified in **vx**.
Pro	loess(**vx**, **vy**, *span*)	A vector required by the *interp* function to find the set of second order polynomials that best fit particular neighborhoods of data points specified in vectors **vx** and **vy**. **vx** is an *m* element vector containing *x* coordinates. **vy** is an *m* element vector containing the *y* coordinates corresponding to the *m* points specified in **vx**. The argument *span*, $span > 0$, specifies how large a neighborhood *loess* will consider in performing this local regression.
	interp(**vs**, **vx**, **vy**, *x*)	Returns the interpolated *y* value corresponding to the *x*. The vector **vs** comes from evaluating *loess* or *regress* using the data matrices **vx** and **vy**.

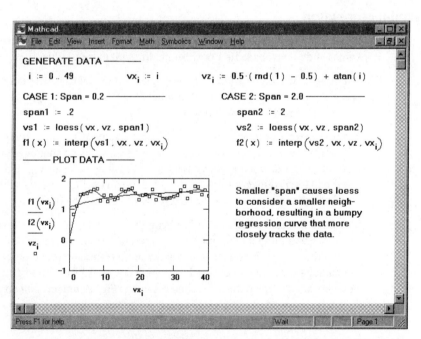

Figure 14-10: Effect of different spans on the loess function. Note that since these are random numbers, it's unlikely you'll be able to reproduce this example exactly as you see here.

Chapter 14 Statistical Functions

Multivariate polynomial regression

The *loess* and *regress* functions discussed in the previous section are also useful when you have set of measured z values corresponding to x and y values and you want to fit a polynomial surface through those z values.

The properties of these functions are described in the previous section. When using these functions to fit z values corresponding to two independent variables x and y, the meanings of the arguments must be generalized. Specifically:

- The argument **vx** which was an m-element vector of x values becomes an m-row and 2 column array, **Mxy**. Each row of **Mxy** contains an x in the first column and a corresponding y value in the second column.

- The argument x for the *interp* function becomes a 2-element vector **v** whose elements are the x and y values at which you want to evaluate the polynomial surface representing the best fit to the data points in **Mxy** and **vz**.

---

regress(**Mxy**, **vz**, k)	A vector required by the *interp* function to find the nth order polynomial that best fits data arrays **Mxy** and **vz**. **Mxy** is an $m \times 2$ matrix containing x-y coordinates. **vz** is an m element vector containing the z coordinates corresponding to the m points specified in **Mxy**.
Pro loess(**Mxy**, **vz**, *span*)	A vector required by the *interp* function to find the set of second order polynomials that best fit particular neighborhoods of data points specified in arrays **Mxy** and **vz**. **Mxy** is an $m \times 2$ matrix containing x-y coordinates. **vz** is an m element vector containing the z coordinates corresponding to the m points specified in **Mxy**. The argument *span*, $span > 0$, specifies how large a neighborhood *loess* will consider in performing this local regression.)
interp(**vs**, **Mxy**, **vz**, **v**)	Returns the interpolated z value corresponding to the point $x = v_0$ and $y = v_1$. The vector **vs** comes from evaluating *loess* or *regress* using the data matrices **Mxy** and **vz**.

You can add independent variables by simply adding columns to the **Mxy** array. You would then add a corresponding number of rows to the vector **v** that you pass to the *interp* function. The *regress* function can have as many independent variables as you want. However, *regress* will calculate more slowly and require more memory when the number of independent variables and the degree are greater than four. The *loess* function is restricted to at most four independent variables.

Keep in mind that for *regress*, the number of data values, m must satisfy

$$m > \binom{n+k-1}{k} \cdot \frac{n+k}{n}$$

where n is the number of independent variables (hence the number of columns in **Mxy**), k is the degree of the desired polynomial, and m is the number of data values (hence the number of rows in **vz**). For example, if you have five explanatory variables and a fourth degree polynomial, you will need more than 126 observations.

Generalized regression

Unfortunately, not all data sets can be modeled by lines or polynomials. There are times when you need to model your data with a linear combination of arbitrary functions, none of which represent terms of a polynomial. For example, in a Fourier series you try to approximate data using a linear combination of complex exponentials. Or you may believe your data can be modeled by a weighted combination of Legendre polynomials, but you just don't know what weights to assign.

The *linfit* function is designed to solve these kinds of problems. If you believe your data could be modeled by a linear combination of arbitrary functions:

$$y = a_0 \cdot f_0(x) + a_1 \cdot f_1(x) + \ldots + a_n \cdot f_n(x)$$

you should use *linfit* to evaluate the a_i. Figure 14-11 shows an example in which a linear combination of three functions: x, x^2, and $(x+1)^{-1}$ is used to model some data.

There are times however when the flexibility of *linfit* is still not enough. Your data may have to be modeled not by a linear combination of data but by some function whose parameters must be chosen. For example, if your data can be modeled by the sum:

$$f(x) = a_1 \cdot \sin(2x) + a_2 \cdot \tanh(3x)$$

and all you need to do is solve for the unknown weights a_1 and a_2, then you have a *linfit* type of problem.

By contrast, if instead your data is to be modeled by the sum:

$$f(x) = 2 \cdot \sin(a_1 x) + 3 \cdot \tanh(a_2 x)$$

and you now have to solve for the unknown parameters a_1 and a_2, you would have a *genfit* problem.

Anything you can do with *linfit* you can also do, albeit less conveniently, with *genfit*. The difference between these two functions is the difference between solving a system of linear equations and solving a system of nonlinear equations. The former is easily done using the methods of linear algebra. The latter is far more difficult and generally must be solved by iteration. This explains why *genfit* needs a vector of guess values as an argument and *linfit* does not.

Figure 14-12 shows an example in which *genfit* is used to find the exponent that best fits a set of data.

linfit(vx, vy, F)   Returns a vector containing the coefficients used to create a linear combination of the functions in **F** which best approximates the data in vectors **vx** and **vy**. **F** is a function which returns a vector consisting of the functions to be linearly combined.

genfit(vx, vy, vg, F)   A vector containing the parameters that make a function f of x and n parameters $u_0, u_1, ..., u_n$ best approximate the data in **vx** and **vy**. **F** is a function that returns an $n + 1$ element vector containing f and its partial derivatives with respect to its n parameters. **vg** is an n-element vector of guess values for the n parameters.

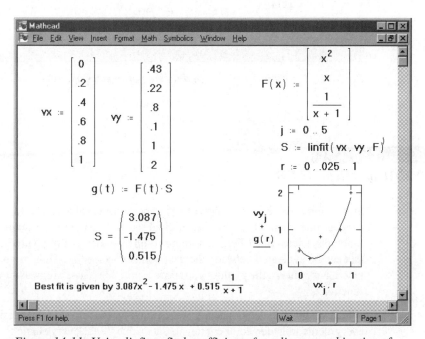

Figure 14-11: Using linfit to find coefficients for a linear combination of functions that best fits the data.

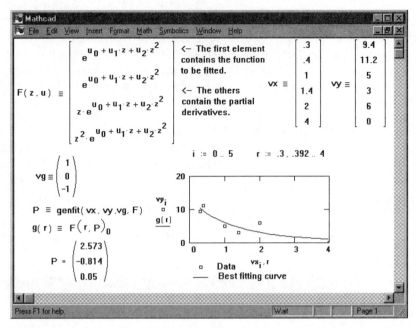

Figure 14-12: Using genfit for finding the parameters of a function so that it best fits the data.

Smoothing functions

Smoothing involves taking a set of *y* (and possibly *x*) values and returning a new set of *y* values that is smoother than the original set. Unlike the regression and interpolation functions discussed earlier, smoothing results in a new set of *y* values, not a function that can be evaluated between the data points you specify. Thus, if you are interested in *y* values *between* the *y* values you specify, you should use a regression or interpolation function.

Whenever you use vectors in any of the functions described in this section, be sure that every element in the vector contains a data value. Since every element in a vector must have a value, Mathcad assigns 0 to any elements you have not explicitly assigned.

The *medsmooth* function is the most robust of the three since it is least likely to be affected by spurious data points. This function uses a running median smoother, computes the residuals, smooths the residuals the same way, and adds these two smoothed vectors together. The details are as follows:

■ Evaluation of medsmooth(**vy**, *n*) begins with the running median of the input vector **vy**. We'll call this **vy′**. The *i*th element is given by:

$$vy'_i = \text{median}(vy_{i-(n-1/2)}, \ldots, vy_i, \ldots, vy_{i+(n-1/2)})$$

■ It then evaluates the residuals: $\mathbf{vr} = \mathbf{vy} - \mathbf{vy'}$.

■ The residual vector, $\mathbf{vr}$, is smoothed using the same procedure described in step 1. This creates a smoothed residual vector, $\mathbf{vr'}$.

■ The *medsmooth* function returns the sum of these two smoothed vectors: $\text{medsmooth}(\mathbf{vy}, n) = \mathbf{vy'} + \mathbf{vr'}$.

Note that *medsmooth* will leave the first and last $(n-1)/2$ points unchanged. In practice, the length of the smoothing window, n, should be small compared to the length of the data set.

The *ksmooth* function in Mathcad Professional uses a Gaussian kernel to compute local weighted averages of the input vector $\mathbf{vy}$. This smoother is most useful when your data lies along a band of relatively constant width. If your data lies scattered along a band whose width fluctuates considerably, you should use an adaptive smoother like *supsmooth*, also available in Mathcad Professional.

For each vy_i in the n-element vector $\mathbf{vy}$, the *ksmooth* function returns a new vy'_i given by:

$$vy'_i = \frac{\sum_{j=1}^{n} K\left(\frac{vx_i - vx_j}{b}\right) vy_j}{\sum_{j=1}^{n} K\left(\frac{vx_i - vx_j}{b}\right)}$$

where:

$$K(t) = \frac{1}{\sqrt{2\pi} \cdot (0.37)} \cdot \exp\left(-\frac{t^2}{2 \cdot (0.37)^2}\right)$$

and b is a bandwidth which you supply to the *ksmooth* function. The bandwidth is usually set to a few times the spacing between data points on the x axis depending on how big a window you want to use when smoothing.

The *supsmooth* function uses a symmetric k nearest neighbor linear least-squares fitting procedure to make a series of line segments through your data. Unlike *ksmooth* which uses a fixed bandwidth for all your data, *supsmooth* will adaptively choose different bandwidths for different portions of your data.

medsmooth(**vy**, *n*)	Returns an *m*-element vector created by smoothing **vy** with running medians. **vy** is an *m*-element vector of real numbers. *n* is the width of the window over which smoothing occurs. *n* must be an odd number less than the number of elements in **vy**.

Pro ksmooth(**vx**,**vy**, *b*) — Returns an *n*-element vector created by using a Gaussian kernel to return weighted averages of **vy**. **vy** and **vx** are *n*-element vectors of real numbers. The bandwidth *b* controls the smoothing window and should be set to a few times the spacing between your *x* data points.

Pro supsmooth(**vx**,**vy**) — Returns an *n*-element vector created by the piecewise use of a symmetric *k*-nearest neighbor linear least-squares fitting procedure in which *k* is adaptively chosen. **vy** and **vx** are *n*-element vectors of real numbers. The elements of **vx** must be in increasing order.

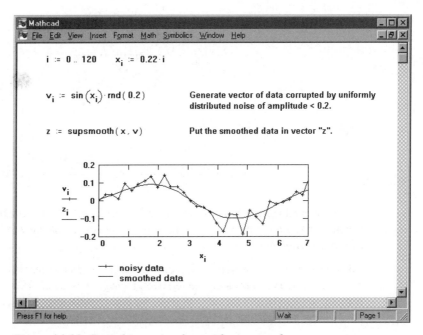

Figure 14-13: Smoothing noisy data with supsmooth.

Chapter 15
Solving Equations

This chapter describes how to solve equations ranging from a single equation in one unknown to systems of up to fifty equations in fifty unknowns. The techniques described here generate numeric solutions. Chapter 17, "Symbolic Calculation," describes a variety of techniques for solving equations symbolically.

The following sections make up this chapter:

Solving one equation

How to use Mathcad's *root* function to numerically solve one equation in one unknown.

Systems of equations

How to use "solve blocks" to solve systems of *n* equations in *n* unknowns.

Using the solver effectively

Examples of how to solve systems of equations efficiently for various values of a parameter.

Solving one equation

To solve a single equation in a single unknown, use the *root* function. This function takes an expression and one of the variables from the expression. It then varies that variable until the expression is equal to zero. Once this is done, the function returns the value that makes the expression equal zero.

---

root($f(z)$), z) Returns the value of z at which the expression or function $f(z)$ is equal to 0. Both arguments to this function must be scalar. The function returns a scalar.

The first argument is either a function defined elsewhere in the worksheet, or an expression. It must return a scalar value.

The second argument is a variable name that appears in the expression. It is this variable that Mathcad will vary to make the expression go to zero. You should assign a number to this variable before using the *root* function. Mathcad uses this as a starting value in its search for a solution.

For example, to define a as the solution to the equation <Insert equation here>, follow these steps:

- Define a guess value for x. Type **x:3**.
  Your choice of guess value determines
  which root Mathcad returns.

$$x := 3$$

- Set the whole expression equal to zero. In other words, rewrite $e^x = x^3$ as $x^3 - e^x = 0$. It is this expression that you give the *root* function.

- Type
  a:root(x^3[Space]-
  e^x[Space],x)
  This defines the variable a to be a root of the desired equation.

$$a := root(x^3 - e^x, x)$$

- Type **a=** to see the root.

$$a = 1.857$$

When you use the root function, keep these suggestions in mind:

- Make sure that the variable is defined with a guess value before you use the *root* function.

- For expressions with several roots, for example $x^2 - 1 = 0$, your guess value determines which root Mathcad will return. Figure 15-1 shows an example in which the *root* function returns several different values, each of which depends on the initial guess value.

■ Mathcad will solve for complex roots as well as real roots. To find a complex root, you must start with a complex value for the initial guess.

■ Solving an equation of the form $f(x) = g(x)$ is equivalent to using the *root* function as follows:

$$\text{root}(f(x) - g(x), x)$$

The root function can solve only one equation in one unknown. To solve several equations simultaneously, use the technique described in the next section, "Systems of Equations." To solve an equation symbolically, or to find an exact numerical answer in terms of elementary functions, choose **Solve for Variable** from the **Symbolic** menu or use the **solve** keyword. See Chapter 17, "Symbolic Calculation."

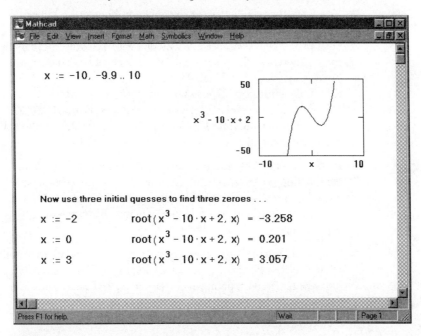

Figure 15-1: Using a plot and the root function to find roots of an expression.

What to do when the root function does not converge

Mathcad evaluates the *root* function using the *secant method*. The guess value you supply for x becomes the starting point for successive approximations to the root value. When the magnitude of $f(x)$ evaluated at the proposed root is less than the value of the predefined variable TOL, the *root* function returns a result.

If after many approximations Mathcad still cannot find an acceptable answer, it marks the *root* function with an error message indicating its inability to converge to a result. This error can be caused by any of the following:

Solving one equation 311

- The expression has no roots.

- The roots of the expression are far from the initial guess.

- The expression has local maxima or minima between the initial guess and the roots.

- The expression has discontinuities between the initial guess and the roots.

- The expression has a complex root but the initial guess was real (or vice versa).

To find the cause of the error, try plotting the expression. This will help determine whether or not the expression crosses the x-axis and if so, approximately where it does so. In general, the closer your initial guess is to where the expression crosses the x-axis, the more quickly the *root* function will converge on an acceptable result.

Hints on using the root function

Here are some hints on getting the most out of the *root* function:

- To change the accuracy of the *root* function, change the value of the built-in variable TOL. If you increase TOL, the *root* function will converge more quickly, but the answer will be less accurate. If you decrease TOL, the *root* function will converge more slowly, but the answer will be more accurate. To change TOL at a specified point in the worksheet, include a definition like $TOL := 0.01$. To change TOL for the whole worksheet, choose **Options** from the **Math** menu, click on the Built-In Variables tab, and replace the number in the text box beside "TOL." After you click "OK," choose **Calculate Worksheet** from the **Math** menu to update the entire worksheet using the new value of TOL.

- If an expression has multiple roots, try different guess values to find them. Plotting the function is a good way to determine how many roots there are, where they are, and what initial guesses are likely to find them. Figure 15-1 shows an example of this. If two roots are close together, you may have to reduce TOL to distinguish between them.

- If $f(x)$ has a small slope near its root, then $\text{root}(f(x), x)$ may converge to a value r that is relatively far from the actual root. In such cases, even though $|f(r)| < TOL$, r may be far from the point where $f(r) = 0$. To find a more accurate root, decrease the value of TOL. Or, try finding $\text{root}(g(x),x)$, where

$$g(x) = \frac{f(x)}{\frac{d}{dx}f(x)}$$

- For an expression $f(x)$ with a known root a, solving for additional roots of $f(x)$ is equivalent to solving for roots of $h(x) = (f(x))/(x-a)$. Dividing out known roots like this is useful for resolving two roots that may be close together. It's often easier to solve for roots of $h(x)$ as defined here than it is to try to find other roots for $f(x)$ with different guesses.

Chapter 15 Solving Equations

Solving an equation repeatedly

Suppose you want to solve an equation many times while varying one of the parameters in the equation. For example, suppose you want to solve the equation $e^x = a \cdot x^2$ for several different values of the parameter a. The simplest way to do this is to define a function:

$$f(a, x) := \text{root}(e^x - a \cdot x^2, x)$$

To solve the equation for a particular value of a, supply both a and a guess value, x, as arguments to this function. Then evaluate the function by typing **f(a,x)=**.

Figure 15-2 shows an example of how such a function can be used to find several solutions to the *root* function. Note that since the guess value, x, is passed into the function itself, there is no need to define it elsewhere in the worksheet.

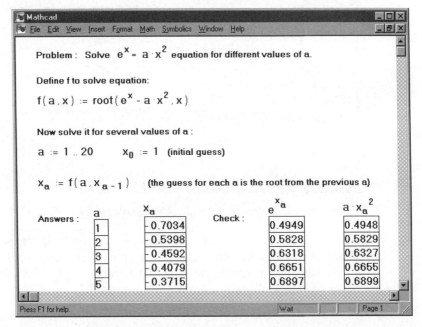

Figure 15-2: Defining a user function with the root function.

Finding the roots of a polynomial

To find the roots of an expression having the form:

$$v_n x^n + \dots + v_2 x^2 + v_1 x + v_0$$

you can use the *polyroots* function rather than the *root* function. Unlike *root*, *polyroots* does not require a guess value. Moreover, *polyroots* returns all roots at once, whether real or complex. Figure 15-3 and Figure 15-4 show examples.

polyroots(**v**) Returns the roots of an *n*th degree polynomial whose coefficients are in **v**, a vector of length $n + 1$. Returns a vector of length *n*.

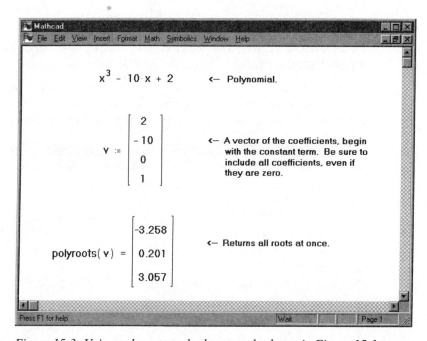

Figure 15-3: Using polyroots to do the example shown in Figure 15-1.

The *polyroots* function will always return numerical values for the roots of a polynomial. To find the roots symbolically, use the **solve** symbolic keyword or choose **Solve for Variable** from the **Symbolic** menu. See Chapter 17, "Symbolic Calculation."

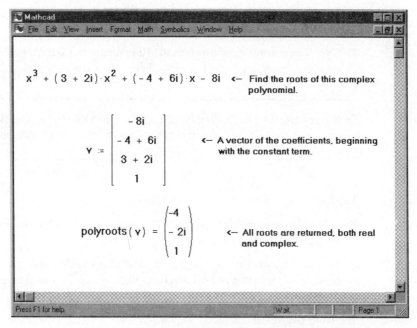

Figure 15-4: Using polyroots to find the roots of a polynomial.

Systems of equations

Mathcad lets you solve a system of up to fifty simultaneous equations in fifty unknowns. The first part of this section sketches the procedure. The remainder contains several examples as well as a discussion of some common errors. The method given here will always return numbers for the unknown variables. To see the unknowns in terms of the other variables and constants, use the symbolic solve blocks discussed in the section "Solving equations symbolically" in Chapter 17.

There are four steps to solving a system of simultaneous equations. These are:

- Provide an initial guess for all the unknowns you intend to solve for. Mathcad solves equations by making a series of guesses which ultimately converge on the right answer. The initial guesses you provide give Mathcad a place to start searching for solutions.

- Type the word *Given*. This tells Mathcad that what follows is a system of equations. You can type *Given* in any combination of upper and lower case letters, and in any font. Just be sure you don't type it while in a text region or paragraph.

- Now type the equations and inequalities in any order below the word *Given*. Make sure you use the symbol "=" to separate the left and right sides of an equation. Press

[Ctrl]= to type "=." You can separate the left and right sides of an inequality with any of the symbols <, >, ≤, and ≥.

■ Type any equation that involves the *Find* function. Like *Given*, you can use any combination of upper and lowercase letters. You can also use any font, size or style.

Find($z1, z2, z3, \dots$) Returns the solution to a system of equations. Number of arguments matches the number of unknowns.

The *Find* function returns values as follows:

■ If *Find* has one argument, it returns the value of that variable that solves the equation between it and the *Given*.

■ If *Find* has more than one argument, it returns a vector of answers. For example, Find($z1, z2$) returns a vector containing the values of $z1$ and $z2$ that solve the system of equations.

The word *Given*, the equations and inequalities that follow, and whatever expression involves the *Find* function, form a "solve block."

Figure 15-5 shows a worksheet that contains a solve block for one equation in one unknown. Since there is only one equation, only one equation appears between the word *Given* and the expression involving *Find*. Since there is only one unknown, the *Find* function has only one argument. For one equation in one unknown, you can also use the *root* function shown below.

$$a := \text{root}(x^2 + 10 - e^x, x)$$

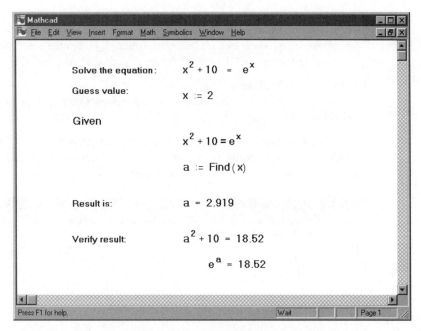

Figure 15-5: A solve block with one equation in one unknown.

Mathcad is very specific about the types of expressions that can appear between the *Given* and the *Find*. The table below lists all the expressions that can be placed in a solve block. These expressions are often called "constraints." In the table below, *x* and *y* represent real-valued scalar expressions, *z* and *w* represent arbitrary scalar expressions.

Condition	Keystroke	Description
$z=w$	[Ctrl]=	Constrained to be equal.
$x>y$	>	Greater than.
$x<y$	<	Less than.
$x\geq y$	[Ctrl]0	Greater than or equal to.
$x\leq y$	[Ctrl]9	Less than or equal to.

Note that Mathcad does not allow the following inside a solve block:

■ Constraints with "≠" in solve blocks.

■ Range variables or expressions involving range variables of any kind.

■ Inequalities of the form $a < b < c$.

If you want to include the outcome of a solve block in an iterative calculation, see the section "Using the solver effectively" on page 325.

Solve blocks cannot be nested inside each other. Each solve block can have only one *Given* and one *Find*. You can however, define a function like $f(x) := \text{Find}(x)$ at the end of one solve block and use this same function in another solve block. This too is discussed in the section "Using the solver effectively" on page 325.

As a rule, you should never use assignment statements (statements like **x := 1**) inside a solve block. Mathcad marks assignment statements inside solve blocks with an appropriate error message.

Figure 15-6 shows a solve block with several kinds of constraints. There are two equations and two unknowns. As a result, the *Find* function contains two arguments, x and y, and returns a vector with two components.

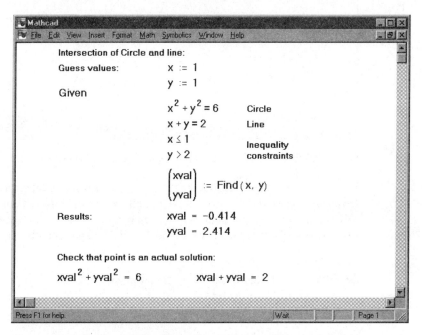

Figure 15-6: A solve block with both equations and inequalities.

What to do with your solution

The *Find* function that terminates a solve block behaves like any other function. There are three things you can do with it:

- You can display it with an equation like $\text{Find}(variable) = $. An example is shown in the top half of Figure 15-7. If you have several variables, you can display a vector of results with an equation like: $\text{Find}(var1, var2, \ldots) = $. An example of how this would look for a system of two equations in two unknowns is shown in Figure 15-8.

- You can define a variable in terms of it by ending the solve block with an equation like $a := \text{Find}(x)$. This is useful when you want to use the solution of a system of equations elsewhere in the worksheet. Once you make this definition, a has the solved value of the variable. An example of this is shown in the lower half of Figure

15-7. If the *Find* returns a vector of values, you can enter an equation like *variable* := Find(*var1*, *var2*, ...). If you do this, *variable* will end up being a vector instead of a scalar. You can also define variables as shown in Figure 15-6.

■ Finally, you can define another function in terms of it by ending the solve block with an equation like $f(a, b, c) := \text{Find}(var1, var2, ...)$. This construction is useful for solving system of equations repeatedly for different values of some parameters $a, b, c, ...$ that appear within the system of equations itself. This method is described in the section"Using the solver effectively" on page 325.

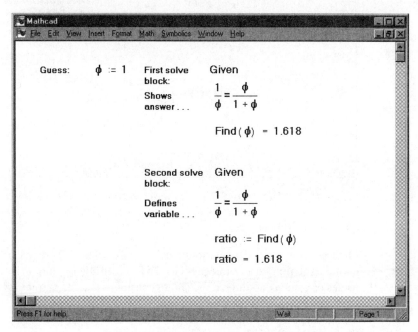

Figure 15-7: You can display the result of a solve block directly, or you can put the result in a variable name for later use.

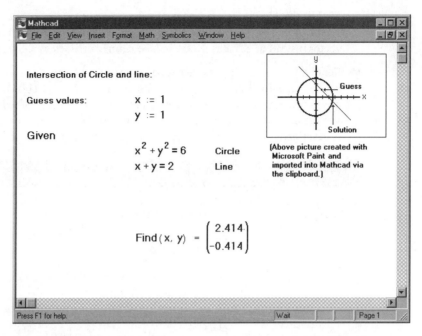

Figure 15-8: When there are two or more unknowns, the Find function no longer returns a scalar. Instead, it returns a vector with as many elements as there are unknowns.

Mathcad can return only one solution for a solve block. There may, however, be multiple solutions to a set of equations. To find a different solution, try different starting values or enter an additional inequality constraint that the current solution does not satisfy. Figure 15-9 shows how different starting values can yield a solution different from that shown in Figure 15-8. Figure 15-10 shows how to add an inequality to force Mathcad to find a different solution.

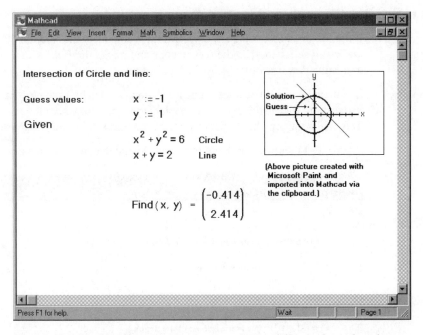

Figure 15-9: A different guess leads to a solution different from that shown in Figure 15-8.

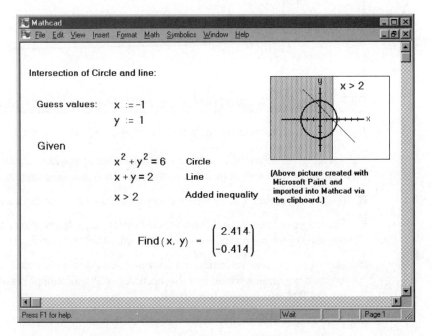

Figure 15-10: Adding a constraint forces a different solution.

What to do when the solver does not reach a solution

If the solver cannot make any further improvements to the solution but the constraints are *not* all satisfied, then the solver stops and marks the *Find* with an error message indicating that it was unable to find a solution.

If you are having difficulty finding a solution, it often helps to plot the curve or curves in question. Plotting can provide graphical insight into where the solution might be. This will help you choose appropriate initial guesses for the variables.

Figure 15-11 shows a problem for which Mathcad could not find a solution.

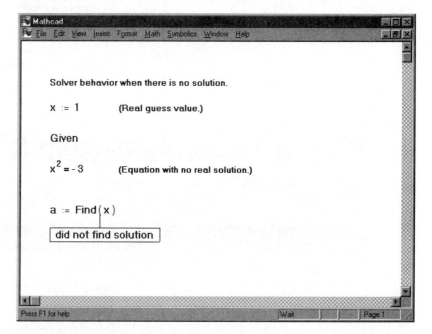

Figure 15-11: A problem in which the solver fails to find a solution.

The solver gives up trying to solve a system of equations whenever the difference between successive approximations to the solution is greater than TOL *and*:

■ The solver reaches a point where it cannot reduce the error any further.

■ The solver reaches a point from which there is no preferred direction. Because of this, the solver has no basis on which to make further iterations.

■ The solver reaches the limit of its accuracy. Roundoff errors make it unlikely that further computation would increase accuracy of the solution. This often happens if you set TOL to a value below 10^{-15}.

The following problems may cause this sort of failure:

■ There may actually be no solution.

- You may have given real guesses for an equation with no real solution. If the solution for a variable is complex, the solver will not find it unless the starting value for that variable is also complex. Figure 15-11 shows an example.

- The solver may have become trapped in a local minimum for the error values. The solving method that Mathcad uses will sometimes reach a point from which it cannot minimize the errors any further. To find the actual solution, try using different starting values or add an inequality to keep Mathcad from being trapped in the local minimum.

- The solver may have become trapped on a point that is not a local minimum, but from which it cannot determine where to go next. The strategies for avoiding this problem are the same as those for avoiding a local minimum: change the initial guesses or add an inequality to avoid the undesirable stopping point.

- It may not be possible to solve the constraints to within the desired tolerance. If the value of TOL is relatively small, Mathcad may have reached something very close to a solution but still be unable to solve all the constraints to an error less than TOL. Try defining TOL with a larger value somewhere above the solve block. Increasing the tolerance changes what Mathcad considers close enough to call a solution.

What to do when there are too few constraints

If there are fewer constraints than variables, Mathcad cannot run the solver at all. Mathcad then marks the *Find* with an appropriate error message.

A problem like that shown in Figure 15-12 is *underdetermined.* The constraints do not give enough information to find a solution. Because there are five arguments in the *Find* function, Mathcad thinks that you want to solve two equations with five unknowns. In general, such a problem has an infinite number of solutions.

To use the solver in Mathcad, you must provide at least as many equations as there are variables to solve for. If you specify the value of some of the variables, you may be able to solve for the remaining variables. Figure 15-13 shows how to fix the problem in Figure 15-12. Because the *Find* function contains only the arguments z and w, Mathcad knows that you want x, y, and v to be held constant at 10, 50 and 0 respectively. A solve block with two equations becomes legitimate because there are now only two unknowns, z and w.

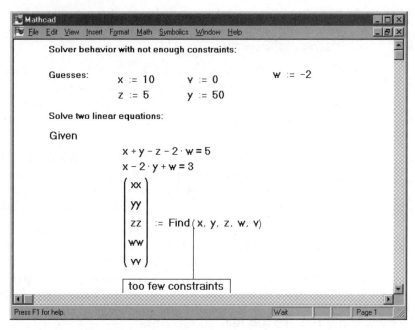

Figure 15-12: Five arguments in the Find make the solver think you want to solve two equations in five unknowns.

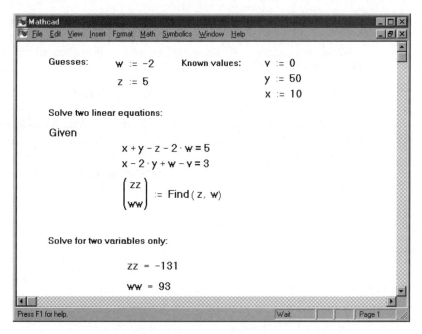

Figure 15-13: The problem can be solved with fewer variables as arguments to Find.

Chapter 15 Solving Equations

Using the solver effectively

This section provides some ideas on how to effectively exploit Mathcad's ability to solve systems of simultaneous equations.

Repeatedly solving an equation

The techniques given thus far, while they are effective for solving a particular system of equations, are limited by two things:

- Every time you use a *Find*, you must have the rest of the solve block to go with it.

- If you want to change some of the parameters or constants in your system of equations to see how these affect the solution, you have to go all the way back to the solve block to change them.

Both these drawbacks are overcome by Mathcad's ability to define a function in terms of a solve block.

If you define a function with *Find* somewhere on the right hand side, this function will solve the system of equations each time you use it. This overcomes the first problem.

If this function has as its arguments the same parameters that you want to vary in the solve block, you can simply change the parameters by changing the numbers you place in the function's argument list. This overcomes the second problem.

Figure 15-14 shows a concrete example. The friction factor, f, of a pipe depends on the pipe's diameter D, its roughness ε, and the Reynolds number R. It's quite conceivable that you would want to experiment with different size pipes (D) made of different types of concrete (ε).

The equation in Figure 15-14 shows the relationship between these parameters. The equation is too complicated to define a function of R, D and ε simply by solving for f in terms of R, D and ε.

You can, however, define a function in terms of a solve block. Whenever you ask Mathcad to evaluate the function $FricFac(\varepsilon, D, R)$, Mathcad takes the ε, D, and R that you supply, replaces the corresponding variables in the solve block, solves for f, and returns the value.

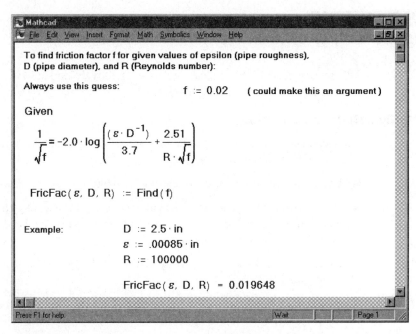

To find friction factor f for given values of epsilon (pipe roughness), D (pipe diameter), and R (Reynolds number):

Always use this guess: $\qquad f := 0.02 \qquad$ (could make this an argument)

Given

$$\frac{1}{\sqrt{f}} = -2.0 \cdot \log\left(\frac{(\varepsilon \cdot D^{-1})}{3.7} + \frac{2.51}{R \cdot \sqrt{f}}\right)$$

FricFac(ε, D, R) := Find(f)

Example: $\qquad$ D := 2.5 · in

$\qquad \varepsilon$:= .00085 · in

$\qquad$ R := 100000

$\qquad$ FricFac(ε, D, R) = 0.019648

Figure 15-14: Defining a function in terms of a solve block.

Suppose that you've settled on a pipe size and material (*D* and ε), and you now want to try several different values of the Reynolds numbers. Although the *FricFac* function in Figure 15-14 was defined in terms of a solve block, it still is a function like any other. As such, you can use it with range variables.

Figure 15-15 shows how to solve for and plot the friction factor for many different values of the Reynolds number. Note that when you use range variables in conjunction with a solve block this way, you are actually solving the system of equations once for each value of the range variable. As a result, this type of calculation has the potential to be quite time consuming.

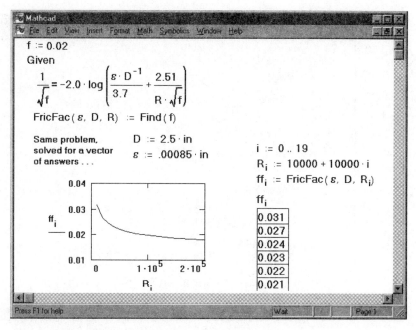

Figure 15-15: A vector of solutions.

The previous example involves only one equation in one unknown. It is possible to solve a system of equations iteratively as well; however, you must be careful not to ask Mathcad to display a table in which each entry in the table is something other than a single number. The example shown in Figure 15-16, a variation of Figure 15-10, shows how you can do this.

Suppose you are looking for the intersection of a line and a circle of varying radius, R. In keeping with the example of Figure 15-15, you could define a function in terms of a solve block. In this case, the appropriate function is $F(R) := Find(x, y)$. This function returns a vector whose elements are the x and y coordinates of the intersection.

The key difference is that this function returns a *vector* of two values for each value of R. Therefore when you ask for the answers by typing **F(R) =**, you are asking not for a table of numbers, but a table in which each element is a vector of two numbers. Since Mathcad has no way to display such a thing on your screen it returns an error message.

The solution is to display a table of the components $F(R)_0$ and $F(R)_1$ separately. By typing **F(R) [0=**, you get a table of all the x values of the intersection points. Similarly, by typing **F(R) [1=**, you get a table of all the y values of the intersection points.

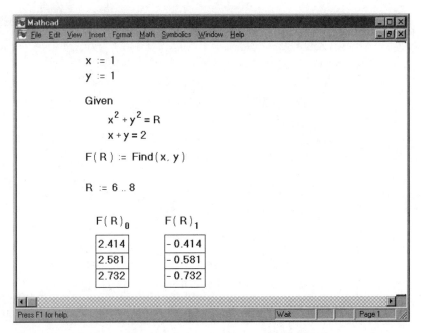

Figure 15-16: How to display three solutions, each of which is a two element vector.

Solving the same problem for different variables

You will occasionally run into a problem in which you want to change the roles of knowns and unknowns in an equation. For example, consider the equation that relates interest rate, loan amount, term of loan, and payments. If you know three of these four quantities, you can solve for the missing one.

The worksheet in Figure 15-17 shows that for a 12% loan on a 30-year mortgage and a payment of $1000 per month, the largest possible loan is $97,218.33.

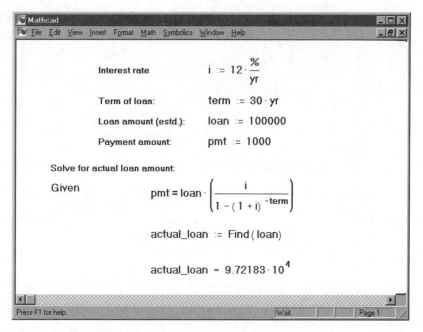

Figure 15-17: Solving for the loan in a mortgage.

With a few simple changes, the same worksheet can be used to solve for the interest rate. Suppose now that the amount of the loan is known to be $120,000. How far would interest rates have to drop to before the payments dropped to $1000 per month? Figure 15-18 shows the answer.

If you compare Figure 15-17 and Figure 15-18, you'll see that they are very much the same. The main difference lies in the argument of the *Find* function. To change what is fixed and what is variable in an equation, simply change the arguments of the *Find* function.

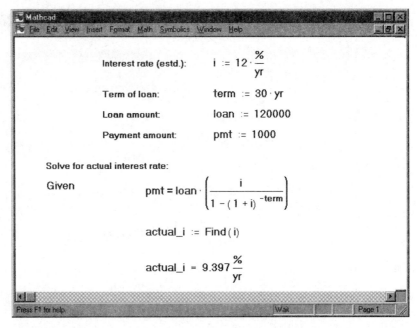

Figure 15-18: Solving for the interest rate in a mortgage.

Approximate solutions

Mathcad supplies a function very similar to *Find* called *Minerr*. This function uses exactly the same algorithm as *Find*. The difference is that if the solver cannot make any further improvements to the solution, *Minerr* returns a value anyway. The *Find* function on the other hand, will return an error message indicating that it could not find a solution. You use *Minerr* exactly the way you would use *Find*.

Minerr($z1, z2, z3, \ldots$)   Returns the solution to a system of equations. Number of arguments matches the number of unknowns.

Minerr usually returns an answer that minimizes the errors in the constraints. However, *Minerr* cannot verify that its answers represent an absolute minimum for the errors in the constraints. If you use *Minerr* in a solve block, you should always include additional checks on the reasonableness of the results. The built-in variable ERR gives the size of the error vector for the approximate solution. There is no built-in variable for determining the size of the error for individual solutions to the unknowns.

Minerr is particularly useful for solving certain nonlinear least-squares problems. Figure 15-19 shows an example in which *Minerr* is used to obtain the unknown parameters in a Weibull distribution. The function *genfit* is also useful for solving nonlinear least-squares problems. See Chapter 14, "Statistical Functions," for more information on *genfit*.

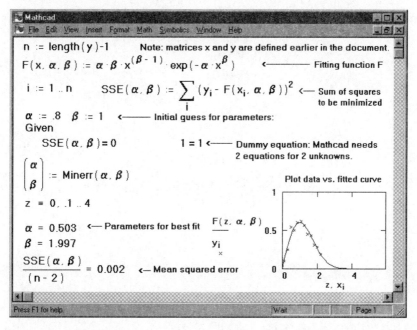

Figure 15-19: Using the minerr function to do nonlinear least-squares fitting.

Using the symbolic solver

You can usually find numerical roots quickly and accurately with Mathcad's *root* function. But there are some circumstances in which you might want to use Mathcad's symbolic solver find exact or approximate roots:

■ If the equation you're solving has a parameter, a symbolic solution may allow you to express the answer directly in terms of the parameter. Then instead of solving the equation over again for each new value of the parameter, you can just substitute its value into your symbolic solution.

■ If you need all the complex roots of a polynomial of degree 4 or less, the symbolic solver will give them to you in a single vector, either exactly or numerically. The symbolic solver will also find complete solutions for *some* polynomials of higher degree.

See the section "Solving equations symbolically" in Chapter 17 for more information about solving equations symbolically.

Chapter 15 Solving Equations

Chapter 16
Solving Differential Equations

This chapter describes how to solve both ordinary and partial differential equations having real-valued solutions. Mathcad Standard comes with the *rkfixed* function, a general-purpose Runge-Kutta solver that can be used on *n*th order differential equations with initial conditions or on systems of differential equations. Mathcad Professional includes a variety of additional, more specialized functions for solving differential equations. Some of these exploit properties of the differential equation to improve speed and accuracy. Others are useful when you intend to plot the solution rather than simply evaluate it at an endpoint.

The following sections make up this chapter:

Solving ordinary differential equations

Using the *rkfixed* function to solve an *n*th order ordinary differential equation with initial conditions. This section is a prerequisite for all other sections in this chapter.

Systems of differential equations

How to adapt the *rkfixed* function to solve systems of differential equations with initial conditions.

Pro **Specialized differential equation solvers**

A description of additional differential equation solving functions and when you may want to use them.

Pro **Boundary value problems**

How to solve boundary value problems involving multivariate functions.

Solving ordinary differential equations

In a differential equation, you solve for an unknown function rather than just a number. For ordinary differential equations, the unknown function is a function of one variable. Partial differential equations are differential equations in which the unknown is a function of two or more variables.

Mathcad has a variety of functions for returning the solution to an ordinary differential equation. Each of these functions solves differential equations numerically. You'll always get back a matrix containing the values of the function evaluated over a set of points. These functions differ in the particular algorithm each uses for solving differential equations. Despite these differences however, each of these functions requires you to specify at least three things:

- The initial conditions.

- A range of points over which you want the solution to be evaluated.

- The differential equation itself, written in the particular form discussed in this chapter.

This section shows how to solve a single ordinary differential equation using the function *rkfixed*. It begins with an example of how to solve a simple first order differential equation and then proceeds to show how to solve higher order differential equations.

First order differential equations

A first order differential equation is one in which the highest order derivative of the unknown function is the first derivative. Figure 16-1 shows an example of how to solve the relatively simple differential equation:

$$\frac{dy}{dx} + 3 \cdot y = 0$$

subject to the initial condition:

$$y(0) = 4$$

The function *rkfixed* in Figure 16-1 uses the fourth order Runge-Kutta method to return a two-column matrix in which:

- The left-hand column contains the points at which the solution to the differential equation is evaluated.

- The right-hand column contains the corresponding values of the solution.

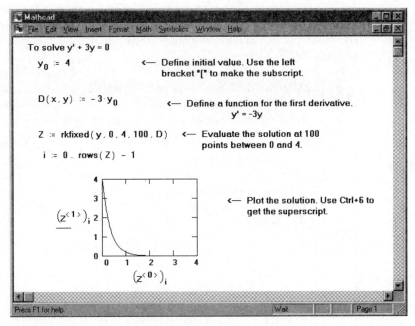

To solve y' + 3y = 0

$y_0 := 4$ <— Define initial value. Use the left
bracket "[" to make the subscript.

$D(x, y) := -3 \cdot y_0$ <— Define a function for the first derivative.
y' = -3y

$Z := rkfixed(y, 0, 4, 100, D)$ <— Evaluate the solution at 100
points between 0 and 4.

$i := 0 .. rows(Z) - 1$

<— Plot the solution. Use Ctrl+6 to
get the superscript.

Figure 16-1: Solving a first order differential equation.

The arguments to the *rkfixed* function are:

rkfixed($\mathbf{y}$, *x1*, *x2*, *npoints*, $\mathbf{D}$)

$\mathbf{y}$ = A vector of *n* initial values where *n* is the order of the differential equation
or the size of the system of equations you're solving. For a first order
differential equation like that in Figure 16-1, the vector degenerates to one
point, $y(0) = y(x1)$.

x1, x2 = The endpoints of the interval on which the solution to the differential
equations will be evaluated. The initial values in $\mathbf{y}$ are the values at *x1*.

npoints = The number of points beyond the initial point at which the solution is to
be approximated. This controls the number of rows ($1 + npoints$) in the
matrix returned by *rkfixed*.

$\mathbf{D}(x, \mathbf{y})$ = An *n*-element vector-valued function containing the first derivatives of the
unknown functions.

The most difficult part of solving a differential equation is solving for the first derivative
so you can define the function $\mathbf{D}(x, \mathbf{y})$. In Figure 16-1 it was easy to solve for $y'(x)$.
Sometimes, however, particularly with nonlinear differential equations, it can be

difficult. In such cases, you can sometimes solve for $y'(x)$ symbolically and paste it into the definition for $\mathbf{D}(x, \mathbf{y})$. To do so, use the **solve** keyword or the **Solve for Variable** command from the **Symbolics** menu as discussed in the section "Solving equations symbolically" in Chapter 17.

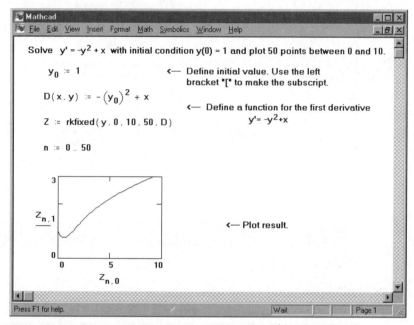

Figure 16-2: A more complicated example involving a nonlinear differential equation.

Second order differential equations

Once you know how to solve a first order differential equation, you're most of the way to knowing how to solve higher order differential equations. We start with a second order equation. The key differences are:

■ The vector of initial values **y** now has two elements: the value of the function and its first derivative at the starting value, *x1*.

■ The function $\mathbf{D}(t, \mathbf{y})$ is now a vector with two elements:

$$\mathbf{D}(t, \mathbf{y}) = \begin{bmatrix} y'(t) \\ y''(t) \end{bmatrix}$$

■ The solution matrix contains three columns: the left-hand one for the *t* values; the middle one for $y(t)$; and the right-hand one for $y'(t)$.

The example in Figure 16-3 shows how to solve the second order differential equation:

$$y'' = y' + 2 \cdot y$$
$$y(0) = 1 \qquad y'(0) = 3$$

Chapter 16 Solving Differential Equations

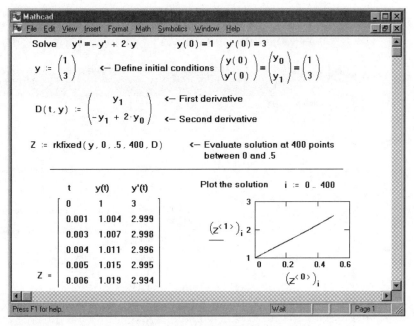

Figure 16-3: Solving a second order differential equation.

Higher order equations

The procedure for solving higher order differential equations is an extension of that used for second order differential equations. The main difference is that:

■ The vector of initial values **y** now has n elements for specifying initial conditions of $y, y', y'', \ldots, y^{(n-1)}$.

■ The function **D** is now a vector with n elements:

$$\mathbf{D}(t, \mathbf{y}) = \begin{bmatrix} y'(t) \\ y''(t) \\ \cdot \\ \cdot \\ \cdot \\ y^{(n)}(t) \end{bmatrix}$$

■ The solution matrix contains n columns: the left-hand one for the t values and the remaining columns for values of $y(t), y'(t), y''(t), \ldots, y^{(n-1)}(t)$.

The example in Figure 16-4 shows how to solve the fourth order differential equation:

$$y'''' - 2k^2 y'' + k^4 y = 0$$

subject to the initial conditions:

$$y(0) = 0 \qquad y'(0) = 1 \qquad y''(0) = 2 \qquad y'''(0) = 3$$

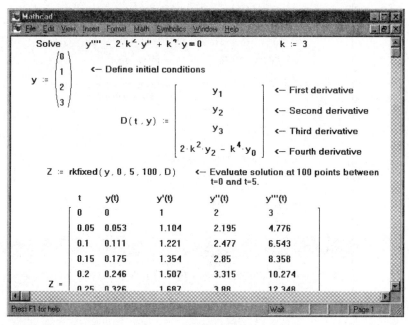

Figure 16-4: Solving a higher order differential equation.

Systems of differential equations

The procedure for solving a coupled system of differential equations follows closely that for solving a higher order differential equation. In fact, you can think of solving a higher order differential equation as just a special case of solving a system of differential equations.

Systems of first order differential equations

To solve a system of first order differential equations:

■ Define a vector containing the initial values of each unknown function.

■ Define a vector-valued function containing the first derivatives of each of the unknown functions.

■ Decide which points you want to evaluate the solutions at.

■ Pass all this information into *rkfixed*.

The *rkfixed* function will return a matrix whose first column contains the points at which the solutions are evaluated and whose remaining columns contain the solution functions evaluated at the corresponding point. Figure 16-5 shows an example solving the equations:

$$x'_0(t) = \mu \cdot x_0(t) - x_1(t) - (x_0(t)^2 + x_1(t)^2) \cdot x_0(t)$$

$$x'_1(t) = \mu \cdot x_1(t) - x_0(t) - (x_0(t)^2 + x_1(t)^2) \cdot x_1(t)$$

with initial conditions:

$$x_0(0) = 0 \qquad x_1(0) = 1$$

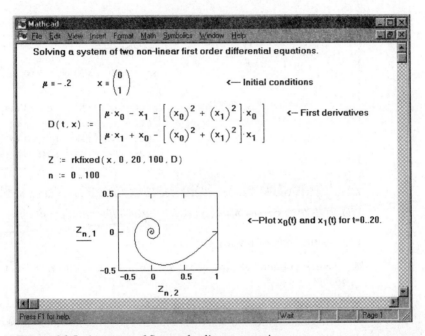

Figure 16-5: A system of first order linear equations.

Systems of higher order differential equations

The procedure for solving a system of nth order differential equations is similar to the procedure for solving a system of first order differential equations. The main differences are:

■ The vector of initial conditions must contain initial values for the $n - 1$ derivatives of each unknown function in addition to initial values for the functions themselves.

■ The vector-valued function must contain expressions for the $n - 1$ derivatives of each unknown function in addition to the nth derivative.

The example in Figure 16-6 shows how to go about solving the system of second order differential equations:

$$u''(t) = 2v(t)$$
$$v''(t) = 4v(t) - 2u(t)$$

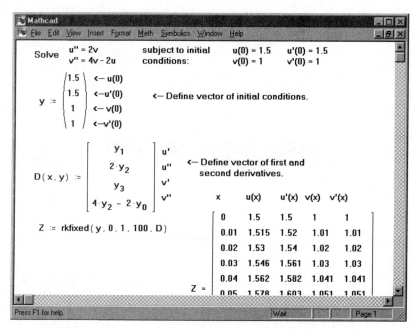

Figure 16-6: A system of second order linear differential equations.

The function *rkfixed* returns a matrix in which:

■ The first column contains the values at which the solutions and their derivatives are to be evaluated.

■ The remaining columns contain the solutions and their derivatives evaluated at the corresponding point in the first column. The order in which the solution and its derivatives appear matches the order in which you put them into the vector of initial conditions that you passed into *rkfixed*.

Specialized differential equation solvers

Pro

The *rkfixed* function discussed thus far is a good general-purpose differential equation solver. Although it is not always the fastest method, the Runge-Kutta technique used by this function nearly always succeeds. Mathcad Professional includes several more specialized functions for solving differential equations, and there are cases in which you may want to use one of Mathcad's more specialized differential equation solvers. These cases fall into three broad categories:

- Your system of differential equations may have certain properties which are best exploited by functions other than *rkfixed*. The system may be stiff (*Stiffb*, *Stiffr*); the functions could be smooth (*Bulstoer*) or slowly varying (*Rkadapt*).

- You may have a boundary value rather than an initial value problem (*sbval* and *bvalfit*).

- You may be interested in evaluating the solution only at one point (*bulstoer*, *rkadapt*, *stiffb* and *stiffr*).

You may also want to try several methods on the same differential equation to see which one works the best. Sometimes there are subtle differences between differential equations that make one method better than another.

The following sections describe the use of the various differential equation solvers and the circumstances in which they are likely to be useful.

Smooth systems

When you know the solution is smooth, use the *Bulstoer* function instead of *rkfixed*. The *Bulstoer* function uses the Bulirsch-Stoer method rather than the Runge-Kutta method used by *rkfixed*. Under these circumstances, the solution will be slightly more accurate than that returned by *rkfixed*.

The argument list and the matrix returned by *Bulstoer* is identical to that for *rkfixed*.

Pro   Bulstoer($\mathbf{y}$, *x1*, *x2*, *npoints*, $\mathbf{D}$)

$\mathbf{y}$ = A vector of *n* initial values.

x1, *x2* = The endpoints of the interval on which the solution to the differential equations will be evaluated. The initial values in $\mathbf{y}$ are the values at *x1*.

npoints = The number of points beyond the initial point at which the solution is to be approximated. This controls the number of rows (1 + *npoints*) in the matrix returned by *Bulstoer*.

$\mathbf{D}(x, \mathbf{y})$ = An *n*-element vector-valued function containing the first derivatives of the unknown functions.

Slowly varying solutions

Given a fixed number of points, you can approximate a function more accurately if you evaluate it frequently wherever it's changing fast and infrequently wherever it's changing more slowly. If you know that the solution has this property, you may be better off using *Rkadapt*. Unlike *rkfixed* which evaluates a solution at equally spaced intervals, *Rkadapt* examines how fast the solution is changing and adapts its step size accordingly. This "adaptive step size control" enables *Rkadapt* to focus on those parts of the integration domain where the function is rapidly changing rather than wasting time integrating a function where it isn't changing all that rapidly.

Note that although *Rkadapt* will use nonuniform step sizes internally when it solves the differential equation, it will nevertheless return the solution at equally spaced points.

Rkadapt takes the same arguments as *rkfixed*. The matrix returned by *Rkadapt* is identical in form to that returned by *rkfixed*.

Pro

Rkadapt(**y**, *x1*, *x2*, *npoints*, **D**)

    y = A vector of *n* initial values.

    x1, *x2* = The endpoints of the interval on which the solution to the differential equations will be evaluated. The initial values in **y** are the values at *x1*.

    npoints = The number of points beyond the initial point at which the solution is to be approximated. This controls the number of rows (1 + *npoints*) in the matrix returned by *Rkadapt*.

    D(*x*, **y**) = An *n*-element vector-valued function containing the first derivatives of the unknown functions.

Stiff systems

A system of differential equations expressed in the form:

$$\mathbf{y} = \mathbf{A} \cdot \mathbf{x}$$

is a stiff system if the matrix **A** is nearly singular. Under these conditions, the solution returned by *rkfixed* may oscillate or be unstable. When solving a stiff system, you should use one of the two differential equation solvers specifically designed for stiff systems: *Stiffb* and *Stiffr*. These use the Bulirsch-Stoer method and the Rosenbrock method, respectively, for stiff systems.

The form of the matrix returned by these functions is identical to that returned by *rkfixed*. However, *Stiffb* and *Stiffr* require an extra argument in the following section:

Stiffb(**y**, *x1*, *x2*, *npoints*, **D**, **J**)
Stiffr(**y**, *x1*, *x2*, *npoints*, **D**, **J**)

> **y** = A vector of *n* initial values.

> *x1*, *x2* = The endpoints of the interval on which the solution to the differential equations will be evaluated. The initial values in **y** are the values at *x1*.

> *npoints* = The number of points beyond the initial point at which the solution is to be approximated. This controls the number of rows (1 + *npoints*) in the matrix returned by *Stiffb* or *Stiffr*.

> **D**(*x*, **y**) = An *n*-element vector-valued function containing the first derivatives of the unknown functions.

> **J**(*x*, **y**) = A function which returns the $n \times (n + 1)$ matrix whose first column contains the derivatives $\partial \mathbf{D}/\partial x$ and whose remaining rows and columns form the Jacobian matrix ($\partial \mathbf{D}/\partial y_k$) for the system of differential equations. For example, if:

$$\mathbf{D}(x, \mathbf{y}) = \begin{bmatrix} x \cdot y_1 \\ -2 \cdot y_1 \cdot y_0 \end{bmatrix} \quad \text{then} \quad \mathbf{J}(x, \mathbf{y}) = \begin{bmatrix} y_1 & 0 & x \\ 0 & -2 \cdot y_1 & -2 \cdot y_0 \end{bmatrix}$$

Evaluating only the final value

The differential equation functions discussed so far presuppose that you're interested in seeing the solution $y(x)$ over a number of uniformly spaced x values in the integration interval bounded by $x1$ and $x2$. There may be times, however, when all you want is the value of the solution at the endpoint, $y(x2)$. Although the functions discussed so far will certainly give you $y(x2)$, they also do a lot of unnecessary work returning intermediate values of $y(x)$ in which you have no interest.

If you're only interested in the value of $y(x2)$, use the functions listed below. Each function corresponds to one of those already discussed. The properties of each of these functions are identical to those of the corresponding function in the previous sections.

bulstoer(**y**, *x1*, *x2*, *acc*, **D**, *kmax*, *save*)
rkadapt(**y**, *x1*, *x2*, *acc*, **D**, *kmax*, *save*)
stiffb(**y**, *x1*, *x2*, *acc*, **D**, **J**, *kmax*, *save*)
stiffr(**y**, *x1*, *x2*, *acc*, **D**, **J**, *kmax*, *save*)

> **y** = A vector of *n* initial values.

> *x1*, *x2* = The endpoints of the interval on which the solution to the differential equations will be evaluated. The initial values in **y** are the values at *x1*.

> *acc* = Controls the accuracy of the solution. A small value of *acc* forces the algorithm to take smaller steps along the trajectory, thereby increasing the accuracy of the solution. Values of *acc* around 0.001 will generally yield accurate solutions.

> **D**(*x*, **y**) = An *n*-element vector-valued function containing the first derivatives of the unknown functions.

> **J**(*x*, **y**) = A function which returns the $n \times (n + 1)$ matrix whose first column contains the derivatives $\partial\mathbf{D}/\partial x$ and whose remaining rows and columns form the Jacobian matrix ($\partial\mathbf{D}/\partial y_k$) for the system of differential equations. See page <Reference>.

> *kmax* = The maximum number of intermediate points at which the solution will be approximated. The value of *kmax* places an upper bound on the number of rows of the matrix returned by these functions.

> *save* = The smallest allowable spacing between the values at which the solutions are to be approximated. This places a lower bound on the difference between any two numbers in the first column of the matrix returned by the function.

Boundary value problems

So far, all the functions discussed in this chapter assume that you know the value taken by the solutions and their derivatives at the beginning of the interval of integration. In other words, these functions are useful for solving initial value problems.

In many cases, however, you may know the value taken by the solution at the endpoints of the interval of integration. A good example is a stretched string constrained at both ends. Problems such as this are referred to as boundary value problems. The first section discusses two-point boundary value problems: one-dimensional systems of differential equations in which the solution is a function of a single variable and the value of the solution is known at two points. The section following this discusses the more general case involving partial differential equations.

Two-point boundary value problems

The functions described so far involve finding the solution to an nth order differential equation when you know the value of the solution and its first $n - 1$ derivatives at the beginning of the interval of integration. This section discusses what happens if you don't have all this information about the solution at the beginning of the interval of integration but you do know something about the solution elsewhere in the interval. In particular:

■ You have an nth order differential equation.

■ You know some but not all of the values of the solution and its first $n - 1$ derivatives at the beginning of the interval of integration, $x1$.

■ You know some but not all of the values of the solution and its first $n - 1$ derivatives at the end of the interval of integration, $x2$.

■ Between what you know about the solution at $x1$ and what you know about it at $x2$, you have n known values.

When this is the case, you should use *sbval* to evaluate the missing initial values at $x1$. Once you have these missing initial values, you will have an initial value problem rather than a two-point boundary value problem. You can then proceed to solve this using any of the functions discussed earlier in this chapter.

The example in Figure 16-7 shows how to use *sbval*. Note that *sbval* does not actually return a solution to a differential equation. It merely computes the initial values the solution must have in order for the solution to match the final values you specify. You must then take the initial values returned by *sbval* and solve the resulting initial value problem as discussed earlier in this chapter.

The *sbval* function returns a vector containing those initial values left unspecified at $x1$. The arguments to *sbval* are:

Pro   sbval(**v**, $x1$, $x2$, **D**, **load**, **score**)

   v = Vector of guesses for initial values left unspecified at $x1$.

   $x1$, $x2$ = The endpoints of the interval on which the solution to the differential equations will be evaluated.

   D(x, **y**) = An n-element vector-valued function containing the first derivatives of the unknown functions.

   load($x1$, **v**) = A vector-valued function whose n elements correspond to the values of

---

the *n* unknown functions at *x1*. Some of these values will be constants specified by your initial conditions. Others will be unknown at the outset but will be found by *sbval*. If a value is unknown you should use the corresponding guess value from **v**.

score(*x2*, **y**) = A vector-valued function having the same number of elements as **v**. Each element is the difference between an initial condition at *x2*, as originally specified, and the corresponding estimate from the solution. The *score* vector measures how closely the proposed solution matches the initial conditions at *x2*. A value of 0 for any element indicates a perfect match between the corresponding initial condition and that returned by *sbval*.

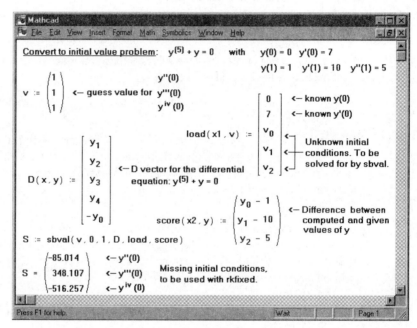

Figure 16-7: Using sbval to obtain initial values corresponding to given final values of a solution to a differential equation.

It's also possible that you don't have all the information you need to use *sbval* but you do know something about the solution and its first *n* − 1 derivatives at some intermediate value, *xf*. This is the exactly the situation contemplated by *bvalfit*.

This function solves a two-point boundary value problem of this type by shooting from the endpoints and matching the trajectories of the solution and its derivatives at the intermediate point.

Pro   bvalfit(**v1**, **v2**, *x1*, *x2*, *xf*, **D**, **load1**, **load2**, **score**)

v1, **v2** = Vector **v1** contains guesses for initial values left unspecified at *x1*. Vector **v2** contains guesses for initial values left unspecified at *x2*.

x1, *x2* = The endpoints of the interval on which the solution to the differential equations will be evaluated.

xf = A point between *x1* and *x2* at which the trajectories of the solutions beginning at *x1* and those beginning at *x2* are constrained to be equal.

D(*x*, **y**) = An *n*-element vector-valued function containing the first derivatives of the unknown functions.

load1(*x1*, **v1**) = A vector-valued function whose *n* elements correspond to the values of the *n* unknown functions at *x1*. Some of these values will be constants specified by your initial conditions. If a value is unknown you should use the corresponding guess value from **v1**.

load2(*x2*, **v2**) = Analogous to *load1* but for values taken by the *n* unknown functions at *x2*.

score(*xf*, **y**) = An *n* element vector valued function used to specify how you want the solutions to match at *xf*. You'll usually want to define *score*(*xf*, **y**) := **y** to make the solutions to all unknown functions match up at *xf*.

This method becomes especially useful when derivative has a discontinuity somewhere in the integration interval as the example in Figure 16-8 illustrates.

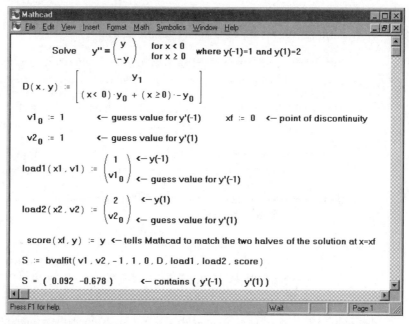

Figure 16-8: Using bvalfit to match solutions in the middle of the integration interval.

Partial differential equations

A second type of boundary value problem arises when you are solving a partial differential equation. Rather than fixing the value of a solution at two points as was done in the previous section, we now fix the solution at a whole continuum of points representing some boundary.

Two partial differential equations that arise often in the analysis of physical systems are Poisson's equation:

$$\frac{\partial^2 u}{\partial x^2} + \frac{\partial^2 u}{\partial y^2} = \rho(x, y)$$

and its homogeneous form, Laplace's equation.

Mathcad has two functions for solving these equations over a square boundary. You should use the *relax* function if you know the value taken by the unknown function $u(x, y)$ on all four sides of a square region.

If $u(x, y)$ is zero on all four sides of the square, you can use *multigrid* function instead. This function will often solve the problem faster than *relax*. Note that if the boundary condition is the same on all four sides, you can simply transform the equation to an equivalent one in which the value is zero on all four sides.

Chapter 16 Solving Differential Equations

The *relax* function returns a square matrix in which:

■ An element's location in the matrix corresponds to its location within the square region, and

■ Its value approximates the value of the solution at that point.

This function uses the relaxation method to converge to the solution. Poisson's equation on a square domain is represented by:

$$a_{j,k} u_{j+1,k} + b_{j,k} u_{j-1,k} + c_{j,k} u_{j,k+1} + d_{j,k} u_{j,k-1} + e_{j,k} u_{j,k} = f_{j,k}$$

The arguments taken by these functions are shown below:

Pro   relax(**a**, **b**, **c**, **d**, **e**, **f**, **u**, *rjac*)

a, b, c, d, e = Square matrices all of the same size containing coefficients of the above equation.

f = Square matrix containing the source term at each point in the region in which the solution is sought.

u = Square matrix containing boundary values along the edges of the region and initial guesses for the solution inside the region.

rjac = Spectral radius of the Jacobi iteration. This number between 0 and 1 controls the convergence of the relaxation algorithm. Its optimal value depends on the details of your problem.

If the boundary condition is zero on all four sides of the square integration domain, use the *multigrid* function instead. An example is shown in Figure 16-9. The same problem solved with the *relax* function instead is shown in Figure 16-10.

Pro   multigrid(**M**, *ncycle*)

M = $(1 + 2^n)$ row square matrix whose elements correspond to the source term at the corresponding point in the square domain.

ncycle = The number of cycles at each level of the *multigrid* iteration. A value of 2 will generally give a good approximation of the solution.

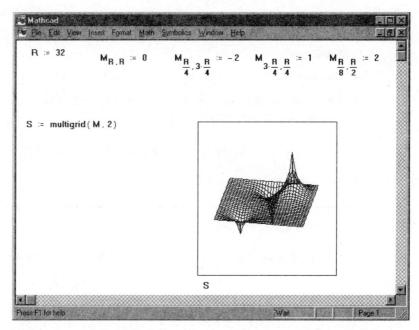

Figure 16-9: Using multigrid to solve a Poisson's equation in a square domain.

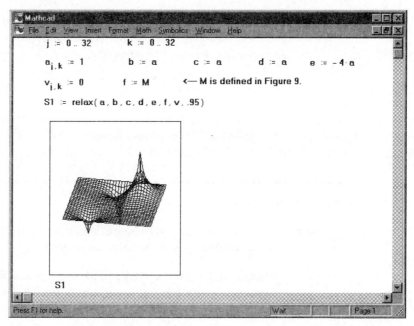

Figure 16-10: Using relax to solve the same problem as that shown in Figure 16-9.

Chapter 17
Symbolic Calculation

This chapter describes symbolic processing in Mathcad. The chapter includes the following sections:

What is symbolic math?

An overview of Mathcad's symbolic math features.

Live symbolic evaluation

Using the symbolic equal sign to perform live symbolic transformations.

Using the Symbolics menu

Using menu commands to perform symbolic transformations.

Symbolic algebra

Manipulating expressions algebraically.

Symbolic calculus

Evaluating indefinite integrals, derivatives, and limits symbolically.

Solving equations symbolically

Algebraic solution of equations or systems of equations.

Symbolic matrix manipulation

Finding the symbolic transpose, inverse, and determinant of a matrix.

Symbolic transforms

Fourier, Laplace and z-transforms.

Symbolic optimization

Symbolically simplifying complex expressions before numerically evaluating them.

Using functions and variables

Differences between the symbolic and numerical processors and how they work with variables and functions.

Limits to symbolic processing

Difficulties you may encounter in symbolic processing.

What is symbolic math?

Elsewhere in this *User's Guide*, you've seen Mathcad engaging in *numerical* mathematics. This means that whenever you evaluate an expression, Mathcad returns one or more *numbers,* as shown at the top of Figure 17-1. Although these numbers are quite useful, they may provide little insight into the underlying relationship between the components in an expression.

When Mathcad engages in *symbolic* mathematics, however, the result of evaluating an expression is generally another expression, as shown in the bottom of Figure 17-1. The form of this second expression is to a great extent under your control. You can factor the original expression, integrate it, expand it into a series, and so on. The way you control the form of that second expression is the subject of this chapter.

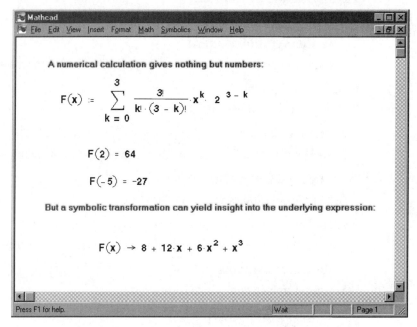

Figure 17-1: A numerical and symbolic evaluation of the same expression.

There are three ways to perform a symbolic transformation on an expression.

■ You can use the symbolic equal sign as described in the section "Live symbolic evaluation" on page 353. This method feels very much as if you're engaging in numerical math.

■ If you need more control over the symbolic transformation, you can use symbolic keywords with the symbolic equal sign, or you can use commands from the **Symbolics** menu.

■ You can make the numerical and symbolic processors work together; the latter simplifying an expression behind the scenes so that the former can work with it more efficiently. This is discussed in the section "Symbolic optimization" on page 388.

Symbolic processing also raises some subtle issues concerning the use of functions and variables. These are described in the section "Using functions and variables" on page 390.

Finally, there are some fundamental limits inherent in computer based symbolic processing generally. These arise because nobody really knows how the human brain does symbolic processing. As a result, nobody really knows how to teach a computer to do it. These limits are discussed in the section "Limits to symbolic processing" on page 395.

Live symbolic evaluation

The symbolic equal sign provides a way to extend Mathcad's live document interface beyond the numerical evaluation of expressions. You can think of it as being analogous to the equal sign "=". Unlike the equal sign, which always gives a number on the right hand side, the symbolic equal sign is capable of giving expressions. You can use it to symbolically evaluate expressions, variables, functions, or programs.

To use the symbolic equal sign:

■ Make sure the **Automatic Calculation** command on the **Math** menu has a check-mark beside it. If it doesn't, choose it from the menu.

■ Make sure the **Automatic Calculation** command on the **Math** menu has a check-mark beside it.

■ Enter the expression you want to evaluate.

$$\frac{d}{dx}\left(x^3 - 2 \cdot y \cdot x\right)$$

■ Press [**Ctrl**]. (the control key followed by a period). Mathcad displays an arrow, "→".

$$\frac{d}{dx}\left(x^3 - 2 \cdot y \cdot x\right) \rightarrow$$

■ Click outside the expression. Mathcad displays a simplified version of the original expression. If an expression cannot be

$$\frac{d}{dx}\left(x^3 - 2 \cdot y \cdot x\right) \rightarrow 3 \cdot x^2 - 2 \cdot y$$

simplified further, Mathcad simply repeats it to the right of the arrow.

The symbolic equal sign is a live operator just like any Mathcad operator. When you make a change anywhere above or to the left of it, Mathcad updates the result. The symbolic equal sign "knows" about previously defined functions and variables and uses them wherever appropriate. You can force the symbolic equal sign to ignore prior definitions of functions and variables by defining them recursively just before you evaluate them as shown in Figure 17-5.

Figure 17-2 shows some examples of how to use the "→". Note that the "→" only applies to an entire expression. You cannot, for example, use the "→" to transform only part of an expression.

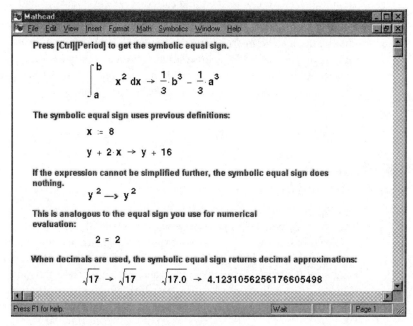

Figure 17-2: Using the symbolic equal sign.

Figure 17-2 also illustrates the fact that the symbolic processor treats numbers containing a decimal point differently from numbers without a decimal point. The general rule is as follows:

- When you send numbers with decimal points to the symbolic processor, any numerical results you get back will be decimal approximations to the exact answer.

- When you send numbers without decimal points to the symbolic processor, any numerical results you get back will be expressed without decimal points whenever possible.

In Figure 17-2, note how $\sqrt{17}$ comes back unchanged since there is no rational square root of 17. But $\sqrt{17.0}$ comes back as a decimal approximation to the irrational number $\sqrt{17}$.

When a symbolic operation gives an approximate decimal answer, this answer is always displayed with 20 significant digits. Although this display is not affected by Mathcad's local or global numerical formats, you can use the **float** keyword described in the next section to control the number of significant digits displayed.

Chapter 17 Symbolic Calculation

Customizing the symbolic equal sign using keywords

The "→" takes the left-hand side and places a simplified version of it on the right-hand side. By default, it simplifies the left-hand side just as if you had chosen **Evaluate⇒Symbolically** from the **Symbolics** menu (see "Using the Symbolics menu" on page 360).

Of course, exactly what "simplify" means is a matter of opinion. As a result, you can, to a limited extent, control how the "→" transforms the expression by using one of the following keywords. To do so:

■ Enter the expression you want to evaluate.

■ Press [Ctrl][Shift]. (hold down the control and shift keys and type a period). Mathcad displays a placeholder to the left of the arrow, "→".

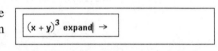

■ Click on the placeholder to the left of the arrow and type any of the keywords from the following table. If the keyword requires any additional arguments, separate the arguments from the keyword with commas.

$$(x + y)^3 \text{ expand} \rightarrow$$

■ Press [Enter] to see the result.

$$(x + y)^3 \text{ expand} \rightarrow x^3 + 3 \cdot x^2 \cdot y + 3 \cdot x \cdot y^2 + y^3$$

Another way to use a keyword is to enter the expression you want to evaluate and click on a keyword button from the Symbolic Keywords palette. This will insert the keyword, placeholders for any additional arguments, and the arrow, "→". You just need to press [Enter] to see the result.

Keyword	Function
complex	Tells Mathcad to carry out symbolic evaluation in the complex domain. Result will usually be in the form $a + i \cdot b$.
float,*m*	Tells Mathcad to display a floating point value with *m* places of precision whenever possible. If the argument *m,* an integer, is omitted, the precision is 20.
simplify	Simplifies an expression, performing arithmetic, canceling common factors, and using basic trigonometric and inverse function identities.
expand,*expr*	Expands all powers and products of sums in an expression except for the subexpression *expr*. The argument *expr* is optional. The entire expression is expanded if the argument *expr* is omitted.
factor,*expr*	Factors an expression into a product, if the entire expression can be written as a product. Factors with respect to *expr*, a

	single radical or a list of radicals separated by commas. The argument *expr* is optional.
solve, *var*	Solves an equation for the variable *var* or solves a system of equations for the variables in a vector *var*.
collect, *var1,* *var2,* ...	Collects like terms with respect to the variables or subexpressions *var1* through *varn*.
coeffs, *var*	Finds coefficients of an expression when it is rewritten as a polynomial in the variable or subexpression *var*.
substitute, *var1=var2*	Replaces all occurrences of a variable *var1* with an expression or variable *var2*. Press [**Ctrl**] = for the equal sign.
series, *var=z,m*	Expands an expression in one or more variables, *var*, around the point *z*. The order of expansion is *m*. Arguments *z* and *m* are optional. By default, the expansion is taken around zero and is a polynomial of order six.
convert,parfrac, *var*	Converts an expression to a partial fraction expansion in the variable *var*.
fourier, *var*	Evaluates the Fourier transform of an expression with respect to the variable *var*.
invfourier, *var*	Evaluates the inverse Fourier transform of an expression with respect to the variable *var*.
laplace, *var*	Evaluates the Laplace transform of an expression with respect to the variable *var*.
invlaplace, *var*	Evaluates the inverse Laplace transform of an expression with respect to the variable *var*.
ztrans, *var*	Evaluates the z-transform of an expression with respect to the variable *var*.
invztrans, *var*	Evaluates the inverse z-transform of an expression with respect to the variable *var*.
assume, *constraint*	Tells Mathcad to impose constraints on one or more variables according to the expression *constraint*.

Note that many of the keywords take at least one additional argument, typically the name of a variable with respect to which you are performing the symbolic operation. Some of the arguments listed with the keywords are optional.

For more information on each of these keywords, see the sections entitled "Symbolic algebra" on page 362, "Symbolic calculus" on page 374, and "Symbolic transforms" on page 384.

Figure 17-3 shows some sample uses of keywords. Note that keywords are case sensitive and must therefore be typed exactly as shown. They are not, however, font sensitive.

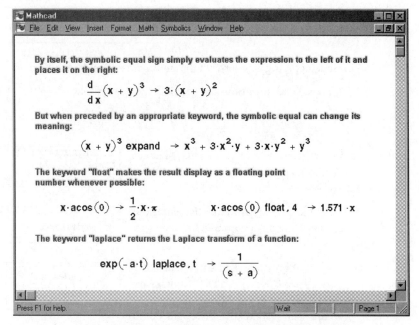

By itself, the symbolic equal sign simply evaluates the expression to the left of it and places it on the right:

$$\frac{d}{dx}(x + y)^3 \rightarrow 3 \cdot (x + y)^2$$

But when preceded by an appropriate keyword, the symbolic equal can change its meaning:

$$(x + y)^3 \text{ expand} \rightarrow x^3 + 3 \cdot x^2 \cdot y + 3 \cdot x \cdot y^2 + y^3$$

The keyword "float" makes the result display as a floating point number whenever possible:

$$x \cdot \text{acos}(0) \rightarrow \frac{1}{2} \cdot x \cdot \pi \qquad x \cdot \text{acos}(0) \text{ float}, 4 \rightarrow 1.571 \cdot x$$

The keyword "laplace" returns the Laplace transform of a function:

$$\exp(-a \cdot t) \text{ laplace}, t \rightarrow \frac{1}{(s + a)}$$

Figure 17-3: Using keywords with a symbolic evaluation sign.

In some cases, you may want to perform two or more types of symbolic evaluation consecutively on an expression. Mathcad allows you to apply several symbolic keywords to a single expression. There are two ways of applying multiple keywords. The method you choose depends on whether you want to see the results from each keyword or only the final result.

To apply several keywords and see the results from each:

■ Enter the expression you want to evaluate.

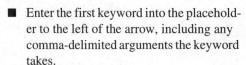

■ Press [**Ctrl**][**Shift**]**.** (hold down the control and shift keys and type a period). Mathcad displays a placeholder to the left of the arrow, "→".

■ Enter the first keyword into the placeholder to the left of the arrow, including any comma-delimited arguments the keyword takes.

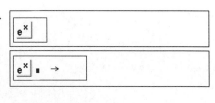

■ Press [**Enter**] to see the result from the first keyword.

■ Click on the result and press [**Ctrl**] [**Shift**]**.** again. The first result disappears temporarily. Enter a second keyword into the placeholder.

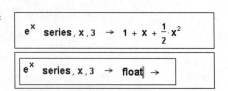

■ Press [Enter] to see the result from the second keyword.

$$e^x \quad \text{series}, x, 3 \;\rightarrow\; 1 + x + \frac{1}{2} \cdot x^2 \;\text{float} \;\rightarrow\; 1. + x + .5 \cdot x^2$$

Continue applying keywords to the intermediate results in this manner.

To apply several keywords and see only the final result:

■ Enter the expression you want to evaluate.

■ Press [Ctrl][Shift]. so that Mathcad displays a placeholder to the left of the arrow, "→".

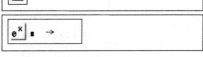

■ Enter the first keyword into the placeholder, including any comma-delimited arguments it takes.

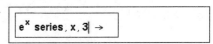

■ Instead of pressing [Enter] to see the result, press [Ctrl][Shift]. again and enter a second keyword into the placeholder. The second keyword is placed immediately below the first keyword.

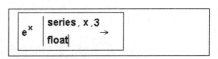

Continue adding keywords by pressing [Ctrl][Shift]. after each one. Press [Enter] to see the final result.

$$e^x \quad \begin{matrix} \text{series}, x, 3 \\ \text{float} \end{matrix} \;\rightarrow\; 1. + x + .5 \cdot x^2$$

These two methods of applying multiple keywords to an expression are demonstrated in Figure 17-4.

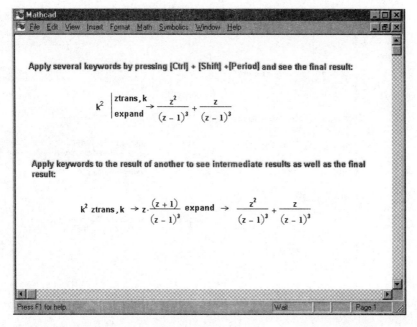

Figure 17-4: Using multiple keywords.

Ignoring previous definitions

When you use the symbolic equal sign to evaluate an expression, Mathcad checks all the variables and functions making up that expression to see if they've been defined earlier in the worksheet. If Mathcad does find a definition, it uses it. Any other variables and functions are evaluated symbolically.

There are two exceptions to this. In evaluating an expression made up of previously defined variables and functions, Mathcad *ignores* prior definitions:

■ when the variable has been defined recursively, or

■ when the variable has been defined as a range variable.

These are illustrated in Figure 17-5.

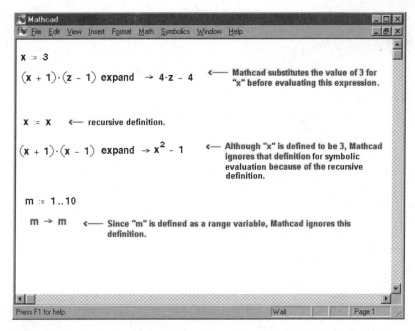

Figure 17-5: Defining a variable in terms of itself makes the symbolic processor ignore any previous definitions.

Using the Symbolics menu

One advantage to using the symbolic equal sign discussed in the last section is that it is "live," just like the numerical processing in Mathcad. That is, Mathcad checks all the variables and functions making up the expression being evaluated to see if they've been defined earlier in the worksheet. If Mathcad does find a definition, it uses it. Any other variables and functions are evaluated symbolically. Later on, whenever you make a change to the worksheet, the results automatically update. This is useful when the symbolic and numerical equations in the worksheet are tied together.

There may be times, however, when a symbolic calculation is quite separate from the rest of your worksheet and does not need to be tied to any previous definitions. In these cases, you can use commands from the **Symbolics** menu. These commands are not live: you apply them on a case by case basis to selected expressions, they do not "know" about previous definitions, and they do not automatically update.

The basic steps for using the **Symbolics** menu are the same for all the menu commands:

■ Place whatever math expression you want to evaluate between the two editing lines or, for some commands, click on a variable in the expression.

■ Choose the appropriate command from the **Symbolics** menu.

■ Mathcad will place the evaluated expression into your document.

For example, to evaluate an expression symbolically using the **Symbolics** menu, follow these steps:

■ Enter the expression you want to evaluate.

$$\frac{d}{dx}\left(x^3 - 2 \cdot y \cdot x\right)$$

■ Surround the expression with the editing lines.

$$\frac{d}{dx}\left(x^3 - 2 \cdot y \cdot x\right)$$

■ Choose **Evaluate⇒Symbolically** from the **Symbolics** menu.

■ Mathcad will place the evaluated expression into your worksheet. The location of the result in relation to the original expression depends on the Evaluation Style you've selected, as described below.

$$3 \cdot x^2 - 2 \cdot y$$

The sections "Symbolic algebra" on page 362, "Symbolic calculus" on page 374, and "Solving equations symbolically" on page 379 describe the various **Symbolics** menu commands in detail.

Displaying symbolic results

If you're using the symbolic equal sign, "→", the result of a symbolic transformation will always go to the right of the "→". However, when you use the **Symbolics** menu, you can tell Mathcad to place the symbolic results in one of the following ways:

■ The symbolic result can go below the original expression.

■ The symbolic result can go to the right of the original expression.

■ The symbolic result can simply replace the original expression.

In addition, you can also choose whether or not you want Mathcad to generate text describing what had to be done to get from the original expression to the symbolic result. This text will go between the original expression and the symbolic result, in effect creating a narrative for the symbolic evaluation. These text regions are referred to as "evaluation comments."

To control both the placement of the symbolic result and the presence of narrative text, choose **Evaluation Style** from the **Symbolics** menu to bring up the "Evaluation Style" dialog box. The check box at the top of the dialog box shows whether Mathcad will automatically generate evaluation comments at each step of the evaluation. Click in this box to toggle these comments on or off.

The three option buttons control where symbolic results are placed. These options do the following:

■ "Show evaluation steps vertically, inserting lines" is useful when you expect lengthy intermediate results and you want to reserve an entire line for them.

■ "Show evaluation steps vertically, without inserting lines" is useful when you want to show two parallel derivations side by side. In this mode, you can position expressions arbitrarily. New answers may, however, overwrite old ones.

■ "Show evaluation steps horizontally" is useful if you want to place the symbolic result to the right of the expression being transformed.

Sometimes you don't care about saving the steps of a derivation. You may just want to transform an expression in place, for example to make a substitution, or to factor the numerator of a fraction. In this case, choose **Evaluation Style** from the **Symbolics** menu and click in the check box for "Evaluate in Place." This tells Mathcad to replace the old expression with the new one. In this mode, evaluation comments are inappropriate and therefore omitted altogether.

See Figure 17-6 for some examples.

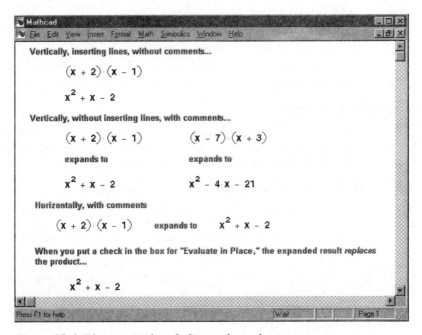

Figure 17-6: Placement of symbolic results and comments.

Symbolic algebra

Mathcad allows you to manipulate an expression algebraically using either keywords and the symbolic equal sign, or menu commands from the **Symbolics** menu. Most of the examples in this section demonstrate "live" symbolic operations using symbolic keywords, but you may apply commands from the Symbolics menu to expressions on a case by case basis if you prefer. Keep in mind that, unlike the keyword-modified expressions, expressions modified by commands from the Symbolics menu do not update automatically, as described in the section "Using the Symbolics menu" on page 360.

Complex evaluation

When evaluating expressions containing complex numbers, you may want to use the keyword **complex**:

- Enter the expression you want to evaluate.

- Press [Ctrl][Shift]. (hold down the control and shift keys and type a period). Mathcad displays a placeholder to the left of the arrow, "→".

- Type complex into the placeholder.

- Press [Enter] to see the result.

Mathcad will assume all the terms in the expression are written in the form $a + b \cdot i$. The results will also be in this form. Figure 17-7 shows an example.

Another way to evaluate an expression in the complex domain is to enclose the expression between the editing lines and choose **Evaluate⇒Complex** from the **Symbolics** menu.

Floating point evaluation

Ordinarily, the symbolic processor returns results by rearranging variables. Thus, when Mathcad evaluates an expression involving π or e, it will usually return another expression involving π or $\exp(x)$. To force Mathcad to return a number instead, use the keyword **float**:

- Enter the expression you want to evaluate.

- Press [Ctrl][Shift]. (hold down the control and shift keys and type a period). Mathcad displays a placeholder to the left of the arrow, "→".

- Type float into the placeholder.

- Press [Enter] to see the result.

Mathcad by default returns a result with up to 20 digits to the right of the decimal point. To specify a different number of digits for the result, follow the keyword **float** with a comma and an integer between 0 and 250. Figure 17-7 shows an example.

Another way to perform floating point evaluation on an expression is to enclose the expression between the editing lines and choose **Evaluate⇒Floating Point** from the **Symbolics** menu. This brings up a dialog box in which you can specify the number of digits to the right of the decimal point.

Constrained evaluation

When evaluating some expressions, you may want to force Mathcad to make certain assumptions about the variables involved. For example, you might want Mathcad to

---

Symbolic algebra

assume x is real when evaluating the square root of x. To impose constraints on the variables in an expression, use the keyword **assume**:

- Enter the expression you want to evaluate.

- Press **[Ctrl][Shift].** (hold down the control and shift keys and type a period). Mathcad displays a placeholder to the left of the arrow, "→".

- In the placeholder, type **assume** followed by a comma and a constraining equation such as **x<10**.

- Press **[Enter]** to see the result.

You can also use the **assume** keyword to tell Mathcad to consider a variable to be real or falling in a certain range of real values. To do so, you can use the following "modifiers":

Modifiers for "assume"

var=**real**	Evaluates the expression on the assumption that the variable *var* is real.
var=**RealRange(*a*,*b*)**	Evaluates on the assumption that all the indeterminates are real and are between *a* and *b*, where *a* and *b* are real numbers or infinity (**[Ctrl]Z**).

To use a modifier, separate it from the **assume** keyword with a comma. For example, to use "x=real" as a modifier with the **assume** keyword on an expression:

- Enter the expression to simplify.

- Press **[Ctrl][Shift].** (hold down the control and shift keys and type a period). Mathcad displays a placeholder to the left of the arrow, "→".

- Enter **assume,x=real** into the placeholder (press **[Ctrl]=** for the equal sign).

- Press **[Enter]** to see the result.

The last example in Figure 17-7 illustrates how an integral can be made to converge by assuming a variable is positive and greater than 1. Note that in order to specify more than one condition, you simply separate the conditions with a comma.

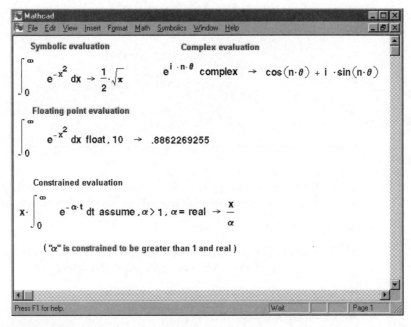

Figure 17-7: Evaluating expressions symbolically.

Simplifying an expression

To force Mathcad to carry out basic algebraic and trigonometric simplification of a selected expression, use the keyword **simplify**:

■ Enter the expression you want to evaluate.

■ Press [Ctrl][Shift] . (hold down the control and shift keys and type a period). Mathcad displays a placeholder to the left of the arrow, "→".

■ Type **simplify** into the placeholder.

■ Press [Enter] to see the result.

When the symbolic processor simplifies an expression, it performs arithmetic, cancels common factors, uses basic trigonometric and inverse function identities, and simplifies square roots and powers.

To control the simplification performed by the **simplify** keyword, you can use the following "modifiers":

Modifiers for "simplify"

assume=real   Simplifies on the assumption that all the indeterminates in the expression are real.

assume=RealRange(*a*,*b*)   Simplifies on the assumption that all the indeterminates are real and are between *a* and *b*, where *a* and *b* are real numbers or infinity ([Ctrl]Z).

trig

Simplifies a trigonometric expression by applying only the following identities:

$$\sin(x)^2 + \cos(x)^2 = 1$$

$$\cosh(x)^2 - \sinh(x)^2 = 1$$

It does not simplify the expression by simplifying logs, powers, or radicals.

To use a modifier, separate it from the **simplify** keyword with a comma. For example, to use the "trig" modifier with the **simplify** keyword on an expression:

■ Enter the expression to simplify.

■ Press [Ctrl][Shift]. (hold down the control and shift keys and type a period). Mathcad displays a placeholder to the left of the arrow, "→".

■ Enter **simplify,trig** into the placeholder.

■ Press [Enter] to see the result.

Figure 17-8 shows some examples using the **simplify** keyword with and without additional modifiers.

Note that you can also simplify an expression by placing it between the two editing lines and choosing **Simplify** from the **Symbolics** menu. This method is useful when you want to simplify parts of an expression. Mathcad may sometimes be able to simplify parts of an expression even when it cannot simplify the entire expression. If simplifying the entire expression doesn't give the answer you want, try selecting subexpressions and choosing **Simplify** from the **Symbolics** menu. If Mathcad can't simplify an expression any further, you'll just get the original expression back as the answer.

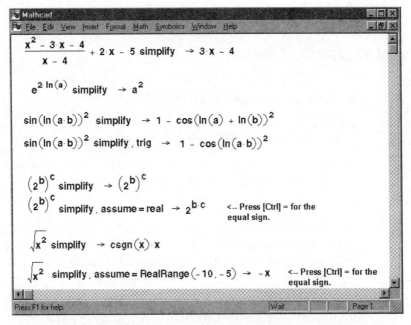

Figure 17-8: Some results of simplifying. Modifiers such as "trig" give more control over the simplification.

In general, when you simplify an expression, the simplified result will have the same numerical behavior as the original expression. However, when the expression includes functions with more than one branch, such as square root or the inverse trigonometric functions, the symbolic answer may differ from a numerical answer. For example, simplifying $\text{asin}(\sin(\theta))$ yields θ, but this equation holds true numerically in Mathcad only when θ is a number between $-\pi/2$ and $\pi/2$.

Expanding an expression

To expand all powers and products of sums in an expression, use the keyword **expand**:

■ Enter the expression you want to expand.

■ Press [**Ctrl**][**Shift**] . (hold down the control and shift keys and type a period). Mathcad displays a placeholder to the left of the arrow, "→".

■ Type **expand** into the placeholder.

■ Press [**Enter**] to see the result.

Mathcad expands all powers and products of sums in the selected expression. If the expression is a fraction, the numerator will be expanded and the expression will be written as a sum of fractions. Sines, cosines and tangents of sums of variables, or integer multiples of variables will be expanded as far as possible into expressions involving only sines and cosines of single variables. If you don't want certain subexpressions to be expanded, follow the **expand** keyword with a comma and the expressions. See Figure 17-10 for some examples.

Another way to expand an expression is to enclose the expression between the editing lines and choose **Expand** from the **Symbolics** menu.

Expanding an expression to a series

To expand an expression to a series, use the keyword **series**:

■ Enter the expression you want to expand.

■ Press [Ctrl][Shift]. (hold down the control and shift keys and type a period). Mathcad displays a placeholder to the left of the arrow, "→".

■ In the placeholder, type **series** followed by a comma and the variable or expression for which you want to find a series expansion.

■ Press [Enter] to see the result.

Mathcad will then generate a series of order 6. To specify a different order of expansion, follow the variable of expansion with a comma and an appropriate integer. The order is the order of the error term in the expansion. For example, if Mathcad expands $\sin(x)$ to a series in x, it returns an expansion of the sine function in powers of x in which the highest power is x^5. The error is thus $O(x^6)$.

Mathcad will find Taylor series (series in nonnegative powers of the variable) for functions that are analytic at 0, and Laurent series for functions that have a pole of finite order at 0. To develop a series with a center other than 0, the argument to the **series** keyword should be of the form $var=z$, where z is any real or complex number. For example, **series, x=1** expands around the point $x=1$. Press [Ctrl] = for the equal sign.

To expand a series around more than one variable, follow the series keyword with a comma and the variables, separated from each other by commas. The last example in Figure 17-9 shows an expression expanded around x and y.

Figure 17-9 shows some examples of expanded expressions.

Another way to generate a series expansion is to enter the expression and click on a variable for which you want to find a series expansion. Then choose **Variable⇒Expand to Series** from the Symbolics menu. A dialog box will prompt you for the order of the series. This command is limited to a series in a single variable; any other variables in the expression will be treated as constants. The results also contain the error term using the O notation. Before you use the series for further calculations you will need to delete this error term.

In using the approximations you get from the symbolic processor, keep in mind that the Taylor series for a function may converge only in some small interval around the center. Furthermore, functions like *sin* or *exp* have series with infinitely many terms, while the polynomials returned by Mathcad have only a few terms (how many depends on the order you select). Thus, when you approximate a function by the polynomial returned by Mathcad, the approximation will be reasonably accurate close to the center, but may be quite inaccurate for values far from the center.

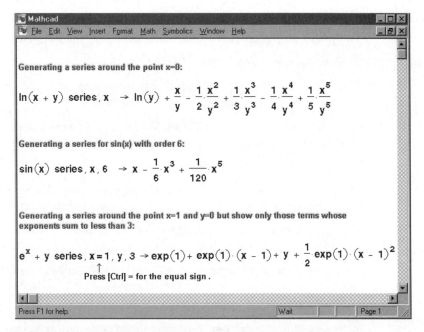

Figure 17-9: Generating a series.

Factoring an expression

To factor an expression, use the keyword **factor**:

■ Enter the expression you want to factor.

■ Press [**Ctrl**][**Shift**]. (hold down the control and shift keys and type a period). Mathcad displays a placeholder to the left of the arrow, "→".

■ In the placeholder, type **factor**.

■ Press [**Enter**] to see the result.

If this expression is a single integer, Mathcad will factor it into powers of primes. Otherwise, Mathcad will attempt to convert the expression into a product of simpler functions. The symbolic processor will combine a sum of fractions into a single fraction and will often simplify a complex fraction with more than one fraction bar.

If you want to factor an expression over certain radicals, follow the **factor** keyword with a comma and the radicals.

When you're simplifying by factoring, you may be able to simplify your expression quite a bit by factoring subexpressions even if the expression taken as a whole can't be factored. To do so, enclose a subexpression between the editing lines and choose **Factor** from the **Symbolics** menu. You can also use this menu command to factor an entire expression, but keep in mind that the **Symbolics** menu commands do not use any previous definitions in your worksheet and do not automatically update.

See the examples in Figure 17-10 for examples of factoring expressions.

Collecting like terms

To simplify an expression by collecting terms containing like powers of a variable:

■ Enter the expression.

■ Press [**Ctrl**][**Shift**]**.** (hold down the control and shift keys and type a period). Mathcad displays a placeholder and the arrow, "→".

■ In the placeholder, type **collect** followed by a comma and the variable or subexpression on which to collect.

■ Press [**Enter**] to see the result.

The result is a polynomial in the variable or subexpression. The subexpression you select must be a single variable or a built-in function together with its argument.

To collect on more than one variable, follow the **collect** keyword with a comma and the variables on which to collect, separated from each other by commas.

See Figure 17-10 for examples of simplifying expressions by collecting like terms. An alternative method for collecting terms of an expression is to click on a variable in an expression and choose **Collect** from the **Symbolics** menu.

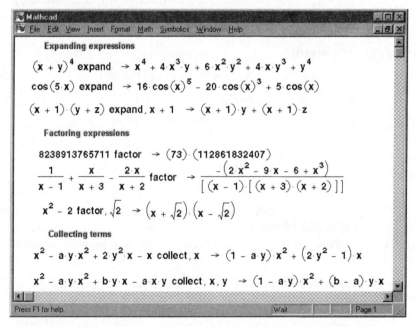

Figure 17-10: Expanding to a polynomial, factoring, and collecting terms.

Partial fraction decomposition

To convert an expression to its partial fraction decomposition, use the keyword **convert**:

■ Enter the expression.

- Press [Ctrl][Shift]. (hold down the control and shift keys and type a period). Mathcad displays a placeholder to the left of the arrow, "→".

- In the placeholder, type `convert,parfrac` followed by a comma and the variable in the denominator of the expression on which to convert.

- Press [Enter] to see the result.

The symbolic processor will try to factor the denominator of the expression into linear or quadratic factors having integer coefficients. If it succeeds, it will expand the expression into a sum of fractions with these factors as denominators. All constants in the selected expression must be integers or fractions; Mathcad will not expand an expression that contains decimal points. See Figure 17-11 for some examples.

Another way to convert an expression to a partial fraction is enter the expression and click on a variable in the denominator. Then choose **Variable⇒Convert to Partial Fraction** from the **Symbolics** menu.

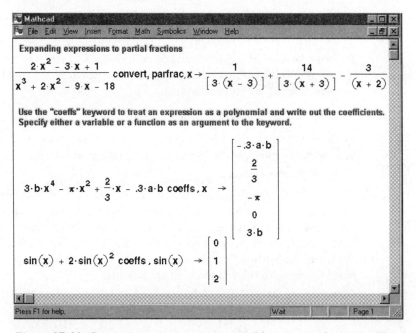

Figure 17-11: Converting expressions to partial fractions and rewriting them as polynomials.

Finding coefficients of a polynomial

Many expressions can be rewritten as polynomials, either in a particular variable or with respect to a subexpression. To force the symbolic processor rewrite an expression as a polynomial and return the coefficients:

- Enter the expression you want to rewrite.

- Press [Ctrl][Shift]. (hold down the control and shift keys and type a period). Mathcad displays a placeholder to the left of the arrow, "→".

- In the placeholder, type **coeffs** followed by a comma and the variable or function in which you want your expression to be regarded as a polynomial.

- Press [**Enter**] to see the result.

Mathcad returns a vector containing the coefficients of the equivalent polynomial. The first element of the vector is the constant term and the last element is the coefficient of the highest order term in the expression. Figure 17-11 shows two examples.

Another way to rewrite an expression as a polynomial is to enclose it between the two editing lines and choose **Polynomial Coefficients** from the **Symbolics** menu.

Substituting an expression for a variable

To replace a variable in an expression with another variable or subexpression, use the keyword **substitute**:

- Enter the expression.

- Press [**Ctrl**][**Shift**] . (hold down the control and shift keys and type a period). Mathcad displays a placeholder to the left of the arrow, "→".

- In the placeholder, type **substitute** followed by a comma and an expression of the form *var1*=*var2* where *var1* is a variable and *var2* is a variable or expression. Press [**Ctrl**] = for the equal sign.

- Press [**Enter**] to see the result.

Mathcad will replace *var1* with *var2*. If *var1* occurs more than once in the expression you are transforming, Mathcad replaces each occurrence. Figure 17-12 shows some examples.

Note that Mathcad will not substitute a variable for an entire vector or a matrix. You can, however, substitute a scalar expression for a variable that occurs in a matrix. To do so, select the expression that will replace the variable and choose **Copy** from the **Edit** menu. Click on an occurrence of the variable you want to replace and choose **Variable⇒Substitute** from the **Symbolics** menu. You can also use this menu command to perform a substitution in any expression.

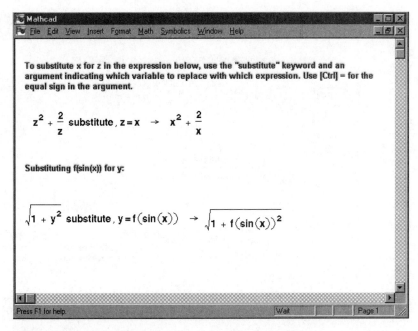

Figure 17-12: Substituting an expression for a variable.

Evaluating a summation

To evaluate a sum symbolically, you can use Mathcad's summation operator and the live symbolic equal sign:

■ Create the summation operator by typing [**Ctrl**][**Shift**]4.

■ Enter the expression you want to sum in the placeholder to the right of the "Σ".

■ Enter the index variable and summation range in the placeholders above and below the "Σ" as shown in Figure 17-13.

■ Press [**Ctrl**]. (the control key followed by a period). Mathcad displays an arrow, "→".

■ Press [**Enter**] to see the result.

The procedure is the same for a product over a range, except that you type [**Ctrl**][**Shift**]3 to get the product operator. If you use numerical limits in a summation or product range, be sure that the upper limit of the range is greater than or equal to the lower limit.

Another way to evaluate a summation is to enclose the summation expression between the editing lines and choose **Evaluate⇒Symbolically** from the **Symbolics** menu.

Figure 17-13 illustrates various results of symbolic evaluation.

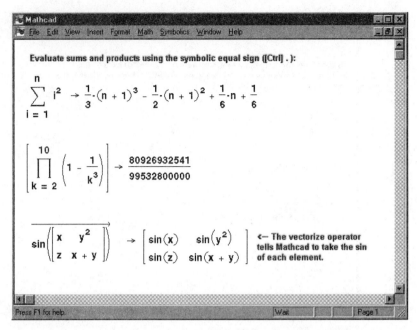

Figure 17-13: Symbolic evaluation of sums, products, and functions.

Symbolic calculus

This section describes how to symbolically evaluate definite and indefinite integrals, derivatives, and limits.

Derivatives

To evaluate a derivative symbolically, you can use Mathcad's derivative operator and the live symbolic equal sign as shown in Figure 17-14:

■ Type **?** to create the derivative operator or type **[Ctrl]?** to create the higher order derivative operator.

■ In the placeholders, enter the expression you want to differentiate and the variable with respect to which you are differentiating.

■ Press **[Ctrl].** (the control key followed by a period). Mathcad displays an arrow, "→".

■ Press **[Enter]** to see the result.

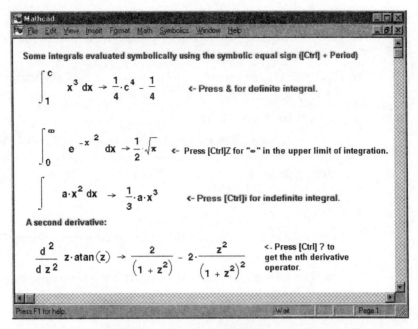

Figure 17-14: Evaluating integrals and derivatives symbolically.

Figure 17-15 shows you how to differentiate an expression without using the derivative operator. The **Symbolics** menu command **Variable⇒Differentiate** differentiates an expression with respect to a selected variable. For example, to differentiate $2 \cdot x^2 + y$ with respect to x:

■ Enter the expression.

■ Click on the x.

■ Choose **Variable⇒Differentiate** from the **Symbolics** menu. Mathcad will display the derivative, $4 \cdot x$.

If you selected the variable y instead of x, you would get the answer 1. Mathcad treats all variables except the one you've selected as constants.

If you've selected neither x nor y the menu command will be gray. Mathcad can't differentiate the expression because you haven't specified a differentiation variable.

If the expression in which you've selected a variable is one element of an array, Mathcad will differentiate only that array element. To differentiate an entire array, differentiate each element individually by selecting a variable in that element and choosing **Variable⇒Differentiate** from the **Symbolics** menu.

Indefinite integrals

Mathcad provides the symbolic indefinite integral operator shown in Figure 17-14. To use this operator:

■ Type [**Ctrl**]**I** to insert the indefinite integral operator and its placeholders.

■ Fill in the placeholder for the integrand.

■ Place the integration variable in the placeholder next to the "*d*." This can be any variable name.

■ Press [**Ctrl**]. (the control key followed by a period). Mathcad displays an arrow, "→".

■ Press [**Enter**] to see the result.

Figure 17-15 shows how to integrate an expression without using the indefinite integral operator. The **Symbolics** menu command **Variable⇒Integrate** integrates an expression with respect to a selected variable. For example, to integrate $2 \cdot x^2 + y$ with respect to *x*:

■ Select the *x*.

■ Choose **Variable⇒Integrate** from the **Symbolics** menu. Mathcad will display the integral.

The **Variable⇒Integrate** command integrates an expression with respect to a selected variable. If you don't have a variable selected, this command will be gray. Mathcad cannot integrate without knowing the variable of integration.

If the symbolic processor can't find a closed-form indefinite integral, you'll see an appropriate error message. Keep in mind that many simple expressions don't have a closed-form indefinite integral that can be written in terms of polynomials or elementary functions. For example, e^{-x^3} has no elementary integral. If the integral is too big to display, Mathcad puts the answer, in text form, on the clipboard. See the section "Long answers" on page 395 to learn what to do when this happens.

When evaluating an indefinite integral, remember that the answer to an integration problem is not unique. If $f(x)$ is an integral of a given function, so is $f(x) + C$ for any constant *C*. Thus, the answer you get from Mathcad may differ by a constant from the answer you find in tables. If you differentiate a function and then integrate the result, you won't necessarily get the original function back as your answer.

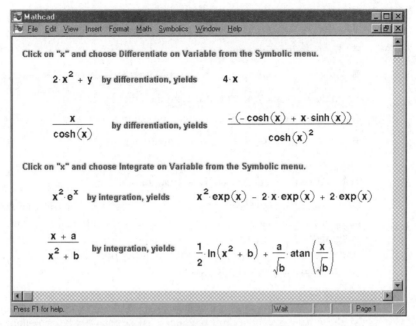

Click on "x" and choose Differentiate on Variable from the Symbolic menu.

$2 \cdot x^2 + y$ by differentiation, yields $4 \cdot x$

$\dfrac{x}{\cosh(x)}$ by differentiation, yields $\dfrac{-(-\cosh(x) + x \cdot \sinh(x))}{\cosh(x)^2}$

Click on "x" and choose Integrate on Variable from the Symbolic menu.

$x^2 \cdot e^x$ by integration, yields $x^2 \cdot \exp(x) - 2 \cdot x \cdot \exp(x) + 2 \cdot \exp(x)$

$\dfrac{x + a}{x^2 + b}$ by integration, yields $\dfrac{1}{2} \cdot \ln(x^2 + b) + \dfrac{a}{\sqrt{b}} \cdot \mathrm{atan}\left(\dfrac{x}{\sqrt{b}}\right)$

Figure 17-15: Differentiating and integrating expressions.

Definite integrals

To symbolically evaluate a definite integral:

■ Type **&** to create the integral operator with its empty placeholders.

■ Fill in the placeholders for the limits of integration. These can be variables, constants, or expressions.

■ Fill in the placeholder for the integrand.

■ Fill in the placeholder next to the "d." This is the variable of integration.

■ Press **[Ctrl].** (the control key followed by a period). Mathcad displays an arrow, "→".

■ Press **[Enter]** to see the result.

The symbolic processor will attempt to find an indefinite integral of your integrand before substituting the limits you specified. See Figure 17-14 for an example. If the symbolic processor can't find a closed form for the integral, you'll see an appropriate error message.

If the symbolic integration succeeds and the limits of integration are integers, fractions, or exact constants like π, you'll get an exact value for your integral. If the integrand or one of the limits contains a decimal point, the symbolic answer will be a number displayed with 20 significant digits. Use the **float** keyword described in "Floating point evaluation" on page 363 to generate a result with a different number of significant digits.

This answer will in general agree with the answer you get by evaluating the same integral numerically. The symbolic and numerical answers are, however, obtained in very different ways. Mathcad's symbolic processor:

■ Finds an indefinite integral.

■ Subtracts its value at the lower limit of integration from its value at the upper limit.

The numerical integration routine, on the other hand:

■ Samples the integrand at many points in the interval of integration.

■ Uses these samples to approximate the integral.

The accuracy of this numerical integration depends on the value you set for the variable TOL and on the smoothness of the function you are integrating.

Of course, many functions do not have a closed form integral, and definite integrals involving these functions can *only* be calculated numerically. Integrals for which the integrand is not smooth (has a discontinuous derivative) might not be evaluated correctly by the symbolic processor. See the section "Integrals" in Chapter 12 for more on Mathcad's numerical integration.

Limits

Mathcad provides three limit operators. These can only be evaluated symbolically. They cannot be evaluated numerically. To use the limit operators:

■ Press [**Ctrl**]**L** to create the limit operator. To create operators for limits from the left or right, press [**Ctrl**]**B** or [**Ctrl**]**A**.

■ Enter the expression in the placeholder to the right of the "lim."

■ Enter the limiting variable in the left-hand placeholder below the "lim."

■ Enter the limiting value in the right-hand placeholder below the "lim."

■ Press [**Ctrl**]**.** (the control key followed by a period). Mathcad displays an arrow, "→".

■ Press [**Enter**] to see the result.

Mathcad will return a result for the limit. If the limit does not exist, Mathcad returns an error message. Figure 17-16 shows some examples of evaluating limits.

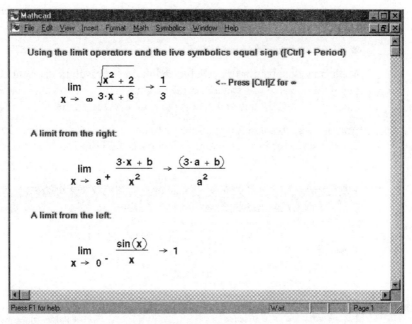

Figure 17-16: Evaluating limits.

Solving equations symbolically

This section discusses how to use either keywords or menu commands from the **Symbolics** menu to symbolically solve an equation for a variable, find the symbolic roots of an expression, and solve a system of equations symbolically. **Most of the examples in this section demonstrate "live" solving using symbolic keywords, but you may apply commands from the Symbolics menu to expressions on a case by case basis if you prefer. Keep in mind that, unlike the keyword-modified expressions, expressions modified by commands from the Symbolics menu do not update automatically, as described in the section "Using the Symbolics menu" on page 360.**

Solving equations symbolically is far more difficult than solving them numerically. You may find that the symbolic solver does not give a solution. This may happen for a variety of reasons discussed in "Limits to symbolic processing" on page 395.

Solving an equation for a variable

To solve an equation symbolically for a variable, use the keyword **solve**:

- Type the equation. Make sure you use [Ctrl]= to create the equal sign.

- Press [Ctrl][Shift] . (hold down the control and shift keys and type a period). Mathcad displays a placeholder to the left of the arrow, "→".

- In the placeholder, type **solve** followed by a comma and the variable for which to solve.

- Press [**Enter**] to see the result.

Mathcad will solve for the variable and insert the result to the right of the "→". Note that if the variable was squared in the original equation, you may get *two* answers back when you solve. Mathcad displays these in a vector. Figure 17-17 shows an example.

Another way to solve for a variable is to enter the equation, click on the variable you want to solve for in an equation, and choose **Variable⇒Solve** from the **Symbolics** menu.

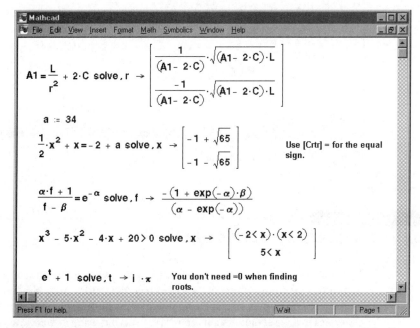

Figure 17-17: Examples of solving equations, solving inequalities, and finding roots.

You can also solve an inequality entered using the symbols $<$, $>$, $\leq$, and $\geq$. Solutions to inequalities will be displayed in terms of Mathcad boolean expressions. If there is more than one solution, Mathcad places them in a vector. A Mathcad boolean expression such as $x < 2$ has the value 1 if it is true and 0 if it is false. Thus the solution "x is less than 2 and greater than -2" would be represented by the expression $(x < 2) \cdot (-2 < x)$.

Finding the roots of an expression

You can use the **solve** keyword to find the roots of an expression in a manner similar to that of solving an equation in a variable:

- Type the expression.

- Press [Ctrl] [Shift] . (hold down the control and shift keys and type a period). Mathcad displays a placeholder to the left of the arrow, "→".

- In the placeholder, type **solve** followed by a comma and the variable for which to solve.

- Press [Enter] to see the result.

Note that there is no need to set the expression equal to zero. When Mathcad doesn't find an equals sign, it assumes you mean to set the expression equal to zero. See Figure 17-17 for an example.

Solving a system of equations symbolically: The "solve" keyword

One way to symbolically solve a system of equations is to use the same **solve** keyword used to solve one equation in one unknown. To solve a system of *n* equations for *n* unknowns:

- Press [Ctrl] M to create a vector having *n* rows and 1 column.

- Fill in each placeholder of the vector with one of the *n* equations making up the system. Make sure you use [Ctrl]= to create the equals sign.

- Press [Ctrl] [Shift] . (hold down the control and shift keys and type a period). Mathcad displays a placeholder to the left of the arrow, "→".

- In the placeholder, type **solve** followed by a comma.

- Press [Ctrl] M to create a vector having *n* rows and 1 column.

- Press [Enter] to see the result.

Mathcad displays the *n* solutions to the system of equations to the right of the arrow. Figure 17-18 shows an example.

Solving a system of equations symbolically: Solve block

Another way to solve a system of equations symbolically is to use a solve block, similar to the numerical solve blocks described in Chapter 15, "Solving Equations."

- Type the word *Given*. This tells Mathcad that what follows is a system of equations. You can type *Given* in any combination of upper and lower case letters, and in any font. Just be sure you don't type it while in a text region or paragraph.

- Now type the equations in any order below the word *Given*. Make sure you press [Ctrl]= to type "=."

- Type the *Find* function as appropriate for your system of equations. This function is described "Systems of equations" on page 315. The arguments of the function are the variables for which you are solving.

- Press [Ctrl] . (the control key followed by a period). Mathcad displays the symbolic equal sign.

- Click outside the *Find* function.

Mathcad displays the solutions to the system of equations to the right of the arrow. If the *Find* function has one argument, Mathcad returns one result. If the *Find* has more than one argument, Mathcad returns a vector of results. For example, Find(*x*, *y*) returns a vector containing the expressions for *x* and *y* that solve the system of equations. Note that if your system is an overdetermined linear system, the *Find* function will not return a solution. Use the *Minerr* function instead of *Find*. *Minerr* will return an answer that minimizes the errors in the constraints.

Most of the guidelines for solve blocks described in Chapter 15, "Solving Equations," apply to the symbolic solution of systems of equations. The main difference is that when you solve equations symbolically, you should not enter guess values for the solutions.

Figure 17-18 shows an example of a solve block used to solve a system of equations symbolically. For more information on solve blocks, see Chapter 15, "Solving Equations."

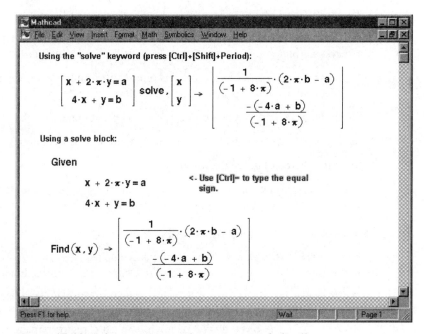

Figure 17-18: Solving a system of equations symbolically.

Symbolic matrix manipulation

This section describes how to find the symbolic transpose, inverse, and determinant of a matrix. The examples in this section demonstrate "live" symbolic matrix manipulation using the matrix operators, described in Chapter 10, "Vectors and Matrices," and the symbolic equal sign. You may, however, apply the Matrix commands from the

Symbolics menu to matrices on a case by case basis if you prefer. Keep in mind that, unlike matrices evaluated with the symbolic equal sign, matrices modified by commands from the Symbolics menu do not update automatically, as described in the section "Using the Symbolics menu" on page 360.

Finding the symbolic transpose

To find the symbolic transpose of a matrix:

- Place the entire matrix between the two editing lines by clicking [**Space**] one or more times.

- **Press [Ctrl] 1 to create the matrix transpose operator.**

- Press [**Ctrl**]. (the control key followed by a period). Mathcad displays an arrow, "→".

- Press [**Enter**] to see the result.

Mathcad returns the matrix with its rows and columns swapped to the right of the "→".

Another way to find the transpose of a matrix is to select the matrix and choose **Matrix⇒Transpose** from the **Symbolics** menu.

Finding the symbolic inverse

To find the symbolic inverse of a square matrix:

- Place the entire matrix between the two editing lines by clicking [**Space**] one or more times.

- **Press ^ -1 to indicate matrix inversion.**

- Press [**Ctrl**]. (the control key followed by a period). Mathcad displays an arrow, "→".

- Press [**Enter**] to see the result.

Mathcad will return a symbolic representation for the inverse of the selected matrix to the right of the "→".

Another way to find the inverse of a matrix is to select the matrix and choose **Matrix⇒Invert** from the **Symbolics** menu.

Finding the symbolic determinant

To find the symbolic determinant of a square matrix:

- Place the entire matrix between the two editing lines by clicking [**Space**] one or more times.

- **Press | to create the matrix determinant operator.**

- Press [**Ctrl**]. (the control key followed by a period). Mathcad displays an arrow, "→".

- Press [**Enter**] to see the result.

Mathcad will return a symbolic representation for the determinant of the selected matrix to the right of the "→". Keep in mind that this is usually a lengthy expression.

Another way to find the determinant of a matrix is to select the matrix and choose **Matrix⇒Determinant** from the **Symbolics** menu.

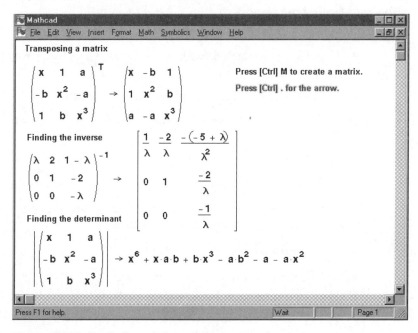

Figure 17-19: Symbolic matrix operations.

Symbolic transforms

This section describes how to perform the Fourier, Laplace, and z-transforms, and their inverses. The examples in this section demonstrate "live" transformations using symbolic keywords, but you may apply the Transforms commands from the Symbolics menu to expressions on a case by case basis if you prefer. Keep in mind that, unlike keyword-modified expressions, expressions modified by commands from the Symbolics menu do not update automatically, as described in the section "Using the Symbolics menu" on page 360.

Figure 17-20 shows some examples of symbolic transforms in Mathcad. Note that the result may contain functions that are recognized by Mathcad's symbolic processor but not by its numeric processor. An example is the function *Dirac* in the middle of Figure 17-20. You'll find numerical definitions for this and other such functions at the end of this chapter and in the on-line Help.

Chapter 17 Symbolic Calculation

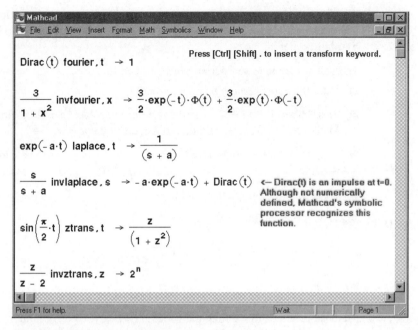

Figure 17-20: Performing symbolic transforms.

When you perform a symbolic transform, Mathcad returns a function in a variable commonly used in the context of the transform. **You can substitute a different variable for the one Mathcad returns by using the substitute keyword. See the section "Symbolic algebra" on page 362 for information on substituting one variable for another.**

Fourier and inverse Fourier transformations

To evaluate the Fourier transform of a function, use the keyword **fourier**:

■ Enter the expression to be transformed.

■ Press **[Ctrl][Shift].** (hold down the control and shift keys and type a period). Mathcad displays a placeholder to the left of the arrow, "→".

■ In the placeholder, type **fourier** followed by a comma and the transform variable.

■ Press **[Enter]** to see the result.

Mathcad returns a function of ω given by:

$$\int_{-\infty}^{+\infty} f(t)e^{-i\omega t}dt$$

where $f(t)$ is the expression to be transformed.

Mathcad returns a function in the variable ω when you perform a Fourier transform since this is a commonly used variable name in this context. If the expression you are transforming already contains an ω, Mathcad avoids ambiguity by returning a function of the variable ωω instead.

Another way to evaluate the Fourier transform of an expression is to enter the expression and click on the transform variable. Then choose **Transform⇒Fourier** from the **Symbolics** menu.

To evaluate the inverse Fourier transform of a function, use the keyword **invfourier**:

- Enter the expression to be transformed.

- Press [Ctrl][Shift]. (hold down the control and shift keys and type a period). Mathcad displays a placeholder to the left of the arrow, "→".

- In the placeholder, type **invfourier** followed by a comma and the transform variable.

- Press [Enter] to see the result.

Mathcad returns a function of *t* given by:

$$\frac{1}{2\pi}\int_{-\infty}^{+\infty} F(\omega)e^{i\omega t}d\omega$$

where $F(\omega)$ is the expression to be transformed.

Mathcad returns a function in the variable *t* when you perform an inverse Fourier transform since this is a commonly used variable name in this context. If the expression you are transforming already contains a *t*, Mathcad avoids ambiguity by returning a function of the variable *tt* instead.

Another way to evaluate the inverse Fourier transform of an expression is to enter the expression and click on the transform variable. Then choose **Transform⇒Inverse Fourier** from the **Symbolics** menu.

Laplace and inverse Laplace transformations

To evaluate the Laplace transform of a function, use the keyword **laplace**:

- Enter the expression to be transformed.

- Press [Ctrl][Shift]. (hold down the control and shift keys and type a period). Mathcad displays a placeholder to the left of the arrow, "→".

- In the placeholder, type **laplace** followed by a comma and the transform variable.

- Press [Enter] to see the result.

Mathcad returns a function of *s* given by:

$$\int_{0}^{+\infty} f(t)e^{-st}dt$$

where $f(t)$ is the expression to be transformed.

Mathcad returns a function in the variable *s* when you perform a Laplace transform since this is a commonly used variable name in this context. If the expression you are transforming already contains an *s*, Mathcad avoids ambiguity by returning a function of the variable *ss* instead.

Another way to evaluate the Laplace transform of an expression is to enter the expression and click on the transform variable. Then choose **Transform⇒Laplace** from the **Symbolics** menu.

To evaluate the inverse Laplace transform of a function, use the keyword **invlaplace**:

■ Enter the expression to be transformed.

■ Press [**Ctrl**] [**Shift**] . (hold down the control and shift keys and type a period). Mathcad displays a placeholder to the left of the arrow, "→".

■ In the placeholder, type **invlaplace** followed by a comma and the transform variable.

■ Press [**Enter**] to see the result.

Mathcad returns a function of t given by:

$$\frac{1}{2\pi}\int_{\sigma - i\infty}^{\sigma + i\infty} F(s)e^{st}dt$$

where $F(s)$ is the expression to be transformed and all singularities of $F(s)$ are to the left of the line $\text{Re}(s) = \sigma$.

Mathcad returns a function in the variable t when you perform an inverse Laplace transform since this is a commonly used variable name in this context. If the expression you are transforming already contains a t, Mathcad avoids ambiguity by returning a function of the variable tt instead.

Another way to evaluate the inverse Laplace transform of an expression is to enter the expression and click on the transform variable. Then choose **Transform⇒Inverse Laplace** from the **Symbolics** menu.

z and inverse *z*-transformations

To evaluate the z-transform of a function, use the keyword **ztrans**:

■ Enter the expression to be transformed.

■ Press [**Ctrl**] [**Shift**] . (hold down the control and shift keys and type a period). Mathcad displays a placeholder to the left of the arrow, "→".

■ In the placeholder, type **ztrans** followed by a comma and the transform variable.

■ Press [**Enter**] to see the result.

Mathcad returns a function of z given by:

$$\sum_{n = 0}^{+\infty} f(n)z^{-n}$$

where $f(n)$ is the expression to be transformed.

Mathcad returns a function in the variable z when you perform a z-transform since this is a commonly used variable name in this context. If the expression you are transforming already contains a z, Mathcad avoids ambiguity by returning a function of the variable zz instead.

Another way to evaluate the z-transform of an expression is to enter the expression and click on the transform variable. Then choose **Transform⇒z-Transform** from the **Symbolics** menu.

To evaluate the inverse z-transform of a function, use the keyword **invztrans**:

■ Enter the expression to be transformed.

■ Press [Ctrl][Shift] . (hold down the control and shift keys and type a period). Mathcad displays a placeholder to the left of the arrow, "→".

■ In the placeholder, type **invztrans** followed by a comma and the transform variable.

■ Press [Enter] to see the result.

Mathcad returns a function of n given by a contour integral around the origin:

$$\frac{1}{2\pi i}\int_C F(z)z^{n-1}dz$$

where $F(z)$ is the expression to be transformed and C is a contour enclosing all singularities of the integrand.

Mathcad returns a function in the variable n when you perform an inverse z-transform since this is a commonly used variable name in this context. If the expression you are transforming already contains an n, Mathcad avoids ambiguity by returning a function of the variable nn instead.

Another way to evaluate the inverse z-transform of an expression is to enter the expression and click on the transform variable. Then choose **Transform⇒Inverse z-Transform** from the **Symbolics** menu.

Symbolic optimization

In general, Mathcad's symbolic processor and Mathcad's numerical processor don't communicate with one another. Because of this, it's possible to set up a complicated numerical calculation without knowing that you could have reduced it to an equivalent but much simpler problem by judicious use of the symbolic processor.

You can, however, make the numerical processor ask the symbolic processor for advice before starting what could be a needlessly complex calculation. In effect, the symbolic processor acts like the numerical processor's consultant, examining each expression and recommending a better way to evaluate it whenever possible. It does this for each expression in the worksheet except for those you specifically tell it to ignore.

For example, if you were to evaluate an expression such as:

$$\int_0^u \int_0^v \int_0^w x^2 + y^2 + z^2 dx\, dy\, dz$$

Mathcad would undertake the laborious task of evaluating a numerical approximation of the triple integral even though one could arrive at an exact solution by first performing a few elementary calculus operations.

This happens because by itself, Mathcad's numerical processor does not know enough to simplify before plunging ahead into the calculation. Although Mathcad's symbolic processor knows all about simplifying complicated expressions, these two processors do not consult with each other. To make these two processors talk to each other, choose **Optimization** from the **Math** menu.

Once you've done this, Mathcad's live symbolic processor steps in and simplifies all expressions to the right of a ":=" *before* the numerical processor gets a chance to begin its calculations. It will continue to do so until you choose **Optimization** from the **Math** menu once more to remove the checkmark.

If Mathcad finds a simpler form for the expression, it responds by doing the following:

■ It marks the region with a red asterisk.

■ It *internally* replaces what you've typed with a simplified form. The expression you typed is left unchanged; Mathcad simply works with an equivalent expression that happens to be better suited for numerical analysis.

■ Mathcad evaluates this equivalent expression instead of the expression you specified. To see this equivalent expression, double-click on the red asterisk beside the region.

If Mathcad is unable to find a simpler form for the expression, it places a *blue* asterisk next to it.

In the previous example, the symbolic processor would examine the triple integral and return the equivalent, but much simpler expression:

$$\frac{1}{3}(w^3 vu + wv^3 u + wvu^3)$$

To see this expression in a pop-up window click on the red asterisk with the right mouse button and choose **Show Popup** from the context menu (see Figure 17-21). To dismiss the pop-up, click the close box in the upper right corner.

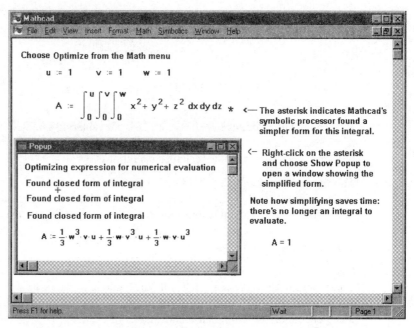

Figure 17-21: A pop-up window showing the equivalent expression that Mathcad actually evaluates.

Since this simplified form contains no integral, Mathcad's numerical processor no longer needs to use a lengthy numerical algorithm to evaluate the integral. This offers two advantages:

■ By avoiding time-consuming integration, Mathcad's numerical processor can evaluate the expression far more quickly.

■ Mathcad avoids all the computation issues inherent in numerical integration.

There may be times when you don't want Mathcad's symbolic processor to examine a particular equation. You may want to evaluate an expression exactly as you've typed it. To do so, right-click on the expression and choose **Optimize** from the context menu. This procedure disables optimization for that expression.

Using functions and variables

Mathcad's symbolic processor does not treat functions and variables in exactly the same way as its numerical processor. These differences revolve around the answers to the following question:

■ Does the symbolic processor "know" that a function or variable is defined elsewhere?

The answer to this depends on two things:

- ■ Is the function or variable built-in or is it defined somewhere on the worksheet?

- ■ Are you using the symbolic equal sign or a menu command?

The next two sections describe what Mathcad does with variables and functions in a symbolic transformation.

A related question is the converse. Symbolic transformations can sometimes return functions and constants which do not exist in Mathcad's list of built-in functions and constants. These are described in the section "Special functions" on page 392.

Built-in functions and variables

As a general rule, built-in functions retain their meanings when used in symbolic transformations provided that it makes sense for them to do so. For example, functions like *sin* and *log* keep their meanings because these have a commonly accepted mathematical meaning. Other functions like *linterp* or *rnd* lack any commonly accepted meaning so Mathcad doesn't attempt to assign one.

Built-in functions that do retain their meanings when used in symbolic calculations include: trigonometric and hyperbolic functions and their inverses; logarithmic and exponential functions; the *Re* and *Im* functions; the *erf* function; the Γ function; the *mod* function; Φ (the Heaviside step function); *max* and *min*; and the *identity* and *eigenvals* functions for matrices.

In general, these functions mean the same thing for both numerical evaluations and symbolic transformations. There are two subtle differences:

- ■ Unlike the numerical *mod* function, the symbolic *mod* function requires an integer modulus, and can accept a polynomial as its first argument.

- ■ Certain of the inverse trigonometric functions use different branches in the complex plane.

As a general rule, built-in constants also retain their meanings when used in symbolic transformations provided that it makes sense for them to do so. The symbolic processor will recognize π, e and ∞. Moreover, these will have their exact meanings when used symbolically. When symbolic transformations are involved, there is no need to limit ∞ to 10^{307} or to limit π to only fifteen digits of precision.

Built-in constants lacking an intuitive mathematical meaning are not recognized by the symbolic processor. For example, TOL and ORIGIN will not have their usual meanings in symbolic transformations. They will be treated like any other undefined variable.

Figure 17-22 shows the difference in the way Mathcad treats functions in symbolic transformations. Note that the symbolic processor will recognize and evaluate the *sin* function, but when asked to evaluate $rnd(3)$ the symbolic processor simply returns $rnd(3)$.

User-defined functions and variables

Functions and variables you define yourself *are* recognized by the symbolic processor when you use the symbolic equal sign discussed in the next section. They *are not*, however, recognized when you use **Symbolics** menu commands. Figure 17-22 shows the difference.

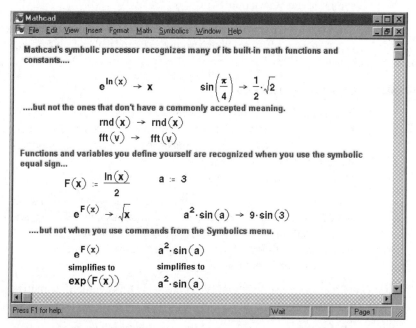

Figure 17-22: The symbolic processor recognizes certain built-in functions. Functions and variables you define yourself are only recognized when you use the symbolic equal sign.

Special functions

A symbolic transformation sometimes comes back in terms of a function which isn't part of Mathcad's list of built-in functions. The list below gives definitions for those special functions. Except for *Ei*, *erf*, and *Zeta*, all of which involve infinite sums, and *W*, you can use these definitions to calculate numerical values.

You can define many of these functions in Mathcad. See the "Special Functions" topic in the Quicksheets of the Resource Center for examples.

γ is Euler's constant, approximately 0.5772156649.

$$\text{Chi}(x) = \gamma + \ln(x) + \int_0^x \frac{\cosh(t) - 1}{t} dt$$

$$\text{Ci}(x) = \gamma + \ln(x) + \int_0^x \frac{\cos(t) - 1}{t} dt$$

$\text{csgn}(z) = 1$ if $\text{Re}(z) > 0$ or $(\text{Re}(z) = 0$ and $\text{Im}(z) \geq 0)$; -1 otherwise.
Define in Mathcad as: $if(\text{Re}(z) \neq 0, 2\Phi(\text{Re}(z)) - 1, 2\Phi(\text{Im}(z)) - 1)$

$$\text{dilog}(x) = \int_1^x \frac{\ln(t)}{1 - t} dt$$

$\text{Dirac}(x) = 0$ if x is not zero. $\int_{-\infty}^{\infty} Dirac(x) dx = 1$

$$\text{Ei}(x) = \gamma + \ln(x) + \sum_{n=1}^{\infty} \frac{x^n}{n \cdot n!} \quad (x > 0)$$

$$\text{erf}(x) = \frac{2}{\sqrt{\pi}} \sum_{n=0}^{\infty} \frac{(-1)^n z^{2n+1}}{n!(2n+1)} \quad \text{(for complex } z\text{)}$$

$$\text{FresnelC}(x) = \int_0^x \cos\left(\frac{\pi}{2} t^2\right) dt$$

$$\text{FresnelS}(x) = \int_0^x \sin\left(\frac{\pi}{2} t^2\right) dt$$

$$\text{LegendreE}(x, k) = \int_0^x \left(\frac{1 - k^2 \cdot t^2}{1 - t^2}\right)^{1/2} dt$$

$$\text{LegendreEc}(k) = \text{LegendreE}(1, k)$$

$$\text{LegendreEc1}(k) = \text{LegendreEc}(\sqrt{1 - k^2})$$

$$\text{LegendreF}(x, k) = \int_0^x \frac{1}{\sqrt{(1 - t^2)(1 - k^2 \cdot t^2)}} dt$$

$$\text{LegendreKc}(k) = \text{LegendreF}(1, k)$$

$$\text{LegendreKc1}(k) = \text{LegendreKc}(\sqrt{1 - k^2})$$

$$\text{LegendrePi}(x, n, k) = \int_0^x \frac{1}{\sqrt{(1 - n^2 \cdot t^2)}\sqrt{(1 - t^2)(1 - k^2 \cdot t^2)}} dt$$

$$\text{LegendrePic}(n, k) = \text{LegendrePi}(1, n, k)$$

$$\text{LegendrePic1}(k) = \text{LegendrePic}(n, \sqrt{1 - k^2})$$

$$\text{Psi}(n, k) = \frac{d^n}{dx^n}\text{Psi}(x)$$

$$\text{Psi}(x) = \frac{d}{dx}\ln(\Gamma(x))$$

$$\text{Shi}(x) = \int_0^x \frac{\sinh(t)}{t}dt$$

$$\text{Si}(x) = \int_0^x \frac{\sin(t)}{t}dt$$

$\text{signum}(x) = 1$ if $x = 0$, $x/|x|$ otherwise; calculate in Mathcad as $(x=0) + x/|x|$.

$W(x)$ is the principal branch of a function satisfying $W(x) \cdot \exp(W(x)) = x$. $W(n, x)$ is the nth branch of $W(x)$.

$$\text{Zeta}(s)(\sum_{n=1}^{\infty} \frac{1}{n^s})\ (s > 1)$$

The functions *arcsec, arccsc, arccot, arcsech, arcscsh, arccoth* can be calculated by taking reciprocals and using the Mathcad built-in functions *acos, asin*, etc. For example:

$$\text{arc sec}(x) := \text{acos}\left(\frac{1}{x}\right)$$

The *Psi* function and Γ appear frequently in the results of *indefinite* sums and products. If you use a single variable name rather than a full range in the index placeholder of a summation or product, and you choose **Evaluate Symbolically** or one of the other symbolic evaluation commands, Mathcad will attempt to calculate an indefinite sum or product of the expression in the main placeholder. The indefinite sum of $f(i)$ is an expression $S(i)$ for which

$$S(i + 1) - S(i) = f(i)$$

The indefinite product of $f(i)$ is an expression $P(i)$ for which

$$\frac{P(i + 1)}{P(i)} = f(i)$$

Limits to symbolic processing

As you work with the symbolic processor, you will undoubtedly discover two things:

■ many problems can *only* be solved numerically, and

■ many more problems yield such lengthy expressions that you'll wish you *had* solved them numerically.

For a computer, symbolic operations are, in general, much more difficult than the corresponding numerical operations. In fact, if you write down a complicated function at random, the chance is very small that either its roots or its integral can be expressed in a simple closed form. For example, there is no formula for the roots of a general polynomial of degree 5 or higher, even though exact roots can be found for some special cases.

Many deceptively simple-looking functions made up of elementary pieces like powers and roots, exponentials, logs, and trigonometric functions have no closed-form integral that can be expressed in terms of these same functions.

When an equation has several solutions, Mathcad sometimes returns only a partial solution and asks if you want this result placed in the clipboard. If you click "OK," Mathcad shows a vector containing the solutions found and the word "Root". In the clipboard, in place of the word "Root" you will see an expression of the form "RootOf (function_of_Z)". The roots of the indicated function are solutions of the original equation.

As with other symbolic operations, the answers you get depend on whether the constants in your equation contain decimal points. If your constants are pure rational numbers like 1/2 or 4, the symbolic solver will try to find an *exact* solution. For example, the solution to the second equation in Figure 17-17 is exact. But if you had defined *a* to be "34.0" instead of "34", Mathcad would have given approximate numerical values.

Long answers

Symbolic calculations can easily produce answers so long that they don't fit conveniently in your window. If the answer consists of the sum of several terms, you can reformat such an answer by using Mathcad's "Addition with line break" operator described in the section "List of operators" in Chapter 12.

To break an expression with plus signs:

■ Click just to the right of the term that appears immediately before the plus sign at which you want to break the expression.

■ Press [**Space**] until the all the terms from the first to the selected on are held between the two editing lines.

■ Press [**Del**]. The plus sign just after the editing lines will disappear.

■ Now type [**Ctrl**][**Enter**] to insert the plus with break.

You can repeat this process if there are several terms connected by plus signs.

Sometimes, a symbolic answer will be so long that you can't conveniently display it in your worksheet. When this happens, Mathcad will ask if you want the answer placed in the clipboard. If you click "OK," Mathcad places a string representing the answer on the clipboard.

When you examine the contents of the clipboard, you'll see an answer written in a Fortran-like syntax as shown in Figure 17-23. This syntax uses the following conventions:

■ The symbols $+, -, *$, and $/$ stand for the basic arithmetic operations. Exponentiation is denoted by "**".

■ The derivative of $f(x)$ with respect to x is written "$\text{diff}(f(x), x)$". The nth derivative is "$\text{diff}(f(x), x\$n)$".

■ A "D" also stands for the partial derivative operator. The nth derivative is "(D, n)". The partial derivative of a function with respect to its nth argument is "$(D[n])$".

■ The integral of $f(x)$ with respect to x is written "$\text{int}(f(x), x)$".

■ The summation and product operators appear as "sum( )" and "product( )".

■ The operator "@" denotes function composition. For example, $(\sin@\exp)(x)$ is the same as $\sin(\exp(x))$. A "@@" represents repeated composition, so $(f@@2)(x)$ is the same as $f(f(x))$.

■ "RootOf(*equation*)" stands for any root of an algebraic equation. (For example, "RootOf(Z**2 + 1)" represents either i or $-i$.)

■ You may see embedded font codes (like "MFNT_03_") preceding the variable name to indicate the font in which the variable name is to appear.

To insert the answer as text into your Mathcad worksheet:

■ Click in an empty area.

■ Choose **Paste** from the **Edit** menu.

To save a long clipboard answer as a separate text file, choose **Save As** from the Clipboard's **File** menu.

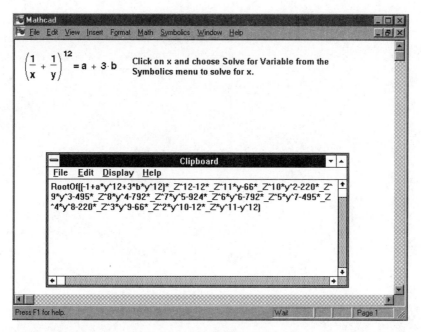

Figure 17-23: A long symbolic answer in the clipboard.

Chapter 17 Symbolic Calculation

Chapter 18
Programming

With Mathcad Professional, you can write your own programs using specialized programming operators. A Mathcad program has many attributes associated with programming languages including conditional branching, looping constructs, local scoping of variables, error handling, the ability to use other programs as subroutines, and the ability to call itself recursively.

Mathcad programs make it easy to do tasks that may be impossible or very inconvenient to do in any other way.

This chapter contains the following sections:

Defining a program

How to create simple programs. Local assignment statements.

Conditional statements

Using a condition to suppress execution of a statement.

Looping

Using **while** loops and **for** loops to control iteration.

Controlling program execution

Using the **break**, **continue**, and **return** statements to modify the execution of a loop or an entire program.

Error handling

Using the **on error** statement to trap errors and the *error* string function to issue error tips.

Programs within programs

Using subroutines and recursion in a Mathcad program.

Evaluating programs symbolically

Using a Mathcad program to generate a symbolic expression.

Programming examples

A sampling of programs displaying some of the power of Mathcad's approach to programming.

Defining a program

A Mathcad program is a special kind of Mathcad expression you can create in Mathcad Professional. Like any expression, a program returns a value—a scalar, vector, array, nested array, or string—when followed by the equal sign. In fact, as described in "Evaluating programs symbolically" on page 416, you can evaluate some Mathcad programs symbolically. And just as you can define a variable or function in terms of an expression, you can also define it in terms of a program.

The main difference between a program and an expression is the way you tell Mathcad how to compute an answer. When you use an expression, you have to describe how to compute the answer in one statement. But when you use a program, you can use as many statements as you want to describe how to compute the answer. You can think of a program as a "compound expression."

The following example shows how to make a simple program to define the function:

$$f(x, w) = \log\left(\frac{x}{w}\right)$$

Although the example chosen is so simple as to render programming unnecessary, it does illustrate how to separate the statements making up the program and how to use the local assignment operator, "←".

- ■ Type the left side of the function definition, followed by a "$:=$". Make sure the placeholder is selected.

- ■ Open the Programming Palette by clicking on the appropriate button in the Math Palette. Then click on the "Add Line" button. Alternatively, press].

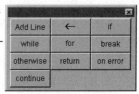

- ■ You'll see a vertical bar with two placeholders. These placeholders will hold the statements making up your program. You can continue adding placeholders for statements as you need them by repeatedly clicking the "Add Line" button.

- ■ Press [**Tab**] to move to the top placeholder. In the top placeholder, type **z**, and click on the "←" button on the Programming Palette. Alternatively, press { to insert a "←."

- In the placeholder to the right of the "←" type **x/w**.

$$f(x, w) := \left| \begin{array}{l} z \leftarrow \dfrac{x}{w} \\ \blacksquare \end{array} \right.$$

- Press [**Tab**] to move to the bottom placeholder.

- The remaining placeholder is the actual value to be returned by the program. Type **log(z)**.

$$f(x, w) := \left| \begin{array}{l} z \leftarrow \dfrac{x}{w} \\ \log(z) \end{array} \right.$$

You can now use this function just as you would any other function. Figure 18-1 shows this function along with an equivalent function defined on one line instead of two. Note that z is undefined everywhere outside the program. The definition of z inside the program is local to the program. It has no effect anywhere else.

A program can have any number of statements. To add a statement, click the "Add Line" button on the toolbar again. Mathcad inserts a placeholder below whatever statement you've selected. To delete the placeholder, click on it and backspace over it.

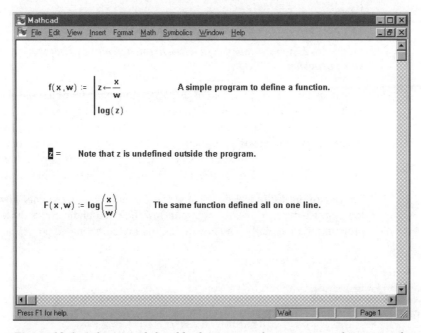

Figure 18-1: A function defined both in terms of a program and in terms of an expression.

Figure 18-2 shows a more complex example involving the quadratic formula. Although you can define the quadratic formula with a single statement as shown in the top half of the figure, you may find it simpler to define it with a series of simple statements as shown in the bottom half. This lets you avoid having to edit very complicated expressions.

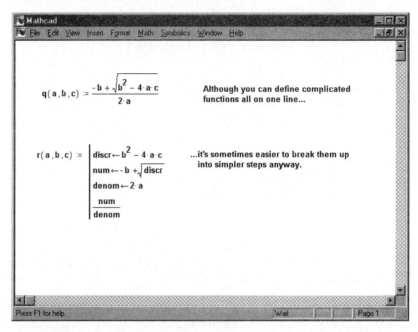

Figure 18-2: A more complex function defined in terms of both an expression and a program.

A Mathcad program, therefore, is an expression made up of a sequence of statements, each one of which is an expression in itself. Like any expression, a Mathcad program must have a value. This value is simply the value of the expression forming the last statement executed by the program. It could be a string expression or a single number, or it could be an array of numbers (see Figure 18-7, for example). It could even be a mixture of types, as described in the section "Nested arrays" in Chapter 10.

The remaining sections describe how to use conditional statements, how to use various looping structures to control program flow, how to handle errors, how to evaluate programs symbolically, and how to build more complicated programs.

Conditional statements

In general, Mathcad evaluates each statement in your program from the top down. There may be times, however, when you want Mathcad to evaluate a statement only when a particular condition is met. You can do this by including an **if** statement in your program. Note that the **if** statement in a Mathcad program is not the same as the *if* function, which you use elsewhere in your worksheet. The *if* function is described in

Chapter 13, "Built-in Functions."

For example, suppose you want to define a function that forms a semicircle around the origin but is otherwise constant. To do this:

- Type the left side of the function definition, followed by a "**: =**". Make sure the placeholder is selected.

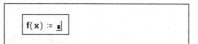

- Click the "Add Line" button on the Programming Palette. Alternatively, press **]**. You'll see a vertical bar with two placeholders. These placeholders will hold the statements making up your program.

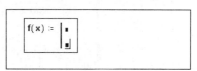

- In the top placeholder, click the "if" button on the Programming Palette. Alternatively, press **}**.

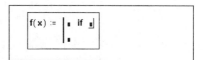

- In the right placeholder, type a boolean expression: an expression that's either true or false. In the left placeholder, type the value you want the expression to take whenever the expression in the right placeholder is true.

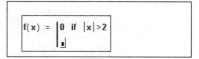

- Select the remaining placeholder and click the "otherwise" button on the Programming Palette.

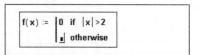

- In the remaining placeholder, type the value you want the program to return if the condition in the first statement is not met.

$$f(x) := \begin{vmatrix} 0 & \text{if } |x| > 2 \\ \sqrt{4 - x^2} & \text{otherwise} \end{vmatrix}$$

Figure 18-3 shows a plot of this function. Note that since this function only has two branches, it's not hard to define it using the *if* function as shown in Figure 18-3. However, as the number of branches exceeds two, the *if* function rapidly becomes unwieldy. An example is shown in Figure 18-4.

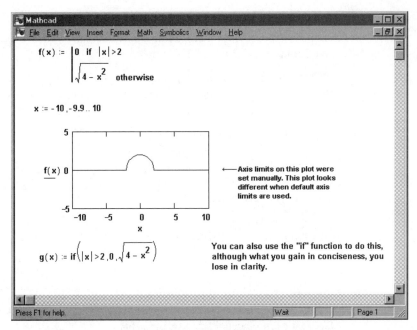

*Figure 18-3: Using the **if** statement to define a piecewise continuous function.*

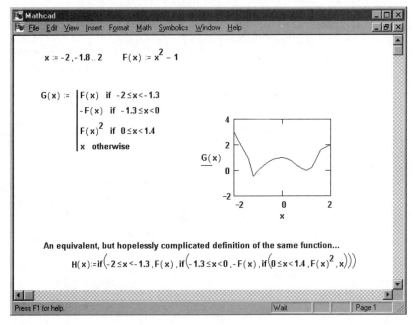

*Figure 18-4: Comparing the **if** statement in a program with the built-in "if" function.*

Chapter 18 Programming   **Pro**

Looping

One of the greatest strengths of programmability is the ability to execute a sequence of statements over and over again in a loop. Mathcad provides two such loops. The choice of which loop to use depends on how you plan to tell the loop to stop executing.

■ If you know exactly how many times a loop is to execute, you can use a **for** loop.

■ If you want the loop to stop upon the occurrence of a condition, but you don't know *when* that condition will occur, use a **while** loop.

"for" loops

A **for** loop is a loop that terminates after a predetermined number of iterations. Iteration is controlled by an iteration variable defined at the top of the loop. While in most cases you want a **for** loop to calculate for the complete number of iterations, you may also interrupt the loop on the occurrence of a particular condition. In such cases stop execution within the body of the loop using one of the methods described in "Controlling program execution" on page 407.

To create a **for** loop:

■ Click the button labeled "for" on the Programming Palette. Do not type the word "for".

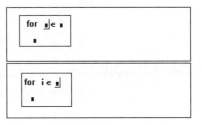

■ In the placeholder to the left of the "∈," type the name of the iteration variable.

■ In the placeholder to the right of the "∈," enter the range of values the iteration variable should take. You usually specify this range the same way you would for a range variable. See Chapter 11, "Range Variables," for more details.

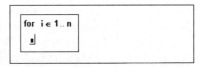

■ In the remaining placeholder, type the expression you want to evaluate repeatedly. This expression generally involves the iteration variable. If necessary, add placeholders by clicking the "Add Line" button on the Programming Palette.

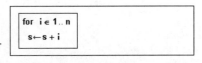

The upper half of Figure 18-5 shows this **for** loop being used to add a sequence of integers. The undefined variable in Figure 18-5 shows that the definition of an iteration variable is local to the program. It has no effect anywhere outside the program.

The lower half shows an example in which the iteration variable is defined not in terms of a range but in terms of the elements of a vector. Although the expression to the right of the "∈" is usually a range, it can also be a vector, a list of scalars, ranges and vectors separated by commas.

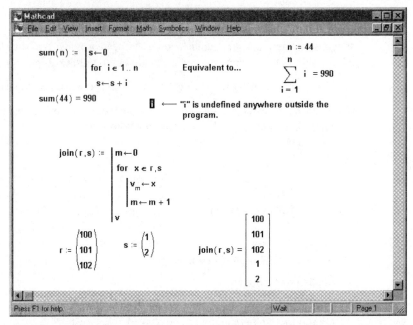

*Figure 18-5: Using a **for** loop with two different kinds of iteration variables.*

"while" loops

A **while** loop is driven by the truth of some condition. Because of this, you don't need to know in advance how many times the loop will execute. It is important, however, to have a statement somewhere, either within the loop or elsewhere in the program, that eventually makes the condition false. Otherwise, the loop will execute indefinitely. If you *do* find yourself in an endless loop or want to interrupt the loop on the occurrence of a particular condition, you can stop execution within the body of the loop using one of the methods described in "Controlling program execution" on page 407.

To create a **while** loop:

■ Click the button labeled "while" on the Programming Palette.

■ In the top placeholder, type a condition. This is typically a boolean expression like the one shown.

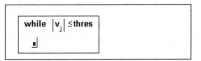

■ In the remaining placeholder, type the expression you want evaluated repeatedly. If necessary, add placeholders by clicking the "Add Line" button on the Programming Palette.

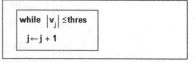

Figure 18-6 shows a larger program incorporating the above loop. Upon encountering a **while** loop, Mathcad checks the condition. If the condition is true, Mathcad executes the body of the loop and checks the condition again. If the condition is false, Mathcad exits the loop.

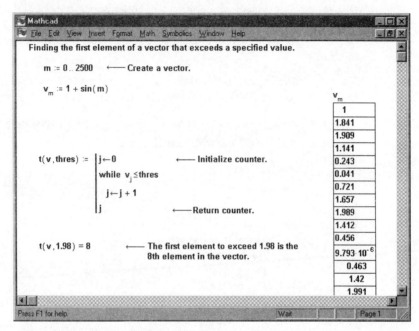

*Figure 18-6: Using a **while** loop to find the first occurrence of a particular number in a matrix.*

Controlling program execution

The Programming Palette in Mathcad Professional includes three statements for controlling program execution:

■ Use the **break** statement within the body of the program to halt execution of the program upon the occurrence of a particular condition. Use **break** also within a **for** or **while** loop to stop the loop and move execution to the next statement outside the loop when a particular condition occurs.

- Use the **continue** statement within a loop to interrupt the current iteration and force program execution to continue with the next iteration of the loop.

- Use the **return** statement to stop a program and return a particular value from within the program rather than from the last statement evaluated.

The "break" statement

It is often useful to break out of a loop or stop program execution completely upon the occurrence of some condition. For example, there is a possibility of a runaway iteration in the program in Figure 18-6. If every element in **v** is less than *thresh*, the condition will never become false and iteration will continue past the end of the vector. This will result in an error message indicating that the index is pointing to a nonexistent array element. To prevent this from occurring, you can use a **break** statement as shown in Figure 18-7.

The program in Figure 18-7 will return 0 if no elements larger than *thresh* are found. Otherwise it returns the index and value of the first element exceeding *thresh*.

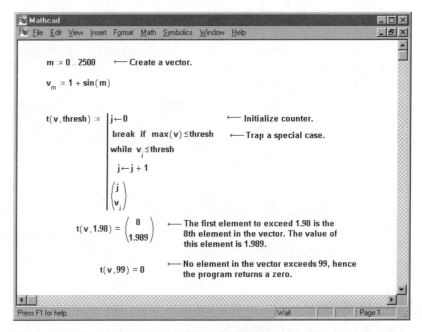

*Figure 18-7: Example in Figure 18-6 modified to return both the index and the actual array value. Note the use of **break** to prevent an error arising when thresh is too large.*

To insert the **break** statement, click on the "break" button in the Programming Palette. Note that to create the program in Figure 18-7, you would click the "break" button first, then click "if".

The "continue" statement

If you use **break** within a **for** or **while** loop, Mathcad stops execution within the loop and resumes execution starting with the next statement after the loop. To interrupt a loop and force calculation to resume at the beginning of the next iteration of the *current* loop, use **continue** instead.

To insert the **continue** statement, click on the "continue" button in the Programming Palette. As with **break**, you typically insert **continue** into the left-hand placeholder of an **if** statement created by clicking on the "if" button in the Programming Palette. The **continue** statement is evaluated only when the right-hand side of the **if** is true.

Figure 18-8 compares the effects of **break** and **continue** on the execution of a loop.

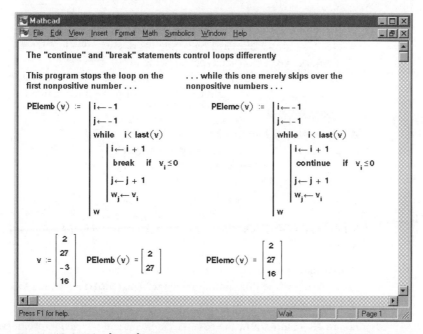

*Figure 18-8: The **break** statement halts the loop, but execution resumes on the next iteration when **continue** is used.*

The "return" statement

A Mathcad program returns the value of the last expression evaluated in the program. In simple programs, the last expression evaluated in the program is in the last line of the program (or, if **break** is used to interrupt a program, the last expression is the one that's evaluated before **break** is called). As you create more complicated programs, you may need more flexibility. The **return** statement allows you to interrupt the program and return particular values other than the default value last computed by the program.

A **return** statement can be used anywhere in a program, even within a deeply nested loop, to force program termination and the return of a scalar, vector, array, or string. As with **break** and **continue**, you typically use **return** on the left-hand side of an **if** statement, and the **return** statement is evaluated only when the right-hand side of the **if** is true.

The following program fragment shows how a **return** statement is used to return a string value upon the occurrence of a particular condition:

■ Click the button labeled "return" on the Programming Palette.

```
return ▪
```

■ Now click the button labeled "if" on the Programming Palette.

```
return ▪   if ▪
```

■ In the placeholder to the right of **return**, create a string expression by typing the double-quote key ("). Then type the string to be

```
return "int"   if ▪
```

returned by the program. Mathcad displays the string between a pair of quotes. See Chapter 8, "Variables and Constants," for more information on creating string expressions.

■ In the placeholder to the right of **if**, type a condition. This would typically be a boolean expression like the one shown. To create the boolean equal sign, type [Ctrl] =.

```
return "int"   if   floor(x) = x
```

In this example, the program returns the string "int" when the expression $floor(x) = x$ is true.

You can add more lines to the expression to the right of **return** by clicking on the "Add Line" button in the Programming Palette. The **return** statement forces the program to return the value of the last expression evaluated.

Figure 18-9 shows how the **return** statement can be used in programs.

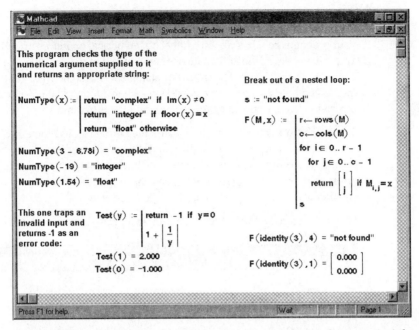

*Figure 18-9: Using **return** to control program execution and return specialized values.*

Error handling

Errors may occur during program execution that will cause Mathcad to stop calculating
the program. For example, because of a particular choice of input, a program may
attempt to divide by 0 in some expression and will encounter a singularity error. In
these cases Mathcad treats the program as it does other math expressions: it marks the
offending expression with an error message and highlights the offending name or
operator in a different color, as described in Chapter 7, "Equations and Computation."

Mathcad Professional gives you two features to improve error handling in programs:

- The **on error** statement on the Programming Palette allows you to "trap" a
  numerical error that would otherwise force Mathcad to stop calculating the program.

- The *error* string function gives you access to Mathcad's error tip mechanism and
  lets you customize error messages issued by your program.

"on error" statement

In some cases you may be able to anticipate program inputs that will lead to a numerical
error (such as a singularity, an overflow, or a failure to converge) that would force
Mathcad to stop calculating the program. As shown in Figure 18-9, the **return**

statement combined with an appropriate boolean test can be used in simple cases to trap values that will lead to program errors. In more complicated cases, especially when your programs rely heavily on Mathcad's numerical operators or built-in function set, you may not be able to anticipate or enumerate all of the possible numerical errors that can occur in a program. The **on error** statement is designed as a general-purpose error trap to compute an alternative expression when a numerical error occurs that would otherwise force Mathcad to stop calculating the program.

To use the **on error** statement, click on the button labeled "on error" on the Programming Palette. In the placeholder to the right of "on error" create the program statement(s) you ordinarily expect to evaluate, but in which you wish to trap any numerical errors. In the placeholder to the left create the program statement(s) you want to evaluate should the default expression on the right-hand side fail.

Figure 18-10 shows **on error** operating in a program to find a root of an expression.

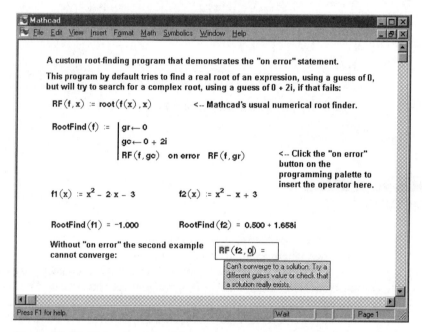

*Figure 18-10: Using the **on error** statement to trap numerical errors in programs.*

Custom error messages

Just as Mathcad automatically produces an appropriate "error tip" when you click on an expression that cannot calculate because of an error (see the bottom of Figure 18-10 for an example), you may want specialized error messages to appear when your programs are used improperly or cannot return answers. Mathcad Professional's *error* string function gives you this capability. For example, you can design custom error tips to appear when incorrect arguments are supplied to the program or when particular conditions are encountered in the program.

The *error* string function, described in the section "String functions" in Chapter 13, evaluates to produce an error tip whose text is simply the string expression it takes as an argument. Typically you will use the *error* string function in the placeholder on the left-hand side of an **if** or **on error** programming statement so that the *error* string function generates an appropriate error tip when a particular condition is encountered.

Figure 18-11 shows how custom error messages can be used even in a small program.

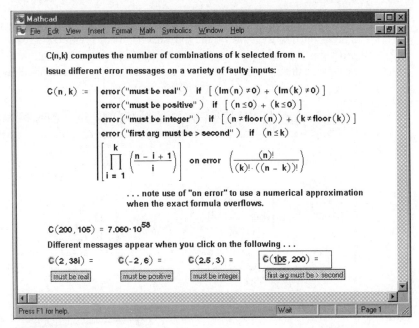

Figure 18-11: Issuing custom error tips via the "error" string function.

Programs within programs

The examples in previous sections have been chosen more for their simplicity than their power. This section shows some examples of more complicated programs capable of performing tasks that would be difficult if not impossible without the availability of these programming features.

Much of the flexibility inherent in programming arises from the ability to embed programming structures inside one another. In Mathcad, you can do this in three ways:

■ You can make one of the statements in a program be another program.

■ You can define a program elsewhere and call it from within another program as if it were a subroutine.

■ You can define a function recursively.

The remainder of this section illustrates these techniques by example.

Subroutines

Recall that a program is just an expression made up of statements, each one of which contains an expression. Since a program statement must be an expression, and since a program is itself an expression, it follows that a program statement can be another program.

Figure 18-12 shows two examples of programs containing a statement which is itself a program. The example on the right-hand side of Figure 18-12 shows how to nest programs even more deeply. In principle, there is no limit to how deeply nested a program can be. As a practical matter, however, programs containing deeply nested programs can become too complicated to understand at a glance.

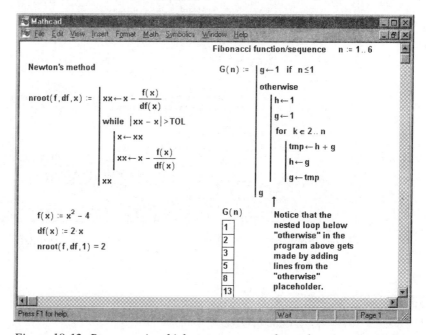

Figure 18-12: Programs in which statements are themselves programs.

One way many programmers avoid overly complicated programs is to bury the complexity in a *subroutine*. Figure 18-13 shows how you can do something similar in Mathcad. By defining *intsimp* elsewhere and using it within *adapt*, the program used to define *adapt* becomes considerably simpler.

The function *adapt* carries out an adaptive quadrature or integration routine by using *intsimp* to approximate the area in each subinterval. If you look at the last line, you'll notice that *adapt* actually calls itself. In other words, it's defined recursively. The following section discusses recursive function definitions in more detail.

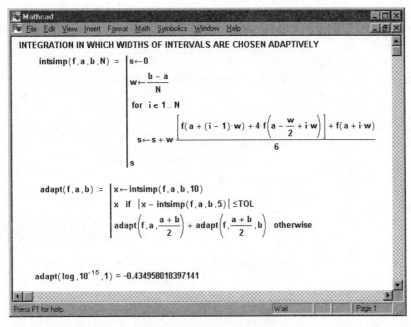

Figure 18-13: Using a subroutine to manage complexity.

Recursion

Recursion is a powerful programming technique that involves defining a function in terms of itself as shown in Figure 18-14. Recursive function definitions should always have at least two parts:

■ An initial condition to prevent the recursion from going forever, and

■ A definition of the function in terms of a previous value of the function.

The idea is similar to that underlying mathematical induction: if you can get $f(n + 1)$ from $f(n)$, and you know $f(0)$, then you know all there is to know about f.

Keep in mind, however, that recursive function definitions, despite their elegance and conciseness, are not always the most computationally efficient definitions. You may find that an equivalent definition using one of the iterative loops described earlier will evaluate more quickly.

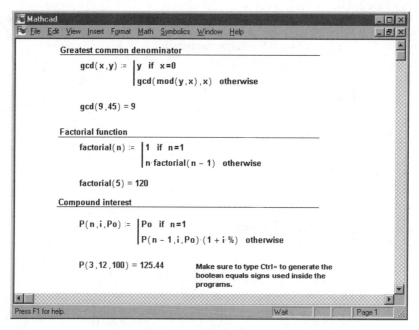

Figure 18-14: Defining a function recursively.

Evaluating programs symbolically

Like any Mathcad expression, a Mathcad program returns a numerical value when followed by the equal sign. You can also write a Mathcad program to return a *symbolic* expression when you evaluate it symbolically using the methods described in Chapter 17, "Symbolic Calculation." For example, when you evaluate a program using the live symbolic operator, "→," Mathcad passes the expression to its symbolic processor and, where possible, returns a simplified symbolic expression. You can use Mathcad's ability to evaluate programs symbolically to generate complicated symbolic expressions, polynomials, and matrices.

The following simple program substitutes one expression for another and returns a simplified symbolic result:

■ Click the button labeled "Add Line" on the Programming Palette.

■ Create a local assignment of variable *a* to *x* in the top placeholder. Type **x**, click on the "←" button on the Programming Palette, and type **a**.

■ In the bottom placeholder, enter an expression that depends on x, such as $(x + y)^2$.

■ Press **[Ctrl].** (the control key followed by a period). Mathcad displays a right arrow, "→," to the right of the program.

■ Click outside the expression to see the simplified result.

Only one of the variables in this example, x, is defined locally in the program, but Mathcad understands the other variables, a and y, as symbols and substitutes a for x in the expression it returns.

Figure 18-15 below shows a function that is defined in terms of a program. Although the function cannot be evaluated numerically in Mathcad, when the function is evaluated symbolically, it generates symbolic polynomials. See "The Treasury Guide to Programming" in the Resource Center for more examples of evaluating a Mathcad program symbolically.

Programs that include the **return** and **on error** statements cannot be evaluated symbolically since the symbolic processor does not recognize these operators.

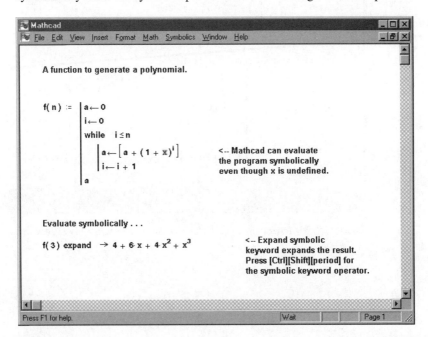

Figure 18-15: Using a Mathcad program to generate a symbolic expression.

Programming examples

With only ten buttons on the Programming Palette, Mathcad's programming environment is easy to use. Nevertheless, this simplicity conceals a surprising amount of programming power. When combined with Mathcad's rich numerical and symbolic functionality and used in conjunction with the abstract data structures provided by Mathcad's nested arrays, these ten operators enable you to write sophisticated programs in Mathcad.

The following figures illustrate just a few of the possibilities. As you experiment with programming in Mathcad, you'll discover many new applications. For further programming examples, see the "Programming" topic in the Resource Center QuickSheets. And in Mathcad Professional the Resource Center includes a special section, "The Treasury Guide to Programming," which includes detailed examples and applications to show you how to get more out of Mathcad programs.

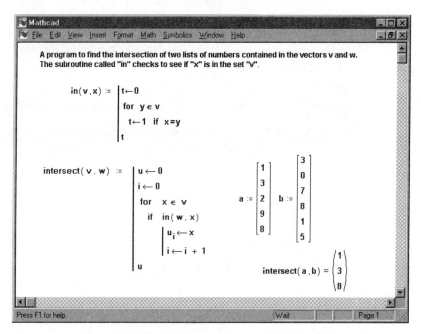

Figure 18-16: Program to find the numbers common to two vectors.

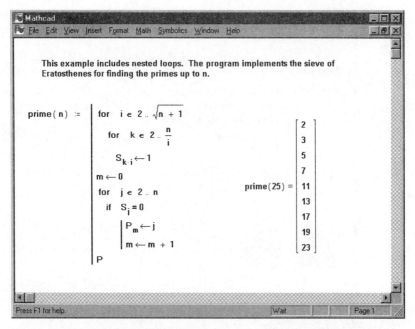

Figure 18-17: Using the sieve of Eratosthenes to find prime numbers.

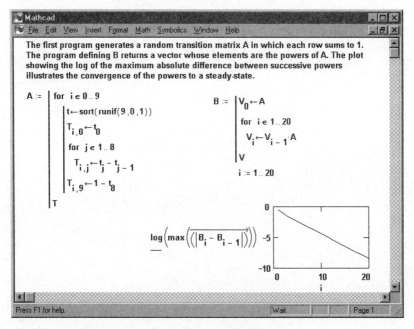

Figure 18-18: Powers of a random transition matrix.

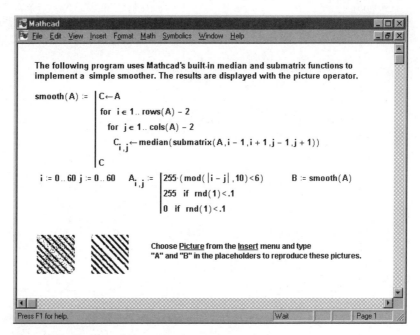

The following program uses Mathcad's built-in median and submatrix functions to implement a simple smoother. The results are displayed with the picture operator.

$$\text{smooth}(A) := \begin{array}{|l}C \leftarrow A \\ \text{for } i \in 1 .. \text{rows}(A) - 2 \\ \quad \text{for } j \in 1 .. \text{cols}(A) - 2 \\ \qquad C_{i,j} \leftarrow \text{median}(\text{submatrix}(A, i-1, i+1, j-1, j+1)) \\ C\end{array}$$

$$i := 0 .. 60 \quad j := 0 .. 60 \quad A_{i,j} := \begin{array}{|l}255 \cdot (\text{mod}(|i-j|, 10) < 6) \\ 255 \text{ if } \text{rnd}(1) < .1 \\ 0 \text{ if } \text{rnd}(1) < .1\end{array} \qquad B := \text{smooth}(A)$$

Choose <u>Picture</u> from the <u>Insert</u> menu and type "A" and "B" in the placeholders to reproduce these pictures.

Figure 18-19: Smoothing a matrix.

Chapter 19
Data Management

Many of Mathcad's built-in functions and operators are useful for manipulating sets of data. Mathcad therefore provides special mechanisms for importing various types of data into a Mathcad worksheet. And, once you've worked with the data, Mathcad allows you to export the results you've generated.

This chapter also discusses a group of Mathcad functions for reading and writing ASCII text files containing numerical data. These functions are primarily available for compatibility with Mathcad worksheets created in earlier versions of Mathcad.

This chapter contains the following sections:

Introduction to components

Overview of *components*, specialized OLE objects used for managing data in Mathcad.

Importing data

Using the File Read/Write component and the Input Table component to import data from a data file. Using the Input Table component to type data in manually or paste it in from the clipboard.

Exporting data

Using the File Read/Write component and the Output Table component to export data to a data file or to the clipboard.

Exchanging data with other applications

Using the Excel, MATLAB, and Axum components to create links between a Mathcad worksheet and these computational applications. Using the Scriptable Object component to script a custom component.

Functions for reading and writing ASCII data files

Description of ASCII file access functions for reading and writing structured and unstructured data.

Introduction to components

Mathcad provides *components* to exchange data between Mathcad and other applications. A component is a specialized OLE object that you insert into a Mathcad worksheet to create a link between the worksheet and either a data source or another application containing data. Unlike other OLE objects you insert into a worksheet, a component communicates with the mathematical equations in Mathcad, linking your Mathcad computations to the rest of your computing environment. This link allows data to flow dynamically between the Mathcad worksheet and a data source or application.

The following components are available in Mathcad for exchanging data between a Mathcad worksheet and other data sources or applications:

■ File Read/Write, for importing and exporting data files in a variety of formats.

■ Input Table and Output Table, for quickly getting data in and out of a Mathcad worksheet.

■ Axum, for creating Axum graphs in a Mathcad worksheet.

Pro   ■ Excel, for creating a link between a Mathcad worksheet and an Excel file.

Pro   ■ MATLAB, for creating a link between a Mathcad worksheet and a MATLAB file.

Pro   ■ Scriptable Object, for creating a custom component via a scripting language.

Some of these components are used to import data, some to export data, and application components, such as Excel, Axum, and MATLAB, allow you to communicate with other applications installed on your computer.

The data going into a component from Mathcad is called *input*. The data coming out of a component is called *output*. The input and output are passed between a Mathcad worksheet and a component by way of a Mathcad variable. The "input variable" is a variable defined in your Mathcad worksheet. It contains the data which will be passed into a component. Output from a component is used to define a Mathcad variable. This variable is referred to as the "output variable."

How to work with components

The basic steps to inserting a component in order to exchange data with Mathcad are as follows:

■ Insert the component.

■ Specify the input variable(s) and output variable(s).

■ Configure the component so that it knows what to do with input and what to send as output.

Since some components only take input or only send output, these steps will differ slightly for each component. The ideas presented in the steps, however, should improve your understanding of how components work.

Step 1: Inserting a component

To insert a component into a Mathcad worksheet:

- Click in a blank spot of your Mathcad worksheet where you would like the component.

- Choose **Component** from the **Insert** menu.

- Choose one of the components from the list and click "Next."

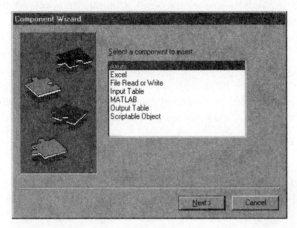

Depending on the component you choose, you may see a Wizard dialog box which lets you specify some properties of the component before it is inserted. Pressing the "Next" buttons continues through the Wizard. You can use the "Back" buttons to go back to a previous page. When you click the "Finish" button, the component will be inserted into your worksheet.

If you don't see a Wizard when you choose one of the components from the Insert Component dialog box, you'll immediately see the component, with some default properties, inserted into your worksheet.

Each component has its own look, so you will see something different for each component you choose. All components have one or more placeholders either to the right of the := or at the bottom of the component. For example, the Excel component might look like this when inserted into your worksheet:

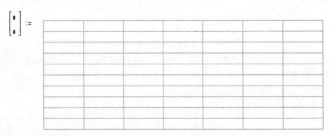

The placeholders you see to the left of the := are for the output variables which will contain the data passed from the component. The placeholder at the bottom of the component is for the name of an input variable the component is getting from Mathcad. The number of placeholders you see to the left or the bottom depend either on the default properties for the component or on the settings you provided in the component's Wizard.

Step 2: Configuring a component

Once you've inserted a component into a worksheet, you usually need to set up the component's properties so that the component knows how to handle any inputs it's getting from Mathcad and what to send as output. To configure the properties for a component:

■ Click on the component once to select it.

■ Click on it with the right mouse button to see a context menu, like the one shown below for the File Read/Write component. The options on the context menu depend on the component you selected, but usually you'll see the commands **Cut**, **Copy**, and **Properties**. Other options are specific to each component.

■ Choose **Properties** from the context menu.

The settings in the Properties dialog box depend on the component you clicked on. The properties dialog for the Output Table component, for example, lets you specify the display format for the numbers in the table. The properties dialog for the Excel component in Mathcad Professional lets you specify the cells in which the input values are stored and the cells from which the output is sent.

Step 3: Exchanging data

Once you've inserted a component into a Mathcad worksheet, filled in the appropriate placeholders, and configured the properties, click away from the component region. At that point, the data exchange takes place: data will pass from the input variable into the component, and the output variable will become defined with the output. This will happen whenever you click on the component and press [**F9**], when the input variables change, or when you choose **Calculate Worksheet** from the **Math** menu.

MathConnex

Pro

The components available in Mathcad are used to connect a Mathcad worksheet to other data sources and applications. If you want to connect these data sources and applications to *each other* as well as to Mathcad, you can use the MathConnex application if you have Mathcad Professional.

In addition to the components available in Mathcad Professional, MathConnex contains a number of other components for manipulating data, such as a Mathcad component for connecting to a Mathcad worksheet. The MathConnex environment lets you connect any of one of the available components to any other component. MathConnex is therefore a tool for controlling data as it flows from one data source or application to another. You can visually design systems of data flow to analyze projects which involve a variety of applications and data sources.

To run MathConnex, click on the MathConnex icon from the Mathcad toolbar, or exit Mathcad and run MathConnex as you would any application. For more information, refer to the *MathConnex Getting Started Guide*.

Importing data

Although you can use Mathcad as a tool for working with variable and function definitions, you can also use Mathcad to perform calculations on data. In order to do so, you first need to import the data into a Mathcad worksheet using either the File Read/Write component or the Input Table component. For a general discussion of components see "Introduction to components" on page 422. You use these components to import data into a Mathcad array. Once the data are in Mathcad as an array, you can use any of Mathcad's built-in functions and operators.

When you import data into Mathcad you should consider where your data is stored:

■ It may be stored in a file created in another application.

■ It may have been copied to the clipboard from another application.

■ It may be on a piece of paper in front of you.

Mathcad therefore allows you to import data by reading from a data file, by pasting it in from the clipboard, or by typing it directly into a Mathcad worksheet.

Importing data from a data file

Mathcad can import data from a file created in any of a variety of applications, such as:

■ Excel (*.xls)

■ Professional edition of MATLAB (*.mat)

■ Lotus 1-2-3 (*.wk*)

■ ASCII editors (*.dat, *.csv, *.prn, *.txt)

When you want to import data from a data file into Mathcad, you should first decide whether you want the data to update automatically in Mathcad whenever it changes later in the data file.

If the data file is likely to change, and you want the changes to be reflected in your Mathcad worksheet whenever it is calculated, you can import and establish a connection between the data file and your Mathcad worksheet. To do so, use the Data File Read/Write component. If you do not want the data to change in Mathcad if the data file changes later on, you can import without establishing a connection between Mathcad and the data file using the Input Table component.

Connecting to a data file

To import data and establish a connection between your Mathcad worksheet and the data file, use the File Read/Write component:

■ Click in a blank spot of your worksheet.

■ Choose **Component** from the **Insert** menu.

■ Choose File Read/Write from the list and click "Next."

This launches the first part of the File Read or Write Wizard. Choose "Read from a data source" and press "Next" to go to the second page of the Wizard, shown below.

■ From the File Format drop-down list in this Wizard, choose the type of data file you want to read.

■ Type the path to the data file you want to read or use the "Browse" button to locate it.

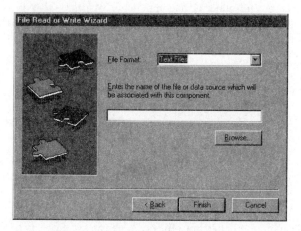

■ Press "Finish." You'll see the File Read/Write component icon and the path to the data file. For example, if you read from a data file called data.txt, you'll see:

$$\blacksquare := \qquad \square$$
$$\text{c:\textbackslash windows\textbackslash data.txt}$$

In the placeholder that appears, enter the name of the Mathcad variable to which the data from the file will be assigned. When you click outside the component, the data file is read in and the data is assigned to the Mathcad variable you entered into the placeholder. Figure 19-1 shows an example of importing data using the File Read/Write component.

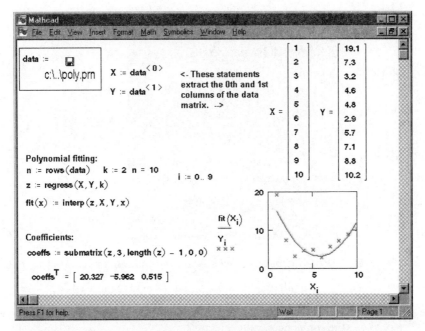

Figure 19-1: Importing data from a data file. Whenever the data file changes, the data will automatically update in Mathcad.

You can now manipulate the Mathcad variable however you'd like using Mathcad's built-in functions and operators. Each time you calculate the worksheet, Mathcad will re-read the data from the file you have specified.

By default, Mathcad will read in the entire data file and assign the values to a matrix with the variable name you provide. To read in only certain rows or columns of a data file:

■ Click once on the component to select it.

■ Click with the right mouse button on the component so that you see the context menu for the component (see example on page 424).

■ Choose **Properties** from the context menu to bring up the Properties dialog box:

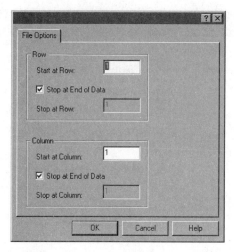

■ Use this dialog box to specify the row and columns at which to start and stop reading.

To read in a different data file or a different type of data file:

■ Click with the right mouse button on the component and select **Choose File** from the component context menu.

■ In the "Files of type" text box, choose the type of file you'd like to import. Use the dialog box to browse to the data file, select the data file, and click "Open."

Importing once from a data file

You can use the Input Table component to import data once from a data file without establishing a connection between a Mathcad worksheet and the data file. To do so:

■ Click in a blank spot of your worksheet.

■ Choose **Component** from the **Insert** menu.

■ Select Input Table from the list and click "Next." The Input Table component will be inserted into your worksheet:

$$\blacksquare := \boxed{0.00}$$

■ In the placeholder that appears to the left, enter the name of the Mathcad variable to which this data will be assigned.

■ Click with the right mouse button on the component so that you see the context menu for the component (see example on page 424).

■ Choose **Import**.

■ The Read from File dialog box appears. In the "Files of type" text box, choose the type of file you'd like to import. Use the dialog box to browse to the data file and click "Open."

The data from the data file will appear in your worksheet in a table. See Figure 19-2 for an example.

When you double-click on the table, you can edit the values in it. You'll see scroll bars which let you scroll through the table. You'll also see handles along the sides of the component region. To resize the table, move the cursor to one of these handles so that it changes to a double-headed arrow, press and hold down the mouse button and drag the cursor in the direction you want the table's dimensions to change.

When you click outside the component, the data is assigned as an array to the Mathcad variable you specified. You can now manipulate this Mathcad array however you'd like using Mathcad's built-in functions and operators. Unlike the File Read/Write component, the Import feature of the Input Table component reads the data only when you choose **Import**, not each time you calculate the worksheet.

Importing data from the clipboard

In some cases, you may have data stored in a spreadsheet or another application, but you don't want to import the data as a file into Mathcad. An alternative to importing a file is to copy the data to the clipboard and paste it into Mathcad. To do so:

■ Select the data in the other application and copy it to the clipboard. In most applications, you do this by choosing **Copy** from the **Edit** menu.

■ Open the Mathcad worksheet in which you want the data to be used.

■ In your Mathcad worksheet, type a variable definition such as $m :=$

■ Click in the placeholder to the right of the := and choose **Paste** from the **Edit** menu. A matrix containing the data you copied will appear.

When you click outside the component, the data you copied will appear in a scrolling table and are assigned as an array to the Mathcad variable you specified. You can manipulate the array however you'd like using Mathcad's built-in functions and operators.

Note that if you paste the copied data into a blank spot of a Mathcad worksheet instead of into a placeholder, you'll also see a matrix containing the data you selected.

When you double-click on the table, you can edit the values in it. You'll see scroll bars which let you scroll through the table. You'll also see handles along the sides of the component region. To resize the table, move the cursor to one of these handles so that it changes to a double-headed arrow, press and hold down the mouse button and drag the cursor in the direction you want the table's dimensions to change.

Entering data manually

It is usually most convenient to have your data stored somewhere on your computer so that you can import the data into Mathcad, either as a file or from the clipboard. However, when you don't have a lot of data and it is not already stored in another application, you can enter your data directly into Mathcad. To do so, create an input table using the Input Table component:

■ Click in a blank spot in your worksheet and choose **Component** from the **Insert** menu.

■ Select **Input Table** from the list and click "Next." The Input Table component will be inserted into your worksheet.

■ In the placeholder that appears, enter the name of the Mathcad variable to which this data will be assigned.

■ Double-click on the component and enter data into the cells. Each row must have the same number of data values. If you do not enter a number into a cell, Mathcad inserts 0 into the cell.

Figure 19-2 shows two input tables. Notice that when you create an input table, you're actually assigning elements to an array that has the name of the variable you entered into the placeholder. Once you've created an array using an input table, you can manipulate the array using Mathcad's built-in functions and operators. Note that if you have a set of X and Y data values, you will probably find it easiest to create one input table for the X's and one for the Y's.

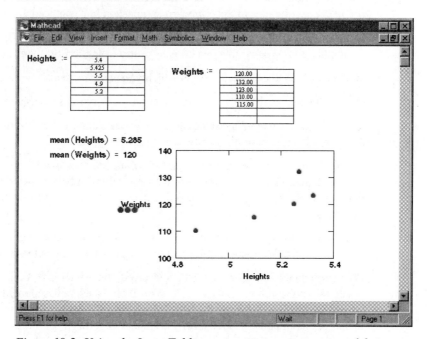

Figure 19-2: Using the Input Table component to create arrays of data.

When you double-click on the table, you can edit the values in it. You'll see scroll bars which let you scroll through the table. You'll also see handles along the sides of the component region. To resize the table, move the cursor to one of these handles so that it changes to a double-headed arrow, press and hold down the mouse button and drag the cursor in the direction you want the table's dimensions to change.

You can copy data from the Input Table component by selecting data, clicking with the right mouse button on the component, and choosing **Copy Data** from the context menu. You can also paste data into the Input Table component by selecting a cell and choosing **Paste Data** from the context menu.

Another way to create an input table is to use a range variables as subscript for another Mathcad variable name. See the section "Entering a table of numbers" in Chapter 11 for more information.

Exporting data

Once you've used Mathcad to perform calculations, you can export the results either to a data file or to the clipboard for pasting into another application. The File Read/Write component and the Output Table component allow you to do this. For a general discussion of components see "Introduction to components" on page 422. You may use any Mathcad variable you have defined in your worksheet as an input variable to the component. The component either sends the data to a data file or lets you copy it to the clipboard.

Exporting to a data file

Mathcad allows you to export the values stored in a Mathcad variable to a variety of file formats, such as the following:

■ Excel (*.xls)

■ MATLAB (*.mat) (Professional edition only)

■ Lotus 1-2-3 (*.wk*)

■ ASCII editors (*.dat, *.csv, *.prn, *.txt)

When you want to export data to a data file, you should first decide whether you want the data to update automatically in the data file when it changes in Mathcad.

If your results are likely to change in Mathcad, and you want to export the new results to a data file whenever the worksheet is calculated, you can export the data and establish a connection between the data file and your Mathcad worksheet. To do so, use the File Read/Write component. If you do not want the data file to change if the results in Mathcad change later on, you can export without establishing a connection between Mathcad and the data file. To do so, use the Output Table component.

Exporting to a connected data file

To export values stored in a Mathcad array or scalar variable to a data file and establish a connection between your Mathcad worksheet and the data file:

■ Click in a blank spot in your worksheet.

■ Choose **Component** from the **Insert** menu.

■ Select File Read/Write from the list and click "Next."

This launches the first part of the File Read or Write Wizard in which you can specify whether the component will read from a data file or write to one. Choose "Write to a data source" and press "Next" to go to the second page of the Wizard:

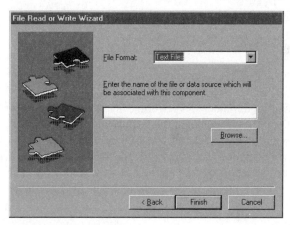

- From the File Format drop-down list in this Wizard, choose the type of data file you want to write.

- Type the path to the data file you want to write or click the "Browse" button to locate it.

Press "Finish." You'll see the File Read/Write component icon and the path to the data file:

c:\windows\data.txt

In the placeholder that appears, enter the name of the Mathcad variable containing the data which will be written to the data file. When you click outside the component, all the values in the input variable will be written to the filename you specified. Each time you calculate the worksheet, the data file is rewritten. See Figure 19-3 for an example.

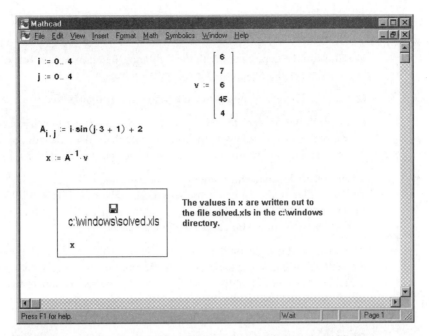

Figure 19-3: Using the File Read/Write component to export data from Mathcad.

To change the name of the data file being created to or to change the type of file being created:

- Click once on the component to select it.

- Click with the right mouse button on the component so that you see the context menu for the component (see example on page 424).

- Select **Choose File.** You will see the Write to File dialog box.

- In the "Files of type" text box, choose the type of file you'd like to create. Use the dialog box to browse to the folder in which the data file will be created and click "Open."

Exporting once to a data file

To export data without establishing a connection between Mathcad and the data file, use the Output Table component:

- Click in a blank spot in your worksheet.

- Choose **Component** from the **Insert** menu.

- Select Output Table from the list and click "Next." The Output Table component will be inserted into your worksheet.

- In the placeholder that appears, enter the name of the Mathcad variable containing the data to be exported.

- Click on the component with the right mouse button so that you see the context menu for the component (see example on page 424).

- Choose **Export**. You will see the Write to File dialog box.

- In the "Files of type" text box, select the format of the file you'd like to create. Use the dialog box to browse to the folder in which the data file will be created and enter the name of the data file you wish to create. Then click "Open."

When you click outside the component, the data you see in the Output Table component will be written to the filename you specified. Unlike the File Read/Write component, the export feature in the Output Table component writes the data only when you choose Export, *not* each time you calculate the worksheet.

When you double-click on the table, you'll see scroll bars which let you scroll through the table. You'll also see handles along the sides of the component region. To resize the table, move the cursor to one of these handles so that it changes to a double-headed arrow, press and hold down the mouse button and drag the cursor in the direction you want the table's dimensions to change.

Changing the format of the numbers in the table

The numbers displayed in the Output Table component will display using a default format specific to the component. Unlike most other values displayed in Mathcad, the values in the Output Table component are not affected by the settings in the Number Format dialog box. To change the way the numbers are displayed in the component:

- Click once on the component to select it.

- Click on the component with the right mouse button so that you see the context menu.

- Choose **Properties** from the context menu.

- Go to the Display tab, which looks like this:

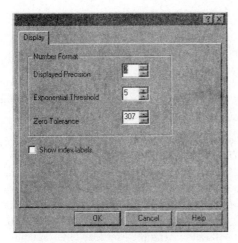

The settings on the Display tab are as follows:

Displayed Precision: Choose or type an integer n. Determines the number of values to the right of the decimal place.

Exponential Threshold: Choose or type an integer n. Values smaller than 10^{-n} or greater than 10^n are displayed in exponential notation.

Zero Tolerance: Choose or type an integer n. Values smaller than 10^{-n} are displayed as zero.

Show index labels: Click this box to display the row and column numbers associated with the values in the table.

Keep in mind that these settings only affect the display of numbers in the Output Table component. They do not affect the values written to a data file if you choose **Export** from the context menu of the Output Table component.

Exchanging data with other applications

As described earlier in this chapter, Mathcad can import and export data files in formats recognized by other applications, including data files saved in spreadsheet programs. This is useful when you simply want to connect to a data file as opposed to the application in which it was created.

For some work, however, you may need access to functionality in the other application as well as the data. It is convenient, then, to set up a link between Mathcad and the other application. A link allows you to exchange data and have immediate access to the other application from within Mathcad.

By linking an application to your Mathcad worksheet, you can:

- Send values from Mathcad to the application.

- Use the application to manipulate the data dynamically without actually leaving the Mathcad environment.

- Send values from the application back to Mathcad.

Although performing tasks of all three kinds takes full advantage of the link, you can also use the link to perform just one or two of them.

To create a connection between Mathcad and another application, you'll use an application component. (For a general discussion of components, see "Introduction to components" on page 422.) When you insert an application component into your Mathcad worksheet, you'll actually see a small window on that application's environment embedded in your Mathcad worksheet. When you double-click on the component, Mathcad's menus and toolbars change to those of the other application. This gives you access to the application without leaving the Mathcad environment.

Mathcad provides components for creating links to Microsoft Excel, MathSoft's Axum (a data analysis and graphics application), and MATLAB from The MathWorks, Inc. The Scriptable Object component allows you to create a custom component to any other application using a scripting language.

The Excel component

Pro

You can use the File Read/Write component to import and export data to and from an Excel file as described in the sections "Connecting to a data file" on page 426 and "Exporting to a connected data file" on page 431. However, there may be times when you want to exchange data between an Excel file and a Mathcad worksheet, and you need brief access to the functionality in Excel, not just the data stored there. For example, you may have some values in Mathcad that you want to send to Excel, use Excel for some manipulation, and send values back to Mathcad to continue working.

The Excel component lets you:

- Pass input variable from Mathcad into an Excel file.

- Double-click on the Excel component to use functionality from Excel.

- Send values from an Excel file which define output variables in Mathcad.

Inserting an Excel component

Before you insert an Excel component into a Mathcad worksheet, Excel needs to be installed on your system, but it does not need to be running.

To insert an Excel component into a Mathcad worksheet:

- Click in a blank spot in your worksheet. If you want to send values to the component from a Mathcad variable defined in your worksheet, make sure you click below or to the right of the variable definition.

- Choose **Component** from the **Insert** menu.

■ Select Excel from the list and click "Next." This launches the first part of the Excel Setup Wizard:

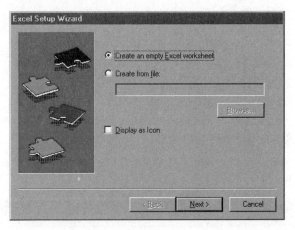

■ If you want to connect a file you've already created, choose "Create from file," and type the path name in the text box or use the Browse button to locate the file; then click "Open." If you don't want to connect to a previously created file, choose "Create an empty Excel Worksheet."

■ Click the Display as Icon box if you want to see an icon in your Mathcad worksheet rather than a portion of the Excel file.

When you click on the "Next" button, the Wizard will bring you through other dialog boxes where you will specify:

■ **The number of input and output variables.** You can supply between 0 and 4 input variables and between 0 and 4 output variables.

■ **Input ranges:** the cells in which the values of each Mathcad input variable will be stored. Enter the starting cell, which is the cell that will hold the element in the upper left corner of an array of values. For example, for an input variable containing a 3×3 matrix of values, you can specify A1 as the starting cell, and the values will be placed in the cells A1 through C3.

■ **Output ranges:** the cells whose values will define the Mathcad output variables. For example, enter C2:L11 to extract the values in cells C2 through L11 and create a 10×10 matrix.

When you finish using the Wizard, you'll see the Excel component in your worksheet with placeholders for the input and output variables. For example, an Excel component that will be sent one input variable and whose output will define two output variables would look like this:

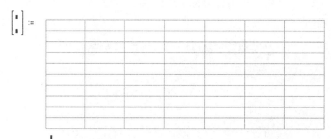

Enter the input variables in the bottom placeholders. Enter the output variables into the placeholders to the left of the :=.

Figure 19-4 shows an example of an Excel component inserted into a Mathcad worksheet.

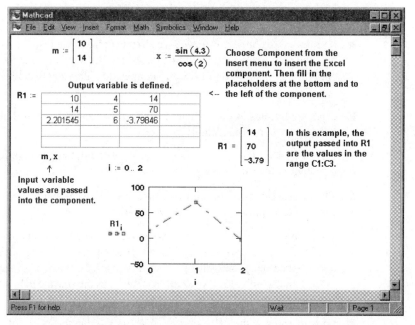

Figure 19-4: Inserting an Excel component into Mathcad to exchange data between an Excel file and a Mathcad worksheet.

When you click outside the component, input variables are sent to Excel from Mathcad and a range of cells are sent from Excel back to Mathcad and assigned to output variables. Once the output variables are defined, you can manipulate them however you'd like using Mathcad's built-in functions and operators.

By default, the Excel component displays only some of the rows and columns. To see more or fewer rows and columns, double-click on the component so that you see handles along the sides of the component region. Move the cursor to one of these handles so that it changes to a double-headed arrow. Press and hold down the mouse button and drag the cursor in the direction you want the component's dimensions to change.

Making changes to the inputs and outputs

Once you set up an Excel component, you may find that you want to add or remove input or output variables, or you may want to change the cell ranges for inputs and outputs which you initially specified in the Setup Wizard. To do so:

- Click once on the component to select it.

- Click on the component with the right mouse button to bring up the context menu.

- To add another output, choose "Add Output Variable." Another placeholder will appear to the left of the :=.

- To add another input, choose "Add Input Variable." Another placeholder will appear at the bottom of the component.

- To eliminate an output, choose "Remove Output Variable." An output placeholder or variable to the left of the := will disappear. If there was more than one output, the last output placeholder or variable will disappear.

- To eliminate an input, choose "Remove Input Variable." An input variable or placeholder at the bottom of the component will disappear. If there was more than one input, the placeholder furthest to the right will disappear.

When you add input or output variables, you'll need to specify which cells in the component will store the new input and which will provide the new output. To do so:

- Click once on the component to select it.

- Click on the component with the right mouse button until you see the context menu.

- Choose **Properties** from the context menu.

- Choose either the Inputs tab or the Outputs tab and specify a range of cells for each input and each output.

You should also follow these steps if you want to change the cell ranges for inputs and outputs you initially specified in the Setup Wizard.

Accessing Excel

After inserting an Excel component into a Mathcad worksheet, you can use the component to perform calculations in Excel, provided you have installed Excel on your system. To do so:

- Double-click on the Excel component in the Mathcad worksheet. The Excel component opens and the menus and toolbars change to Excel menus and toolbars.

- Edit the Excel component however you'd like.

- Click back in the Mathcad worksheet to have the component recalculate and to resume working in Mathcad.

The MATLAB component

Pro   You can use the File Read/Write component to import and export data to and from a MATLAB file as described in the sections "Connecting to a data file" on page 426 and

"Exporting to a connected data file" on page 431. However, there may be times when you want to exchange data between a MATLAB worksheet and a Mathcad worksheet, and you need brief access to MATLAB's functionality, provided you have installed MATLAB (Professional edition) on your system. For example, you may have some values in Mathcad that you want to send to MATLAB, use MATLAB to manipulate them, and send values back to MATLAB.

A MATLAB component lets you:

■ Pass values stored in variables in Mathcad into MATLAB variables.

■ Double-click on the MATLAB component to use MATLAB to process the data.

■ Send data from MATLAB variables into Mathcad variables.

Before you insert an MATLAB component into a Mathcad worksheet, MATLAB needs to be installed on your system, but it does not need to be running.

Inserting a MATLAB component

To insert a MATLAB component into a Mathcad worksheet:

■ Click in a blank spot in your worksheet. If you want to send values to the MATLAB component from a Mathcad variable, make sure you click below or to the right of the variable definition.

■ Choose **Component** from the **Insert** menu.

■ Select MATLAB from the list and click "Next." The MATLAB component will be inserted into your worksheet.

■ In the placeholder that appears at the bottom, enter the name of the Mathcad input variables to pass into the MATLAB component. In the placeholder that appears to the left of the component, enter the names of the Mathcad output variables to be defined. You can add more placeholders or remove some in the same way that you add and remove inputs and outputs for the Excel component as described in the section "Making changes to the inputs and outputs" on page 439.

By default, the input variables will be sent into MATLAB variables named `in0`, `in1`, `in2`, and so on refer. The MATLAB variables `out0`, `out1`, `out2`, and so on will define the output variables to be created in Mathcad. To change these names:

■ Choose **Properties** from the component's context menu.

■ Use the Outputs and Inputs tabs to type in new names for the inputs and outputs.

Accessing MATLAB

Once you know what MATLAB variable names take the input and provide the output, you should set up your MATLAB component just as you would create a file in MATLAB. Be sure to define the variables which will be passed as output. To use the MATLAB component to perform calculations in MATLAB:

■ Double-click on the MATLAB component in the Mathcad worksheet.

■ The MATLAB component opens a text window for entering MATLAB commands.

■ Edit the MATLAB worksheet however you'd like.

When you click outside the component, input variables are sent to MATLAB and arrays are assigned to output variables in Mathcad. Once the output variables are created in Mathcad, you can manipulate them however you'd like using Mathcad's built-in functions and operators.

The Axum component

Axum is a technical graphing and data analysis application available from MathSoft. Axum gives you access to over 75 2D and 3D graph types. You also get complete control over the look of your graphs because you can point and click to make just about any change you want.

If you have Axum 5 (patch level 5.03 or higher) installed on your system, the Axum component brings some of this graphing power to your Mathcad worksheet and gives you the power to create publication-quality graphs from your Mathcad data without leaving the Mathcad environment. (For a general discussion of components, see "Introduction to components" on page 422.)

Using the Axum component you can:

■ Create over 50 different types of 2D and 3D graphs using Mathcad data. For example, the Axum component lets you create the following: a 2D Area Chart, a 2D Grouped Bar Chart, and a 3D Regression Plot.

■ Double-click on the Axum component to use Axum to format every detail of your graph.

Inserting an Axum Graph

Before you insert an Axum component into a Mathcad worksheet, Axum needs to be installed on your system, but it does not need to be running.

To insert an Axum component into a Mathcad worksheet:

■ Create the arrays which will provide input to the Axum component and which Axum will display in a graph. For information on the number and type of arrays required for each type of graph, choose **Mathcad-Axum Link** from Axum's **Help** menu and go to the section titled "Mathcad data specifications for creating Axum graphs."

■ Click in a blank spot in your worksheet. Make sure you click below or to the right of the arrays.

■ Choose **Component** from the **Insert** menu.

■ Select Axum from the list and click "Next." This launches the first part of the Axum Setup Wizard.

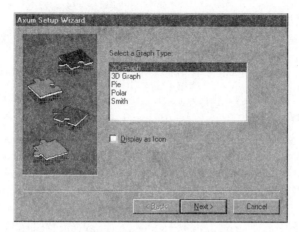

■ Choose they type of graph you would like to insert and click "Next" to go to the next page of the Wizard.

■ Choose a plot type. The available choices depend on the type of graph you selected.

■ Click "Finish." The Axum component will be inserted into your worksheet.

■ Enter the appropriate array variables in the placeholders that appear.

When you click outside the component, the array data will be displayed in the Axum plot type you selected in the Wizard. Each time you calculate the worksheet, the data is redisplayed in Axum. See Figure 19-5 for an example.

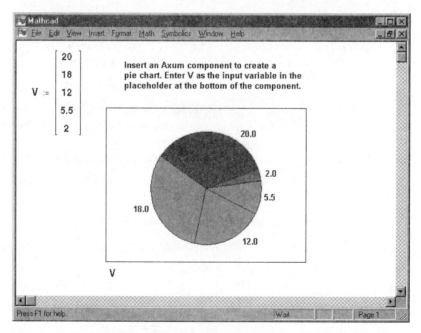

Figure 19-5: The Axum component lets you create graph types that aren't directly available in Mathcad.

Editing an Axum Graph

After inserting an Axum component into a Mathcad worksheet, you can format the graph using Axum's formatting options. To do so:

- Double-click on the Axum graph in the Mathcad worksheet.

- The menus and toolbars change to Axum's menus and toolbars. Edit the Axum graph however you'd like.

- Click back in the Mathcad worksheet to recalculate the component and to resume working in Mathcad.

The Scriptable Object component

Pro   Although Mathcad has components for exchanging data between a Mathcad worksheet and Excel, MATLAB, and Axum, you can actually exchange data between a Mathcad worksheet and any other application that supports OLE Automation, even if Mathcad does not have a specific component to do so. You can use the Scriptable Object component to create a custom component that:

- Sends values from Mathcad to the application.

- Uses the application to manipulate the data without actually leaving Mathcad.

- Sends values from the other application back to Mathcad.

You can create a custom scriptable object from any object you can insert into a Mathcad worksheet. For example, you may want to send some values from Mathcad to Lotus 1-2-3, manipulate the values there, and send results back to the Mathcad worksheet.

To create a Scriptable Object component, you must:

- Be proficient in a supported scripting language, such as Microsoft VBScript or JScript, that is installed on your system.

- Have some knowledge of the way the other application has implemented OLE.

- Have the other application available on your system.

More on scripting languages

Before you insert a Scriptable Object component into a Mathcad worksheet, you need to have a scripting language installed on your system. As this *User's Guide* goes to press, the following two scripting languages are supported: Microsoft VBScript (Visual Basic Scripting Edition) version 2 and Microsoft JScript (an implementation of JavaScript) version 2. Both of these scripting languages can currently be downloaded at no charge from Microsoft, Inc.'s Web sites:

<code>http://www.microsoft.com/vbscript</code>
<code>http://www.microsoft.com/jscript</code>

VBScript is a strict *subset* of the Visual Basic for Applications language used in Microsoft Excel, Project, Access, and the Visual Basic 4.0 development system. VBScript is designed to be a lightweight interpreted language, so it does not use strict types (only Variants). Also, because VBScript is intended to be a safe subset of the language, it does not include file input/output or direct access to the underlying operating system.

JScript is a fast, portable, lightweight interpreter for use in applications that use ActiveX Controls, OLE automation servers, and Java applets. JScript is directly comparable to VBScript (not Java). Like VBScript, JScript is a pure interpreter that processes source code rather than producing stand-alone applets.

The syntax and techniques used in the scripting language you choose are beyond the scope of this *User's Guide*. For more information about Microsoft VBScript and JScript, consult Microsoft, Inc.'s Web sites.

Inserting a Scriptable Object

To insert a Scriptable Object component into a Mathcad worksheet:

■ Click in a blank spot in your worksheet. If you want to send values to the object from a Mathcad variable, make sure you click below or to the right of the variable definition.

■ Choose **Component** from the **Insert** menu.

■ Select Scriptable Object from the list and click "Next."

This launches the Scripting Wizard. The Wizard first prompts you to specify the OLE server application from which you want to create a Scriptable Object. The Object to Script scrolling list shows the available applications on your system. Choose an application that supports the OLE2 automation interface (consult the documentation for the application for details).

You must specify:

■ Whether the component will be a new file or whether you will insert a file that already exists.

■ Whether you will see the actual file in your Mathcad worksheet or if you'll see an icon.

When you click the "Next" button, the Wizard will bring you through other dialog boxes where you will specify:

■ Which scripting language you will use.

■ The type of object you want to script.

■ The name of the object.

■ The number of inputs and outputs the object will accept and provide.

When you finish using the Wizard, you'll see a Scriptable Object component in your worksheet with placeholders for the input and output variables. Enter the input variables in the bottom placeholders. Enter the output variables into the placeholders to the left of the :=.

Figure 19-6 shows a simple example of a scripted object—in this case, a picture of a face. The object accepts two input values and sends out two output values. The input values determine whether the face smiles or winks.

Object model

The Scriptable Object component has the following predefined objects, properties, and methods that enable you to configure it to work as a Mathcad component.

Collections

- **Inputs** and **Outputs** are predefined *collections* of DataValue objects (see below) containing the Scriptable Object's inputs and the outputs, respectively.

- The **Count** property can be used to query the total number of elements in the collection. For example, **Outputs.Count** returns the number of output ports.

- The **Item** method is used to specify an individual element in the collection. To refer to a particular input or output, use the notation **Inputs.Item(*n*)** or **Outputs.Item(*n*)**, where *n* is the index of the input or output. The index *n* always starts from 0. Since **Item** is the default method, languages such as VBScript and JScript let you drop the method name to imply the default method. For example, **Inputs(0)** is equivalent to **Inputs.Item(0)** and references the first input.

DataValue objects

- The **Value** property accesses a DataValue's real part. For example, in VBScript or JScript **Inputs(0).Value** returns the real part of the first input.

- The **IValue** property accesses a DataValue's imaginary part. For example, in VBScript or JScript **Outputs(1).IValue** returns the imaginary part of the second output. If there is no imaginary part, the **IValue** portion returns "NIL."

- The **IsComplex** property returns "TRUE" if a DataValue has a valid imaginary part; this property returns "FALSE" otherwise. For example, the expression **(inputs(0).IsComplex)** returns "FALSE" if the first input has only a real part.

- The **Rows** and **Cols** properties yield the number of rows and columns.

Global methods

- The **alert** function takes a single string parameter that is presented to the user as a standard modal Windows message box with an "OK" button.

- The **errmsg** function takes a single string parameter as its first argument that displays as an error message from within the script and causes the script to stop execution. The second parameter is also a string, but it is optional. It is used to display the source of the error.

Note: In JScript, the names of functions, methods, objects, and properties are case sensitive, while in VBScript they are not.

Scripting the object

To start scripting an object:

■ Click once on the component to select it.

■ Click on the component with the right mouse button.

■ Choose **Edit Script** from the context menu.

You'll see a new window called the Script Editor containing three subroutine stubs in which you insert your own scripting code. Figure 19-6 shows a portion of the completed VBScript script for an object called **SmileyEvent**.

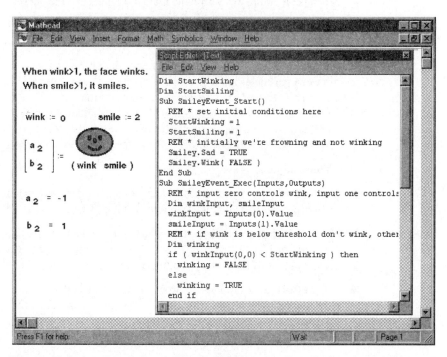

Figure 19-6: A scripted object. The Script Editor window shows a portion of the VBScript code used to configure the object.

The script you write will usually contain at a minimum the following three subroutines:

■ A *starting* routine, called once when execution of the component begins. This is a good place to initialize variables, open files for reading and writing, etc.

■ An *execution* routine that by default takes as arguments the collections **Inputs** and **Outputs**.

■ A *stopping* routine, called once when execution of the component stops.

The commands in each section are executed in sequence whenever the Mathcad worksheet is calculated. What you will include in these subroutines is determined largely by the properties of the OLE object you are scripting; consult the documentation for the server or control.

Choose **Close & Return** from the Script Editor's **File** menu when you have completed your script and want to resume working in the Mathcad worksheet.

Functions for reading and writing ASCII data files

If the data file you want to import or export to is a plain ASCII file, you can use components for importing and exporting data as described in the first three sections of this chapter. Alternatively, you can use Mathcad's built-in functions for reading plain ASCII data files. These built-in functions are provided mainly for compatibility with worksheets created in earlier versions of Mathcad, but you can use them in a Mathcad 7 worksheet if you like.

Files in plain ASCII format consist only of numbers separated by commas, spaces, or carriage returns. The following are some examples of files that the built-in functions can read, assuming the data are in ASCII format:

■ A file containing experimental data captured with data-acquisition hardware and software.

■ A file created by printing from a spreadsheet program to the disk.

■ A column of numbers typed into a word processor and saved in plain ASCII format.

■ Output from a BASIC program.

■ Data downloaded from a mainframe database.

The numbers in the data files can be integers like **3** or **-1**, floating-point numbers like **2.54**, or E-format numbers like **4.51E-4** (for $4.51 \cdot 10^{-4}$).

For example, this list of numbers would be a valid line in an ASCII data file:

        200, 50 25.1256, 16E-2, -16.125E15

Mathcad also has functions for saving data in ASCII files. Data files saved by Mathcad with these functions contain numbers separated by spaces and carriage returns.

ASCII data files can be either *structured* or *unstructured*. Structured data files contain the data organized in rows and columns. Unstructured data files contain numbers, but not necessarily in rows and columns. Mathcad has file access functions for reading and writing both structured and unstructured ASCII data files.

Note: Mathcad documents themselves are not valid data files.

Arguments to file access functions

The argument you supply to any Mathcad file access function described in this section is a *string expression*—or a variable to which a string is assigned—that corresponds either to:

- the name of a data file in the working directory of the Mathcad worksheet you're currently working on; or

- a full or relative path to a data file located elsewhere on a local or network file system.

As described in Chapter 8, "Variables and Constants," a string in Mathcad is a special kind of math expression that always appears between double quotes, and you start a string expression in an *empty math placeholder* by typing the double-quote (") key.

If the data file you want to use is located in the working directory of the current Mathcad worksheet, the string expression you supply to a file access function can simply contain the name of the file you are reading from or writing to. For example, the string expression "**data2.prn**" (quotes included) refers to the file **data2.prn** located in the working directory of the current Mathcad worksheet. Any worksheet containing such string expressions in file access functions can be safely moved to another file system with a different directory structure, provided that you move any required data files along with your worksheet.

Pro

If you have Mathcad Professional, you may use the *concat* function (described in Chapter 13, "Built-in Functions,") to concatenate the Mathcad built-in variable CWD, which is a string corresponding to the current directory of the worksheet, with any string argument to a file access function. In this way you will ensure that any file access functions in your worksheet will work properly should you move your worksheet and data files to another file system.

If the file to read from or write to is not in the working directory, the argument to a file access function must be a string expression containing a full or relative path to the data file. For example, you could use the string expression "**C:\data\trial1.dat**" to identify the file **trial1.dat** located in the **C:\data** folder. If you include path information in your string expressions, your file access functions may not work if you move your worksheet to another file system that does not have a similar directory structure.

See the section "Strings" in Chapter 8 for more information about creating and editing strings. For examples of how to use string expressions as arguments to data file access functions, see Figure 19-7 though Figure 19-13.

ASCII data file access functions

Mathcad includes six functions for accessing numerical data stored in ASCII data files: *READ, WRITE, APPEND, READPRN, WRITEPRN*, and *APPENDPRN*. They each take as an argument a string expression as described above.

These functions have the following properties:

- You must type the function name all in uppercase. Alternatively, you may insert the function into your document by choosing **Function** from the **Insert** menu and double-clicking on the function name.

- If Mathcad cannot find a data file, it marks the file-access function with an error message indicating that it could not find the file you specified. If Mathcad tries to read a file and the format is incorrect, it marks the function with an error message.

- The *WRITE*, *APPEND*, *WRITEPRN*, and *APPENDPRN* functions must appear alone on the left side of a definition.

- Each new equation reopens the data file. When you read data, for example, each new equation starts reading at the beginning of the file.

- If two equations in the same document use *WRITE* or *WRITEPRN* with the same file, the data from the second equation will overwrite the data from the first. Use *APPEND* or *APPENDPRN* when you don't want to overwrite data. These functions add to an existing file instead of overwriting it.

The table below describes these six functions. In this table:

- **A** represents an array, either vector or matrix.

- v_i represent the individual elements of vector **v**.

- *file* is a string expression containing the name of a file in the working directory or a path to a file outside the working directory. For more information, see section "Arguments to file access functions" on page 448.

- *i* is a range variable.

The functions *READ*, *WRITE* and *APPEND* can be used with range variables. The remaining functions never use range variables.

Function	Meaning
READ(*file*)	Read a value from a data file. Returns a scalar. Usually used as follows: $v_i := \text{READ}(file)$
WRITE(*file*)	Write a value to a data file. If file already exists, replace it with new file. Must be used in a definition of the following form: $\text{WRITE}(file) := v_i$
APPEND(*file*)	Append a value to an existing file. Must be used in a definition of the following form: $\text{APPEND}(file) := v_i$
READPRN(*file*)	Read a structured data file. Returns a matrix. Each line in the data file becomes a row in the matrix. The number of elements in each row must be the same. Usually used as follows: $\mathbf{A} := \text{READPRN}(file)$
WRITEPRN(*file*)	Write a matrix into a data file. Each row becomes a line in the file. Must be used in a definition of the form: $\text{WRITEPRN}(file) := \mathbf{A}$

APPENDPRN(*file*)   Append a matrix to an existing file. Each row in the matrix becomes a new line in the data file. Must be used in a definition of the following form:

APPENDPRN(*file*) := **A**

Existing data must have as many columns as **A**.

Reading and writing data in unstructured files

This section discusses how to use *READ*, *WRITE*, and *APPEND* to read and write data in unstructured files: files containing numbers, but not necessarily in rows and columns.

Figure 19-7 shows two ways to use *READ* to read data from a file.

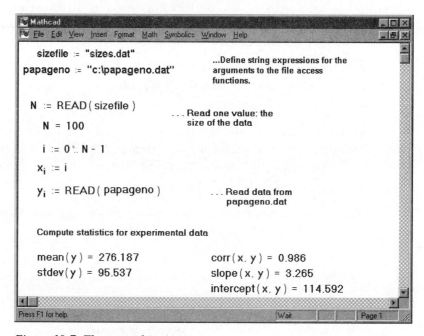

Figure 19-7: The READ function.

The first *READ* equation defines N as the first value in the data file **sizes.dat**. The second *READ* equation fills the array **y** with the first 100 numbers in the data file **papageno.dat** located in the root directory.

When Mathcad reads data with the *READ* function:

■ Each new equation reopens the file and starts reading from the beginning. You cannot read two successive sets of data from the same file by using two separate *READ* equations.

■ In an equation with *READ* and a range variable, Mathcad reads one value for each value of the range variable. If the data runs out before the range variable, Mathcad just stops looking for more data. If the range variable ends before the end of the data, Mathcad ignores the extra data in the file.

Figure 19-8 shows how to use the *WRITE* function to write data to a data file.

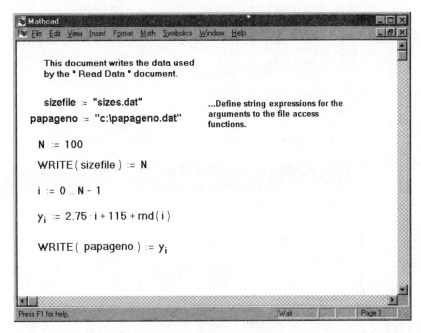

Figure 19-8: Writing data with the WRITE function.

The first *WRITE* equation writes a single number to the data file **sizes.dat**. The second *WRITE* equation writes *N* numbers to the data file **papageno.dat**, one number for each value of the range variable *i*.

When Mathcad writes data to a file, it separates successive numbers with spaces. Mathcad also inserts line breaks to keep the lines shorter than 80 characters. When you use *WRITE*, all values are saved to the file with maximum precision, regardless of the global format of the document.

Mathcad ignores units when it writes data to a data file.

Like the *READ* function, the *WRITE* function reopens the file and starts at the beginning for each new equation. If you want to write data to a file from several different equations, use the *APPEND* function instead of the *WRITE* function in the second and subsequent equations.

Warning: If you use the *WRITE* function on the same file in two separate equations, the data from the second equation will overwrite the data from the first equation.

Reading and writing data in structured files

This section discusses how to use *READPRN*, *WRITEPRN*, and *APPENDPRN* to read and write data in structured files. A structured data file is a data file with a fixed number of values per line. For example, if you print a rectangular area from a spreadsheet into a file, the resulting rows and columns of numbers will be a structured file.

Suppose you have an ASCII text file containing the data shown below. These numbers could come from a spreadsheet or from any other source.

0.25	0.91	0.72	1.8
0.77	2.18	1.63	4.4
2.74	8.08	5.46	16.63
3.94	16.33	7.92	33.63
3.82	13.82	7.52	28.5
2.79	8.09	5.58	16.73
6.84	24.04	13.86	49.63
4.68	12.68	9.76	26.06

Figure 19-9 shows a Mathcad worksheet in which these numbers are read into a matrix.

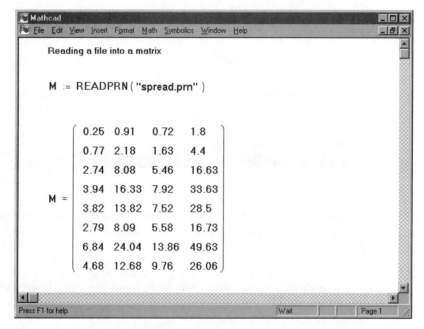

Figure 19-9: Reading spreadsheet data into a matrix.

The *READPRN* function reads the entire data file, determines the number of rows and columns, and creates a matrix out of the data.

When Mathcad reads data with the *READPRN* function:

■ Each instance of the *READPRN* function reads an entire data file.

■ All lines in the data file must have the same number of values. (Lines containing no values are ignored.) If the lines in the file have differing numbers of values, Mathcad marks the *READPRN* equation with an error message.

■ The *READPRN* function ignores text in the data file.

■ The result of reading the data file is an *m*-by-*n* matrix, where *m* is the number of lines containing data in the file and *n* is the number of values per line. To define a matrix out of the numbers in a data file, type an equation like **M** := **READPRN**("**file.prn**"). *Do not use subscripts on* **M**. *READPRN returns a* matrix, so no subscripts are necessary.

Warning: Each line in the data file must contain the same number of values. If you leave gaps where Mathcad expects numbers, the *READPRN* function will not be able to read the file. Mathcad determines where one number ends and the next begins by looking for spaces or commas.

Sometimes each column of values in a data file represents a different variable. Figure 19-10 shows how to use superscripts to create a vector from each column in the data file.

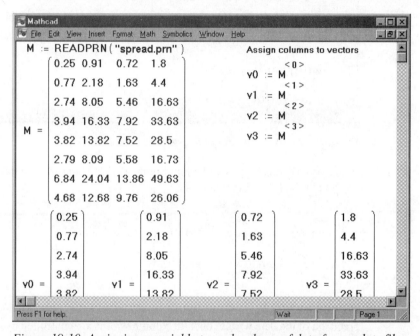

Figure 19-10: Assigning a variable to each column of data from a data file.

Figure 19-11 shows how to use the *WRITEPRN* function to write data to a structured data file.

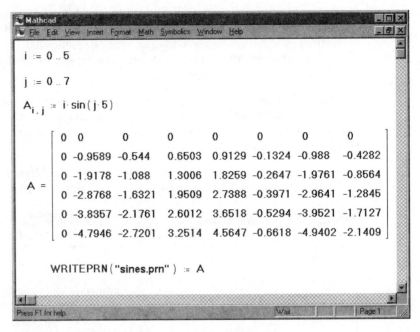

Figure 19-11: Writing data to a structured data file.

When you calculate the document in Figure 19-11, Mathcad creates a data file containing the following numbers:

```
0       0       0       0       0       0       0       0
0      -0.9589 -0.544  0.6503  0.9129 -0.1324 -0.988 -0.4282
0      -1.918  -1.088  1.301   1.826  -0.2647 -1.976 -0.8564
0      -2.877  -1.632  1.951   2.739  -0.3971 -2.964 -1.285
0      -3.836  -2.176  2.601   3.652  -0.5294 -3.952 -1.713
0      -4.795  -2.72   3.251   4.565  -0.6618 -4.94  -2.141
```

Unlike the *WRITE* function, the *WRITEPRN* function writes out the data in columns. The precision of the data written out and column widths are controlled by PRNPRECISION and *PRNCOLWIDTH* which you can set by choosing **Options** from the **Math** menu and clicking on the Built-in Variables tab. In the example above, note that since the *PRNPRECISION* is set to four, the numbers are written to four decimal places. Since *PRNCOLWIDTH* is set to eight, each column has space for eight characters. Since *PRNPRECISION* and *PRNCOLWIDTH* can be varied independently, you must take care to choose them in such a way that the column width can accommodate all the digits, together with a space to separate the columns.

When you use *WRITEPRN*:

■ Equations using *WRITEPRN* must be in a specified form as follows: On the left should be WRITEPRN(*file*), where *file* is a string expression containing a filename or a pathname. This is followed by a definition symbol (:=) and a matrix expression. *Do not use range variables or subscripts with WRITEPRN.*

■ Each new equation writes a new file. If two equations write to the same file, the data written by the second equation will overwrite the data written by the first. Use *APPENDPRN* if you want to append values to a file instead of overwriting the file.

■ The built-in variables *PRNCOLWIDTH* and *PRNPRECISION* determine the format of the data file that Mathcad creates. The current value of *PRNCOLWIDTH* specifies the width of the columns (in characters). The current value of *PRNPRECISION* specifies the number of significant digits used. By default, *PRNCOLWIDTH*=8 and *PRNPRECISION*=4. To change these values, choose **Options** from the **Math** menu and edit the numbers on the Built-In Variables tab, or enter definitions in your Mathcad document above the *WRITEPRN* function, as shown in Figure 19-12.

■ If the array you are writing is either a *nested* array (an array whose elements are themselves arrays) or a complex array (an array whose elements are complex) then *WRITEPRN* will *not* create a simple ASCII file. Instead, *WRITEPRN* creates a file using a special format unlikely to be readable by other applications. This file can, however, be read by Mathcad's *READPRN* function.

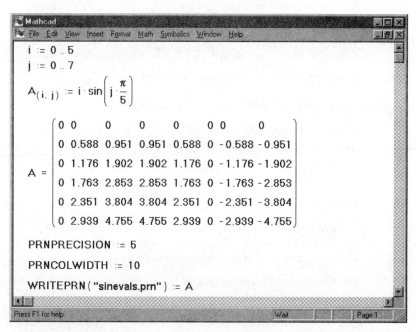

Figure 19-12: A document that creates a data file with columns 10 characters wide containing numbers with 5 significant digits.

By using the *augment* function, you can concatenate several variables and write them all to a data file. Figure 19-13 demonstrates how to do this.

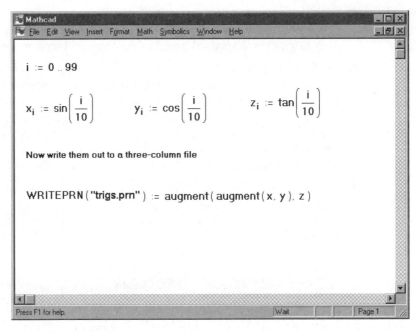

Figure 19-13: Writing several concatenated vectors.

Advantages of using READPRN and WRITEPRN

READPRN is generally preferable to *READ*. When the data values are regularly listed out in columns, *READPRN* brings the data into Mathcad in a readily accessible form.

If some lines in a data file have more data values than others, data values may be missing. Use a text editor to replace the missing values with zeros before you use *READPRN*.

READ is required for files in which numbers for a single variable are scattered across several lines in the file. This includes files created by the *WRITE* function, in which there are as many numbers on each line as will fit.

Remember: use a range variable subscript to read with *READ*; do *not* use a subscript to read with *READPRN*.

WRITEPRN generally produces more readable files than *WRITE* because the data values are neatly lined up in rows and columns. However, *WRITE* produces smaller files than *WRITEPRN* because it doesn't have to add spaces to line up the numbers.

Use *WRITE* instead of *WRITEPRN* when you want to crowd as many values as possible into a small data file. *WRITE* creates a data file with only one space between each value and the next.

Pro   *WRITEPRN* and *READPRN* allow you to write out and read in nested arrays created in Mathcad Professional. For more information on nested arrays, see the section "Nested arrays" in Chapter 10.

Graphics Features

Chapter 20
Graphs

Mathcad graphs are both versatile and easy to use. To create a graph, click where you want to insert the graph, choose **Graph**⇒**X-Y Plot** from the **Insert** menu, and fill in the placeholders. You can modify the format extensively, including reformatting the axes and curves and using a variety of different types of labels.

The following sections describe the use of Mathcad graphs:

Creating a graph

Basic steps in creating and editing a graph. QuickPlots versus graphs where you explicitly specify the range of values over which to plot.

Graphing functions

Procedures for graphing functions.

Graphing a vector

Procedures for graphing vectors.

Graphing more than one expression

Procedures for creating graphs with multiple traces.

Formatting the axes

Procedures for modifying the formats of the x- and y-axes.

Formatting individual curves

Procedures for modifying the formats of curves or traces in a graph.

Setting default formats

Procedures for using default format settings.

Labeling your graph

Procedures for working with titles, axis labels, and other labels.

Modifying your graph's perspective

Procedures for changing the size of the graph, zooming in on a portion of the graph, and finding coordinates in it.

Gallery of graphs

A set of sample graphs illustrating options for creating graphs.

Creating a graph

You create X-Y graphs in Mathcad using the *X-Y plot operator*. The X-Y plot operator, like other Mathcad operators, has placeholders for you to fill in that specify expressions to be computed and displayed.

You can insert the X-Y plot operator into your worksheet in one of three ways; although these methods are equivalent, only the first is mentioned in the rest of this chapter. Click in your worksheet where you want your graph to appear and either:

■ Choose **Graph⇒X-Y Plot** from the **Insert** menu; or

■ Press the @ key; or

■ Click on the X-Y Plot button in the Graph Palette.

The X-Y plot operator is very flexible, letting you either:

■ Create a *QuickPlot* based only on one or more expressions of a single variable, the dependent variable. Once you have entered the expression(s) in the placeholder on the *y*-axis, Mathcad automatically creates the plot over a range of –10 to 10 for the dependent variable on the *x*-axis.

■ Explicitly enter expressions on both the *y*-axis *and* *x*-axis that specify the range of values over which to plot. Usually these expressions depend on range variables you have previously defined in your worksheet. If the range variables aren't previously defined, Mathcad will generate appropriate range variables for the plot.

This section outlines the difference between these two uses of the X-Y plot operator. The sections "Graphing functions" on page 464, "Graphing a vector" on page 465, and "Graphing more than one expression" on page 470 describe the kinds of expressions you can plot in greater detail. See "Formatting the axes" on page 472 and "Formatting individual curves" on page 478 for an introduction to Mathcad's plot formatting options.

QuickPlots

You can quickly and easily create X-Y graph from a single Mathcad expression. To do so:

■ Enter the expression or function of a single variable you want to plot. Make sure the editing lines remain in the expression.

$\sin(x)$

- Choose **Graph⇒X-Y Plot** from the **Insert** menu.

- Press [**Enter**] or click away from the graph.

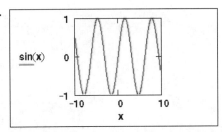

Mathcad automatically produces a plot over a default range of the dependent variable on the *x*-axis: –10 to 10. You can change the axis range by editing the upper and lower limits on the *x*-axis. See "Setting limits for axes" on page 474.

To graph more than one expression using a QuickPlot:

- Enter the expressions or functions of a single variable you want to plot, separated by commas. Make sure the editing lines remain in the expression.

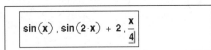

- Choose **Graph⇒X-Y Plot** from the **Insert** menu.

- Press [**Enter**] or click away from the graph.

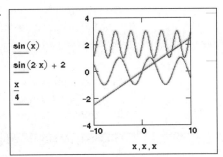

Mathcad produces a plot of all the expressions or functions, again over a range of –10 to 10. You can change the axis range by editing the upper and lower limits on the *x*-axis as described in "Setting limits for axes" on page 474.

Notice that you can create a QuickPlot in one of two ways. You can either:

- First type the expression(s) and then choose **Graph⇒X-Y Plot** from the **Insert** menu, in which case your expression appears automatically in the *y*-axis placeholder; or

- First choose **Graph⇒X-Y Plot** from the **Insert** menu and then enter the expression(s) in the *y*-axis placeholder.

Explicitly specifying the range on the *x*-axis

When you want to specify the *x*-axis argument or the range variable used, you can create a graph following these steps:

- Click in your worksheet wherever you want the graph to appear.

- Choose **Graph⇒X-Y Plot** from the **Insert** menu. Mathcad creates an empty graph with six placeholders, three on each axis.

Creating a graph

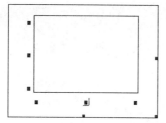

To see the graph, fill in the placeholders:

- The placeholder at the middle of the horizontal axis holds the variable or expression to graph against. Enter a range variable, a subscripted variable, or any other expression involving a range variable in this placeholder.

- The placeholder at the middle of the vertical axis holds an expression to graph. Enter a range variable, subscripted variable, or any other expression involving the range variable on the horizontal axis.

- The other four placeholders can be used to override Mathcad's automatic choices of axis limits. For more information about axis limits, see "Setting limits for axes" on page 474.

Mathcad graphs one point for each value of the range variable. If you don't define the range variable in your worksheet, as described above, Mathcad automatically generates an appropriate range for the dependent variable in your plot. Range variables are discussed in Chapter 11, "Range Variables."

Graphs typically have one or more expressions involving range variables on each axis. Be aware that it's usually an error to use two different range variables in the same curve, or *trace*, on a graph. If you use two range variables in the same trace, Mathcad tries to graph one point for each value of each range variable. For example, if i ranges through 20 points and j through 30, and you try to plot y_i against x_j, Mathcad tries to graph a total of 600 points. It is, however, permissible to use different range variables in different traces on the same graph.

Just as with an equation, Mathcad does not process a graph until you click outside the graph region. When Mathcad processes the graph, it draws one point for each value of each range variable in the x or y axis expressions and, unless you specify otherwise, connects them with straight lines.

Figure 20-1 shows some typical graphs with the placeholders filled in. Note the line that appears under the y-axis arguments. This indicates the trace type and color used to display the curve. See the section "Formatting individual curves" on page 478 to learn how to control this.

The graph in the upper left corner of Figure 20-1 is an example of a *parametric* plot: one in which the expressions you are plotting on the x-axis and y-axis are both functions of a single variable. If you do not explicitly define a range variable for the parameter in such a plot, Mathcad uses a default range for this variable to create the graph.

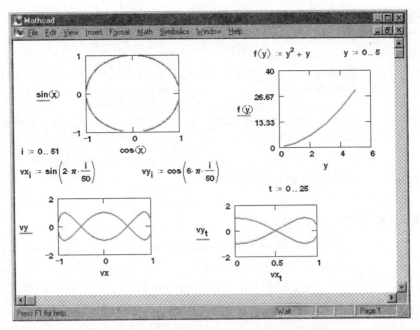

Figure 20-1: X-Y graphs of expressions, functions, and vectors.

If an expression is complex, Mathcad graphs only the real part. The imaginary part is ignored. Note that no error message will be displayed.

Working with graph regions

You can drag, cut, copy, and paste a graph just as you would any other math region. See Chapter 3, "Editing Equations," for details.

To delete a graph from your worksheet:

■ Press and hold down the mouse button just outside the plot.

■ With the button still pressed, drag the mouse cursor so as to enclose the graphics region in a selection rectangle.

■ Choose **Cut** from the **Edit** menu.

To move a graph, follow the instructions above for deleting it. Then click the mouse wherever you want the graph and choose **Paste** from the **Edit** menu. Alternatively, you can drag a plot as you would an equation.

See "Modifying your graph's perspective" on page 484 for Mathcad's options for resizing graphs, zooming in on graphs, and reading coordinates from graphs.

Graphing functions

Each trace on a graph depends on a range variable, and Mathcad graphs one point for each value in the range variable. As mentioned in the previous section, however, Mathcad automatically generates a default range for the dependent variable of an expression you type in the y-axis and creates the graph over it if you do not explicitly define a range variable.

If you want to specify exactly what range of values the range variable has, you can define a range variable in your worksheet. This method is described in the following sections.

Graphing a function

To graph a function over a range, as shown in Figure 20-2, do the following:

■ Define a range variable, such as x, that ranges over the values you want to graph. (The range variable need not be called x; you can use any valid Mathcad name.) See Chapter 11 for instructions on defining a range variable.

■ Type the expression you want to plot in the middle placeholder of the y-axis and type x in the middle placeholder of the x-axis.

■ Click anywhere outside the graph region to see the plot.

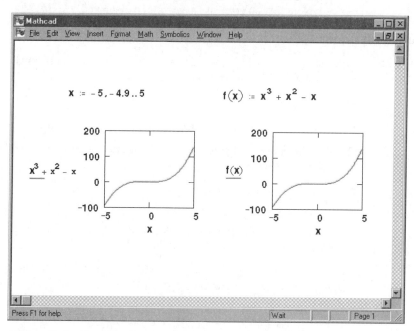

Figure 20-2: Graphing an expression against a range variable.

Chapter 20 Graphs

You can also define a function $f(x)$ and place it in the middle placeholder of the y-axis. This is particularly useful when the expression you want to plot becomes large and unwieldy. The second graph in Figure 20-2, above, shows the same plot as the first graph in the figure, except that it is made with a function definition.

Using functions for polar plots

By creatively using the tools presented in this chapter, you can plot a wide variety of closed curves. The example in Figure 20-3 illustrates how to transform polar into rectangular coordinates. This technique lets you create polar plots, or even paths in the complex plane. In Figure 20-3, the equation for the cardioid in polar coordinates is given by $r(\theta)$. The equations for $x(\theta)$ and $y(\theta)$ are the usual transformation from polar to rectangular coordinates. See Chapter 21, "Polar Plots," for a description of Mathcad's built-in polar plotting capabilities.

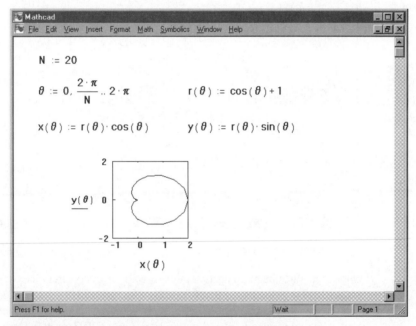

Figure 20-3: Two functions computed independently.

Graphing a vector

To graph the elements of a vector, you need to use the vector subscript operator to specify which elements to plot. A graph of a vector is shown in Figure 20-4. To create this graph, do the following:

■ Define a range variable i that references the subscript of each element you want to plot.

- Define a vector y_i. Use the left bracket key, [, to create the subscript.

- Press @ to create an empty plot region.

- Place y_i in the middle placeholder of the vertical axis and i in the middle placeholder of the horizontal axis.

- Click anywhere outside the graph region to see the plot.

A graph created using these steps is shown in Figure 20-4.

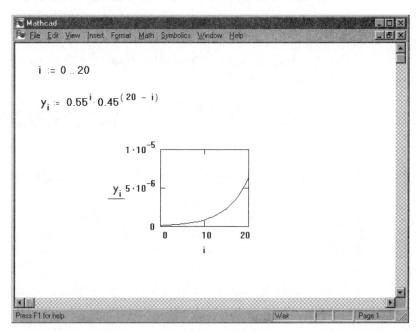

Figure 20-4: Graphing a vector.

Subscripts must be non-negative integers (or integers greater than or equal to ORIGIN, if ORIGIN≠0.) This means that the *x*-axis variable used in a graph like Figure 20-4 can run through whole-number values only. If you want to graph fractional or negative values on the *x*-axis, graph a function as in Figure 20-2, or graph two vectors as described in the next section.

If you have a handful of data points that don't have a convenient functional relationship as in Figure 20-4 but there are too few of them for you to use data files, you might want to use an input table to create a vector. For more information, see "Entering data manually" on page 429.

Graphing one vector against another

To graph all the elements of one vector against all the elements in another, enter the names of the vectors in the *x*- and *y*-axis placeholders on the graph. For example, to create the first graph shown in Figure 20-5:

- Define *x* and *y* as shown in the figure.

- Press @ to create an empty graph region.

- Place y in the middle placeholder of the y-axis and x in the middle placeholder of the x-axis.

- Click anywhere outside the graph region to see the plot.

Mathcad plots all the elements in the vector x against the elements in the vector y. If the vectors are not the same length, Mathcad will plot the number of elements in the shorter vector.

In some cases, you may prefer to explicitly tell Mathcad which elements of the vectors to plot. This is useful when you want to only plot some of elements. To plot certain elements as opposed to all of them, you must define a range variable and use it as a subscript on the vectors. The subscript references the elements to graph. A graph produced using this method is shown in Figure 20-1. The vectors do not need to be the same length. The only requirements are:

- The two vector must share the same subscript. For example, you cannot plot x_i against y_j because i and j are not the same subscript.

- Each value of the subscript must correspond to an element in each vector. For example, if x has only two elements and y has eight elements, and the range variable goes from 0 through 7, you will get an error.

To create the plot shown in the bottom right of Figure 20-1, do the following:

- Define a range variable t that references on the subscript of each element you want to plot.

- Define the arrays vx_t and vy_t. Use the left bracket key, [, to create the subscript.

- Press @ to create an empty graph region.

- Place vy_t in the middle placeholder of the y-axis and vx_t in the middle placeholder of the x-axis.

- Click anywhere outside the graph region to see the plot.

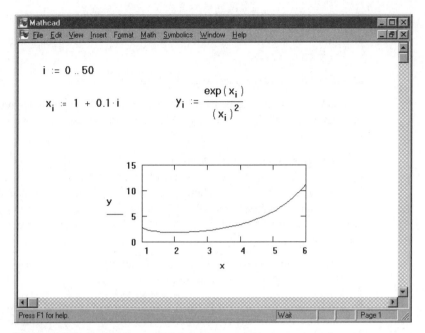

Figure 20-5: Graphing two vectors.

Although the *x* vector in Figure 20-5 is a list of evenly spaced values, this need not be the case. Only the *i* values are required to be evenly spaced integers. No such restriction exists for the x_i. This allows you to plot something besides integers on the *x*-axis while still satisfying the requirement for integers as subscripts.

In Figure 20-5, the y_i came directly from the x_i. Other applications might compute *x* and *y* independently from a third variable. As long as the two vectors use the same range variable, you can graph them on the same graph. Figure 20-6 shows a polar graph in which both *x* and *y* depend on the variables *r* and θ. Figure 20-6 uses vectors to do what was done with functions in Figure 20-3.

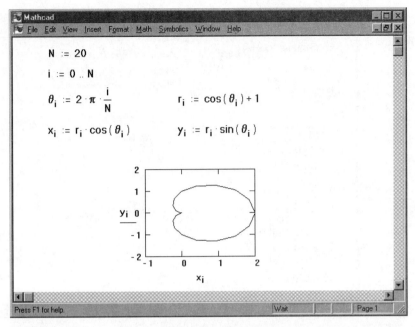

Figure 20-6: Two vectors computed independently.

Note that in Figure 20-6, the range variable *i* must have integer values and must be used to define a vector, namely θ, of equally spaced non-integer values. In Figure 20-3, however, we could define θ directly as a range variable. This is because functions do not require integer arguments the way vectors require integer subscripts.

Graphing data

You don't have to use Mathcad to generate the vectors that you plot, as was done for the example in Figure 20-5. You can create vectors by reading in data from a data file, by pasting in the data from the clipboard, or by typing data directly into an input table. These techniques are described in Chapter 19, "Data Management." Once you create vectors from data—for example, by extracting columns from a matrix—you can plot the vectors just as you would plot any vectors, as discussed in the previous section. See Figure 20-7 for an example of plotting vectors from data imported from an external file.

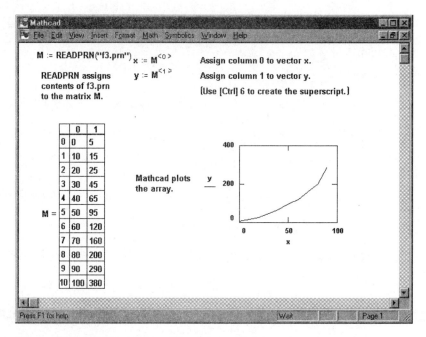

Figure 20-7: Plotting vectors from imported data.

Graphing other expressions

The examples in Figure 20-2 through Figure 20-7 show some of the most common types of graphs. However, graphs are not limited to these examples. You can graph any expression against any other expression, as long as they share the same range variables. For example, see Figure 20-12 for an example of graphing a constant to be used as a marker on the graph of another function.

Graphing more than one expression

You can graph several traces on the same graph. A graph can show several *y*-axis expressions against the same *x*-axis expression, or it can match up several *y*-axis expressions with corresponding *x*-axis expressions. One way to graph several expressions is to create a QuickPlot as described in the first section of this chapter.

Alternatively, you can graph several *y*-axis expressions versus one *x*-axis expression, using a conventional graph. To do so, choose **Graph⇒X-Y Plot** from the **Insert** menu and enter the first *y*-axis expression in the *y*-axis placeholder followed by a comma. You'll see a placeholder immediately below this first expression. Enter the second expression here, followed by another comma to get another empty placeholder. Enter the next expression. All the expressions should use the same range variable, as shown in Figure 20-8.

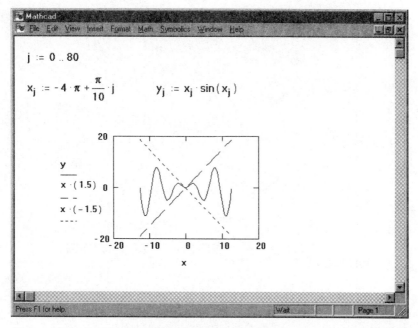

Figure 20-8: Graph with multiple y-axis expressions.

To graph several independent curves on the same set of axes, enter two or more expressions separated by commas on the *x*-axis and the same number of expressions on the *y*-axis. Mathcad matches up the expressions in pairs—first *x*-axis expression with first *y*-axis expression, the second with the second, and so on. It then draws a trace for each pair. Each matching pair of expressions should use the same range variable. The range variable for one pair need not match the range variables for the other pairs.

You can plot up to 16 arguments on the *y*-axis against 1 argument on the *x*-axis.

Figure 20-9 shows an example in which the range variables differ for each pair. Note however, that all traces on a graph share the same axis limits. For each axis, all expressions and limits on that axis must have compatible units.

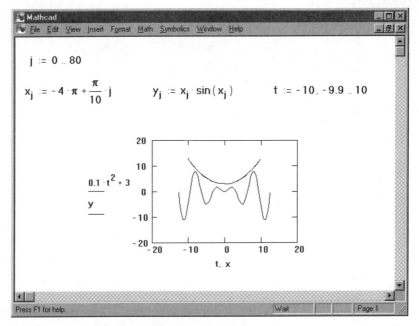

Figure 20-9: Graph with multiple expressions on both axes.

Formatting the axes

You can reformat your graph's axes, using the X-Y Axes page of the Formatting Currently Selected X-Y Plot dialog box.

To change a graph's format:

■ Click in the graph to select it.

■ Double-click in the graph. Alternatively, choose **Graph⇒X-Y Plot** from the **Format** menu. You'll see the dialog box for formatting X-Y plots.

■ If necessary, click the X-Y Axes tab to display the X-Y Axes page, shown below.

■ There is a complete group of settings for each axis. Change the appropriate settings.

■ Click "OK" to accept your changes and close the dialog box. Mathcad redraws the graph with the new settings in effect. Alternatively, click "Apply" to see the graph redrawn without closing the dialog box. Click "Close" to close the dialog box.

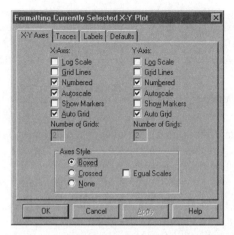

If you initiate this process by double-clicking on an axis, you'll see an equivalent dialog box for that axis alone.

The rest of this section describes the settings on the X-Y Axes page of the dialog box for formatting X-Y Plots. It then provides detailed discussions about options for setting axis limits and for adding horizontal and vertical reference lines to your graph.

Axis settings

Each axis has the following settings associated with it:

Log Scale

When this box is checked, the selected axis is logarithmic and the axis limits must be positive. The bottom-right-hand graph in Figure 20-16 on page 489 illustrates a graph with a logarithmic axis.

Grid Lines

When this box is checked, the tick marks on the selected axis are replaced by grid lines. The top-right-hand graph in Figure 20-16 on page 489 illustrates a graph that uses grid lines rather than tick marks.

Numbered

When this box is checked, the tick marks on the selected axis are numbered.

Autoscale

This controls axis limits that you don't otherwise specify. When this box is checked, Mathcad rounds the axis limit to the next major tick mark. When unchecked, Mathcad sets the axis limit to the data limit. For a discussion of Autoscale and the other ways to set axis limits, see "Setting limits for axes" later in this section.

Show Markers

When this box is checked, you can add reference lines to your graph. For a discussion of Show Markers and another way to create horizontal and vertical reference lines, see "Adding horizontal and vertical lines" later in this section.

Auto Grid

When this box is checked, Mathcad automatically selects the number of grid intervals created by tick marks or grid lines on the axes. When the box is unchecked, you choose the number of grid intervals by typing in the box labeled "No. of Grids". Enter a number from 2 to 99. You can specify the number of grid intervals only when Log Scale is unchecked. Figure 20-21 on page 491 illustrates the effect of Auto Grid.

In addition to these check boxes, the X-Y Axes page contains the following:

No. of Grids

When available, this text box indicates the number of grid intervals on the associated axis. You can enter a number between 2 and 99, inclusive. This box is only available when Auto Grid and Log Scale are unchecked.

Axes Style

These buttons define the style in which the graph will show the axes. Boxed axes are crossed in the bottom left corner of the graph. Crossed axes are crossed in the center of the graph. If you select None, no axes will be displayed on the graph. Figure 20-22 on page 492 illustrates the use of crossed axes. If you choose Equal Scale, both axes will use the same limits.

See the section "Setting default formats" on page 479 to learn how to:

■ Quickly restore the graph to its default format settings.

■ Use a particular graph as a model for all future graphs.

Setting limits for axes

Mathcad provides the following ways to set limits for axes:

■ Automatically, with Autoscale turned on.

■ Automatically, with Autoscale turned off.

■ Manually, by entering the limits directly on the graph.

By default, a plot you create in Mathcad is autoscaled. With Autoscale on, Mathcad automatically sets each axis limit to the first major tick mark beyond the end of the data. This will be a reasonably round number large enough to display every point being graphed. With Autoscale off, Mathcad automatically sets the axis limits exactly at the data limits.

Figure 20-10 shows how turning Autoscale on and then off changes the way the graph looks.

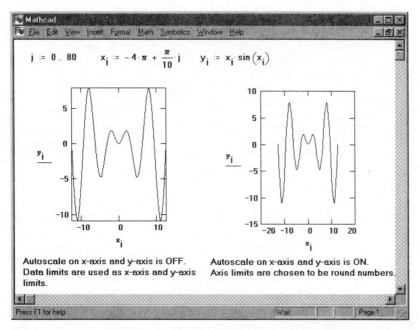

Figure 20-10: The effects of having Autoscale turned on and off.

To turn Autoscale off and have the axis limits automatically coincide with the end of the data:

■ Click on the graph to select it and then choose **Graph⇒X-Y Plot** from the **Format** menu. Mathcad displays the dialog box for formatting X-Y graphs, shown on page 472. Click the X-Y Axes tab if the X-Y Axes page is not displayed. (You can also double-click on the axis itself to see a similar dialog box.)

■ Click on Autoscale for the appropriate axis to remove the check and to toggle Autoscale off.

You may want to use axis limits other than those set by Mathcad. You can override Mathcad's automatic limits by entering limits directly on the graph. To do so:

■ Click the graph to select it. Mathcad displays four additional numbers, one by each axis limit. These numbers are enclosed within corner symbols, as illustrated in the selected plot in Figure 20-11.

■ To set the axis limit on the horizontal axis, click on the number underneath the appropriate x-axis limit and type the number at which you want the axis to end. To set an axis limit for the vertical axis, do the same thing to the number to the left of the appropriate y-axis limit.

■ Click outside the graph. Mathcad redraws it using the axis limits you specified. The corner symbols below the limits you changed will disappear. Figure 20-11 shows the effect of manually setting limits on a graph.

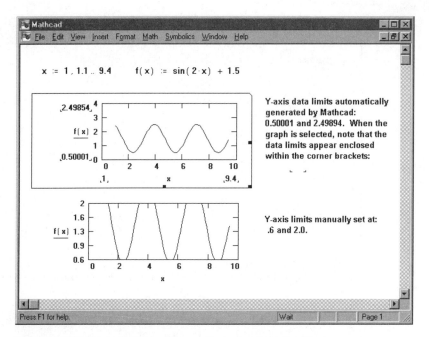

Figure 20-11: Data limits set manually and automatically.

Adding horizontal and vertical lines

Mathcad places linearly or logarithmically spaced tick marks or grid lines on a graph. The spaces between these markings are relatively round numbers that span the range of values on each axis. There may, however, be occasions when you need to place a line somewhere other than where Mathcad would normally place a grid line.

To add a horizontal or vertical line to a plot:

■ Click in the plot to select it.

■ Choose **Graph⇒X-Y Plot** from the **Format** menu or double-click on the graph to bring up the dialog box for formatting X-Y graphs.

■ If necessary, click on the X-Y Axes tab to display the X-Y Axes page, as shown on page 472.

■ For a vertical line, click on Show Markers in the X-axis column to add a check; for a horizontal line, click on Show Markers in the Y-axis column to add a check. Click "OK". Mathcad shows two additional placeholders on each axis for which you have Show Markers checked.

■ To add a vertical line, click on one of the placeholders under the *x*-axis and type in a value at which you want a line drawn. For a horizontal line, do the same thing in one of the placeholders under the *y*-axis.

When you click outside the graph, Mathcad draws a dashed line at each number you specify. The number you type appears at the end of the line. To move the dashed line, click on the number in the placeholder and change it. To delete the line, delete this number or click on Show Markers for the appropriate axis to uncheck it.

By using the Show Markers function, you can add to each axis one or two dashed lines stretching across the plot. When you need to place more than two lines or you need more control over the appearance of a line, you can add lines by plotting a constant expression.

■ To create a horizontal line, place a range variable on the middle placeholder of the *x*-axis and the constant expression on the *y*-axis. Mathcad will plot a horizontal line across the plot at whatever value the constant value happens to be. The expression you place on the *y*-axis need not depend on the range variable you place on the *x*-axis.

■ To create a vertical reference line, reverse the roles of the *x*- and *y*-axes. Place a range variable on the middle placeholder of the *y*-axis and the constant expression on the *x*-axis.

Figure 20-12 compares graphs having reference lines created by plotting constant expressions and by using the Show Markers option.

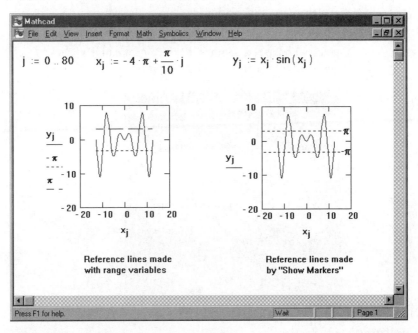

Figure 20-12: Graphs with reference lines.

Formatting individual curves

You can reformat the traces on your graph, using the Traces page of the dialog box for formatting X-Y graphs.

To reformat a graph's traces:

- Click in the graph to select it.

- Double-click in the graph. Alternatively, choose **Graph⇒X-Y Plot** from the **Format** menu. Mathcad displays the dialog box for formatting X-Y graphs.

- If necessary, click the Traces tab to display the Traces page.

- Click on the line in the scrolling list box for that trace. To change the name of the trace, type the new name in the text box under the "Legend Label" column. To change the symbol or marker, line type, color, trace type, or line weight of this trace, click on the arrow beside each text box to see a drop-down list of options, and then click on the option you want. See the next section, "Trace settings," for complete explanations of the various options in these lists.

- Click "OK" to accept your changes and close the dialog box. Mathcad redraws the graph with the new settings in effect. Alternatively, click "Apply" to preview your changes without closing the dialog box.

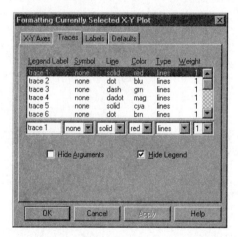

Trace settings

A graph can have up to sixteen individual traces. Each trace is described by a line in the scrolling list. Mathcad uses these lines as needed, assigning one for each trace in your graph. Each line has six fields:

Legend Label
This is the name of the trace as it would appear in the legend beneath the plot. See the section "Displaying or hiding arguments and legends" on page 484 for more

information about legends.

Symbol

This controls whether each point on the curve is marked with a symbol. You can mark each point with either an "×," a "+," a hollow box, a hollow diamond, a circle, or no symbol at all. If you have a lot of points packed closely together, you should probably select "none." Figure 20-19 on page 490 shows an example in which each data point is marked by with an "×."

Line

This controls whether the line is solid, dotted, dashed, or whether it consists of alternating dashes and dots. This feature provides a useful way to distinguish unmarked curves in black and white printouts.

Color

This controls whether the selected trace is red, blue, green, magenta, cyan (a light blue), brown, black, or white. Mathcad ignores this on monochrome displays.

Type

This controls the type of trace that will be displayed. Mathcad can generate the following types of plots: curves, bar graphs, stepped curves, error bars, stem graphs, and points. Figure 20-17 on page 489 has examples of step graphs and error bars. Figure 20-18 on page 490 has examples of stem graphs and bar graphs.

Weight

This controls the weight or thickness of the trace. Select from 1 to 9 (thinnest to thickest). Select "p" for a trace that is one device pixel wide. Although this may look like weight 1 on your screen, a high resolution printer will print it as a very fine line. This field also controls the size of the symbols marking data points, if you have selected a symbol other than "none". If you have selected trace type points, this field sets the weight of the dot plotted at each data point.

See "Setting default formats" on page 479 to learn how to:

■ Quickly restore the graph to its default format settings.

■ Use a particular graph as a model for all future graphs.

In addition to the scrolling list and its associated text box and lists, the Trace page has two check boxes: Hide Arguments and Hide Legend. These are explained fully in the "Displaying or hiding arguments and legends" on page 484.

Setting default formats

Mathcad uses default settings to format the axes and traces of new graphs as you create them. You can change these defaults in two ways:

■ By saving as defaults the settings of your current graph.

■ By using the Setting Default Formats for X-Y Plots dialog box, if you don't want to use an existing graph.

Changing defaults only affects new graphs; previously existing graphs are unaffected.

Copying defaults from an existing graph

One way to create a new set of defaults is to use the format settings of an existing graph. The advantage of this method is that you can actually see how the format settings look as you define them.

To use the format of a particular graph as the default graph format:

■ Click in the graph to select it.

■ Choose **Graph⇒X-Y Plot** from the **Format** menu or double-click on the selected graph. Mathcad displays the dialog box for formatting X-Y graphs. If necessary, click on the Defaults tab to see the Defaults page.

■ If the Use for Defaults check box doesn't contain a check, click on it to add one. When you close the dialog box, Mathcad saves these settings as your default settings.

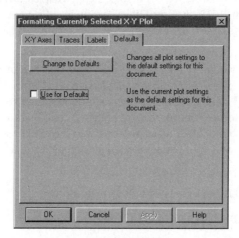

Setting defaults without using a graph

You don't have to use an existing graph to create or revise default formats. Instead, you can use the X-Y Axes page on the dialog box for setting X-Y plot defaults. To set defaults this way:

■ Make sure that you don't have any graphs selected.

■ Choose **Graph⇒X-Y Plot** from the **Format** menu. You'll see the dialog box for setting X-Y graph defaults. The following figure shows an example of this dialog box with the X-Y Axes page displayed.

■ Change the appropriate settings on the X-Y Axes and Traces pages.

■ Click "OK" to accept your changes and close the dialog box.

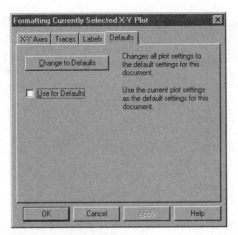

Using default graph settings

If you want to reverse the format changes that have been made to a graph since it was created, you can restore its original default settings. To restore the original defaults:

■ Click the Defaults tab on the dialog box for formatting X-Y graphs. (See the figure on page 480.)

■ Click "Change to Defaults."

■ Click "OK" to close the dialog box.

Mathcad redraws the graph, using the default format settings that were in place when the graph was first created.

Labeling your graph

Mathcad provides several ways to help you to identify what it is that you've plotted. You can choose to display:

■ A *title*, either above or below the graph.

■ *Axis labels* to describe what's plotted on each axis.

■ *Legends* to identify the individual traces.

■ *Arguments* showing what you typed into the *x*- and *y*-axis place holders.

Figure 20-13 shows the relative locations of each of these types of labels on a boxed axes graph and on a crossed axes graph.

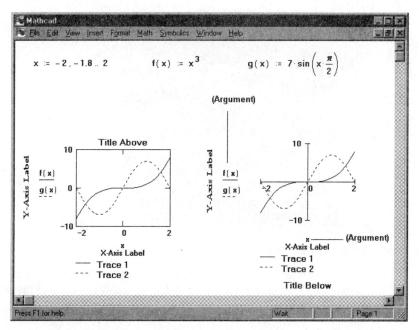

Figure 20-13: Graphs with different labels.

You can use these labels all together or in any combination. By default, Mathcad shows neither title nor axis labels, displays the arguments, and hides legends.

Working with titles

To add a title to a graph, follow these steps:

- Click in the graph to select it.

- Choose **Graph⇒X-Y Plot** from the **Format** menu or double-click on the selected graph. Mathcad displays the dialog box for formatting X-Y graphs. If necessary, click on the Labels tab.

- Type a title for your graph into the Title text box.

- Click on either the Above or Below button, depending upon where you want to put the title. Note, however, that Mathcad doesn't display the title until you click "Apply" or close the dialog box.

- Make sure that the Show Title check box is checked. If it isn't, Mathcad still remembers the title but won't display it.

- Click "OK" to accept your changes. Mathcad redraws the graph with the title in place. Alternatively, click "Apply" to preview your title without closing the dialog box.

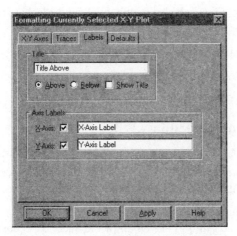

To edit a graph's title, follow these steps:

■ Click in the graph to select it.

■ Choose **Graph⇒X-Y Plot** from the **Format** menu or double-click on the selected graph. Mathcad displays the dialog box for formatting X-Y graphs. If necessary, click the Labels page. (You can also double-click on the title itself to display an equivalent dialog box.)

■ Edit the information for the title as appropriate or backspace over the title to delete it.

■ Click "OK" to close the dialog box.

Labeling axes on a graph

You can also label one or both axes of a graph in much the same way as you add a title to a graph. The x-axis label appears directly below the x-axis, and the y-axis label appears just to the left of the y-axis. To label an axis, follow these steps:

■ Click in the graph to select it.

■ Choose **Graph⇒X-Y Plot** from the **Format** menu or double-click on the selected graph. Mathcad displays the dialog box for formatting X-Y graphs. If necessary, click on the Labels tab to see that page, as shown in the preceding section.

■ Type the axis labels into the appropriate text boxes.

■ To save the label name without having it appear on the graph, click X-Axis or Y-Axis to remove the check.

■ Click "OK" to accept your changes and close the dialog box. Mathcad redraws the graph with the new settings in effect. Alternatively, click "Apply" to preview your changes without closing the dialog box.

To edit an axis label, follow these steps:

■ Click in the graph to select it.

■ Choose **Graph⇒X-Y Plot** from the **Format** menu or double-click on the selected graph. Mathcad displays the dialog box for formatting X-Y graphs. If necessary, click the Labels page. (You can also double-click on the label itself to display an equivalent dialog box.)

- Edit the information for the title as appropriate.

- To remove a label, delete it from the text box.

- Click "OK" to close the dialog box.

Displaying or hiding arguments and legends

Mathcad provides both arguments and legends for identifying specific traces on a graph:

- Arguments are the expressions that you typed into the placeholders of the x- and y-axes to create the graph. By default, Mathcad displays arguments.

- Legends are labels that appear underneath the graph containing a name and an example of the line and symbols used to draw the trace. By default, legends are hidden.

To display or hide arguments and legends:

- Click on the graph to select it.

- Choose **Graph**⇒**X-Y Plot** from the **Format** menu or double-click on the graph. Mathcad displays the dialog box for formatting X-Y graphs, as shown below. If necessary, click on the Traces tab.

- To suppress the display of the arguments, click on Hide Arguments to add a check.

- To show the legend, click on Hide Legend to remove the check.

Modifying your graph's perspective

Mathcad provides options for manipulating the presentation of your graph:

- You can resize the graph, making it proportionally larger or smaller or stretching the x-axis or y-axis for emphasis.

- You can zoom in on a portion of the graph.

- You can get the coordinates for any point that was plotted to construct the graph.

- You can get the coordinates for any location within the graph.

The rest of this section shows how to use these features.

Resizing a graph

Resizing a graph is very much like resizing a window:

- Click in the graph to select it.

■ Move the mouse pointer to one of the three handles along the edge of the graph. The pointer will change to a double-headed arrow.

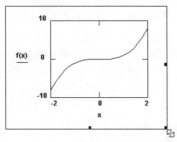

■ Press and hold down the mouse button and move the mouse in the direction that you want the graph's dimension to change.

■ Once the graph is the right size, let go of the mouse button.

■ Click outside the graph to deselect it.

Note that when you change the size of a graph for which the Auto Grid is set, Mathcad may add or delete tick marks or grid lines or change axis limits to maintain the default spacing.

Zooming in on a graph

Mathcad allows you to select a region of a graph and magnify it. To zoom in on a portion of a graph, follow these steps:

■ Click in the graph to select it.

■ Choose **Graph⇒Zoom** from the **Format** menu, or click on the Zoom button on the Graph Palette. The X-Y Zoom dialog box appears.

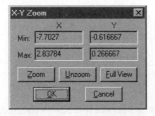

■ If necessary, reposition the X-Y Zoom dialog box so that you can see the entire region of the graph you want to zoom.

■ In the graph region, click the mouse at one corner of the region you want to magnify.

■ Press and hold down the mouse button and drag the mouse. A dashed selection rectangle emerges from the anchor point.

■ When the selection rectangle just encloses the region you want to magnify, let go of the mouse button. If necessary, you can click on the selection rectangle, hold the mouse button down, and move the rectangle to another part of the graph.

■ The coordinates of the selected region are listed in the Min: and Max: text boxes of the X-Y Zoom dialog box. Click the "Zoom" button to redraw the graph. The axis limits are temporarily set to the coordinates specified in the X-Y Zoom dialog box. To make these axis limits permanent, click "Accept."

Before you make these axis limits permanent, you can select another region to zoom by enclosing another selection rectangle around a new region. Press "Unzoom" to undo the zoom you've just made. If you're working with a graph that has already been zoomed, you may want to view the original graph as it was before any zooming took place. To do so, click on "Full View."

Figure 20-14 shows the effects of zooming in on a portion of a graph.

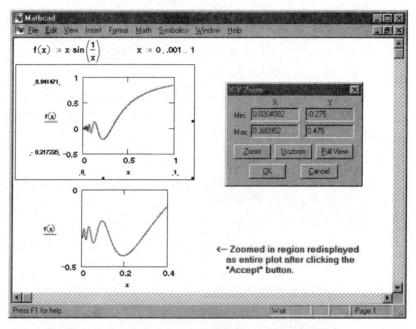

Figure 20-14: A zoomed-in region of a graph.

Getting a readout of graph coordinates

To see a readout of graph coordinates of the specific points that make up a trace, follow these steps:

■ Click in the graph to select it.

■ Choose **Graph**⇒**Trace** from the **Format** menu, or click on the Trace button on the Graph Palette, to show the X-Y Trace dialog box.

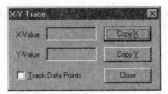

■ If necessary, reposition the X-Y Trace dialog box so that you can see the entire region of the graph. Note that the Track Data Points check box is checked.

■ In the graph region, click and drag the mouse along the trace whose coordinates you want to see. A dotted crosshair jumps from one point to the next as you move the pointer along the trace.

■ If you release the mouse button, you can now use the left and right arrows to move to the previous and next data points. Use the up and down arrows to move to other traces.

■ As the pointer reaches each point on the trace, Mathcad displays the x and y values of that point in the X-Value and Y-Value boxes.

■ The x and y values of the last point selected are shown in the X-Value and Y-Value boxes. The crosshair remains until you click outside the graph.

To copy a coordinate to the clipboard:

■ Click "Copy X" or "Copy Y". You can then paste that value into a math region or a text region on your Mathcad worksheet, into a spreadsheet, or into any other application that allows pasting from the clipboard.

■ Double-click on the control box in the upper-left-hand corner to close the X-Y Trace dialog box. The crosshair will remain on your graph until you click anywhere outside the graph or click the "Close" button.

To see a readout of graph coordinates for any location in a graph:

■ Follow the above procedures to call up the X-Y Trace dialog box.

■ Click on Track Data Points to uncheck it.

■ In the graph region, click and drag the mouse pointer over the points whose coordinates you want to see. A dotted crosshair follows the pointer as you drag it over the graph. Mathcad displays the coordinates of the pointer in the X-Value and Y-Value boxes. The x and y values change continuously to reflect the current pointer position.

■ When you release the mouse button, the X-Value and Y-Value boxes show the x and y values of the last pixel selected.

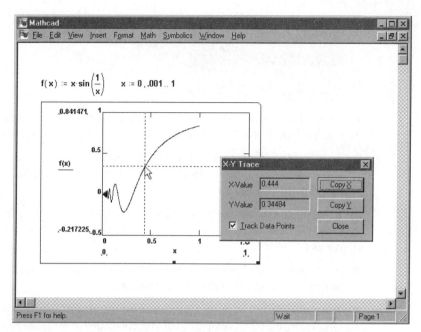

Figure 20-15: Reading coordinates from a graph.

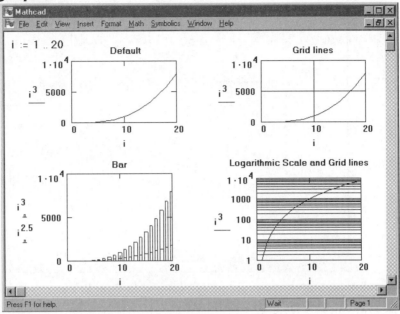

Figure 20-16: Different graph formats on the same graph.

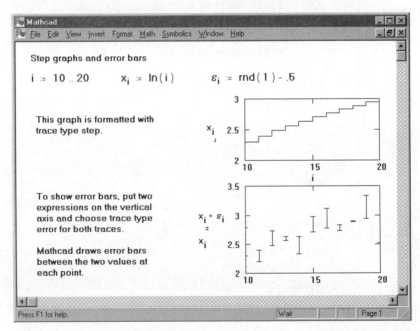

Figure 20-17: Step graphs and error bars from the scrolling list under "Trace type."

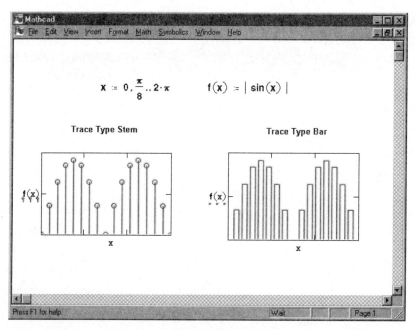

Figure 20-18: Stem graphs and bar graphs from the scrolling list under "Trace type."

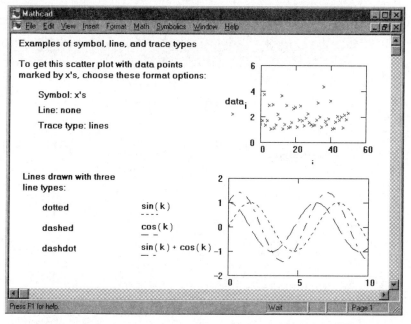

Figure 20-19: Choosing from the scrolling lists under "Line" and "Symbol."

     Chapter 20 Graphs

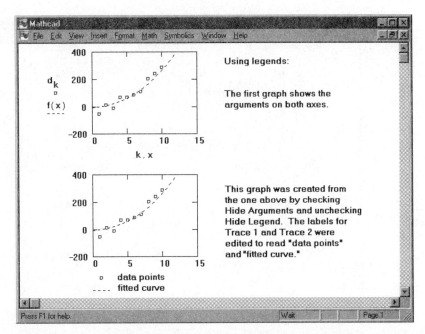

Figure 20-20: Hiding and showing the legend on the same graph.

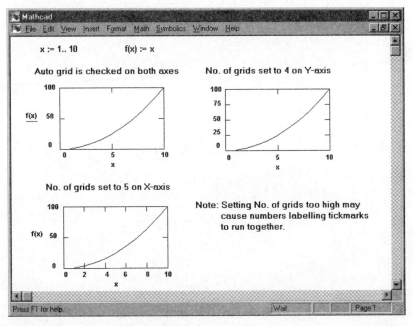

Figure 20-21: Unchecking Auto Grid option to vary the number of tick marks.

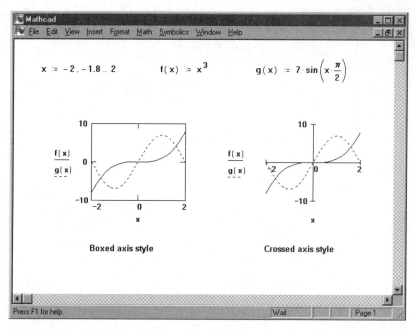

Figure 20-22: Using the "Crossed Axes" option to cross axes in the center of the plot.

Chapter 20 Graphs

Chapter 21
Polar Plots

In addition to X-Y plots, Mathcad worksheets can contain polar plots. Using polar coordinates, you can quickly and easily display angle-dependent data.

The following sections describe how to create, use, and format polar plots:

Creating a polar plot

Basic steps in creating a polar plot. QuickPlots versus plots where you explicitly specify the range on the angular axis.

Graphing more than one expression

Procedures for creating polar plots with multiple traces.

Formatting the axes

Procedures for modifying the radial and angular axes.

Formatting individual curves

Procedures for modifying curves or traces in a polar plot.

Setting default formats

Procedures for using default format settings for polar plots.

Labeling your polar plot

Procedures for working with titles, legends, and other labels.

Modifying your polar plot's perspective

Procedures for changing the size of the plot, zooming in on a portion of the plot, and finding coordinates in it.

Gallery of polar plots

A set of sample polar plots illustrating the options for creating polar plots.

Creating a polar plot

Mathcad's *polar plot operator* lets you plot functions that do not lend themselves well to Cartesian (*x-y*) coordinates. A typical polar plot shows the value of a radial expression *r* versus an angular expression θ. For example, you could use a polar plot to graph circular antenna patterns or electric field intensities around an object.

Mathcad draws polar plots by mapping *r* and θ onto *x* and *y* using the standard transformations $x = r\cos(\theta)$ and $y = r\sin(\theta)$. *r* and θ can assume positive or negative values.

You insert the polar plot operator into a blank space in your worksheet by choosing any one of three equivalent methods: by choosing **Graph⇒Polar Plot** from the **Insert** menu, by typing [**Ctrl**]7, or by clicking the Polar Plot button in the Graph Palette. Like the X-Y plot operator described in Chapter 20, "Graphs," the polar plot has placeholders on its axes for you to fill in that specify expressions to be computed and displayed, and it automatically chooses a default range for the angular axis variable if you do not specify one. In the case where you do not specify the angular axis variable, Mathcad creates a polar *QuickPlot*.

Polar QuickPlot

You can quickly and easily create a polar plot from a single Mathcad expression. To do so:

■ Enter the expression or function of a single variable you want to plot. Make sure the editing lines remain in the expression.

■ Choose **Graph⇒Polar Plot** from the **Insert** menu.

■ Press [**Enter**] or click away from the graph.

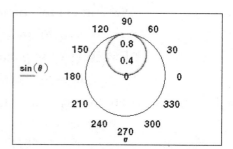

Mathcad automatically produces a polar plot over a default range of the dependent variable on the angular axis: 0 to 360 degrees (0 to 2π radians). You can graph multiple expressions on the radial axis, generating several traces on the polar plot, by entering them as described in "Graphing more than one expression" on page 496.

Notice that you can create a QuickPlot in one of two ways. You can either:

■ First type an expression and then choose **Graph⇒Polar Plot** from the **Insert** menu, in which case your expression appears automatically in the radial axis placeholder; or

- First choose **Graph**⇒**Polar Plot** from the **Insert** menu and then enter an expression in the radial axis placeholder.

Explicitly specifying the range on the angular axis

When you want to specify the angular axis argument or the range variable used, use the following steps to create a polar plot:

- Click where you want the polar plot to appear.

- Choose **Graph**⇒**Polar Plot** from the Insert menu. Mathcad shows a circle with four placeholders as shown below:

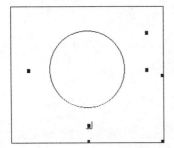

- Above the plot region, define an angle θ and a function of the angle, $r(\theta)$.

- The bottom placeholder holds the angle variable to plot against. Enter a range variable or any expression involving a range variable in this placeholder.

- The left placeholder holds a radial expression to plot.

- The two placeholders to the right hold the upper and lower radial limits. Mathcad fills in these placeholders by default. If you want, you can modify these limits. See the section "Formatting the axes" on page 498.

Just as with an equation or other plot types, Mathcad will not process the polar plot until you click outside the plot.

You can specify many of the characteristics of the polar plot including the size, the number of grid lines, and the upper and lower radial axis limits. The procedures for specifying these characteristics are described later in this chapter.

Here are the typical steps in plotting a function like the one shown in Figure 21-1:

- Define a range and an increment for θ. If you don't, Mathcad generates a polar plot over a default range of 0 to 360 degrees.

- Define $r(\theta)$, a function of θ.

- Show $r(\theta)$ in a polar plot.

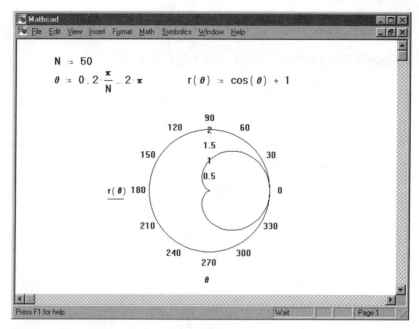

Figure 21-1: Polar plot of a function of θ.

Graphing more than one expression

Just as you can graph several expressions on a single Cartesian (X-Y) plot, you can graph several expressions on the same polar plot. Each expression generates a *trace*. A polar plot can show several *r* expressions against the same θ expression, or it can match up several *r* expressions with corresponding θ expressions.

To graph several *r* expressions versus one θ expression, enter the first *r* expression followed by a comma. You'll see a placeholder immediately below this first expression. Enter the second expression here, followed by another comma to get another empty placeholder. All the expressions should use the same range variable, as shown in Figure 21-2. Figure 21-2 also shows how to define an angular range in degrees.

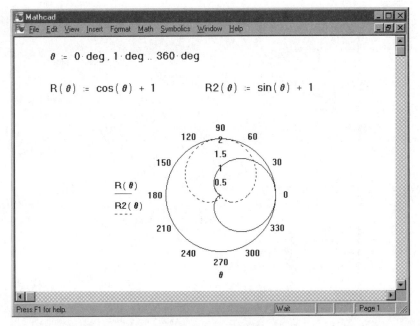

Figure 21-2: Polar plot with multiple expressions.

To graph several independent curves on the same polar plot, enter two or more expressions separated by commas in the angular axis placeholder and the same number of expressions in the radial axis placeholder. For example, to plot $r(\theta)$ against θ and $s(\phi)$ against ϕ you could type "$r(\theta)$, $s(\phi)$" in one placeholder and "θ, ϕ" in the other. Mathcad matches the expressions in pairs—$r(\theta)$ with θ and $s(\phi)$ with ϕ. It then draws a trace for each pair. Each matching pair of expressions should use the same range variable. The range variable for one pair need not match the range variables for the other pairs.

As with x-y plots, you can plot one vector of values against another, using a range variable to index the two vectors. This is illustrated in Figure 21-3.

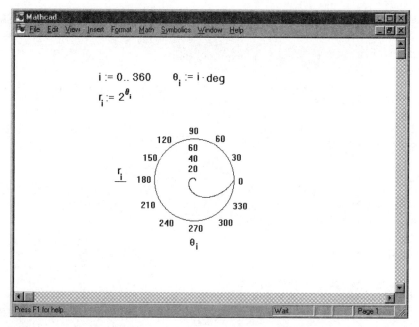

Figure 21-3: Plotting one vector against another.

Formatting the axes

You can reformat your polar plot's axes, using the Polar Axes page of the dialog box for formatting polar plots.

To change a polar plot's format:

■ Click in the polar plot to select it.

■ Double-click in the polar plot. Alternatively, choose **Graph⇒Polar Plot** from the **Format** menu. You'll see the dialog box for formatting polar plots, shown below.

■ If necessary, click the Polar Axes tab.

■ There is a complete group of settings for each axis. Change the appropriate settings.

■ Click "OK" to accept your changes and close the dialog box. Mathcad redraws the polar plot with the new settings in effect. Alternatively, click "Apply" to see the plot redrawn without closing the dialog box.

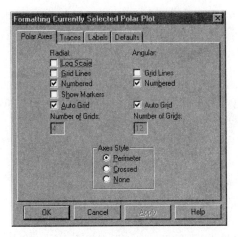

Axis settings

Each axis has the following settings associated with it:

Log Scale

When this box is checked, the radial axis is logarithmic. Axis limits must be positive. This setting is available only for the radial axis. Figure 21-10 on page 513 illustrates a polar plot with a logarithmic axis.

Grid Lines

When this box is checked, the tick marks on the selected axis are replaced by grid lines. If the axis is logarithmic, then logarithmically spaced grid lines are added if space permits. Radial grid lines are circles of fixed radius; angular grid lines radiate out from the origin at a fixed angle. Figure 21-8 on page 512 compares a plot with tick marks to the same plot with grid lines.

Numbered

When this box is checked, the selected grid lines are numbered. Figure 21-8 on page 512 illustrates numbers being used with grid lines.

Show Markers

When this box is checked, you can add reference lines to your polar plot. See "Adding radial reference lines" on page 501.

Auto Grid

When this box is checked, Mathcad automatically selects the number of grid markings (tick marks or grid lines). When the box is unchecked, you choose the number of grid markings (from 2 to 99) by typing a number in the No. of Grids text box. You can specify the number of grid markings only when Log Scale is unchecked. Figure 21-9 on page 512 illustrates the effect of Auto Grid.

In addition to these check boxes, the dialog boxes contain the following:

No. of Grids

When available, this text box indicates the number of tick marks or grid lines on the associated axis. You can enter a number between 2 and 99, inclusive. This box is only available when Auto Grid and Log Scale are unchecked. Figure 21-9 on page 512 shows the effects of defining the number of grid lines on both the radial and the angular axes.

Axes Style

These buttons let you choose between crossed axes, no axes at all, and a plot enclosed by a circle (perimeter). Figure 21-11 on page 513 illustrates the difference between perimeter and crossed axes.

See the section "Setting default formats" below to learn how to:

■ Quickly restore a polar plot to its default format settings.

■ Use a particular plot as a model for all future polar plots.

Setting limits for axes

Mathcad sets the upper and lower radial axis limits by default. For a linear scale, the upper limit is the maximum radial value of whatever is plotted. The lower limit is zero. For a logarithmic scale, the upper limit is set to the next higher integer power of ten above the maximum of the data. The lower limit on a logarithmic scale is set to the next integer power of ten below the minimum of the data.

You may want to use axis limits other than those set by Mathcad. You can override Mathcad's limits by entering limits directly on the graph. To do so:

■ Click in the polar plot to select it. Mathcad shows two additional numbers on the upper right of the polar plot. These numbers are enclosed within corner symbols, as illustrated by the selected plot in Figure 21-4, below.

■ Mathcad treats a negative radial limit as a positive value. To set the maximum value of the radial axis, click on the number in the top placeholder and type in a new number. While there's rarely a reason to change the minimum value, you can do this by clicking on the lower number and typing a new number.

■ Click outside the plot, Mathcad immediately redraws it using the axis limits you specify. Figure 21-4 shows the effect of manually setting limits on a polar plot.

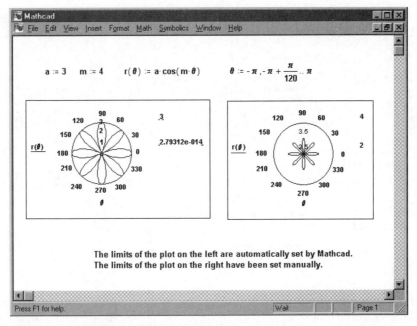

Figure 21-4: Manually setting axis limits.

Adding radial reference lines

Mathcad places linearly or logarithmically spaced radial grid lines on a polar plot. The spaces between grid lines are relatively round numbers that span the range of values on the angular axis. There may, however, be occasions when you need to place a radial line somewhere other than where Mathcad would normally place a grid line.

To add a radial reference line to the polar plot:

■ Click in the polar plot to select it.

■ Choose **Graph⇒Polar Plot** from the **Format** menu or double-click on the plot to display the dialog box for formatting polar plots. If necessary, click on the Polar Axes page.

■ Click the Show Markers check box in the radial axis column to add a check. Click "OK". Mathcad shows two additional placeholders on the upper-left side of the plot.

■ Click on one of the placeholders and type in the value at which you want the radial reference line drawn. Repeat this process with the other placeholder to add two radial reference lines.

When you click outside the graph, Mathcad draws a dashed circle at each number that you specified. The number that you typed appears on this dashed circle. To move the dashed circle, click on the appropriate number and change it. To delete the circle, delete this number or click on the Show Markers check box to remove the check. Figure 21-5 illustrates the use of radial reference lines.

Formatting the axes

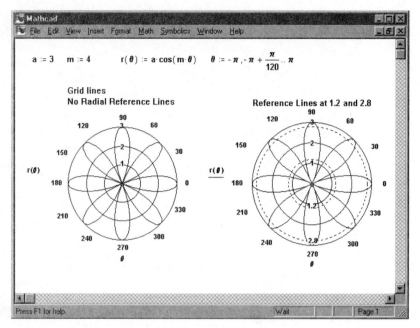

Figure 21-5: Adding radial reference lines to a polar plot.

Formatting individual curves

You can reformat the traces on your polar plot, using the Traces page of the dialog box for formatting polar plots.

To reformat a plot's traces:

- Click in the polar plot to select it.

- Double-click in the polar plot. Alternatively, choose **Graph⇒Polar Plot** from the **Format** menu. Mathcad displays the dialog box for formatting polar plots.

- If necessary, click the Traces tab.

- Click on the appropriate line in the scrolling list box to select a trace. To change the name of the trace, type the new name in the text box under the "Legend Label" column. To assign a symbol or marker, line type, color, trace type, and line weight to this trace, click on the arrow beside each text box to see a drop-down list of options, and then click on the option you want. See the next section, "Trace settings," for complete explanations of these fields.

- Click "OK" to accept your changes and close the dialog box. Mathcad redraws the plot with the new settings in effect. Alternatively, click "Apply" to preview your changes without closing the dialog box.

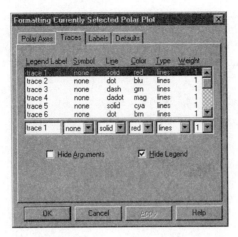

Trace settings

A graph can have up to sixteen individual traces. Each trace is described by a line in the scrolling list. Mathcad uses these lines as needed, assigning one for each trace in your plot. Each line has six fields:

Legend Label

This is the name of the trace as it would appear in the legend beneath the plot. See the section "Displaying or hiding arguments and legends" on page 507 for more information about legends.

Symbol

This controls whether each point on the curve is marked with a symbol. If y you choose, you can mark each point with either an "×," a "+," a hollow box, or a hollow diamond. If you have a lot of points packed closely together, you should probably select "none." Figure 21-12 on page 514 shows an example in which each data point is marked by with an "×."

Line

This controls whether the line is solid, dotted, or dashed or whether it consists of alternating dashes and dots. This feature provides a useful way to distinguish unmarked curves in black and white printouts.

Color

This controls whether the selected trace is red, blue, green, magenta, cyan (a light blue), brown, black, or white. Mathcad ignores this on monochrome displays.

Type

This controls the type of trace that will be displayed. Mathcad can generate the following types of plots: curves, bar graphs, stepped curves, error bars, stem graphs, and points. (You must have at least two traces to use error bars.) Figure 21-13 on page 514 illustrates the same polar plot, displayed with a variety of trace types.

Weight

This controls the weight or thickness of the trace. Select from 1 to 9 (thinnest to thickest). Select "p" for the lightest (single-pixel) trace. Although this may look like weight 1 on your screen, a high resolution printer will print it as a very fine line. This field also controls the size of the symbols marking data points, if you have selected a symbol other than "none". If you have selected trace type points, this field sets the weight of the dot plotted at each data point.

See "Setting default formats" below to learn how to:

■ Quickly restore a polar plot to its default format settings.

■ Use a particular plot as a model for all future polar plots.

In addition to the scrolling list and its associated text box and lists, the Trace page has two check boxes: Hide Arguments and Hide Legend. These are explained fully in the "Displaying or hiding arguments and legends" on page 507.

Setting default formats

Mathcad uses default settings to format the axes and traces of new polar plots as you create them. You can change these defaults in two ways:

■ By saving as defaults the settings of your current plot.

■ By using the Setting Default Formats for Polar Plots dialog box to set defaults, if you don't want to use an existing plot.

Changing defaults only affects new polar plots; previously existing plots are unaffected.

Copying defaults from an existing plot

One way to create a new set of defaults is to use the format settings of an existing polar plot. The advantage of this method is that you can use "Apply" to see how the format settings look while you define them.

To use the format of a particular polar plot as the default polar plot settings:

■ Select the graph by clicking on it.

■ Click the Defaults tab on the dialog box for formatting polar plots. The Defaults page appears, as shown below.

■ If the Use for Defaults check box isn't checked, click on it to add one. When you close the dialog box, Mathcad saves these settings as your default settings.

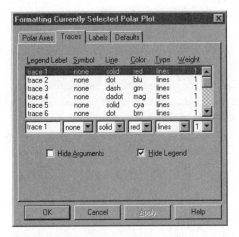

Setting defaults without using a polar plot

You don't have to use an existing polar plot to create or revise default formats. Instead, you can use the dialog box for polar plot defaults. To set defaults this way:

■ Make sure that you don't have any plots selected.

■ Choose **Graph**⇒**Polar Plot** from the **Format** menu. You'll see the dialog box for polar plot defaults. The following figure shows an example of this dialog box with the Polar Axes page displayed.

■ Change the appropriate settings on the Polar Axes and Traces pages.

■ Click "OK" to accept your changes and close the dialog box.

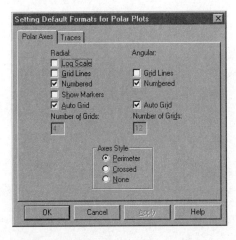

Using default graph settings

If you don't want the format changes made to your polar plot since creating the last set of default settings, you can restore the plot to its current default settings. To do so:

- Click the Defaults tab on the dialog box for polar plots.

- Click "Change to Defaults".

- Click "OK" to close the dialog box.

Mathcad redraws the plot, using the most recent set of default format settings. Mathcad does not use any defaults you might have set using the Use for Defaults check box at any time after the creation of this plot.

Labeling your polar plot

Mathcad provides several ways to help you to identify what it is you've plotted. You can display:

- A *title* centered above or below the polar plot.

- A *legend* identifying each trace.

- The arguments you used to create the plot.

Figure 21-6 shows the relative locations of each of these labels on a perimeter graph and on a crossed axes graph.

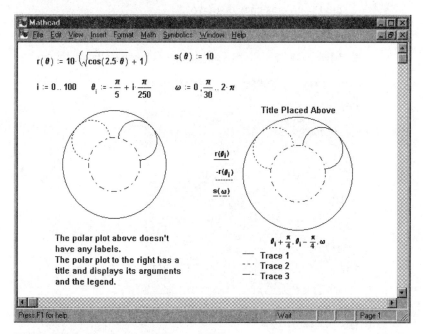

Figure 21-6: Graphs with different labels.

You can use these labels all together or in any combination. By default, Mathcad hides the title, displays arguments, and hides the legend.

Working with titles

To add a title to a polar plot, follow these steps:

■ Click in the polar plot to select it.

■ Choose **Graph⇒Polar Plot** from the **Format** menu or double-click on the selected plot. Mathcad displays the dialog box for formatting polar plots. If necessary, click on the Labels tab to see the Labels page, as shown below.

■ Type a title for your polar plot into the Title text box.

■ Click on either the Above or Below button, depending upon where you want to put the title.

■ Make sure that the Show Title check box is checked. If it isn't, Mathcad still remembers the title but won't display it.

■ Click "OK" to accept your changes. Mathcad redraws the polar plot with the title in place. Alternatively, click "Apply" to preview your title without closing the dialog box.

To change the title's text or position, edit the information in the Title group as appropriate. To delete the title, highlight it in the text box and press [Del].

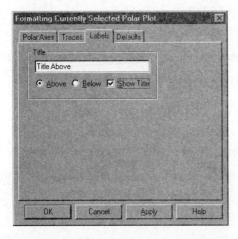

Displaying or hiding arguments and legends

Mathcad provides both arguments and legends for identifying specific traces on a polar plot:

■ Arguments are the expressions that you typed into the placeholders to create the polar plot. By default, Mathcad displays arguments.

- Legends are labels that appear underneath the polar plot. They contain a name and an example of the line and symbols used to draw the trace. By default, Mathcad hides legends.

To display or hide arguments and legends:

- Click in the polar plot to select it.

- Choose **Graph⇒Polar Plot** from the **Format** menu or double-click on the graph. Mathcad displays the dialog box for formatting polar plots. If necessary, click on the Traces tab.

- To suppress the display of the arguments, click on the Hide Arguments check box to add a check.

- To show the legend, click on the Hide Legend check box to remove the check.

Modifying your polar plot's perspective

Mathcad provides options for manipulating the presentation of your polar plot:

- You can make the plot larger or smaller.

- You can zoom in on a portion of the plot.

- You can get the coordinates for any point that was plotted to construct the plot.

- You can get the coordinates for any location within the plot.

The rest of this section shows how to use these features.

Resizing a polar plot

Resizing a polar plot is very much like resizing a window:

- Click in the polar plot to select it.

- Move the mouse pointer to one of the three handles along the edge of the polar plot. The pointer will change to a double-headed arrow.

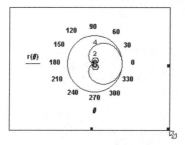

- Press and hold down the mouse button and move the mouse in the direction in which you want the polar plot's dimensions to change.

- Once the polar plot is the right size, let go of the mouse button.

- Click outside the polar plot to deselect it.

Zooming in on a polar plot

Mathcad allows you to select a region of a polar plot and magnify it. To zoom in on a portion of a plot, follow these steps:

- Click in the polar plot to select it.

- Choose **Graph**⇒**Zoom** from the **Format** menu, or click on the Zoom button in the Graph Palette. The Polar Zoom dialog box appears.

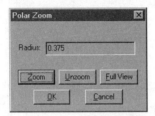

- If necessary, reposition the Polar Zoom dialog box so that you can see the entire region of the graph you want to zoom.

- Click in the polar plot region and drag the mouse while holding down the mouse button. A dashed selection circle is centered in the plot.

- When the selection circle just encloses the region you want to magnify, let go of the mouse button.

- The radius of the selected region is shown in the Radius box of the Polar Plot Zoom dialog box. Click the "Zoom" button to redraw the plot. The axis limits are temporarily set to the coordinates specified in the Polar Plot Zoom dialog box.

Before you make these axis limits permanent, you can select another region to zoom by enclosing another selection circle around the new region. Click "Unzoom" to start the zooming process over. If you're working with a plot that has already been zoomed, you may want to view the original plot as it looked before any zooming took place. To do so, click on "Full View".

Figure 21-7 shows the effects of zooming in on a portion of a polar plot.

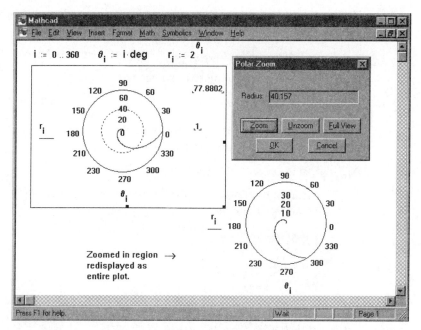

Figure 21-7: A zoomed-in region of a polar plot.

Getting a readout of polar plot coordinates

To see a readout of polar plot coordinates of the specific points that make up a trace, follow these steps:

- Click in the polar plot to select it.

- Choose **Graph⇒Trace** from the **Format** menu to show the Polar Trace dialog box.

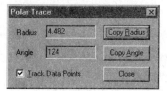

- If necessary, reposition the Polar Trace dialog box so that you can see the entire region of the graph.

- Drag the mouse along the trace whose coordinates you want to see. A dotted crosshair jumps from one point to the next as you move the pointer along the trace.

- Use the left and right arrows to move to the previous and next data points. Use the up and down arrows to move to other traces.

- As the pointer reaches each point on the trace, Mathcad displays the coordinates of the pointer location in the Radius and Angle boxes.

- When you release the mouse button, the radius and angle settings of the last point selected are shown in the Radius and Angle boxes. The crosshair remains until you click outside the polar plot.

- Double-click on the control box in the upper-left-hand corner to close the Polar Trace dialog box. The crosshair will remain on your plot until you click anywhere outside it.

To copy a coordinate to the clipboard:

- Click "Copy Radius" or "Copy Angle".

- You can then paste that value into either a math or text region of your Mathcad worksheet, into a spreadsheet, or into any other application that allows pasting from the clipboard.

To see a readout of coordinates for any location in a polar plot:

- Follow the above procedures to call up the Polar Trace dialog box.

- Click on Track Data Points to uncheck it.

- In the polar plot region, click and drag the mouse pointer over the points whose coordinates you want to see. A dotted crosshair follows the pointer as you drag it over the plot. Mathcad displays the coordinates of the pointer in the Radius and Angle boxes. The radius and angle values change continuously to reflect the current pointer position.

- When you release the mouse button, the Radius and Angle boxes show the r and θ values of the last pixel selected.

Gallery of polar plots

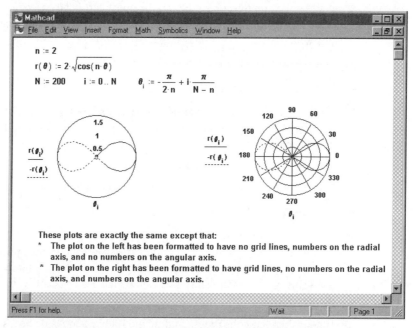

Figure 21-8: Different axis formats on the same polar plot.

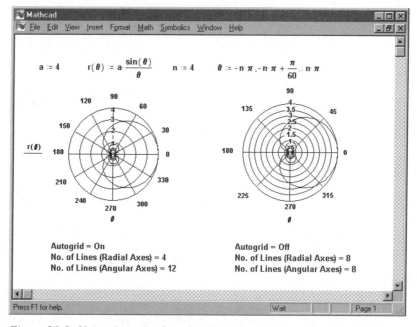

Figure 21-9: Using Auto Grid on the same polar plot.

Chapter 21 Polar Plots

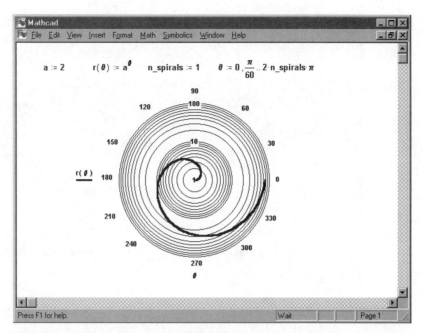

Figure 21-10: Polar plot with a logarithmic axis.

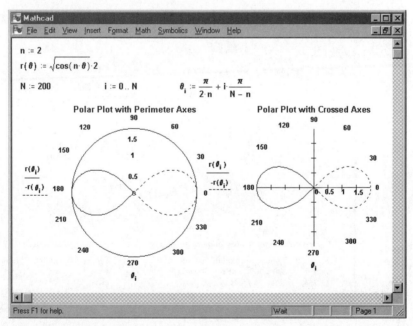

Figure 21-11: Using perimeter and crossed axes styles on the same polar plot.

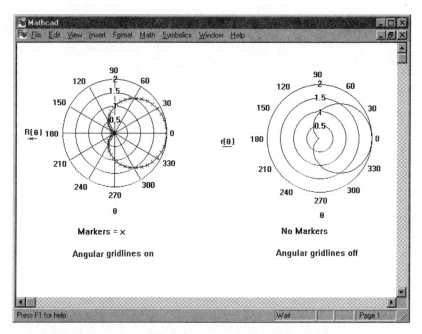

Figure 21-12: Using symbols and lines on the same polar chart.

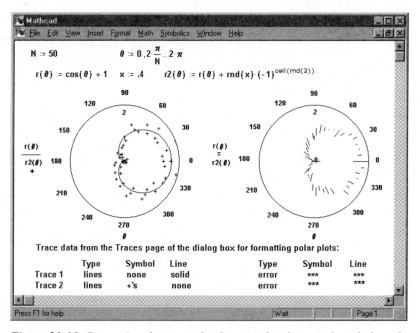

Figure 21-13: Presenting the same plot formatted as lines and symbols and then as error bars.

Chapter 22
Surface Plots

Mathcad worksheets can include both two-dimensional plots and three-dimensional plots. Unlike the two-dimensional plots, which work with range variables and functions, three-dimensional plots require a matrix of values. This chapter shows how a matrix can be represented as a surface plot in which you see a three-dimensional illustration of its values.

This chapter describes how to create, use, and format three-dimensional surface plots. The chapters that follow describe how to work with other types of three-dimensional plots.

This chapter contains the following sections:

Creating a surface plot

Basic steps for creating surface plots; procedures for creating surface plots for functions of two variables and for creating parametric surface plots.

Resizing surface plots

Procedures for changing the size of surface plots.

Formatting surface plots

Procedures for changing surface plots: setting the viewpoint, size, and magnification; adding labels; and formatting lines, colors, and axes.

Creating a surface plot

To create a surface plot:

■ Define a matrix of values to plot. Mathcad will use the rows and column numbers of the matrix as *x*- and *y*-axes. The matrix elements will be plotted as heights above or below the *xy* plane.

■ Choose **Graph⇒Surface Plot** from the **Insert** menu. Mathcad shows a box with a single placeholder, as shown below:

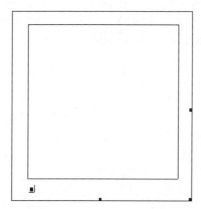

■ Type the name of the matrix in the placeholder. Just as with an equation, Mathcad will not process the surface plot until you click outside the plot.

What you see is a visual representation of the matrix. Mathcad draws a perspective view of the matrix as a two-dimensional grid lying flat in three-dimensional space. Each matrix element is represented as a point at a specified height above or below this grid. The height is proportional to the value of the matrix element. In the default perspective, the first row of the matrix extends from the back left corner of the grid to the right, while the first column extends from the back left corner out toward the viewer.

Mathcad draws lines to connect the points in the plot. These lines define the surface. The perspective for this rendering of the surface depends on the location of the viewer with respect to the surface. You can specify this view by changing the plot's tilt or rotation, as described in "Changing your view of the surface plot" on page 520.

Plotting a function of two variables

A typical surface plot shows the values of a function of two variables. To see such a plot, you must first create a matrix that holds the values of the function, then create a surface plot of that matrix. Here are the typical steps in plotting a function of two variables such as that shown in Figure 22-1:

■ Define a function of two variables.

■ Decide how many points you want to plot in the *x* and *y* directions. Set up range variables *i* and *j* to index these points. For example, if you want to plot 10 points in each direction, enter:

$$i := 0 .. 9 \qquad j := 0 .. 9$$

■ Define x_i and y_j as evenly spaced points on the *x*- and *y*-axes.

■ Fill the matrix **M** with the values of $f(x_i, y_j)$.

■ Choose **Graph⇒Surface Plot** from the **Insert** menu.

■ Type **M** in the placeholder and click outside the region.

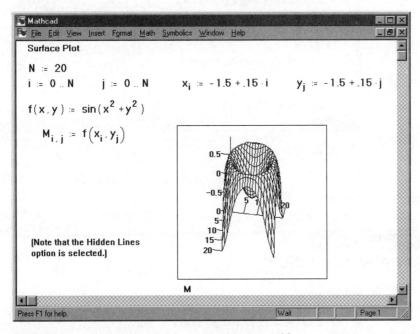

Figure 22-1: Surface plot of a function of two variables.

Creating parametric surface plots

To use Mathcad's surface plot operator to draw parametric surface plots:

■ Type the names of three matrices having the same number of rows and columns into the placeholders at the bottom of the surface plot.

■ Mathcad interprets these three matrices as the *x*-, *y*-, and *z*-coordinates of points on a surface and draws this surface from the viewing angle prescribed by the Rotation and Tilt settings.

The underlying parameter space is a rectangular sheet covered by a uniform mesh. In effect, the three matrices map this sheet into three-dimensional space. For example, the matrices **X**, **Y**, and **Z** defined in Figure 22-2 carry out a mapping that rolls the sheet into a tube and then joins the ends of the tube to form a torus.

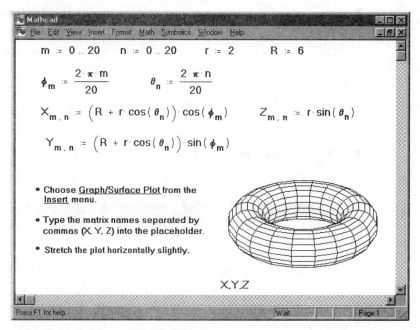

$$m := 0 .. 20 \qquad n := 0 .. 20 \qquad r := 2 \qquad R := 6$$

$$\phi_m := \frac{2 \cdot \pi \cdot m}{20} \qquad \theta_n := \frac{2 \cdot \pi \cdot n}{20}$$

$$X_{m,n} := \left(R + r \cdot \cos(\theta_n) \right) \cdot \cos(\phi_m) \qquad Z_{m,n} := r \cdot \sin(\theta_n)$$

$$Y_{m,n} := \left(R + r \cdot \cos(\theta_n) \right) \cdot \sin(\phi_m)$$

- Choose <u>Graph/Surface Plot</u> from the <u>Insert</u> menu.
- Type the matrix names separated by commas (X, Y, Z) into the placeholder.
- Stretch the plot horizontally slightly.

X,Y,Z

Figure 22-2: Parametric surface plots.

You can't convert parametric surface plots into any other type of 3D plot.

Resizing surface plots

To change the size of a surface plot, follow these steps:

■ Click in the surface plot to select it.

■ Move the mouse pointer to one of the three handles along the edge of the surface plot. The pointer will change to a double-headed arrow.

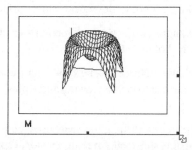

■ Press and hold down the mouse button. While holding down the button, move the mouse. The surface plot region will stretch in the direction of motion.

- Once the surface plot is the right size, let go of the mouse button.
- Click outside the surface plot to deselect it.

Formatting surface plots

Mathcad provides many ways to change the way a surface plot looks. These can be categorized in four groups:

- Viewing characteristics: the type of plot being displayed; the perspective or point of view from which you see the surface; how "bumpy" the surface looks; and the presence or absence of borders, enclosing boxes, axes, and coordinate planes.

- Color and line formatting: whether the z-coordinates of the surface are indicated by shades of gray or by color; whether the surface is opaque or transparent; and whether the surface patches form a smooth surface or form parallel patches.

- Axis formatting: whether to show tick marks or grid marks on each axis.

- Title characteristics: how the surface plot will display titles.

To change any of these plot characteristics, start with the 3D Plot Format dialog box:

- Choose **Graph⇒3D Plot** from the **Format** menu. Alternatively, double-click on the plot itself. Mathcad brings up the 3D Plot Format dialog box. The View Page of this dialog box is shown below. The remaining three tabs take you to three additional pages.

- If necessary, click the tab for the page you want to work with.

- Make the appropriate changes in the dialog box.

- To see the effect of your changes *without* closing the dialog box, click "Apply."

- When you're finished, close the dialog by clicking "OK."

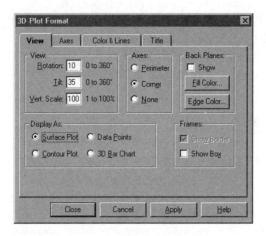

Changing your view of the surface plot

The View page of the 3D Plot Format dialog box lets you modify the general presentation of your plot.

To change your plot from a surface plot to another type of 3D plot, click on the appropriate button in the Display As group. You can convert any surface plot (except for parametric plots) into a contour plot or a 3D bar chart. These plot types are fully discussed in the corresponding chapters of this *User's Guide*. You can also display just the points making up the surface without displaying the surface itself. To do so, click on Data Points. You can change how the points look by using the Colors and Lines tab of this dialog box.

To change the perspective, or point of view, from which you see the surface of your plot, adjust the numbers in the Rotation and Tilt text boxes. Use an integer between 0 to 360 degrees. Figure 22-3 shows the effects of varying the rotation and tilt (as well as the scale) of a surface plot.

■ Increasing the rotation turns the plot clockwise. When the rotation is set to 0, you look straight down the first column of the matrix. The first row of the matrix points to the right. When the rotation is set to 90, you look straight down the first row of the matrix. The first column points to the left.

■ Increasing the tilt raises you higher above the plot's surface. When the tilt is set to 0, you look edge on at the plane of the matrix. When the tilt is set to 90, you look straight down on the surface. Think of how a mountain range looks when you're on the ground (tilt equals 0) and when you're flying directly above (tilt equals 90).

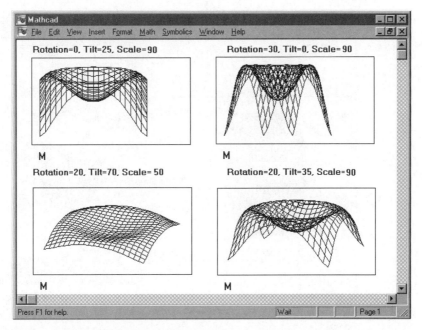

Figure 22-3: Different views of a surface.

To control how bumpy the plot looks, adjust the magnification of the vertical scale by changing the number in the Vert. Scale text box. This is an integer between 1 and 100. When the vertical scale is small, the variations in height of the surface will be barely perceptible. At 100, the variations are shown at full scale. Figure 22-3 shows the effects of varying the scale (as well as the rotation and tilt) of a surface plot.

To add or remove a border around the surface plot region, click on Show Border in the Frames group to add or remove a check. The border is a two-dimensional frame around the surface plot region.

To enclose the surface and the axes within a three-dimensional bounding box, click on Show Box in the Frames group to add a check.

You can add back planes to your surface plots:

■ To show the *xy*, *xz*, and *yz* back planes, click on "Show" in the Back Planes group.

■ To color the surface of the back planes, click on "Fill Color."

■ To outline the edges of the back planes in a particular color, click on "Edge Color."

Figure 22-4 shows a surface plot with a border around it and with back planes showing and the same plot enclosed within a box without showing back planes.

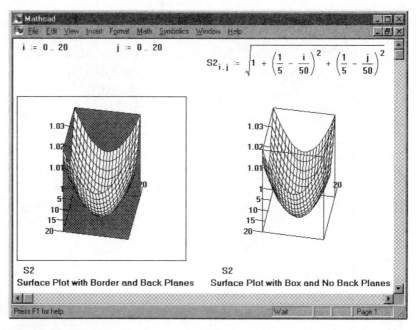

Figure 22-4: Using a border or a bounding box on a surface plot.

Changing the shading of the surface

You can often make a surface plot communicate more effectively by using different colors to represent different values of z. Alternatively, if you intend to print on a black and white printer, you can achieve a similar effect by using different shades of gray to represent the different values of z. Use the Color and Lines page of the 3D Plot Format dialog box.

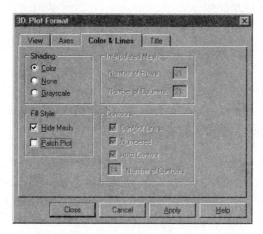

To specify the shading of your plot, click the appropriate button in the Shading group:

■ None: The surface won't have any shading, regardless of where it is.

- Grayscale: The largest values of the matrix will be in white and the smallest values will be in black. Intermediate values will be in shades of gray.

- Color: The largest values of the matrix will be in red and the smallest values will be in blue. Intermediate values will range from yellow through green.

Figure 22-5 shows the same surface plot displayed without shading and in grayscale.

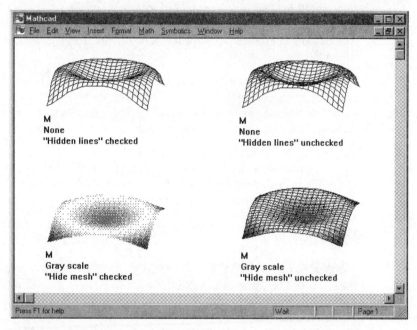

Figure 22-5: Surface plots showing display options for lines and meshes.

If you've chosen to leave the surface without shading ("None"), you'll be able to see through the surface as if it were transparent. Depending on the surface and on your viewpoint, you may find it distracting to see through the surface. When this happens, you may want to render the surface opaque. Note that this option is unnecessary when a surface is rendered in color or in shades of gray. Such surfaces are inherently opaque.

- To make the surface opaque, click Hidden Lines to add a check. Mathcad hides any lines that are behind the surface. Such a plot takes longer to draw since Mathcad has to determine which parts of the surface are concealed.

- To make the surface transparent, click Hidden Lines to remove the check. If you uncheck Hidden Lines, the surface shows lines that are behind it. Such a plot will draw more quickly than if lines were hidden, but it may be more difficult to interpret.

The upper two surface plots in Figure 22-5 show the same surface with and without lines showing.

By default, Mathcad overlays a mesh on colored and grayscale surfaces. The intersections of the lines making up this mesh correspond to the elements of the underlying matrix. Each patch created by this mesh gets a color corresponding to the value of the underlying matrix element.

As the number of matrix elements increases, this mesh can become so dense that it begins to obscure the colors. When this happens you may want to hide the mesh. To do so, click Hide Mesh in the Fill Style group to add a check.

Note that Hide Mesh is only available for colored and grayscale plots. Hiding the mesh of a plot that doesn't have any shading would make that plot invisible. The lower two surface plots in Figure 22-5 show the same surface plot with the mesh showing and with it hidden.

By default, the patches making up the surface are free to tilt in whatever direction necessary to connect them to their neighboring patches. The result is a continuous surface. In this case, each point at which grid lines intersect is associated with a matrix element. This means that for an $m \times n$ matrix, there will be $(m-1)(n-1)$ patches.

To constrain these patches to be horizontal, click Patch Plot in the Fill Style group for regular surface plots and Alternative Mesh for parametric surface plots to add a check. The resultant discontinuous surface shows a patch for each matrix element. This means that for an $m \times n$ matrix, there will be mn patches.

Figure 22-6 shows an example of the same matrix being plotted with Patch Plot checked and not checked.

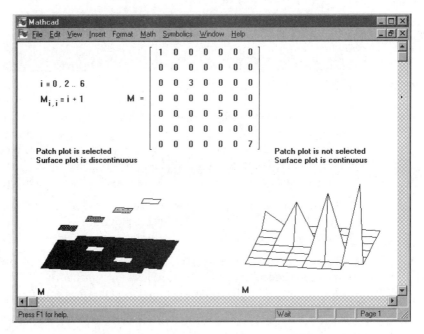

Figure 22-6: Patch plots.

Chapter 22 Surface Plots

Formatting the axes

The Axes page of the 3D Plot Format dialog box lets you modify the format of the axes of your plot. Each axis is described by its own set of check boxes and text boxes.

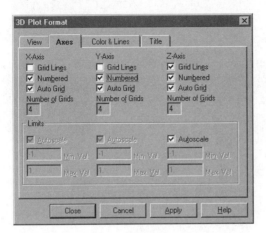

Mathcad generates grid lines for surface plots by extending tick marks up and down the two back planes adjacent to a given axis. Thus, x-axis grid lines represent lines of constant x drawn on the xz plane and the xy plane, the two orthogonal planes whose intersections form the x-axis. The y-axis grid lines and z-axis grid lines are defined similarly.

Note that this makes it impossible to draw lines of constant x on only the xz plane. Clicking Grid Lines always results in grid lines being drawn on two of the three back planes.

To choose between using tick marks or grid lines on a selected axis, use the Grid Lines check box for that axis. When Grid Lines is checked, Mathcad will extend the tick marks on the selected axis into grid lines on each adjacent back plane. For example, checking this on the z-axis will result in lines of constant z on both the yz and the xz back planes. If you are showing grid lines, you should seriously consider showing back planes as well. See "Changing your view of the surface plot" on page 520. Figure 22-7 shows an example of a surface plot that uses grid lines rather than tick marks.

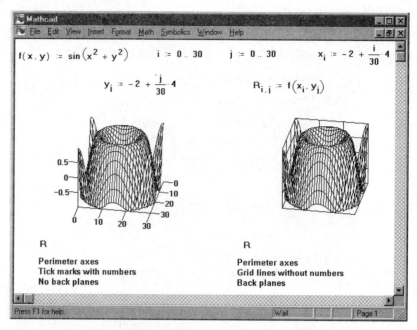

Figure 22-7: Using the different options for tick marks.

To add or remove numbers for the tick marks on an axis, use the Numbered check box for that axis. Figure 22-7 shows the differences between having numbers on the tick marks and not having numbers.

You can have Mathcad automatically select the number of grid intervals on an axis or you can specify the number yourself. Grid intervals are the spaces between tick marks or grid lines.

■ To have Mathcad select the number of grid intervals, use the Auto Grid check box. When Auto Grid is checked, Mathcad will automatically select the number of grid intervals on the specified axis.

■ To specify the number of grid intervals on an axis *yourself*, enter an integer from 1 to 99 in the No. of Grids text box. This text box is only available when Auto Grid is unchecked.

By default, Mathcad autoscales the z-axis according to the range of values in the matrix you are plotting. Sometimes you will want to fix the scaling yourself, for example, if you are comparing views of related data or setting up a surface animation sequence. To set the z-axis limits manually, click on the Autoscale box in the z-axis column of the Axes page to uncheck it. Then enter the maximum and minimum values in the Max. Val. and Min. Val. text boxes.

Since a surface plot is made by plotting the elements of a matrix, Mathcad cannot "know" anything about x and y coordinates. By default, the coordinates on the x- and y-axes of a surface plot will simply be rows and columns. The Max. Val. and Min. Val. text boxes are therefore grayed out on the x- and y-axes for an ordinary surface plot. If you've made a parametric surface plot, however, you will be able to modify the Max. Val. and Min. Val for all three axes.

Labeling the surface plot

The Title page of the 3D Plot Format dialog box, shown below, lets you add and modify a title for your surface plot.

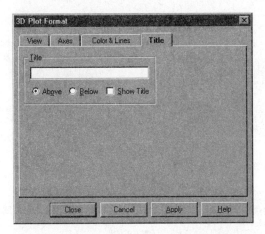

To add or edit a title for your surface plot:

■ Type the title for your plot into the Title text box.

■ To display the title, click on Show Title to insert a check. To conceal the title without deleting it, click on Show Title to remove the check.

■ To position the title, click on either the Above or Below button. Mathcad places the title either directly above or below your plot. Figure 22-8 shows the options for positioning labels on your plot.

■ To change the title's text or position, edit the information in the Title group as appropriate.

■ Click "OK" to close the dialog box when you have finished.

■ To delete the title, highlight it in the Title text box and press [**Del**].

If you initiate this process by double-clicking on the title itself, you'll see an equivalent dialog box.

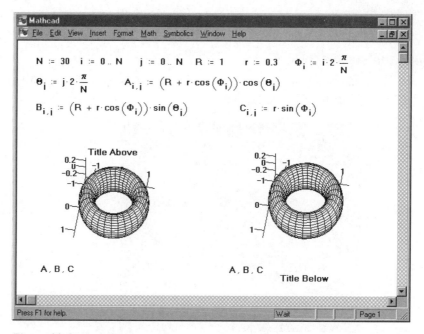

Figure 22-8: Positioning a title on a surface plot.

Chapter 23
Contour Plots

A contour plot lets you quickly visualize level curves—curves along which a particular quantity is constant. Using Mathcad, you make a contour plot in the same way you make a surface plot: by passing a matrix of z values in which each row and column corresponds to a particular x and y value. This chapter describes how a matrix can be represented as a contour plot.

This chapter contains the following sections:

Creating a contour plot

Basic steps in creating a contour plot; what the plot actually shows.

Resizing a contour plot

Procedures for changing the size of contour plots.

Formatting contour plots

Procedures for changing contour plots: formatting contours and axes and adding labels.

Creating a contour plot

To create a contour plot:

■ Define a matrix of values to plot. Mathcad will assume that the rows and columns represent equally spaced intervals on the axes. Mathcad then linearly interpolates the values of this matrix to form level curves. Such level curves can represent isotherms, isobars, equipotentials, streamlines, and many other physical phenomena.

■ Choose **Graph⇒Contour Plot** from the **Insert** menu. Mathcad shows a box with a single placeholder as shown below:

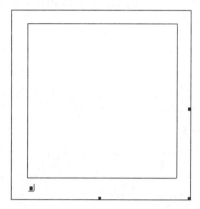

■ Type the name of the matrix in the placeholder. Just as with an equation, Mathcad will not process the contour plot until you click outside the region.

What you see is a visual representation of the matrix's level curves. Each level curve, or contour, is formed in such a way that no two cross. By default, the contours are labeled with their height above or below the *xy* plane. Mathcad plots the matrix by rotating it so that the (0,0) element is at the lower-left corner. Thus the rows of the matrix correspond to values on the *x*-axis, increasing to the right, and the columns correspond to values along the *y*-axis, increasing toward the top.

You can specify whether or not the contours are to be numbered, how many contours there are, and what labels and grid lines appear on the axes by formatting the contour plot. This is described in "Formatting contour plots" on page 532.

Level curves of a function of two variables

A typical contour plot shows the level curves of a function of two variables. To see such a plot, you must first create a matrix that holds the values of the function, then create a contour plot of that matrix. Here are the typical steps in plotting a function of two variables such as that shown in Figure 23-1:

■ Define a function of two variables.

- Decide how many points you want to plot in the x and y directions. Set up range variables i and j to index these points. For example, if you want to plot 10 points in each direction, enter:

$$i := 0 \, .. \, 9 \qquad j := 0 \, .. \, 9$$

- Define x_i and y_j as evenly as evenly spaced points on the x- and y-axes.
- Fill the matrix **M** with the values of $f(x_i, y_j)$.
- Show **M** in a contour plot.

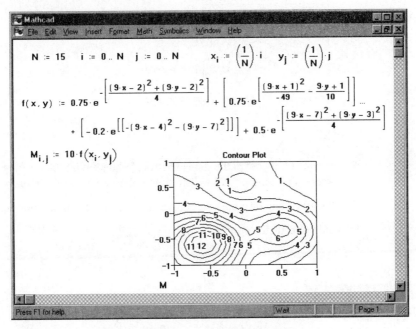

Figure 23-1: Contour plot of a function of two variables.

Note that if you plot a function as described here, the positive x-axis of the plot extends to the right and the positive y-axis extends toward the top of the window. Since the contour plot is created by putting the heights above the xy plane into a matrix, Mathcad has no way of knowing the actual values of the x and y axes. For this reason, the axes on contour plots are by default normalized to extend from 1 to -1. You can manually change the axis limits from these default values by choosing **Graph$\Rightarrow$3D Plot** from the **Format** menu with the contour plot selected or by double-clicking on the plot. Then set the values you want in the Min. Val. and Max. Val. text boxes on the Axes page.

Resizing a contour plot

To change the size of a contour plot, follow these steps:

- Click in the contour plot to select it.

- Move the mouse pointer to one of the three handles along the edge of the plot. The pointer will change to a double-headed arrow.

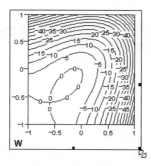

- Press and hold down the mouse button. While holding down the button, move the mouse. The contour plot will stretch in the direction of motion.

- Once the contour plot is the right size, let go of the mouse button.

- Click outside the contour plot to deselect it.

Formatting contour plots

Mathcad gives you control over many of the visual characteristics of contour plots. These can be categorized in four groups:

- Viewing characteristics: the type of plot being displayed.

- Axis formatting: whether to show tick marks or grid lines on each axis.

- Color and line formatting: whether the plot uses grayscale or color to show the height of a section and how the plot shows contours.

- Title characteristics: how the plot will display titles.

To change any of these plot characteristics, start with the 3-D Plot Format dialog box:

- Click on the plot to select it.

- Choose **Graph⇒3D Plot** from the **Format** menu. Alternatively, double-click on the plot itself. Mathcad brings up the 3D Plot Format dialog box. The View Page of this dialog box is shown below. The remaining three tabs take you to three additional pages.

- If necessary, click the tab for the page you want to work with.

- Change the appropriate characteristics in the dialog box.

- To see the effect of your changes *without* closing the dialog box, click "Apply."

- When you're finished, close the dialog by clicking "OK."

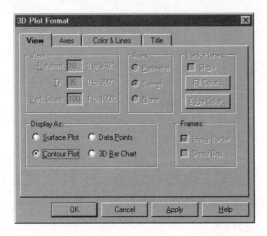

Changing your view of the contour plot

The View page of the 3D Plot Format dialog box lets you modify the general presentation of your plot.

To change your plot from a contour plot to another type of 3-D plot, click on the appropriate button in the Display As group. You can convert a contour plot into a Surface Plot or a 3D Bar Chart. These plot types are fully discussed in the corresponding chapters in this *User's Guide*. You can also display just the points making up the contours without displaying the contours themselves. To do so, click on Data Points. You can then change how the points look by using the Colors & Lines tab of this dialog box. For more information, see Chapter 25, "3D Scatter Plots."

Figure 23-2 shows the same matrix being plotted as a surface plot and as a contour plot.

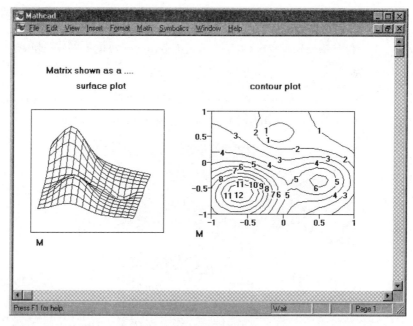

Figure 23-2: Matrix shown as both a surface plot and as a contour plot.

Changing the shading of the contours

You can often make a contour plot communicate more effectively by using different colors to represent different values of *z*. Alternatively, if you intend to print on a black and white printer, you can achieve a similar effect by using different shades of gray to represent different values of *z*. Use the Color and Lines page of the 3D Plot Format dialog box.

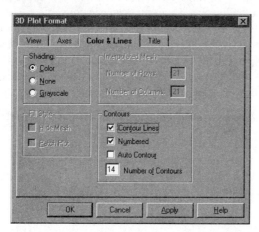

To specify the shading of your plot, click the appropriate button in the Shading group:

■ Color: The bands between contour lines are colored. The largest values of the matrix will be in red and the smallest values will be in blue. Intermediate values will range from yellow through green.

■ None: The bands between contour lines don't have any shading. Be sure the Contour Lines check box is checked or you won't see any contours at all.

■ Grayscale: The bands between contour lines are in shades of gray. The largest values of the matrix will be in white and the smallest values will be in black. Intermediate values will be in shades of gray.

Figure 23-3 shows the same contour plot displayed without shading and in grayscale.

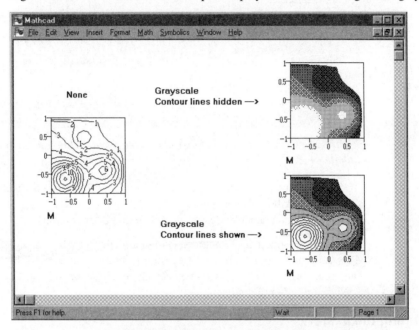

Figure 23-3: No shading and grayscale versions of a contour plot.

Besides varying the colors of a contour plot, you can also choose to hide the contours themselves. If you've chosen to leave the surface without shading ("None"), you should have the contour lines showing. If the plot is colored or grayscale, you can hide the contour lines and let the colors or gray shades show the contours. To show or hide the contour lines, click Contour Lines to add or remove the checkmark. Figure 23-3 shows the same contour plot with the contour lines hidden and showing.

Contours can be numbered to indicate the value associated with that contour. To add or remove numbers on most contours, use the Numbered check box. Figure 23-4 shows the same contour plot with numbered and unnumbered contour lines. Note that Mathcad doesn't number every contour when to do so would result in overcrowding.

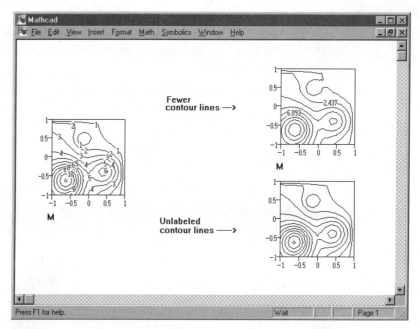

Figure 23-4: Changing the number of contours and turning off contour labeling.

To have Mathcad automatically select the number of contours to display, use the Auto Contour check box. When checked, Mathcad will automatically select the number of contours. When unchecked, you select the number of contours.

To specify the number of contours, enter an integer into the No. of Contours text box. This text box is only available when Auto Contour is unchecked. Figure 23-4 shows the same contour plot with contours automatically selected by Mathcad and with a specified number of contours.

Formatting the axes

The Axes page of the 3D Plot Format dialog box, shown below, lets you modify the format of the *x*- and *y*-axis of your plot. Each axis is described by its own set of check boxes and text boxes.

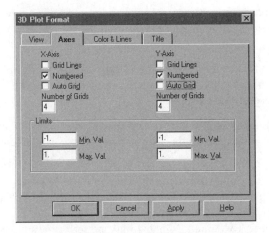

Mathcad generates grid lines on the plot at the same positions as the tick marks. To choose between seeing tick marks or grid lines on a selected axis, use the Grid Lines check box. When Grid Lines is checked, Mathcad adds grid lines to the plot. Figure 23-5 shows the same contour plot with and without grid lines.

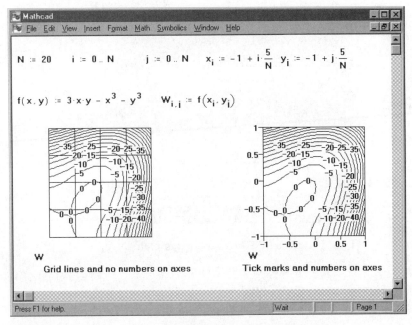

Figure 23-5: Effect of using the different options for tick marks.

To add or remove numbers for the tick marks on an axis, use the Numbered check box for that axis. The plot with grid lines in Figure 23-5 doesn't have numbers on the axes while the plot without grid lines does have them.

You can have Mathcad automatically select the number of grid intervals on an axis or you can specify the number yourself. Grid intervals are the spaces between tick marks or grid lines.

■ To have Mathcad select the number of grid intervals, use the Auto Grid check box. When Auto Grid is checked, Mathcad will automatically select the number of grid intervals on the specified axis.

■ To specify the number of grid intervals on an axis *yourself*, enter an integer from 1 to 99 in the No. of Grids text box. This text box is only available when Auto Grid is unchecked.

To set limits on the maximum or minimum values of the *x*- or *y*-axis, enter the limit in the Max. Val. or Min. Val. text box. However, since the surface of the plot is stored as rows and columns in a matrix, these numbers have no significance as coordinates. They affect the display only. By default, Min and Max are set to −1 and 1 respectively.

Labeling the contour plot

The Title page of the 3D Plot Format dialog box, shown below, lets you add and modify labels on your contour plot.

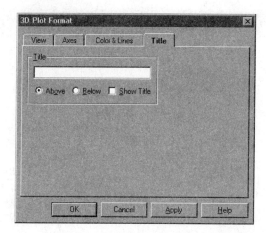

To add or edit a title for your contour plot:

■ Type the title for your plot into the Title text box.

■ To display the title, click on Show Title to insert a check. To conceal the title without deleting it, click on Show Title to remove the check.

■ To position the title, click on either the Above or Below button. Mathcad places the title either directly above or below your plot.

■ Click "OK" or "Close" to close the dialog box when you have finished.

To change the title's text or position, edit the information in the Title group as appropriate. To delete the title, highlight it in the text box and press [Del].

Figure 22-8 on page 528 shows how Mathcad positions a title on a 3D plot.

Chapter 24
3D Bar Charts

Three-dimensional bar charts offer you additional flexibility when displaying data. You can use them to visualize a matrix not as a surface plot but as bars of varying heights. You can show the bars either where they are in the matrix, stacked one on top of another, or laid out side-by-side.

This chapter contains the following sections:

Creating a 3D bar chart

Basic steps for creating bar charts and for creating bar charts for functions of two variables.

Resizing 3D bar charts

Procedures for changing the size of bar charts.

Formatting 3D bar charts

Procedures for changing bar charts: setting the viewpoint, size, and magnification; adding titles; and formatting lines, colors, and axes.

Creating a 3D bar chart

To create a bar chart:

■ Define a matrix of values to display. Mathcad will use the rows and column numbers of the matrix as *x*- and *y*-axes. The matrix elements will be shown as columns extending from the *xy* plane to the appropriate height.

■ Choose **Graph⇒3D Bar Chart** from the **Insert** menu. Mathcad shows a box with a single placeholder, as shown below:

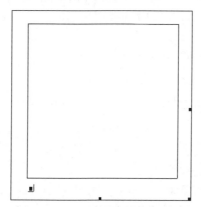

■ Type the name of the matrix in the placeholder. Just as with an equation, Mathcad will not display anything until you click outside the plot region.

What you see is a visual representation of the matrix. Mathcad draws a perspective view of the matrix as a two-dimensional grid lying flat in three-dimensional space. Each matrix element is represented as a column extending above or below this grid by an amount proportional to the value of the matrix element. In the default perspective, the first row of the matrix extends from the back left corner of the grid to the right, while the first column extends from the back left corner out toward the viewer.

The perspective on the bar chart depends on the location of the viewer with respect to the surface. You can specify this view by changing the chart's tilt or rotation, as described in "Changing your view of the 3D bar chart" on page 543.

Displaying a function of two variables

A typical 3D bar chart shows the values of a function of two variables. To see such a chart, you must first create a matrix that holds the values of the function, then create a bar chart of that matrix. Here are the typical steps in plotting a function of two variables such as that shown in Figure 24-1:

■ Define a function of two variables.

- Decide how many points you want to display in the *x* and *y* directions. Set up range variables *i* and *j* to index these points. For example, if you want to display 10 points in each direction, enter:

$$i := 0 .. 9 \qquad j := 0 .. 9$$

- Define x_i and y_j as evenly as evenly spaced points on the *x*- and *y*-axes.

- Fill the matrix **M** with the values of $f(x_i, y_j)$.

- Choose **Graph⇒3D Bar Chart** from the **Format** menu.

- Type **M** in the placeholder. Then click outside the plot region.

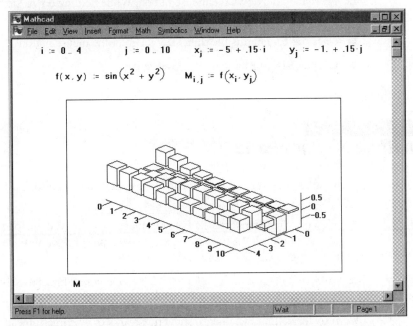

Figure 24-1: 3D bar chart of a function of two variables.

Resizing 3D bar charts

To change the size of a bar chart, follow these steps:

- Click in the bar chart to select it.

- Move the mouse pointer to one of the three handles along the edge of the bar chart. The pointer will change to a double-headed arrow.

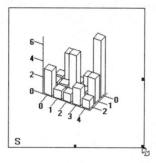

- Press and hold down the mouse button. While holding down the button, move the mouse. The bar chart will stretch in the direction of motion.

- Once the bar chart is the right size, let go of the mouse button.

- Click outside the bar chart to deselect it.

Formatting 3D bar charts

Mathcad provides many ways to change the way a bar chart looks. These can be categorized in four groups:

- Viewing characteristics: the type of plot being displayed; the perspective or point of view; how tall the tallest bars are; and the presence or absence of borders, enclosing boxes, axes, and coordinate planes.

- Color and line formatting: how the bars are colored; how the bars are laid out; spacing between the bars.

- Axis formatting: whether to show tick marks or grid lines on each axis.

- Title characteristics: how the bar chart will display titles.

To change any of these characteristics, start with the 3D Plot Format dialog box:

- Click on a bar chart to select it.

- Choose **Graph⇒3D Plot** from the **Format** menu. Alternatively, double-click on the chart itself. Mathcad brings up the 3D Plot Format dialog box. The View Page of this dialog box is shown below. The remaining three tabs take you to three additional pages.

- If necessary, click the tab for the page you want to work with.

- Make the appropriate changes in the dialog box.

- To see the effect of your changes *without* closing the dialog box, click "Apply".

- When you're finished, close the dialog by clicking "OK."

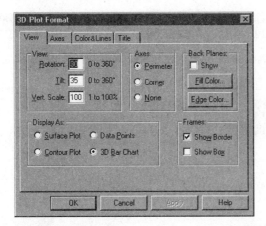

Changing your view of the 3D bar chart

The View page of the 3D Plot Format dialog box lets you modify the general presentation of your bar chart.

To change from a bar chart to another type of 3D plot, click on the appropriate button in the Display As group. You can convert a bar chart into a surface plot or a contour plot. These plot types are fully discussed in the corresponding chapters of this *User's Guide*. You can also display just the points at the top of the bars. To do so, click on Data Points. You can change how the points look by using the Colors & Lines tab of this dialog box. For more information, see Chapter 25, "3D Scatter Plots."

To change the perspective, or point of view, from which you see the bars on your chart, adjust the numbers in the Rotation and Tilt text boxes. Use an integer between 0 to 360 degrees. Figure 24-2 shows the effects of varying the rotation and tilt (as well as the vertical scale) of a bar chart.

■ Increasing the vertical rotation turns the chart clockwise. When the rotation is set to 0, you look straight down the first column of the matrix. The first row of the matrix points to the right. When the rotation is set to 90, you look straight down the first row of the matrix. The first column points to the left.

■ Increasing the tilt raises you higher above the chart's surface. When the tilt is set to 0, you look edge on at the plane of the matrix. When the tilt is set to 90, you look straight down on the tops of the bars. Think of how tall buildings look when you're on the ground (tilt equals 0) and when you're flying directly above (tilt equals 90).

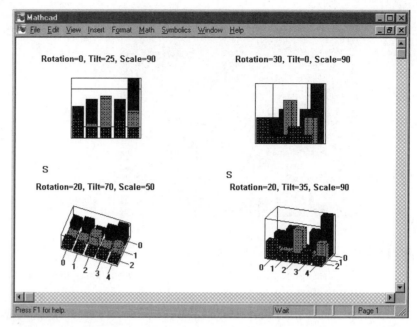

Figure 24-2: Different views of a bar chart.

To control how tall the tallest bars look, adjust the vertical scale by changing the number in the Vert. Scale text box. This is an integer between 1 and 100. When the vertical scale is small, the variations among the bars will barely be perceptible. At 100, the variations are such that the chart fills almost the entire frame. Figure 24-3 shows the effects of varying the scale (as well as the rotation and tilt) of a bar chart.

To add or remove a border around the bar chart, click on Show Border in the Frames group. The border is a two-dimensional frame around the bar chart.

To enclose the surface and the axes within a three-dimensional bounding box, click on Show Box in the Frames group.

To show the *xy*, *xz*, and *yz* back planes:

■ Click on "Show" in the Back Planes group.

■ To color the surface of the back planes, click on "Fill Color".

■ To outline the edges of the back planes in a particular color, click on "Edge Color".

Figure 24-3 shows the same bar chart with back planes, with a border, and with a bounding box.

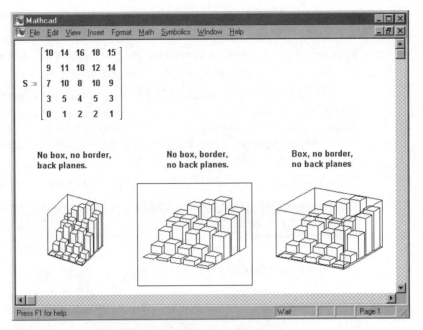

Figure 24-3: Using a border or a bounding box on a bar chart.

Changing the color and layout of the bars

You can often make a 3D bar chart communicate more effectively by using different colors. In addition, you can switch among several layouts of the bars to show your data most effectively. Use the Color & Lines page of the 3D Plot Format dialog box.

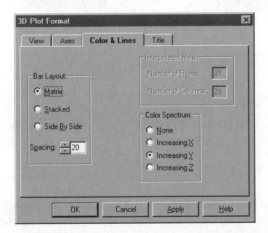

To specify the color of your chart, click the appropriate button in the Color Spectrum group:

■ None: The bar chart doesn't show any colors.

■ Increasing X: The largest values along the *x*-axis will be in red and the smallest values will be in blue. Intermediate values will range from yellow through green.

■ Increasing Y: The largest values along the *y*-axis will be in red and the smallest values will be in blue. Intermediate values will range from yellow through green.

■ Increasing Z: The largest values along the *z*-axis will be in red and the smallest values will be in blue. Intermediate values will range from yellow through green.

Use the Spacing text box to increase the space between adjacent bars on your plot. This text box measures spacing as the percentage of the size of the grid on which the bars are placed. The default spacing is 20%; the maximum spacing is 99%. As you increase the percentage, Mathcad makes the bars progressively skinnier. Figure 24-4 shows different spacing for plots of the same matrix.

Figure 24-4 shows the same bar chart using each of the Color Spectrum options.

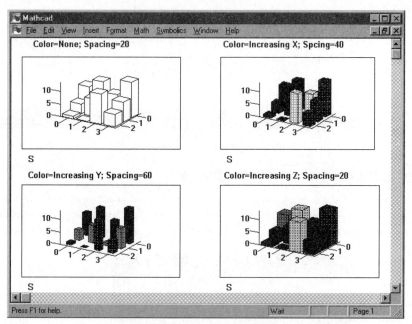

Figure 24-4: Color and spacing options for bar plots.

You can also control the placement of the bars relative to one another using the Bar Layout buttons. The three options are:

■ Matrix: The bars are arranged exactly as the corresponding numbers in the underlying matrix.

■ Stacked: All the bars coming from the same column of the matrix are stacked one on top of another. An $m \times n$ matrix would therefore appear as n bar clusters, each formed by stacking m bars one on top of another.

■ Side by Side: All the bars coming from the same column of the matrix are clustered together side-by-side. An $m \times n$ matrix would therefore appear as n bar clusters, each of which contains m bars.

Figure 24-5 shows an $m \times n$ matrix being displayed using each of these three layout options. Note that if you want to swap rows and columns, you can simply plot the transpose of the matrix.

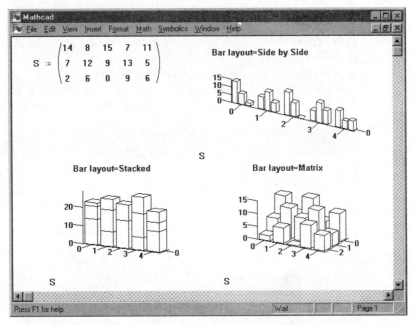

Figure 24-5: Different bar layouts with the same bar chart matrix.

Formatting the axes

The Axes page of the 3D Plot Format dialog box lets you modify the format of the axes of your plot. Each axis is described by its own set of check boxes and text boxes.

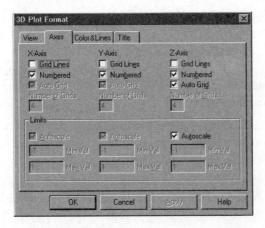

Mathcad generates grid lines for bar charts by extending tick marks up and down the two back planes adjacent to a given axis. Thus, x-axis grid lines represent lines of constant x drawn on the xz plane and the xy plane, the two orthogonal planes whose intersections form the x-axis. The y-axis grid lines and z-axis grid lines are defined similarly.

To choose between using tick marks or grid lines on a selected axis, use the Grid Lines check box for that axis. When Grid Lines is checked, Mathcad will extend the tick marks on the selected axis into grid lines on each adjacent back plane. For example, checking this on the z-axis will result in lines of constant z on both the yz and the xz back planes. If you are showing grid lines, you should seriously consider showing back planes as well. See "Changing your view of the 3D bar chart" on page 543. Figure 24-6 shows an example of a bar chart that uses grid lines rather than tick marks.

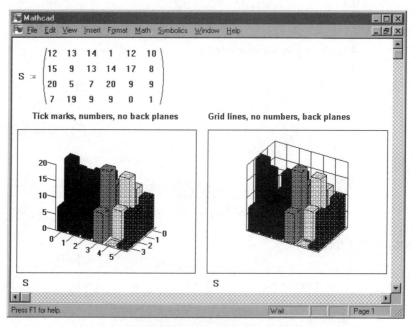

Figure 24-6: Using the different options for tick marks.

To add or remove numbers for the tick marks on an axis, use the Numbered check box for that axis. Figure 24-6 shows the differences between having numbers on the tick marks and not having numbers.

For bar charts, you can have Mathcad automatically select the number of grid intervals on the z-axis. The grid intervals on the x and y axes always match the rows and columns of the matrix whose elements constitute the bars being plotted.

- To have Mathcad select the number of grid intervals on the z-axis, use the Auto Grid check box. When Auto Grid is checked, Mathcad will automatically select the number of grid intervals on the specified axis.

- To specify the number of grid intervals on an axis *yourself*, enter an integer from 1 to 99 in the No. of Grids text box. This text box is only available when Auto Grid is unchecked.

By default, Mathcad autoscales the *z*-axis according to the range of values in the matrix you are plotting. Sometimes you will want to fix the scaling yourself, for example, if you are comparing views of related data or setting up a surface animation sequence. To set the *z*-axis limits manually, click on the Autoscale box in the *z*-axis column of the Axes page to uncheck it. Then enter the maximum and minimum values in the Max. Val. and Min. Val. text boxes.

Labeling 3D bar charts

The Title page of the 3D Plot Format dialog box, shown below, lets you add and modify the title on your bar chart.

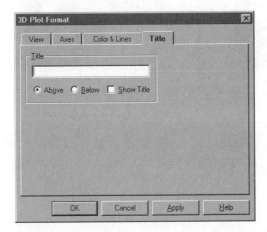

To add or edit a title for your bar chart:

■ Type the title for your plot into the Title text box.

■ To display the title, click on Show Title to insert a check. To conceal the title without deleting it, click on Show Title to remove the check.

■ To position the title, click on either the Above or Below button. Mathcad places the title either directly above or below your plot.

■ To change the title's text or position, edit the information in the Title group as appropriate.

■ Click "OK" to close the dialog box when you have finished.

■ To delete the title, highlight it in the Title text box and press [Del].

If you initiate this process by double-clicking on the title itself, you'll see an equivalent dialog box.

Figure 24-7 shows how Mathcad positions a title on a 3D bar chart.

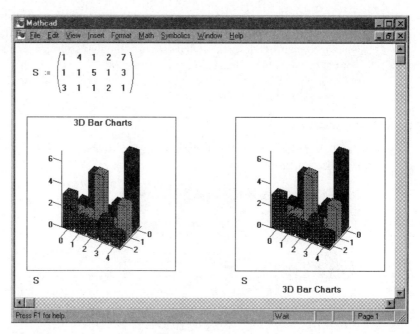

Figure 24-7: Titles on a bar chart.

Chapter 25
3D Scatter Plots

When using other types of 3D plots, you need to make a matrix in which rows and columns correspond to x and y values and the value of the matrix element is the z value. Scatter plots, on the other hand, let you specify x, y, and z coordinates directly. This makes them useful for drawing parametric curves or for observing clusters of data in a 3D space. This chapter shows how three vectors can be used to build a scatter plot.

This chapter contains the following sections:

Creating a 3D scatter plot

Basic steps in creating a scatter plot.

Resizing scatter plots

Procedures for changing the size of scatter plots.

Formatting scatter plots

Procedures for changing scatter plots: setting the viewpoint and the presentation; adding labels; and formatting markers, lines, and axes.

Creating a 3D scatter plot

Scatter plots allow you to plot an arbitrary collection of points in a three-dimensional space. This is particularly useful for such tasks as identifying data clusters or tracing a trajectory of a point. Scatter plots differ from all other 3D plots as follows:

- In all other 3D plots, you create a matrix in which the rows and columns correspond to x and y coordinates and the value of the matrix element is the corresponding z coordinate.

- In scatter plots, you create three vectors with as many elements as there are points to plot. The x, y, and z coordinates of a point go into the three elements of the corresponding vectors.

Unlike other 3D plots, you can easily have several z values corresponding to the same x and y value. This is often necessary in statistical applications in which you take the same measurement more than once. You can also easily create parametric curves through a three-dimensional space since the indices of the vectors are themselves natural parameters to use.

To create a 3D scatter plot:

- Define three vectors, each having as many elements as you have points to plot. Each vector contains either the x, y, or z coordinates of all the points.

- Choose **Graph⇒3D Scatter Plot** from the **Insert** menu. Mathcad shows a box with a single placeholder as shown below:

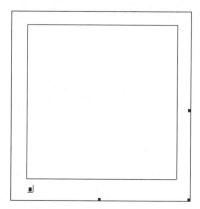

- Type the names of the vectors, separated by commas, in the placeholder.

Just as with an equation, Mathcad will not process the scatter plot until you click outside the region.

If you have a matrix of rows and columns corresponding to the x and y coordinates that you want to show as a set of points, create a *surface plot*, double-click on it to bring up the 3D Plot Format dialog box, and select Data Points in the Display As group on the View page. See "Changing your view of the surface plot" on page 520.

Resizing scatter plots

To change the size of a scatter plot, follow these steps:

■ Click in the scatter plot to select it.

■ Move the mouse pointer to one of the three handles along the edge of the scatter plot. The pointer will change to a double-headed arrow.

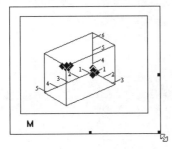

■ Press and hold down the mouse button. While holding down the button, move the mouse. The scatter plot will stretch in the direction of motion.

■ Once the scatter plot is the right size, let go of the mouse button.

■ Click outside the scatter plot to deselect it.

Formatting scatter plots

Mathcad gives you control over many of the visual characteristics of scatter plots. These can be categorized in four groups:

■ Viewing characteristics: the type of plot being displayed, the perspective or point of view from which you see the plot, and the presence or absence of borders, enclosing boxes, axes, and back planes.

■ Color and line formatting: how the plot will mark points; how markers will be connected; and the format of any lines connecting markers.

■ Axis formatting: whether to show tick marks or grid lines on each axis.

■ Title characteristics: how the plot will display titles.

To change any of these plot characteristics, start with the 3D Plot Format dialog box:

■ Click on the plot to select it.

■ Choose **Graph⇒3D Plot** from the **Format** menu. Alternatively, double-click on the plot itself. Mathcad brings up the 3D Plot Format dialog box. The View Page of this dialog box is shown below. The remaining three tabs take you to three additional pages.

■ If necessary, click the tab for the page you want to work with.

■ Make the appropriate changes in the dialog box.

■ To see the effect of your changes *without* closing the dialog box, click "Apply."

■ When you're finished, close the dialog by clicking "OK."

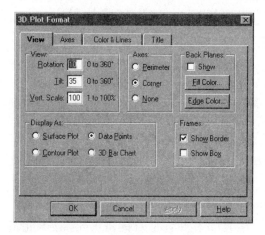

Changing your view of the scatter plot

The View page of the 3D Plot Format dialog box lets you modify the general presentation of your 3D scatter plot.

To change your plot from a scatter plot to another type of 3D plot, click on the appropriate button in the Display As group. You can convert a scatter plot into a Surface Plot, Contour Plot, or a 3D Bar Chart. These plot types are fully discussed in the corresponding chapters in this *User's Guide*.

When you view a scatter plot as a surface or contour plot or a 3D bar chart, Mathcad actually *interpolates* a surface that approximates your scatter data, using a 21 by 21 mesh by default. To change the density of this mesh, click on the Color & Lines tab and edit the number of rows and columns in the Interpolated Mesh group. If your data is not well approximated by a surface, Mathcad may be unable to compile a useful interpolation. If this occurs, Mathcad will signal this fact with a message in the status line.

As you view your scatter plot, you may not be able to perceive any patterns in your data. However, by examining the plot from another perspective, you may be able to isolate clusters of data. To change the perspective, or point of view, from which you see the scatter plot, change the numbers in the Rotation and Tilt text boxes. Use an integer between 0 to 360 degrees. Figure 25-1 shows the effects of varying the rotation and tilt (as well as the scale) of a scatter plot.

- Increasing the rotation turns the plot clockwise.

- Tilt controls whether you see the data edge on or whether you look down from directly overhead.

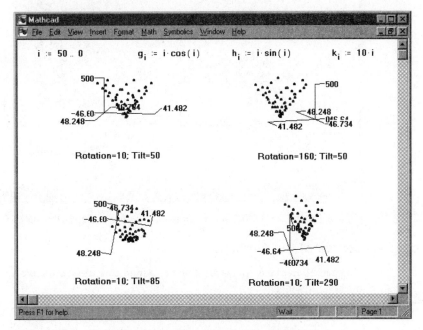

Figure 25-1: Changing the rotation and tilt of a scatter plot.

To add or remove a border around the scatter plot region, click on Show Border. The border is a two-dimensional frame around the scatter plot region.

To enclose the plot and the axes within a three-dimensional bounding box, click on Show Box in the Frames group to add a check.

To show the *xy*, *xz*, and *yz* back planes:

- Click on Show in the Back Planes group.

- To color the surface of the back planes, click on "Fill Color."

- To outline the edges of the back planes in a particular color, click on "Edge Color."

Figure 25-2 shows a scatter plot with a border around it and with back planes showing together with the same plot enclosed within a box without showing back planes.

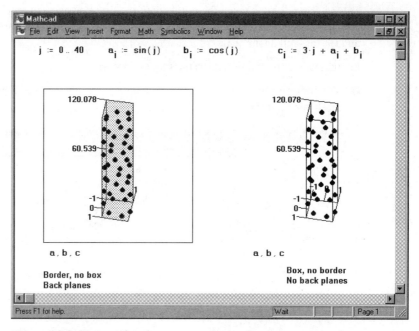

Figure 25-2: Using a border or an enclosing box on a scatter plot.

Changing the format of the markers

You can often make your scatter plot communicate more effectively by changing one of the following:

■ You can mark the points with a symbol.

■ You can connect the points with a line.

To do either of these, use the Color & Lines page of the 3D Plot Format dialog box.

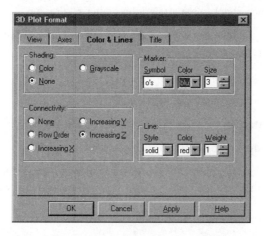

To specify the type of marker your plot will use, select an option from each of the following drop-down lists:

- Symbol: Each point in the scatter plot is marked by a symbol. Select among o's, ×'s, +'s, boxes, and diamonds. You can also select "none"; however, if you do and you aren't using a connecting line, your plot will be blank.

- Color: The markers can be any of the colors listed on the drop-down list, for example, red, blue, green, magenta, cyan, brown, black, and white.

- Size: Markers can range in size from 1 (thinnest) to 10 (thickest).

Figure 25-3 shows the same plot with markers formatted in several ways.

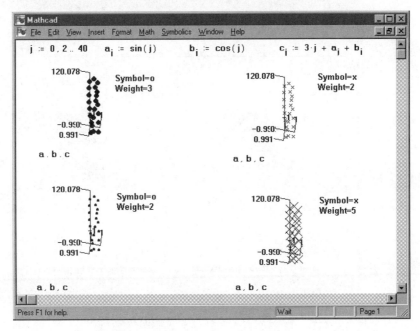

Figure 25-3: Different formatting options for markers on a scatter plot.

If you are plotting data that shows progressive movement in a direction (for example, points in a trajectory), you may want to connect the data points with a line. Mathcad provides several options for connecting the data points:

- No line

- The order in which the points occur in the matrix (row order)

- Increasing x values

- Increasing y values

- Increasing z values

Use the buttons in the Connectivity group to choose which of these options Mathcad should use to connect the data points.

Once you've decided on the order for connecting the points, you can specify the way the line connecting them will look. Use the buttons in the Line group to choose:

- Style: The connecting line can be solid, dashed, dotted, or alternately dashed and dotted. You can also select "none"; however, if you do so and aren't using markers, your plot will be blank.

- Color: The lines can be any of the colors on the drop-down list.

- Weight: Lines can range in size from 1 (lightest) to 10 (the heaviest).

Figure 25-4 shows the same plot connected in different orders.

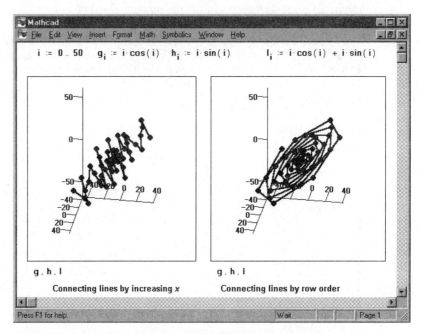

Figure 25-4: Passing a line through points on a scatter plot.

Formatting the axes

The Axes page of the 3D Plot Format dialog box lets you modify the format of the x, y, and z axes of your plot. Each axis is described by its own set of check boxes and text boxes.

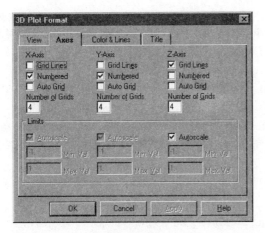

Mathcad generates grid lines on the plot at the same positions as the tick marks. To choose between using tick marks or grid lines on a selected axis, use the Grid Lines check box. When Grid Lines is checked, Mathcad adds grid lines to the plot. Figure 25-5 shows the same scatter plot with and without grid lines.

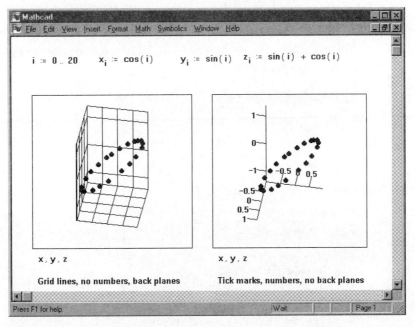

Figure 25-5: Using the different options for axes on a scatter plot.

To add or remove numbers for the tick marks on an axis, use the Numbered check box for that axis. The plot with grid lines in Figure 25-5 doesn't have numbers on the axes while the plot without grid lines does have them.

You can have Mathcad automatically select the number of grid intervals on an axis or you can specify the number yourself. Grid intervals are the spaces between tick marks or grid lines.

■ To have Mathcad select the number of grid intervals, use the Auto Grid check box. When Auto Grid is checked, Mathcad will automatically select the number of grid intervals on the specified axis.

■ To specify the number of grid intervals on an axis *yourself*, enter an integer from 1 to 99 in the No. of Grids text box. This text box is only available when Auto Grid is unchecked.

By default, Mathcad sets the axis limits according to the data ranges in the three input vectors. However, you can set these limits by hand as follows:

■ Click on the Autoscale box in the appropriate axis columns of the Axes page to uncheck it.

■ Enter the maximum and minimum values in the Max. Val. and Min. Val. text boxes.

Fixing the axis limits in this way is useful when you are comparing plots of related data sets or setting up an animation sequence.

Labeling the scatter plot

The Title page of the 3D Plot Format dialog box, shown below, lets you add and modify labels on your scatter plot.

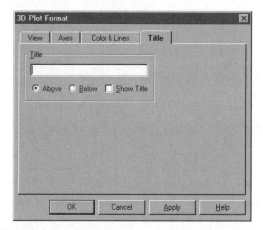

To add or edit a title for your scatter plot:

■ Type the title for your plot into the Title text box.

■ To display the title, click on Show Title to insert a check. To conceal the title without deleting it, click on Show Title to remove the check.

■ To position the title, click on either the Above or Below button. Mathcad places the title either directly above or below your plot.

■ To change the title's text, edit the information in the Title group as appropriate.

- Click "OK" to close the dialog box when you have finished.

- To delete the title, highlight it and press **[Del]**.

If you initiate this process by double-clicking on the title itself, you'll see an equivalent dialog box.

Figure 25-6 shows how Mathcad positions titles on a scatter plot.

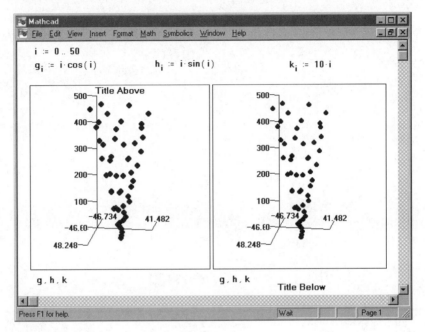

Figure 25-6: Titles on a scatter plot.

Chapter 26
Vector Field Plots

This chapter describes how to plot a two-dimensional vector field by representing x and y components of a vector as complex numbers.

This chapter contains the following sections:

Creating a vector field plot

Basic steps in creating a vector field plot.

Resizing vector field plots

Procedure for changing the size of vector field plots.

Formatting vector field plots

Procedures for changing vector field plots: formatting the vector fields and axes and adding labels.

Creating a vector field plot

In a vector field plot, each point in the *xy* plane is assigned a two-dimensional vector. To create a vector field plot, you must define a rectangular array of points and assign a vector to each point. You can do this by creating a matrix of complex numbers in which:

- The rows and columns represent *x* and *y* coordinates.

- The real part of each matrix element is the *x* component of the vector associated with that row and column.

- The imaginary part of each element is the *y* component of the vector associated with that row and column.

To create a vector field plot:

- Create a matrix as described above.

- Choose **Graph⇒Vector Field Plot** from the **Insert** menu. Mathcad shows a box with a single placeholder as shown below:

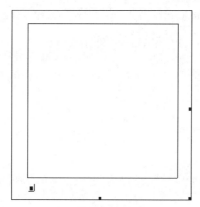

- Type the name of the matrix in the placeholder.

Just as with an equation, Mathcad will not process the vector field plot until you click outside of it.

Mathcad plots the matrix by rotating it so that the (0,0) element is at the lower-left corner. Thus the rows of the matrix correspond to values on the *x*-axis, increasing to the right, and the columns correspond to values along the *y*-axis, increasing toward the top.

What you'll see is a collection of $m \cdot n$ vectors as shown in Figure 26-1. The base of each vector sits on the *x* and *y* values corresponding to its row and column. The magnitude and direction of each vector are derived from the real and imaginary parts of the matrix element.

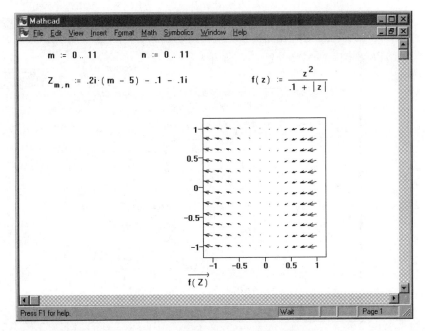

Figure 26-1: A sample vector plot from a complex matrix.

You can also create a vector field plot by using two matrices of real numbers rather than a single matrix of complex members. The two matrices must have the same number of rows and columns. The first matrix should have the x components of the vectors; the second should have the y components. Figure 26-2 shows the same vector field as that shown in Figure 26-1, but it is plotted using two real matrices rather than a single complex matrix.

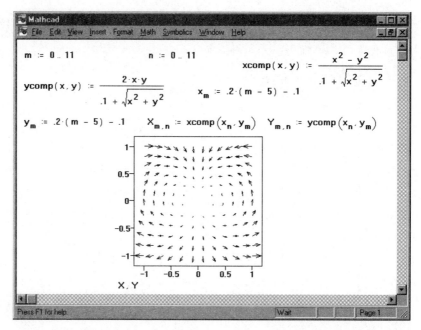

Figure 26-2: A sample vector plot from two matrices of real numbers.

You can specify what labels and grid lines appear on the axes by formatting the vector field plot. This is described in "Formatting vector field plots" on page 567.

Resizing vector field plots

To change the size of a vector field plot, follow these steps:

■ Click in the vector field plot to select it.

■ Move the mouse pointer to one of the three handles along the edge of the plot. The pointer will change to a double-headed arrow.

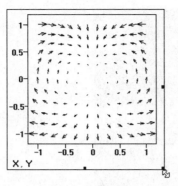

- Press and hold down the mouse button. While holding down the button, move the mouse. The plot will stretch in the direction of motion.

- Once the plot is the right size, let go of the mouse button.

- Click outside the vector field plot to deselect it.

Formatting vector field plots

Mathcad gives you control over many of the visual characteristics of vector field plots. These can be categorized in three groups:

- Axis formatting: whether to show tick marks or grid lines on each axis.

- Title characteristics: how the plot will display titles.

To change any of these plot characteristics, start with the 3D Plot Format dialog box:

- Click on the plot to select it.

- Choose **Graph**⇒**3D Plot** from the **Format** menu. Alternatively, double-click on the plot itself. Mathcad brings up the 3D Plot Format dialog box. The Axes Page of this dialog box is shown below. The remaining tab takes you to the Title page. The View and the Color & Lines pages are not used for these plots.

- If necessary, click the tab for the page you want to work with.

- Change the appropriate characteristics in the dialog box.

- To see the effect of your changes *without* closing the dialog box, click "Apply."

- When you're finished, close the dialog by clicking "OK."

Formatting the axes

The Axes page of the 3D Plot Format dialog box, shown below, lets you modify the format of the x- and y-axis of your plot. Each axis is described by its own set of check boxes and text boxes.

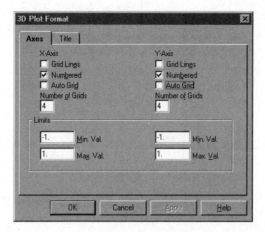

Mathcad generates grid lines on the plot at the same positions as the tick marks. To choose between using tick marks or grid lines on a selected axis, use the Grid Lines check box. When Grid Lines is checked, Mathcad adds grid lines to the plot. Figure 26-3 shows the same vector field plot with and without grid lines.

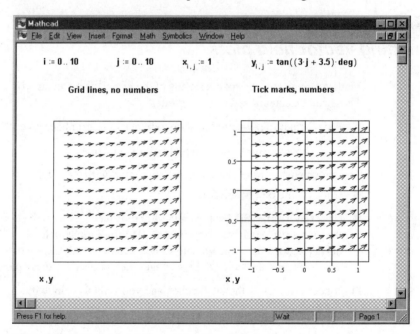

Figure 26-3: Using grid lines and tick marks.

To add or remove numbers for the tick marks on an axis, use the Numbered check box for that axis. The plot with grid lines in Figure 26-3 doesn't have numbers on the axes while the plot without grid lines does have them.

You can have Mathcad automatically select the number of grid intervals on an axis or you can specify the number yourself. Grid intervals are the spaces between tick marks or grid lines.

■ To have Mathcad select the number of grid intervals, use the Auto Grid check box. When Auto Grid is checked, Mathcad will automatically select the number of grid intervals on the specified axis.

■ To specify the number of grid intervals on an axis *yourself,* enter an integer from 1 to 99 in the No. of Grids text box. This text box is only available when Auto Grid is unchecked.

Since a vector field plot is made by plotting the elements of a matrix, Mathcad cannot "know" anything about *x* and *y* coordinates. All it knows is the vector associated with a particular row and column. By default, the coordinates on the *x*- and *y*-axes of a vector field plot will simply be rows and columns.

To change the limits on the maximum or minimum values to be plotted on the *x*- and *y*-axis, enter the new limit in the Max. Val. or Min. Val. text box.

Labeling the vector field plot

The Title page of the 3D Plot Format dialog box lets you add and modify a title on your vector field plot.

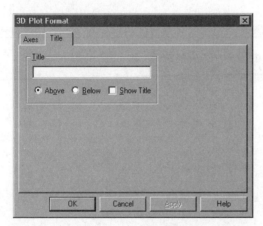

To add or edit a title for your vector field plot:

■ Type the title for your plot into the Title text box.

■ To display the title, click on Show Title to insert a check. To conceal the title without deleting it, click on Show Title to remove the check.

■ To position the title, click on either the Above or Below button. Mathcad places the title either directly above or below your plot.

■ Click "OK" to close the dialog box when you have finished.

To change the title's text or position, edit the information in the Title group as appropriate. To delete the title, highlight it in the text box and press [**Del**].

If you initiate this process by double-clicking on the title itself, you'll see an equivalent dialog box.

Figure 26-4 shows how Mathcad positions a title on a vector field plot.

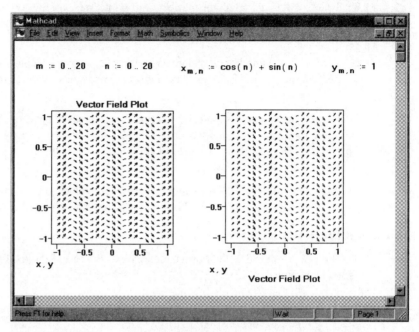

Figure 26-4: Titles on a vector field plot.

Chapter 27
Animation

This chapter describes how to use Mathcad to create and play short animation clips by using the built-in variable FRAME. Anything that can be made to depend on this variable can be animated. This includes not only plots but numerical results as well. You can play back the animation clips at different speeds or save them for use by other applications.

The following sections make up this chapter:

Creating an animation clip

How to use the FRAME variable to create a sequence of images and how to string this sequence together into a movie.

Playing an animation clip

Using Mathcad's animation player to play back your movie. Embedding animations in your worksheet.

Gallery of animations

A collection of examples showing what you can do with animation.

Creating an animation clip

Mathcad comes with a predefined constant called FRAME whose sole purpose is to drive animations. The steps in creating any animation are as follows:

■ Create an expression or plot whose appearance ultimately depends on the value of FRAME as shown in Figure 27-1. This expression need not be a graph as shown. It can be anything at all.

■ Choose **Animate** from the **View** menu to bring up the following dialog box.

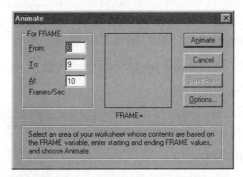

■ Select the portion of your worksheet you want to animate as shown in Figure 27-2.

■ In the dialog box, set the upper and lower limits for FRAME. The FRAME variable will increment by one as it proceeds from the lower limit to the upper limit.

■ In the Frames/Sec. text box, enter the playback speed.

■ Click the "Animate" button in the dialog box. You'll see a miniature rendition of your selection inside the dialog box as shown in Figure 27-3. Mathcad redraws this once for each value of FRAME. This won't necessarily match the playback speed since at this point, you're just *creating* the animation, you're not yet playing it back.

At this point, an animation has been created. You can now do one of two things with it:

■ You can save it as a Windows AVI file for use by other Windows applications.

■ You can play it back immediately.

To save your animation clip as a Windows AVI file, click the Save As button in the dialog box. You'll see the usual Save As dialog box. Since animation clips tend to take considerable disk space, Mathcad saves them in compressed format. Before creating the animation, you may want to choose what compression method to use or whether to compress at all. To do so, click on the Options button.

To play the animation sequence back, follow the instructions in the next section.

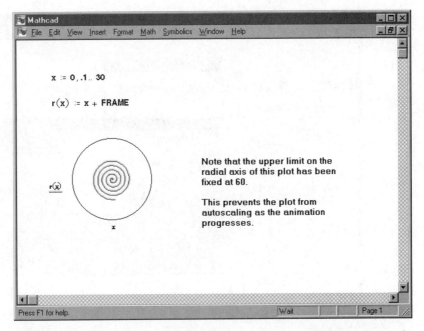

Figure 27-1: An expression suitable for animation. Note the dependence of the plot on FRAME.

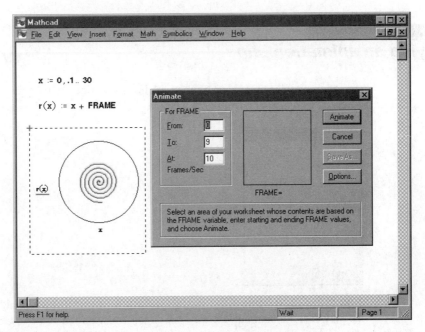

Figure 27-2: The region to be animated has been selected.

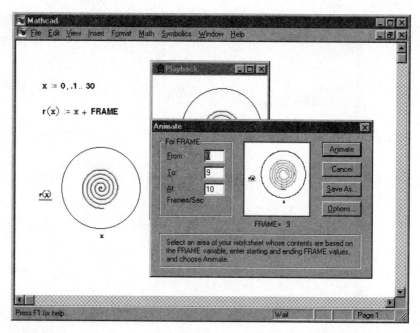

Figure 27-3: The animation clip has been created and is ready for playback.

Playing an animation clip

As soon as you've created an animation clip as described in the previous section, Mathcad brings up the following window:

Note that the first frame of the animation clip you just created is already in the window. To play back the animation clip, click on the arrow button at the lower left corner of the window. The arrow will turn into a square and the animation will begin to play. You can control the playback speed by clicking on the button to the right of the play button, which then displays the context menu shown below:

Choose **Speed** from the menu and adjust the slider control.

You can also play back the animation clip on a frame by frame basis, either forward or backward. To do so, drag the slider below the animated picture to the left or right.

You can resize this window the way you would any window, by dragging a corner in the appropriate direction. Keep in mind, however, that the image in the window is a bitmap and therefore subject to distortion when resized. You can minimize this distortion by keeping the aspect ratio (height to width) constant when you resize. To do this conveniently, click on the button to the right of the play button and choose **View** from the context menu.

Playing a previously saved animation

If you have an existing Windows AVI file on your disk, you'll be able to play it within Mathcad. To do so:

■ Choose **Playback** from the **View** menu to bring up the following dialog box:

The window is collapsed shut since no animation clip has been opened. To open one, click on the button to the right of the play button and choose **Open** from the menu. You'll see an Open File dialog box which you can use to locate and open the Windows AVI file you want to play.

Once you've loaded a Windows AVI file, you can proceed as described in the previous section.

Launching an animation directly from your worksheet

Once you have created an animation, you may want to launch it directly from your worksheet without having to choose **Playback** from the **View** menu, as described above. You may also wish to embed it or link it directly to your worksheet so that it can be played "in place."

Here are three ways to associate a particular animation file with your worksheet:

■ Insert a hyperlink in your worksheet to an AVI file by choosing **Hyperlink** from the **Insert** menu. You may attach the hyperlink to a plot, a graphic, a text region, or any other region in the worksheet, and the AVI file you link to may be located on a local or network disk drive or on the Internet. Once you have specified an AVI file as the target of the hyperlink, you launch it simply by double-clicking on the

---

hyperlink in the worksheet. The AVI file then plays in its own window. See Chapter 4, "Worksheet Management," for information about creating hyperlinks.

■ Create a *shortcut* to the AVI file in your worksheet by dragging the icon for the AVI file from the Windows Explorer and dropping it into your worksheet at a blank space where you want the animation to appear. The first frame of the animation will appear as a picture in your worksheet. To activate the shortcut, click on the picture of the first frame and click on the play button that appears at the bottom of the picture. Although the AVI file remains external to your Mathcad worksheet, it plays in place in your worksheet. See Figure 27-4 for an example.

■ Embed or link an OLE object in your worksheet by choosing **Object** from the **Insert** menu and selecting "Video Clip" from the list in the Insert Object dialog box. See Chapter 4, "Worksheet Management," for details about embedding versus linking OLE objects in Mathcad worksheets and how to edit OLE objects in place.

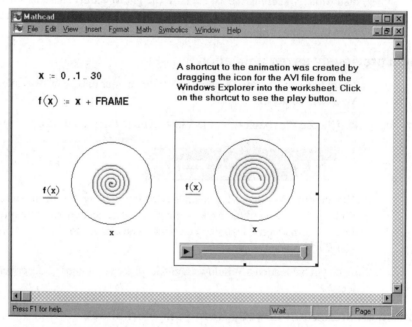

Figure 27-4: A Mathcad worksheet containing a shortcut to an animation.

Gallery of animations

The following figures show some of the things you can do with animation using Mathcad's different plot types (polar, X-Y, 3D scatter, vector field, parametric surface, bar, and contour). Choose **Resource Center** from the **Help** menu and look for "Animations" in the QuickSheets to see some more.

Note that since Mathcad's plots autoscale by default, you'll almost always have to change the plot format to show the animation you want. For example, when animating an X-Y plot or a polar plot you should enter values into the axis limit placeholders to fix the extent of each axis and preserve the plot scaling throughout the course of the animation. Similarly, when an animation involves a 3D plot, you should fix the axis limits by double-clicking on the plot to bring up the 3D Plot Format dialog box, unchecking Autoscale on the Axes page, and setting the axis limit on each axis in such a way that all points generated in the course of the animation are within the axis limits.

In the examples in this chapter, Figure 27-1 has a maximum radius in the placeholder for the radial axis limit; Figure 27-7 and Figure 27-9 have autoscale turned off on all axes and appropriate limits entered.

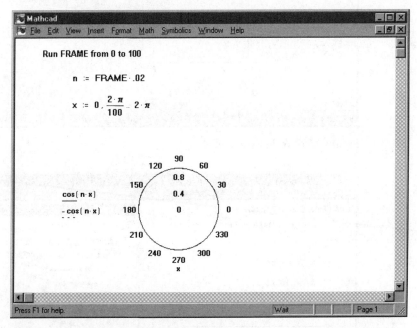

Figure 27-5: Growing a four-leaf clover.

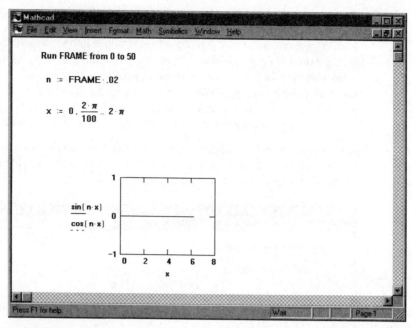

Figure 27-6: Roller coaster.

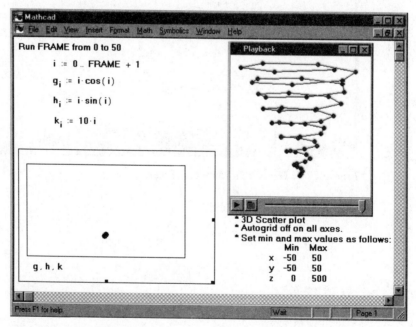

Figure 27-7: Tornado.

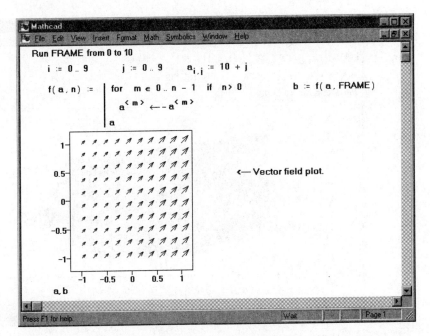

Figure 27-8: Diffusion of one field across another.

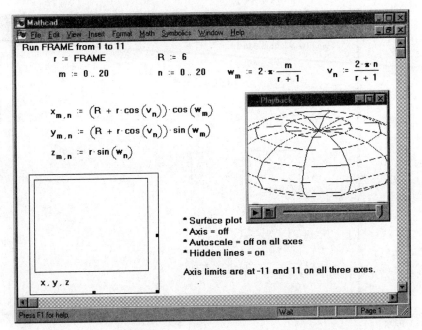

Figure 27-9: Nested spheroids.

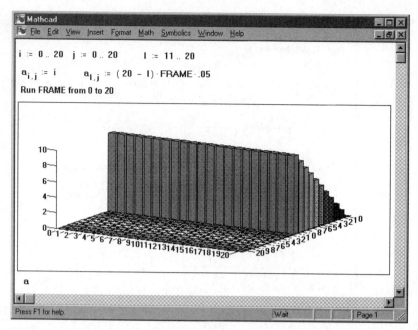

Figure 27-10: Barn raising. This one may take a few minutes.

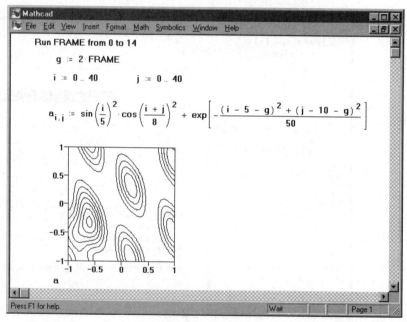

Figure 27-11: Animated contour map. This one may take a few minutes.

Chapter 27 Animation

Chapter 28
Importing and Exporting Graphics

Mathcad can read in graphic image files as data for you to manipulate mathematically and to view as pictures. You can process images as arrays in Mathcad and export arrays as image files to graphics editors or other applications. This chapter also describes how to create pictures in a Mathcad worksheet by reference to bitmap files, and how to import graphic images by copying them from another application and pasting them into Mathcad.

This chapter contains the following sections:

Reading and writing graphics files

Reading and writing grayscale BMP image files with *READBMP* and *WRITEBMP* and color BMP image files with *READRGB* and *WRITERGB*; viewing images in the picture operator. Additional image reading and writing functions in Mathcad Professional.

Creating pictures

Using the **Picture** command from the **Insert** menu to create a picture based on a matrix or bitmap file. Pasting in a graphic image from the clipboard.

Formatting pictures

Changing the positioning and size of existing pictures, and working with the palettes of 256-color bitmaps.

Reading and writing graphics files

Mathcad includes functions that allow you to read in a grayscale or color image as data. Once you have read an image into a Mathcad matrix, you can view it in Mathcad's picture operator or apply image processing techniques or other mathematical manipulations. And once you finish processing a matrix, you may save the data to disk as an image for later use in Mathcad or in graphics applications.

While the functions described in this section are designed specifically to read and write image files, they share many of the general behaviors of the functions for reading and writing ASCII data described in Chapter 19, "Data Management."

Reading, viewing, and writing BMP files

To import a bitmap (BMP format) file as data into Mathcad, use one of these functions:

Function	Meaning
READBMP(*file*)	Create a matrix containing a grayscale representation of the bitmap image in *file*. Each element in the matrix corresponds to a pixel. The value of a matrix element determines the shade of gray associated with the corresponding pixel. Each element is an integer between 0 (black) and 255 (white).
READRGB(*file*)	Create a matrix in which the color information in *file* is represented by the appropriate values of red, green, and blue. This matrix consists of three submatrices, each with the same number of columns and rows. Three matrix elements, rather than one, correspond to each pixel. Each element is an integer between 0 and 255. The three corresponding elements, when taken together, establish the color of the pixel.

You must use all uppercase letters to type these function names; alternatively, choose **Function** from the **Insert** menu and double-click on the function name in the scrolling list.

The argument you supply to *READBMP* or *READRGB* is a string expression—or a variable to which a string is assigned—as described in "Arguments to file access functions" on page 448. The string can correspond to either:

■ the name of a bitmap (BMP format) file in the working directory of the Mathcad worksheet you're currently working on; or

■ a full or relative path to a bitmap file located elsewhere on a local or network file system.

Each function returns a matrix of numbers used to represent the image.

For example, to create a matrix **M** of numbers corresponding to the image in the color image file **data2.bmp**, type either

$$M := \texttt{READBMP("data2.bmp")} \text{ or}$$

$$M := \texttt{READRGB("data2.bmp")}$$

In the first case **M** will be a grayscale representation of the image; in the second, **M** will consist of three submatrices corresponding to the red, green, and blue components of the color image.

As a second example, to read the grayscale image **blur.bmp** in the **C:\DATA** directory into the matrix **B**, pass the following string expression to *READBMP*:

$$B := \texttt{READBMP("C:\DATA\blur.bmp")}$$

See Chapter 8, "Variables and Constants," for more information about creating string expressions.

To divide the matrix for a color image into its red, green, and blue components, use the formulas shown in Figure 28-1 that use the *submatrix* function. In this example the color bitmap file **monalisa.bmp** is read into a grayscale matrix **gray** as well as the packed RGB matrix **packed** and then converted into three submatrices called **red**, **green**, and **blue**.

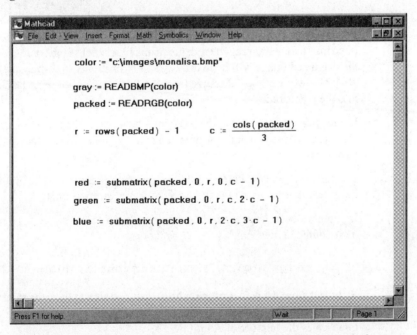

Figure 28-1: Reading in a color image as both grayscale and packed RGB matrices.

Once you have read an image file into Mathcad, you can use the *picture operator* to view it. First click in a blank part of your worksheet and then:

- Choose **Picture** from the **Insert** menu.

- Type the name of the matrix in the place-holder at the bottom left of the picture operator.

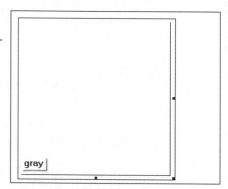

- Click outside the picture region to see the image.

To display an image in color, you must provide the picture operator with the names of three matrices containing the red, green and blue color values of the image. Otherwise, the displayed image will be in grayscale. For example, to display the image in Figure 28-1, you would choose **Picture** from the **Insert** menu and type `red,green,blue` into the placeholder:

If you want to display only the red components of the image that was used for Figure 28-1, you still must include the green and blue submatrices, but they both should contain only zeros.

Keep in mind that the colors of the image that you ultimately see may be distorted to the extent that you don't display 256 colors on your monitor.

If you have been working with submatrices for a color file, you can recombine them by defining an *augment3*(**X**, **Y**, **Z**) function:

```
augment3(X, Y, Z) := augment(X, augment(Y, Z))
```

X, **Y**, and **Z** are the names of the submatrices and should have the same number of rows and columns. The resulting matrix will then have the same number of rows as **X** but three times the number of columns.

Once you finish processing a matrix, you may want to save it to disk for later use. To do this, use one of the following functions:

Function	Meaning
WRITEBMP(*file*)	Create a grayscale BMP file from the matrix.
WRITERGB(*file*)	Create a color BMP file from a matrix in which the image is stored in RGB format.

You can use Mathcad's *augment* function (or the *augment3* function defined above) to combine submatrices at the time you are saving a file to your disk. For example, the following saves the submatrices that were created in Figure 28-1 as one 24-bit color image file called **nucolor.bmp**:

```
WRITERGB("nucolor.bmp"):=augment(red,augment(green,blue))
```

WRITEBMP and *WRITERGB* each take a string expression as described in "Arguments to file access functions" on page 448. The string can correspond to either:

■ the name of a bitmap (BMP format) file in the working directory of the Mathcad worksheet you're currently working on; or

■ a full or relative path to a bitmap file located elsewhere on a local or network file system.

Additional image reading and writing functions

Pro   In addition to the functions for reading and writing bitmap files described above, Mathcad Professional includes an assortment of more specialized functions for reading images or image components, including functions for reading images in GIF, JPG, and TGA formats. Your choice of which function to use will depend on:

■ Whether you want to create a Mathcad matrix in which the image is separated into: red, green, and blue (RGB); hue, lightness, and saturation (HLS); or hue, saturation, and value (HSV) components.

■ Whether you want to read in the entire image or just one component (for example, only the red values) of the image.

The functions used to read images work in exactly the same way as *READBMP* described in the previous section, but each recognizes images in the following formats: BMP, GIF, JPG, and TGA. Each function a string expression as described in "Arguments to file access functions" on page 448. The string can correspond to either:

■ the name of an image (BMP, GIF, JPG, or TGA format) file in the working directory of the Mathcad worksheet you're currently working on; or

■ a full or relative path to an image file located elsewhere on a local or network file system.

Each function returns a matrix of numbers used to represent the image.

Function	Meaning
Pro READ_IMAGE(*file*)	Creates a matrix containing a grayscale representation of the image in *file*. To read an image in color, use one of the functions below.
Pro READ_HLS(*file*) READ_HSV(*file*)	Creates a matrix in which the color information in *file* is represented by the appropriate values of hue, lightness, and saturation (HLS) or hue, saturation, and value (HSV).
Pro READ_RED(*file*) READ_GREEN(*file*) READ_BLUE(*file*)	Extracts only the red, green, or blue component from a color image. The result has one-third the number of columns that the matrix returned by *READ_RGB* would have had.
Pro READ_HLS_HUE(*file*) READ_HLS_LIGHT(*file*) READ_HLS_SAT(*file*)	Extracts only the hue, lightness, or saturation component from a color image. The result has one-third the number of columns that the matrix returned by *READ_HLS* would have had.
Pro READ_HSV_HUE(*file*) READ_HSV_SAT(*file*) READ_HSV_VALUE(*file*)	Extracts only the hue, saturation, or value component from a color image. The result has one-third the number of columns that the matrix returned by *READ_HSV* would have had.

In addition to the *WRITEBMP* and *WRITERGB* functions described in the previous section, Mathcad Professional has functions for creating color BMP files out of matrices in which the image is stored in HLS or HSV format.

Function	Meaning
Pro WRITE_HLS(*file*)	Create a color BMP file out of a matrix in which the image is stored in HLS format.
Pro WRITE_HSV(*file*)	Create a color BMP file out of a matrix in which the image is stored in HSV format.

Like *WRITEBMP* and *WRITERGB*, these functions each take a string expression as described in "Arguments to file access functions" on page 448. The string can correspond to either:

■ the name of a bitmap (BMP format) file in the working directory of the Mathcad worksheet you're currently working on; or

■ a full or relative path to a bitmap file located elsewhere on a local or network file system.

To use these functions, you write an assignment expression with the left-hand side containing the call to the *WRITE_HLS* or *WRITE_HSV* function and the right-hand side containing a matrix expression. For example, to create the 24-bit color image file **process.bmp** in the current directory from matrices **H**, **L**, and **S** corresponding to the hue, light, and saturation components of the image, enter:

```
WRITE_HLS("process.bmp"):=augment(H,augment(L,S))
```

Creating pictures

You can create a picture in a Mathcad worksheet in the following ways:

- By using the picture operator and supplying it either the name of a Mathcad matrix or the name of an external bitmap file as a string expression, or

- By pasting in a graphic image from another application via the clipboard.

Creating a picture from a matrix

You can view any matrix in Mathcad as a picture by using the picture operator:

- Click in a blank space in your Mathcad worksheet.

- Choose **Picture** from the **Insert** menu.

- Type the name of a matrix in the placeholder at the bottom of the operator.

This is most useful when you import graphics files into Mathcad as matrices as described in "Reading and writing graphics files" on page 582. For example, you can use the *READBMP* function to read a bitmap file into a matrix, and then use the picture operator to see the picture in Mathcad. See the figure on page 584 for an example.

Creating a picture by reference to a bitmap file

To create a picture directly from a bitmap file without reading it first into a matrix, click in a blank space in your worksheet and then:

- Choose **Picture** from the **Insert** menu to insert the picture operator.

- In the placeholder, type a string expression containing the name of a bitmap file in the current directory, or type a full path to a bitmap file.

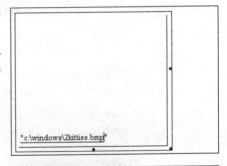

"c:\windows\2kitties.bmp"

- Click outside the picture operator and the bitmap will appear in your worksheet.

Each time you open the worksheet or calculate the worksheet, the bitmap file will be read into the picture operator. If you modify the source bitmap file, you must recalculate your worksheet to see the modified image. If you move the source bitmap file, Mathcad will not be able to display the picture.

Importing graphic images from the clipboard

You can copy any image from another application to the clipboard and paste it into Mathcad in one of the formats put on the clipboard at the time of copying. If you use the **Paste** command on Mathcad's **Edit** menu to paste in an image from the clipboard (or use drag-and-drop from another application), you will often paste a linked *OLE object* into your Mathcad worksheet, as discussed in Chapter 4, "Worksheet Management." When you double-click on a linked OLE object, you activate the application that created the object and are able to edit the object in your Mathcad worksheet.

This section describes using the **Paste Special** command on the **Edit** menu to paste graphic images into Mathcad worksheets in noneditable formats: as pictures (metafiles) or bitmaps. A metafile, which is strictly a Windows graphic format, can be resized in Mathcad without undue loss of resolution, whereas a bitmap is usually viewed best only at its original size. A device-independent bitmap, or DIB, is stored in a bitmap format that is portable to other operating systems.

To paste a graphics image from the clipboard into Mathcad, do the following:

■ Place the graphics image on the clipboard, usually via a **Copy** command on the **Edit** menu. Many Windows applications have this feature.

■ Click the mouse wherever you want the image in your Mathcad worksheet.

■ Choose **Paste Special** from the **Edit** menu, and choose one of the available formats. If you do not wish to paste a linked OLE object, choose "Picture (metafile)" or "Device Independent Bitmap" from the list in the Paste Special dialog box.

■ Click "OK." Mathcad creates a picture region and puts into it the image stored on the clipboard.

The format choices in the Paste Special dialog box will vary, depending on the application from which you originally copied a selection.

Mathcad stores the color depth—the number of colors in the image—at the time you paste it into a worksheet. This means that you can safely resave any worksheets that contain color images on systems that have different color displays, either fewer or more colors. The images will continue to display at the proper color depth on the systems that created the worksheets.

When you import directly from the clipboard, the picture information is stored as part of the Mathcad worksheet. This makes the document take up more disk space. It also means that when you copy the worksheet, the picture information travels along with it.

Formatting pictures

As discussed in previous sections of this chapter, you create pictures in a Mathcad worksheet from matrices, bitmap files, or graphic images pasted from the clipboard. This section describes your options for formatting a picture once you've created it.

Resizing pictures

To resize a picture region, do the following:

■ Click the mouse inside the picture region to select it.

■ Move the mouse pointer to one of the handles along the edge of region. The pointer will change to a double-headed arrow.

■ Press and hold down the left mouse button. With the button still held, drag the mouse in the direction you want the picture region to be stretched.

When you change the size of the picture region, the picture inside may be distorted. If you resize the picture by dragging diagonally on the handle in the lower right corner, you will preserve the aspect ratio—the ratio of height to width—of the original picture.

You can also avoid distortion by restoring the original size of the picture region:

■ Double-click on the picture itself, or choose **Properties** from the **Format** menu. This brings up the Properties dialog box.

■ Click on the box labeled "Display at Original Size."

■ Click the "OK" button. Mathcad changes the size of the picture to match that of the original image.

Framing a picture

Mathcad allows you to place a border all the way around a picture region. To do so:

■ Double-click on the picture itself, or choose **Properties** from the **Format** menu. This brings up the Properties dialog box.

■ Click on the box labeled "Show Border."

■ Click the "OK" button. Mathcad draws a border around the picture region.

Deleting and moving pictures

Use the **Edit** menu commands to cut, delete, or copy a picture region.

To cut or delete a picture region:

■ Click inside the region to select it. This will place a selection box around the picture.

■ Press [**Ctrl**]**X** or choose **Cut** from the **Edit** menu. Choose **Delete** from the **Edit** menu to leave the clipboard unaffected.

To copy a picture region:

- Click inside the region to select it. This will place a selection box around the picture.

- Press [Ctrl]C or choose **Copy** from the **Edit** menu.

- Click the mouse wherever you want to place a copy of the region and press [Ctrl]V or choose **Paste** from the **Edit** menu.

To move a picture region:

- Click inside the region to select it. This will place a selection box around the region.

- Place the pointer on the border of the box. The pointer will turn into a small hand.

- Press and hold down the mouse button.

- Without letting go of the button, move the mouse to where you'd like the picture region.

Note that unlike some applications, Mathcad treats the picture region and the image within it as a single region, not as separate frames. Therefore, when you press [Ctrl]C or [Ctrl]X, Mathcad places both the image and the picture region into the clipboard.

Controlling color palettes

If you are using a 256-color display and have color bitmaps in your Mathcad worksheets, Mathcad by default uses a single 256-color palette to display all the bitmaps in your worksheets. This is the same default color palette Mathcad uses for displaying the rest of the Mathcad screen, and is suitable for most pictures.

This default color palette, however, may not be the exact one that any color bitmaps in a worksheet were designed to use. To improve the appearance of bitmaps in your worksheet, you can tell Mathcad to optimize its default color palette so that it chooses the best possible 256 colors to display bitmaps in the worksheet. To do so:

- Choose **Color ⇒Optimize Palette** from the **Format** menu. Now Mathcad will survey the pictures in the worksheet and generate an optimal 256-color palette to use for all of them.

- Make sure that **Color ⇒Use Default Palette** in the **Format** menu has a check mark. Then Mathcad will use the new default palette it generates.

If you don't want Mathcad to use one color palette for all color bitmaps, choose **Color ⇒Use Default Palette** in the **Format** menu. The check mark next to this option will be removed, and Mathcad will use whatever color palette is best for each picture. The disadvantage to unchecking **Use Default Palette** is that the screen may flash as you scroll through a Mathcad worksheet and each 256-color bitmap loads a new palette. We therefore recommend that you keep a check mark next to the **Color ⇒Use Default Palette** option in the **Format** menu if you are working in 256-color mode.

If your display driver supports a greater number of colors, the palette setting options on the **Format** menu are grayed out.

Appendices

Appendices

Appendix A
Reference

This appendix lists functions, operators, menu commands, special key-strokes, and other reference material. It is made up of the following sections:

Menu commands

Function keys

Greek letters

Operators

Built-in functions listed alphabetically

Predefined variables

Suffixes for numbers

Arrow and movement keys

ASCII codes

Menu commands

File menu

New	[Ctrl]N	Open new worksheet based on available templates.
Open...	[Ctrl]O	Open existing worksheet or template.
Save	[Ctrl]S	Save current worksheet or template.
Save As...		Save current worksheet or template under new name.
Close	[Ctrl][F4]	Close current worksheet or template.
Collaboratory...		Open a dialog box for downloading and uploading messages and Mathcad worksheets from MathSoft's Collaboratory server on the Internet.
Internet Setup...		Change various settings associated with Internet access.
Send...		Mail current worksheet.
Page Setup...		Set margins, suppress printing beyond right margin.
Print Preview...		Show worksheet as it will appear when printed.
Print...		Print worksheet or selected regions.
Exit	[Alt][F4]	Exit Mathcad.

Edit menu

Undo	[Alt][BkSp]	Undo most recent edit.
Redo		Undo the last undo.
Cut	[Ctrl]X	Cut selection.
Copy	[Ctrl]C	Copy selection.
Paste	[Ctrl]V	Insert selection most recently copied or cut.
Paste Special		Insert selection most recently copied or cut in other available formats.
Delete	[Ctrl]D	Delete selection.
Select All		Select every region in the worksheet.

Find...	[Ctrl][F5]	Search for math or text characters.
Replace...	[Shift][F5]	Search for and replace math or text characters.
Go to Page...		Position the top of a specified page at the top of your window.
Check Spelling...		Search text for misspelled words.
Links...		Edit OLE links in the worksheet.

View menu

Math Palette		Hide Math Palette. When Palette is hidden, this menu item is checked.
Toolbar		Hide Toolbar. When Toolbar is hidden, this item is checked.
Format Bar		Hide Format bar. When Format Bar is hidden, this menu item is checked.
Regions		Toggle between boxed and unboxed display of regions.
Zoom...		Zoom in for a close-up or out for an overall view.
Refresh	[Ctrl]R	Force screen redraw.
Animate...		Create an animation clip.
Playback...		Play an existing animation clip.

Insert menu

Graph ⇒

X-Y Plot	@	Create two-dimensional Cartesian plot.
Polar Plot	[Ctrl]7	Create a plot for plotting radius against angle.
Surface Plot	[Ctrl]2	Create a plot for displaying a surface in three dimensions.
Contour Plot	[Ctrl]5	Create a plot for displaying the level curves of a surface.
3D Scatter Plot		Create a three-dimensional scatter plot.
3D Bar Chart		Create a three-dimensional bar chart.
Vector Field Plot		Create a vector field plot for two-dimensional vectors.

Matrix...	[Ctrl]M	Create a new matrix or insert and delete rows or columns from an existing matrix.
Function...	[Ctrl]F	Show a scrolling list of available built-in functions.
Unit...	[Ctrl]U	Show a scrolling list of available units.
Picture...	[Ctrl]T	Insert a region for graphics import.
Math Region		Create a math region inside a text region or at the crosshair location.
Text Region	"	Start a new text region at the crosshair location.
Page Break		Insert a hard pagebreak.
Hyperlink $\Rightarrow$		
New		Create a hypertext link from the current region to another worksheet on a local file system or on the World Wide Web.
Erase		Deactivate any hypertext links associated with the current selection.
Edit		Edit a hypertext link associated with the current selection.
Reference...		Make variable and function definitions from another worksheet available in the current worksheet.
Component...		Insert a data or application component into the worksheet at the crosshair.
Object...		Embed or link an OLE object from an OLE server on your system.

Format menu

Number...	Change precision displayed, threshold for scientific notation, and other similar characteristics.
Equation...	Choose font, size, color, and style used to display math expressions.
Text...	Choose font, size, color, and style of selected text.
Paragraph...	Choose indenting and justification style of selected text region.
Style...	Apply, modify, create, or delete text style.

Properties...	Change background color or surrounding box of selected region. Apply calculation options to math region.
Color $\Rightarrow$	
Background...	Change color of worksheet background.
Highlight...	Change color of highlighted regions.
Annotation...	Change color of any changes made to an Electronic Book.
Use default palette...	Enable or disable the display of all bitmap images using a default color palette to reduce screen flashing on 256-color displays. When the default palette is used, this menu item is checked.
Optimize palette...	Create optimal 256-color default palette for display of all bitmap images in the worksheet.
Graph $\Rightarrow$	
X-Y Plot...	Change characteristics for all Cartesian plots in current worksheet. If a plot is selected, changes will affect only the selected plot.
Polar Plot...	Change characteristics for all polar plots in current worksheet. If a plot is selected, changes will affect only the selected plot.
3D Plot...	Change characteristics for the currently selected three-dimensional plot.
Trace...	Read coordinates directly from the currently selected graph.
Zoom...	Magnify view of a portion of the currently selected graph.
Separate Regions	Separate overlapping regions.
Align Regions $\Rightarrow$	
Across	Align selected regions to a horizontal line midway between the highest and the lowest region.
Down	Align selected regions to a vertical line midway between the rightmost and the leftmost region.
Lock Regions $\Rightarrow$	
Set Lock Area	Define extent of a write-protected area on the worksheet.
Lock Area...	Write protect selected area.

| Unlock Area... | | Permit editing in a locked area. |
| Headers/Footers... | | Specify headers and footers for printouts. |

Math menu

Calculate	[F9]	Update all results on screen.
Calculate Worksheet		Update all results in worksheet.
Automatic Calculation		Toggle between automatic calculation mode in which Mathcad updates screen continuously, and manual mode.
Optimization		Turn optimize feature on and off. This feature causes Mathcad to attempt to simplify any expression to the right of ":=" or "=". When the optimize feature is on, this menu item is checked.
Options ⟹		
Built-In Variables...		Set values of built-in variables. Reset random numbers.
Unit System...		Choose unit system for the default display of results.
Dimensions...		Choose the names of the fundamental dimensions for the current system of units.

Symbolics menu

Evaluate ⟹		
Symbolically	[Shift][F9]	Carry out symbolic evaluation of an expression.
Floating Point...		Return a floating point number for constants rather than a symbolic expression. A dialog box allows you to choose the floating point precision.
Complex		Carry out symbolic evaluation of a complex expression. The result is expressed in the form $a + b \cdot i$.
Simplify		Simplify the selected expression, performing arithmetic, canceling common factors, and using basic trigonometric and inverse function identities.

Expand	Expand all powers and products of sums in the selected expression.
Factor	Factor the selected expression into a product, if the entire expression can be written as a product. To factor a subexpression of a larger expression, select the subexpression.
Collect	Collect terms containing like powers of the selected subexpression, which may be a single variable or a function together with its argument. The result is a polynomial in the selected expression.
Polynomial Coefficients	Find the coefficients of the expression when written as a polynomial in the selected variable or function.
Variable ⇒	
Solve	Find the value of the selected variable that makes the expression containing the variable equal to zero. If you select a variable in an equation or inequality, this command solves the equation or inequality for the selected variable.
Substitute	Substitute the contents of the clipboard for each occurrence of a selected variable in an expression. To use this menu command, first put the expression being substituted in the clipboard by selecting and choosing **Copy** or **Cut**. Then select an occurrence of the variable you are substituting for and choose this menu command.
Differentiate	Differentiate the entire expression containing the selected variable with respect to that variable. Other variables are treated as constants.
Integrate	Integrate the entire expression containing the selected variable with respect to that variable.
Expand to Series...	Derive an expansion series for an expression with respect to the variable you have selected. A dialog box allows you to choose the order of the series.
Convert to Partial Fraction	Generate a partial fraction expansion for an expression by factoring the numerator and denominator with respect to the selected variable.
Matrix ⇒	
Transpose	Return transpose of the selected matrix.

Invert	Return symbolic inverse of the selected square matrix.
Determinant	Return symbolic determinant of the selected square matrix.
Transform $\Rightarrow$	
Fourier	Evaluate Fourier transform of expression with respect to the selected variable. Result is in terms of ω.
Inverse Fourier	Evaluate the inverse Fourier transform of the expression with respect to the selected variable. Result is in terms of t.
Laplace	Evaluate the Laplace transform of the expression with respect to the selected variable. Result is in terms of s.
Inverse Laplace	Evaluate the inverse Laplace transform of the expression with respect to the selected variable. Result is in terms of t.
Z	Evaluate the z-transform of the expression with respect to the selected variable. Result is in terms of z.
Inverse Z	Evaluate the inverse z-transform of the expression with respect to the selected variable. Result is in terms of n.
Evaluation Style...	Choose the format for symbolic results. A dialog box presents the options, which include vertically stacked display of results and comments, horizontal display, and display without evaluation comments.

Window menu

Cascade	Stack all worksheet windows neatly, with title bars showing.
Tile Horizontal	Arrange all worksheet windows horizontally so that they don't overlap.
Tile Vertical	Arrange all worksheet windows vertically so that they don't overlap.
Arrange Icons	Arrange worksheet icons neatly along lower left edge of application window

Help menu

Mathcad Help...	[F1]	Show index for on-line help.
Resource Center...		Open a window for browsing reference content, QuickSheets, and Web-based worksheets and information.
Tip of the Day...		Show a series of helpful hints. Displays automatically at Mathcad start-up unless disabled.
Open Book...		Open a Mathcad Electronic Book you have installed.
Using Help...		Show instructions for using Help.
About Mathcad...		Display version number, serial number, and copyright information.

Function keys

Keys	Actions
[**F1**]	Help.
[**Shift**][**F1**]	Context sensitive help.
[**F2**]	Copy selected region to clipboard.
[**F3**]	Cut selected region to clipboard.
[**F4**]	Paste contents of clipboard.
[**Ctrl**][**F4**]	Close worksheet or template.
[**F5**]	Open a worksheet or template.
[**Ctrl**][**F5**]	Search for text or math characters.
[**Shift**][**F5**]	Replace text or math characters.
[**F6**]	Save current worksheet.
[**Ctrl**][**F6**]	Make next window active.
[**F7**]	Open a new worksheet.
[**F9**]	Recalculate everything on the screen. With *READ*, *WRITE* or other file I/O function selected, forces Mathcad to read or write to disk.

Greek letters

To type a Greek letter into an equation or into text, press the corresponding roman equivalent from the table below, followed by [Ctrl]G. Alternatively, use the Greek Symbol Palette.

Name	Uppercase	Lowercase	Roman equivalent
alpha	A	α	A
beta	B	β	B
chi	X	χ	C
delta	Δ	δ	D
epsilon	E	ε	E
eta	H	η	H
gamma	G	γ	G
iota	I	ι	I
kappa	K	κ	K
lambda	L	λ	L
mu	M	μ	M
nu	N	ν	N
omega	W	ω	W
omicron	O	o	O
phi	F	φ	F
phi (alternate)		φ	J
pi	P	π	P
psi	Y	ψ	Y
rho	R	ρ	R
sigma	S	σ	S
tau	T	τ	T
theta	Q	θ	Q
theta (alternate)	J		J
upsilon	U	υ	U
xi	X	ξ	X
zeta	Z	ζ	Z

Note: The Greek letter π is so commonly used that it has its own keyboard shortcut: [Ctrl]P.

Operators

In this table:

- **A** and **B** represent arrays, either vector or matrix.

- **u** and **v** represent vectors with real or complex elements.

- **M** represents a square matrix.

- z and w represent real or complex numbers.

- x and y represent real numbers.

- m and n represent integers.

- i represents a range variable.

- S and any names beginning with S represent string expressions.

- t represents any variable name.

- f represents a function.

- X and Y represent variables or expressions of any type.

For information about programming operators in Mathcad Professional, see Chapter 18, "Programming." For information about symbolic operators and keywords, see Chapter 17, "Symbolic Calculation."

Operation	Appearance	Keystroke	Description
Parentheses	(X)	'	Grouping operator.
Vector Subscript	$\mathbf{v}_n$	[	Returns indicated element of a vector.
Matrix Subscript	$\mathbf{A}_{m,n}$	[	Returns indicated element of a matrix.
Superscript	$\mathbf{A}^{\langle n \rangle}$	[Ctrl]6	Extracts column n from array **A**. Returns a vector.
Vectorize	$\vec{X}$	[Ctrl]-	Forces operations in expression X to take place element by element. All vectors or matrices in X must be the same size.
Factorial	$n!$	!	Returns $n \cdot (n-1) \cdot (n-2)\ldots$ The integer n cannot be negative.
Complex conjugate	$\overline{X}$	"	Inverts the sign of the imaginary part of X. This keystroke creates a string expression in a blank placeholder.
Transpose	$\mathbf{A}^{\mathsf{T}}$	[Ctrl]1	Returns a matrix whose rows are the columns of **A** and whose columns are the rows of **A**. **A** can be a vector or a matrix.

Power	z^w	^	Raises z to the power w.
Powers of matrix, matrix inverse	$\mathbf{M}^n$	^	nth power of square matrix $\mathbf{M}$ (using matrix multiplication). n must be a whole number. $\mathbf{M}^{-1}$ is the inverse of $\mathbf{M}$. Other negative powers are powers of the inverse. Returns a square matrix.
Negation	$-X$	–	Multiplies X by -1.
Vector sum	$\Sigma \mathbf{v}$	[Ctrl]4	Sums elements of vector v; returns a scalar.
Square root	$\sqrt{z}$	\	Returns positive square root for positive z; principal value for negative or complex z.
nth root	$\sqrt[n]{z}$	[Ctrl]\	Returns nth root of z; returns a real valued root whenever possible.
Magnitude, Absolute value	$\|z\|$	|	Returns $\sqrt{\mathrm{Re}(z)^2 + \mathrm{Im}(z)^2}$.
Magnitude of vector	$\|\mathbf{v}\|$	|	Returns the magnitude of the vector v: $\sqrt{\mathbf{v} \cdot \mathbf{v}}$ if all elements in v are real. Returns $\sqrt{\mathbf{v} \cdot \overline{\mathbf{v}}}$ if any element in v is complex.
Determinant	$\|\mathbf{M}\|$	|	Returns the determinant of the square matrix $\mathbf{M}$. Result is a scalar.
Division	$\dfrac{X}{z}$	/	Divides the expression X by the non-zero scalar z. If X is an array, divides each element by z.
Multiplication	$X \cdot Y$	*	Returns the product of X and Y if both X and Y are scalars. Multiplies each element of Y by X if Y is an array and X is a scalar. Returns the dot product (inner product) if X and Y are vectors of the same size. Performs matrix multiplication if X and Y are conformable matrices.
Cross product	$\mathbf{u} \times \mathbf{v}$	[Ctrl]8	Returns cross-product (vector product) for the three-element vectors u and v.
Summation	$\displaystyle\sum_{i\,=\,m}^{n} X$	[Ctrl] [Shift]4	Performs summation of X over $= m, m + 1, ..., r. X$ can be any expression. It need not involve i but it usually does. m and n must be integers.
Product	$\displaystyle\prod_{i\,=\,m}^{n} X$	[Ctrl] [Shift]3	Performs iterated product of X for $= m, m + 1, ..., r. X$ can be any expression. It need not involve i but it usually does. m and n must be integers.
Range sum	$\displaystyle\sum_{i} X$	$	Returns a summation of X over the range variable i. X can be any expression. It need not involve i but it usually does.
Range product	$\displaystyle\prod_{i} X$	#	Returns the iterated product of X over the range variable i. X can be any expression. It need not involve i but it usually does.

Integral	$\int_{a}^{b} f(t)dt$	&	Returns the definite integral of $f(t)$ over the interval $[a, b]$. a and b must be real scalars. All variables in the expression $f(t)$, except the variable of integration t, must be defined. The integrand, $f(t)$, cannot return an array.
Derivative	$\frac{d}{dt}f(t)$	?	Returns the derivative of $f(t)$ evaluated at t. All variables in the expression $f(t)$ must be defined. The variable t must be a scalar value. The function $f(t)$ must return a scalar.
nth Derivative	$\frac{d^n}{dt^n}f(t)$	[Ctrl]?	Returns the nth derivative of $f(t)$ evaluated at t. All variables in $f(t)$ must be defined. The variable t must be a scalar value. The function $f(t)$ must return a scalar. n must be an integer between 0 and 5 for numerical evaluation or a positive integer for symbolic evaluation.
Addition	$X + Y$	+	Scalar addition if X, Y, or both are scalars. Element by element addition if X and Y are vectors or matrices of the same size. If X is an array and Y is a scalar, adds Y to each element of X.
Subtraction	$X - Y$	−	Performs scalar subtraction if X, Y, or both are scalars. Performs element by element subtraction if X and Y are vectors or matrices of the same size. If X is an array and Y is a scalar, subtracts Y from each element of X.
Addition with line break	$X...$ $+ Y$	[Ctrl] [↵]	Same as addition. Line break is purely cosmetic.
Greater than	$x > y$, $S1 > S2$	>	For real scalars x and y, returns 1 if $x > y$, 0 otherwise. For string expressions $S1$ and $S2$, returns 1 if $S1$ strictly follows $S2$ in ASCII order, 0 otherwise.
Less than	$x < y$, $S1 < S2$	<	For real scalars x and y, returns 1 if $x < y$, 0 otherwise. For string expressions $S1$ and $S2$, returns 1 if $S1$ strictly precedes $S2$ in ASCII order, 0 otherwise.
Greater than or equal	$x \geq y$, $S1 \geq S2$	[Ctrl]0	For real scalars x and y, returns 1 if $x \geq y$, 0 otherwise. For string expressions $S1$ and $S2$, returns 1 if $S1$ follows $S2$ in ASCII order, 0 otherwise.
Less than or equal	$x \leq y$, $S1 \leq S2$	[Ctrl]9	For real scalars x and y, returns 1 if $x \leq y$, 0 otherwise. For string expressions $S1$ and $S2$, returns 1 if $S1$ precedes $S2$ in ASCII order, 0 otherwise.
Not equal to	$z \neq w$, $S1 \neq S2$	[Ctrl]3	For scalars z and w, returns 1 if $z \neq w$, 0 otherwise. For string expressions $S1$ and $S2$, returns 1 if $S1$ is not character by character identical to $S2$.
Equal to	$X = Y$	[Ctrl]=	Returns 1 if $X = Y$, 0 otherwise. Appears as a bold = on the screen.

Built-in functions listed alphabetically

This section lists Mathcad's built-in functions alphabetically, with a short description of each one. Functions labeled **Pro** are available only in Mathcad Professional. For more information, see Chapter 13, "Built-in Functions." Matrix and vector functions are covered in detail in Chapter 10, "Vectors and Matrices." And for more information on Mathcad's differential equation solvers, see Chapter 16, "Solving Differential Equations."

In this table,

- x and y represent real numbers.

- z represents either a real or a complex number.

- m, n, i, j and k represent integers.

- S and any names beginning with S represent string expressions.

- **v, u** and any names beginning with **v** represent vectors.

- **A** and **B** represent matrices or vectors.

- **M** and **N** represent square matrices.

- **F** represents a vector-valued function.

- *file* is a string variable that corresponds to a filename or path.

Any function that expects an angle as an argument expects that angle in radians. Similarly, any function that returns an angle as a result, returns the angle in radians. Complex or multivalued functions always return the principal value.

Function names are case sensitive. You must type them as shown here. Names of built-in functions are not, however, font sensitive.

Function	Returns . . .
acos(z)	Inverse cosine. Result in radians. Principal value for complex z.
acosh(z)	Inverse hyperbolic cosine. Result in radians. Principal value for complex z.
angle(x, y)	Angle from x-axis to (x, y). x and y real. Result in radians.
APPEND(*file*)	Single value to append to data file *file*.
APPENDPRN(*file*)	Matrix to append to structured data file *file*.
arg(z)	Angle in complex plane to number z.
asin(z)	Inverse sine. Result in radians. Principal value for complex z.
asinh(z)	Inverse hyperbolic sine. Result in radians. Principal value for complex z.
atan(z)	Inverse tangent. Result in radians. Principal value for complex z.

	atanh(z)	Inverse hyperbolic tangent. Principal value for complex z.
	augment($\mathbf{A}$, $\mathbf{B}$)	A matrix formed by putting the two argument matrices side by side. $\mathbf{A}$ and $\mathbf{B}$ must have the same number of rows. Either or both arguments may be vectors.
Pro	bulstoer($\mathbf{y}$, $x1$, $x2$, acc, $\mathbf{D}$, kmx, sv)	Smooth Bulirsch-Stoer differential equation solver, where $\mathbf{y}$ is the vector of n initial values, n is the order of the DE or size of the system of DEs, $x1$ and $x2$ are endpoints of the solution interval, acc controls accuracy, $\mathbf{D}(x, \mathbf{y})$ prescribes the derivatives, kmx is the maximum number of intermediate points, and sv is the minimum distance between x values (which needn't be equally spaced). Provides good DE solution estimate at $x2$.
Pro	Bulstoer($\mathbf{y}$, $x1$, $x2$, $npts$, $\mathbf{D}$)	Smooth Bulirsch-Stoer differential equation solver, where $\mathbf{y}$ is the vector of n initial values, n is the order of the DE or size of the system of DEs, $x1$ and $x2$ are endpoints of the solution interval, $npts$ controls the number of rows in the matrix output, and $\mathbf{D}(x, \mathbf{y})$ prescribes the derivatives. Provides DE solution at equally spaced x values by repeated calls to bulstoer.
Pro	bvalfit($\mathbf{v1}$, $\mathbf{v2}$, $x1$, $x2$, xf, $\mathbf{D}$, $\mathbf{ld1}$, $\mathbf{ld2}$, $\mathbf{sc}$)	Converts a boundary value differential equation to initial/terminal value problems. $\mathbf{v1}$ is the guess vector for missing initial values at $x1$, $\mathbf{v2}$ is the guess vector for missing terminal values at $x2$, $x1$ and $x2$ are endpoints of the solution interval, the n-vector $\mathbf{D}(x, \mathbf{y})$ prescribes the derivatives, n is the order of the DE, the n-vector $\mathbf{ld1}(x1, \mathbf{v1})$ contains both known initial conditions and guess values from $\mathbf{v1}$, the n-vector $\mathbf{ld2}(x2, \mathbf{v2})$ is similar, the n-vector $\mathbf{sc}(xf, \mathbf{y})$ measures solution discrepancy at xf, where $x1 < xf < x2$. Useful when derivatives have a single discontinuity at xf.
	ceil(x)	Least integer $\geq x$. x must be real.
	cfft($\mathbf{A}$)	Fast Fourier transform of complex data. Returns an array of same size as its argument.
	CFFT($\mathbf{A}$)	Identical to cfft($\mathbf{A}$), except uses a different normalizing factor and sign convention. Returns an array of same size as its argument.
Pro	cholesky($\mathbf{M}$)	A lower triangular matrix $\mathbf{L}$ such that $\mathbf{L} \cdot \mathbf{L}^{\mathbf{T}} = \mathbf{M}$. This function assumes $\mathbf{M}$ is symmetric and uses only the upper triangular part of $\mathbf{M}$.
	cnorm(x)	Cumulative normal distribution. Same as pnorm(x, 0, 1)
	cols($\mathbf{A}$)	Number of columns in array $\mathbf{A}$. Returns a scalar.
Pro	concat($S1$, $S2$)	The string formed by appending string $S2$ to the end of string $S1$.
Pro	cond1($\mathbf{M}$)	Condition number of the matrix $\mathbf{M}$ based on the L_1 norm.
Pro	cond2($\mathbf{M}$)	Condition number of the matrix $\mathbf{M}$ based on the L_2 norm.
Pro	conde($\mathbf{M}$)	Condition number of the matrix $\mathbf{M}$ based on the Euclidean norm.
Pro	condi($\mathbf{M}$)	Condition number of the matrix $\mathbf{M}$ based on the infinity norm.

corr(**A**, **B**)	Correlation (Pearson's r) of two arrays **A** and **B** having the same number of rows and columns. Returns a scalar.
cos(z)	Cosine. Argument in radians.
cosh(z)	Hyperbolic cosine.
cot(z)	Cotangent. Argument in radians.
coth(z)	Hyperbolic cotangent.
csc(z)	Cosecant. Argument in radians.
csch(z)	Hyperbolic cosecant.
csort(**A**, n)	Sort rows so as to put column n in ascending order.
cspline(**vx**, **vy**)	Coefficients of cubic spline with cubic ends. **vx** and **vy** are real vectors of same size. Elements of **vx** must be in ascending order.
cspline(**Mxy**, **Mz**)	Vector of second derivatives for data arrays **Mxy** and **Mz**. This vector becomes the first argument of the *interp* function. The resultant surface is cubic at the edges of the region spanned by **Mxy**.
cvar(**A**, **B**)	Covariance of elements in **A** and **B**. **A** and **B** must have the same number of rows and columns.
dbeta(x, s_1, s_2)	Probability density for a beta distribution.
dbinom(k,n,p)	Binomial distribution of a random variable.
dcauchy(x,l,s)	Probability density for the Cauchy distribution.
dchisq(x, d)	Probability density for the chi-squared distribution.
dexp(x, r)	Probability density for the exponential distribution.
dF(x, $d1$, $d2$)	Probability density for the F distribution.
dgamma(x, s)	Probability density for the gamma distribution.
dgeom(k, p)	$P(X = k)$ when the random variable X has the geometric distribution.
Pro diag(**v**)	Diagonal matrix containing on its diagonal the elements of **v**.
dlnorm(x, μ, σ)	Probability density for the lognormal distribution.
dlogis(x, l, s)	Probability density for the logistic distribution.
dnbinom(k, n, p)	$P(X = k)$ when the random variable X has the negative binomial distribution.
dnorm(x, μ, σ)	Probability density for the normal distribution.
dpois(k, λ)	$P(X = k)$ when the random variable X has the Poisson distribution.
dt(x, d)	Probability density for Student's t distribution.
dunif(x, a, b)	Probability density for the uniform distribution.
dweibull(x, s)	Probability density for the Weibull distribution.

	eigenvals(**M**)	A vector of eigenvalues for the matrix **M**.
	eigenvec(**M**, z)	A vector containing the normalized eigenvector corresponding to the eigenvalue z of the square matrix **M**.
Pro	eigenvecs(**M**)	A matrix containing the normalized eigenvectors corresponding to the eigenvalues of the matrix **M**. The nth column of the matrix is the eigenvector corresponding to the nth eigenvalue returned by *eigenvals*.
	erf(z)	Error function.
Pro	error(S)	The error message string S.
	exp(z)	Exponential: e^z
	find(*var1, var2, . . .*)	Values of *var1, var2,* . . . that solve the system of equations. Returns a scalar if only one argument; otherwise, returns a vector of answers.
	fft(**v**)	Fast Fourier transform of real data. **v** must be a real vector with 2^n elements, where n is an integer. Returns a vector of size $2^{n-1} + 1$.
	FFT(**v**)	Identical to fft(**v**), except uses a different normalizing factor and sign convention. **v** must be a real vector with 2^n elements, where n is an integer. Returns a vector of size $2^{n-1} + 1$.
	floor(x)	Greatest integer $\leq x$. x must be real.
	genfit(**vx, vy, vg, F**)	A vector containing the parameters that make a function f of x and n parameters $u_0, u_1, \ldots, u_t$ best approximate the data in **vx** and **vy**. **F** is a function that returns an $n + 1$ element vector containing f and its partial derivatives with respect to its n parameters. **vx** and **vy** must be the same size. **vg** is an n element vector of guess values for the n parameters.
Pro	geninv(**A**)	Matrix **L**, the left inverse of matrix **A**, such that $\mathbf{L} \cdot \mathbf{A} = \mathbf{I}$, where **I** is the identity matrix having the same size as **A**. Matrix **A** is an $m \times n$ real-valued matrix, where $m \geq n$.
Pro	genvals(**M, N**)	Vector **v** of computed eigenvalues each of which satisfies the generalized eigenvalue problem $\mathbf{M} \cdot \mathbf{x} = v_i \cdot \mathbf{N} \cdot \mathbf{x}$. Matrices **M** and **N** contain real values. Vector **x** contains the corresponding eigenvectors.
Pro	genvecs(**M, N**)	A matrix containing the normalized eigenvectors corresponding to the eigenvalues in **v**, the vector returned by *genvals*. The nth column of this matrix is the eigenvector **x** satisfying the generalized eigenvalue problem $\mathbf{M} \cdot \mathbf{x} = v_n \cdot \mathbf{N} \cdot \mathbf{x}$. Matrices **M** and **N** contain real values.
	hist(**intervals, data**)	Histogram. **intervals** is a vector of interval limits, in ascending order. **data** is an array of data. Returns a vector of size one less than the size of **intervals**, showing how many points of **data** fall in each interval.
	I0(x)	Bessel function $I_0(x)$. Argument must be real.

I1(*x*)	Bessel function $I_1(x)$. Argument must be real.
In(*m*, *x*)	Bessel function $I_m(x)$. *x* must be real; $0 \leq m \leq 100$.
icfft(**A**)	Inverse Fourier transform corresponding to *cfft*. Returns an array of the same size as its argument.
ICFFT(**A**)	Inverse transform corresponding to *CFFT*. Returns an array of the same size as its argument.
identity(*n*)	Identity matrix of size *n*. *n* must be a positive integer.
if(*cond*, *x*, *y*)	Conditional: returns *x* or *y* depending on value of *cond*. If *cond* is true (non-zero), returns *x*. If *cond* is false (zero), returns *y*.
ifft(**v**)	Inverse Fourier transform corresponding to *fft*. Takes a vector of size $1 + 2^{n-1}$, where *n* is an integer. Returns a real vector of size 2^n.
IFFT(**v**)	Inverse transform corresponding to *FFT*. Takes a vector of size $1 + 2^{n-1}$, where *n* is an integer. Returns a real vector of size 2^n.
Im(*z*)	Imaginary part of complex number *z*. Also works on vectors and matrix arguments.
intercept(**vx**, **vy**)	Intercept of regression line. Takes two vector arguments **vx** and **vy** of same size. The elements of **vx** must be in ascending order. Returns a scalar: the *y*-intercept of the regression line.
interp(**vs**, **vx**, **vy**, *x*)	Interpolated value from spline coefficients. Takes three vector arguments **vs**, **vx**, and **vy** of same size and a scalar *x* at which to interpolate; returns a scalar. The elements of **vx** should be in ascending order. **vs** should be a vector computed with *cspline*, *lspline*, or *pspline*.
interp(**vs**, **Mxy**, **Mz**, *v*)	Spline interpolated value of **Mz** at the *x* and *y* coordinates specified in **v**.
Pro iwave(**v**)	Inverse wavelet transform corresponding to *wave*. Takes a 2^n element vector of real data, where *n* is an integer.
J0(*x*)	Bessel function $J_0(x)$. Argument must be real.
J1(*x*)	Bessel function $J_1(x)$. Argument must be real.
Jn(*m*, *x*)	Bessel function $J_m(x)$. *x* must be real; $0 \leq m \leq 100$.
K0(*x*)	Bessel function $K_0(x)$. Argument must be positive.
K1(*x*)	Bessel function $K_1(x)$. Argument must be positive.
Kn(*m*, *x*)	Bessel function $K_m(x)$. *x* must be positive; $0 \leq m \leq 100$.
Pro ksmooth(**vx**,**vy**, *b*)	An *n*-element vector created by using a Gaussian kernel to return weighted averages of **vy**. **vy** and **vx** are *n*-element vectors of real numbers. The bandwidth *b* controls the smoothing window and should be set to a few times the spacing between your *x* data points.
last(**v**)	Index of last element in vector **v**. Returns a scalar.
length(**v**)	Number of elements in vector **v**. Returns a scalar.

	linfit(**vx**, **vy**, **F**)	A vector containing the coefficients used to create a linear combination of the functions in **F** which best approximates the data in **vx** and **vy**. **F** is a function that returns a vector.
	linterp(**vx**, **vy**, *x*)	Linearly interpolated value. Takes two vector arguments **vx** and **vy** of same size and a scalar *x* at which to interpolate; returns a scalar. The elements of **vx** should be in ascending order.
	ln(*z*)	Natural logarithm of *z* (to base *e*). Returns principal value (imaginary part between π and $-\pi$) for complex *z*.
Pro	loess(**vx**, **vy**, *span*)	Vector required by the *interp* function to find the set of second order polynomials that best fit particular neighborhoods of data points specified in arrays **vx** and **vy**. **vx** is an *m* element vector containing *x* coordinates. **vy** is an *m* element vector containing the *y* coordinates corresponding to the *m* points specified in **vx**. The argument *span* (*span* > 0) specifies how large a neighborhood *loess* will consider in performing this local regression.
Pro	loess(**Mxy**, **vz**, *span*)	Vector required by the *interp* function to find the set of second order polynomials that best fit particular neighborhoods of data points specified in arrays **Mxy** and **vz**. **Mxy** is an $m \times 2$ matrix containing *x-y* coordinates. **vz** is an *m* element vector containing the *z* coordinates corresponding to the *m* points specified in **Mxy**. The argument *span* (*span* > 0) specifies how large a neighborhood *loess* will consider in performing this local regression.
	log(*z*)	Common logarithm of *z* (to base 10).
Pro	lsolve(**M**, **v**)	Solution vector **x** such that $\mathbf{M} \cdot \mathbf{x} = \mathbf{v}$.
	lspline(**vx**, **vy**)	Coefficients of cubic spline with linear ends. **vx** and **vy** are real vectors of same size. Elements of **vx** must be in ascending order.
	lspline(**Mxy**, **Mz**)	Vector of second derivatives for data arrays **Mxy** and **Mz**. This vector becomes the first argument of the *interp* function. The resultant surface is linear at the boundaries of the region spanned by **Mxy**.
Pro	lu(**M**)	One matrix containing the three square matrices **P**, **L**, and **U**, all having the same size as **M** and joined together side by side, in that order. These three matrices satisfy the equation $\mathbf{P} \cdot \mathbf{M} = \mathbf{L} \cdot \mathbf{U}$. **L** and **U** are lower and upper triangular respectively.
	matrix(*m*, *n*, *f*)	Creates a matrix in which the *ij*th element contains $f(i, j)$ where $= 0, 1, ..., m - 1$ and $= 0, 1, ..., n - 1$.
	max(**A**)	Largest element in **A**. Returns a scalar. If **A** is complex, returns max(Re(**A**)) + *i*.max(Im(**A**)).
	mean(**A**)	Mean of elements of an array **A**. Returns a scalar.
	median(**A**)	Median of elements in array **A**. Returns a scalar.
	medsmooth(**vy**,*n*)	An *m*-element vector created by smoothing **vy** with running medians. **vy** is an *m*-element vector of real numbers. The smoothing window has size *n*.

	min(**A**)	Smallest element in **A**. Returns a scalar. If **A** is complex, returns $\min(\mathrm{Re}(\mathbf{A})) + i.\min(\mathrm{Im}(\mathbf{A}))$.
	minerr(*var1, var2, . . .*)	Values of *var1, var2, . . .* coming closest to solving the system of equations. Returns a scalar if only one argument; otherwise, returns a vector of answers.
	mod(*x, modulus*)	Remainder on dividing *x* by *modulus*. Arguments must be real. Result has same sign as *x*.
Pro	multigrid(**M**, *ncycle*)	Solves the Poisson partial differential equation over a planar square region. The $n \times n$ matrix **M** gives source function values, where $n - 1$ is a power of 2 and zero boundary conditions on all four edges are assumed. Cycle control variable *ncycle* is usually 1 or 2. Different algorithm and faster than relax, which is more general.
Pro	norm1(**M**)	The L_1 norm of the matrix **M**.
Pro	norm2(**M**)	The L_2 norm of the matrix **M**.
Pro	norme(**M**)	The Euclidean norm of the matrix **M**.
Pro	normi(**M**)	The infinity norm of the matrix **M**.
Pro	num2str(*z*)	The string whose characters correspond to the decimal value of the number *z*.
	pbeta(*x*, s_1, s_2)	Cumulative beta distribution with shape parameters s_1 and s_2. $s_1, s_2 > 0$
	pbinom(*k, n, p*)	Cumulative binomial distribution for *k* successes in *n* trials.
	pcauchy(*x, l, s*)	Cumulative Cauchy distribution with scale parameters *l* and *s*.
	pchisq(*x, d*)	Cumulative chi-squared distribution in which $d > 0$ is the degrees of freedom and $x > 0$.
	pexp(*x, r*)	Cumulative exponential distribution in which $r > 0$ is the rate and $x > 0$.
	pF(*x*, d_1, d_2)	Cumulative F distribution in which $d_1, d_2 > 0$ are the degrees of freedom. $x > 0$.
	pgamma(*x, s*)	Cumulative gamma distribution in which $s > 0$ is the shape parameter. $x > 0$.
	pgeom(*k, p*)	Cumulative geometric distribution. *p* is the probability of success. $k \geq 0$ and $0 < p \leq 1$.
	plnorm(*x*, μ, σ)	Cumulative lognormal distribution in which μ is the logmean, σ is the logdeviation, and $x > 0$.
	plogis(*x, l, s*)	Cumulative logistic distribution. *l* is the location parameter. $s > 0$ is the scale parameter.
	pnbinom(*k, n, p*)	Cumulative negative binomial distribution in which $n > 0$ and $0 < p \leq 1$.
	pnorm(*x*, μ, σ)	Cumulative normal distribution with mean μ and standard deviation σ.

polyroots(**v**)	Roots of the nth degree polynomial whose coefficients are in **v**, a vector of length $n + 1$.
ppois(k, λ)	Cumulative Poisson distribution. $\lambda > 0$.
Pro predict(**v**, m, n)	A vector of n predicted values based on m consecutive elements in **v**, a vector whose values represent samples taken at equal intervals.
pspline(**vx**, **vy**)	Coefficients of cubic spline with parabolic ends. **vx** and **vy** are real vectors of same size. Elements of **vx** must be in ascending order.
pspline(**Mxy**, **Mz**)	Vector of second derivatives for data arrays **Mxy** and **Mz**. This vector becomes the first argument of the *interp* function. The resultant surface is parabolic at the boundaries of the region spanned by **Mxy**.
pt(x, d)	Cumulative Student's t distribution. d is the degrees of freedom. $x > 0$ and $d > 0$.
punif(x, a, b)	Cumulative uniform distribution. b and a are the endpoints of the interval. $a < b$.
pweibull(x, s)	Cumulative Weibull distribution. $s > 0$.
qbeta(p, s_1, s_2)	Inverse beta distribution with shape parameters s_1 and s_2. $0 \le p \le 1$ and $s_1, s_2 > 0$.
qbinom(p, n, q)	Number of successes in n trials of the Bernoulli process such that the probability of that number of successes is p. q is the probability of success on a single trial. $0 \le q \le 1$ and $0 \le p \le 1$.
qcauchy(p, l, s)	Inverse Cauchy distribution with scale parameters l and s. $s > 0$ and $0 < p < 1$.
qchisq(p, d)	Inverse chi-squared distribution in which $d > 0$ is the degrees of freedom. $0 \le p < 1$.
qexp(p, r)	Inverse exponential distribution in which $r > 0$ is the rate. $0 \le p < 1$.
qF(p, d_1, d_2)	Inverse F distribution in which $d_1, d_2 > 0$ are the degrees of freedom. $0 \le p < 1$.
qgamma(p, s)	Inverse gamma distribution in which $s > 0$ is the shape parameter. $0 \le p < 1$.
qgeom(p, q)	Inverse geometric distribution. q is the probability of success on a single trial. $0 < p < 1$ and $0 \le q < 1$.
qlnorm(p, μ, σ)	Inverse log normal distribution in which μ is the log of the mean, $\sigma > 0$ is the log of the standard deviation. $0 \le p < 1$.
qlogis(p, l, s)	Inverse logistic distribution. l is the location parameter. $s > 0$ is the scale parameter. $0 \le p < 1$.
qnbinom(p, n, q)	Inverse negative binomial distribution with size n and probability of failure q. $0 \le q \le 1$ and $0 \le p \le 1$.

	qnorm(p, μ, σ)	Inverse normal distribution with mean μ and standard deviation σ. $0 < p < 1$ and $\sigma > 0$.
	qpois(p, λ)	Inverse Poisson distribution. $\lambda > 0$ and $0 \le p \le 1$.
Pro	qr(**A**)	A matrix whose first n columns contain the square, orthonormal matrix **Q**, and whose remaining columns contain the upper triangular matrix, **R**. Matrices **Q** and **R** satisfy the equation $\mathbf{A} = \mathbf{Q} \cdot \mathbf{R}$, where **A** is a real-valued array.
	qt(p, d)	Inverse Student's t distribution. d is the degrees of freedom. $d > 0$ and $0 < p < 1$.
	qunif(p, a, b)	Inverse uniform distribution. b and a are the endpoints of the interval. $a < b$ and $0 \le p \le 1$.
	qweibull(p, s)	Inverse Weibull distribution. $s > 0$ and $0 < p < 1$.
	rank(**A**)	The rank of real-valued matrix **A**.
	rbeta(m, s_1, s_2)	Vector of m random numbers having the beta distribution. $s_1, s_2 > 0$ are the shape parameters.
	rbinom(m, n, p)	Vector of m random numbers having the binomial distribution. $0 \le p \le 1$. n is an integer satisfying $n > 0$.
	rcauchy(m, l, s)	Vector of m random numbers having the Cauchy distribution. l and $s > 0$ are scale parameters.
	rchisq(m, d)	Vector of m random numbers having the chi-squared distribution. $d > 0$ is the degrees of freedom.
	Re(z)	Real part of complex number z.
	READ(*file*)	Single value read from data file *file*.
Pro	READ_BLUE(*file*)	Matrix corresponding to the blue color component in image file *file*.
	READBMP(*file*)	Matrix containing a grayscale representation of the image in BMP image file *file*.
Pro	READ_GREEN(*file*)	Matrix corresponding to the green color component in image file *file*.
Pro	READ_HLS(*file*)	Matrix in which the color information in image file *file* is represented by the appropriate values of hue, saturation, and value.
Pro	READ_HLS_HUE(*file*)	Matrix corresponding to the hue color component in image file *file*.
Pro	READ_HLS_LIGHT(*file*)	Matrix corresponding to the lightness color component in image file *file*.
Pro	READ_HLS_SAT(*file*)	Matrix corresponding to the saturation color component in image file *file*.
Pro	READ_HSV(*file*)	Matrix in which the color information in image file *file* is represented by the appropriate values of hue, lightness, and saturation.
Pro	READ_HSV_HUE(*file*)	Matrix corresponding to the hue color component in image file *file*.

Pro	READ_HSV_SAT(*file*)	Matrix corresponding to the saturation color component in image file *file*.
Pro	READ_HSV_VALUE(*file*)	Matrix corresponding to the value color component in image file *file*.
Pro	READ_IMAGE(*file*)	Matrix containing a grayscale representation of the image file *file*. *file* may be in BMP, GIF, JPG, or TGA format.
	READPRN(*file*)	Matrix read from structured data file *file*.
Pro	READ_RED(*file*)	Matrix corresponding to the red color component in image file *file*.
	READRGB(*file*)	Array in which the color information in image file *file* is represented by the appropriate values of red, green, and blue. This array is formed by combining the three arrays giving the red, green, and blue components of the image into a single array with three times as many columns as the image.
	regress(**vx**, **vy**, *n*)	Vector required by the *interp* function to find the *n*th order polynomial that best fits data arrays **vx** and **vy**. **vx** is an *m* element vector containing *x* coordinates. **vy** is an *m* element vector containing the *y* coordinates corresponding to the *m* points specified in **vx**.
	regress(**Mxy**,**vz**, *n*)	Vector required by the *interp* function to find the *n*th order polynomial that best fits data arrays **Mxy** and **vz**. **Mxy** is an $m \times 2$ matrix containing *x-y* coordinates. **vz** is an *m* element vector containing the *z* coordinates corresponding to the *m* points specified in **Mxy**.
Pro	relax(**A, B, C, D, E, F, U**, *rjac*)	Solves the Poisson partial differential equation over a planar square region. $n \times n$ matrices **A**, **B**, **C**, **D**, and **E** specify coefficients for linearly approximating the Laplacian operator at each of n^2 gridpoints, $n \times n$ matrix **F** gives source function values, $n \times n$ matrix **U** prescribes boundary values along all four edges and guesses for interior values, and $0 < rjac < 1$ is the Jacobi spectral radius. More general than multigrid, which is faster.
	reverse(**v**)	Reverse order of elements in **v**.
	rexp(*m*, *r*)	Vector of *m* random numbers having the exponential distribution. $r > 0$ is the rate.
	rF(*m*, d_1, d_2)	Vector of *m* random numbers having the F distribution. $d_1, d_2 > 0$ are the degrees of freedom.
	rgamma(*m*, *s*)	Vector of *m* random numbers having the gamma distribution. $s > 0$ is the shape parameter.
	rgeom(*m*, *p*)	Vector of *m* random numbers having the geometric distribution. $0 < p \le 1$.

Pro	rkadapt(**y**, *x1, x2, acc*, **D**, *kmx, sv*)	Slowly varying Runge-Kutta differential equation solver, where **y** is the vector of *n* initial values, *n* is the order of the DE or size of the system of DEs, *x1* and *x2* are endpoints of the solution interval, *acc* controls accuracy, **D**(*x*, **y**) prescribes the derivatives, *kmx* is the maximum number of intermediate points, and *sv* is the minimum distance between *x* values (which needn't be equally spaced). Provides good DE solution estimate at *x2*.
Pro	Rkadapt(**y**, *x1, x2, npts*, **D**)	Slowly varying Runge-Kutta differential equation solver, where **y** is the vector of *n* initial values, *n* is the order of the DE or size of the system of DEs, *x1* and *x2* are endpoints of the solution interval, *npts* controls the number of rows in the matrix output, and **D**(*x*, **y**) prescribes the derivatives. Provides DE solution at equally-spaced *x* values by repeated calls to rkadapt.
	rkfixed(**y**, *x1, x2, npts*, **D**)	Standard Runge-Kutta differential equation solver, where **y** is the vector of *n* initial values, *n* is the order of the DE or size of the system of DEs, *x1* and *x2* are the endpoints of the solution interval, *npts* controls the number of rows in the matrix output, and **D**(*x*, **y**) prescribes the derivatives. Provides DE solution at equally spaced *x* values.
	rlnorm(*m*, μ, σ)	Vector of *m* random numbers having the lognormal distribution in which μ is the logmean and $\sigma > 0$ is the logdeviation.
	rlogis(*m*, *l*, *s*)	Vector of *m* random numbers having the logistic distribution in which *l* is the location parameter and $s > 0$ is the scale parameter.
	rnbinom(*m*, *n*, *p*)	Vector of *m* random numbers having the negative binomial distribution. $0 < p \leq 1$. *n* is an integer satisfying $n > 0$.
	rnd(*x*)	Random number between 0 and *x*, *x* real. Identical to runif(1, 0, *x*) if $x > 0$.
	rnorm(*m*, μ, σ)	Vector of *m* random numbers having the normal distribution with mean μ and standard deviation $\sigma > 0$.
	root(*expr*, *var*)	Value of *var* where *expr* is zero.
	rows(**A**)	Number of rows in array **A**. Returns a scalar.
	rpois(*m*, λ)	Vector of *m* random numbers having the Poisson distribution. $\lambda > 0$.
	rref(**A**)	A matrix representing the row-reduced echelon form of **A**.
	rsort(**A**, *n*)	Sort columns so as to put row *n* in ascending order.
	rt(*m*, *d*)	Vector of *m* random numbers having Student's *t* distribution. $d > 0$.
	runif(*m*, *a*, *b*)	Vector of *m* random numbers having the uniform distribution in which *b* and *a* are the endpoints of the interval and $a < b$.
	rweibull(*m*, *s*)	Vector of *m* random numbers having the Weibull distribution in which $s > 0$ is the shape parameter.

Pro	sbval(**v**, *x1*, *x2*, **D**, **ld**, **sc**)	Converts a boundary value differential equation to an initial value problem. **v** is the guess vector for missing initial values, *x1* and *x2* are endpoints of the solution interval, the *n*-vector **D**(*x*, **y**) prescribes the derivatives, *n* is the order of the DE, the *n*-vector **ld**(*x1*, **v**) contains both known initial conditions and guess values from **v**, and the *n*-vector **sc**(*x2*, **y**) measures solution discrepancy at *x2*. Good when derivatives are continuous throughout.
	sec(*z*)	Secant. Argument in radians.
	sech(*z*)	Hyperbolic secant.
Pro	search(*S1*, *SubS*, *m*)	The starting position of the substring *SubS* in *S1* beginning from position *m*. Returns −1 if the substring is not found. $m \geq 0$.
	sin(*z*)	Sine. Argument in radians.
	sinh(*z*)	Hyperbolic sine.
	slope(**vx**, **vy**)	Slope of regression line. Takes two vector arguments **vx** and **vy** of the same size. The elements of **vx** must be in ascending order.
	sort(**v**)	Sort elements in vector **v**.
	stack(**A**, **B**)	Array formed by placing **A** above **B**. The arrays **A** and **B** must have the same number of columns.
	stdev(**A**)	Standard deviation of elements of **A**. Uses *n* in the denominator. Returns a scalar.
	Stdev(**A**)	Sample standard deviation of elements of **A**. Uses $n - 1$ in the denominator. Returns a scalar.
Pro	stiffb(**y**, *x1*, *x2*, *acc*, **D**, **J**, *kmx*, *sv*)	Stiff Bulirsch-Stoer differential equation solver, where **y** is the vector of n initial values, *n* is the order of the DE or size of the system of DEs, *x1* and *x2* are endpoints of the solution interval, *acc* controls accuracy, **D**(*x*, **y**) prescribes the derivatives, **J**(*x*, **y**) is the Jacobian matrix prescribing the second derivatives, *kmx* is the maximum number of intermediate points, and *sv* is the minimum distance between *x* values (which needn't be equally spaced). Provides good DE solution estimate at *x2*.
Pro	Stiffb(**y**, *x1*, *x2*, *npts*, **D**, **J**)	Stiff Bulirsch-Stoer differential equation solver, where **y** is the vector of *n* initial values, *n* is the order of the DE or size of the system of DEs, *x1* and *x2* are endpoints of the solution interval, *npts* controls the number of rows in the matrix output, **D**(*x*, **y**) prescribes the derivatives, and **J**(*x*, **y**) is the Jacobian matrix prescribing the second derivatives. Provides DE solution at equally-spaced *x* values by repeated calls to stiffb.
Pro	stiffr(**y**, *x1*, *x2*, *acc*, **D**, **J**, *kmx*, *sv*)	Stiff Rosenbrock differential equation solver, where **y** is the vector of n initial values, *n* is the order of the DE or size of the system of DEs, *x1* and *x2* are endpoints of the solution interval, *acc* controls accuracy, **D**(*x*, **y**) prescribes the derivatives, **J**(*x*, **y**) is the Jacobian matrix prescribes the second derivatives, *kmx* is the maximum number of intermediate points, and *sv* is the minimum distance between *x* values (which needn't be equally spaced). Provides good DE solution estimate at *x2*.

Pro	Stiffr(**y**, *x1*, *x2*, *npts*, **D**, **J**)	Stiff Rosenbrock differential equation solver, where **y** is the vector of *n* initial values, *n* is the order of the DE or size of the system of DEs, *x1* and *x2* are endpoints of the solution interval, *npts* controls the number of rows in the matrix output, **D**(*x*, **y**) prescribes the derivatives, and **J**(*x*, **y**) is the Jacobian matrix prescribing the second derivatives. Provides DE solution at equally spaced *x* values by repeated calls to stiffr.
Pro	str2num(*S*)	A numerical constant formed by converting the characters in *S* into a number. Characters in *S* must constitute a real, complex, floating point, or e-format number. Spaces are ignored.
Pro	str2vec(*S*)	A vector of ASCII codes corresponding to the characters in string *S*.
Pro	strlen(*S*)	The number of characters in string *S*.
	submatrix(**A**, *ir*, *jr*, *ic*, *jc*)	Submatrix of **A** consisting of all elements common to rows *ir* through *jr* and columns *ic* through *jc*. To maintain order of rows and/or columns, make sure $ir \leq jr$ and $ic \leq jc$, otherwise order of rows and/or columns will be reversed.
Pro	substr(*S*, *m*, *n*)	A substring of *S* beginning with the character in the *m*th position and having at most *n* characters. $m, n \geq 0$.
Pro	supsmooth(**vx**, **vy**)	An *n*-element vector created by the piecewise use of a symmetric *k*-nearest neighbor linear least square fitting procedure in which *k* is adaptively chosen. **vy** and **vx** are *n*-element vectors of real numbers. The elements of **vx** must be in increasing order.
Pro	svd(**A**)	One matrix containing two stacked matrices **U** and **V**, where **U** is the upper $m \times n$ submatrix and **V** is the lower $n \times n$ submatrix. Matrices **U** and **V** satisfy the equation $\mathbf{A} = \mathbf{U} \cdot \mathrm{diag}(\mathbf{s}) \cdot \mathbf{V}^{\mathbf{T}}$, where **s** is the vector returned by svds(**A**). **A** is an $m \times n$ array of real values, where $m \geq n$.
Pro	svds(**A**)	A vector containing the singular values of the $m \times n$ real-valued array **A**, where $m \geq n$.
	tan(*z*)	Tangent. Argument in radians.
	tanh(*z*)	Hyperbolic tangent.
	tr(**M**)	Trace of square matrix **M**: sum of diagonal elements.
	until(*x*, *y*)	Returns *y* until *x* is negative.
	var(**A**)	Variance of elements of **A**. Uses *n* in the denominator. Returns a scalar.
	Var(**A**)	Sample variance of elements of **A**. Uses $n - 1$ in the denominator. Returns a scalar.
Pro	vec2str(**v**)	The string formed by converting the vector **v** of ASCII codes to characters. The elements of **v** must be integers between 0 and 255.
Pro	wave(**v**)	Discrete wavelet transform of real data using Daubechies four-coefficient wavelet filter. Vector **v** must contain 2^n real values, where *n* is an integer.

	WRITE(*file*)	Single value written to a data file *file*.
	WRITEBMP(*file*)	Grayscale BMP image file *file* out of a matrix.
Pro	WRITE_HLS(*file*)	Color BMP image file *file* out of an array formed by juxtaposing the three arrays giving the hue, lightness, and saturation values of an image.
Pro	WRITE_HSV(*file*)	Color BMP image file *file* out of an array formed by juxtaposing the three arrays giving the hue, saturation, and value components of an image.
	WRITEPRN(*file*)	Structured data file out of a matrix.
	WRITERGB(*file*)	Colored BMP file out of an array formed by juxtaposing the three arrays giving the red, green, and blue values of an image.
	Y0(x)	Bessel function $Y_0(x)$. Argument must be positive.
	Y1(x)	Bessel function $Y_1(x)$. Argument must be positive.
	Yn(m, x)	Bessel function $Y_m(x)$. x must be positive; $0 \le m \le 100$.
	$\delta(x, y)$	Kronecker delta function. Returns 1 if $x=y$; otherwise, returns 0. (To type δ, press **d[Ctrl]G**)
	$\varepsilon(i, j, k)$	Completely antisymmetric tensor of rank three. i, j, and k must be integers between 0 and 2 (or between ORIGIN and ORIGIN+2). Result is 0 if any two are the same, 1 if the three arguments are an even permutation of (0 1 2), and –1 if the arguments are an odd permutation of (0 1 2). (To type ε, press **e[Ctrl]G**)
	$\Gamma(z)$	Euler's gamma function. (To type Γ, press **G[Ctrl]G**)
	$\Phi(x)$	Heaviside step function. Returns 1 if $x \ge 0$; otherwise, returns 0. (To type Φ, press **F[Ctrl]G**)

Predefined variables

Mathcad's predefined variables are listed here, together with their default starting values.

Constant=Value	Meaning
$\pi = 3.14159...$	Pi. Mathcad uses the value of π to 15 digits. To type π, press [Ctrl]p.
$e = 2.71828...$	The base of natural logarithms. Mathcad uses the value of e to 15 digits.
$\infty = 10^{307}$	Infinity. This symbol represents values larger than the largest real number representable in Mathcad (about 10^{307}). Do not use this variable in place of actual infinities in numerical formulas. To type ∞, press [Ctrl]Z.
$\% = 0.01$	Percent. Use in expressions like 10*% (appears as $10 \cdot \%$) or as a scaling unit at the end of an equation with an equals sign.
TOL $= 10^{-3}$	Tolerance. The tolerance Mathcad uses in numerical approximation algorithms (integrals, equation solving, etc.). For more information, see the section on the specific operation in question.
ORIGIN $= 0$	Array origin. Specifies the index of the first element in arrays.
PRNCOLWIDTH $= 8$	Column width used in writing files with *WRITEPRN* function.
PRNPRECISION $= 4$	Number of significant digits used when writing files with the *WRITEPRN* function.
FRAME $= 0$	Used as a counter for creating animation clips.
CWD = "<system path>"	String corresponding to the working directory of the worksheet.
in$n = 0$, out$n = 0$	Input and output variables (in0, in1, out0, out1, etc.) in a Mathcad component in a MathConnex system. See the *MathConnex Getting Started Guide* for details.

Pro (CWD row)
Pro (in$n$ row)

Suffixes for numbers

The table below shows how Mathcad interprets numbers. (A number is any sequence of characters beginning with a digit.)

Suffix	Examples	Meaning
i *or* j	4i, 1j, 3 + 1.5j	Imaginary
H *or* h	0aH, 8BCh	Hexadecimal
O *or* o	57O, 100o	Octal
L	−2.54L	Standard length unit
M	2.2M	Standard mass unit
T	3600T	Standard time unit
Q	−100Q	Standard charge unit
K	−273K	Standard absolute temperature unit
U	125U	Standard luminosity unit in SI unit system
S	6.97S	Standard substance unit in SI unit system

Arrow and movement keys

Keys	Actions
[↑]	Move crosshair up. In math: move editing lines up. In text: move insertion point up to previous line.
[↓]	Move crosshair down. In math: move editing lines down. In text: move insertion point down to next line.
[←]	Move crosshair left. In math: select left operand. In text: move insertion point one character to the left.
[→]	Move crosshair right. In math: select right operand. In text: move insertion point one character to the right.
[Shift][↑]	In math: move crosshair outside and above equation. In text: highlight from insertion point up to previous line.
[Shift][↓]	In math: move crosshair outside and below equation. In text: highlight from insertion point down to next line.
[Shift][←]	In math: move crosshair outside and to the left of equation. In text: highlight towards the left of the insertion point, character by character.
[Shift][→]	In math: move crosshair outside and to the right of equation. In text: highlight towards the right of the insertion point, character by character.
[Ctrl][↑]	In text: move insertion point to the beginning of a line.
[Ctrl][↓]	In text: move insertion point to the beginning of next line.
[Ctrl][←]	In text: move insertion point left to the beginning of a word.
[Ctrl][→]	In text: move insertion point to the beginning of next word.
[Ctrl][Shift][↑]	In text: highlight from insertion point up to the beginning of a line.
[Ctrl][Shift][↓]	In text: highlight from insertion point to end of the current line.
[Ctrl][Shift][←]	Highlight left from insertion point to the beginning of a word.
[Ctrl][Shift][→]	Highlight from insertion point to beginning of the next word.

Keys	Actions
[Space]	In math: cycles through different states of the editing lines.
[Tab]	In text: inserts a five-character space. In array or plot: move to next placeholder.
[Shift][Tab]	In array or plot: move to previous placeholder.
[PgUp]	Move up 5 lines.
[PgDn]	Move down 5 lines.
[Ctrl][PgUp]	Move 80% up the window.
[Ctrl][PgDn]	Move 80% down the window.
[Shift][PgUp]	Move up to previous pagebreak.
[Shift][PgDn]	Move down to next pagebreak.
[Home]	In equation, move to beginning previous region. In text, move to beginning of current line.
[End]	In equation, move to next region. In text, move to end of current line.
[Ctrl][Home]	Scroll to beginning of worksheet. In text, move insertion point to beginning of text region or paragraph.
[Ctrl][End]	Scroll to end of worksheet. In text, move insertion point to end of text region or paragraph.
[↵]	In text: start new line. In equation or plot: move crosshair below region, even with left edge of region.

ASCII codes

Decimal ASCII codes from 32 to 255. Characters corresponding to codes 0–31 are nonprinting, as are characters in the table indicated by "*npc*."

Code	Character	Code	Character	Code	Character	Code	Character	Code	Character
32	[space]	80	P	130	‚	182	¶	230	æ
33	!	81	Q	131	ƒ	183	·	231	ç
34	"	82	R	132	„	184	¸	232	è
35	#	83	S	133	…	185	¹	233	é
36	$	84	T	134	†	186	º	234	ê
37	%	85	U	135	‡	187	»	235	ë
38	&	86	V	136	^	188	¼	236	ì
39	'	87	W	137	‰	189	½	237	í
40	(	88	X	138	Š	190	¾	238	î
41	)	89	Y	139	‹	191	¿	239	ï
42	*	90	Z	140	Œ	192	À	240	ð
43	+	91	[	141–4	*npc*	193	Á	241	ñ
44	,	92	\	145	'	194	Â	242	ò
45	-	93	]	146	'	195	Ã	243	ó
46	.	94	^	147	"	196	Ä	244	ô
47	/	95	_	148	"	197	Å	245	õ
48	0	96	`	149	•	198	Æ	246	ö
49	1	97	a	150	–	199	Ç	247	÷
50	2	98	b	151	—	200	È	248	ø
51	3	99	c	152	~	201	É	249	ù
52	4	100	d	153	™	202	Ê	250	ú
53	5	101	e	154	š	203	Ë	251	û
54	6	102	f	155	›	204	Ì	252	ü
55	7	103	g	156	œ	205	Í	253	ý
56	8	104	h	157–8	*npc*	206	Î	254	þ
57	9	105	i	159	Ÿ	207	Ï	255	ÿ
58	:	106	j	160	*npc*	208	Ð		
59	;	107	k	161	¡	209	Ñ		
60	<	108	l	162	¢	210	Ò		
61	=	109	m	163	£	211	Ó		
62	>	110	n	164	¤	212	Ô		
63	?	111	o	165	¥	213	Õ		
64	@	112	p	166	¦	214	Ö		
65	A	113	q	167	§	215	×		
66	B	114	r	168	¨	216	Ø		
67	C	115	s	169	©	217	Ù		
68	D	116	t	170	ª	218	Ú		
69	E	117	u	171	«	219	Û		
70	F	118	v	172	¬	220	Ü		
71	G	119	w	173	-	221	Ý		
72	H	120	x	174	®	222	Þ		
73	I	121	y	175	¯	223	ß		
74	J	122	z	176	°	224	à		
75	K	123	{	177	±	225	á		
76	L	124	|	178	²	226	â		
77	M	125	}	179	³	227	ã		
78	N	126	~	180	´	228	ä		
79	O	127–9	*npc*	181	µ	229	å		

Reference

Appendix B
Unit Tables

Mathcad comes with four built-in systems of units and uses the SI system by default. You can select a system of units by choosing **Options** from the **Math** menu as discussed in Chapter 9, "Units and Dimensions."

Once you make a selection, several dozen variable names are automatically reserved for unit definitions unique to whatever system of units you chose. This appendix lists the unit definitions associated with each of the available unit systems.

If you choose a system of units, you should try not to use the predefined variables listed in this appendix as anything but units.

This appendix includes the following sections:

SI units
CGS units
U.S. customary units
MKS units
Alphabetical list of units

SI units

Base units

m (meter), *length*

kg (kilogram), *mass*

s (second), *time*

A (ampere), *current*

K (kelvin), *temperature*

cd (candela), *luminosity*

mole, *substance*

Angular measure

$rad = 1$

$deg = \dfrac{\pi}{180} \cdot rad$

$str = 1 \cdot str$

Length

$cm = 0.01 \cdot m$

$km = 1000 \cdot m$

$mm = 0.001 \cdot m$

$ft = 0.3048 \cdot m$

$in = 2.54 \cdot cm$

$yd = 3 \cdot ft$

$mi = 5280 \cdot ft$

Mass

$gm = 10^{-3} \cdot kg$

$tonne = 1000 \cdot kg$

$lb = 453.59237 \cdot gm$

$mg = 10^{-3} \cdot gm$

$ton = 2000 \cdot lb$

$slug = 32.174 \cdot lb$

$oz = \dfrac{lb}{16}$

Time

$min = 60 \cdot s$

$hr = 3600 \cdot s$

$day = 24 \cdot hr$

$yr = 365.2422 \cdot day$

Area, Volume

$hectare = 10^4 \cdot m^2$

$acre = 4840 \cdot yd^2$

$L = 0.001 \cdot m^3$

$mL = 10^{-3} \cdot L$

$fl\_oz = 29.57353 \cdot cm^3$

$gal = 128 \cdot fl\_oz$

Velocity, Acceleration

$mph = \dfrac{mi}{hr}$

$kph = \dfrac{km}{hr}$

$g = 9.80665 \cdot \dfrac{m}{s^2}$

Force, Energy, Power

$N = kg \cdot \dfrac{m}{s^2}$

$dyne = 10^{-5} \cdot N$

$lbf = g \cdot lb$

$kgf = g \cdot kg$

$J = N \cdot m$

$erg = 10^{-7} \cdot J$

$cal = 4.1868 \cdot J$

$kcal = 1000 \cdot cal$

$BTU = 1.05506 \cdot 10^3 \cdot J$

$W = \dfrac{J}{s}$

$kW = 1000 \cdot W$

$hp = 550 \cdot \dfrac{ft \cdot lbf}{s}$

Pressure, Viscosity

$$Pa = \frac{N}{m^2}$$

$$psi = \frac{lbf}{in^2}$$

$$atm = 1.01325 \cdot 10^5 \cdot Pa$$

$$in\_Hg = 3.38638 \cdot 10^3 \cdot Pa$$

$$torr = 1.33322 \cdot 10^2 \cdot Pa$$

$$stokes = 10^{-4} \cdot \frac{m^2}{s}$$

$$poise = 0.1 \cdot Pa \cdot s$$

Electrical

$$C = A \cdot s$$

$$V = \frac{J}{C}$$

$$mV = 10^{-3} \cdot V$$

$$KV = 10^3 \cdot V$$

$$\Omega = \frac{V}{A}$$

$$k\Omega = 10^3 \cdot \Omega$$

$$M\Omega = 10^6 \cdot \Omega$$

$$S = \frac{1}{\Omega}$$

$$mho = \frac{1}{\Omega}$$

$$H = \frac{V}{A} \cdot s$$

$$\mu H = 10^{-6} \cdot H$$

$$mH = 10^{-3} \cdot H$$

$$\mu A = 10^{-6} \cdot A$$

$$mA = 10^{-3} \cdot A$$

$$kA = 10^3 \cdot A$$

$$F = \frac{C}{V}$$

$$pF = 10^{-12} \cdot F$$

$$nF = 10^{-9} \cdot F$$

$$\mu F = 10^{-6} \cdot F$$

$$Wb = V \cdot s$$

$$Oe = \frac{1000}{4 \cdot \pi} \cdot \frac{A}{m}$$

$$T = \frac{Wb}{m^2}$$

$$gauss = 10^{-4} \cdot T$$

Frequency, Activity

$$Hz = \frac{1}{s}$$

$$kHz = 10^3 \cdot Hz$$

$$MHz = 10^6 \cdot Hz$$

$$GHz = 10^9 \cdot Hz$$

$$Bq = \frac{1}{s}$$

Temperature

$$R = 0.556 \cdot K$$

Dose

$$Gy = \frac{J}{kg}$$

$$Sv = \frac{J}{kg}$$

Luminous flux, illuminance

$$lm = cd \cdot str$$

$$lx = \frac{cd \cdot str}{m^2}$$

CGS units

Base units

cm (centimeter), *length*   gm (gram), *mass*   sec (second), *time*

coul (coulomb), *charge*   K (kelvin), *temperature*

Angular measure

$$\mathrm{rad} = 1$$

$$\deg = \frac{\pi}{180} \cdot \mathrm{rad}$$

Length

$$m = 100 \cdot cm$$

$$km = 1000 \cdot m$$

$$mm = 0.1 \cdot cm$$

$$ft = 30.48 \cdot cm$$

$$in = 2.54 \cdot cm$$

$$yd = 3 \cdot ft$$

$$mi = 5280 \cdot ft$$

Mass

$$kg = 1000 \cdot gm$$

$$tonne = 1000 \cdot kg$$

$$lb = 453.59237 \cdot gm$$

$$mg = 10^{-3} \cdot gm$$

$$ton = 2000 \cdot lb$$

$$slug = 32.174 \cdot lb$$

$$oz = \frac{lb}{16}$$

Time

$$min = 60 \cdot sec$$

$$hr = 3600 \cdot sec$$

$$day = 24 \cdot hr$$

$$yr = 365.2422 \cdot day$$

Area, Volume

$$hectare = 10^4 \cdot m^2$$

$$acre = 4840 \cdot yd^2$$

$$liter = 1000 \cdot cm^3$$

$$mL = cm^3$$

$$fl\_oz = 29.57353 \cdot cm^3$$

$$gal = 128 \cdot fl\_oz$$

Velocity, Acceleration

$$mph = \frac{mi}{hr}$$

$$kph = \frac{km}{hr}$$

$$g = 980.665 \cdot \frac{cm}{sec^2}$$

$$c = 2.997925 \cdot 10^{10} \cdot \frac{cm}{sec}$$

$$c\_ = c \cdot \frac{sec}{m}$$

Force, Energy, Power

$$\text{dyne} = \text{gm} \cdot \frac{\text{cm}}{\text{sec}^2}$$

$$\text{newton} = 10^5 \cdot \text{dyne}$$

$$\text{lbf} = g \cdot \text{lb}$$

$$\text{kgf} = g \cdot \text{kg}$$

$$\text{erg} = \text{dyne} \cdot \text{cm}$$

$$\text{joule} = 10^7 \cdot \text{erg}$$

$$\text{cal} = 4.1868 \cdot 10^7 \cdot \text{erg}$$

$$\text{BTU} = 1.05506 \cdot 10^{10} \cdot \text{erg}$$

$$\text{kcal} = 1000 \cdot \text{cal}$$

$$\text{watt} = \frac{\text{joule}}{\text{sec}}$$

$$\text{kW} = 1000 \cdot \text{watt}$$

$$\text{hp} = 550 \cdot \frac{\text{ft} \cdot \text{lbf}}{\text{sec}}$$

Pressure, Viscosity

$$\text{Pa} = 10 \cdot \frac{\text{dyne}}{\text{cm}^2}$$

$$\text{psi} = \frac{\text{lbf}}{\text{in}^2}$$

$$\text{atm} = 1.01325 \cdot 10^5 \cdot \text{Pa}$$

$$\text{in\_Hg} = 3.38638 \cdot 10^3 \cdot \text{Pa}$$

$$\text{torr} = 1.33322 \cdot 10^2 \cdot \text{Pa}$$

$$\text{stokes} = \frac{\text{cm}^2}{\text{sec}}$$

$$\text{poise} = 0.1 \cdot \text{Pa} \cdot \text{sec}$$

Electrical

These are CGS-esu units, based only on mass, length, and time. The "stat" units are defined in terms of dyne, cm, and sec.

$$\text{statamp} = \text{dyne}^{0.5} \cdot \text{cm} \cdot \text{sec}^{-1}$$

$$\text{statcoul} = \text{dyne}^{0.5} \cdot \text{cm}$$

$$\text{statvolt} = \text{dyne}^{0.5}$$

$$\text{statohm} = \text{sec} \cdot \text{cm}^{-1}$$

$$\text{statsiemens} = \text{cm} \cdot \text{sec}^{-1}$$

$$\text{statfarad} = \text{cm}$$

$$\text{statweber} = \text{dyne}^{0.5} \cdot \text{cm}$$

$$\text{stathenry} = \text{sec}^2 \cdot \text{cm}^{-1}$$

$$\text{statesla} = \text{dyne}^{0.5} \cdot \text{cm} \cdot \text{sec}^{-2}$$

Frequency

$$\text{Hz} = \frac{1}{\text{sec}}$$

$$\text{KHz} = 10^3 \cdot \text{Hz}$$

$$\text{MHz} = 10^6 \cdot \text{Hz}$$

$$\text{GHz} = 10^9 \cdot \text{Hz}$$

Temperature

$$R = 0.556 \cdot K$$

Conversions to SI Units

$$\text{amp} = \frac{c}{10} \cdot \text{statamp}$$

$$\text{volt} = \frac{\text{watt}}{\text{amp}}$$

$$\text{ohm} = \frac{\text{volt}}{\text{amp}}$$

$$\text{coul} = \text{amp} \cdot \text{sec}$$

$$\text{farad} = \frac{\text{coul}}{\text{volt}}$$

$$\text{henry} = \text{volt} \cdot \frac{\text{sec}}{\text{amp}}$$

U.S. customary units

Base units

ft (foot), *length*   lb (pound), *mass*   sec (second), *time*

coul (coulomb), *charge*   K (kelvin), *temperature*

Angular measure

$$rad = 1$$

$$deg = \frac{\pi}{180} \cdot rad$$

Length

$$in = \frac{ft}{12}$$

$$m = \frac{ft}{0.3048}$$

$$yd = 3 \cdot ft$$

$$cm = 0.01 \cdot m$$

$$mi = 5280 \cdot ft$$

$$km = 1000 \cdot m$$

$$mm = 0.001 \cdot m$$

Mass

$$slug = 32.174 \cdot lb$$

$$oz = \frac{lb}{16}$$

$$ton = 2000 \cdot lb$$

$$kg = \frac{lb}{0.45359237}$$

$$tonne = 1000 \cdot kg$$

$$gm = 10^{-3} \cdot kg$$

$$mg = 10^{-3} \cdot gm$$

Time

$$min = 60 \cdot sec$$

$$hr = 3600 \cdot sec$$

$$day = 24 \cdot hr$$

$$yr = 365.2422 \cdot day$$

Area, Volume

$$acre = 4840 \cdot yd^2$$

$$hectare = 10^4 \cdot m^2$$

$$fl\_oz = 29.57353 \cdot cm^3$$

$$liter = (0.1 \cdot m)^2$$

$$mL = 10^{-3} \cdot liter$$

$$gal = 128 \cdot fl\_oz$$

Velocity, Acceleration

$$mph = \frac{mi}{hr}$$

$$kph = \frac{km}{hr}$$

$$g = 32.174 \cdot \frac{ft}{sec^2}$$

Force, Energy, Power

$$lbf = g \cdot lb$$

$$newton = kg \cdot \frac{m}{sec^2}$$

$$dyne = 10^{-5} \cdot newton$$

$$kgf = g \cdot kg$$

$$joule = newton \cdot m$$

$$erg = 10^{-7} \cdot joule$$

$$cal = 4.1868 \cdot joule$$

$$kcal = 1000 \cdot cal$$

$$BTU = 1.05506 \cdot 10^3 \cdot joule$$

$$watt = \frac{joule}{sec}$$

$$hp = 550 \cdot \frac{ft \cdot lbf}{sec}$$

$$kW = 1000 \cdot watt$$

Pressure, Viscosity

$$psi = \frac{lbf}{in^2}$$

$$Pa = \frac{newton}{m^2}$$

$$atm = 1.01325 \cdot 10^5 \cdot Pa$$

$$in\_Hg = 3.38638 \cdot 10^3 \cdot Pa$$

$$torr = 1.33322 \cdot 10^2 \cdot Pa$$

$$stokes = \frac{cm^2}{sec}$$

$$poise = 0.1 \cdot Pa \cdot sec$$

Electrical

$$volt = \frac{watt}{amp}$$

$$mV = 10^{-3} \cdot volt$$

$$KV = 10^3 \cdot volt$$

$$ohm = \frac{volt}{amp}$$

$$mho = \frac{1}{ohm}$$

$$siemens = \frac{1}{ohm}$$

$$\Omega = ohm$$

$$K\Omega = 10^3 \cdot ohm$$

$$M\Omega = 10^6 \cdot ohm$$

$$henry = \frac{weber}{amp}$$

$$\mu H = 10^{-6} \cdot henry$$

$$mH = 10^{-3} \cdot henry$$

$$amp = \frac{coul}{sec}$$

$$\mu A = 10^{-6} \cdot amp$$

$$mA = 10^{-3} \cdot amp$$

$$KA = 10^3 \cdot amp$$

$$farad = \frac{coul}{volt}$$

$$pF = 10^{-12} \cdot farad$$

$$nF = 10^{-9} \cdot farad$$

$$\mu F = 10^{-6} \cdot farad$$

$$weber = volt \cdot sec$$

$$oersted = \frac{1000}{4 \cdot \pi} \cdot \frac{amp}{m}$$

$$tesla = \frac{weber}{m^2}$$

$$gauss = 10^{-4} \cdot tesla$$

Frequency

$$Hz = \frac{1}{sec}$$

$$KHz = 10^3 \cdot Hz$$

$$MHz = 10^6 \cdot Hz$$

$$GHz = 10^9 \cdot Hz$$

Temperature

$$R = 0.556 \cdot K$$

MKS units

Base units

m (meter), *length*   kg (kilogram), *mass*   sec (second), *time*

coul (coulomb), *charge*   K (kelvin), *temperature*

Angular measure

$rad = 1$ $deg = \dfrac{\pi}{180} \cdot rad$

Length

$cm = 0.01 \cdot m$ $km = 1000 \cdot m$ $mm = 0.001 \cdot m$

$ft = 0.3048 \cdot m$ $in = 2.54 \cdot cm$ $yd = 3 \cdot ft$

$mi = 5280 \cdot ft$

Mass

$gm = 10^{-3} \cdot kg$ $tonne = 1000 \cdot kg$ $lb = 453.59237 \cdot gm$

$mg = 10^{-3} \cdot gm$ $ton = 2000 \cdot lb$ $slug = 32.174 \cdot lb$

$oz = \dfrac{lb}{16}$

Time

$min = 60 \cdot sec$ $hr = 3600 \cdot sec$ $day = 24 \cdot hr$

$yr = 365.2422 \cdot day$

Area, Volume

$hectare = 10^4 \cdot m^2$ $acre = 4840 \cdot yd^2$ $liter = (0.1 \cdot m)^3$

$mL = 10^{-3} \cdot liter$ $fl\_oz = 29.57353 \cdot cm^3$ $gal = 128 \cdot fl\_oz$

Velocity, Acceleration

$mph = \dfrac{mi}{hr}$ $kph = \dfrac{km}{hr}$ $g = 9.80665 \cdot \dfrac{m}{sec^2}$

Force, Energy, Power

$newton = kg \cdot \dfrac{m}{sec^2}$ $dyne = 10^{-5} \cdot newton$ $lbf = g \cdot lb$

$kgf = g \cdot kg$ $joule = newton \cdot m$ $erg = 10^{-7} \cdot joule$

$cal = 4.1868 \cdot joule$ $kcal = 1000 \cdot cal$ $BTU = 1.05506 \cdot 10^3 \cdot joule$

$watt = \dfrac{joule}{sec}$ $kW = 1000 \cdot watt$ $hp = 550 \cdot \dfrac{ft \cdot lbf}{sec}$

Pressure, Viscosity

$$Pa = \frac{newton}{m^2}$$

$$psi = \frac{lbf}{in^2}$$

$$atm = 1.01325 \cdot 10^5 \cdot Pa$$

$$in\_Hg = 3.38638 \cdot 10^3 \cdot Pa$$

$$torr = 1.33322 \cdot 10^2 \cdot Pa$$

$$stokes = 10^{-4} \cdot \frac{m^2}{sec}$$

$$poise = 0.1 \cdot Pa \cdot sec$$

Electrical

$$volt = \frac{watt}{amp}$$

$$mV = 10^{-3} \cdot volt$$

$$KV = 10^3 \cdot volt$$

$$ohm = \frac{volt}{amp}$$

$$mho = \frac{1}{ohm}$$

$$siemens = \frac{1}{ohm}$$

$$\Omega = ohm$$

$$K\Omega = 10^3 \cdot ohm$$

$$M\Omega = 10^6 \cdot ohm$$

$$henry = \frac{weber}{amp}$$

$$\mu H = 10^{-6} \cdot henry$$

$$mH = 10^{-3} \cdot henry$$

$$amp = \frac{coul}{sec}$$

$$\mu A = 10^{-6} \cdot amp$$

$$mA = 10^{-3} \cdot amp$$

$$KA = 10^3 \cdot amp$$

$$farad = \frac{coul}{volt}$$

$$pF = 10^{-12} \cdot farad$$

$$nF = 10^{-9} \cdot farad$$

$$\mu F = 10^{-6} \cdot farad$$

$$weber = volt \cdot sec$$

$$oersted = \frac{1000}{4 \cdot \pi} \cdot \frac{amp}{m}$$

$$tesla = \frac{weber}{m^2}$$

$$gauss = 10^{-4} \cdot tesla$$

Frequency

$$Hz = \frac{1}{sec}$$

$$KHz = 10^3 \cdot Hz$$

$$MHz = 10^6 \cdot Hz$$

$$GHz = 10^9 \cdot Hz$$

Temperature

$$R = 0.556 \cdot K$$

Alphabetical list of units

Unless otherwise specified, all units are available in the SI, CGS, U.S., and MKS systems.

Unit	Measures...	Available in . . .
A	current	SI
acre	area	
amp	current	
atm	pressure	
Bq	activity	
BTU	energy	
c	velocity	CGS
c_	dimensionless	CGS
C	charge	SI
cal	energy	
cd	luminous intensity	
cm	length	
coul	charge	
day	time	
deg	angle	
dyne	force	
erg	energy	
F	capacitance	SI
farad	capacitance	
fl_oz	volume	
ft	length	
g	acceleration	
gal	volume	
gauss	magnetic flux density	SI, U.S., MKS
GHz	frequency	
gm	mass	
Gy	dose	
H	inductance	SI
hectare	area	
henry	inductance	
hp	power	

Unit	Measures...	Available in . . .
hr	time	
Hz	frequency	
in	length	
in_Hg	pressure	
J	energy	SI
joule	energy	
K	temperature	
kA	current	SI
KA	current	
kcal	energy	
kg	mass	
kgf	force	
kHz	frequency	SI
KHz	frequency	
km	length	
kph	velocity	
kV	potential	SI
KV	potential	
kW	power	
kΩ	resistance	SI
L	volume	SI
lb	mass	
lbf	force	
liter	volume	
lm	luminous flux	
lx	illuminance	
μA	current	
μF	capacitance	
μH	inductance	
m	length	
MΩ	resistance	
mA	current	
mg	mass	
mH	inductance	
mho	conductance	

Unit	Measures...	Available in . . .
MHz	frequency	
mi	length	
min	time	
mL	volume	
mm	length	
mole	substance	
mph	velocity	
mV	potential	
N	force	SI
newton	force	
nF	capacitance	
Oe	magnetic field strength	SI
oersted	magnetic field strength	MKS, U.S., SI
ohm	resistance	
oz	mass	
Pa	pressure	
pF	capacitance	
poise	viscosity (dynamic)	
psi	pressure	
R	temperature	
rad	angle	
s	time	SI
S	conductance	SI
sec	time	
siemens	conductance	MKS, U.S., SI
slug	mass	
statamp	current	CGS
statcoul	charge	CGS
statfarad	capacitance	CGS
stathenry	inductance	CGS
statohm	resistance	CGS
statsiemens	conductance	CGS
stattesla	magnetic flux density	CGS
statvolt	potential	CGS
statweber	magnetic flux	CGS

Unit	Measures...	Available in . . .
stokes	viscosity (kinematic)	
str	angle	
Sv	dose	
T	magnetic flux density	SI
tesla	magnetic flux density	MKS, U.S., SI
ton	mass	
tonne	mass	
torr	pressure	
V	potential	SI
volt	potential	
Ω	resistance	
W	power	SI
watt	power	
Wb	magnetic flux	SI
weber	magnetic flux	MKS, U.S., SI
yd	length	
yr	time	

Note: For certain units that have many different definitions—such as hp, cal, BTU, and Hz—Mathcad adopts one common definition but allows you to choose from among several alternatives in the Insert Unit dialog box.

Unit Tables

Appendix C
Creating a User DLL

Extend Mathcad Professional's power by writing your own customized functions. Your functions will have the same advanced features as Mathcad built-in functions, such as customized error messages, interruption, and exception handling in case of overflow and divide by zero. Your functions will appear in the **Insert Function** dialog box like all built-in functions. The functions may operate on complex scalars and complex arrays and they may return complex scalars, complex arrays, and error messages.

This appendix describes how to create 32-bit DLLs for Mathcad Professional. The following sections make up this appendix:

Creating dynamically linked libraries

An overview of how to write your function and fill out the `FUNCTIONINFO` structure.

A sample DLL

A simple example of a user-created DLL with extensive comments. This sample can be used as a template for your own DLL.

Examining a sample DLL

A detailed examination of a simple example DLL, explaining the `COMPLEXARRAY` and `COMPLEXSCALAR` structures, error handling and function registration.

Handling arrays

Using the `COMPLEXARRAY` structure to handle arrays.

Allocating memory

Allocating and freeing memory.

Exception handling

How Mathcad traps the floating point exceptions.

Structure and function definitions

A reference guide to the structures and functions used.

Creating dynamically linked libraries

To create customized functions, you will first need to create source code in C or C++, then compile the source code with a 32-bit compiler. Next, you will link the object files together with the MathSoft-provided `mcaduser.lib` library to create a DLL. Finally, you will place your DLL into the `userefi` subdirectory.

Writing your DLL source code

Provided below is an overview of the steps involved in creating a DLL. Refer to the rest of this appendix for specific details on how to do each step.

Writing a DLL entry point routine

When you start Mathcad Professional, it looks in the `userefi` directory for library files with a `.dll` extension. Mathcad attempts to load all such files. During this loading process, your DLL must supply Mathcad with information about your library, including the names of the functions in the library, the types of arguments the functions take, the types of values they return, and the text of possible error messages. To supply this information, your DLL must have an entry point routine. A DLL entry point routine is called by the operating system when the DLL is loaded. Because the way to specify the DLL entry point routine is linker specific, refer to the `readme.mcd` file in the `userefi` directory for linking instructions.

Registering your function

For each function in your library, there must be a `FUNCTIONINFO` structure. The `FUNCTIONINFO` structure contains the information that Mathcad uses to register a user function. `FUNCTIONINFO` structure is an argument of `CreateUserFunction`. A call to `CreateUserFunction` inside the DLL entry point routine registers your function with Mathcad.

Writing your function

You must, of course, write a C or C++ function which implements your Mathcad user function. The parameters of your C/C++ function are pointers to the return value and to the arguments. The C/C++ function returns 0 if successful, otherwise it returns an error code. The address of the C/C++ function is passed to Mathcad inside a `FUNCTIONINFO` structure. In this way, Mathcad knows to execute your code when the function is called from a Mathcad document. Refer to the description of `MyCFunction` in the reference section at the end of this appendix.

Error Handling

C/C++ functions which return error messages require an error message table in the DLL code. A call to `CreateUserErrorMessageTable` inside the DLL entry point routine informs Mathcad of the meaning of error codes returned by the C/C++ functions from the DLL.

Compiling and linking your DLL

To create your DLL you will need a 32-bit compiler such as Microsoft Visual C++ (32-bit version), Borland C++ version 4.5, or Watcom C++32 version 10.0. Instructions on compiling and linking your DLL are given in a `readme.mcd` file located in the `userefi` directory. For more specific instructions on how to link and compile your source code, refer to the user guide provided with your compiler.

A sample DLL

To get you started writing DLLs for Mathcad we include a number of code samples. The example below is the file `multiply.c` located in the `userefi\microsoft\sources\simple` subdirectory.

The file contains a function which returns the result of multiplying an array by a scalar. This code implements the Mathcad user function *multiply*(*a*, **M**), which returns the result of an array **M** multiplied by a scalar *a*. The source code is explained in detail in later sections.

Sample code

```
#include "mcadincl.h"
#define INTERRUPTED1
#define INSUFFICIENT_MEMORY2
#define MUST_BE_REAL3
#define NUMBER_OF_ERRORS3

// tool tip error messages
// if your function never returns an error, you do not need to create this table
char * myErrorMessageTable[NUMBER_OF_ERRORS] =
{
    "interrupted",
    "insufficient memory",
    "must be real"
};

// this code executes the multiplication
// see the information on MyCFunction  to find out more
LRESULT MultiplyRealArrayByRealScalar(
    COMPLEXARRAY * const Product,
    const COMPLEXSCALAR * const Scalar,
    const COMPLEXARRAY * const Array )
{
    unsigned int row, col;
    // check that the scalar argument is real
    if ( scalar->imag != 0.0
    )
```

```
        // if not, display "must be real" under scalar argument
        return MAKELRESULT( MUST_BE_REAL, 1 );

    // check that the array argument is real
    if ( Array->hImag != NULL )

        // if not, display "must be real" under array argument
        return MAKELRESULT( MUST_BE_REAL, 2 );

    // allocate memory for the product
    if( !MathcadArrayAllocate( Product, Array-rows,
    Array-cols,

        // allocate memory for the real part
        TRUE,

        // do not allocate memory for the imaginary part
        FALSE ))

        // if allocation is not successful, return with the appropriate error code
        return  INSUFFICIENT_MEMORY;

    // if all is well so far, perform the multiplication
    for ( col = 0; col < Product-> cols; col++ )
    {
        // check that a user has not tried to interrupt the calculation
        if ( isUserInterrupted() )
        {
            // if user has interrupted, free the allocated memory
            MathcadArrayFree( Product );

            // and return with an appropriate error code
            return INTERRUPTED;
        }
        for ( row = 0; row < Product-> rows; row++ )
            Product->hReal[col][row] =
                Scalar-> real*Array-> hReal[col][row];
    }
    // normal return
    return 0;
}
// fill out a FunctionInfo structure with
// the information needed for registering the function with Mathcad
FUNCTIONINFO multiply =
{
// name by which Mathcad will recognize the function
"multiply",

// description of "multiply" parameters for the Insert Function dialog box
"a,M",
```

// description of the function for the Insert Function dialog box
```
"returns the product of real scalar a and real array M",
```

// pointer to the executable code
// i.e. code that should be executed when a user types in "`multiply(a,M)=`"
```
(LPCFUNCTION)MultiplyRealArrayByRealScalar;
```

*// multiply(a, **M**) returns a complex array*
```
COMPLEX_ARRAY,
```

*// multiply(a, **M**) takes on two arguments*
```
2,
```

// the first is a complex scalar, the second a complex array
```
{ COMPLEX_SCALAR, COMPLEX_ARRAY}
};
```

// all Mathcad DLLs must have a DLL entry point code
// the `_CRT_INIT` *function is needed if you are using Microsoft's 32-bit compiler*
```
BOOL WINAPI _CRT_INIT(HINSTANCE hinstDLL, DWORD dwReason, LPVOID
lpReserved);
BOOL WINAPI DllEntryPoint (HINSTANCE hDLL, DWORD dwReason, LPVOID
lpReserved)
{
    switch (dwReason)
    {
        case DLL_PROCESS_ATTACH:
```
            // DLL is attaching to the address space of the current process.
            // the next two lines are Microsoft-specific
```
            if (!_CRT_INIT(hDLL, dwReason, lpReserved))
                return FALSE;
```

            // register the error message table
            // if your function never returns an error,
            // you don't need to register an error message table
```
            if ( CreateUserErrorMessageTable( hDLL,
                NUMBER_OF_ERRORS, myErrorMessageTable ) )
```
                // and if the errors register OK, register the user function
```
                CreateUserFunction( hDLL, &multiply );

        break;
        case DLL_THREAD_ATTACH:
        case DLL_THREAD_DETACH:
        case DLL_PROCESS_DETACH:
```

            // the next two lines are Microsoft-specific
```
            if (!_CRT_INIT(hDLL, dwReason, lpReserved))
                return FALSE;
        break;
    }
```

```
            return TRUE;
}
#undef INTERRUPTED
#undef INSUFFICIENT_MEMORY
#undef MUST_BE_REAL
#undef NUMBER_OF_ERRORS
```

Compiling and linking the sample DLL

If you are using a Microsoft 32-bit compiler you can compile this file with the following command

```
cl -c -I..\..\include -DWIN32 multiply.c
```

This creates an object file **MULTIPLY.OBJ**. You can use the following command to link **MULTIPLY.OBJ** with the appropriate library and place **MULTIPLY.DLL** in the **userefi** directory.

```
link -out:..\..\..\multiply.dll -dll
-entry:"DllEntryPoint" multiply.obj
..\..\lib\mcaduser.lib
```

Check to make sure the **MULTIPLY.DLL** file is in the **userefi** subdirectory. Start Mathcad and verify that *multiply* appears in the Insert Function dialog box. You are now ready to use *multiply* in Mathcad.

Examining a sample DLL

This section will examine the source code of the simple example in the previous section. Refer to the code in the sample DLL.

MyCFunction

The heart of the program is **MyCFunction**, called **MultiplyRealArrayByRealScalar** function. It performs the actual multiplication. When the user types **multiply(a,M)=**, Mathcad executes the **MultiplyRealArrayByRealScalar** routine. The value of *a* is passed to the **MultiplyRealArrayByRealScalar** function in the **Scalar** argument. The value of **M** is passed in the **Array** argument. A pointer to the return value **Product** is the first argument of the **MultiplyRealArrayByRealScalar** function.

COMPLEXSCALAR structure

The scalar value *a* is passed to the **MultiplyRealArrayByRealScalar** function in a *COMPLEXSCALAR* structure. The structure has two members, *real* and *imag*. The real part of *a* is stored in **Scalar-> real**, the imaginary part in **Scalar-> imag**.

COMPLEXARRAY structure

The array value **M** is passed to the `MultiplyRealArrayByRealScalar` function in a *COMPLEXARRAY* structure. The `COMPLEXARRAY` structure has four members, *rows, cols, hReal,* and *hImag.* The number of rows in **M** is found in `Array-> rows`, the number of columns is found in `Array-> cols`. The real part of the element $\mathbf{M}_{row,col}$ is found in `Array-> hReal[col][row]` and the imaginary part in `Array-> hImag[col][row]`. If no element of **M** has an imaginary part, `Array-> hImag` is equal to NULL. If all elements of **M** are purely imaginary, `Array-> hReal` is equal to NULL.

The result of the multiplication of **M** by *a* is stored by the program in the `COMPLEXARRAY` structure pointed to by the argument `Product`. Note the memory for the multiplication result is allocated inside the `MultiplyRealArrayByRealScalar` function with a call to the `MathcadArrayAllocate` function.

Error Messages

If the multiplication was successful, `MultiplyRealArrayByRealScalar` stores the result in the `COMPLEXARRAY` structure pointed to by the argument `Product` and returns 0. In the case of an error, its return value has two components. One is the error code and the other is the location in which to display the error message.

Look at the error message table from the top of the file:

```
char * myErrorMessageTable[NUMBER_OF_ERRORS] =
{
    "interrupted",
    "insufficient memory",
    "must be real"
};
```

The function `MultiplyRealArrayByRealScalar` returns `MAKELRESULT(3,1)` to display string number 3, "must be real," under the first argument of `multiply(a,M)`. If `MathcadArrayAllocate` is unable to allocate memory, `MultiplyRealArrayByRealScalar` returns 2 to display string number 2, "insufficient memory," under the function name.

As shown in the sample DLL code, the following steps are involved in producing an error message:

■ creation of an array of error message strings.

■ registering the error message strings with Mathcad via a call to `CreateUserErrorMessageTable`. This call is made within the DLL entry point routine.

■ returning an appropriate error code from the user function.

DLL entry point function

The DLL entry point is called by the operating system when the DLL is loaded. Mathcad requires that you register your user functions and your error message table while the DLL is being loaded. Note how this is done in the following code lines.

```
BOOL WINAPI DllEntryPoint (HINSTANCE hDLL, DWORD dwReason, LPVOID
lpReserved)
{
    switch (dwReason)
    {
        case DLL_PROCESS_ATTACH:

            if ( CreateUserErrorMessageTable( hDLL,
                NUMBER_OF_ERRORS, myErrorMessageTable ) )
                // if the errors register OK, register user function
                CreateUserFunction( hDLL, &multiply );

            break;
        case DLL_THREAD_ATTACH:
        case DLL_THREAD_DETACH:
        case DLL_PROCESS_DETACH:
            break;
    }
    return TRUE;

}
```

CreateUserErrorMessageTable registers the error messages. CreateUserFunction registers the function. You can register only one error message table per DLL,
but you can register more than one function per DLL.

FUNCTIONINFO structure

The FUNCTIONINFO structure, *multiply*, is used for registering the DLL function with
Mathcad. It contains information about the name by which Mathcad recognizes the
function, the description of the function parameters, its arguments, its return value, and
the pointer to the code which executes the function.

```
FUNCTIONINFO multiply =
{
    "multiply",
    "a,M",
    "returns the product of real scalar a and real array M",
    (LPCFUNCTION)MultiplyRealArrayByRealScalar;
    COMPLEX_ARRAY,
    2,
    {COMPLEX_SCALAR, COMPLEX_ARRAY}
};
```

Precision

Data is passed between Mathcad and MyCFunction in double precision. Use the
appropriate conversion inside MyCFunction for different data types.

mcadincl.h

MathSoft provides the mcadincl.h include file. This file contains the prototypes for
the following functions: CreateUserFunction, CreateUserErrorMessageTa-

ble, MathcadAllocate, MathcadFree, MathcadArrayAllocate, MyCFunction, MathcadArrayFree, isUserInterrupted. mcadincl.h also includes the type definitions for the structures COMPLEXSCALAR, COMPLEXARRAY, and FUNCTIONINFO.

Handling arrays

If your function takes an array as its argument or returns an array, refer to the COMPLEXARRAY structure description in "Structure and function definitions" on page 650. Note that the arrays are two-dimensional and the structure contains information about the size of the arrays and the pointers to the real and imaginary parts of the array. Refer to the next section "Allocating Memory" below for how to allocate memory inside COMPLEXARRAY structures.

Allocating memory

The first argument of MyCFunction is a pointer to a return value. If it points to a COMPLEXARRAY structure, you will need to allocate memory for the members of this structure using MathcadArrayAllocate. If MyCFunction is returning an error, free the memory allocated for the return value using MathcadArrayFree. In the case of an error-free return, do not free the memory allocated for the return value.

Use the MathcadAllocate and MathcadFree functions to allocate and free memory inside MyCFunction.

Exception handling

Mathcad traps the following floating point exceptions; overflow, divide by zero, and invalid operation. In the case of these exceptions, Mathcad will display a floating point error message under the function. Mathcad will also free all the memory allocated inside MyCFunction with MathcadArrayAllocate and MathcadAllocate.

Structure and function definitions

This section describes in more detail the structures and functions used in creating your own dynamically linked library.

The COMPLEXSCALAR Structure

```
typedef struct tagCOMPLEXSCALAR {
    double real;
    double imag;
} COMPLEXSCALAR;
```

The **COMPLEXSCALAR** structure is used to pass scalar data between Mathcad and a user DLL. The real part of a scalar is stored in the *real* member of a **COMPLEXSCALAR**, and the imaginary in the *imag* member.

Member	Description
real	Contains the real part of a scalar.
imag	Contains the imaginary part of a scalar.

The COMPLEXARRAY Structure

```
typedef struct tagCOMPLEXARRAY {
    unsigned int rows;
    unsigned int cols;
    double **hReal;
    double **hImag;
} COMPLEXARRAY;
```

The **COMPLEXARRAY** structure is used to pass array data between Mathcad and a user DLL. It contains the information about the size of the array and whether any of the elements in the array has an imaginary or a real component.

Member	Description
rows	Number of rows in the array.
cols	Number of columns in the array.
hReal	Points to the real part of a complex array *hReal[i][j]* contains the element in the *i*th column and the *j*th row of the array. *hReal* is equal to NULL if the array has no real component.
hImag	Points to the imaginary part of a complex array *hImag[i][j]*, contains the element in the *i*th column and the *j*th row of the array. *hImag* equals NULL if the array has no imaginary component.

Comments

hReal and *hImag* members of the argument array are indexed as two-dimensional array of the range $[0 .. cols - 1][0 .. rows - 1]$.

The FUNCTIONINFO Structure

```
typedef struct tagFUNCTIONINFO{
    char * lpstrName;
    char * lpstrParameters;
    char * lpstrDescription;
    LPCFUNCTION lpfnMyCFunction;
    long unsigned int returnType;
    unsigned int nArgs;
    long unsigned int argType[MAX_ARGS];
} FUNCTIONINFO;
```

The **FUNCTIONINFO** structure contains the information that Mathcad uses to register a user function. Refer below for each member and its description.

Member	Description
lpstrName	Points to a NULL-terminated string that specifies the name of the user function.
lpstrParameters	Points to a NULL-terminated string that specifies the parameters of the user function. The string is used by the Insert Function dialog box.
lpstrDescription	Points to a NULL-terminated string that specifies the function description for the Insert Function dialog box.
lpfnMyCFunction	Pointer to the code that executes the user function.
returnType	Specifies the type of value returned by the function. The values are **COMPLEX_ARRAY** or **COMPLEX_SCALAR**.
nArgs	Specifies the number of arguments expected by the function. Must be between 1 and **MAX_ARGS**.
argType	Specifies an array of long unsigned integers containing input parameter types.

CreateUserFunction

```
const void * CreateUserFunction(hDLL, functionInfo)
HINSTANCE hDLL;
FUNCTIONINFO * functionInfo;
```

CreateUserFunction is called when the DLL is attaching to the address space of the current process in order to register the user function with Mathcad.

Parameter	Description
hDLL	Handle of the DLL supplied by the DLL entry point routine.
functionInfo	Points to the **FUNCTIONINFO** structure that contains information about the function. The **FUNCTIONINFO** structure has the following form:

```
typedef struct tagFUNCTIONINFO{
    char * lpstrName;
    char * lpstrParameters;
    char * lpstrDescription;
    LPCFUNCTION lpfnMyCFunction;
    long unsigned int returnType;
    unsigned int nArgs;
    long unsigned int argType[MAX_ARGS];
} FUNCTIONINFO;
```

Return value

The return value is a non-NULL handle if the registration is successful. Otherwise, it is NULL.

CreateUserErrorMessageTable

```
BOOL CreateUserErrorMessageTable(hDLL, n, ErrorMessageTable)
HINSTANCE hDLL;
unsigned int n;
char * ErrorMessageTable[ ];
```

`CreateUserErrorMessageTable` is called when the DLL is attaching to the address space of the current process in order to register the user error message table with Mathcad.

Parameter	Description
hDLL	Handle of the DLL supplied by the DLL entry point routine.
n	Number of error messages in the table.
ErrorMessageTable	An array of *n* strings with the text of the error messages.

Return value

The return value is TRUE if the registration is successful. Otherwise, it is FALSE.

MathcadAllocate

```
char * MathcadAllocate(size)
unsigned int size;
```

Should be used to allocate memory inside the `MyCFunction`. Allocates a memory block of a given size (in bytes) of memory.

Parameter	Description
size	Size (in bytes) of memory block to allocate. Should be non-zero.

Return value

Returns a pointer to the storage space. To get a pointer to a type other than char, use a type cast on the return value. Returns NULL if the allocation failed or if size is equal to 0.

MathcadFree

```
void MathcadFree(address)
char * address;
```

Should be used to free memory allocated with **MathcadAllocate**. The argument address points to the memory previously allocated with **MathcadAllocate**. A NULL pointer argument is ignored.

Parameter	Description
address	Address of the memory block that is to be freed.

Return value

The function does not return a value.

MathcadArrayAllocate

```
BOOL MathcadArrayAllocate(array, rows, cols, allocateReal,
allocateImaginary)
COMPLEXARRAY* const array;
unsigned int rows;
unsigned int cols;
BOOL allocateReal;
BOOL allocateImaginary;
```

Allocates memory for a **COMPLEXARRAY** of *cols* columns and *rows* rows. Sets the *hReal*, *hImag*, *rows* and *cols* members of the argument array.

Parameter	Description

array	Points to the **COMPLEXARRAY** structure that is to be filled with the information about an array.
	The **COMPLEXARRAY** structure has the following form:
	
	`typedef struct tagCOMPLEXARRAY {`
	`    unsigned int rows;`
	`    unsigned int cols;`
	`    double **hReal;`
	`    double **hImag;`
	`} COMPLEXARRAY;`

rows	Row dimension of the array that is being allocated. After a successful allocation, the *rows* member of the argument array is set to the value of *rows*.
cols	Column dimension of the array that is being allocated. After a successful allocation, the *cols* member of the argument array is set to the value of *cols*.
allocateReal	Boolean flag indicating whether a memory block should be allocated to store the real part of the array. If *allocateReal* is FALSE the function does not allocate storage for the real part of array and sets the *hReal* member to NULL.
allocateImag	Boolean flag indicating whether a memory block should be allocated to store the imaginary part of the array. If *allocateImag* is FALSE the function does not allocate storage for the imaginary part of array and sets the *hImag* member to NULL.

Return value

Returns TRUE if the allocation is successful, FALSE otherwise.

Comments

hReal and *hImag* members of the argument array are allocated as 2-dimensional array of the range $[0 .. cols - 1][0 .. rows - 1]$.

MyCFunction

```
LRESULT MyCFunction(returnValue, argument1,...)
void * const returnValue;
const void * const argument1;
...
```

MyCFunction is the actual code which executes the user function. Mathcad arguments and a pointer to a return value are passed to this function. It puts the result of the calculation in the return value.

Parameter	Description
returnValue	Points to a COMPLEXARRAY or a COMPLEXSCALAR structure where the function result is to be stored. If you are implementing a Mathcad user function which returns a scalar, *returnValue* is a pointer to a COMPLEXSCALAR structure. If you are implementing a Mathcad user function that returns an array, *returnValue* points to a COMPLEXARRAY structure.
argument1	Points to a read-only COMPLEXARRAY or a COMPLEXSCALAR structure where the first function argument is stored. If you are implementing a Mathcad user function that has a scalar as its first argument, *argument1* is a pointer to a COMPLEXSCALAR structure. If you are implementing a Mathcad user function that has an array as its first argument, *argument1* points to a COMPLEXARRAY structure.

... If you are implementing a Mathcad user function that has more than one argument, your `MyCFunction` will have additional arguments. The additional arguments will be pointers to the read-only `COMPLEXARRAY` or a `COMPLEXSCALAR` structures where the data for the corresponding Mathcad user function argument is stored.

Return value

`MyCFunction` should return 0 to indicate an error-free return. To indicate an error `MyCFunction` should return an error code in the low word of the returned `LRESULT`, and in the high word the number of the argument under which the error box should be placed. If the high word is zero the error message box is placed under the function itself. See the section on error handling to find out more about error codes.

Comments

`MyCFunction` is a placeholder for the library-supplied function name. You can name the function that executes your Mathcad user function anything you would like, but you must register the address of your executable code with Mathcad by setting the `lpfnMyCFunction` member of the `FUNCTIONINFO` structure.

MathcadArrayFree

```
void MathcadArrayFree(array)
COMPLEXARRAY * const array;
```

Frees memory that was allocated by the `MathcadArrayAllocate` function to the *hReal* and *hImag* members of the argument array.

Parameter	Description

array	Points to the `COMPLEXARRAY` structure that is to be filled with the information about an array.
	The `COMPLEXARRAY` structure has the following form:
	
	``typedef struct tagCOMPLEXARRAY {
	    unsigned int rows;
	    unsigned int cols;
	    double **hReal;
	    double **hImag;
	} COMPLEXARRAY;```

Return value

The function does not return a value.

isUserInterrupted

```
BOOL isUserInterrupted(void)
```

The `isUserInterrupted` function is used to check whether a user has pressed the [Esc] key. Include this function if you want to be able to interrupt your function like other Mathcad functions.

Parameter

The function does not take any parameters.

Return value

Returns TRUE if the [Esc] key has been pressed, FALSE otherwise.

DLL interface specifications, contained in the documentation, may be used for creating user-written external functions which work with Mathcad for your personal or internal business use only. These specifications may not be used for creating external functions for commercial resale, without the prior written consent of MathSoft, Inc.

Index

↵ (Enter key) 6
∫ (integral) 236, 606
→ (symbolic equals sign) 353
× (vector product) 235, 605
Σ (vector sum) 235, 605
→ (vectorize operator) 195, 204–205, 234, 604
Σ and ∏ (summation and product) 235, 605
! (factorial) 235, 604
% 158
() (parentheses) 61
+ (with line break) 236, 606
+, −, ·, and / 236, 606
:= (definition) 132
<, >,≤, ≥ (inequalities) 236, 606
= (boolean equals) 237, 606
= (evaluating expression) 141
| · | (determinant) 235, 605
| · | (magnitude/absolute value) 235, 605
∞ (infinity) 158
≠ (not equal to) 237, 606
≡ (global assignment) 139
√ (square root) 235, 605
3D Plot Format dialog box
    Axes page for 3D bar charts 547
    Axes page for 3D scatter plots 558
    Axes page for contour plots 536
    Axes page for surface plots 525
    Axes page for vector field plots 567
    Color & Lines page for 3D bar charts 545
    Color & Lines page for 3D scatter plots 556
    Color & Lines page for contour plots 534
    Color & Lines page for surface plots 522
    Title page for 3D bar chart 549
    Title page for 3D scatter plots 560
    Title page for contour plots 538
    Title page for surface plots 527
    Title page for vector field plots 569
    View page for 3D bar charts 543
    View page for 3D scatter plots 554
    View page for contour plots 533
    View page for surface plots 520

A

aborting calculations in progress 146
absolute value 235, 605
    See also magnitude 235
acosh function 261
adaptive smoothing of data 307
addition 236, 606
algorithms
    See numerical methods 246
aligning regions 67
aligning text 105
anchor points 137
angle function 265
Animate command 572
animation 576
    compressing AVI files 572
    creating 572
    launching from worksheet 575
    playback 574
    playback context menu 575
    saving 572
    saving with worksheet 575
    See also AVI files 576
    speed 572, 575
annotating Electronic Books 45
annotation color 45
annotations
    deleting from Electronic Books 46
    highlighting 45
    inserting in Electronic Books 45
antisymmetric tensor function 275
APPEND function 447, 449, 451
APPENDPRN function 447, 450, 455
approximations
    Minerr function 316
    root of expression 310
arg function 265
argument of complex number 265
arguments
    hiding in graphs 484
    hiding in polar plots 508
    of functions 133
arrays
    as arguments to user functions 208
    calculating with 183, 222
    calculations by element 204
    creating 182
    defining 180, 183, 210

definition of 180
displaying results 190
extracting a column 187
extracting a subarray 199–200
functions for 196
matrices 180
nested 209
operators for 193
ORIGIN used with 188
setting starting index 188
size limits 192
subscripts 185
vectors 180
when to use subscripts 230
arrow keys
for editing 623
for scrolling 13
ASCII codes
entering in strings 165
table 625
asinh function 261
assume keyword 356, 359
atanh function 261
augment function 199, 585
used to write several variables to file 455
augmenting matrices 585
Auto (on status bar) 144
Auto Contour
using 536
Auto Grid
contour plots 538
graphs 474
polar plots 499
automatic mode 144
Autoscale
3D bar charts 548
3D scatter plots 560
contour plots 538
graphs 473–474
polar plots 502
surface plots 526
autoscroll 66
AVI files
compression 572
creating 572
hyperlinking from worksheet 575
playback 575
saving 572
Axes page
3D bar charts 547
3D scatter plots 558

contour plots 536
surface plots 525
vector field plots 567
X-Y Plot defaults dialog box 480
X-Y plots 472, 475
axes style
graphs 474
polar plots 500
axes, formatting
3D bar charts 547
3D scatter plots 558
contour plots 536
surface plots 525
vector field plots 567
axis limits 462
Axum component 441

B

back planes
3D bar charts 544
3D scatter plots 555
surface plots 521
bandpass filter 275
bar charts (2D)
graphs 479
polar plots 503
bar charts (3D) 539
adjusting spacing between bars 546
Autoscale 548
back planes 544
bar configurations 547
borders 544
boxes 544
changing bar colors 545
converting 543
creating 540
formatting 542
formatting axes 547
grid intervals 548
grid lines 548
of function of two variables 540
perspective 542–543
resizing 541
setting axis limits 548
tick marks 548
titles 549

vertical scale 544
base of results (decimal/hex/octal) 118
base units 175
Bessel functions 262
beta distribution 284
binomial distribution 284
bitmaps
    color palettes 590
    functions for reading 582
blank lines, inserting or deleting 69
blank pages in printouts 80
blank space between regions 20
BMP files 582
boilerplate math 38
bookmarks 39
Books context menu 42
boolean operators 250, 272
    and strings 252
borders
    3D bar charts 544
    3D scatter plots 555
    surface plots 521
bottom margin 77
boundary value problems 345
boxed axes 474
boxes
    3D bar charts 544
    3D scatter plots 555
    surface plots 521
break statement 408
breaking equations 236, 395, 606
built-in functions 258
    alphabetical list 607
    listed by type 258
    symbolic only 392
Built-In Variables page on Math Options dialog box
        159
bulstoer function 341
bvalfit function 347

C

Calc on message line 145
calculation 17, 144
    disabling for individual equation 148
    equations 17, 141
    interrupting 146

    locking 83, 85
    order in worksheets 137
    restarting after interrupting 146
    units in 171
    unlocking 86
calculator, using Mathcad as 15
carriage returns in text 99
cauchy distribution 284
ceil function 265
centigrade 174
CFFT function 266, 269
cfft function 266, 268
CGS units 176
character
    deleting 55
    inserting 55
chemistry notation 157
Chi function 392
chi-squared distribution 284
cholesky decomposition function 202
Ci function 393
clipboard 62, 396
cnorm function 284
coeffs keyword 356, 371
Collaboratory 10
    forums 33
    server URL 33
    topics 33
    using to open a file from the Internet 74
Collect command 370
collect keyword 356, 370
colon (:) as definition symbol 16, 132
color
    3D bar charts 545
    3D scatter plots 557
    changes to Electronic Books 45
    contour plots 534
    equation highlights 127
    graphs 479
    in equations 123
    in text 105
    polar plots 503
    surface plots 522
    text highlights 113
Color & Lines page
    3D bar charts 545
    3D scatter plots 556
    contour plots 534
    surface plots 522
color images
    displaying 584

reading 582
    unpacking and packing 585
    writing to file 584
color palettes for bitmaps 590
cols function 196
column vectors
    See vectors 182
comments in Electronic Books 45
common log 262
complementary error function 264
complex
    conjugate 162, 235, 604
    fast Fourier transform 266
    tolerance 119
Complex command 363
complex keyword 355, 363
complex numbers 161
    conjugate 162
    determining angle 162
    display of 118–119
    imaginary unit symbol 118
    in graphs 463
    magnitude of 162
    operators and functions for 162, 264
    real and imaginary parts 162
    vector field plots 563–564
components
    inserting 423
    overview of 422
computing results 17
concat function 276
condition number of matrix 198
conditional
    functions 271, 276
    statement 403
conjugate (complex) 162, 235, 604
constants
    See numbers 122
    See predefined variables 122
Constants math style 122
constraints
    defined 317
    in solve blocks 317
    too few 323
context menu
    animation playback 574
    component 424
    Electronic Book 42
    Excel component 439
    Input Table component 430
    Scriptable Object component 446

Web browsing 39
continue statement 409
contour integrals 248
contour plots 529
    Auto Grid 538
    Autoscale 538
    changing the shading 534
    converting plot type 533
    creating 530
    displaying as points 533
    formatting 532
    formatting axes 536
    grid intervals 538
    hiding the contours 535
    numbering the contours 535
    of function of two variables 530
    resizing 532
    setting axis limits 538
    specifying how many contours 536
    specifying tick marks and grid lines 537
    titles 538
convert keyword 356, 370
Convert to Partial Fraction command 370
converting 3D plots
    from 3D bar charts 543
    from 3D scatter plots 554
    from contour plots 533
    from surface plots 520
converting to partial fractions 356
copy and paste 92
copying
    arrays 142
    from Electronic Book 43
    regions 65
    results 142
    text 103
    to clipboard 62
correlation (*corr*) function 281
cosecant (*csc*) function 260
cosh function 261
cosine (*cos*) function 260
cosine integral 393
cotangent (*cot*) function 260
coth function 261
covariance (*cvar*) function 280
creating
    3D bar charts 540
    3D scatter plots 552
    contour plots 530
    graphs 460
    hyperlinks 88

polar plots 494
pop-up window 89
surface plots 516
text regions 98
vector field plots 564
worksheet templates 72
cross product 195, 235, 605
crossed axes 474, 500
csch function 261
csgn function 393
csort function 270
cspline function 295, 297
Ctrl+M
    to create matrix 182
    to create vector 180
    to edit matrix 182
Ctrl+P for pi 155
cube root 163, 235, 605
cubic spline interpolation 293, 296
cumulative distribution functions 284
cumulative distributions 281
curve fitting
    functions for 299
    linear 300
    polynomial 301, 303
    using cubic splines 293
curves, finding area under 246
customer registration 40
cutting text 103
cvar function 280
CWD variable 158, 448

D

δ function 275
d/dx
    See derivatives 241
dashed selection rectangle 64
data
    entering into a table 429
    graphing 469
    importing into Mathcad 425
data exchange 10
data files 447
    column width 455
    format for data in 447
    PRNCOLWIDTH used with 455

PRNPRECISION used with 455
    reading data from 425
    reading into a matrix 425, 452
    significant figures 455
    spreadsheet 447
    structured 452–453
    unstructured 450
    writing a matrix to a file 431, 453
    writing data to 431, 451
    writing rows and columns of data 431, 453
data input 220, 428
data input tables 220
data output tables 217
Data Points, display as
    3D bar plots 543
    contour plots 533
    surface plots 520
date
    in headers and footers 79
    inserting on a page 79
dbeta function 281
dbinom function 281
dcauchy function 282
dchisq function 282
decimal places
    See precision 119
decimal points
    symbolic calculation 354, 363, 395
decomposition
    matrix 202
    partial fraction 370
    singular value 202
default formats
    graphs 480
    polar plots 504
    template 72
    worksheet layout 72
Defaults page
    polar plots 504
    X-Y plots 480
defining
    functions 133
    global 139
    multiple definitions of variable 138
    operators 252
    programs 400
    range variables 214
    recursive functions 416
    See also creating 16
    several variables at once 207
    strings 164

units 171, 175
variable in program 400
variables 16, 132
definition symbol (:=) 132
degrees, converting to radians 174
deleting
annotations from Electronic Books 46
blank lines 69
characters 55
equations 67
graphs 463
hyperlinks 90
line breaks from text 99
lockable area 86
operators 59
pagebreaks 78
parentheses 62
parts of an expression 63
regions 67
text 98, 103
delta function 275, 393
density functions 281
derivative and nth derivative 236, 241, 245, 606
derivatives 236, 241, 606
higher order 245
symbolic 374
determinant 195, 235, 383, 605
Determinant command 383
device-independent bitmap 588
dexp function 282
dF function 282
dgamma function 282
dgeom function 282
diagonal matrix (*diag*) function 197
DIB
See device-independent bitmap 588
dictionaries (spell-checker) 116
did not find solution (error)
in solve block 322
differential equations 334
higher order 337
partial 348
second order 336
slowly varying solutions 341
smooth systems 341
specialized solvers 341
stiff systems 342
systems 338
Differentiate on Variable command 374
differentiation
See derivatives 245

differentiation variable 242, 245
digamma function 394
dilog function 393
dilogarithmic integral 393
dimensions 160, 167
common sources of error 170
consistency 170
Dimensions page on Math Options dialog box 178
Dirac delta function 393
disabling equations 101, 148
Display as Matrix 119
displayed precision 119
displaying
color images 584
full numerical precision 119
grayscale images 584
distribution functions 281
division 235, 605
DLLs
creating 642
custom 642
linking to mcaduser.lib library 642
dlnorm function 283
dlogis function 283
dnbinom function 283
dnorm function 283
dot product 194
double integrals 249
dpois function 283
drag and drop 43, 92, 94
dragging regions 65–66
drawings
See pictures 587
dt function 283
dunif function 283
dweibull function 284
dynamic-link libraries for Mathcad 642

E

ε function 275
e, base of natural logarithms 158
Edit Links command 95
editing equations
annotated example 53
compared to word-processors 53
deleting ()'s from around expression 62

deleting an operator 59
deleting parts of expression 63
existing expressions 55
inserting an operator 56
making expression an argument to a function 60
math 53
moving parts of an expression 62
moving/rearranging equations 64
numbers 55
putting ()'s around an expression 61
variable or function names 55
editing lines 55
Ei function 393
eigenvals function 391
eigenvalues 200–202, 391
eigenvectors 200–202
Electronic Book
annotating 45
annotation color 45
bookmark 43
browsing history 43
copying information from 43
deleting annotations 46
hyperlinks 42
moving around in 42
navigation 42
opening 41
printing section 45
saving section 45
searching for information in 43
toolbar 42
Electronic Books 11, 31, 40, 89–90
available titles 41
Mathcad Treasury 41
elements, vector and matrix 185
e-mail address 32
endpoints for ranges 216
Enter key 6
epsilon function 275
equal sign (=)
as boolean operator 237, 606
in numerical calculations 141
in solve blocks 316–317
symbolic calculations 353, 379, 381
equality constraints 317
equations
as constraints in solve blocks 317
breaking 236, 395, 606
calculating results 17, 141
changing font 122
color 123

commenting out 101, 148
definition 132
disabling calculation for 101, 148
effect of range variables in 216
errors in 148
font 122
global definitions 139
in text 100
locking 83, 85
order of evaluation 137, 144
processing and calculating 16, 144
properties 101, 148
solving for root 310
solving symbolically 379, 381
solving with solve blocks 315
unlocking 86
using units in 168
wrapping 236, 606
erf function 263, 391, 393
ERR variable and *minerr* 330
error (*erf*) function 263, 393
error bars
graphs 479, 489
polar plots 503
error function 278
in programs 412
error messages
and user functions 150
correcting 149
custom 278
in equations 148
in programs 412
not detected with 0 as factor/numerator 149
with units 170
Euler's constant 392
Euler's gamma function 264
Evaluate Floating Point command 363
Evaluate in Place option 361
Evaluate Symbolically command 360–361
Evaluation and Boolean Palette 253
Excel component 436
Expand command 367
expand in series 356
expand keyword 355, 367–368
Expand to Series command 368
exponent 235, 605
exponential
function 261
notation, entering 161
notation, in displayed results 119
threshold 119

exponential (*exp*) function 262
exponential distribution 284
exponential integral 393
exponential threshold
    in components 435
exporting
    data 431
    text 107
    worksheets as RTF 75
expressions
    applying a function to 60
    collecting like terms of 370
    converting to partial fractions 370
    correcting errors in 149
    deleting parts of 63
    error messages in 148
    evaluating 141
    expanding 367–368
    factoring 369
    finding the coefficients of 371
    moving parts of 62
    range variables in 216
    selecting several 64
    simplifying 365
    symbolic evaluation of 353, 363

F

F (function) keys, table of 602
F distribution 284
Φ function 275
Factor Expression command 369
factor keyword 355, 369
factorial (!) 235, 604
fahrenheit 174
fast Fourier transform
    alternate forms of 269
    See Fourier transforms 269
FFT
    See Fourier transforms 269
FFT function 266, 269
fft function 266–267
File Read/Write component 426, 431
File Send command 83
file-access functions 447
filename
    in headers/footers 79

files
    reading data from 447
    saving 28
    writing data to 447
filters 275
    for exporting data 431
    for importing data 425
    signal processing 275
Find function
    at end of solve block 316, 381
    user functions defined with 325
    values returned by 316
first order differential equation 334
fitting a surface
    using cubic splines 296
float keyword 355, 363
Floating Point command 363
floor function 265
font
    changing in math 122
    changing in text 104
    sensitivity 126
    used to display equations 122
for loop 405
Format Bar 104–105, 123
    defined 13
    math styles 124
    text styles 109
Format Properties command 101, 112, 589
Format Style command 109
formatting
    3D bar charts 542
    3D scatter plots 553
    contour plots 532
    numbers in matrices 121
    results 118
    surface plots 519
    symbolic 361
    vector field plots 567
    worksheets 76
Fourier keyword 385
fourier keyword 356
Fourier transforms 356
    alternate form 269
    symbolic 385
    two-dimensional 269
    using *fft* 266
FRAME for animation 572
Fresnel cosine integral 393
Fresnel sine integral 393
FTP 32

functions
    applying to an expression 60
    boolean 273
    built-in 258, 607
    complex arithmetic 162
    defined in terms of solve blocks 325
    defining 22, 133
    error message 276
    file-access 447
    Fourier transform 266
    graphing 464
    hyperbolic 261
    inverse trigonometric 260
    piecewise continuous 271, 276, 404
    plotting function of two variables 516, 530, 540
    plotting in polar plot 500
    population statistics 280
    prediction 298
    probability distribution 281
    real and imaginary part 264
    recursive 136, 416
    regression 299
    See also built-in functions 258
    series for 368
    statistical 280
    symbolic calculation 392
    tensor 275, 278
    that take vector arguments 196
    to combine arrays 199
    to combine vectors or matrices 199
    to compute angle to a point 265
    to create arrays 199
    to find roots of expressions 310
    to manipulate strings 276
    trigonometric 260
    user function names 154
    user-defined 133
    vector and matrix 196

G

gamma (Euler's constant) 392
gamma distribution 285
gamma function 264, 391
Gaussian distribution 284
generalized
    eigenvalues 200
    eigenvectors 201
    inverse of a matrix 197
genfit function 305
geninv function 197
genvals function 200
geometric distribution 285
Given, in solve blocks 315, 381
global definitions 139
Go to Page command 14
Gopher 32
Graph Palette 460
graphs 441, 459
    Auto Grid 474
    Autoscale 473–474
    axes style 474
    axis labels 483
    axis limits 462
    axis settings in dialog box 473
    bar charts (2D) 479
    changing perspective 484
    color of traces 479
    complex numbers 463
    copying format from existing plot 480
    creating 24, 460
    deleting 463
    error bars 479, 489
    formatting 27, 472
    formatting traces 478
    graphing functions 464
    graphing several curves 470
    graphing vectors 466
    grid lines 473
    hiding arguments 484
    horizontal and vertical lines 476
    labels and titles 481
    legends 479, 484, 491
    line charts 479
    logarithmic axes 473, 489
    markers 479
    moving 463
    polar coordinates 465, 468
    QuickPlot 24
    read out of coordinates 486
    resizing 25, 484
    setting axis limits 475
    setting defaults with no plot 480
    Show Markers 476
    stem 479
    step 479, 489
    tick marks 473–474, 491
    titles 482

trace settings in dialog box 478
traces on 470
what to graph 464
with dots 479
zooming 485
grayscale images
displaying 584
reading 582
writing to file 584
grayscale plots
3D bar charts 545
contour 534
surface 522
greatest integer 265
Greek letters
in equations 154
table of 155, 603
Greek Symbol Palette 155
grid intervals
3D bar charts 548
3D scatter plots 560
contour plots 538
surface plots 526
vector field plots 569
grid lines
3D bar charts 548
3D scatter plots 559
graphs 473
on contour plots 537
polar plots 499
surface plots 525
vector field plots 568
guess
for *root* function 311
for solve blocks 315

H

halting iteration on a condition 273
handbook
See Electronic Books 40, 42
hard line breaks in text 99
hard pagebreaks 78
HBK (Electronic Book) file 41
headers and footers 78
heaviside step function 275, 391
help 10

context sensitive 46
on-line 46
QuickSheets 37
hexadecimal numbers 118, 160
highlighting
annotations in Books 45
equations 127
text regions 112
highpass filter 275
histogram (*hist*) function 287
history of browsing in Electronic Book 43
HTML 39
HTTP 32
hyperbolic cosine integral 392
hyperbolic functions 261
hyperbolic sign integral 394
hyperlinks
and relative paths 90
deleting 90
to other file types 90
to worksheets 88

I

i (imaginary unit) 160
I0, *I1*, and *In* Bessel functions 263
ICFFT function 269
icfft function 268
identity function 197, 391
identity matrix 197
if function 271–272, 276
if statement 403
IFFT and *ICFFT* functions 266
ifft and *icfft* functions 266–267
IFFT function 269
Im function 265, 391
image components
HLS 585
HSV 585
RGB 585
image file format
BMP 582, 585
GIF 585
JPG 585
TGA 585
imaginary numbers 160–161
choosing *i* or *j* for display 118

symbol for 118
imaginary part of a complex number 265
implied multiplication 53, 160, 168
importing
    data 425
    text 107
impulse function 275
in0, in1, etc., variables 158
incompatible units error 170
increments for ranges 216
indefinite
    integral 375
    sum 373
indented paragraphs 105
index variables
    See range variables 214
inequalities 236–237, 606
    as constraints in solve blocks 317
infinity (∞) 154, 158
inner product 194
in-place activation 92, 96
Input Table component 428–429
input to a component 422
Insert Function command 449
Insert Function dialog box 258
Insert Hyperlink command 88, 575
insert key 56, 98
Insert Link command 86
Insert Math Region command 101
Insert Matrix dialog box 180, 182–183
Insert Object command 92, 576
Insert Reference command 86–87
Insert Unit dialog box 168, 639
inserting
    annotations in Electronic Books 45
    blank lines 69
    characters 55
    equations in text 100
    functions 61
    hyperlinks 88
    line break in text 99
    math region 101
    minus sign in front of expression 60
    parentheses around expression 61
    text 98
    units 168
    worksheet 87
insertion point 15
integral transforms
    Fourier 385
    Laplace 386

integrals 236, 246, 606
    contour 248
    double 249
    indefinite 375
    numerical approximations used 247
    symbolic evaluation of 377
    tolerance for numeric approximation 247
    variable limits 247
integrand, of definite integral 246
Integrate on Variable command 375
integrating variable, of definite integral 246
integration
    See integrals 236
intercept function 300
International System of units 176
Internet 74
    access 32
    Collaboratory 33
Internet Setup command 32
interp function 295, 298, 302–303
interpolation 291
    cubic splines 293
    for a vector of points 295
    linear 292
    using cubic splines 296
interrupted (error) 147
interrupting calculations in progress 146
inverse
    cumulative distributions 285
    Fourier transform 266, 385
    hyperbolic functions 261
    Laplace transform 386
    matrix 195, 235, 383, 605
    trigonometric functions 260
    wavelet transform 270
    z-transform 387
inverse Fourier transforms 356
inverse Laplace transforms 356
inverse of matrix 383
inverse z-transforms 356
Invert command 383
invfourier keyword 356, 385
invlaplace keyword 356, 386
invztrans keyword 356, 387
iterated product 235–237, 605
iterated sum 237
iteration 222
    faster without subscripts 231
    halting 273
    on a vector 228
    over a range 222

program loops 405
recursive 226
See also range variables 222
with seed value 226
with several variables 227
iwave function 270

J

j (imaginary unit) 160
J0, *J1*, and *Jn* Bessel functions 263
Jacobian matrix 343
JavaScript 443
JScript 443

K

K0, *K1*, and *Kn* Bessel functions 263
keywords 355
keywords, symbolic 355
Kronecker's delta function 275
ksmooth function 307

L

labels
    graph axes 483
    graphs 481
    polar plots 506
Labels page
    polar plots 507
    X-Y plots 482
Lambert's *W* function 394
laplace keyword 356, 386
Laplace transforms 356, 386
Laplace's equation 348
last function 196
Laurent series 368
least integer function 265

left inverse of a matrix 197
left page margin 77
legends
    graphs 479, 484, 491
    polar plots 503, 507
length function 196
level curves 551
limits on array sizes 192
limits, evaluating 378
line break
    in equation 236, 606
    in text 99
line charts
    polar plots 503
    X-Y plots 479
linear
    interpolation 292
    prediction 298
    regression 299–300
    systems of differential equations 338
    systems of equations 203
lines
    polar plots 503
    X-Y plots 479
linfit function 305
link
    See also hyperlinks 575
    to animation file 575
    to Internet 74
    to other worksheets 86
    to World Wide Web 74
linterp function 292
Lissajous figures 463
literal subscripts 156
ln (natural log) function 262
local result format 24, 120
Lock Area command 85
Lock Regions command 84
lockable area 83
    deleting 86
    specifying 84
locked calculations 83, 85–86
loess function 302–303
log function 261–262
log normal distribution 285
logical operators
    See boolean operators 272
logistic distribution 285
looping
    for loop 405
    while loops 406

looping in programs 405
Lorczak, Paul R. 41
lowpass filter 275
lsolve function 203
lspline function 295, 297
LU decomposition (*lu*) function 202

M

Macintosh Mathcad 6 files 72
magnitude 235, 605
    complex numbers 162
    vector 195
mailing worksheets 83
mantissa 264
manual mode
    starting in 147
    updating in 145
margins 76–77
markers
    3D scatter plots 556
    graphs 479
    polar plots 503
marking changes in Electronic Books 45
Markov processes 228
Math Options dialog box
    Built-In Variables page 159
    Unit System page 175
Math Palette 10, 12, 155, 193, 234
math styles
    applications 125
    applying 124
    Constants 122
    editing 122
    saving 126
    Variables 122
Mathcad
    quitting 29
    starting 11
Mathcad 6 for Macintosh 72
Mathcad 6 for Windows 72
Mathcad Treasury 38, 41
MathConnex 86, 424
MathSoft home page 39
MATLAB component 439
matrices
    adding/deleting rows or columns 182

    as arguments to user functions 208
    as array elements 209
    calculations by element 204
    combining 199
    combining with *augment* function 199
    combining with stack function 199
    condition number 198
    creating 182
    creating from bitmaps 582
    creating with components 422
    defining 183
    defining by formula 225
    defining with two range variables 225
    definition of 180
    determinant 195, 235, 383, 605
    displayed as pictures 583
    displayed as scrolling output tables 190
    extracting a column 185
    extracting a submatrix 199–200
    extracting elements 185, 209
    functions for 196
    inverting 195, 235, 383, 605
    limits on size 192–193
    matrix arithmetic 195
    norm 198
    numbering elements 185, 188
    operators for 193
    ORIGIN used with 188
    plotting in 3D bar chart 540
    plotting in contour plot 530
    plotting in surface plot 516
    plotting in vector field plots 564
    raising to a power 195, 235, 605
    rank 198
    sorting by row or column 270
    start with row and column zero 188
    subscripts 187
    transpose 195, 235, 383, 604
    when to use subscripts 230
    writing to data files 453
matrix function 199
matrix subscript 234, 604
max function 196, 391
MCD file 72
MCT file 72
mean function 280
median function 280
medsmooth function 306
menu commands
    See also individual commands 594
    table 594

messages
    removing from the Collaboratory 36
    sending to the Collaboratory 35
metafile 588
Microsoft Internet Explorer 38, 40
Microsoft Office 95
min function 196, 391
Minerr function
    at end of solve block 330, 381
    values returned by 316, 330
minus sign 235, 605
    inserting in front of expression 60
MKS units 176
mod function 265, 391
mode
    See automatic mode, manual mode 145
moving
    crosshair 623
    editing lines 623
    graphs 463
    insertion point 623
    regions 66
    scrollbar 13
    to bottom of worksheet 14
    to top of worksheet 14
multigrid function 349
multiple integrals 249
multiple roots, finding with solve blocks 320
multiple summations 238, 240
multiplication 53, 235, 605
    implied 53, 160, 168
multivalued functions 163, 262
multivariate cubic spline interpolation 296

differential equations 336
    regression 304
    systems of equations 315
nonscalar value (error message) 215
norm
    functions 198
    of matrix 198
    of vector 195, 235, 605
norm1 and *norm2* functions 198
normal distribution 284–285
norme and *normi* functions 198
not converging (error)
    integrals 247–248
    root function 311
notation used in manual 5
nth order derivative 245
nth root 163, 235, 605
num2str function 277
numbering pages 79
numbers 159
    complex 160–161
    dimensional values 160
    displayed as zero 119
    exponential notation for 119, 161
    format for computed results 118
    formatting 23, 118
    hexadecimal 160
    imaginary 160–161
    octal 160
    radix (base) for results 118
numerical methods
    differentiation 241, 245
    integration 246

N

O

names
    font sensitive 126
    operators in 156
    variable and function names 154
    vectors and scalars use same names 184
natural log 262
negating an expression 60, 235, 605
negative binomial distribution 285
nested arrays 209
noisy data 306
nonlinear

object linking and embedding
    See OLE 92
objects
    embedding 92
    linking 92
octal numbers 118, 160
OLE 10, 444
    drag and drop 94
    editing links 95
    in-place activation 92, 95
    used in components 422

on error statement 411
on-line resources 31
opening
    Electronic Books 41
    worksheets 74
operator palettes 237
operators
    as parts of variable name 156
    boolean 272
    complete list of 604
    defined 50
    defining 252
    derivative 241, 374
    for complex numbers 162
    for vectors and matrices 193
    how to type 234
    indefinite integral 375
    inserting 56
    integral 246
    iterated product 237
    iterated sum 237
    listed in order of precedence 234
    logical 250, 272
    nth order derivative 245
    palettes 10, 12, 234, 237
    vector sum 241
Optimize command 389
Optimize Palette command 590
order of calculation of equations 144
order of derivative 245
order of evaluation 139
ORIGIN variable 158, 188, 222
output from a component 422
Output Table component 433
overlapping regions 69
overtyping text 98

P

page
    boundary 77
    headers and footers 78
    length 78
    numbering 79
Page Setup dialog box 76–77, 80
pagebreaks, inserting and deleting 78
palettes 10, 12, 237

palettes, color, for bitmaps 590
paper size for printing 77
paper source for printing 77
paragraphs 98
    alignment 105
    indenting 105
    properties 105
parametric plots 462
parametric surface plots 518
parentheses 61
    deleting from expression 62
partial differential equations 348
partial fractions 370
password
    locked areas 85
Paste command 94
Paste Special command 94, 588
pasting
    arrays 142
    bitmaps 588
    device-independent bitmaps 588
    from clipboard 62, 588
    metafiles 588
    numerical results 142
    OLE objects 94
    text 103
patch plots 524
pbeta function 284
pbinom function 284
pcauchy function 284
pchisq function 284
Pearson's correlation coefficient 281
pending computations 144–145
percent 158
perimeter axes 500
permutations 275
personal dictionary (spell-checker) 116
perspective for 3D bar charts 543
perspective, changing
    3D bar charts 542
    3D scatter plots 554
    surface plots 520
    vector field plots 567
pexp function 284
pF function 284
pgamma function 285
pgeom function 285
pi ($\prod$, product symbol) 237
pi (3.14159...) 54, 158
picture operator 192, 583–584
pictures

border on 589
created from bitmap file 587
created from matrix 587
formatting 589
importing into an array 582
pasted from clipboard 588
resizing 589
piecewise continuous functions 271, 276, 404
placeholder 15
in graph regions 462
units 172
Playback command 575
plnorm function 285
plogis function 285
plots
3D bar charts 539
3D scatter plots 551
contour plots 529
graphs 459
polar plots 493
read out of coordinates 510
surface plots 515
vector field plots 563
pnbinom function 285
pnorm function 285
points, plotting 552
poisson distribution 285
Poisson's equation 348
Polar Axes page
polar plot defaults 505
polar plots 498
polar coordinates 493
Polar Plot dialog box
Defaults page 504
Labels page 507
Polar Axes page 498
Traces page 502
polar plots 493
Auto Grid 499
Autoscale 502
axes style 500
axis settings in dialog box 499
bar charts 503
changing perspective 508
color of traces 503
copying coordinates to clipboard 511
copying format from existing plot 504
creating 494
error bars 503
formatting 498
formatting traces 502–503

graphing several curves 496
grid lines 499
hiding arguments 508
horizontal and vertical lines 501
labels and titles 506
legends 503, 507
line charts 503
lines 503
logarithmic axes 499
logarithmic axis limits 500
markers 503
QuickPlot 494
radial reference lines 501
relation to rectangular plots 465
resizing 508
setting axis limits 500
setting defaults with no plot 505
Show Markers 501
step 503
tick marks 499
titles 507
trace settings in dialog box 502
traces on 496
using default settings 505
with dots 503
zooming 509
Polar Trace dialog box 510
Polar Zoom dialog box 509
polygamma function 394
polynomial
finding the roots of 313
regression 301, 303
Polynomial Coefficients command 371
polyroots function 313
population standard deviation 280
population statistics 280
population variance 280
pop-up window, creating 89
power 235, 605
ppois function 285
precedence among operators 234
precision
in components 435
in displayed results 119
predefined variables 158
predict function 298
prediction 291
principal branch of function 163, 262
Print Preview command 82
printing 29, 79
blank pages in 76, 80

calculate worksheet first 146
color 113, 127
current worksheet 80
Electronic Book section 45
extra pages 80
landscape 78
portrait 78
print preview 82
selected pages 80
selected regions 80
to a file 80
wide worksheets 80
PRN files 453
PRNCOLWIDTH variable 158, 455
PRNPRECISION variable 158, 455
probability density functions 281
probability distribution
    beta 284
    binomial 284
    cauchy 284
    chi-squared 284
    exponential 284
    F 284
    gamma 285
    geometric 285
    log normal 285
    logistic 285
    negative binomial 285
    normal 285
    poisson 285
    Student's t 285
    uniform 285
    Weibull 285
probability distributions 281
processing equations 16, 144, 146
    results of 144
product 235–237, 605
    cross product 195
    dot product 194
    over a range 237
    symbolic 373
product registration 40
program
    if statement 403
Programming Palette 400
programs
    adding lines 400
    break statement 408
    continue statement 409
    controlling or interrupting 407
    defining 400

error handling 411
error messages in 412
for loop 405
for loops 405
generating symbolic results 417
if statement 403
local assignment 400
looping 405
nested 414
on error statement 411
output of 400
palette for creating 12
recursion 415–416
return statement 409
statements 400
subroutines 414–415
symbolic evaluation of 416
while loop 406
properties
    equation region 127
    of components 424
    text region 112
proxy server 32
Psi functions 394
pspline function 295, 297
pt function 285
pulse function 275
punif function 285
pweibull function 285

Q

qbeta function 285
qbinom function 285
qcauchy function 285
qchisq function 286
qexp function 286
qF function 286
qgamma function 286
qgeom function 286
qlnorm function 286
qlogis function 286
qnbinom function 286
qnorm function 286
qpois function 286
QR decomposition (*qr*) function 202
qt function 286

QuickPlot 24, 460, 494
QuickSheets 11, 37
    See also Resource Center 38
    storing custom operators 255
quitting Mathcad 29
qunif function 286
qweibull function 286

R

radians
    converting to degrees 174
    trig functions 259
radix of displayed results 118
random number generators 288
range variables 21, 214
    creating 21
    defining 214, 216
    fundamental principle for 216
    how Mathcad evaluates equations with 216
    in expressions 216
    setting endpoints and increments 216
    using two in one equation 226
rank function 198
rbeta function 288
rbinom function 288
rcauchy function 288
rchisq function 288
Re function 265, 391
READ function 449–450
READ_BLUE function 586
READ_GREEN function 586
READ_HLS function 586
READ_HLS_HUE function 586
READ_HLS_LIGHT function 586
READ_HLS_SAT function 586
READ_HSV function 586
READ_HSV_HUE function 586
READ_HSV_SAT function 586
READ_HSV_VALUE function 586
READ_IMAGE function 586
READ_RED function 586
READBMP function 582
readout of coordinates
    graphs 486
    plots 510
READPRN function 449, 452

    compared to *READ* 456
READRGB function 582
real part of a complex number 265
rectangle to indicate disabled equation 148
recursion 136, 226, 416
reduced view 64
reduced-row echelon form 197
reference existing worksheet 87
reference lines in graphs 476
reference tables
    See Resource Center 38
references
    and relative paths 88
regions 20
    3D bar charts 539
    3D scatter plots 551
    aligning 67
    blank space between 20
    contour plot 529
    copying 65
    deleting 67
    dragging 65–66
    dragging across documents 66–67
    equation 20
    graphs 459
    locking 83, 85
    moving 66
    overlapping 69
    polar plots 493
    selecting 16
    separating 69
    surface plot 515
    text 98
    unlocking 86
    vector field plots 563
    viewing 20, 69
registration 40
regress function 302–303
regression
    linear 300
    nonlinear 304
    polynomial 301, 303
    using linear combinations of functions 304
regression functions 299
relational operators 272
relative paths
    for hyperlinks 90
    for references 88
relax function 349
replacing characters in math or text 114
resizing

3D bar charts 541
3D scatter plots 553
    contour plot 532
    graphs 484
    pictures 589
    polar plots 508
    surface plot 518
    text regions 99
    vector field plots 566
Resource Center 11
    accessing worksheets on Web 38
    bookmarks 39
    contents 38
    QuickSheets 38
    reference tables 38
    tutorial 38
    Web browsing in 38
    Web library 38
resources, on-line 31
result format 118
    global 118
    local 120
results
    calculating 17
    calculating with equations 141
    copying 142
    dimensions in 171
return statement 409
reverse function 270
rexp function 289
rF function 289
rgamma function 289
rgeom function 289
rich text format (RTF) 75, 107
right page boundary 77
right page margin 76–77
rkadapt function 341
rkfixed function 334
rlnorm function 289
rlogis function 289
rnbinom function 289
rnd function 288–289
rnorm function 289
Romberg integration 246
root function 310
    defining user function in terms of 313
    displayed in a symbolic result 395
    failure of 311
    initial guess for 311
    secant method and 311
    tolerance for numeric approximation 311

roots
    finding 310
    finding multiple with solve blocks 320
    finding symbolically 380
    of polynomials 313
    using plots to find 312
rounding off 264
row vectors
    See vectors 182
rows function 196
rpois function 289
rref function 197
rsort function 270
rt function 289
RTF file 72
    See also rich text format 72
runif function 289
rweibull function 289

S

sample standard deviation 281
sample variance 280
Save As dialog box 28
saving
    annotations in Electronic Books 45
    Electronic Book section 45
    new file 28
    worksheets 28, 75
sbval function 345
scalar
    addition 195
    definition of 180
    division 194
    multiplication 194
scatter plots 490
scatter plots (2D) 490
scatter plots (3D) 551
    Autoscale 560
    back planes 555
    borders 555
    boxes 555
    changing marker formats 556
    connecting by lines 557
    converting 554
    creating 552
    formatting 553

formatting axes 558
grid intervals 560
grid lines 559
perspective 554
resizing 553
setting axis limits 560
tick marks 559
titles 560
Scriptable Object component 443
Scripted Object component
object model 445
scrolling 13
autoscroll 66
scrolling output table 190
copying values from 143
setting numerical format for 119
search
Electronic Book 43
in equations 113
in text 113
Search Book command 43
search function 277
secant (*sec*) function 260
secant method 311
sech function 261
second derivatives
calculating 245
for spline functions 296
second order differential equations 336
seed for random number generator 290
seeded iteration 226
with a vector 228
with several variables 227
selecting
graphs 25
math expression 57
pagebreak 78
regions 16, 64
several equations 65
text 103
selection rectangle 64
semicolon, in range variable definitions 214
separating overlapping regions 69
series 368
series keyword 356
Set Lockable Area command 84
shading
contour plots 534
surface plots 522
Shi function 394
Show Border option 589

Show Markers
graphs 476
polar plots 501
Si function 394
sigma (summation symbol) 237
for vector 195
sign function (complex) 393
sign function (real) 394
signum function 394
Simplify command 365
simplify keyword 355, 365
simultaneous definitions 207
simultaneous equations
solving numerically 315
sine (*sin*) function 260
sine integral 394
singular value decomposition 202
singular values of a matrix 203
singularities in trig functions 260
sinh function 261
slope function (linear regression) 300
smooth systems (differential equations) 341
smoothing data 306
soft pagebreaks 78
solve blocks 315
cannot be nested 318
constraints in 317
defining a function that uses 325
defining variables in terms of 319
definition of 316
did not find solution error 322
displaying results of 318
end with *Find* or *Minerr* 330
expressions allowed in 317
finding multiple solutions 320
finding vector of results 326
Given in 315
solving for different variables 328
too few constraints in 323
using effectively 325
using to solve symbolically 381
values returned by 316, 330
Solve command 380
Solve for Variable command 379
solve keyword 356, 379–381
solving equations 315
differential equations 335
See also solve blocks 315
with *lsolve* 203
with *root* function 310
with solve blocks 315, 381

with Solve for Variable 379
with solve keyword 379
sort function 270
sorting vectors and matrices 270
spaces, inserting or deleting 69
spell-checking 115
spline functions 293, 296
    end conditions for 295, 297
    example using 294
    multivariate 296
    second derivatives for 296
spreadsheets
    ASCII data from 447
    exchanging data with 435
    reading data from 452
square root 235, 605
    estimating arithmetically 226
stack function 199
stack overflow error 151
standard deviation (*stdev*) function 280–281
standard normal distribution 284
statistics
    cubic spline interpolation 293
    cumulative distribution functions 284
    density functions 281
    functions 280
    generalized linear regression 304
    histograms 287
    interpolation 291
    inverse cumulative distributions 285
    linear interpolation 292
    linear prediction 291, 298
    linear regression 299
    multivariate cubic spline 296
    multivariate polynomial regression 303
    nonlinear regression 304
    polynomial regression 301
    random number generation 288
    smoothing data 306
Stdev function 281
stdev function 280
stem graphs 479
step function 275
step graph
    graphs 479, 489
    polar plots 503
step-size for iteration 216
stiffb function 341
stiffr function 341
str2num function 277
str2vec function 277

string expressions
    See strings 164
string literals
    See strings 164
strings
    arguments to file access functions 448
    arguments to graphics read/write functions 582, 585–586
    as elements of vectors 164
    comparing 236, 252
    converting to numbers and vectors 277
    defining 164
    editing 165
    evaluating 164
    manipulating 276
    variables 164
strlen function 277
structured data 453
Student's t distribution 285
styles
    math 122
    text 108
submatrix function 199–200, 583
subroutines 414–415
subscripted variables
    calculating with 222
    entering values in input tables 220
subscripts
    in text 105
    last element function 196
    left bracket used to type 185
    literal 156
    non-numeric 156
    ORIGIN used with 188
    start with zero 188
    vector and matrix 185, 234, 604
    when to use 230
Substitute for Variable command 372
substitute keyword 356, 372
substr function 277
subtraction 236, 606
summation 235–236, 605
    multiple 238, 240
    of vector elements 195
    symbolic evaluation of 373
    variable upper limit 240
summations, over a range 237
superscript
    array 234, 604
    example of array superscript in use 228
    to get column from matrix 187

supsmooth function 307
surface plots 515
    Autoscale 526
    back planes 521
    borders 521
    boxes 521
    changing the shading 522
    changing view 520
    controlling how bumpy 521
    converting 520
    creating 516
    discontinuous 524
    formatting 519
    formatting axes 525
    grid intervals 526
    grid lines 525
    mesh on the surface 524
    of function of two variables 516
    parametric 518
    patch plots 524
    perspective 520
    resizing 518
    setting axis limits 526
    tick marks 525
    titles 527
    vertical scale 521
svd function 202
svds function 203
symbolic
    equal sign 353
    evaluation 353
    evaluation of programs 416
    evaluation returns long answers 395
    keywords 355
    transforms 384
Symbolic Keywords palette 355
Symbolics menu commands 359–360
System of Units dialog box 175
system of units, choosing 175

T

tables
    input 220
    output 217
    show only 50 elements 219
tangent (*tan*) function 260

tanh function 261
Taylor series 368
TCP/IP 32
technical support 40
temperature 174
templates 72
    calculation mode 147
    creating new 73
    for math 38
    modifying 75
    used to save calculation mode 147
    using to create a worksheet 72
text 97
    alignment 105
    changing font 104
    color 105
    cut and paste in 103
    deleting 103
    editing 102
    entering 18
    exporting to other programs 107
    Greek letters in 105
    importing from other programs 107
    inserting equations in 100
    moving 100
    moving insertion point in 102
    regions 98
    selecting 103
    selecting a word 103
    spell-checking 115
    styles 108
text box 18, 98
text regions 98
    changing width 99
    creating 18, 98
    editing 102
    hard line breaks 99
    how to exit 19, 98
text styles 108
    applying 109
    creating 111
    modifying 110
tick marks 474
    3D bar charts 548
    3D scatter plots 559
    contour plots 537
    graphs 473
    polar plots 499
    surface plots 525
    vector field plots 568
tilde (~), used in global definitions 139

time in headers and footers 79
time, inserting on a page 79
Tip of the Day 46
Title page
    3D bar chart 549
    3D scatter plots 560
    contour plots 538
    surface plots 527
    vector field plots 569
titles
    3D bar charts 549
    3D scatter plots 560
    contour plots 538
    graphs 481–482
    polar plots 506–507
    surface plots 527
    vector field plots 569
TOL variable 158
    used in symbolic calculations 391
    used with integrals 247
    used with *root* function 312
    used with solve blocks 322
tolerance
    See TOL variable 158
too few constraints (error) 323
toolbar 13
    Electronic Book 42
    Web 39
top margin 77
top-to-bottom evaluation 137
trace (*tr*) function 198
traces
    graphs 470
    polar plots 496
Traces page
    polar plots 502, 505
    X-Y plots 478
trailing zeros 119
transcendental functions 259
transforms
    Fourier (numerical) 266
    Fourier (symbolic) 385
    Laplace 386
    symbolic 384
    wavelet 270
    z 387
Transpose command 383
transpose of matrix 195, 235, 383, 604
trig keyword modifier 366
trigonometric functions 259–260
    with degrees and radians 174

truncation
    See floor function 264
truncation functions 264–265
tutorial 38
two-point boundary value problems 345
typing over text 98

U

U.S. Customary units 176
undefined variables 137, 140
uniform distribution 285
Uniform Resource Locator
    See URL 38
unit impulse function 275
unit step function 275
units 167
    alphabetical list 636
    alternative definitions 169
    base units 175
    CGS system 176
    changing dimension names 177
    common sources of error 170
    converting calculated results 172
    default 168
    defining 171, 175
    dimensional consistency 170
    dimensional values 160
    errors in dimensions 170
    in calculated values 171
    in equations 168
    in tables 219
    metric 176
    MKS system 175
    placeholder 172
    prefixes 176
    SI 176
    U.S. customary 176
Unlock Area command 86
until function 271, 273
update
    file access functions 449
    results in window 144
    window manually 145
    worksheet 146
    worksheet window 146
URL

Collaboratory 33
for worksheet 74
MathSoft home page 39
Use Default Palette command 590
user functions 133
array arguments 208
defined in terms of *root* 313
defined in terms of solve blocks 325
errors in 150
evaluating variables in 135
valid names 154

V

Var function 280
var function 280
variables
complex 161
defining 16, 132
defining several at once 207
global definitions of 139
in red 140, 149
matrices 180
names 154
predefined 158
range variables 21, 214
string 164
substituting for 372
vectors 180
variance function 280
VBScript 443
vec2str function 277
vector field plots 563
creating 564
formatting 567
formatting axes 567
from complex matrices 564
from real matrices 565
grid intervals 569
grid lines 568
perspective 567
resizing 566
tick marks 568
titles 569
vector product 235, 605
vector subscript 234, 604
vector sum operator 241

vectorize operator 204–205, 234, 604
effect of 205
how to type 205
properties of 207
when to use 231
vectors
as arguments to user functions 208
as array elements 209
calculations by element 204
column vectors 182
combining 199
combining with *augment* function 199
combining with *stack* function 199
computing with 183
cross product 195
defining 180, 183
defining several variables at once 207
displayed as scrolling output tables 190
dot product 194
functions for 196
graphing 466
limit on size 193
magnitude 195, 235, 605
norm 195, 235, 605
numbering elements 185, 188
operators for 193
ORIGIN used with 188
row 182
solve blocks applied to 326
sorting elements 270
start with element zero 188
subscripts 185
sum elements of 235, 605
sum of elements operator 195
undefined elements filled with zeros 186, 188
vector arithmetic 195
vectorize operator 204
when to use subscripts 230
vertical scale
3D bar charts 544
surface plots 521
video clips 576
View page
3D bar charts 543
3D scatter plots 554
contour plots 533
surface plots 520
Visual Basic Scripting Edition 443

W

W function 394
wait message 145
wave function 270
wavelet transforms 270
Web
    See World Wide Web 39
Web library 38
Web toolbar 39
Weibull distribution 285
while loops 406
windows
    generally 13
    multiple 14
    scrolling 13
    update results automatically 144
    update results manually 145
    zooming in and out of 13, 64
Wizards
    for inserting a component 423
worksheets
    definition of 11
    exporting as RTF 75
    formatting 76
    hyperlinking 86, 89
    in pop-up window 89
    including by reference 86
    mailing 10
    opening 74
    opening from Internet 36, 40, 74
    order of evaluation 137
    posting on the Collaboratory 35
    printing 29, 79
    referencing in another worksheet 87
    removing from the Collaboratory 36
    retrieving from the Collaboratory 34
    saving 28, 72, 75
    saving as Mathcad 6 format 76
    sending by e-mail 83
World Wide Web 11, 74
    accessing 39
    bookmarks for browsing 39
    browsing 39
    Collaboratory 33
    HTML browsing 39
    library 38
    MathSoft home page 39–40
    MathSoft store 40

toolbar 39
wrapping equations 236, 606
WRITE function 447, 449
WRITEBMP function 585–586, 620
WRITEPRN function 447, 449, 453
    compared to *WRITE* 456
WRITERGB function 585–586, 620
WWW
    See World Wide Web 39

X

X-Y Plot default dialog box 480
X-Y Plot dialog box
    Axes page 472, 475
    Defaults page 480
    Labels page 482
    Traces page 478
X-Y plots
    data 469
    parametric 462
    QuickPlot 24, 460
    stem 479
X-Y Trace dialog box 486
X-Y Zoom dialog box 485

Y

$Y0$, $Y1$, and Yn Bessel functions 263
y-intercept 300

Z

zero tolerance 119
    in components 435
zeros of expressions or functions
    See roots 310
Zeta function 394
Zoom command 13

zooming
   graphs 485
   polar plots 509

windows 13, 64
ztrans keyword 356, 387
z-transforms 356, 387